Life in a Mexican Village:

TEPOZTLÁN RESTUDIED

by Oscar Lewis

To Robert Redfield

contents

Preface / ix

Introduction / xi

part 1: The Village and Its Institutions

part 2: The People

preface

THIS STUDY was begun as a joint project of the Inter-American Indian Institute of Mexico and the National Indian Institute of the United States. The project was originally conceived as a pilot study for a contemplated series of studies in various parts of Latin America, to provide government agencies working in rural areas with a better understanding of the psychology and needs of the people. John Collier, as head of the National Indian Institute, and Manuel Gamio, director of the Inter-American Indian Institute, were instrumental in organizing the project and seeing it through its first year. Financial assistance was provided by the Viking Fund.

As field representative of the National Indian Institute, I was director of the project and had the assistance from time to time of personnel provided by various Mexican government agencies. Field work began in Tepoztlán in December, 1943, and was carried on through June, 1944, when it was abruptly terminated because of lack of funds. In the summer of 1947 I returned to the village to continue field work for a period of three months, with the aid of research grants from the American Philosophical Society and Washington University. In the summer of 1948 I again returned to the village with the aid of research grants from the American Philosophical Society and the University of Illinois.

With Dr. Gamio's aid, and through the courtesy of Dr. Alfonso Caso and Dr. D. F. Rubín de la Borbolla, of the Museo Nacional de Historia y Antropología, four anthropology students were assigned to this project for field work training. The students were Angélica Castro de la Fuente, Isabel Pozas, Anselmo Marino Flores, and Francisco Lima. The Departamento de Educación also generously assigned Esperanza Dominguez Reina as a student assistant. In addition we had the assistance of two social workers and two doctors from the Departamento de Salubridad y Asistencia, and two agronomists from the Departamento Agrario.

The Departamento de Asuntos Indígenas took an active interest in the project, and contributed personnel and aid in other ways, during all three field trips. In 1943 and 1944, when Asuntos Indígenas was under the direction of Isidro Candia, we enjoyed the field assistance of Dr. Emanuel Palacios, anthropologist. Later, through the courtesy of Dr. Gonzalo Aguirre Beltrán and Julio de la Fuente, in their capacity as directors of Asuntos Indígenas, we received the services of Alberto Beltrán, artist. To Alberto Beltrán I am especially grateful for his fine drawings which illustrate this book, and for his enthusiastic cooperation and keen interest in anthropology. To him and to all those mentioned above I extend my thanks.

To Dr. Alejandro D. Marroquín, of El Salvador, I am deeply grateful for capable assistance during all three of my field trips. He has generously shared with me his broad knowledge of Latin America and has contributed much to this study. In addition to his over-all assistance he did a special study of village politics and government in 1944, and in 1947 he worked with me on an intensive family case study. At present, as my colleague at the University of Illinois, he has continued to assist me in the organization of portions of the field data.

I am indebted to Luis Chávez Orozco, outstanding Mexican historian, for locating and making available to me much unpublished archive materials pertaining to Tepoztlán. He also permitted me to use his excellent private library and files on uncataloged documents in the Archivo General y Pública de la Nación. Had it not been for his cooperation and generosity, the historical sections of this study would have suffered.

In the course of my work in Mexico, my family and I were shown kindnesses by many people. I wish particularly to thank Julio de la Fuente, Emanuel Palacios, Angélica Castro de la Fuente, Amelia Fox, Alfonso Villa Rojas, Wigberto Jiménez Moreno, and Antonio Pompa y Pompa. It was also my special privilege to work with Manuel Gamio, Mexico's elder statesman among social scientists.

Our friends in Tepoztlán are too numerous for mention here, and I must thank them as a group. Needless to say, this study was made possible only by their kind cooperation. Well over one hundred Tepoztecans contributed directly as informants, and a few were among my best assistants.

To Dr. Robert Redfield I am indebted for his continued interest in this study. Correspondence and discussions with him have always been stimulating and helpful. He graciously aided me in securing funds for my last two field trips. Moreover, his encouragement in this critical restudy of his own work, in the interest of science, has been a source of moral support.

Dr. Theodora M. Abel and Dr. Renata A. Calabresi have been most kind to take time out from their busy schedules to analyze the Rorschach protocols and to produce Chapter 13—"The People Seen from Their Rorschach Tests." Dr. Edgar Anderson, of Washington University and the Missouri Botanical Gardens, has graciously helped with an intensive study of Tepoztecan corn. His report, "An Intensive Survey of Maize in Tepoztlán," appears as Appendix A. To my colleagues at the University of Illinois, Dr. John Albig, Dr. Erich Ahrens, Dr. J. E. Hulett, Dr. Margaret Reid, Dr. Frederick Will, and Dr. O. H. Mowrer, I am grateful for their reading of portions of the manuscript and their helpful suggestions. To Dr. George P. Murdock, Dr. Melville J. Herskovits, Dr. Paul Radin, Dr. Howard Becker, and Dr. Jules Henry, I am also grateful for their comments on portions of the manuscript. I would like to thank Dr. Vera L. Maslow for her careful and critical reading of the entire manuscript.

To my wife, Ruth Maslow Lewis, I am deeply indebted for her collaboration in all aspects of the field work and for her aid in the preparation of the manuscript.

introduction

In 1926 Robert Redfield, a young American anthropologist, first studied the village of Tepoztlán and gave us his pioneer work, *Tepoztlán—a Mexican Village*.[1] This book has since become a standard reference and a classic in the field of community studies.[2] It is of particular importance in the history of community studies in that it contains Redfield's first statement on the nature of the folk society, and, at least implicitly, the concept of the folk-urban continuum, a hypothesis of societal change later made explicit in *The Folk Culture of Yucatan*.[3] The folk-urban conceptualization of culture change now enjoys great prestige among sociologists and anthropologists, and has served as the theoretical frame of reference for many of the community studies done by Redfield's students.[4]

In the same year in which Redfield's first book appeared, Stuart Chase visited Tepoztlán for a short while and later described it in his book, *Mexico, a Study of Two Americas*.[5] His account, based largely on Redfield's work, was, in effect, a popularized version of the folk-urban dichotomy. In it Tepoztlán was compared very favorably with Middletown, U.S.A.

Seventeen years after Redfield's study, I went to Tepoztlán to do a broad ethnographic and historical study of the social, economic, political, and religious life of the community, with special emphasis upon an analysis of the changes which had occurred in the village since 1926. This involved a restudy of the village and a comparison of our findings.[6] Special attention, however, was given to those aspects of village life which Redfield had merely touched upon, such as demography, the land problem, systems of agriculture, the distribution of wealth, standards of living, politics and local government, the life cycle of the individual, and interpersonal relations. The bulk of the materials presented in this book is therefore new data.[7]

Upon my arrival in the village it seemed to be in many respects as Redfield had described it. In physical appearance it had changed but little. Once off the highway which runs to the plaza, there were the same unpaved streets and adobe houses, the barrio chapels, the people carrying water to their homes from the nearest fountain, the men wearing their ancient white *calzones* and huaraches, the bare-

---

[1] Robert Redfield, *Tepoztlán—a Mexican Village* (Chicago: University of Chicago Press, 1930).

[2] It is interesting to note that at the time of publication Redfield viewed it as a preliminary investigation which he hoped to continue. *Ibid.*, p. vii.

[3] Redfield, *The Folk Culture of Yucatan* (Chicago: University of Chicago Press, 1941).

[4] See, for example, Julio de la Fuente, *Yalalag, Una Villa Zapoteca Serrana* (Mexico: Museo Nacional de Antropología, 1949); and Horace Miner, *St. Denis, a French Canadian Parish* (Chicago: University of Chicago Press, 1939).

[5] Stuart Chase, *Mexico—a Study of Two Americas* (New York: Macmillan Co., 1931).

[6] Originally it was planned to use Redfield's monograph as an ethnographic base for a personality study. It soon became apparent, however, that because of the many changes which had occurred since 1926, a restudy of the village was necessary. The importance of restudies in the social sciences and the implications of the differences in our findings are treated in Chapter 21, "Summary and Conclusions," p. 427.

[7] It was not necessary for our purposes to restudy certain aspects of village life adequately covered by Redfield, such as the material culture, the fiesta system, the *corridos*, magic, and medicine.

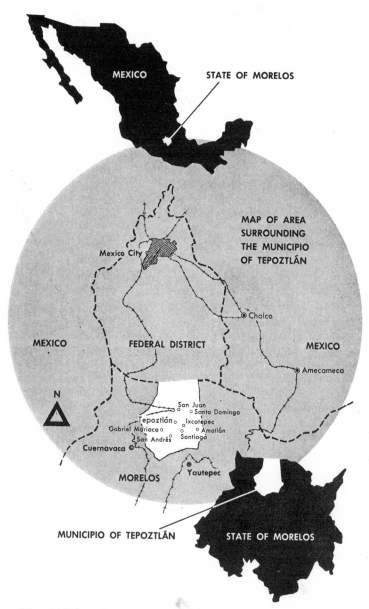

Fig. 1. Map of Mexico.

foot women with braids and long skirts. But signs of change could also be seen. There were the new asphalt road, the buses, the tourist cars, the Coca-Cola and aspirin signs, the Sinarquist placards on a roadside wall, the queue of women and children waiting to have their corn ground at the mills, the new stores and poolrooms in the plaza, and a few women with bobbed hair and high-heeled shoes. Moreover, school enrollment had increased from the "few score" of Redfield's time, to over six hundred, and the village had obtained *ejidos* under the national *ejido* program.

What had really happened in these past seventeen years? How profound were these changes? How had native institutions been affected? What old problems had been resolved and what new problems had been created? To what extent had the villagers become incorporated into the main stream of national life? How did the increase in trade and the influx of wealth affect the cultural habits of the people, their standards of living, their aspirations, their thinking? In short, had the people and their way of life really changed?

These questions are of much more than local interest. The changes which had occurred in Tepoztlán were taking place over wide areas of Mexico and the world. It was hoped that an intensive study of a single village might enable us to get at some of the fundamental processes and principles of culture change, and at the same time be useful to administrators concerned with the task of carrying out welfare programs in the so-called backward areas of the world.

The conditions for such a study seemed especially propitious in Tepoztlán for a number of reasons. Most of the changes noted above had come after 1926. We could therefore use Redfield's study as a base line from which to measure and analyze these changes. We could also work with some of Redfield's informants and with others who had lived through this period. Here was an unusual opportunity for an anthropologist.

As the field work progressed, other problems arose. It became apparent that many of the changes which had taken place in the village, particularly in social organization and attitudes of the people, were part and parcel of a larger process of culture change which dated back at least before the Mexican Revolution of 1910-20. We therefore had to go back some time, preceding Redfield's visit, and study the effects of the Mexican Revolution upon the village.

But the historical focus could not be limited to the Revolution. It was desirable to study the history of the village from pre-Hispanic times if we were to appreciate the contemporary scene and to interpret the pattern of change. Indeed, one of the advantages of studying a peasant community like Tepoztlán, as compared with a truly isolated and non-literate society, is the possibility of getting historical perspective. For this purpose the following sources were used: archaeological findings, legends, unpublished archive materials on the village covering a period from the sixteenth to the nineteenth centuries; comparative data on pre-Hispanic Mexico and colonial Mexico from sixteenth-century chroniclers and other sources; the files of the national and state government agencies which had contacts with the village; and finally, the reconstruction of conditions before the Revolution of 1910-20 from the accounts of informants who had lived through that time.

The intensive historical study served a number of ends. It served to check the validity of some generalizations made by historians and other scholars concerning various aspects of Mexican history. For example, there has been some disagreement among scholars about the size of the pre-Hispanic population and the rate of depopulation after the Conquest.[8] As we shall see, the data on Tepoztlán throw some light on this subject. Similarly, there have been divergent interpretations of the Mexican Revolution. Here we have a village which was in the heart of it. What can an intensive study of a single village tell us about the results of the Revolution? How does it fit in with the general picture? How did the *ejido* program work out in this particular case, and what clarification does this offer on the larger agrarian problem? In this study I attempt to answer these and other questions. A sufficient number of similarly detailed local studies might provide new insights which could be used in the formulation of more accurate broad generalizations.[9]

The field techniques used in this study were those of the current anthropological repertory, and included participant-observers, interviews, autobiographies, case studies, and a battery of psychological tests including the Rorschach. A study of a relatively large and complex village like Tepoztlán, with a population of approximately 3,500,[10] with differences in the size of barrios, the degree of wealth, and the attitude of the older and younger generation, and with a rapidly changing culture, presented formidable problems. Assistance was necessary; furthermore, the traditional anthropological reliance upon a few informants for obtaining a picture of the culture was obviously inadequate in this situation. Sampling and securing data and informants representative of all the significant differences in the village seemed just as important here as in a study of a modern urban community. We therefore employed quantitative procedures wherever possible, utilizing census data, local government records and documents, schedules, and questionnaires. Numerous village surveys were made with the assistance of local informants and a small staff of field workers.

Two aspects of the field study deserve special mention. Intensive case studies of representative families were carried·on, by living with a family and applying to this family all of the techniques and conceptual categories traditionally used by the anthropologist in studying a larger social unit. Seven families were studied intensively in this manner, with the aid of student assistants. Much of the detailed information on inter-personal relations contained within this volume was obtained from these family studies.[11] Two of these studies will appear in a later publication.

[8] Cf. the conservative estimate of Bailey W. Diffie, *Latin-American Civilization: Colonial Period* (Harrisburg: Stackpole Sons, 1945), pp. 179-80; and Sherburne F. Cook and Lesley B. Simpson, "The Population of Central Mexico in the Sixteenth Century," *Ibero-Americana,* Vol. XXXI (1948).

[9] Intensive historical studies of small areas are increasing. See, for example, Sherburne F. Cook, "The Historical Demography and Ecology of the Teotlalpan," *Ibero-Americana,* Vol. XXXIII (1949).

[10] The population of some other Mexican communities for which we have anthropological studies are as follows: Chan Kom, 251 (1930); Tzintzuntzan, 1,231 (1945); Mitla, 2,500 (1936); and Cherán, 5,000 (1945).

[11] For a discussion of some of the possibilities of this kind of family study, see Oscar Lewis, "An Anthropological Approach to Family Studies," *American Journal of Sociology,* Vol. LV, No. 5 (March, 1950).

Because this project in its early phase was under the sponsorship of the Inter-American Indian Institute, we wanted to learn about the practical problems of the people. It occurred to me that it might be an interesting technique to call meetings of the heads of families in each of the barrios of the village, to explain our mission, and to ask them to discuss their problems.[12] The response of the people was instructive and led quite unexpectedly to the organization of a program of services as a corollary to the research project.

At each of the meetings men rose to state that if it was an understanding of their problems we wanted, we would not have to stay very long, for they knew their problems only too well. They complained that their lands were becoming more sterile and their yields progressively lower, and that they could only harvest a single crop a year because of lack of rainfall—they asked for an irrigation program. Some men complained that each year they were losing a large part of their corn because of insects—they asked for help on insect control. Others complained, "We have a new road and many tourists, but our children are dying"—they asked for a doctor. Still others stressed the need for a new school building. It was made clear to us that they would be interested in helping us in our study of the village only if we would help them with these problems. One dignified, elderly Tepoztecan rose and said, "Many people have come here to study us, but not one of them has helped us."

It was clear that if we were to establish good rapport with these people we would have to help them. After explaining the situation to Dr. Gamio and consulting with members of the sponsoring committee for our research project, we decided to ask Mexican government agencies for help. Further consultations followed, and we finally obtained two agronomists, two doctors, and two social workers for the village.

The details of the operation of this program of service have been described in another report.[13] Here I should like to point out that we gained some of our best insights into the nature of Tepoztecan character and institutions through this experiment.[14] It was as if we had set up an experimental situation to study the reactions of the villagers to outside influences.

---

[12] The difference between asking people about their history and customs and asking about their problems may be very significant in the total view of the culture a field worker gets.

[13] Lewis, *The Tepoztlán Project: A Report on Administrative Problems* (Washington, D.C.: National Indian Institute, 1945).

[14] On the basis of our Tepoztecan experience, it seems that the combination of research and service programs might be an excellent way of integrating the fields of applied and theoretical anthropology. I realize that this may sound heretical to the purists. But the history of other disciplines may be instructive in this regard. O. H. Mowrer pointed out to me that in the history of psychology some of the greatest progress in the development of psychological theory has come as a result of the clinical treatment of patients. The experience of English anthropologists with action programs in Africa also points in this direction. Malinowski has commented on this as follows:

"The pose of academic detachment and persistent blindness to the fact that theoretical anthropology can learn quite as much from practical issues as it can teach in return, have considerably handicapped modern developments in the Science of Man. . . . In my opinion there is no doubt that whole-hearted concern with practical matters will more directly lead the theoretical student into the understanding of the dynamic aspect of culture change than any

Field work was begun with several preliminary visits to Tepoztlán and the surrounding villages of the municipio.[15] On one of these visits I brought letters of recommendation from the governor of the state of Morelos to the local municipal authorities, who were very helpful and who became our first informants. With their aid we rented a house in the village where I lived with my family. It was my purpose during the first month to establish rapport, locate informants, select representative families to be studied, and generally prepare the way for the coming of the student assistants from the Museo Nacional de Historia y Antropología who were to help with the field work.

Establishing ourselves in the village presented few difficulties. Because of the frequent coming and going of tourists, the presence of a few outsiders created no particular stir. However, during the first few months we heard rumors that we were spies from the U. S. A. with imperialistic designs,[16] that we were Protestant missionaries come to change the religion,[17] that we were agents of the Mexican government studying the economy for the purpose of raising taxes, and that we were trying to locate all youths eligible for conscription, a burning issue in the village at that time. Fortunately for the project, the rumors never became widespread and did not present any serious obstacles. With the exception of a single incident which occurred after the investigation had been going smoothly for four months, there were many manifestations of good will and cooperativeness on the part of Tepoztecans. Throughout the study, rapport with our selected families and other informants was excellent.

The circle of our acquaintances and informants in the village was extended considerably because our Mexican student assistants lived with families in each of the barrios and made many friends on their own initiative. Also, some of Redfield's informants were still alive, remembered him well, and were eager to work with us. On our return to the village in 1947 after an absence of three years, we were impressed by the enthusiasm with which we were greeted. The very fact that we had returned seemed to have automatically increased their confidence in us. In our last two summer field trips we were therefore able to obtain data of a much more personal and intimate nature than before.

---

other avenue of research. What is practically urgent to man, whether it be desirable or detestable, whether inspiring or galling, soon becomes a collective drive, that is, a relevant social force." Bronislaw Malinowski, "The Anthropology of Changing African Cultures," *Methods of Study of Culture Contact in Africa,* International Institute of African Languages and Cultures, Memo. XV (Oxford, England: Oxford University Press, 1938).

[15] I am indebted to Julio de la Fuente for accompanying me on these first visits; it was partly on the basis of his counsel that Tepoztlán was selected for study.

[16] We learned later that this rumor was begun by a Sinarquist agent from Mexico City who visited the village regularly during our stay and had succeeded in organizing a small Sinarquist unit in the village.

[17] Shortly after we moved into Tepoztlán we were visited by a delegation of Tepoztecans who wanted to know if we were connected with the YMCA project that was operating nearby in the municipio of Tepoztlán, and we were asked pointedly if we had come to change the religion. We explained that we were in no way connected with a religious organization, and that our purpose was to study the customs of the people and to learn of their needs. Apparently they were satisfied with our answer. The leader of this group later became one of our friends and informants.

The excellent rapport of our staff with Tepoztecans deserves some comment, because it was in such sharp contrast to the poor quality of inter-personal relations among the villagers themselves. I mention this point here because it has an important bearing upon the question of methodology and the reliability of impressions of rural Mexico. There is a natural tendency on the part of anthropologists as well as tourists to judge people by how they act in relationship to oneself. To do this in the case of Tepoztlán (and I suspect that this holds true for much of Mexico) would be to miss some of the essential character traits of the people.

When an anthropologist with the title "el doctor" and university students enter a village like Tepoztlán, they are treated in a special manner. Tepoztecans are sensitive to status distinctions, and many are eager to cultivate people who, they believe, have connections and may be in a position to help them. Many also enjoy talking with outsiders who are *gente de cultura* (cultured people); it gives them a sense of importance. By the same token, this sensitivity to status made others, who for one reason or another were not selected as informants, envious and even vindictive. In short, I should like to emphasize that despite the fact that doors were opened to us and that we have formed many close friendships in the village, Tepoztecans are not always pleasant to each other.

Early in the project I decided to use the barrio [18] and the family as the basic units of research. The seven barrios were still, as in Redfield's time, important locality groupings; and as we have indicated earlier, we considered the study of families fundamental to our research. The first few weeks were therefore spent in an analysis of a population census of the village which had been made a year before by the local authorities with the aid of the schoolteachers. The census data were reorganized first on a barrio basis. Barrio lists of families were drawn up, and each family was assigned a number which thereafter was used to identify that family. In addition, alphabetical lists of all men and women in each barrio were made, with the corresponding family number after each name. In this way we were able to identify all individuals in the village with respect to their barrio and family membership.

As a preliminary to obtaining families that would represent the various socio-economic groupings in the village, several informants ranked the families in each of the barrio lists according to relative wealth and social position. The criteria used in this tentative classification were the ownership of (1) a house, (2) land, or (3) cattle. In this way we obtained a rough idea of the relative economic standing of all the families in the village. On the basis of this, three families, each representing different socio-economic levels, were tentatively selected for study in each of the seven barrios.

After I had been in the village for about a month, the student assistants began to come one at a time. By December there were five students and a field worker in the village, each of whom was placed with a family in a different barrio. While we had some success in placing these student assistants with families that represented differences in socio-economic levels, size, composition, and degree of ac-

---

[18] Redfield's emphasis upon barrio differences led me to use them in this way, although they were not as important as I had anticipated.

culturation, we found that there was a greater willingness among the better-to-do and more acculturated families on our list to have one of our staff live with them. Some of the poorer families who expressed willingness to accept a student were unable to do so because of very crowded living conditions. Many of these poorer families were large and lived in a single room.

We were now ready to begin the accumulation of a great variety of information on every family in the village. Each assistant was made responsible for gathering the data in his barrio. In the three smaller barrios, none of which had over forty families, it was possible to get a few informants who knew quite intimately most families in their barrios. In these smaller barrios, for instance, practically any male adult knew quite well who did or did not own land or other property. In the larger barrios no single informant was well acquainted with more than a small percentage of the families, and we therefore had to use many more informants. In effect, we were doing a census in each barrio, with the number of items investigated progressively increasing as our rapport improved, and as we felt free to ask more questions. Among the items of information which we eventually obtained for each family were (1) ownership of property, such as house, land, cattle and other animals, fruit trees, and sewing machines; (2) occupation and sources of income; (3) marital status, number of marriages, barrio of origin or birthplace of each spouse, kinship of all persons then living on the same house site, and other related items; (4) social participation and positions of leadership; (5) educational level and whether or not any of the children had attended school outside the village. These items were obtained on all families and were supplemented by a number of partial surveys on other items. In addition to the information which we obtained ourselves, we also utilized and checked much of the information contained in the census of 1940. We had obtained a special breakdown of the municipio census by individual villages from the Federal Department of Statistics. The information on all these items was checked independently by at least two informants.

Getting accurate data on land-ownership in Tepoztlán was a difficult and delicate matter because of general suspicion of the motives of anyone who undertakes such a study. Our staff worked for many weeks copying the property listing in the local property register for every family in the village. These findings were then compared with the information independently obtained from informants. Many discrepancies were found. The information which we obtained from informants indicated that approximately fifteen of the people who owned land according to our informants were not registered as landowners. On the other hand, we found several cases of land registered in the name of individuals who were not known by our informants to be landowners. By checking all cases in which there was a discrepancy between the data in the register and those of our informants, we believe that we arrived at a reasonably accurate picture of the real situation. In this connection we learned that there was a higher incidence of unregistered land in the outlying villages of the municipio, where such matters are less easily controlled by local authorities.

The question of the size of land plots presented much more difficult problems than the question of land-ownership. Tepoztecans still do not think basically in terms of hectares, but rather in terms of the amount of seed needed to plant a plot. Thus a peasant will say he planted so many *cuartillos* of corn or beans, rather than so many hectares or *tareas*. In Tepoztlán the number of *cuartillos* of corn that will cover one hectare varies according to the size of seed and the type of terrain. By and large, however, Tepoztecans consider that ten *cuartillos* of *maíz ancha,* the prevalent type of corn used, make up one hectare in lands used for plow agriculture, which are the only privately owned lands and the only ones we were concerned with. We measured and paced numerous milpas with the aid of the two Mexican agronomists, and found that the quantity of seed for one hectare of land varied between nine and one-half to twelve *cuartillos* of corn. On this basis we accepted the Tepoztecan figure of ten *cuartillos* as reasonably accurate and have used it throughout the study. In checking sample plots for size, we found that the size of plots registered was quite accurate. However, the value of land registered had no relationship to its current value.

With the help of the agronomists, we mapped all the village sites as well as some of the outlying agricultural lands near some of the barrios. On my later visits to the village in 1947 and 1948, I did a study of land types and land use with the assistance of Alberto Beltrán, who drew the maps and aided in surveys. We also carefully examined the municipal records, from which we obtained data on births and deaths over a ten-year period, the number of marriages over an eight-year period, the municipal income and expenditures for a fifteen-year period, and the number and types of court cases from 1926 to 1944.

We would like to say a word about our use of Tepoztecans as assistants. We took advantage of the presence of a number of intelligent and fairly well-educated Tepoztecans in the village by employing them as assistants in many of the surveys. This saved us a great deal of time and effort, and we were able to collect a wider variety of data than would otherwise have been possible. In addition to surveys, we obtained autobiographies, written accounts of experiences during the Revolution, a daily record over a short period of all visitors to the Municipal Palace and the purpose of the visits, written accounts of the local political situation by various political figures in the village, collections of stories, jokes, and sayings, and case histories of quarrels among neighbors and among relatives. We were gratified that several of our Tepoztecan assistants proved to be such helpful and reliable workers.

While we were gathering this information for the village as a whole, each of our student assistants was recording data and observations on the families with which they were living. A long, detailed guide for observing and recording behavioral data and for the writing of life histories was prepared by Ruth Lewis as an aid to the students. Again, we secured the cooperation of the more educated members of families in keeping daily records, in answering special questionnaires, or in writing up special subjects.

The testing program was carried out in the school, and the testing group was made up of fifty children of school age selected from our list of twenty-one representative families. The families represented each of the socio-economic levels and each of the barrios. The psychological tests which we endeavored to give to each child in the testing group were the Rorschach, the Grace-Arthur Performance Scale, the Goodenough Draw-a-Man, the Emotional Response Test, the Moral Judgment Test, an adapted form of Thematic Apperception, free drawings, and written themes. The Rorschach tests were given by Ruth Lewis; the Performance Scale, the drawing tests, and the written themes, by Angélica Castro de la Fuente; the Thematic Apperception, by Esperanza Dominguez Reina; and the others, by local assistants.[19]

The methodological orientation of this study combines the historical, the functional, and the configurational points of view. In the first instance we have studied Tepoztecan culture as a changing phenomenon, responding to different influences at various times in its complicated history. In the second, we have examined the institutions of the village as they function at the present time, and have shown the inter-relationships between the social, economic, and political aspects of life. In the third, we have sought to understand Tepoztecan culture as a whole, as an integrated way of life, as well as part of the larger Mexican scene.

Tepoztlán is discussed from two points of view: first, as an entity in itself, with its internal organization which includes the family, the barrio, the village-wide institutions like the church, the school, and the local government; and second, as part of the units larger than itself such as the municipio, the state, the nation, and the world. These internal and external aspects of village organization and village life are, of course, closely inter-related and together constitute a continuum of social and economic organization. In the case of Tepoztlán, its relationship with the Mexican nation is particularly important, as the context within which its history, economics, politics, and other aspects of life have developed. Mexico was therefore one of our basic configurations in this study.

Broadly speaking, studies of Mexico by social scientists have been of two types: one, studies of the nation as a whole; and two, studies of single communities. The former have been done primarily by historians, geographers, economists, and sociologists; [20] the latter by anthropologists. The relationship between these two types of studies has tended to be one-sided. Whereas the writers of national studies, of necessity, have had to draw upon local studies, anthropologists for the most part have carried on their work with little effort to place it within a national or even a regional framework.[21] Indeed, anthropological studies of communities in Mexico and, for that matter, in other parts of Latin America, have been characterized by what might be called an ideological localism whereby each little community is

---

[19] We have drawn upon the results of most of the tests in writing up the sections on Tepoztecan character. However, with the exception of the Rorschach results, which are published here, the other test data will be published later.

[20] A few examples of the type of national studies I have in mind are Eyler N. Simpson, *The Ejido, Mexico's Way Out* (Chapel Hill: University of North Carolina Press, 1937); Ernest Gruening, *Mexico and Its Heritage* (New York: Century Co., 1928); Frank Tannenbaum, *The Mexican Agrarian Revolution* (New York: Macmillan Co., 1929); Nathan L. Whetten, *Rural Mexico* (Chicago: University of Chicago Press, 1948).

[21] The work that Redfield and the Carnegie Institute of Washington carried on in Yucatán represents an exception. However, the primary orientation of the community studies in this program was to use Yucatán as a convenient laboratory for the study of theoretical problems concerning the nature of society and social change rather than toward a better understanding of Mexico and its problems.

treated as self-sufficient and isolated.[22] Undoubtedly, this is a carry-over from an older anthropological tradition which was concerned with salvaging cultural data from rapidly disappearing primitive peoples. While such an approach might still have some justification in dealing with an isolated tribe in the jungles of New Guinea, it has little justification in studies of modern nations like Mexico.

The common cultural heritage of Spain has reached into the most distant corners of Mexico since early colonial times; and since the Revolution of 1910-20, even the more isolated villages have become increasingly drawn into the main stream of national life and have felt the impact of national policies and programs. Tepoztlán is subject to national Mexican law, its *ejido* program is part of a national program, its school system is regulated by the Federal Department of Education, its forests are protected by the Federal Department of Forestry, and in a more general way its economic life is part of the larger economy of the state of Morelos and the nation. In this sense, then, the culture of Tepoztlán is part of the larger culture of Mexico and must be examined in that context.

In studying communities in Mexico it is important that the anthropologist become a student not merely of the single community but of the region and nation as well. The anthropologist must be sufficiently versed in the more important historical, geographical, economic, and cultural characteristics of the region and nation to be able to place his community in relation to each of them, and to indicate just what the community is representative of in the larger scene. Like the sociologist, the anthropologist must become skilled in the use of census data and comparative statistics to relate and compare population trends, standards of living, health and education, and types of agricultural problems. In the matter of cultural characteristics the anthropologist must know what is unique to his community and what it shares with broader areas, what is new and what is old, what is primitive and what is modern.

It seems to me that such a procedure makes for a better sense of perspective in understanding the local scene, and helps to distinguish more clearly between what is local and what is widespread.[23] It makes local materials more useful to other social scientists as well as to government administrators concerned with action programs. Furthermore, it offers an excellent opportunity to study the way in which national events and programs such as the Revolution and the *ejido* program have worked out under local conditions. One of the questions to be considered in this study, therefore, is: What is Tepoztlán representative of in rural Mexico?

It has become commonplace in writing about Mexico to begin by emphasizing the great diversity in geography, language, and the cultural levels of the people. Diversity is undoubtedly one of the important characteristics of the country, but we must not overlook the fact that within this diversity there are underlying similarities in trends and problems as well as in culture. These similarities are the result

---

[22] For a similar criticism see Julian Steward's paper, "Some Limitations of Anthropological Community Studies," read at the American Anthropological Association Meeting, 1948.

[23] A recent monograph on a Tarascan village devotes considerable space to describing children's games, which are known throughout most of Mexico and in other parts of Latin America, as though these games were a distinctively local Tarascan phenomenon.

of widespread contacts of the Indian peoples among themselves before the Spanish Conquest, and the common influence of Spanish colonial institutions since the Conquest.

Tepoztlán parallels, to a remarkable degree, many of the characteristics of Mexico as a whole. Within the relatively limited area of the municipio of Tepoztlán [24] we find practically the entire range of climatic zones of Mexico, from the *tierra fría* to *tierra caliente,* with their accompanying variety of natural resources. It is a striking fact that over fifty per cent of the total land area of Mexico falls within the range of altitudes found within this single municipio, that is, from approximately 3,500 to 9,500 feet. Tepoztlán is also distinctive in the way in which its statistical indices follow national figures for such items as the percentage of its arable land to total land, the percentage of its forest land to total land, and the average size of landholdings. The rate of population growth as well as the distribution of age groups also closely parallels the national figures.

In Tepoztlán, as in Mexico as a whole, we find contrasting elements of the primitive and the modern, the old and the new, the Spanish colonial and the contemporary. Tepoztlán has a strong Indian heritage; many pre-Columbian traits persist in the village today. The system of communal land-ownership, an important aspect of the economy and social organization of the municipio, has remained practically intact. Many elements of pre-Hispanic agriculture are found; corn, beans, and squash remain the staple products. Pre-Columbian traits of material culture have also persisted, particularly in house construction, furnishings, cookery, foods, and clothing. Among the more important of these items we find adobe walls, the sweathouse (*temascal*) made of stone and mortar, clay plastered granaries for corn (*cuescomatl*), the hearth (*tlequilitl*), the three-legged grinding stone (*metate*), the clay griddle (*comal*), the mortar and pestle (*molcaxitl* and *texolotl*), huaraches, tortillas, chile, and pulque. In non-material culture there are also survivals, especially in curing and magic, and in customs pertaining to birth and other stages of the life cycle.[25] The Náhuatl language has also persisted. As late as 1927 Náhuatl was spoken by nearly all the inhabitants, although most of the villagers also spoke Spanish.

The large number of Spanish colonial elements which still exist in the village culture today were introduced early in the sixteenth century soon after the Spanish Conquest. The most important of these traits are the physical layout of the village with its barrios, streets, and central plaza; Catholicism and the churches; the Spanish language; a money economy; domestic animals, the plow and other agricultural tools; and the greater part of the beliefs and customs of the people.

Side by side with the pre-Columbian and Spanish colonial elements are many significant items of modern industrial civilization, such as corn mills and sewing

[24] While the village of Tepoztlán is the primary subject of this study, the village cannot be understood except within the framework of the municipio of Tepoztlán, of which it is the *cabecera* (head), a status roughly equivalent to our county seat. In this study, therefore, there will be frequent references both to the village and the municipio.

[25] Many of Bernardino de Sahagún's descriptions of native Aztec diseases and their cures are still remarkably accurate descriptions of present-day customs in Tepoztlán. Indeed, many sections of Sahagún read as if he had been relying upon Tepoztecan informants.

machines, a modern highway and buses, clocks, poolrooms, patent medicines, powdered milk, a few battery radios, and one or two automobiles. The existence of these old and new traits, and the varying degree in which they are combined from family to family, makes for cultural complexity and heterogeneity in Tepoztlán.

Tepoztlán, like Mexico, has had a long and complicated history of mingling of peoples and cultures, and has never been a truly isolated village. The marginal position of Tepoztlán between the high plateau area to the north and the lower valleys of the south, as well as its proximity to the major roads of travel, has subjected it since pre-Hispanic times to influences from many areas.[26] Tepoztlán has been inhabited continuously since early archaic horizons, and the various ceramic levels unearthed in the village show a variety of influences which include Olmec, Toltec, and Aztec.[27] In the more recent pre-Hispanic times it was a center of religious pilgrimages, some of which came from distant Chiapas and Guatemala, and the fame of El Tepozteco, the legendary culture hero of the village, seems to have been known far and wide.

Since the Spanish Conquest the village of Tepoztlán has had even more contact with the outside and, in fact, has been closer to the main stream of national life. The great scenic beauty of Tepoztlán and its proximity to Mexico City and Cuernavaca, two key political and administrative centers, have played an important part in the history of Tepoztlán. Martín Cortés, the son of Hernán Cortés, and members of the Cortés family over a few generations, lived in the village in the present-day barrio of La Santísima. The barrio chapel was reputedly built by Martín Cortés just opposite his house so that he could hear morning Mass without going to church. The forced labor of the Tepoztecans in the mines of Taxco and in the neighboring haciendas of the Marqués del Valle, during the sixteenth and seventeenth centuries, brought Tepoztecans into contact with Negro slaves

---

[26] Edgar Anderson's study of Tepoztecan corn (see Appendix A, p. 449) also shows the marginal position of Tepoztlán.

[27] In the thirteenth century, the nearby towns of Chalco, Amecameca, and portions of Morelos were inhabited by the Olmecs, who were a Popoloco-Mixteca group. Wigberto Jiménez Moreno suggests that some of these Olmecs were later Nahuatlized. It is perhaps significant that to this day Tepoztecans make religious pilgrimages to both Chalco and Amecameca. Undoubtedly Tepoztecans had frequent contacts with both towns prior to the Conquest. Shortly after the fall of the Toltec empire some of the dispersed Toltec groups fled to Cholula which was an Olmec center.

Jiménez Moreno has suggested that the pre-Hispanic history of Mexico might be divided into two great periods. In the first, the coastal or Olmec influence predominated and in the second, the plateau predominated, particularly after the founding of Tula. The valley of Morelos seems from the earliest times to have been a meeting place for both the eastern and northern influence and its culture therefore represents a synthesis of both. As evidence of eastern influence in Tepoztlán, Jiménez points to the square shields of El Tepozteco, clearly not a highland trait. Square shields are an Olmec trait and are also shown in relief work in the room of the ball courts in Chichen Itzá. Furthermore, the ax shown in the figure of Ometochtli is called *itztopolli*, which is like the Olmec *macteputztli* shown in the Olmec codices. Wigberto Jiménez Moreno, "El Enigma de los Olmecas," *Cuadernos Americanos*, Vol. V, No. 5 (Sept.–Oct., 1942), pp. 122-25.

For ceramic evidence on this point, see the work of Florencia Muller, *Chimalacatlan, Acta Antropológica*, Vol. 3, No. 1 (March, 1948).

of Cortés in Cuernavaca and on nearby haciendas. This is suggested by the local physical type as well as by local lore. There is a tradition in the village that Negro slaves from Cuernavaca worked as day laborers in the construction of the church. It is said that a Negro lies buried in each of the pillars of the church and that is the reason why the church is so strong.[28]

The village of Tepoztlán well illustrates the Mexican pattern of the domination of the center over the periphery. Since the sixteenth century, Tepoztlán, as the principal village, has dominated the surrounding villages politically, economically, and socially. Tepoztecans today feel superior to the people of the outlying villages, and, by and large, have superior educational facilities, better means of communication, and a higher standard of living. Going from Tepoztlán, the center, to the smaller surrounding villages of the municipio, we find a greater persistence of older customs, less literacy, and more people who speak only Náhuatl.

Tepoztecans, at various times in the history of the village, have achieved positions of prominence in many fields and have had personal contacts with men in the highest political circles of the state of Morelos and the nation. Many young men have left Tepoztlán, especially in the middle of the last century, to become doctors, lawyers, teachers, engineers, and priests. Tepoztlán boasts of having produced, within the last fifty years, two governors of the state of Morelos, three justices to the state court, a state senator, and more than half a dozen deputies to the state legislature. Many of these men have kept in touch with their relatives in the village and have been a constant stimulus for culture change.

One of the early Tepoztecans to become a distinguished figure and an important influence in the village was Professor Mariano Jacobo Rojas, who was born in Tepoztlán in 1842. This schoolteacher became a champion of bilingual education

---

[28] I am indebted to Dr. Gonzalo Aguirre Beltrán for calling to my attention a number of seventeenth-century documents, which indicate the presence of Negroes and mulattoes in Tepoztlán. These documents also show that the Inquisition prosecuted the Negroes for taking *peyote* and for their practices of magic and divination. The following declaration of the Negress Louisa, made available to me by Aguirre Beltrán, is typical: "Asked if she knew or presumed the reason for her being called before the board of Inquisition she said that she presumed that it was to learn what she knew about magic performed by a Negro called Domingo Angola who had fled from the jurisdiction of Zacatecas, and that she, having fled from her master, went to the village of Temimilcingo in the jurisdiction of Cuauhnahuac and there ran across him and was in his company for three months since last July; and in this time she saw many times this Negro Domingo talk to some little sticks or dolls dressed as men and others as women, and the sticks talked to him in the presence of everyone; and we heard that they were speaking in Spanish and in the Congo language and they did no less than dance the dances of both nations and sang songs of both nations, clearly and distinctly, so that all of us heard them; and the dolls asked for food; and food was carried to where they were, and after a little while they said; we have eaten, now you eat; and when it was time to steal they said, go it is time [propitious] to steal now, and when it was not time, and they were asked, they would say, now is not time. This darkie Moreno also had two snakes, one of which he took with him when he was going to steal, and the other was left in the house to guard the clothing and the Negro women. And once when I wanted to flee, the snake grabbed out for my foot and bit me as you can see by the mark it has left (which mark she showed us near the heel bone); and this witness continued to say that the other snake which he took along when he went to steal was of the same size and color as the one at home, about half a *vara* long and of two colors, yellow and black, and she heard say that the snake silenced them (the victims of the robbery?)."
From Archivo General de la Nación, Section on Inquisición, 486.254 (Tepoztlán, 1621). (Courtesy of Gonzalo Aguirre Beltrán.)

and had an interview with Emperor Maximilian at Acapantzingo to impress upon him the need for such education in Mexico. In 1878 Rojas was appointed secretary of the Department of Public Education of the state of Morelos by Francisco Leyva, the first constitutional governor of the state. Later Rojas returned to the village and published a newspaper in Náhuatl called "Xocoyotzin" (*El Menor*), and also a paper in Náhuatl and Spanish called *El Grano de Arena*. In the eighties he organized a chapter of the Lancaster Society, an educational society which had been making inroads in Mexico at the time. Rojas also had many personal contacts with President Porfirio Díaz, and in 1908 was appointed professor of Náhuatl at the National Museum of Archaeology.

Shortly before the Revolution, a small Museum of Antiquities was founded in Tepoztlán, a public library was opened, and night classes for adult education were held. This cultural florescence, though short-lived and limited to a small group of Tepoztecan intellectuals, most of whom came from well-to-do *cacique* families, earned for Tepoztlán the reputation of being the Athens of Morelos. This group of intellectuals had considerable influence despite their small number, and were instrumental in sending many young Tepoztecans to schools outside and in setting a precedent for higher education which has inspired Tepoztecans to this day.

A landmark in the history of the development of Tepoztlán was the building of the railroad in 1897 through the upper part of the municipio, with a station at El Parque—which is about an hour's climb from the village of Tepoztlán. The building of the railroad was opposed by most Tepoztecans, and set off a sharp struggle between the local *cacique*s and the population at large who accused the former of selling out the communal resources to the gringos. Despite this opposition, Tepoztecans participated in the benefits which came with the building of the railroad. Many of them worked as day laborers and received the then phenomenal wage of $1.50 a day, or well over three times the prevailing wages at haciendas. In addition there were hundreds of laborers from other villages, many of whom came down to Tepoztlán to buy supplies.

Trade flourished, and it is said that there were more stores and artisans in the village at that time than in the years between 1920 and 1930. This source of income, though temporary and favoring primarily the merchants, was one of the factors which contributed to the cultural florescence which was going on during this time. Tepoztecans came into contact with laborers from all over Mexico and with Americans. The first wire fencing and steel plows came into the village with the railroad, and the advent of freight trains stimulated the charcoal-making industry.

Tepoztlán is typical of another major current in Mexican history, the relationship and the struggles between the so-called free Indian villages and the haciendas. Because of the marginal location of Tepoztlán to the hacienda area, and because most of its lands were unsuitable for sugar and rice plantations, Tepoztlán managed to escape the aggrandizement of the haciendas, except for a portion of its southern lands which were lost to the Hacienda of Oacalco. But while Tepoztlán was able to retain most of its communal lands since the Conquest, it was close enough to the haciendas to serve as a convenient source of labor supply, and its economy was therefore intimately tied up with that of the hacienda system.

The Mexican Revolution of 1910-20 was a turning point in the history of Tepoztlán as well as of the nation, and was a major influence in breaking down any remaining isolation of the village. Tepoztlán was in the heart of Zapatista country, and few villages suffered greater upheavals. The village was alternately occupied by opposing Zapatista and federal forces recruited from all parts of the country, and both left their progeny in the village, further adding to the mixture of physical types. At one time or another during this period the entire population fled to the hills or to Mexico City, Guerrero, Puebla, and other parts of the country, and as a result there is a large proportion of adults who have lived outside of Tepoztlán.

The Revolution also brought about the overthrow of the ruling *cacique* group in Tepoztlán and a general lessening of social and economic class differences. The communal lands which had been under the control of local *caciques* were now freely available to all Tepoztecans. Furthermore, the municipio regained the land it had lost to a neighboring hacienda and thus participated in the benefits of the national *ejido* program. In addition, the Revolution has meant a general rise in the standard of living, the expansion of educational facilities, as well as a weakening of the older concepts of authoritarianism and a corresponding strengthening of democratic values.

Tepoztlán mirrors many national trends and brings into sharp focus some of the most pressing problems of Mexico as a nation. The changes which have occurred in Tepoztlán since the Revolution, such as the introduction of corn mills, the building of modern highways, and the establishment of bus service to Cuernavaca, are typical of changes that are taking place over wide areas throughout Mexico. The poor agricultural resources, the relative importance of forest and grazing lands in the agricultural economy, soil erosion and exhaustion, deforestation, the small size of both private and *ejido* landholdings, population pressure, and low productivity are among the problems which stand out in Tepoztlán as in the nation. One of the advantages of studying these problems within the framework of a single municipio and village is that we can better understand the inter-relationship between geographic, historic, economic, social, political, and psychological factors; and above all, it is possible to know better what these problems and changes mean to the people themselves.

It is important, also, to consider the ways in which Tepoztlán is distinctive. If we compare Tepoztlán with other villages in Mexico, rather than with the nation as a whole, we find that in many ways it is atypical. Tepoztlán is a large village, larger than ninety per cent of the villages of Mexico, making for a greater complexity of social organization. Tepoztlán has been a political and administrative center of the municipio since the Conquest and even under Moctezuma; it has retained its communal lands,[29] a long tradition of literacy, and a local intelligentsia

---

[29] Simpson, in connection with an otherwise excellent critique of Chase's romantic version of Tepoztlán, has written that Tepoztlán cannot be considered a "typical" Mexican village or municipio because, according to Helen Phipps (*Some Aspects of the Agrarian Question in Mexico —A Historical Study* (Austin: University of Texas Press, 1925), p. 120) it was the only village in the entire state of Morelos which maintained its communal lands. It seems to me that Phipps' statement is a considerable exaggeration. At least three of the municipios surrounding Tepoztlán did not lose all of their communal lands before the Revolution; their lands, like those

since the middle of the last century; specialized industries or handicrafts are absent or have disappeared; and it is situated not far from Mexico City. These are the facts that tend to differentiate Tepoztlán from many Mexican villages.

In the foregoing pages I have attempted to place Tepoztlán in the broader Mexican scene in terms of its geography, history, population trends, agrarian problems, and other aspects, and have pointed out in what ways Tepoztlán is representative of the nation as a whole. Obviously, in a country of such great diversity as Mexico it would be impossible to find any single village or municipio which would represent the entire range of variations and differences. Tepoztlán is not here presented as *the* synthesis of Mexico but rather as *one* synthesis.

---

of Tepoztlán, were not suitable for plantation purposes. This undoubtedly was also the case in many other mountainous areas in Mexico. On this basis I would be inclined to follow Tannenbaum's findings which indicate that in 1910 approximately 16 per cent of all villages and 51 per cent of all rural population could be classified as of the "free-village" type. (See Tannenbaum, *Mexican Revolution*, pp. 30-37.) Simpson, *The Ejido*, p. 36, considers this figure as a "considerable over-estimate." In any case, Tepoztlán would be typical of the free-village type.

part 1: THE VILLAGE AND ITS INSTITUTIONS_____

the setting: 1

THE VILLAGE of Tepoztlán is in the state of Morelos, about sixty miles south of Mexico City. It is connected by a paved road with the Mexico City–Cuernavaca highway and is fifteen miles northeast of Cuernavaca. The village forms part of the municipio of Tepoztlán which embraces an area of 60,000 acres and consists of eight villages: San Juan, Santo Domingo, Amatlán, Ixcatepic, Gabriel Mariaca, San Andrés, Santiago, and Tepoztlán proper. The northern section of the municipio coincides in part with the boundary line between the state of Morelos and the Federal District. (See Fig. 2.)

PHYSICAL ENVIRONMENT

The topography of the state of Morelos can be described as a sugar bowl, tilted to the southeast, with mountains forming the outer rim and the level, fertile lands of the sugar plantations forming the center. The municipio of Tepoztlán is on the northern rim of this bowl. It extends from the rugged, mountainous, and heavily wooded country in the north, down the slope of the Ajusco Mountain range to the level, fertile lands of the sugar plantation area near Yautepec. From the northern limits near Milpa Alta to the southern limits near Yautepec, a distance of about seventeen miles, there is a drop in altitude from about 10,500 feet [1] to about 3,700. While most of the villages tend to cluster near the center of the municipio (none are found in the extreme northern or southern portions), there is nevertheless a wide range in altitude among them. Indeed, the villages are located at seven different levels. The widest range is between San Juan in the north at about 7,000 feet, and San Andrés in the south at about 4,300 feet. But even in the case of Tepoztlán and San Juan, which are less than four miles apart, one is 2,000 feet above the other. (See Fig. 3.)

The northern part of the municipio is in *tierra fría* or the cold zone; the middle part is in *tierra templada* or the temperate zone; and the southern part is in *tierra*

---

[1] Otlayuca, the highest point in the northern portion of the municipio, is 3,151 meters or about 10,335 feet. See *Carta General del Estado de Morelos,* Secretaría de Fomento (Mexico, D.F., 1910).

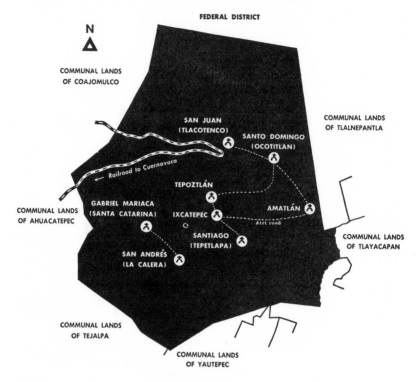

Fig. 2. Tepoztlán and surrounding municipios.

caliente or the hot zone. San Juan, the highest village, is at the lower limit of *tierra fría* while San Andrés, the lowest village, is at the upper limit of *tierra caliente*. Three of the villages, Tepoztlán proper, Ixcatepec, and Amatlán, are at approximately the same level within the temperate zone. Santo Domingo is about intermediate between the cold zone and the temperate zone, and Santiago is about intermediate between the hot zone and the temperate zone.

To the north of the village is the mountainous and heavily wooded area locally known as the monte, which constitutes approximately fifty per cent of the total area of the municipio. The predominant trees are pine, fir, oak, and madroña.[2] The monte with its forest constitutes the greatest single natural resource of the municipio. It has traditionally been the source of firewood, lumber, and charcoal; and, as we shall see later, the monte has been the subject of bitter inter-village

---

[2] The species of trees in the monte are as follows: oak or *encino* (*Quercus reticulata*), (*Quercus albocinato*), and (*Quercus Laurinea*); fir or *ayamel* (*Abies religiosa*); pine or *ocote*, (*Pinus patula*); *Cuaxochitl* (unidentified).

quarrels and many political struggles within the municipio and the village. Most of the monte is in *tierra fría*. Here the rainy season begins a few weeks earlier than in the lower regions, and the atmosphere is more humid because of the low hanging clouds. Here the soil is porous and unsuitable for adobe.

Most of the houses are therefore made of cane, straw, or wattle, and the majority of the roofs are made of wooden boards instead of tile as in Tepoztlán. Wooden boards are also put on the floor by those who can afford them for protection against the damp and cold. In the village of San Juan, which is in this region, corn is planted earlier, ripens later, and is less subject to the ravages of insects than in Tepoztlán

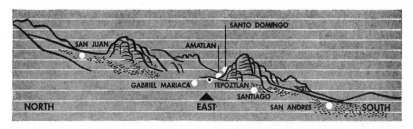

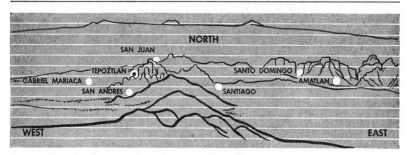

Fig. 3. Altitude of Tepoztlán and surrounding villages.

and the lower, warmer villages. Here there are no coffee trees, no hog plum, no banana, nor other tropical and semi-tropical fruits. But unlike the other villages, a little wheat, barley, lima beans, and some potatoes may be grown in San Juan. Also, *capulín, tejocote,* peaches, pears, and other fruits grow much better than in Tepoztlán and the lower villages. Furthermore, San Juan has no malaria.

The southern half of the municipio is divided into two parts by a ridgelike chain of hills or *cerros* which extends from the southern wall of the valley of Tepoztlán and continues south to divide the entire state of Morelos into its two major topographic regions, the valley of Cuernavaca and the valley of Amilpas. Within the municipio of Tepoztlán the large area of land to the west of this divide slopes gently to the southwest where it merges with the valley of Cuernavaca. This region contains the greater portion of the arable land of the municipio; and two villages, Gabriel Mariaca and San Andrés, are located here. Here, too, is the land known as *texcal,* an area covered with volcanic rock and a thorny scrub forest with a pre-dominating flora of copal gum, mimosalike legumes, a tree "sweet potato," and silk cotton trees.[3] *Texcal* covers a strip of land approximately two kilometers wide on the eastern limits of the municipio and constitutes about ten per cent of the total land area of the municipio. To the east of the divide is an area of rounded hills covered with scrub forest. These lands are known as *terrenos cerriles.* The predominating flora is *vera blanca, agualisca,* and scrub oak. Both the hill land and the land of the divide itself are used for grazing and for the planting of corn by the primitive cutting and burning method; and the trees from the cleared land are used for firewood. The villages of Santiago and Ixcatepec are located in the lower levels of this area, and the villages of Amatlán and Santo Domingo are found in pockets in the mountain chain which forms the eastern boundary of the municipio.

In viewing the land resources and types of land use in the municipio as a whole, we find there are five distinct types according to Tepoztecan categories: monte, *texcal, cerros, terrenos cerriles,* and *terrenos de temporal.* Each of these land types, with the exception of the *cerros,* plays an important role in the Tepoztecan econ-omy. Their distribution is shown in Fig. 4. The approximate area of each of these land types and their uses are shown in Table 1.

TABLE 1.   Tepoztecan Land Types and Land Uses.

Land Types	Land Uses	Percentage of Total Land Area of Municipio
Monte	Lumber, firewood, charcoal	45
Texcal	*Tlacolol* (hoe culture), firewood	10
Terrenos cerriles	Grazing, *tlacolol,* firewood	18
Cerros	Some grazing and *tlacolol* but mostly of no use	12
Terrenos de temporal	Plow agriculture	15
Total		100

The foregoing data are based on a survey made by the writer with the aid of Tepoztecan informants. A survey of the land resources of the municipio made by the Departamento Agrario in 1937 agrees quite closely with our own study (see Table 2), except that the categories used in classifying the lands are not those used by Tepoztecans.

It can be seen from Table 1 that the forest lands and grazing lands together ac-count for the largest portion of the lands of the municipio, approximately sixty-three per cent. The agricultural poverty of the municipio as well as of the village of Tepoztlán can be seen from the fact that only about fifteen per cent of the total land area is available for plow agriculture. Furthermore, most of the cultivable land is highly eroded and of poor productive quality. Tepoztecans distinguish three

---

[3] The flora of the *texcal* consists primarily of *huaje blanco—Leucaena* (Leguminosae); *copal—Elaphrium* (Burseraceae); *Casahuate—Ipomoea* (Convolvulaceae); and *palo mulato—Elaphrium* (Burseraceae).

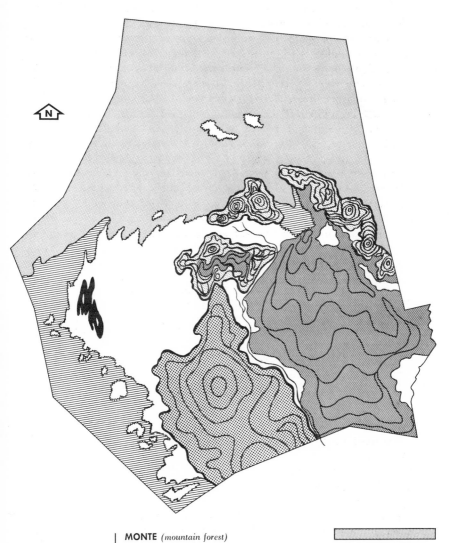

Fig. 4. Land-use map, municipio of Tepoztlán.

MONTE *(mountain forest)*

TEXCAL *(scrub forest on recent volcanic material)*

ROCAS *(buttes)*

CERROS *(scrub forest on steep hilly land)*

TERRENOS CERRILES *(scrub forest on rolling hills)*

TEPETATE *(highly eroded area)*

Area used in plow agriculture

types of categories of cultivable land according to productivity. The distribution of these land classes is shown in Fig. 5.

First-class land produces an average of about two *cargas* of corn on the cob for every *cuartillo* of seed planted. This is by far the best land, and it is located in the valley bottoms where seasonal streams bring down the rich fertilizing materials from the monte and forests. The soil on this land is dark brown to black. Less than five per cent of the land of plow agriculture is of this type. Second-class land produces on the average of one *carga* of corn on the cob for every *cuartillo* of seed planted. This land slopes more and is more eroded; it accounts for about forty-five per cent of the cultivable land.[4] The soils are sandier and vary from light brown to reddish. Third-class lands produce on the average of about one-half a *carga* of corn on the cob for every *cuartillo* of seed planted, and account for another forty-five per cent of the cultivable land. These lands have the steepest slope and are the most eroded. It is on these lands that rock terraces, said to be of pre-Conquest times, are used to prevent the complete washing away of the soils. The soil on this land is yellowish and very stony. Frequently the rock-bottom *tepetate* is only a few inches from the surface. (See Fig. 6.)

TABLE 2.   Land types and areas according to agrarian Census of 1937.

Land Types	Areas (in Hectares)	Percentage of Total Land Area of Municipio
Monte Alto	11,400	44.0
Monte Bajo	5,750	22.0
En cerril accidental inútil para la agricultura	3,010	11.0
Terrenos de temporal de primero	675	3.8
Terrenos de temporal de segundo y tercero	5,075	19.1
Total	25,910	

From the foregoing materials we can see that the municipio of Tepoztlán is not a single natural or geographic unit.[5] Hills and mountains break it up and form barriers between the villages. Thus Tepoztlán is separated from the village of San Juan to the north by one group of hills and from San Andrés to the southwest by another. Sahto Domingo, to the southeast of Tepoztlán, is nestled high up in a pocket in the mountain wall and is more or less isolated from all the other villages of the municipio. Only three of the villages, Ixcatepec, Santiago, and Tepoztlán proper, are located within a single valley and drained by the same stream. The re-

---

[4] Although there is some evidence in early sixteenth-century documents examined by the writer which points to a greater productivity of the land at that time, it is interesting to note that the description of the lands of the municipio in the first land title of 1548 describes the lands as rocky, sterile, and ill suited for agriculture. Furthermore, the greater portion of the lands was described as "sitios de ganado menor" and "sitios de ganado mayor" which may indicate that the Spaniards viewed the land resources of Tepoztlán as best suited for grazing.

[5] Redfield's references to the municipio as "a natural community" and as a "valley community" tend to give the municipio a geographic unity which it does not in fact have. Redfield, *Tepoztlán*, p. 59.

Fig. 5. Land classes, municipio of Tepoztlán.

FIRST-CLASS LAND
SECOND-CLASS LAND
THIRD-CLASS LAND

maining villages must depend upon springs which in some cases are a mile distant. The fact that the municipio has existed for hundreds of years as a political and social entity in the face of this lack of geographic unity raises interesting questions which will be discussed later.

THE VILLAGE

Centrally located within the municipio, and nestled in a broad alluvial valley surrounded by hills and massive rock outcroppings of fantastic and beautiful for-

Fig. 6. Rock terrace in Tepoztlán.

mations, lies the village of Tepoztlán.[6] (See Fig. 7.) These hills and rock out-croppings constitute two fairly well defined units. One begins just north of the village and curves toward the southeast, reaching to the neighboring municipio of Tlayacapan, a distance of about fifteen miles. The other begins just south of the village and extends to the east for a short distance to form the southern wall of the valley of Tepoztlán. The valley runs northwest-southeast and then turns directly south. The upper or northwestern end of the valley is considerably narrower than the lower end. The valley is drained by a small perennial stream locally known as the Río Atenco, which flows through the village and then turns east and south where it flows into the Yautepec River which in turn joins the Balsas River.

The spectacular peaks and buttes of the rock outcroppings which rise to 1,200 feet above the village are locally known as *cerros* and are important landmarks to the people of Tepoztlán. Each *cerro* is known by its Náhuatl name and has an ancient legend associated with it. Among the more important *cerros* are *El Tlahuitepetl*

---

[6] In the early sixteenth-century documents Tepoztlán is called "Tepuztlan." Writers on the history of the village have suggested that the term is derived from the Náhuatl *tepoztli* (iron) and *tlan* (abundance); that is, Tepoztlán means "place of abundant iron." But there are no iron deposits in Tepoztlán, nor is there evidence of any in the past. More recently, Muller has suggested another interpretation which would seem to be more in accord with all the facts. She suggests that Tepoztlán is the Hispanicized version of the older Nahua term *Tepoztectla,* which means "place of the broken rocks." This is derived from *tetl* (rock) and *postectli* (broken), and is an accurate description of the village site. Muller claims that some of the early chroniclers used this term for Tepoztlán. There would still remain the problem of explaining the use of a copper ax as the glyph for Tepoztlán in the Codex Mendocino. It may be that this glyph was used because they had no other way of showing broken rock. Certainly copper axes may have been imported by the village.

(peak of light), *El Ehecatepetl* (peak of air), *El Cihuapapolotzin* (peak of the butterfly), *El Tlamintepetl* (peak of the wounded), *El Chalchitepetl* (peak of the treasure), and *El Ocelotepetl* (peak of the tiger). One of these *cerros* has been an important archaeological site since 1895, when a stone temple of a Tepoztecan deity was unearthed. This temple and the great scenic beauty of the village has attracted many tourists in recent years.

The *cerros* which surround the village form a natural fortress, and the rugged hilly country of which they are a part has served as a refuge from attack at various times in the history of Tepoztlán and is ideally suited for guerrilla warfare. According to ancient Tepoztecan legend the *cerros* served as defensive outposts against hostile peoples long before the Conquest. When the Spaniards first came to the village in 1521, Tepoztecans fled to the *cerros;* and more recently during the Revolution of 1910-20, when Tepoztlán was the scene of intermittent guerrilla warfare between Zapatista and federal soldiers, Tepoztecans again sought refuge in the *cerros.*

The location of Tepoztlán in an intermediate position between *tierra fría* and *tierra caliente* gives it the advantages of an excellent climate and a rich semi-tropical flora without the disadvantages of the cold to the north or the tropical heat to the south. Tepoztecans are aware of these advantages and consider themselves

Fig. 7. Tepoztlán, seen from cliffs to the north.

fortunate in this respect. Tepoztlán is just above the malaria area, and although some malaria occurs it is generally contracted by Tepoztecans who have been working in the lowlands. The climate of Tepoztlán is one of the most healthful in the state of Morelos, and Tepoztlán has one of the lowest death rates in the state.

The average annual temperature for the village is about 65° F. However, there are marked daily and seasonal variations. In the rainy season mornings are usually humid and cool but by midday the temperature is up to 65°. The evenings are cool. During the months of November, December, and January the nights and early mornings are much colder, and the temperature drops to 35° to 40°. The cold works hardships on the people because of the lack of warm clothing. However, even during these months the temperature rises to 65° and 70° by midday. At no time does the temperature rise above 80°. While it gets hot in the open fields under the sun, it is generally comfortable in the village because of the many shade trees on almost every house site. The daily variations in temperature and humidity are partially responsible for the high frequency of rheumatic complaints and respiratory diseases.

The rainy season begins toward the end of May or early June and generally lasts to mid-October.[7] The average annual rainfall in the village is about 60 inches, most of which comes during the five months from June to October. In June and July the rains generally come in the afternoon and last for a few hours. During these months the working day in the fields ends at about 2:00 P.M. In August and September the rains generally begin later in the afternoon and frequently last through the night. However, there is much variation within this general pattern. Although droughts are not uncommon, excessive rainfall is the more common complaint. Sometimes Tepoztecans cannot cultivate their crops with plow and oxen because of the mud.

The crucial months for the corn crop are August and September when the ears of corn are filling out. The occasional lack of rain during these months is attributed by some of the older folks to the failure of the dancers, at the fiesta in honor of the deity El Tepozteco, to carry out correctly the traditional ceremonies. The coexistence of pagan and Catholic elements in beliefs concerning rain is shown by the fact that the saints of the central church, as well as those of the barrios, are taken in procession through the village to pray for rain when necessary. Hailstorms occur in the rainy season but they are generally brief. It is a common belief among Tepoztecans that the setting off of firecrackers or the shooting of guns will stop the hail.

The dry season begins in October or November and lasts for seven long months. The earth becomes parched and many of the semi-deciduous trees lose their leaves. Water must be hauled in greater quantities for the animals, the flowers, and the young trees on the house sites. Winds from the north cause small dust storms in the village and sometimes damage the ripening corn. Respiratory diseases are more frequent during this time of the year. Because of the dry season, only one crop a

---

[7] See Redfield, *Tepoztlán,* p. 121, for description of the rains.

year can be grown in Tepoztlán. Lack of water for irrigation is one of the most frequent complaints. Tepoztecans speak of the irrigated farming area of nearby Yautepec, where a few crops a year are grown, as an agricultural paradise.

A rich semi-tropical flora grows in the village. On almost any house site a great variety of plants and trees are found. The more common ones are *papaya,* coffee, *ciruela* (hog plum), *guaje, aguacate, chayote, mango,* banana, *maguey,* and some prickly pear. Most families grow a variety of flowers and herbs which are used for cooking and as medicines.

Like the municipio, the village of Tepoztlán is located on a slope (Fig. 8) and the resulting diversity of topography and climate noted for the municipio is also

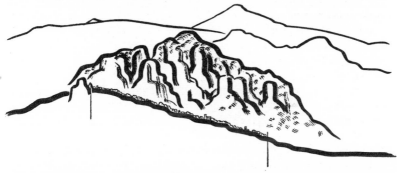

Fig. 8. Tepoztlán lies on a steep incline.

characteristic of the village itself, except that the contrasts are less sharp. The upper part of the village is steeper, rockier, and somewhat cooler; the lower part is warmer and, being closer to the surrounding hills and better watered, has a richer flora and more abundant growth of *ciruela* and coffee trees. The incline runs from the northwest to the southeast, for the northern or upper part of the village is several hundred feet higher than the southern part.

The streets running north and south slope steeply. During the rainy season these streets are often converted into cascading streams which rush, knee-deep, downward toward the center. To avoid erosion many streets are stone-paved and terraced. The Aztec system of terracing by means of an ascending series of platforms and inclines is still conserved. (See Fig. 9.) However, many streets, particularly those in the outlying barrios, are neither paved nor terraced and are turned into slippery mud-holes or badly eroded gorges by the rains. Other streets are rough, boulder-strewn pathways which must be climbed rather than walked; still others are covered with weeds and scattered stones and resemble dried-out stream beds more than streets. (See Fig. 10.) The streets running east and west also tend to be hilly and irregular because of the streams, arroyos, and gorges which cut across the village. Only the paved road and the plaza in the center are on a more or less level plane.

The village is large, spread out, and roughly rectangular in shape. (See Fig. 11.) It is approximately two kilometers in length and one and one-half in width. Al-

Fig. 9. Terrace street, Aztec style.

though the village contains 662 house sites, it does not have the compact or crowded appearance of some Mexican towns. For the most part, the houses are separated from each other by gardens, patios, corrals, and sometimes milpas. These are enclosed by low-lying stone walls which do not block the view from the street and which permit overhanging trees to shade the street. Only a few houses in the center are built contiguously in Spanish style and are enclosed by high, concealing walls.

Tepoztlán has the traditional square plaza around which are grouped the more important public buildings. On one side of the plaza is the small public park, complete with bandstand, shade trees, benches, and brick walks. The paved road, which runs along the other side of the park, ends at this point, and here, too, is the last stop on the bus line.

North of the park is the courthouse which houses the office of the president, secretary, and other local officials. A guard in soldier's uniform is frequently seen pacing up and down before the steps. The new school house was built next to the courthouse and is now one of the important edifices of the center. Between these two buildings and the plaza itself is the Portales, a semi-enclosed street where most of the stores and permanent vending places are located. The street has a roof supported by columns and provides merchants and buyers protection from the sun and

Fig. 10. A street, resembling a dried-out stream bed.

rain. To the east is the large cathedral and convent, the most imposing and hand-some buildings in the village. The convent is now a historical monument and is visited by tourists. Between the cathedral and the plaza is a row of whitewashed, flat-roofed stores. West of the plaza is a dirt road leading to the lower part of the village, to the cemetery, and to the village of Ixcatepec and more stores. The mills and some of the finer old houses of former *caciques* are also located on the plaza.

This part of the village presents the appearance and some of the hustle and bustle of a town, but the streets off the center are uniformly quiet and rustic and stamp Tepoztlán as a rural village. (See Fig. 12.) But even the center does not give the impression of an active, thriving community. The park, plaza, and public buildings show evidence of chronic neglect. Only for the annual Carnaval is the area well swept and the main fountain cleaned. The park is seldom occupied by the native population and, except when there are tourists, usually looks abandoned.

The stores are small and dark and have unattractive displays. On market days the few vendors and the small variety of goods available betray little commercial activity and a general air of decline. (See Fig. 13.)

The streets just off the plaza bear names indicated by placards. As is customary in Mexico the street names commemorate important historical events and outstand-ing local figures. Thus in Tepoztlán we find such street names as The Fifth of May, Aniceto Villamar, and No Reelección.[8] Only those houses in the center are

---

[8] Some of the street names are in Náhuatl and refer to pre-Hispanic figures, for example, Avenida del Tepozteco and Netzahualcoyotl.

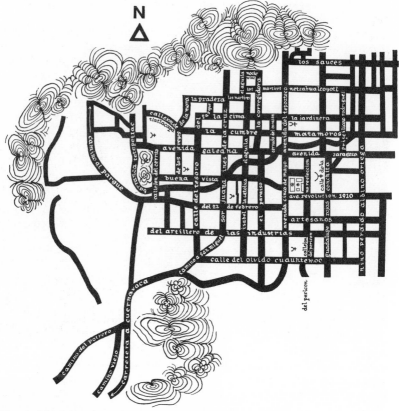

Fig. 11. Tepoztlán, showing streets, plaza, and barrio chapels.

numbered, but not in any systematic manner. Street names and house numbers are not used by the local population nor do they appear on letters addressed to the villagers from the outside. Since mail remains in the post office until called for, this does not present a problem.

At night the village appears even less sophisticated than during the day because of the lack of public street lighting. When there is no moon it is difficult, even dangerous, to walk through the rough streets without a flashlight or candle. Normally only young men venture out at night. Most people retire early, and the streets are dark and quiet. During the day the village also tends to be quiet, but many sounds can be heard: voices from within the houses, children crying or playing, housewives slapping tortillas into shape, people and animals walking over the stones, church bells, buses honking and racing loudly along the main thoroughfare, and an occasional lone peddler crying his wares. At night the only sounds heard are the serenades of romantic youths, an occasional drunken peasant being taken home, and the animals.

Drinking water is supplied by a spring in one of the surrounding hills. The water is carried to street fountains by iron pipes which were first laid in 1902. Every barrio except San Pedro has one or more of these fountains. In the large barrios, fountains are placed at strategic street corners and are more numerous. In all there

Fig. 12. The end of the main street, Tepoztlán.

are twenty-six public fountains in the village. Most of them are made of clay and cement; some are semi-enclosed and protected by a roof, generally topped by a cross; others are merely open tanks. (See Fig. 14.)

A few homes near the center have water piped directly into their patios or kitchens. For this privilege a small tax is paid to the municipio. There is no attempt to control private use of the public water supply, and this has in the past caused some conflict. In several instances, persons with a private water supply permit relatives, friends, or *compadres* to take as much water as they wish; sometimes a neighbor will connect his water pipe to that of another, thus avoiding the tax. This uncontrolled use sometimes greatly decreases the flow of water into the nearest public fountain, particularly during the dry season when water is scarce. There have been

Fig. 13. The market place, Tepoztlán.

Fig. 14. Public fountain, Tepoztlán.

occasions when groups of angry residents, headed by a political leader, have broken into houses to cut off the private water supply that was draining the public one.

THE BARRIOS

The village is divided into seven barrios or named locality groupings, each with its own church, patron saint, and internal religious organization.[9] (See Fig. 15.) The barrios of today are essentially religious organizations, but also have important social functions. Redfield believed the barrios were pre-Hispanic survivals of the ancient *calpulli,* an interpretation to be questioned in the light of our data. He wrote:

The *barrio* is plainly recognizable as the pre-Columbian *calpolli.* From the accounts we have of the social organization of Tenochtitlan (Mexico City) and of Texcoco, it

Fig. 15. The barrios of Tepoztlán.

appears that each *pueblo* in the Nahua area was divided into units which bore this name. These units were originally, it has been supposed, based on kinship, but at the time of the Conquest, in Tenochtitlan at least, the kinship tie had largely disappeared, and the *calpolli* was a local unit. Each had its own god, religious structure, courts and judges, and military organization; and the members of each *calpolli* owned in common lands apart and distinct from the lands of the other *calpolli.*

With the destruction of the tribal organization following the Conquest, the military,

[9] In the following pages I have listed *eight* barrios rather than *seven,* because families on twenty-nine house sites in the barrio of Santo Domingo think of themselves as a separate unit owing allegiance to the barrio of Santa Cruz. I have therefore treated these twenty-nine house sites as a separate unit and have referred to them as Santa Cruz (small) in distinction to Santa Cruz (large), since Santa Cruz is the barrio to which they pay taxes.

political, and judicial functions of the *calpolli* fell into desuetude. But the social and re-ligious functions, conflicting with none of the Spanish forms, and coinciding in some measure with the current Spanish notion of a church parish, continued in Tepoztlán, as no doubt in other *pueblos*, to this day.[10]

The evidence cited by Redfield in support of this speculation is a portion of a recitation in Náhuatl which reads, "Here I am surrounded by my four mountains, seven hills, seven wells and seven stony hillsides." From this Redfield concludes, "This is clearly a reference, in topographic terms, to the *barrios*." [11] This interpre-tation is not acceptable, since the seven barrios are not each associated with a stony hillside. Nor does each barrio have its own well.

While there can be no doubt that the village is pre-Hispanic, I believe that the present-day layout with its barrio divisions is almost certainly post-Conquest. This conclusion is based primarily upon an analysis of sixteenth-century documents in which the seven barrios are not mentioned, and is partially confirmed by local tradition and some recent archaeological work. These sources suggest that before the Spanish Conquest the village was much more spread out, with numerous small population clusters settled along the valley near the *cerros* where there was an adequate water supply. In a document of 1580,[12] we find that the seat of the village was at a site called *Tetlán*, a site which is known today as being outside of the village limits, to the west. When the road to Cuernavaca was being built in 1935 and 1936, ceramic deposits and other evidence of habitation were unearthed at this spot. In the map (Fig. 16), I have located a number of sites which show some evi-dence of having been inhabited and which are believed to be pre-Hispanic settle-ment sites. Some of these sites are mentioned in a document of 1550 which gives the *sitios* and *estancias* which paid tribute to Tepoztlán. I have identified many of these house site names within the village today, but others are known only as the names of sites out in the fields and near the *cerros* as shown in Fig. 16. Still others could not be identified at all.

On the basis of this evidence, it is suggested that the Spaniards brought together the population clusters from the outlying settlements to control the people and to facilitate taxation.[13] That this was a general Spanish policy is clear from other sources.[14] A few informants felt certain that this is what had happened in

[10] Redfield, *Tepoztlán*, pp. 76–77.

[11] *Ibid.*, p. 72.

[12] Francisco del Paso y Troncoso, *Relación de la Villa de Tepuztlan* in *Papeles de Nueva España*, Segunda Serie, Geografía y Estadística, Tomo VI (Madrid, 1905), p. 244—this valuable document will be referred to as *Relación* in the pages that follow. It is one of our best sources for the culture of Tepoztlán prior to the Spanish Conquest. It was prepared in 1580 by village officials with the aid of Tepoztecan informants, in response to a questionnaire sent out to all villagers of New Spain by Philip II.

[13] In a document—*Hospital de Jesús*, Leg. 289, Exp. 100—dated March 2, 1551, we find a complaint, made by an investigator sent to Tepoztlán, to the effect that there were still some outlying "barrios" not listed in the Tepoztlán census. It was explained that this was done by the natives to cheat the government of taxes.

[14] See Dan Stanislowski, "Early Spanish Town Planning in the New World," *Geographical Review*, 37 (1947), 94-105.

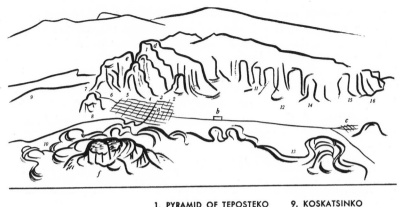

	1. PYRAMID OF TEPOSTEKO	9. KOSKATSINKO
a. **Tepoztlan**	2. TLAKWAPA	10. TEKWESKONTITLA
b. **Cementerio**	3. AXITLA	11. MEETSTITLA
c. **Ixcatepec**	4. MAKPALOSTOK	12. TEXKATSO
d. **Tlawiltepetl**	5. TENECHKALKO	13. TLAXOMOLKO
e. **Ocelotsin**	6. TLATLAKAPA	14. TEMASATITLA
f. **Chachitepetl**	7. TEXOHKO	15. ACHICHIPIKO
	8. TEOPANSOLKO	16. MESOHKILA

Fig. 16. Possible sites of pre-Hispanic settlements.

Tepoztlán and suggested some of the settlement sites from which the present-day barrios were formed.

The *Relación* describes the village in some detail and gives the names and legends associated with each of the villages of the municipio, but it says nothing of barrios within the village itself. In fact none of the sixteenth-century documents mention the present-day barrios. However, in a document of 1579 [15] there is mention of four barrios of Tepoztlán: Atenco, Teycapan, Olac, and Pochitlán. These are listed as separate from the "capital" or Tepoztlán proper, suggesting that they were settlements outside of the village which were later incorporated into the village.[16] Atenco is identified by informants as the present-day barrio of Santo Domingo. The other barrios could not be identified by our informants but they are mentioned repeatedly in the early documents, appearing for the first time in a document dated 1551.[17]

[15] *Indios*, Vol. 1, Exp. 251.

[16] This interpretation is also suggested by documents which make it clear that the term "barrio" was used to designate a settlement outside of the village which did not have independent status. For the latter they used "estancia." A plaque in the church of the outlying village of Ixcatepec tells that the village was a "barrio" of Tepoztlán until 1732 when the church was built and an independent community established.

[17] *Hospital de Jesús*, Leg. 289, Exp. 100. The fact that *four* barrios are mentioned is particularly significant, for it agrees with the account of Durán and other chroniclers who describe the early Nahua tribes as being divided into four units. The four barrios, rather than the present-day barrios, may well have been the ancient *calpulli*.

The first mention of some of the present-day barrios is found in a document of 1807, which is a census of the villages by barrios and by house sites within each barrio.[18] The fact that the barrios of San Sebastián and San Pedro are not mentioned suggests that these two are the most recent additions. This is also in accord with a vague local tradition. Unfortunately the barrio chapels do not carry any dates. The census of 1807 is especially useful in that it gives the names of the house sites in Náhuatl and thereby makes possible a comparison of the house sites with those found today, since they are still known by the same names. The remarkable discovery that results from such a comparison is that the barrio boundaries have not changed much in the past 150 years. The major difference is that the present-day house sites are much smaller, probably reflecting the process of division by inheritance. From all of the foregoing it seems probable that the present-day barrios, with their churches, were built up gradually during the seventeenth and eighteenth centuries, and that two of the barrio chapels were built in the nineteenth century.

During the colonial period the barrio must have been an extremely important unit in the social organization of the village, since it served both as a politico-administrative unit as well as a religious unit. From the document of 1579, we learn that each barrio had its own *tequitlatos* (officials who spoke for the barrio) and *alguaciles*. It is possible that the *tequitlatos* were leaders of labor groups who were recruited in the *repartimiento* system on a barrio basis. Before the separation of church and state, the assignment of the village *cuatequitl* must have been done on a barrio basis. The barrio lost some of its functions after the time of Juárez when the village was divided up into eight *demarcaciones* (political wards), each with a delegate responsible to the local government. The *demarcaciones* cut across barrios. Since that time the *demarcación* rather than the barrio is used in organizing local census data, in assigning labor tasks for the village *cuatequitl,* in making public announcements, and in organizing elections. But despite the loss of some of its functions, the barrio continues to have great religious and social importance. The barrio is considered as an old and native institution, the *demarcación* as something imposed from the outside. Any school child knows his barrio, but very few adults or children know what *demarcación* they belong to.

The barrio names and the number of house sites by barrio are shown in the following:

TABLE 3. Number of Barrios and House Sites, 1944.

Barrio	House Sites
Santo Domingo	174
San Miguel	163
La Santísima	139
Santa Cruz (large)	67
Los Reyes	37
San Sebastián	34
Santa Cruz (small)	29
San Pedro	19
Total	662

[18] *Ibid.*, Leg. 356, Exp. 8.

With the exception of Santa Cruz (small) which, strictly speaking, is not an independent barrio but is about to become one, there are three large barrios: Santo Domingo, La Santísima, and San Miguel; and four smaller ones: Santa Cruz, Los Reyes, San Sebastián, and San Pedro. While topographic factors have played some role in fixing barrio boundaries, the larger barrios are grouped around the central plaza and the smaller ones are located above these on the ascending slope. However, the outer portions of the larger barrios are almost as distant from the center of the village as is the barrio of San Pedro. Since the entire village is built on a slope, the smaller barrios are called "los de arriba" and the larger ones "los de abajo."

Some Tepoztecans now use the road as a convenient dividing line between the upper and lower portions of the village. But the road cuts through the three larger barrios. The boundaries of the barrios are not always clearly defined, and we found considerable disagreement among informants concerning the limits. "Sometimes a boundary runs in the middle of a street and sometimes the houses on both sides pertain to the same *barrio,* the boundary then running just behind a row of houses. Occasionally there are irregular jogs which take a few houses out of a block and include them in another *barrio.* A whole block of houses, geographically in San Miguel, belong to the *barrio* of Santa Cruz, although almost at the opposite end of the town." [19]

Barrio membership is primarily determined by the ownership of a house site in a barrio and the payment of the tax for the upkeep of the barrio. In this fashion, barrio stability is assured despite the considerable changes in residence which occur in the village. For it is the house site that traditionally belongs to one barrio or another, and whoever lives on it, whether he obtained it by inheritance or purchase, becomes a member of that barrio. In most cases a person belongs to the barrio in which he was born and raised. However, a man who was born and raised in the barrio of San Pedro may purchase a site in Santa Cruz and establish his home there. If he pays his tax and participates in the affairs of the barrio he automatically becomes a member of Santa Cruz. He may, for reasons of sentiment, continue to support his barrio of origin and will probably also attend the barrio fiesta of San Pedro, since many of his relatives will still be there. But this is voluntary. Since patrilocal residence after marriage predominates, the men of any barrio are generally more closely related than the women. A woman upon marriage becomes a member of her husband's barrio. However, women, more than men, maintain cross-barrio loyalties; they help their relatives in the barrio of origin to prepare the fiesta.

It should be noted that some persons own house sites in two or three barrios. In these cases they must pay the tax in each but participate in the religious and social life of the barrio in which they reside or where they were raised and born. Widows, as heads of families, pay the tax on their house sites and are considered as members in the barrio of their house site. Young couples sometimes buy a house

---

[19] Redfield, *Tepoztlán,* p. 70.

site in a barrio to which neither spouse belongs and thereby acquire membership in a barrio new to both of them.

Each barrio elects a *mayordomo* who is in charge of barrio affairs. To be eligible for *mayordomo* one must be a native of the village, a member of the barrio and a married man, though exceptions to the latter are known. A reputation for honesty and a willingness to serve the barrio are of course essential. The position of *mayordomo* is one that takes a lot of time and expense. As a rule the rich families do not seek this position, though there may be some pressure upon them to accept. Normally the *mayordomo* is elected for one year, but during recent years there has been a paucity of candidates, especially in the smaller barrios, and some *mayordomo*s have had to serve for as long as five years at a time. Recently the barrio of San Sebastián had to get a member of the adjoining barrio of San Miguel for a *mayordomo* because they could find no one within the barrio who wanted the job. The election for *mayordomo* takes place the evening before the Day of the Dead, when the barrio members meet in the churchyard. Only the men participate. A bonfire is made, punch is served, and likely candidates are briefly discussed. A few speeches in Náhuatl may be made and the *mayordomo* is selected by mutual agreement. There is no formal voting. Barrio elections come the closest to truly democratic processes in the village. The elections are not controlled by the priest of the central church.

The incumbent receives from the former *mayordomo* a list of the contributors of the barrio, the key to the church and to the trunk or chest where the religious objects and ornaments are kept. Some of the more valuable jewels are entrusted by the *mayordomo* to a barrio member *de confianza*. The *mayordomo* also receives the funds of the barrio. Most barrios have a fund of a few hundred pesos. In 1943 Los Reyes had 150 pesos and Santo Domingo had 450 pesos.

The *mayordomo* is responsible for the collection of *limosnas,* the organization of the barrio *cuatequitl* or collective labor for the upkeep of the chapel, the preparation and organization of the barrio fiesta, and the maintenance of the church. To do all of this he appoints assistant *mayordomos* and committees who are responsible to him. The *mayordomo* has no authority beyond his personal appeal and prestige. During the twenties when the Cristeros attacked the village, the *mayordomos* organized defense corps for the protection of the barrio chapels.

The most important role of the barrio is religious and social. The barrio saint is a symbol of the collective spirit of the barrio, and the barrio organization—with its *mayordomos,* collective labor on the communally owned plot of land, and the annual barrio fiesta—acts as a unifying influence. This aspect of the barrio was well described by Redfield and, except for a few changes, still holds today.

But it is at the time of the fiesta that the collective importance of the *barrio* members reaches its highest importance, and the chapel becomes the great focus of interest for the entire *pueblo* and even for neighboring villages. The decoration of the chapel, the ceremonial bringing of the candles, the burning of the candles, the erection and burning of the *castillo,* the preparation and consumption of festal dishes, the playing of the ancient flute or the *teponaztli* on the roof of the chapel, one or more sacred dances and sometimes *toros*—all constitute a program of ritual and entertainment which occupies from one to seven days. Although members of other *barrios* take part in the entertainment, the *barrio* whose *santo* is celebrated acts as host, and its members very much feel their collective importance.[20]

Barrio *esprit de corps* is also reflected in the inter-barrio competition, especially at the Carnaval, in the claims of superior miraculousness of some barrio saints as over against others, and in the traditional nicknames of each of the barrios. More recently, the soccer teams were organized on an inter-barrio basis, but this did not last.

Yet it would be easy to overestimate the strength of this *esprit de corps*[21] and the differences between the barrios. For example, Redfield wrote:

The *barrios* have, indeed, obviously different cultures, or what is the same thing, different personalities. The varying characteristics of the *barrios* are recognized by the Tepoztecans themselves, and at least the more reflective of them can express the differences they feel. Thus, Santo Domingo is the most civilized *barrio* and the most patriotic (i.e., most nearly conscious of national feeling). . . . Santa Cruz is strongly primitive —Catholic, exclusive, and independent. . . . San Pedro is a *barrio* of poor, illiterate people who preserve to a marked extent ancient mentality and resent the presence of outsiders in their midst. . . .[22]

The consciousness of *barrio* personalities receives an expression in names which are applied to the *barrios*. These names are in Náhuatl and are in every case names of animals. The names are

Santo Domingo	Cacame [Toads]
La Santísima	Tzicame [Ants]
San Miguel	Techihehicame [Lizards]
Santa Cruz and San Sebastián	Tapemaxtlame [*Cacomixtles*]
Los Reyes	Metzalcuanime [Maguey Worms]
San Pedro	Tlacuatzitzin [*Tlacuaches*] [23]

This account does not describe present-day conditions as observed by the informants and me, and would seem to be a considerable exaggeration of barrio differences even for 1926. At best it would perhaps apply to conditions before 1900 when barrio differences were greater. Barrio nicknames were remembered by our informants, but they are rarely used and have little function in the life of the community. We were also told that a man's barrio could be determined by small differences in dress or manner, but we could observe no such differences, nor were they explained to us. This is not to deny the existence of some barrio differences. It is true, for example, that Santa Cruz has the reputation of being the

[20] *Ibid.*, p. 78.
[21] Some of the symptoms of weakness are the very poor turnout of barrio members for the planting and harvesting of the barrio milpa, the lack of candidates willing to serve as *mayordomo*, and the renting out of the barrio milpas on a cash basis.
[22] *Ibid.*, p. 80.
[23] *Ibid.*, p. 81.

most religious and conservative and, according to our study of wealth distribution, it is also the poorest. This does not justify Redfield's statement that the barrios have "obviously different cultures," or that "the members of a barrio tend to think and act alike." Indeed, the absence of distinct barrio traditions was striking. No one could be found who knew the history of his barrio. No one knew when the barrio chapel had been built or when the milpa of the chapel had been obtained.

During the Díaz regime, the distinction between the larger and smaller barrios in terms of those of the center and those of the periphery corresponded in some degree to class distinction, since most of the well-to-do *caciques* and merchants lived in the center. Strictly speaking, however, even this distinction was not accurate, since all the larger barrios had their share of the poor and illiterate; and, as we have already seen, parts of the larger barrios are almost as far from the plaza as the most distant smaller ones.

The general tendency since the Revolution, especially during the past twenty years, has been the diminishing of barrio differences. Today an approximately equal distribution of well-to-do and acculturated families are to be found in all the barrios. In fact, Los Reyes, one of the smaller barrios, showed the highest proportion of landholding families. The various barrios now participate much more equally in village life. The distribution of services is no longer limited to the center. By 1943 there were about ten small stores and a few barber shops scattered among the barrios. Similarly, in contrast to Redfield's finding in 1926 that no letters went to the outlying barrios, San Pedro and Los Reyes now receive their share of the mail. It is also doubtful whether there are at present any significant differences in literacy on a barrio basis. Today the contacts between the outlying barrios and the outside is much less mediated through the center. We discovered just as large a percentage of young people from the smaller barrio as from the larger who have gone to study outside of the village. And certainly Redfield's characterization—the smaller as barrios of *tontos,* the larger as barrios of *correctos*—does not apply now.[24]

POPULATION

Tepoztlán had a population of 3,230 according to the Mexican Federal Census of 1940. In 1942 a local census of the village taken by schoolteachers and officials showed a population of 3,517, and by 1947 the population was well over four thousand. It is apparent that the Tepoztecan population, like that of Mexico as a whole, is increasing rapidly.

SIZE AND GROWTH

While we have no exact data on the size of the Tepoztecan population at the time of the Conquest, there is evidence which suggests that it was considerably larger than the present-day population and in fact larger than at any time since the Conquest. The earliest materials from which a reliable population estimate can

---

[24] For a critical discussion of Redfield's distinction between *tontos* and *correctos,* see Chapter 21, "Summary and Conclusions," p. 430.

be made date back to about forty years after the Conquest and are found in an unpublished document in the archives of the Indies, cited by Cook and Simpson in their recent study of population changes in central Mexico.[25] These writers give the tribute value for Tepoztlán for 1560 and 1567 as 1,150 and 2,718½ pesos, respectively. Since the assessment at this time was one peso per family head, it is possible to calculate the population. The figure for 1567 is taken as the more reliable one by Cook and Simpson, who point out that the earlier figure was purposely depressed by the Marqués del Valle and his agents to rob the Crown of income.[26] Following the procedure of these same authors in assuming four as the average size of a family, we find that Tepoztlán had a total population of 10,874 in about 1567.[27] This population of 10,874 must refer to the municipio as a whole, rather than to the village of Tepoztlán proper, because it was customary at the time to include the surrounding villages as tributaries of Tepoztlán. But even so, it is the highest figure for Tepoztecan population that has ever been recorded. If we were to judge Tepoztlán by the findings of Cook and Simpson, which indicate that the population of central Mexico as a whole declined by sixty per cent from 1519 to 1570, then the pre-Conquest population of Tepoztlán would have to be put at over 17,000. However, this seems improbable, considering the limited natural resources of the municipio of Tepoztlán.[28] In all probability the decline in the Tepoztecan population during the first forty years after the Conquest was not nearly as great as in other parts of this area, for Tepoztlán suffered no military losses from the Conquest itself, and it was not until the middle thirties and forties that they began to feel seriously the impact of Spanish rule. As we shall see, the large population losses in Tepoztlán occurred later.

Our next bit of evidence on population is found in the work of López de Velasco[29] for the years 1571-73, when Tepoztlán is said to have had 2,600 tributaries, which would give it a population of 10,400. Although Velasco specifically writes of "la villa de Tepuztlan," the number of tributaries undoubtedly refers to Tepoztlán and its surrounding villages. In a document dated 1576 (in the Archivo General de la Nación, México, General de Parte L, 238) quoted by Zavala[30] we

---

[25] Cook and Simpson, "The Population of Central Mexico," *Ibero-Americana*, Vol. XXXI (1948).

[26] *Ibid.*, p. 5.

[27] Cook and Simpson believe the 1567 date refers to conditions at about 1560. They write, "The inventory is based upon the real assessments made prior to 1567, and the values there given may, with no great risk of overstatement, be taken as the real values of 1560." *Ibid.*

[28] Recent studies of sample areas in central Mexico suggest an amazingly high pre-Conquest population. Areas which presumably had a population density of almost 600 persons per square mile now show a population density of 38 persons per square mile. See Cook, "Soil Erosion and Population in Central Mexico, *Ibero-Americana*, Vol. XXXIV, 1949.

[29] Juan López de Velasco, *Geografía y Descripción Universal de las Indias* (Madrid, 1894), p. 204. It is interesting to note how Tepoztlán compared in size with some of the nearby towns. Cuernavaca had 26,800 inhabitants; Yautepec, 18,000; Huaxtepec, 36,000. All of these towns, smaller today, are still larger than Tepoztlán.

[30] Silvio Zavala y María Castelo, *Fuentes para la Historia del Trabajo en Nueva España,* Bk. I (México: Fondo de Cultura Económica, 1939), pp. 144–45.

are told that the villages of Tepoztlán had 3,000 taxpaying Indians. However, this estimate appears in a petition by nearby *hacendados* for additional labor from the Indian villages and can therefore be presumed to be an overstatement of the actual number.

A much more reliable source of data is a document dated 1580 which gives the number of heads of families, widows, and single adults in each of the six surrounding villages of the municipio. From this document we find that the population of Tepoztlán proper was 5,865 and that of the entire municipio, 7,613.[31] This indicates either a considerable loss in population during the seventies, or that the earlier estimates were excessive. However, other sources tend to confirm the fact that the population was declining rapidly. For example, a document dated July 11, 1590, states, "In the last recount made among the people of the mentioned village there were fifteen hundred and eighty-one taxpayers, including widows and old maids." [32] The same document states that sixty-three Indians would have to give service, based on the tax rate of four men out of every hundred, which means 1,575 taxpayers or a total population of about 6,300. Thus, within the thirty-year period from 1560 to 1590 the population had decreased by over forty per cent. The major causes of this decline were epidemics, reported during the sixties, seventies, and eighties; the losses from the work in the mines of Taxco and Cuautla; and the moving away of Tepoztecans who sought to avoid the high taxes.

Our next data on population are for 1807, when a local census of the village of Tepoztlán was made. This census is especially interesting because of its inclusiveness; it gives us our first mention of the present-day barrios and the names of individuals and house sites by barrios.[33] This census shows a population of 2,540. This means that in the 228-year period from 1579 to 1807 the population of the village of Tepoztlán dropped by 3,284 or 56 per cent.

The nineteenth century was a period of population increase for Tepoztlán, in fact, for the first time since the Conquest. In 1890 the population of the village had risen to 4,163 and that of the municipio as a whole to 8,589.[34] This was the nearest approach to the early colonial and pre-Hispanic population. However, this remarkable comeback was destined to be short-lived, for the Revolution of 1910-20 was especially hard on Tepoztlán. According to the census of 1921 the village population was down to 2,156 and that of the municipio was three thousand.

Since 1921 the population has been increasing rapidly. By 1930 the population of the village was up to 2,580, an increase of 19.7 per cent, and from 1930 to 1940 there was a 29 per cent increase. This rate of increase was much higher than that of Mexico as a whole, which was 18.7 for the same period, and the highest re-

---

[31] *Indios*, Vol. 1, Exp. 252.

[32] *Ibid.*, Vol. 4, Exp. 797.

[33] *Hospital de Jesús*, Leg. 356, Exp. 8. A careful search of the census of 1793 of Revillagigedo failed to bring to light any data on Tepoztlán. However, the Ramo de Censo does show a map of the municipio of Tepoztlán with its seven surrounding villages.

[34] Alfonso Luis Velasco, *Geografía y Estadística de la República Mexicana*, Bk. VIII (1890), p. 57.

corded for a ten-year period. However, it was not quite as high as the increase for the state of Morelos, which was 36.3 for the same ten-year period.[35]

In analyzing the reasons for the recent rapid rise in the Tepoztecan population we must consider the decades 1920-30 and 1930-40 separately, for the factors at work were distinct. During 1920-30 Tepoztlán was going through a transition period, struggling to get back to normalcy after the devastating effects of the Revolution when practically the entire population was forced to flee. It is therefore probable that the 19 per cent increase in population during 1920-30 was due to the influx of returning families from their forced exile, in addition to the rate of natural increase. After 1930 few families returned to the village. On the contrary individuals began to leave, especially after the construction of the new road in 1936 and increased contacts with the outside. The increase of 29 per cent between 1930-40 must therefore be explained primarily in terms of the sharp decline in the mortality rates, especially infant mortality. This point will be treated later.

In reviewing the history of population growth in Tepoztlán we can distinguish four major periods: two of decline and two of increase. The first period was one of decline following the Conquest. We have suggested that, unlike the findings for central Mexico as a whole where the sharpest decline occurred within the first fifty years after the Conquest, this process in Tepoztlán was delayed and decline did not set in heavily until after 1560. From 1560 to 1804 there was a decline of over 70 per cent. The reasons for this decline have already been mentioned. The second period was one of rapid growth during the nineteenth century and up to 1910. The third period was again one of sharp decline until 1921. And the fourth period has been one of rapid increase. By and large the population curve for Tepoztlán is very much like that of Mexico as a whole and is stark testimony to the many upheavals suffered by Tepoztlán and the nation.

TABLE 4. Population of Tepoztlán and Surrounding Villages of the Municipio.

Village	1579	1890	1940
Tepoztlán	5,824	4,163	3,230
Santa Catarina	238	1,214	991
San Andrés	235	781	317
Santiago	385	276	216
Amatlán	481	211	162
Santo Domingo	233	1,114	444
San Juan	176	676	499
Ixcatepec	—[a]	154	111
El Parque	—	—	64
Total	7,572	8,589	6,034

[a] Ixcatepec became a separate village in the early part of the eighteenth century. Formerly it was considered a barrio of Tepoztlán.

Before leaving the subject of population changes, it might be well to summarize and compare the relative concentration of the population of Tepoztlán proper and the surrounding villages since the sixteenth century. This is shown in Table 4.

[35] Whetten, *Rural Mexico*, p. 39.

It can be seen from Table 4 that the population history of each of the villages has been quite varied. Perhaps the most striking thing about these figures is the much greater concentration of population in Tepoztlán (76 per cent of the total in 1579 as against 48 per cent of the total in 1890 and as compared with 1940). This difference may reflect the early Spanish policy of attempting to concentrate as many people as possible in a central administrative town where control was easier.

SEX AND AGE DISTRIBUTION

The 1940 sex and age distribution of the population shows a perfectly even distribution by sexes, with 1,615 men and 1,615 women. These figures do not agree with data from the local village census of 1943 with which I have worked and which seem much more reliable. According to this census there was a total population of 3,517, with 1,851 men and 1,666 women. That there are more men than women in the population is also supported by the data on the distribution of recorded births by sex in the village over a ten-year period from 1933 through 1942. From a total of 2,676 recorded births, 1,391 or 52 per cent were male and 1,285 or 48 per cent were female.

A comparison of the age distribution of Tepoztlán with that of rural Mexico as a whole reveals some interesting factors. (See Table 5.)

TABLE 5. Comparison of Distribution of Tepoztecan Population with Population of Rural Mexico by Age Group.

Age Group	Per Cent of Total Population	
	Tepoztlán	Rural Mexico
Under 5	13.03	15.3
5-9	15.75	15.1
10-14	14.24	12.5
15-19	10.17	10.0
20-24	4.48	7.6
25-29	5.47	7.9
30-34	5.94	6.5
35-39	7.23	6.8
40-44	4.54	4.6
45-49	4.24	3.7
50-54	3.86	2.9
55-59	3.28	2.1
60-64	2.66	2.1
65-69	1.79	1.1
70-74	0.98	0.8
75-79	0.74	0.4
80-84	0.68	0.3
85-89	0.27	0.1
90 and over	—	0.1

On the whole, Tepoztecan figures follow national figures closely. Thus, 28.8 per cent of the Tepoztecan population is less than ten years of age as compared with 30.4 for all of rural Mexico. However, there is a striking difference in the distribution for the age groups from 20 to 30 years. The Tepoztecan figures are slightly less than 10 per cent while the national figures are about 15 per cent. The fact that there are relatively few people in Tepoztlán between the ages from 20 to 30 reflects the high mortality rate in Tepoztlán during the years of the Revolution.

Another interesting difference is the much larger percentage of people over age 50 in Tepoztlán, 15.5 per cent for Tepoztlán as compared with 9.9 per cent for rural Mexico. In 1940 there were 95 individuals over age 70 and 39 individuals over 80. The longer age span in Tepoztlán is even more striking when compared with a Tarascan village like Tzintzuntzan, where only one person over 80 was reported.[36] I believe this is related to the relatively higher standard of living in Tepoztlán and to its healthful climate.

BIRTH AND MORTALITY RATES

The birth rates and death rates are shown in Tables 6 and 7.

TABLE 6. Birth Rate, from 1930 to 1940.

Year	Births per 1,000 Inhabitants
1930	43.8
1931	61.0
1932	64.8
1933	61.6
1934	54.7
1935	51.1
1936	37.2
1937	47.3
1938	41.5
1939	47.0
1940	41.3

TABLE 7. Mortality Rate, from 1930 to 1940.[a]

Year	Total Deaths	Mortality by Age		Infant Mortality (Deaths per 1,000 Live Births)	General Mortality
		Less than 1 year	More than 1 year		
1930	105	41	64	198.1	22.2
1931	132	40	92	134.7	27.1
1932	81	21	60	64.8	16.2
1933	133	27	106	85.4	25.9
1934	97	25	72	86.8	18.4
1935	89	23	66	83.3	16.5
1936	71	21	50	101.9	12.8
1937	88	22	66	82.1	15.5
1938	66	15	53	62.2	11.7
1939	130	18	112	64.5	21.9
1940	85	15	70	59.8	14.0

ᵃ Based on data from the Departamento de Estadística, Mexico, D.F.

It can be seen from Table 6 that the average birth rate for the eleven-year period from 1930 to 1940, inclusive, was 55.1 per cent. This is considerably higher

[36] See George M. Foster, *Empire's Children: The People of Tzintzuntzan* (México: Imprenta Nuevo Mundo, 1948), p. 29.

than the national average of 48.6 for the same period. It should be noted, however, that the birth rate varies considerably from year to year. The data in Tables 6 and 7 were obtained from the Federal Department of Statistics in Mexico City, which in turn gets its data from the municipal registry in Tepoztlán. To check on the reliability of these data I examined the local registry for the five-year period from 1939 to 1943. I found that not all births are recorded, and that many births are recorded years after the event. For example, three births which had taken place in 1926 were included in the record for 1941. Out of 284 births recorded in the register of 1939, 45 were born in other years; 42 out of 251 in 1940; 63 out of 245 in 1941; 68 out of 299 in 1942; and 64 out of 245 in 1943. In other words, of 1,324 births recorded during this five-year period, 282 were not born in the year in which they were recorded. It should be noted, however, that most of the cases were only one year late. And the fact that the procedure of including births from other years is a regular one tends to reduce the margin of error. Thus, while these statistics leave much to be desired, they do indicate general trends.

The average rate of infant mortality for the eleven-year period 1930 to 1940, inclusive, was 102.3 and the general mortality for the same period was 20.2. While both figures are high when compared with death rates in rural areas in the United States, it must be noted that they are considerably lower than the figures for the state of Morelos as a whole, for which the comparable figures were 133.6 and 30.2, respectively. The general mortality rates for the 31 municipios of the state of Morelos shows the municipio of Tepoztlán to be in the lowest quartile, third from the bottom, again indicating the relatively healthful location of the village. Furthermore, the infant mortality rate for Tepoztlán was also lower than for rural Mexico, which was 121 for the five-year period 1939 to 1943, inclusive.[37]

The mortality figures, like the birth figures, show a marked variation from year to year. However, the general trend for Tepoztlán was toward a sharp lowering of the mortality rate, especially in the case of infant mortality, witness the drop from 198.1 of 1930 to 59.8 in 1940. How can we explain this trend?

Probably the most important factor in the decrease of the infant mortality rate has been the increase in and greater availability of medical services. Tepoztlán has received a good deal of attention from the Mexican Department of Health, which has carried out a fairly intensive program of inoculation. While the health officials have not succeeded in eliminating the sources of infection and epidemics in the village—witness the serious typhoid epidemic in 1940, and the measles epidemic of 1947 which killed off many children—they have taken energetic measures to control the epidemics.

Since 1930 there have been doctors residing temporarily in Tepoztlán for short periods.[38] There have been at least two *pasantes* (graduate medical students) who,

---

[37] Whetten, *Rural Mexico*, p. 328.

[38] From the doctors' reports on file at the Department of Health in Mexico City, it appears that rheumatism is the most frequent disease and accounted for 50 per cent of all illnesses treated. Next in frequency was benign goiter, followed by tuberculosis and enteritis.

in accord with government regulations, must spend a six-month training period in the field to qualify for the medical degree. In addition, some Tepoztecans visit private doctors and the free health clinic in Cuernavaca. The presence of five mid-wives with some training in modern hygienic methods is also to be noted. Finally, the trend toward a lower general mortality rate may be related to the steadily increasing standard of living in the village. As will be seen later, the consumption of meat, eggs, milk, and bread has risen considerably over the last twenty years.

In Table 8 is presented the average mortality rate by age groups for the entire municipio of Tepoztlán over a twelve-year period from 1930 to 1941, inclusive.

TABLE 8. Average Mortality Rate by Age Group, from 1930 to 1941, Inclusive.

Age Group	Mortality Rate
Less than 1 year	96.94
1-4	44.24
5-9	7.24
10-14	10.31
15-19	11.22
20-39	5.60
40-59	15.75
60 and over	56.80

These figures show that the age of lowest mortality rate in Tepoztlán is from twenty to thirty-nine. The death rate from forty to fifty-nine, though increased, is not unusually high, indicating that many individuals live to a fairly ripe old age.

LANGUAGE AND LITERACY

Two languages are spoken in Tepoztlán, Spanish and the indigenous Náhuatl. Twenty years ago when Redfield was there, nearly all the inhabitants spoke Náhuatl. Since that time there has been a marked decrease in the use of Náhuatl and a corresponding increase in the use of Spanish. The data in Table 9, based on the Federal Census of 1930 and 1940, indicate this trend.

TABLE 9. Languages Spoken in the Municipio and Tepoztlán.

Languages	Municipio		Tepoztlán
	1930	1940	1940
Spanish	14%	40%	52%
Náhuatl	4	5	1
Spanish and Náhuatl	82	55	47

Although about one-half of all Tepoztecans are still bilingual, the drop from 82 to 55 per cent for the municipio and to 47 per cent for Tepoztlán proper is striking. The decrease of those who speak only Náhuatl in the entire municipio was from 144 individuals in 1930 to 29 in 1940. In 1944 there were five persons in Tepoztlán who spoke only Náhuatl. The significance of this trend is unmistakable. It would be safe to predict that within the next few generations the number of bilingual persons will become negligible.

Among the younger generation today we noted a distinctly negative attitude toward Náhuatl. People under thirty-five tend to be ashamed to speak Náhuatl in the presence of outsiders and will frequently deny knowledge of the language, although the majority are able to understand it and speak it to some degree. Within most homes, parents and members of the older generation customarily speak in Spanish but resort to Náhuatl to tell secrets, jokes, and especially during quarrels when they wish to be more expressive. Thus, many children have come to associate speaking Náhuatl at home with quarreling, insulting, and scolding. Náhuatl is also preferred at the barrio meetings for the election of the *mayordomo* and during the ceremonial address on the festive celebration in honor of El Tepozteco. It is also spoken by the *huehuechiques* (ceremonial figures) at other fiestas.

The rapid decrease in the use of Náhuatl has occurred in the face of the persistent efforts of some Tepoztecans to preserve the native language. One of the primary objectives of the Colonia Tepozteco, founded in 1920 in Mexico City by Tepoztecans who had been forced to seek refuge there during the years of the Revolution, was "to bring about the preservation of our native tongue for transmission to future generations." Even before the Revolution a group of Tepoztecan intellectuals had published a paper in Náhuatl. There still exists a pro-Náhuatl society in Mexico City composed primarily of middle-class Tepoztecans who periodically visit the village and proclaim the importance of using the native tongue. When the bus companies were founded in Tepoztlán in the middle thirties, they were given Náhuatl names, one bus cooperative being called Ometochtli and the other El Tepozteco. Similarly, in sports events like track the runners will sometimes take Náhuatl names.

The greater use of Spanish in the village has not been accompanied by a corresponding increase in literacy. The decline in illiteracy in the municipio during the ten-year period from 1930 to 1940 has been from 66 to 55 per cent. We have no data for illiteracy for the village of Tepoztlán for 1930. However, in 1940 it was down to 42 per cent, which is considerably lower than for the municipio as a whole. By and large there is a high correlation between membership in the middle economic group and literacy. Many in the upper economic group are illiterate.[39]

There has been a considerable increase in the reading of newspapers in recent years. In Redfield's time no newspapers came regularly to the village, and only a few individuals occasionally read newspapers. In 1944 there were fifty-six people who bought newspapers on an average of twice a week. Forty read *El Universal, Novedades,* and *Excelsior,* the conservative Mexican papers; one read *El Popular,* the left wing labor paper; and fifteen read the pro-Sinarquista sheets, *El Sinarquista, Hombre Libre, Omega,* and *La Pluma,* a local weekly published in Cuernavaca. These individuals played an important role in determining public opinion in the village on local, national, and international issues. It was my impression in 1944 that most of the more vocal villagers were sympathetic to the Axis powers.

---

[39] See Chapter 9, "Wealth Differences and Levels of Living," p. 173.

MEANS OF COMMUNICATION

Tepoztlán has relatively good means of communication. It has a railroad, a modern highway, bus service, mail service, and one telephone. As we have seen earlier, the railroad was built about 1900. The building of the railroad was particularly significant, for it encouraged the commercial exploitation of certain natural resources on a scale formerly impossible. The railroad is used primarily for the transportation of wood and charcoal to Mexico City.

In 1936 the asphalt road connecting Tepoztlán with the Mexico City–Cuernavaca Highway was completed, and shortly thereafter a bus cooperative was organized.[40] The line was successful and expanded. At present there are two bus lines to Cuernavaca, both owned and operated by Tepoztecans and in bitter competition with each other. In 1944 each line operated four buses which ran every hour from seven in the morning to seven at night, seven days a week. The round-trip fare to Cuernavaca was 90 centavos. Both lines carried more than 1,600 Tepoztecan passengers to Cuernavaca and back each week. Four days a week there was an average of 175 passengers. On Tuesdays and Thursdays, the market days in Cuernavaca, there was an average of 300 a day, and 300 to 400 on Sundays.

Before the construction of the road, communication between Tepoztlán and surrounding regions was primarily by burro and by foot. The most frequent trading and social contacts were with Yautepec, about three hours' distance, and with Cuernavaca, about four hours' distance. Since the road has been built it takes about forty-five minutes to Cuernavaca by bus and about twenty minutes by private car. Since the coming of the road, Cuernavaca has replaced Yautepec in importance. This shift is significant because the greater cultural sophistication of Cuernavaca has accelerated the rate of change in Tepoztlán. The road has had many other far-reaching effects which will be discussed later.

Tepoztlán has had mail service since 1926, and mail is delivered daily. Redfield reported in 1926 that there was an average of about twelve letters a day, most of which were for families living in the center. In 1944 there were about thirty letters daily. This increase was relatively small considering the great increase in literacy, trade, and population.

Tepoztlán has had a telephone and telegraph since before the Revolution, but the lines have rarely functioned. In the early thirties the telephone was repaired, but there is little occasion for its use, except for official business. The bus lines have changed this situation somewhat, for the bus line officials have more frequent occasion to communicate with Cuernavaca.

---

[40] The first bus line was established by a man from Cuernavaca but it was soon taken over by Tepoztecans.

the village and the world outside: 2

IF WE WERE to ask almost any Tepoztecan adult for his conception of the geography of the world, we would find that it is vague and spotty and limited to only a few countries.[1] He would know that there is a country called the United States which is close to Mexico and whose people are the light-skinned gringos who speak a different language, are Protestants, and manufacture machines. He knows that to the south of Mexico there are other countries like Guatemala which are Spanish speaking and Catholic. He also knows that some place in the world there is Spain, the land from which the *gachupines* came.[2] Many Tepoztecans know that in a distant land there is a city called Rome where the Pope, the "King of the Catholics," lives. Some have heard of Germany and Japan, the countries which were at war with the gringos.

In general their knowledge of peoples other than Mexicans is very slight. They think of any stranger who has a light complexion and blue eyes as a gringo or *norteamericano*. A German anthropologist who lived in the village was constantly referred to as a gringo. Tepoztecans have seen some Negroes and Chinese, the latter primarily as peddlers. Tepoztecans do not seem to be aware of nationality differences and simply call most strangers "foreigners"; even light-skinned native-born Mexicans from other states, cities, and towns are included in this classification.

Most Tepoztecans have never been beyond the borders of Mexico, but in recent years there have been some exceptions. During the last war about fifteen Tepoztecan men worked as laborers in the United States and all returned to the village. Among this group were some comparatively well-educated men who were able to express their impressions and experiences and did much to impart new information about

---

[1] Until the middle thirties when the road was built, Tepoztecans thought of distances primarily in terms of the amount of time it took to walk a certain distance. Thus they knew that it took about a day to get to Mexico City, two days to Jojutla. A five-day trip was about the greatest distance they could conceive. Now that most Tepoztecans ride the bus to Cuernavaca, their notions of distance are changing. However, they still do not think in terms of kilometers and find it difficult to conceive of the great distances between their village and the U.S.A. or Europe.

[2] *Gachupín* is a deprecatory term used to designate Spaniards.

the U.S.A. to the villagers. In addition, one Tepoztecan fought in the Mexican squadron which went to the Philippines and he, too, spoke of his experiences.

Tepoztecans have not escaped the repercussions of international events in recent years. World War II led to conscription, toward which Tepoztecans reacted negatively. During the first few months of our field work in the village in 1943-44 an incident occurred which illustrates the local attitude. The son of the president of the municipio had been recruited and was on his way to Cuernavaca to report for duty. His bus was stopped and the boy was "kidnapped" by several men. It was common gossip that this act was planned by the boy's father who, as a result of it, was imprisoned in Cuernavaca for some time. Federal troops were sent into the village and there was much tension among the people. However, the affair blew over, and the villagers resigned themselves to conscription and military training for their sons.

Another way in which current international events influence the village is in the intensified campaign of the Roman Catholic Church throughout the Catholic world. Acción Católica has almost doubled its membership in Tepoztlán since 1943 as a result of the increased activity of the church. The sermons of the priest sometimes include warnings against the threat of Communism, a theme which was also heard in the local church immediately after the Mexican Revolution and in the twenties. Other than this, most Tepoztecans have no information about international trends or problems; they are ignorant of the United Nations, the Marshall Plan, the Atlantic Pact, and even of national loans.

The geographical horizon of most Tepoztecans becomes a little more concrete when they think of Mexico. While the shape of the country and its boundaries may still be hazy, they know that Mexico is their country, that it has coasts on the east and west, that the Isthmus of Tehuantepec is very hot, while the north is cold. They also know that the people of Monterrey are "stingy" and that the Yucatecans have "square-heads." They have heard of Tampico and Vera Cruz as important ports, and that Mexico produces oil and minerals. They also know some of the names of the states of Mexico, and many have had occasion to deal personally not only with people from Mexico City and with other Morelenses, but also with Mexicans from different states. During the Revolution they came into contact with soldiers from diverse parts of the country; the Norteños del Coahuila camped in Tepoztlán for months, and the people still speak of their strange customs.

Of course, the geographic horizons of the younger generation which has had some years of schooling are quite different. The children study a little world geography and know the continents and major countries of the world. Most have studied the map of Mexico, and some of the youth are beginning to demonstrate a real nationalism.

The average Tepoztecan's notion of the geography of the state of Morelos is much more precise than his notion of the geography of the nation. Many Tepoztecans have traveled over large portions of the state, as well as neighboring regions, during the years of the Revolution. Others have taken trips for economic purposes, religious pilgrimages, or political reasons. Tepoztecans know what towns are to the north of the state of Morelos and have a pretty good notion of the products produced in the various parts of the state. Their work on haciendas to the south has also given them some familiarity with this part of the state. Some Tepoztecans are related by ties of marriage and *compadrazgo* with families in other parts of the state of Morelos.

There is an increasing identification of Tepoztecans with the Mexican nation and with the state of Morelos. The factors which relate the villagers to these larger entities are cultural, administrative, religious, political, and economic.

CULTURAL FACTORS

Perhaps the most important and decisive of the several cultural factors—the school, cultural missions, books and newspapers, the literacy campaign, and the movies—which tend to make for the formation of a sentiment of *mexicanidad* or Mexican nationalism is the school, where the younger generation learn about the history, geography, and economy of the country as a whole, and where a conscious effort is made to instill love of country.

THE SCHOOL

The school became more effective after the early twenties when the schools of the state of Morelos were federalized by means of a special agreement between the state and the nation. This led to the standardization of texts and teaching methods. But more important, the school personnel was recruited from various parts of Mexico rather than, as formerly, only from the state of Morelos. Since that time, Tepoztlán has had teachers from Yucatán, Jalisco, Nuevo León, and many other states. These teachers have different backgrounds and expose the children to the customs and sentiments of their respective regions. Thus, in the programs organized in the school, pupils have had the opportunity of seeing teachers dance the *jarabe tapatío,* the *raspa veracruzana,* and the *jarana yucateca.*

Squadron 201, the new school building named after a squadron of Mexican aviators who fought in the Philippines in World War II, stands as a symbol of *mexicanidad* to Tepoztecans. The school was constructed with national funds upon the direct order of President Avila Camacho in response to the request of a Tepoztecan who was a member of Squadron 201. Upon the return of the squadron to Mexico, President Camacho organized a public reception and at this time invited each member to ask for what he desired. The majority of the men asked for subsidies for their families, but Angel Bocanegra asked for a school for his village. Because of this he has become a great hero in the village, and among the younger generation has taken the place of the older regional and village heroes of the Revolution.

The school not only stimulates Mexican nationalism, but is also a powerful factor in developing the feeling of being a Morelense. The school teaches the geography and economy of the state in some detail. The text on the geography of the state of Morelos is excellent and covers all the municipios of the state. Excursions organized by the school give the younger generation an opportunity to know their state.

The proximity of Cuernavaca, the state capital, also plays some part in developing a consciousness of being Morelenses. In Cuernavaca there are secondary and preparatory schools to which some Tepoztecan parents send their children, since the local school reaches only to the sixth grade.

STUDENT SCHOLARSHIPS

Each year the secretary of education makes available a number of student scholarships for advanced study outside the village. About fifty Tepoztecans have received such scholarships during the past fifteen years, and many of these students have returned to the village to teach or to carry on their work as farmers. The experience away from home makes for many changes in habits and customs, and must be reckoned as another source of culture change, though obviously a limited one.

CULTURAL MISSIONS

Paralleling the work of the school is that of the cultural missions, also a federal service, which travel throughout the country visiting peasant and Indian communities and giving instruction for adults. Tepoztlán has had a cultural mission for two years, and in 1947 the mission worked in one of the surrounding villages of the municipio. All of the members of the mission were non-Tepoztecans, again making for increased opportunities to become familiar with customs from different parts of the country. The mission taught Tepoztecans how to make beds, chairs, and other furniture; it taught the girls knitting, sewing, and crocheting; it encouraged social dancing and sports such as volleyball; it taught the women how to make inexpensive candies and preserves; it worked on improving the homes by getting a few families to build privies and to raise the hearth off the floor for more sanitary cooking. In addition, there was a doctor attached to the mission who administered inoculations and gave advice on baby care.

BOOKS AND NEWSPAPERS

Most of the books which reach Tepoztlán are textbooks used in the school. One of the innovations of the Mexican government since the Revolution has been the elimination of most texts written by foreigners, and the substitution of texts written by Mexicans, which seek to arouse Mexican nationalism. Stories of the Mexican Indians have been substituted for those of children of other lands, and national heroes receive an important place in most texts dealing with history. The secretary of education has printed millions of copies of history texts which are distributed free, and some of these books have reached Tepoztecan homes.

Among other publications which occasionally reach Tepoztlán are leaflets put out by the Partido Revolucionario Mexicano (now the Partido Revolucionario

Institucional) presidential messages, propaganda leaflets from the League of Agrarian Communities, the Confederación de Trabajadores Mexicanos, and the Sinarquistas. However, the reading public is still very small, and for the most part such leaflets go unnoticed.

Twenty years ago the few literate persons in the village read novels, such as the popular *Génova de Brabante* or *María el Hada del Bosque* and, among the youth, the *Secretario de los Amantes*. Today one finds the youth reading the popular comics "Paquín" and "Chamaco." The principal characters in these comics are Mexicans and the jokes are full of Mexicanisms associated with city life.

Other fairly common items read by young Tepoztecans are the *cancioneros* (song sheets), some of which are distributed free by the Bayer Aspirin Company as part of their advertising. These songs are written by Mexicans and generally reflect much of the life of the countryside in different regions of Mexico. It is not unusual on a moonlit night to hear groups of young men singing of a legend of Mayab, or a *danzón* from Vera Cruz, or a song from Jalisco. American tunes such as "Begin the Beguine," sung in Spanish, are also occasionally heard. Many of the songs exalt the virtues of the Mexicans and of Mexico, and reflect the growing sense of nationalism. Thus, we were not surprised to hear a young Tepoztecan on his way to the fields singing, "Soy puro mexicano, nacido en esta tierra que es mi linda nación." This song is a symbol of Tepoztecan localism slowly giving way to identification with the Mexican nation.

Because of the proximity of the state capital to Mexico City, local newspapers are overshadowed by the national dailies. However, two small papers are published in Cuernavaca, and these carry local notices, news, and many advertisements of the commercial houses of Cuernavaca. Some of these newspapers reach Tepoztlán, but they are read primarily by the local government officials. On fiesta days the paper is sometimes sold by a hawker who may announce some sensational murder in the state. The paper is very Morelos-conscious and uses slogans such as, "Every good Morelense buys these products" or "Morelos advances towards agricultural progress," etc. The only other local periodical which reaches a few Tepoztecans is the *Diario Oficial del Estado,* read primarily by the courthouse officials.

LITERACY CAMPAIGN

Another federal service which reached Tepoztlán and contributed toward the identification of Tepoztecans with the nation was the campaign against illiteracy, carried out by the Department of Education. The slogans used included, "Mexico must be great because of its culture" and "The Fatherland must have citizens who can read." Slogans such as these were posted on billboards in the village, and representatives from the Department of Education came to Tepoztlán, gave talks, and showed movies. It was recognized that in a village like Tepoztlán the original idea of each literate teaching at least one illiterate how to read would not work. The program was therefore organized by the schoolteachers in terms of adult evening classes for illiterates.

NATIONAL AND STATE HOLIDAYS

The commemoration of the dates of national independence is assuming more and more importance in Tepoztlán. Thanks to the labor of the school, the national holidays of September fifteenth and sixteenth have become outstanding fiestas in the village—only the Carnaval is still more popular. Preparations are begun at least two months prior to September fifteenth. The children are the first to begin the campaign in the homes, for they are told by their teachers to ask for new uniforms for the parade. Despite the burden of such expense, many parents purchase the uniforms. All the local officials, the president, the councilmen, the judges, the director of the school, and the collector of rents, prepare for the event and all attend. Speakers from the governor's office in nearby Cuernavaca are usually invited, and the populace turns out to hear them.

The state of Morelos has its own civic fiestas which are celebrated with considerable flourish. Among the most important are the celebration of the birthday of Father Morelos, after whom the state was named, and the birth and death of the great General Emiliano Zapata, the most popular hero in the state. As in the case of the national fiestas, the school is the organizing and driving force in the celebration of these fiestas; however, they are not on as large a scale as national fiestas. The teachers and the school director generally make speeches, reviewing the great achievements of the hero Zapata, and they do not fail to point out that at least five of Zapata's generals were from Tepoztlán. In addition to these local celebrations, Tepoztecans often send a delegate to the official state celebration of Zapata's birthday.

The state also has its popular song writers, and its songs dwell on local history or local scenes, easily recognized as Morelos songs by the lyrics if not by the music.

MOVIES

Mexican movies have also broadened the Tepoztecan view of Mexico and the world. More and more the younger generation see an occasional movie in Cuernavaca, and sometimes a movie comes to Tepoztlán to be shown in the plaza at a small cost.

ADMINISTRATIVE FACTORS

At least half a dozen federal government agencies have files on Tepoztlán. These files contain correspondence with the village and provide us with a more or less objective record of Tepoztlán and national agencies. Most of the files date from the early twenties and reflect the increasing role of these agencies in village life in the post-Revolutionary period. The agencies which have the fullest records are the Departamento Agrario, Forestal, Asuntos Indígenas, Economía Nacional, Salubridad, and Asistencia Social.

It is not my purpose to give a detailed account of all the federal agencies which may directly or indirectly influence Tepoztlán. However, the more salient ways in which the national administrative apparatus affects the daily lives of Tepoztecans will be considered here.

TAXATION

Federal taxation touches most Tepoztecans directly and is a common subject of complaint. Most Tepoztecans view it as an imposition and do not readily understand the need for taxation nor what is done with the money. In fact, Tepoztecans pay relatively little in federal taxes, primarily on the sale of charcoal, on the slaughter of animals, and on trade. Tepoztecans accept fatalistically the necessity of paying taxes, but it develops a negative and critical attitude toward the national government.

HEALTH SERVICES

The federal government has a health center in Cuernavaca which is frequented by some Tepoztecans. However, the majority, particularly the older people, do not use it because they still prefer *curanderos* and are not yet accustomed to the idea of receiving services from the state. Even the federal health workers who come into the village from time to time to administer inoculations against communicable disease are endured by most villagers out of "respect" for the great power of the government, rather than because of an understanding of their services.

AGRICULTURAL SERVICES

The Departamento Agrario intervenes directly in the affairs of Tepoztecans who hold land under the *ejido* program. Federal authority is the final authority which resolves problems or conflicts concerning *ejido* lands. But here, too, many Tepoztecans see in the agrarian authorities an imposition rather than a system of public service. As we have shown earlier, the nationalization of the communal lands has lessened local control, and this has not been well accepted. Tepoztecans do not yet understand the need for national control of forest resources, especially when such control conflicts with their local interests.

NATIONAL DEFENSE

Perhaps the clearest form in which the Tepoztecan peasant sees the power of the federal government is in the federal troops. Almost as a matter of tradition, Tepoztecans have viewed soldiers with strong suspicion and dislike, and have fought attempts to conscript their sons. However, the attitude toward federal troops today is quite different from that shown toward the Federales of the Díaz regime. Today the troops stationed in the village fraternize with the population; and though they are "respected" there is less of the fear that existed during the Díaz regime. Federal troops have been sent to the village on a number of occasions in recent years, once in connection with resistance to conscription during the early part of World War II, and again when local political contests resulted in violence.

The negative reactions of the peasants to conscription stem from a number of causes. Many recalled the hateful system of forced recruiting which had existed under the Díaz regime and feared that this system was now being reinstituted. Parents were distrustful of the care and food their sons would receive in the army and worried about their fate among strangers in the hostile outside world. Also, the absence of an eighteen-year-old son for a year often meant a serious economic loss to the family. Tepoztecans do not identify national problems of defense or internal order with their own interests, and they resent having to fight other people's (i.e., Mexicans') battles. Local feeling against conscription reached its climax when it was rumored that the young men were being prepared to fight against the Germans at the orders of the United States. This rumor was spread throughout Mexico by the Sinarquistas.

JUSTICE AND THE DEPARTAMENTO DE GOBERNACIÓN

There are very few occasions when local court cases reach the federal courts. However, federal intervention was sought during the hectic political campaigns of the twenties, when Tepoztecans who were imprisoned for political reasons appealed for federal injunctions to set them free. More recently a boundary conflict between Tepoztlán and Tejalpa reached the Federal Supreme Court, and Tepoztecans have sent many delegations to visit the justices of this court to explain their case.

Another federal department with which Tepoztecans have had some contact is *Gobernación* which is responsible for preserving public order throughout Mexico and for the smooth functioning of political campaigns and elections.

As we have seen, the attitude of Tepoztecans toward most federal agencies is a negative one. The outstanding exception is the school, which was built with federal funds and which is appreciated by the populace. The fact is that Tepoztecans might obtain more aid from federal agencies if they sought it out. However, the attitude of suspicion and self-sufficiency of the older generation militates against this. Now that the younger generation is beginning to take over positions of power, the situation may change. Angel Bocanegra, president of the municipio, is a good example of this. Bocanegra did not hesitate to go to Mexico City and visit the various federal departments soliciting aid for the village. In preparing for the celebration of the national holidays in 1949, Bocanegra borrowed an electric generator from one agency to provide electricity for the occasion, a movie projector from another agency, and from still another agency he received the promise of help in improving the quality of the local water supply.

Dealings of Tepoztecans with the administrative apparatus of the state government are quite frequent and are facilitated by the proximity of Cuernavaca. The governor of the state is an important figure to Tepoztecans. It would be difficult to find Tepoztecans who do not know the name of the present governor, and many can recall at least a few past governors. Indeed, some even remember the names of some of the governors of the Díaz epoch. The governor is thought of as "almost the president." However, the fact that they have seen the governor more often than the president and that he generally visits the village before elections makes the villagers feel less distant toward him. There is less hesitancy about sending a delegation to the governor than to the president. On the other hand, Tepoztecans are much more critical of the governor and the state government than of the president. Tepoztecans recognize the necessity of a federal government to maintain order and "to protect us from the foreigners." They see much less reason for the existence of the state government, but they fear and respect its powers and authority.

Bodies such as the Procuraduría General del Estado and the Receptoría General de Rentas del Estado have enormous meaning to the Tepoztecan. The first is the body in charge of all cases of violation of the public order, and their agents have frequently come to Tepoztlán to make arrests or to track down offenders. The Procuraduría settles property cases and often sends summons to Tepoztecans to appear at a certain hour and day for hearings. Tepoztecans complain bitterly about the fact that the Procuraduría accepts no excuses and will summon a man during the height of the agricultural season just as readily as any other time. Whether a man has bus fare or not, he must appear in Cuernavaca or an order for his arrest and detention will be forthcoming and a fine will be imposed. The Tepoztecan therefore fears the Procuraduría, which appears to him to have arbitrary power. He also fears the public jails and the courts, both of which are related to the Procuraduría. The state office of rents in Cuernavaca is also disliked, since it collects the bulk of the taxes taken from Tepoztlán.

In Cuernavaca there are such services as a state hospital and state supported medical clinics. But Tepoztecans are under the impression that the hospital is inferior, and rarely go there. A few have more faith in the hospitals of Mexico City and occasionally go there for serious operations.

RELIGIOUS FACTORS

Just as Tepoztecans are aware of an administrative hierarchy whose seat is in Mexico City, so they are aware of a religious hierarchy headed by the archbishop in Mexico City. Of course, they realize that the final authority is the Pope in Rome. The local priest often mentions the Pope and his messages, as well as the messages from the archbishop. The church in Tepoztlán has taken an active part in all the recent campaigns of the national church organization. For example, the four hundredth anniversary of the Virgin of Guadalupe, which was celebrated throughout the nation, was also celebrated in Tepoztlán and was the occasion for the visitation of church dignitaries who explained the great miracle of the apparition of the Virgin to Juan Diego shortly after the Conquest. In their sermons the priests generally identify the Virgin as a symbol of Mexican nationalism. And of course there are Tepoztecans who go on the annual pilgrimages to the shrine of the Virgin. In addition there are other religious cults of widespread popularity in Tepoztlán and other parts of the nation. One such cult is the Holy Saint of Chalma, who is visited annually by many Tepoztecans.

The Catholic Church within the state has its regional seat in Cuernavaca, where the bishop resides. The priest in Tepoztlán is under his supervision and carries out his instructions. Periodic religious pilgrimages establish important ties with other parts of the state. Within Tepoztlán there are the following *mayordomías,* each of which organizes at least one annual visit to another town. The *mayordomías* in Tepoztlán proper include Mazatepec, Jiutepec, Tejalpa, Tlayacapan, all in Morelos, and Chalma in the state of Guerrero. Four of the seven villages of the municipio of Tepoztlán also have *mayordomías* that relate them to the state. Santiago goes to Oacalco and Yautepec; Gabriel Mariaca to Ixcatepec, Tlayacapan, Cuautla, Jojutla, Jiutepec, and Mazatepec, all in Morelos, to Amecameca in the state of Mexico, to Chalma in Guerrero, and to the Villa de Guadalupe in the Federal District. Ocotitlán goes to the Villa de Guadalupe, Chalma, and Amecameca. San Juan goes to Mazatepec, Chalma, the Villa de Guadalupe, and Amecameca.

POLITICAL FACTORS

The Mexican Revolution of 1910-20 has been one of the most important factors in developing a sense of nationalism among Tepoztecans. Many Tepoztecans joined the ranks of the Zapatistas and had occasion to travel widely with the guerrilla forces. As we have pointed out, the rest of the population was forced to flee to other parts of the nation. All of this meant more extensive contacts with the outside.

During the years of the Revolution and thereafter, many of the *caudillos* of the Revolution, such as Zapata and Obregón, established the custom of visiting the peasants personally and discussing local problems. Contact with the rural population has been one of the policies of the post-Revolution presidents since Calles. Tepoztecans now think of the president of Mexico not only as a representative of the powerful government, but also as a popular figure, a friend of the peasants.

It is not uncommon for Tepoztecans to send requests or protests directly to the president. This has happened in almost every case of conflict between factions in the village or in cases of boundary quarrels with neighboring villages or municipios. This attitude toward the president was reinforced by the personal visit of General Lázaro Cárdenas to the village during his presidency. Cárdenas arrived in the village on foot, without any previous announcement or preparation, and accompanied only by a small contingent of friends and officials. The president set up a temporary office in the atrium of the church, where he consulted Tepoztecans about their problems. The big request from the village was for aid with the construction of a road to Cuernavaca. The president acceded, and the road was quickly completed with federal help.

The national elections for the president, which come every six years, also give Tepoztecans an opportunity to discuss political themes of nation-wide scope. Before the elections, delegates and politicians visit the village to organize local committees in favor of their particular group or candidate. During such campaigns Tepoztecans become more keenly aware that they are acting not only as Tepoztecans and as Morelenses, but also as members of the Mexican nation.

To a lesser degree the election of federal senator and deputies also touches the Tepoztecan population. On these occasions politicians from the capital come to the village to electioneer and to organize sympathizers for their candidates. However, the intervention of the governor of the state is much more direct in these elections, and so Tepoztecans tend to view them as state or regional elections. On the whole, the younger generation participates very little in politics, since this is a matter for the older men.

Some indication of the Tepoztecan sense of belonging to the Mexican nation may be gathered from their reaction to the question of Mexico's participation in World War II. Most Tepoztecans were opposed to Mexican entrance into the war on the side of the democracies. Under the influence of Sinarquist propaganda, sympathy with the Axis powers developed in the village. Rumors began to circulate that Zapata was not really dead but was fighting with Hitler, and that that explained why the Germans were winning so many victories. The latent and widespread anti-U.S.A. sentiment was encouraged by rumors that the Mexicans were being asked to fight to save the gringos. Nevertheless, the Tepoztecans accepted the Mexican declaration of war as one of those decisions of the omnipotent federal government, about which nothing can be done. This Tepoztecan attitude of passivity was typical of the attitude of most Mexicans toward the war.

Since the Revolution the state of Morelos has developed an intense political life that has reached into Tepoztlán. After the thirties, constitutional government was instituted and the governor and local officials were elected, rather than imposed. Political campaigns and electioneering became important; and Tepoztlán, because of its proximity to the state capital, received much attention from prospective candidates. In the attempt to get votes, speakers appealed to state loyalty with such slogans as, "First the Morelenses and then the Mexicans," and made typical demagogic preelection speeches. A good number of Tepoztecans show enthusiasm and interest in state politics, and several hundred men generally turn out to hear the speeches. The election of a new governor always means the possibility of some advantage to the village, or at least to a few Tepoztecans who have actively supported him.

ECONOMIC FACTORS

The Tepoztecan economy is not self-sufficient, and is an integral part of the larger national economy. Tepoztlán exports corn, charcoal, and plums to Mexico City, and in turn imports manufactured goods and some foods. Trading relations involve contacts with individuals in the big city, and occasionally Tepoztecans go directly to Mexico City to make purchases. Since the construction of the road, trade and economic contacts with Mexico City have been much more frequent. The tourist trade has also made for increased contacts with outsiders.

Trade between Tepoztlán and other towns in the state of Morelos develops knowledge of the region and its peoples. Tepoztlán carries on most of its trade with Cuernavaca and Yautepec, but also with smaller towns and villages in the state.

THE VILLAGE AND THE MUNICIPIO

The relations of the village with the municipio are closer and more personal than those with any of the larger units discussed so far. Tepoztecans know the municipio intimately—they know its topography, history, legends, natural resources, people, and villages. Even small children can name the seven villages, and know the way to each. The limits of the municipio are also well known, as are the details of the many recurring boundary disputes with neighboring municipios. It is within the bounds of the municipio that the every-day world of the Tepoztecan exists. Here the farmers work the communal lands, cut and burn the communal forests, graze their cattle, hunt for medicinal herbs, and attend village fiestas.

The fact that the village of Tepoztlán is the *cabecera* of the municipio gives Tepoztecans a sense of pride and superiority over residents of the remaining villages. Tepoztlán has for centuries had a dominant position in relation to the other villages.

In treating of the units larger than the municipio, we have spoken about cultural factors and have dealt with history within that category. In the case of the municipio, the historical factor is much more important and deserves special consideration. Although the state of Morelos is a relatively recent political entity dating from 1867, the political and geographical unit equivalent to the present-day municipio dates back over four hundred years to the pre-Hispanic era.

According to a legend in Tepoztlán concerning the formation of the municipio, the surrounding villages were originally defensive military outposts of the central village of Tepoztlán where political control rested. Before the Spanish Conquest, Tepoztlán was frequently at war with the surrounding towns and, therefore, needed outposts to hold off surprise attacks. Only in this way can present-day Tepoztecans explain the location of San Juan in a place that has no water supply.

While we have no reliable historical data on the origins of the municipio as such, there is no question but that six of the seven present-day villages existed before the Conquest and that the present-day boundaries of the municipio are about the same as those before the Conquest. The geographical unit represented by the present-day municipio is therefore an ancient one.[3]

Before the Conquest, Tepoztlán was a semi-independent *señorío* (kingdom) which was administratively subject to Huaxtepec. Tepoztlán with its surrounding

---

[3] In *Relación*, pp. 238-39, the six outlying villages are referred to as *estancias* of Tepoztlán and are named and described as follows:

"The *estancia* of Santiago, called Tepetlapan, which is one of the six *estancias* of the said town, is toward the south, in the direction of Yautepeque. They say it is so named because it is built on coarse rock, which is called Tepetate. . . .

"The *estancia* of Santa María Magdalena, which is the second *estancia* of the six, and is a little to the east of this town, they say is called Cimatlen (Amatlán) because in ancient times they had there an idol which they worshipped which they called Ometecatl, and which acknowledged homage to the devil (*sic*) of Tepoztlán.

"And the *estancia* of Santo Domingo, third of the six, which stands sloping a little to the north of this town, they say is called Xocotitlán now and formerly Elosuchitlan, which means land of

villages is always listed as a single unit in the tax lists and in the early colonial documents. It appears as such in the *Matrículo de Tributos de Moctezuma,* a copy of which was obtained by the first viceroy of Mexico, Mendoza. Its relation to "Huastepeque" is also given in the *Relación de Tepuztlan* of 1580 and in later documents. After the Conquest, the older administrative lines were altered and Tepoztlán became subject to Cuernavaca, its ancient enemy.

We know very little about the relations between Tepoztlán and the other villages of the municipio after the Conquest, but some documents suggest considerable friction. In a document from the *Hospital de Jesús,* dated January 19, 1774, we learn that the governor of Tepoztlán complained to the authorities in Cuernavaca that four of the villages traditionally subject to Tepoztlán had recently rebelled and had obtained the privilege of paying taxes separately.

The bonds between Tepoztlán and the surrounding villages of the municipio are numerous. The communal lands which belong to the municipio, the inter-village trade, the bi-weekly market at Tepoztlán are the strongest economic bonds. Administratively, Tepoztlán is the center to which the other villagers must come to register births, marriages, and deaths; to pay taxes, federal and state; or to get a certificate of good conduct. The villagers are also dependent upon Tepoztlán for their religious services, baptisms, communions, Mass, and confession, for only Tepoztlán has a resident priest. The priest visits each village once or twice a year on the occasion of the village fiesta. The fiesta system also brings the villagers together, for there is much inter-village visiting on such occasions.

Tepoztlán is also related to the surrounding villages by ties of *compadrazgo.* In almost all cases, however, the dominant position of Tepoztlán is reflected by the fact that the other villagers seek out Tepoztecans as godparents and not vice versa. Although Tepoztecans have many godchildren in the surrounding villages, the converse is not true.

Ties of marriage within the municipio are surprisingly weak. In all there are less than a dozen individuals from other villages in the municipio married into Tepoztlán. Cases of Tepoztecans going to live in the smaller villages are practically unheard of. There are more marriages between Tepoztecans and people from villages outside of the municipio than within it.

---

flowers like ears of corn, which in the Mexican language are called *elotl,* and Xocotitlán because there are some fruits there which are called *guayabas.*

"The *estancia* of San Juan, which is in the direction of Mexico City and at the northern part of this town, is called Tepecuytlapilco, as they say because it is situated at the top of a hill, for so it signifies in the Spanish language.

"And the *estancia* of Santa Catalina, which is in the direction of Cuernavaca and at the eastern part of this town, they say it is called Cacatepetlac because it is built upon coarse rock and as it is of little use for growing things; the grass is short and this is what it means in the Spanish language.

"The *estancia* of San Andrés, which is the sixth and last of all, and stands among some hills to the south of this town, they say is called Alacueyacan (Atlacueyacan) in the Mexican tongue, which in the Spanish means land which was surrounded by reeds or place where many reeds grow, for it appears that formerly there were many there."

The feeling of superiority of Tepoztecans is also revealed in their characterizations of the other villagers. The people from Ocotitlán are described as "bad" people, as "assassins," or as "poor Indians"; of the people of Gabriel Mariaca, Tepoztecans say, "son tontitos" (they are foolish), or "they are rich but they don't know how to spend because of their ignorance." The women of Gabriel Mariaca are looked down upon because they work in the fields, wear straw hats, and carry heavy loads "like men." Some of the traditional nicknames applied to the surrounding villages are also revealing in this connection. Thus, Gabriel Mariaca is referred to as *cuatlalteme* (heads of earth, dull heads, or backward), La Calera as *cuatichtizatin* (white-headed people, because they make lime).

The political dominance of Tepoztlán over the other villages is clear. Although in theory any adult from any one of the eight villages of the municipio can become president, in practice it is almost always a Tepoztecan. The only exception known to me is the case of José Hernández from the village of Gabriel Mariaca, but he was imposed by the state governor. Rarely, a lesser office, like councilman's, may be filled from one of the surrounding villages, but this happens only as a result of a political deal.

status distinctions and family organization: 3

In the pre-Hispanic period Tepoztlán was a highly stratified society, with a few *principales* (ruling families) on the top of the social pyramid and the mass of *maceguales* (commoners) at the bottom. The *Relación* tells us something about class relations and gives us a picture that agrees quite closely with our knowledge of the structure of Aztec society at the time of the Conquest.[1]

The [Tepoztecans] recognized only two *principales;* one called *chichemeca hueytzin tecutli* and the other *cacameteutli,* until they became a *señorío* of Moctezuma, a fact recognized by their tribute of paper; and to the two *principales* they paid no regular tribute, except what they asked. They worked their lands, built houses and made clothing and gave them fowl and all that they needed.

When the lords who governed them went into the street [carried in litters] no one, man, woman, or child, was to appear on the street, except for the *principales* who accompanied them, and if perchance someone passed by, he was ordered punished; and in case this was not feasible, the said Indian threw himself to the ground, and asked pardon . . . and to have any dealings [with the lords] they did not approach them directly, but went to one of their *principales* who had the position of judges, one of whom was called *Tlacuhcalcatzintle* and the other *Tecpanecatzintle* and the other *Cuacoatzintle.* . . .

After the Spanish Conquest the social structure was modified considerably, but the old hierarchal arrangements persisted—except that the political and religious power was transferred to the new ruling group represented by the Spaniards. In Tepoztlán many of the old *principales* were maintained in power by the conquerors and were incorporated into the new administrative apparatus. Judging from early colonial documents, the local bureaucracy during the second half of the sixteenth century was very large, certainly much larger than the present bureaucracy, and in all probability larger than the pre-Hispanic one. In 1579 we find almost one hundred individuals on the official payroll of the municipio, as compared to less than twenty today.

The independence of Mexico from Spain in the early part of the nineteenth cen-

---

[1] *Relación*, pp. 241, 242.

tury seemed to have little effect on Tepoztecan internal structure. The political life of the village continued in the hands of families who represented a mixture of the old *principales* and the new Spanish elite.

During the Díaz regime the domination of the village by the upper *cacique* group reached its peak, and class distinctions were marked. The *caciques* owned most of the privately held land, controlled the communal lands of the municipio and the local government, and formed an elite group who had social contacts with the elite of Cuernavaca and even of Mexico City. They were set apart from the rest of the village population by their large and more elaborate homes located in the center of the village, their urban styled clothing, their literacy and superior education. Vicente Ortega, the *cacique* in power almost until the outbreak of the Revolution, was a *compadre* of the governor of the state of Morelos, and served as a representative to the state legislature; and other leading Tepoztecans achieved high positions in the state administrative hierarchy.

The Revolution transformed the social structure of the village. The upper or *cacique* families fled the village for their lives and lost most of their wealth, particularly their cattle and artisan shops. The poor who remained also had to leave the village repeatedly, and sought refuge in the surrounding *cerros* when government troops were approaching. Once peace was restored, the families slowly began to return to the village. Some of the *caciques* or their sons also returned to take up residence in their battered or burned homes. It was necessary for all, rich and poor, to begin life anew and build back to normalcy. But they were building within a new social framework. The participation of the villagers in the ranks of the Zapatista forces, the revolutionary slogans of "land and liberty" and "down with the *caciques*" had left its imprint on the psychology of the people and acted as a distinct levelling influence. The political dominance of the *caciques* was gone. And a fundamental economic change had occurred, for the communal lands of the municipio, which constituted about eighty per cent of all the lands, were again available to the villagers. By 1930 the village had also recovered its *ejido* from one of the nearby haciendas, further broadening the land base in the village.

FACTORS IN STATUS

Today, class distinctions in Tepoztlán are much less marked; the former economic and social bases for class distinctions are gone.[2] But there are numerous status distinctions in the village, and the possibility of some future development of sharper stratification on the basis of wealth can be seen. It might be more accurate to describe present-day Tepoztlán as an incipient class society.[3] Sex, age, and kinship

---

[2] Memory of former class distinctions remains and exerts some influence. The expression, "He is the son of a *cacique* family," was used repeatedly by our informants.

[3] The term "class" is used here in the traditional sense to distinguish between broad social groupings differentiated from other groupings by their relationship to the process of production, by occupational distinctions, income levels, and a sense of social distance that makes for cohesive social groups over a period of time. In this definition I follow MacIver who writes, "It is the sense of status, sustained by economic, political, or ecclesiastical power and by the distinc-

are the basic factors in social differentiation, while differences in wealth, education, and living standards distinguish individuals but not cohesive social groups.

SEX AND AGE

Sex and age differences are the basic factors in the ascription of status and in the structuring of inter-personal relations. Male superiority is accepted as part of the order of things. Women are expected to show deference and respect to men; wives to husbands, sisters to brothers. Sexual differentials are marked in the rearing of children, in the division of labor, and in the privileges and responsibilities of individuals at each stage of the life cycle. Men assume all important leadership roles, economic, political, social, and religious. The double standard in sexual relations is practiced by men, and is generally accepted by women. However, women have comparatively high status; they may own and inherit property, participate in religious life, and as mothers enjoy an important role within the home.

The principle of respect for age is second only to that of male superiority. Young people must address older people by the respectful *Vd.*, and in turn are addressed by the more familiar *tú*. The basic age divisions or statuses recognized in the village are five: (1) *criatura* (infant), until about age two or weaning time; (2) *niño* (child), from two to about twelve; (3) *jóvenes, muchacho, muchacha,* or señorita, from about twelve until marriage; (4) *adulto* or *hombre* (man) and *mujer* (woman), from marriage in the case of a man, and after having one or two children in the case of a young married girl; (5) *anciano* or *viejo* (the aged).

The infant status is by far the most privileged. Infants get a great deal of attention and care. Notwithstanding the widespread preference for boys, there are practically no sexual differentials in the treatment accorded infants.

The child status is an extended one, and the development of the child is viewed as a slow process which must not be unduly hurried. In the early years the child is expected to learn the all-important virtues of obedience and respect for parents, older siblings, and other adults. Responsibilities and work are assumed earlier by girls than by boys, but in both cases it is generally gradual. Nevertheless, the period of childhood is a relatively difficult one. It is a time when punishments are given, when play must be gradually restricted and finally eliminated. It is also the period of greatest demands and least rewards.

The period of youth is the time when both boys and girls assume adult work roles. They are not viewed as adults, however, and do their work under the supervision of their parents. The sexual differentials in this stage are very sharp, and boys have much more personal freedom than girls. This period of youth is generally longer for boys than girls, since the latter marry earlier. Young men, however, may not hold public office or be entrusted with positions of responsibility in the barrio.

---

tive modes of life and cultural expressions corresponding to them, that draws class apart from class, gives cohesion to each class and stratifies a whole society." Cf. Robert M. MacIver and Charles H. Page, *Society* (New York: Rinehart and Co., Inc., 1949), p. 349. It will become apparent to the reader that Tepoztlán has no classes in the above sense. However, in terms of the Warner approach, many classes and subclasses might be found in Tepoztlán.

The *adultos* consist of married adults and heads of families. Marriage is important as initiating the adult status, and it is the most productive one for both men and women. The adults are the most important group both economically and politically and they run the society. If adult males carry most of the responsibilities, they also enjoy many privileges. They may smoke and drink, have affairs with women, beat their wives, and otherwise exercise male prerogatives. These prerogatives are not supposed to apply to unmarried youths, but when young men begin to get drunk and run around with women, it is said that they "are becoming men."

The status of the aged is, theoretically, one of great respect. Old men and women can address anyone in the familiar *tú* and in return are to be addressed by *Vd*. But sometimes the more endearing *abuelito* or *papacito* is used. To contradict an *anciano* and certainly to beat an old man is an outrage; "it is like beating your own father." The status of the aged, however, is by no means an enviable one, particularly when old people can no longer support themselves. Children are supposed to support aged parents but there are cases of extreme neglect and the theme, "I would rather die than depend upon my children" is frequently heard. The old people do not take part in politics and in general do not have positions of leadership. Because of the rapidly changing culture, the *ancianos* are out of step with the times. Many speak Spanish poorly and have difficulty even in communicating with their grandchildren. In some cases the younger generation, particularly those who have been away to school, are embarrassed by the old-fashioned dress, speech, and manners of their grandparents.

RACE

Race is not an important factor in status in Tepoztlán, and racial prejudice hardly exists. Although Tepoztecans are quite sensitive to color differences, there are no distinct racial groups as such recognized in the village. The three distinctions most commonly made are *blanco, prieto,* and *indio.* The *blancos* are those with light skin and light eyes, characteristics which are definitely favored. The *prietos* are those with dark skin. The term *indio* has various connotations. Sometimes it is used as the equivalent of *campesino* as opposed to the city man; thus it may be said, "Here in Tepoztlán we are all *indios* and we get along on very little, whereas the city people are very demanding." At other times the word *indio* is used to designate low socio-cultural status, "el pobre, como es indito, no sabe ni siquiera hablar bien" (because the poor thing is Indian he can't even speak well). In this sense, many refer to the inhabitants of the smaller and poorer barrios of San Pedro, Los Reyes, and San Sebastián as *indios. Indio* is also used as a term of criticism in reference to one who has poor self-control and is capable of violence. Thus Tepoztecans will say, "In Amatlán they are very Indian, if one is not careful he may be assassinated."

Basically, the term "Indian" is used to designate social status rather than physical type. A wealthy dark person who dresses in city style may not be considered *blanco,* but neither will he be called *indio.* On the other hand, a rich person who continues to dress in the white *calzones* and huaraches like most Tepoztecans, may be called "un indio platudo," a wealthy Indian, or literally "a silvered Indian." Thus, the residents of Gabriel Mariaca are often described as "esos inditos tienen harta lana, son platudos."

The term *negro* or *negra* is sometimes used as a term of abuse. An irate husband may call his wife *negra* or *cambuca* if she is a shade darker than he. But similarly, he may call her *gringa*, if she is somewhat lighter; both terms are intended as insults.

Many of the sons and daughters of the old *cacique* families seem to be lighter than the rest of the population, suggesting that the *caciques* of the Díaz epoch may have had a stronger admixture of Spanish blood than did the rest of the population. However, groupings do not run along racial lines. About an equal sprinkling of light-skinned people is found among the rich and poor, the *cultos*, the *ignorantes*, etc.

WEALTH

The concepts of rich and poor are frequently used designations of social status in Tepoztlán. But the terms are used in a relative way, are not easily defined, and are applied, as a rule, to individuals rather than to groups. All Tepoztecans tend to characterize themselves as poor, and there is no ostentatious display of wealth on the part of the rich. Concealing wealth is a deep-seated trait, done to avoid envy, claims of friends, taxes, and contributions to the church and public affairs. This attitude tends to limit the function of wealth as a factor for social differentiation. And, by and large, the rich in Tepoztlán are not easily distinguishable from the poor.

Both rich and poor work the land dressed in the same white *calzones* and huaraches; both rich and poor hire day laborers when necessary; and men who own property, as well as those who do not, hire themselves out as laborers when cash is needed. Many of the present-day rich families were once poor, and they cling to the habits of hard work and frugality with which they improved their economic status. However, in varying degrees the rich have a higher standard of living than the poor and can be said to eat better, dress better, and live in more comfortable and better equipped homes. But a man's wealth is not judged by the way in which he lives; rather it is estimated in the amount of land, cattle, plow-oxen, and money he has.

In general there is no sharp social distance between the rich and poor, although there is much sensitivity and awareness of differences in economic status. People in Tepoztlán prefer the company of their equals or inferiors, rather than those who are in a superior economic status. But although a rich man may explain the poverty of a neighbor in terms of his being backward and ignorant, he will treat him with due respect.

LAND-OWNERSHIP

The expression, "He has many lands" (land parcels) is the simplest way the Tepoztecan has of designating wealth and high social status. Conversely, when one says, "He has no land" it is the equivalent of stating that a man is poor. But the contrast between landless and landholders from a purely economic point of view is not sharp, because most landholders have tiny holdings and do not live any better than many who are landless.[4] Yet, even the ownership of a small parcel adds to a man's social standing because of the positive value associated with land-ownership. The acquisition of even a small parcel of land gives the Tepoztecan a feeling of well being and security. It should be noted that the landholders and the landless do not constitute distinct social classes, and there is no conflict of ideologies between them.

Within the category of landholders a distinction is made between (1) *proprietarios,* those who own private land; (2) *ejidatarios,* those who hold *ejido* parcels; and (3) *tlacololeros,* those who work communal lands. The economic aspects of these three distinct tenurial types will be treated later.[5] Here it should be noted that, in a sense, each represents a distinct status group, with the greatest prestige attached to *proprietarios* and the least to the *tlacololeros.* In addition, each group has different and sometimes conflicting interests, and as such is developing distinctive group consciousness.

The *tlacololeros,* for example, organized themselves during the thirties and have taken the leadership in defending the communal lands in boundary disputes with other municipios, because these are the lands upon which they depend. The *tlacololeros* as a group have been opposed to the nationalization of the communal lands of the municipio and the creation of a municipal *ejido.* They view the transfer of *tlacolol* land to *ejidatarios* as a threat to their interests. Thus, the *tlacololeros* are the staunchest defenders of the ancient Indian system of communal land-ownership.

The *ejidatarios,* on the other hand, do not share the collectivist tendencies of the *tlacololeros.* On the contrary, they seem motivated by a strong sense of individualism and would like to become private owners of the *ejido* parcels assigned them. The *ejidatarios* are perhaps the most politically conscious group in the village, for their welfare depends in large measure on political considerations, and particularly on maintaining cordial relations with the *ejido* commissioner.

LABOR RELATIONS

Most landowners in Tepoztlán have occasion to be both employers and employees during the year. As employers they hire *peones* to help with the planting and harvesting, and as employees they hire themselves out to other landowners or artisans when work on their own land is over. This double role is a common one and blurs whatever class lines there are in Tepoztlán. Even those who are *peones* the whole year round hope some day to be landowners and employers. Also, employees are frequently relatives, *compadres,* or friends with whom there is a reciprocal arrangement of aid or labor exchange. There are no men who employ many workers on a large scale; three or four *peones* who are hired for short periods

---

[4] The contrast between landholder and landless was much sharper before the Revolution.
[5] See Chapter 6, "Land Tenure," p. 113.

during the busiest parts of the agricultural cycle are considered a good number.

The relations between employer and employee are generally characterized by a spirit of mutual cooperation as well as by a recognition of equality of status. The employer usually works side by side with his workers, addressing them in *tú* if they are his own age and in *Vd.* if they are older. In most cases a *peón* works for another only if he receives good treatment, and frequently feels that by working he is conferring a favor upon the employer. It is common for a laborer to quit a job if the employer is too imperious, demanding, or vigilant. Even in Cuernavaca, Tepoztecan workers have a reputation of being "too independent" and sensitive to slights.

There are few full-time domestic servants in Tepoztlán. Women may be hired to assist in households during fiestas, at the birth of a child, or when the mother is seriously ill. Several well-to-do families hire a laundress regularly. The absence of a servant class is in striking contrast with European rural villages and is evidence of the essential classlessness of Tepoztecan society. When domestic help is needed, it is common to call upon relatives and friends. There is a reluctance to hire maid-servants because it reduces the privacy of the home. When it is unavoidable, servants are sought from among the other villages of the municipio rather than within Tepoztlán itself. Conversely, women consider it humiliating to be servants. Orphans or the daughters of the very poorest families seek such employment, and they prefer to work in Cuernavaca or Mexico City rather than in their own village.

EDUCATION

Less than twenty years ago the distinction between the *cultos* (educated) and the *ignorantes* (ignorant) was based on the ability to read and write. With the spread of education this no longer holds. The graduates of the local school and even of the secondary schools are no longer considered *cultos*. The status of *culto* is now applied primarily to lawyers, doctors, and dentists, who live in the city, and to a few local residents who dress in city clothes, write a good letter, run a typewriter, use big or unusual words, and are intelligent and well informed. A *culto* does not necessarily have to be citified or schooled in modern ways, for one of the best known *cultos* is an old candlemaker famous for his study of Náhuatl and for his skill in speaking that ancient language. *Cultos* generally receive respect and admiration, although they are not above criticism if they have undesirable personality traits. For example, one of Redfield's principal informants was described by many of my informants as a man who was *culto* but who was also *chiflado* (lightheaded).

POLITICS

The *políticos* are the local leaders who are active in politics, and as such have a special status in the village. They have many "friends" and *compadres,* and have influence with local and state officials. They generally know how to talk well, and often act as representatives for the more retiring and humble villagers in their dealings with state or federal agencies.

There are about fifty *políticos* in the village, drawn from various groups. Some are *cultos,* others are *ignorantes.* Most of the leaders can read and write and might qualify for what Redfield designated the *correctos,* although no such social grouping is recognized in the village. Some of the *políticos* are poor, others rich; most are Catholic, but two important ones are Protestant. Some represent the older generation, others the younger. The attitude of the villagers toward the *políticos* is ambivalent. On the one hand, *políticos* are admired for their ability and popularity; on the other hand, they are criticized for neglecting their farm work and for spending and drinking excessively. The majority of the villagers are not active in politics and are called *apartados.* The *políticos* often refer to them as "niños miedosos" (fearful children).

Within the category of *políticos* there are other distinctions made, particularly between the *caciques* or *hijos de caciques* on the one hand, and the Zapatistas and *revolucionarios* on the other. The *hijos de caciques* are the descendants of the "best" families of prerevolutionary days. The term *cacique* is also applied to anyone who opposed the Revolution, irrespective of family background. The term has become a general term of opprobrium used against political enemies, especially if they are of an independent or haughty character.

Zapatista refers to all those who took an active part in the ranks of Zapata during the Revolution. Since most of the villagers sympathized with Zapata, the term "Zapatista" is now limited to those who actually fought with the guerrilla armies. For this reason they generally speak of "an old Zapatista" to differentiate between a sympathizer and a true fighter in the cause.

The term "revolutionary" is less used in Tepoztlán than either *cacique* or Zapatista, and was imported from Mexico City. The terms "revolution" and "revolutionary" are part of the official designations of the political parties in power since the Revolution. Despite the changes in structure and ideology, the word "revolutionary" remains in the titles of the leading parties. In the time of Calles it was called Partido Nacional Revolucionario; under Cárdenas and Avila Camacho, Partido de la Revolución Mexicana; and now, Partido Revolucionario Institucional. Since Tepoztecans have become increasingly exposed to political propagandists, they have come to associate the term "revolutionary" with anyone who works for the government party in power.

RELIGION

The first awareness of a religion other than Catholicism came to Tepoztecans at about 1900 when a group of Mormon missionaries converted a few families in the village of San Andrés. In the early thirties, exposure to another religion came closer to home when about twenty Tepoztecan families became Seventh Day Adventists. The leading figure in this break with Catholicism was a Tepoztecan from the poor barrio of San Sebastián. He was an ex-Zapatista and a local leftist *político* who had been forced to flee the village after the massacres of 1927. While in Mexico City he was converted. He returned to Tepoztlán in 1927, and by 1930 had won many families in his barrio to the new religion. Thus, for the first time in the history of the village there were Catholics and Protestants.

The Protestant families were ostracized and on a number of occasions their homes were stoned. The fact that the Protestants were among the poorer families, and primarily *tlacololeros,* did not add to the prestige of the new cult. In the face of the hostility against them their number dwindled. Today there are less than a dozen families who continue as Seventh Day Adventists. They have managed to adapt themselves by continuing to pay the barrio *limosnas,* supporting local fiestas, and not being too strict about keeping their Sabbath (Saturday) when working for a Catholic employer. Though no longer persecuted they still have very low status in the village. The children of these families have suffered a great deal. They are the butt of bitter comments and jokes in the school and have very few friends in the village. Nevertheless, the leader of the Seventh Day Adventists has again become active in village politics and has been accepted again by his Catholic political colleagues. This has meant a departure from Seventh Day Adventist tenets, in that he has returned to drinking and smoking. Now he says of himself, "I am half-Catholic again."

This experience with Protestantism within their own ranks has made Tepoztecans wary of outsiders who may be identified as Protestants. This was further reinforced by the establishment of the Hatch Demonstration Project under the auspices of the YMCA. The church has waged a sucessful propaganda campaign against the project, denouncing it as a Protestant missionary center working under the guise of a scientific program.

THE FAMILY

Tepoztlán is a family-centered society. The biological family consisting of parents and unmarried children constitutes the basic economic and social unit, and is by far the predominant type. The Tepoztecan family has a strong patriarchal emphasis and patrilocal residence is preferred. Families are strong, cohesive units held together by traditional bonds of loyalty, common economic strivings, mutual dependence, stability of marriage, the prospect of inheritance, and finally, the absence of other social groups to which the individual can turn in time of need. Family unity and stability is further assured by the pattern of child training and the nature of parent-child relationships, which will be discussed later.

Some Tepoztecan families work smoothly with a minimum of tensions. In others there is much conflict and tensions resulting from drunkenness of the husband, adultery of one of the spouses, sibling rivalry, favoritism on the part of the parents, and difficulties with in-laws. Even in these cases, however, the negative or disruptive aspects of family life are generally counterbalanced by the positive ones, and the family remains the strongest and most cohesive unit. Moreover, despite the many social and economic changes of recent years and the rather sharp differences between generations, we find little decline in parental authority and little evidence of family disorganization.

Independence, self-reliance, and a strong sense of privacy are among the cherished values of Tepoztecan family life. Relations with the extended family are limited; there is a reticence in borrowing and calling upon others for help and, by the same token, reticence in giving help. Yet, in times of emergency a Tepoztecan turns most often to relatives, uncles, aunts, brothers, sisters, godparents, and *compadres*. Favors are carefully remembered and usually returned. There are no formal councils of the extended family, but relatives are generally well informed about one another and there is much gossip and unsolicited advice. Visiting among relatives is infrequent and for the most part is limited to special occasions, such as the annual barrio fiesta, illness, births, weddings, and deaths.

THE FAMILY AND THE HOUSE SITE

There are 662 occupied house sites in the village. Most sites contain a single house but some have two, three, and four. The number of persons per house site ranges from 1 (45 cases) to 17 (1 case). The distribution of persons per house site is shown in Table 10.

TABLE 10. Distribution of Persons per House Site.

No. of Persons	No. of House Sites
1	45
2	82
3	76
4	76
5	68
6	80
7	78
8	60
9	55
10	20
11	10
12	7
13	2
14	1
15	1
16	0
17	1
Total	662

Smaller households predominate over larger ones, reflecting the fact that most households consist of the biological family. The large number of house sites occupied by a single individual is very striking for this peasant community. It reflects the weakness of the extended family and reminds us of conditions in the urban centers.

An analysis of the kinship composition of each of the house sites is shown in Table 11.

It can be seen from Table 11 that over seventy per cent of all house sites are occupied by the biological family. When a niece or nephew lives with the family, it is almost always because the child was orphaned or abandoned. Such a child

TABLE 11. Kinship Composition by Households, 1943.

Type of Composition	House Sites
I Simple biological family with variations	
a) Husband, wife, and unmarried children	421
b) Type I-a and niece or nephew	12
c) Type I-a and brother or sister of one of the spouses	24
Total	457
II The biological family with married children	
a) Husband, wife, unmarried children, and one married son and his family	56
b) Husband, wife, unmarried children, and one married daughter and her family	26
c) Husband, wife, unmarried children, and married sons or daughters and their families	8
Total	90
III Married siblings with their families	
a) Two married brothers and their families	3
b) Two married sisters and their families	5
c) Married brother and sister and their families	6
Total	14
IV Unrelated families	5
V Persons living alone	45
VI Miscellaneous composition	51
Total	662

may be taken in by the godparents, but living with an aunt or uncle is generally preferred. Usually an unwed or widowed brother or sister lives with a married sibling when the parents are no longer alive.

Approximately sixteen per cent of the house sites are occupied by multiple families, some of which are extended families. When a young married son lives with his parents as an *hijo de familia,* he continues to work for his father and is subject to his authority. In such cases there is a single fireplace with the daughter-in-law working under the supervision of the mother-in-law. This is clearly the older pattern of family life. Traditionally, the married son continues to live with his father until the next son marries, after which the older son may set up his own house or at least establish his own kitchen. However, the present tendency in the village is for the young couple to become independent as soon as possible, often after one or two years. In fact, many of the younger generation would prefer to set up their own house immediately after marriage and those who have the wherewithal do so. The majority of the cases under Type II and all in Types III and IV are multiple families each with their separate kitchens and separate budgets.

Although residence is preferably patrilocal, there are twenty-six cases of married daughters living with the parents. About one-third of these cases include the daughters' husbands, the others are either widows, abandoned wives, or women who have separated from their husbands. There are only eight families in which more than one married son and daughter continue to live with their parents, again indicating the few cases of large extended families living together. Cases of married siblings living with their families are also few.

Because of the absence of the custom of renting houses, it is unusual to find unrelated families living on the same house site. The five cases indicated in Table 11 were those in which an unused house on a house site was loaned to a family or a newly wed couple without a home.

Under "Miscellaneous Composition" we have included those cases which did not fall under our classifications. A variety of types are covered by this category. For example, cases of an old widowed brother and sister; a widow and son plus the family of her deceased husband's nephew; parents with the first and second wives of their dead son and his children, with a widowed daughter, and with a daughter separated from her husband.

THE FAMILY AS AN ECONOMIC UNIT

In Tepoztlán, as in most peasant societies, the family is the basic cooperative unit of production, and each member is expected to contribute to its support and welfare. The biological family seeks to be independent and self-sufficient. There are no institutionalized day-to-day cooperative endeavors between families, and normally little aid is given or received. Nevertheless, some mutual assistance between families exists in the form of borrowing and labor exchange. For example, a man who owns a small parcel of land but no plow-oxen may arrange to work as a *peón* for an uncle, brother, *compadre,* or neighbor, in exchange for the plowing of his own land. But there is a minimum of such cooperation, for Tepoztecans are essentially individualists.

Most work, whether it be agriculture, trade, or some special occupation, is carried on individually rather than cooperatively. Even within the family the division of labor is such that each individual does a separate task instead of working together on the same task. For example, the mother may do all the marketing, one daughter may wash all the clothes, another daughter may grind all the corn. Although such a division of labor may seem quite natural, it contrasts with that of a more cooperative society like the Zuni Indians where, for example, three women of a single household grind corn in unison.

Much of the men's work is also done on an individual basis. It is common to see men working alone in the fields and returning alone in the evening. Similarly, a man will go alone to cut wood, burn charcoal, or transport goods to distant villages. The care of cattle by young men and boys is also frequently done by a single individual, although brothers or cousins sometimes go together. On cattle buying trips to Guerrero, two or three men will go together for mutual protection but each carries on his own business.

On a number of occasions during the year the entire family may work together on a single project. This occurs sometimes during the corn harvest, but more frequently in picking plums during September and October. The shelling of large quantities of corn for sale also may be done by the whole family. This occurs more often in the smaller outlying barrios where the women are less reluctant to do men's work. Finally, the barrio fiesta generally requires a great deal of cooperative endeavor within the family.

The daily division of labor within the household reveals how the family functions as an economic unit. We present in Chart 1 a synchronic record of the activities of each member of a family which we observed for this purpose over a period of four days. This family is a member of the upper economic group and owns several plots of land and some cattle. The parents are in their early fifties and the age of the three daughters ranges from thirteen to twenty-four. Another daughter and a son are away at boarding schools and contribute little to the family in the form of labor. The record was made from March 28 to March 31, 1944, during the dry season when the father had little work in the fields. In addition, the father was slightly ill with chills and fever during part of the recorded period. This was not a disadvantage since it served to keep him at home where his activities could be more readily observed. The picking of *guajes* (acacia pods) fortunately began during this period and gave us an opportunity to record in detail how that work is carried on.

The following record, though covering only four days, shows in detail how the general work patterns operate during this season of the year. The father is at home and does many chores normally done by his wife. His illness does not prevent him from working; in Tepoztlán a man remains in bed only when seriously ill. However, he rests a good deal and reads, which is something the father in our observed family rarely does.

The mother is generally the first to rise and make the fire. She serves the meals, "cures" her husband, visits her mother, and is the only one of the women in the family to take an afternoon nap with more or less regularity. The item "Visits woman," which appears among her activities on Thursday, was listed because she had learned that this woman would visit the boarding school where the absent daughter was studying, and the mother wished to send her daughter a package by this woman.

CHART 1. A Synchronic Record of the Activities of Each Member of a Tepoztecan Family.

Time (March 28)	Father	Mother	Eldest Daughter	Second Daughter	Youngest Daughter
A.M. 6:00– 6:30	In bed	Rises, makes fire and coffee	In bed	In bed	In bed
6:30– 7:00	Rises, feeds cattle, takes them to pasture	Goes to buy bread, sweeps patio	Rises, sweeps kitchen, prepares utensils	Rises, goes for milk	"
7:00– 7:30	Drinks coffee	Serves husband and self coffee	Grinds corn, makes tortillas	Drinks coffee, cuts and stores dried fish	Rises, washes, combs hair
7:30– 8:00	Hauls water, shells corn for mules	Resumes sweeping patio	"	Smooths and folds laundered clothes	Breakfasts
8:00– 8:30	Breakfasts	Combs hair, breakfasts, serves others	"	Breakfasts	Goes to school
8:30– 9:00	Talks with investigator	Cuts squash for animals, cooks squash, shells corn	"	Makes beds	At school
9:00– 9:30	Goes to bed	Arranges squash in market basket	Breakfasts	Sweeps porch	"
9:30–10:00	In bed	"	Washes dishes	Washes arms and feet, combs hair	"
10:00–10:30	" "	Goes to market to sell corn and squash	Prepares corn for grinding	Accompanies mother to market to make purchases	"
10:30–11:00	" "	At market	Prepares and cooks stew	At market	"
11:00–11:30	" "	" "	"	" "	"
11:30–12:00	" "	" "	"	Returns home, polishes nails	"

Chart 1. A Synchronic Record of the Activities of Each Member of a Tepoztecan Family (*Cont.*).

Time P.M.	Father	Mother	Eldest Daughter	Second Daughter	Youngest Daughter
12:00–12:30	Feeds mules	At market	Grinds corn	Talks with recorder	Returns home
12:30– 1:00	Rests	" "	Makes tortillas	Feeds chickens	Does nothing
1:00– 1:30	"	Returns home, prepares lunch	" "	Helps making tortillas	" "
1:30– 2:00	Eats and talks with recorder	Serves and eats	" "	Eats	Eats
2:00– 2:30	" "	"	Eats	"	Goes to school
2:30– 3:00	Reads prayers	"	"	Sews	At school
3:00– 3:30	Goes to bed	Hauls water for animals	Washes dishes	"	"
3:30– 4:00	In bed	In bed	" "	"	"
4:00– 4:30	" "	Cleans dried gourds	Shells corn, prepares dough	"	"
4:30– 5:00	Reads prayers	"	" "	"	"
5:00– 5:30	In bed	"	Mends her clothes	"	Returns home
5:30– 6:00	" "	Feeds turkeys	" "	"	Reads
6:00– 6:30	" "	Cuts squash for animals	Knits	"	Talks to friends
6:30– 7:00	" "	Mends blouse	"	"	"
7:00– 7:30	" "	Goes to visit mother	Grinds corn	Goes for bread	Knits

CHART 1. A Synchronic Record of the Activities of Each Member of a Tepoztecan Family (*Cont.*).

Time	Father	Mother	Eldest Daughter	Second Daughter	Youngest Daughter
P.M.					
7:30– 8:00	In bed	Sits in kitchen, talks with girls	Makes tortillas	Prepares coffee	Knits
8:00– 8:30	Gets up to drink coffee	Serves coffee to family and self	Eats	Eats	Eats
8:30– 9:00	Goes to bed, **takes medicine and foot bath**	Prepares medicinal drink and foot bath for husband	Washes dishes	Knits	Knits
9:00– 9:30	In bed	Goes to bed	Goes to bed	"	"
9:30	" "	In bed	In bed	Goes to bed	Goes to bed
(March 29) A.M.					
6:00– 6:30	Rises, feeds cattle	Rises, puts up coffee	Rises, makes fire, sweeps kitchen	In bed	In bed
6:30– 7:00	Drinks coffee	Hauls water, goes for bread	Grinds corn	Rises, goes for milk	" "
7:00– 7:30	Hauls water	Has coffee and bread	"	Waters plants, has coffee and bread	Rises, washes
7:30– 8:00	Takes cattle to pasture	Goes to wash clothes at *lavaderos*	Makes tortillas	Sweeps, makes beds	Eats
8:00– 8:30	Breakfasts and talks with family	Washes clothes	"	Goes to pick flowers	Goes to school
8:30– 9:00	Feeds animals	"	Breakfasts	"	At school
9:00– 9:30	Looks for carpenter's tools	"	Prepares beans	"	" "

CHART 1. A Synchronic Record of the Activities of Each Member of a Tepoztecan Family (*Cont.*).

Time A.M.	Father	Mother	Eldest Daughter	Second Daughter	Youngest Daughter
9:30–10:00	Cuts wood for making chairs	Looks over trees in patio, plans to plant more	Washes dishes	Goes to pick flowers	At school
10:00–10:30	"	"	Smooths dirt floor and fills in holes with earth	Washes, combs hair	"
10:30–11:00	"	Hauls water for plants	"	Sews	"
11:00–11:30	"	Feeds chickens	"	"	"
11:30–12:00	Goes to bed	Washes, combs hair	Grinds corn and makes tortillas	"	"
P.M. 12:00–12:30	Continues work on chairs	Prepares lunch	"	"	Returns home
12:30– 1:00	"	"	"	"	Sits in kitchen
1:00– 1:30	"	"	"	"	"
1:30– 2:00	Eats	Serves and eats	Grinds corn and makes tortillas	Eats	Eats
2:00– 2:30	Rests	Shells corn	Eats	Sews	Goes to school
2:30– 3:00	Works on chairs	"	Washes dishes	Goes to doctor for cure	At school
3:00– 3:30	"	"	"	"	"
3:30– 4:00	"	Goes to plaza to buy *rebozo*	Knits	"	"
4:00– 4:30	"	"	"	"	"

CHART 1. A Synchronic Record of the Activities of Each Member of a Tepoztecan Family (*Cont.*).

Time	Father	Mother	Eldest Daughter	Second Daughter	Youngest Daughter
P.M.					
4:30– 5:00	Works on chairs	Goes to plaza to buy *rebozo*	Knits	Goes to doctor for cure	At school
5:00– 5:30	"	Returns, goes for bread	"	Returns, cuts out dress	Returns home
5:30– 6:00	"	Visits mother	"	" "	Visits friend
6:00– 6:30	"	Shells corn	Takes image of Virgin to friend's house	Accompanies eldest daughter	" "
6:30– 7:00	Completes one chair	" "	" "	" "	" "
7:00– 7:30	Cleans up, puts away tools	Prepares supper	" "	" "	" "
7:30– 8:00	Rests	" "	Grinds corn, makes tortillas	Knits	" "
8:00– 8:30	Eats	Serves and **eats**	" "	Eats	Eats
8:30– 9:00	Goes to bed	Talks in **kitchen**	Eats	Talks in kitchen	Talks in kitchen
9:00– 9:30	In bed	Mends skirt	Washes dishes	Goes to bed	Goes to bed
9:30	" "	Goes to bed	Goes to bed	In bed	In bed
(March 30)					
A.M.					
5:30– 6:00	Rises, feeds cattle	Rises, makes fire and coffee, sweeps patio	In bed	Rises, sweeps corridor	" "
6:00– 6:30	Drinks coffee, hauls water	Takes cattle to **pasture**	Rises, works in kitchen	Goes for milk	" "
6:30– 7:00	Hauls water	Takes cattle to **pasture**, shells **beans**	Makes tortillas, grinds corn	Makes beds	" "

Chart 1. A Synchronic Record of the Activities of Each Member of a Tepoztecan Family (*Cont.*).

Time	Father	Mother	Eldest Daughter	Second Daughter	Youngest Daughter
A.M.					
7:00– 7:30	Hauls water	Takes cattle to pasture, shells beans	Makes tortillas, grinds corn	Breakfasts	Rises, washes, combs hair
7:30– 8:00	Breakfasts	Breakfasts	" "	Feeds chickens, treats one	Breakfasts
8:00– 8:30	Hauls more water	Shells corn for mules	Breakfasts, washes dishes	Goes to buy beans for Lent	Goes to school
8:30– 9:00	Looks for tools to pick guajes	Helps look for tools	" "	Cleans beans	At school
9:00– 9:30	Makes new handles for ax and hoe	Waters plants	Cleans kitchen	Washes feet, combs hair	" "
9:30–10:00	"	Prepares stew	Washes feet, combs hair	Changes dress	" "
10:00–10:30	"	Picks over plants, shells corn, takes it to market to sell, washes clothes on way,	Goes to church	Goes to church with sister	" "
10:30–11:00	"		"	" "	" "
11:00–11:30	"	prepares lunch	"	" "	" "
11:30–12:00	"	"	"	" "	" "
P.M.					
12:00–12:30	"	"	"	" "	Returns home
12:30– 1:00	"	"	"	" "	At home
1:00– 1:30	"	"	Grinds corn, makes tortillas	Helps prepare meal	" "
1:30– 2:00	Eats	Serves and eats	" "	Eats	Eats
2:00– 2:30	Continues work with tools	Combs hair	" "	Cuts out blouse	Goes to school

CHART 1. A Synchronic Record of the Activities of Each Member of a Tepoztecan Family (*Cont.*).

Time	Father	Mother	Eldest Daughter	Second Daughter	Youngest Daughter
P.M.					
2:30– 3:00	Continues work with tools	Visits mother	Grinds corn, makes tortillas	Cuts out blouse	At School
3:00– 3:30	"	"	Eats	Goes to bed	"
3:30– 4:00	"	Goes to bed	Washes dishes	Sews	"
4:00– 4:30	"	In bed	"	"	"
4:30– 5:00	"	Selects leaves for tamales	Knits	"	"
5:00– 5:30	Goes to bed	Visits woman	"	Goes to church for Rosario	Returns home
5:30– 6:00	Continues work	"	"	"	At home
6:00– 6:30	"	"	"	"	"
6:30– 7:00	Picks *guajes*	"	Goes to get image of Virgin	Sews	"
7:00– 7:30	"	Gathers *guajes*	Grinds corn	Lights candles	"
7:30– 8:00	Eats	Serves and eats	Lies down with headache	Eats	Eats
8:00– 8:30	Talks with family	Talks, washes dishes	In bed	Talks with family	Talks with family
8:30– 9:00	Goes to bed	"	" "	"	"
9:00– 9:30	In bed	Goes to bed	" "	Goes to bed	Goes to bed
(March 31) A.M.					
5:00– 5:30	Rises, feeds cattle	Rises, picks *guajes*	" "	In bed	In bed

CHART 1. A Synchronic Record of the Activities of Each Member of a Tepoztecan Family (*Cont.*).

Time	Father	Mother	Eldest Daughter	Second Daughter	Youngest Daughter
A.M.					
5:30– 6:00	Picks *guajes*	Picks *guajes*	Rises, sweeps	In bed	In bed
6:00– 6:30	"	"	Grinds corn, makes tortillas	Rises, goes for milk	Rises
6:30– 7:00	"	"	"	Picks *guajes*	Combs hair, washes
7:00– 7:30	"	"	"	"	
7:30– 8:00	"	"	"	Breakfasts	Breakfasts
8:00– 8:30	Breakfasts	Breakfasts	Breakfasts	Picks *guajes*	Goes to school
8:30– 9:00	Picks *guajes*	Picks *guajes*	Washes dishes	Makes beds, sweeps	At school
9:00– 9:30	"	"	Bathes feet	Sews	" "
9:30–10:00	"	"	Goes to church	"	" "
10:00–10:30	"	"	"	"	" "
10:30–11:00	"	"	"	Shells corn	" "
11:00–11:30	Feeds cattle	"	"	Sews	" "
11:30–12:00	Picks *guajes*	"	"	"	" "
P.M.					
12:00–12:30	"	"	Grinds corn, makes tortillas	"	" "
12:30– 1:00	"	"	"	"	" "
1:00– 1:30	"	Prepares lunch	"	"	Returns home

CHART 1. A Synchronic Record of the Activities of Each Member of a Tepoztecan Family.

Time P.M.	Father	Mother	Eldest Daughter	Second Daughter	Youngest Daughter
1:30– 2:00	Eats lunch	Serves and eats	Eats	Eats	Eats
2:00– 2:30	Picks *guajes*	Sorts *guajes*	Washes dishes	Goes to cousin's house to bathe	Does school work
2:30– 3:00	" "	"	" "	" "	Goes to school
3:00– 3:30	Waters cattle	"	Shells corn	Picks *guajes*	At school
3:30– 4:00	Picks *guajes*	"	"	"	"
4:00– 4:30	"	"	Irons clothes	"	"
4:30– 5:00	"	"	"	"	"
5:00– 5:30	"	"	"	"	"
5:30– 6:00	"	"	"	"	Returns home
6:00– 6:30	"	"	"	"	At home
6:30– 7:00	Sorts *guajes*	"	"	Fixes dress	"
7:00– 7:30	"	"	"	" "	"
7:30– 8:00	Eats	Irons clothes	Makes tortillas	Lights candles	"
8:00– 8:30	Talks with wife	Eats	Eats	Eats	Eats
8:30– 9:00	Goes to bed	Talks with daughters	Washes dishes	Talks with mother and sisters	Talks with mother and sisters
9:00– 9:30	In bed	Goes to bed	Goes to bed	Goes to bed	Goes to bed

The eldest daughter is also an early riser. She does not pick *guajes* with the others, but instead takes over her mother's task of ironing. Her daily routine changes little throughout the year and is broken only by knitting or going to church. She frequently lies down in the afternoon because of a headache.

The second daughter does a variety of work, much of which is pleasurable, like going to the plaza or picking flowers. She spends much more time on her personal appearance than does her elder sister.

The youngest daughter always rises last and leaves for school without doing chores as other girls of her age commonly do. Her day is principally devoted to school and varies little during the school year.

The record also reveals some interesting details concerning the division of labor among the women. Limiting ourselves to a discussion of the mother and the two older daughters, we find that their activities fall under the following categories: housework, farm work, marketing, sewing and knitting, and church attendance. Table 12 summarizes the number of hours spent by the women of this family on each of these activities during the four days we observed them.

TABLE 12. Hours Spent by Women of Tepoztecan Family at Various Activities During Four-Day Period.

Type of Activity	Hours		
	Mother	Eldest Daughter	Second Daughter
Housework	15	39	9
Farm work	21½	—	8
Trading or selling	8½	—	—
Marketing	3	—	4½
Sewing and knitting	—	5	18
Church attendance	—	7	5½

Of sixty-three hours of housework, forty-eight were done by the daughters, and thirty-nine of these forty-eight hours were done by the eldest daughter alone. She spent approximately five hours each day kneeling at the *metate* or over the *comal,* grinding corn and making tortillas, since this family lives too far from the mill to carry the corn there daily. The second daughter spent on the average of four and one-half hours a day at the sewing machine. This work varies considerably during the year, however, depending upon the fiesta cycle.

The mother's emphasis on farm work is clear, though this also varies with the time of the year. She devotes more time to trading than this four-day record indicates, since she frequently spends one or two full days a week at the Cuernavaca market, where she gets a slightly higher price for her corn and where she can make certain purchases at a lower price. It is interesting to note that although the youngest daughter goes to the plaza twice a day to school, she is rarely asked to do the marketing because the mother and second daughter enjoy this activity and prefer to do it themselves. The mother goes to the plaza once or twice a day and the second

daughter four or five times a week. In the four-day period seven ,
hours were consumed in marketing trips.

The daughters spend more time than the mother in sewing and knittin,
going to church. These tend to be regarded as leisure activities, and the mo.
does not indulge in them except when necessary because she "doesn't want to lose
time." However, she devotes more time to going to church and to other religious
activities than this record indicates. Both sisters, but particularly the eldest, have
the reputation of being devout and spend much time going to church. Almost the
only occasion for the older girl to leave the house is because of some religious
activity.

In the daily routine the women of the household have many more opportunities
of working together than does the family as a whole. They may work together
in the kitchen, accompany one another to the plaza as chaperones, and exchange
instruction in sewing and knitting. Cooperation is at its highest in preparing fiesta
meals, particularly the annual barrio fiesta.

The division of labor varies from family to family and depends chiefly upon
the number of sons to the number of daughters; the number of grown children to
the number of small children; the amount of land, livestock, fruit trees, and other
property the family owns; and the ambition and enterprise of the parents.

MARRIAGE

There are three types of marriage in Tepoztlán, namely, *por lo civil* (civil marriage), *por la iglesia* (church marriage), and *uniones libres* (free unions). According to the Mexican Census of 1940 ten per cent of all married couples in
Tepoztlán were married by civil law alone, twenty-five per cent by church alone,
and fifty per cent by both civil law and church; and fifteen per cent had entered into
free unions. To understand the distribution of these types of marriage it must be
remembered that since 1928 civil marriage has been obligatory by law. Before that
time most people in Tepoztlán married only by church, or lived in free union.
Church marriage still carries the greatest prestige and, as in most of Mexico, is considered the only true form of marriage by the majority—but especially by the older
folk. Civil marriage is viewed as a preliminary to church marriage; the priest is not
supposed to marry anyone who does not have a legal marriage certificate. But marriage by civil law alone is increasing. A study of all Tepoztecan marriages recorded
in Tepoztlán between 1941 and 1946 showed that a little over twenty per cent were
civil marriages not followed by church marriages. The reasons for this trend will be
discussed later.

The relatively low status of civil marriage is reflected in the types of people who
marry only *por lo civil*: (1) orphaned girls with no family to press for a church
marriage; (2) girls who become pregnant before marriage; (3) women who have
had one or more children out of wedlock; (4) second marriages; (5) elopements;
(6) poor boys who cannot afford a church wedding. In these cases there is an
absence of elaborate preparation for the marriage. The couple generally appear

before the local municipal authorities in the same clothing they wear daily. They obtain a marriage certificate for which they pay a fee which varies with the economic status and political connections of the groom. Some pay as little as five or ten pesos; others pay as much as fifty pesos. After they get their marriage certificate the couple may go to the home of the groom where chocolate, bread, wine, and *ponche* may be served. However, the simplicity of the civil marriage is in sharp contrast with the elaborate and expensive preparations for the church marriage.[6]

Less than a generation ago, girls commonly married between the age of twelve and fifteen and boys anywhere from sixteen to thirty, but most often in their middle and late twenties. Today there is a definite trend toward later marriage for girls and earlier marriage for boys. An analysis of 133 Tepoztlán marriages recorded in the municipio marriage registry from 1941 to 1946, inclusive, reveals that most girls marry between fifteen and seventeen and most boys between nineteen and twenty. (See Table 13.)

TABLE 13. Frequency Distribution of Age of Marriage for Men and Women in 133 Cases Recorded During 1941-1946, Inclusive.

Age	No. of Men	No. of Women	Age	No. of Men	No. of Women
12	0	1	26	2	2
13	0	0	27	1	1
14	0	5	28	2	0
15	0	22	29	3	1
16	0	28	30	2	3
17	8	27	31	0	0
18	11	15	32	1	2
19	17	11	33	1	0
20	27	1	34	2	0
21	10	0	35	3	0
22	11	4	36	3	0
23	9	3	37	3	0
24	4	0	38	2	0
25	4	0	39	0	0
			40	1	0

Eighty per cent of the women and twenty-seven per cent of the men married at nineteen or earlier, whereas only ten per cent of the women and fifty-four per cent of the men married in their twenties. There are many more marriages of men than women in their thirties and forties. The few women who marry after twenty-nine represent cases of second marriage. In the past a girl who was not married by the time she was twenty had little chance of getting married; and it was said of such girls, "She might as well enter a convent," and "She is ready to dress saints." More and more girls are delaying marriage in order to go through secondary school and become teachers. It is interesting to note that many of the Tepoztecan school-

---

[6] In the past there were two stages in the civil marriage, the *presentación* and the actual marriage.

teachers in the village who are now in their early twenties are still unmarried and are already considered "old maids."

A study of the age difference between spouses in the 133 couples mentioned above showed that the husband was older than the wife in all but three cases. In one of these cases the husband and wife were of the same age, and in the other two the wives were one and six years older than the husbands. Table 14 shows the distribution of the age differences between spouses in which the husbands were older.

TABLE 14. Age Differences Between Husbands and Wives, 1944.

Age Difference (in years)	No. of Cases
1	20
2	13
3	24
4	15
5	11
6	15
7	11
8	3
9	5
10	2
11	1
12	2
13	1
14	1
15	2
16	0
17	1
18	1
19	1
20	4

The qualities looked for in a spouse vary considerably between boys and girls. In selecting a wife, boys generally choose a girl for romantic reasons, beauty, or personality. Girls tend to be more realistic about selecting a husband and will often refuse to marry a boy who is known to drink, chase women, be violent, or be lazy. However, status factors are very important in marriage. It is usual for boys to seek out a girl who is poorer and who has the same or less education, so that "the man can be the boss" and his family need not be ashamed before her. Tepoztecan boys tend to "respect" and avoid having affairs with girls from the more important and prosperous families, for fear of incurring reprisals from the parents of such girls. Girls, on the other hand, seek to improve their economic status with marriage, and it is rare for a girl to marry a man with less education. As a result of these attitudes, the daughters of the families in the upper economic group in the village have difficulty finding husbands. They tend to marry later, and to marry more educated men or men from the outside. Occasionally a wealthy girl in her late twenties will marry a boy poorer than herself rather than remain unmarried.

An analysis of twenty-five marriages that occurred in two of the smaller barrios within the last ten years revealed that in fifteen cases the wife was poorer than the husband at the time of marriage, in five cases husband and wife had approximately the same economic status, and in five cases the wife was from a wealthier family than the husband. In each of the five marriages in the last group there was some extenuating factor which explained the fact that a rich girl married a poor boy. Two of the girls were known to have had affairs previous to the marriage; one girl was thirty years old and married a boy of seventeen; one girl was from a small nearby village and married "up" socially, if not economically, into Tepoztlán; and one girl married for love over the objections of her parents.

Parents, in giving their blessings to a marriage, are more concerned with practical considerations of the health of the prospective mate and the family's reputation. The boy's mother and godmother will make inquiries about the girl and will oppose her if she is found to have a reputation for being lazy or disobedient at home, having many *novios,* going out alone, or being sickly. If the women in the girl's family frequently suffer from lack of milk at the birth of a child, she will be considered a bad risk. Mothers are also wary of their son's marrying a girl who is the favorite at home. These factors are of prime importance to the boy's mother since she will be closely associated with her future daughter-in-law. If the mother strongly disapproves of the girl, she will do everything she can to break up the relationship. If the son insists on the marriage, his parents will be obligated to carry out his wishes but will do so grudgingly and will make a poor wedding.

The girl's parents seek a son-in-law who owns or who will inherit some property and who knows how to work hard. They are not so demanding about personal qualities as are his parents, since their son-in-law will, for the most part, not live with them, although they generally disapprove of a man who drinks a great deal or who is *muy enamorado.* A boy who is discovered to be their daughter's *novio* will almost always be strongly disapproved of by the girl's parents, because of their anger over being deceived and because it is taken to be evidence of the boy's lack of respect for them.

Marriage restrictions in Tepoztlán follow the usual Catholic tradition of western culture. Marriage between all but distant relatives is forbidden. First and second cousins do not marry, and marriage between third and fourth cousins is discouraged. However, relationships beyond second cousins are often not carefully kept track of so that in practice there are many marriages between relatives. There are also marriages between individuals of the same surname. An interesting aspect of marriage restrictions is that children of *compadres* cannot marry each other, for they are "spiritual brothers and sisters." Since the *compadre* terminology is also extended to the sibling of the *compadre,* this marriage restriction also includes their children, and many families are therefore ruled out from those eligible for marriage. There was not a single case of marriage between children of *compadres.*

The great majority of Tepoztecans marry within their own village. Of 585 married couples in the village in 1944 only 58 were marriages with outsiders. Of those marrying into the village, 35 were women and 23 were men, reflecting the predominance of patrilocal residence. Eighteen of the outsiders married to Tepoztecans came from the surrounding villages within the municipio of Tepoztlán; forty came from rural regions of nearby states such as Guerrero, Puebla, and Mexico, D.F. The relatively few marriages between Tepoztecans and other villages within the municipio are probably due to the attitudes of superiority of Tepoztecans.

Forty-two per cent of the marriages in the village are between members of the same barrio. (See Table 15.) This is a much higher proportion than might be

TABLE 15. Inter- and Intra-Barrio and Village Marriages, 1944.

Barrio	Men Married to Women of Other Barrios	Men Married to Women of Other Villages or Towns	Women Married to Men of Other Barrios	Women Married to Men of Other Villages or Towns	Intra-Barrio Marriages	Couples From Other Barrios or Villages	Total
Santo Domingo	39	11	13	10	70	4	147
La Santísima	44	6	19	6	38	20	133
San Sebastián	12	4	4	1	10	8	39
San Pedro	2	2	2	. .	4	1	11
San Miguel	33	7	10	4	52	21	127
Santa Cruz (large)	26	2	7	1	26	3	65
Santa Cruz (small)	15	2	1	. .	3	4	25
Los Reyes	15	4	6	1	10	2	38
Total	186	38	62	23	213	63	585

inferred from Redfield's statement on this point in 1926-27. As might be expected, the highest percentage of intra-barrio marriages occurs in the larger barrios where there is a wider choice of eligible mates. The relatively high incidence of intra-barrio marriage means that one's affinal relatives are within one's own barrio. Since visiting and other social activities tend to follow kinship lines, this type of marriage strengthens the barrio as a social unit.

Inter-barrio marriages constitute approximately 49 per cent of all marriages. By far the greater number are cases in which the women leave their own barrio and go to live in the barrio of their husband, again reflecting the preference for patrilocal residence. However, the fact that 85 cases (representing 16 per cent of all couples) were those in which the men went to live in the barrio of their wives, is significant. Tepoztecans speak with deprecation of matrilocal residence. When a young man goes to live with his wife's people after marriage, it is said, "se regaló como perro" (he was given away like a dog). Another common expression is, "se fué como 'nuero'" (he went as a male daughter-in-law). Matrilocal residence occurs for the most part in the case of poor orphans or in the case of younger men marrying older and more dominating women.

It can be seen in Table 15 that most intermarriages are between the large ad-

joining barrios of the center, namely Santo Domingo, San Miguel, and La Santís-
·ima. Table 15 also shows that individuals from the smaller barrios of San Pedro,
Los Reyes, and San Sebastián marry very little with individuals of the larger barrios.
It is noteworthy that there was not a single marriage between the barrio of San
Pedro and Santo Domingo. These two barrios represent the extremes in size and
are also at opposite ends of the village.

Divorce and Separation: On the whole, marriage is quite stable in Tepoztlán.
Divorce as such is practically unknown. However, separations occur and may be
initiated by either spouse. In the cases we have studied there were about as many
wives who left their husbands as vice versa. The most frequent cause for separation
on the part of the husband is that he finds another woman more attractive. Since
it is common for men to have mistresses, permanent attachments are often formed
and the wife and children may be abandoned. Most of the cases of abandonment
are those of free unions. A man will feel greater hesitation at leaving his wife if he
has been married by church. Infidelity on the part of the wife is considered a just
cause for beating her but it is rarely a cause for separation. A wife may leave her
husband if he drinks too much or if he is lazy or beats her too often. Of course,
wives are supposed to put up with these things, but some do not. Interference by
parents often leads to separations. The local judge, who has heard many cases of
marital discord, considers parental interference as the primary factor in most separations.

When a separation occurs, the children invariably stay with the mother. The
husband takes no responsibility for his family and makes no contribution for their
support. Indeed, it is so unusual for a man to support an abandoned wife that when
it does happen it is said that he must have been bewitched. However, when a man
continues to help support his wife (*pasar los gastos*) after he has left her, he still
retains sexual rights and may treat her as a *querida* (sweetheart). Godparents of
the spouses may make some effort to reconcile the couple but this is not always
effective. In the past few years the *monjas* (Catholic nuns) who have come to the
village have been making a house-to-house campaign to try to unite separated
couples and to marry couples who have been "living in sin." They have met with
little success, for Tepoztecans resent their activities as undue interference in their
personal matters.

As might be expected in a village of this size, separations invariably lead to a
great deal of gossip, accusations, and bitterness, and usually involve many more
individuals than just the spouses.

Changes in Marriage: The principal changes which have occurred in marriage
in Tepoztlán since 1910 are as follows: (1) delay in the age of marriage for girls,
earlier marriage for boys, and the consequent development of a period of adoles-
·cence and courtship; (2) transition from a system of marriage arranged by the
parents, with or without the consent of the children, to one in which the individuals
choose their spouses but may follow the formal procedures of having their parents
act as intermediaries for the marriage arrangements; (3) elimination of the bride

price and services to the in-laws; [7] (4) increase in letter-writing as a prelude to courtship; (5) marked increase in elopements, which may be indicative of the breakdown of parental authority in these matters; (6) introduction of civil marriage by national law; (7) desire of young couples to become independent of their parents and their in-laws and to set up their own home; (8) decreasing importance in the role of godparents in marriage, in many cases the girl no longer sleeps at the home of her godparents the night before the wedding but stays at home; and (9) the increased expenses in marriage.

---

[7] See Chapter 18, "Adolescence, Courtship, and Marriage," p. 406.

economics: general aspect and historical background: 4

THE CONTEMPORARY economy of Tepoztlán is essentially a household economy of small producers, peasants, artisans, and merchants, whose primary motive for production is subsistence. But it is not a self-sufficient economy and probably was not even in pre-Conquest days. The Tepoztecan economy today forms part of the larger national economy of Mexico and, to a more limited degree, of the world economy. The price of corn, the most important local product, is as much determined by international markets as by local conditions of supply and demand. Tepoztlán depends heavily on trade with the outside for basic elements of diet, such as salt, sugar, and chile, which are obtained from nearby regions, and for sewing machines, patent medicines, pool tables, water pipes, steel plows, and buses which are obtained from more distant urban centers. Tepoztlán has few handicrafts, there is no pottery, no weaving, no basketmaking. Household utensils, cloth, baskets, and many other items are obtained by purchase.

From the point of view of agriculture, the basic source of livelihood, the resources of Tepoztlán are poor indeed. As we have seen, only about fifteen per cent of the total land area of the municipio is cultivable by plow and oxen. Furthermore, there is no irrigation, which means only one harvest a year. The village could not support itself by farming alone. Tepoztecans therefore seek other sources of income, and are busy doing a variety of jobs during different parts of the year. Some work on nearby plantations, others engage in trade, make rope, produce charcoal, raise livestock, or have some other part-time activity. But with all of this the fundamental problem for most Tepoztecans is that of subsistence.

The Tepoztecan economy, though that of a peasant society, is neither simple nor primitive. It has many qualities well known to the student of rural society in western civilization. Among the more important are well-developed concepts of private property; a high degree of individualism; a free market; the definition of wealth in terms of land, cattle, and other forms of property; a relatively wide range in wealth differences; the use of money; a highly developed system of marketing and trade, interest on capital, work for wages, pawning of property, renting of land, and the use of plow-oxen; and specialization in part-time occupations.

But despite this roster of familiar traits, the Tepoztecan economic system is quite distinctive and defies easy classification in terms of our traditional categories, such as capitalistic or feudal. For side by side with the above traits are less familiar ones such as communal land-ownership, collective labor, hoe culture, production primarily for subsistence, barter, the absence of credit institutions, the lack of capital, the fear of displaying wealth, and the continued importance of religion and ritual in economic pursuits.

A complicating factor, and in terms of our own society a differentiating one, is that the Tepoztecan economy and technology represent a fusion of elements from three distinct historical levels: the pre-Hispanic, the Spanish colonial, and the modern western European. Furthermore, it is not always possible to ascertain with assurance which trait belongs to which level. While some traits are found in both the pre-Hispanic and post-Conquest periods, the function and meaning of the trait would seem to have been so different in the total economies of these distinct periods that equating the two is hardly justified. For example, while private property in land may have existed before the Conquest, it is questionable whether it was widespread or played the same role in the total economy and in the aspirations of the people that it does today. And though wealth differences undoubtedly existed at that time, the criteria of wealth as well as its distribution were probably very different from the present. Also, while the market system is probably pre-Hispanic there is a world of difference between the present-day market, which reflects international price changes, and the more localized pre-Hispanic markets.

PRE-CONQUEST AND SPANISH-COLONIAL ECONOMY

Specific data on the pre-Conquest economics of Tepoztlán are quite limited. The archeological evidence indicates the presence of potsherds from distant areas of Mexico and would therefore suggest wide trading contacts.

Archaeological research carried out in Tepoztlán in 1942-43 by Miss Florencia Muller revealed six ceramic levels and indicated similarities in ceramics with southern Morelos, Vera Cruz, Teotihuacan, Monte Alban, and points even farther south.[1]

The *Relación* suggests that Tepoztlán was a stratified society of nobles and commoners, not unlike Aztec society, with class differences affecting diet, clothing, marriage customs, and other aspects of life. It also contains scattered references which give us some idea of local foods, industries, and other economic pursuits. The following excerpts contain the pertinent data.

. . . and they had wars with those of the town of *Capihtlan* and of the town of *Cuauhunava,* and they fought with their feathered weapons and beneath their *escuahupiles* of quilted cotton, and the garments of feathers, some like lions and others like tigers, and others like birds, with their wide wooden sabres, like swords, and the blades were of flint that they might cut, and their bucklers of feathers and others with their bows and

---

[1] I am grateful to Miss Muller for the summary of her findings; see Appendix B, p. 453.

arrows, and others with their slings with which they threw very large stones and others with *maporros,* and others fought with weapons like pikes made of oaken staves, four-cornered, and those who were vassals wore only cloths of *nequen,* which is made from the maguey, and their wide breeches on their *verguilacos,* and the chieftain wore a cloth of white cotton, with his fine cloak, and he who wore such had to be a brave man, and if he were not known for such, they killed him straightway, and they wore nothing else, and the garment which they now wear is of cloth covered with painted stripes, each one according to his ability and opportunity, and their shirts of linen either of cotton of the land or of Ruan, and their *caraguelles* of linen and the stripes of the stuffs worked in feathers, and the same with the women who wear skirts and *guaypies* [outer garments] according to the possibilities of each, of colored cotton and feathers, and the foods that they used were what are used now such as *tamales,* and *tortillas,* and their chickens and venison and rabbit and their *chile;* this was the diet of the *principales* [nobles]; but the *maceguales* [commoners], [ate] tortillas, chile, and some rabbit, gruels, beans, *chian* and other vegetables which they had to eat, which are same as they have now, and the quail and doves were kept as greatly prized food for their idol, and demon, and formerly they lived a much longer time and died very old, and when three or four died, they considered it a great pestilence and did not allow them to be buried, but burned them and winnowed their ashes in the air; they say that the reason why there was no pestilence, and why they now live a short time and many, many die regularly, what is understood to be the reason is that at that time they went naked, and slept on the ground, and bathed twice each day, and lived in health, and now they go about in shirts, and sleep in beds, with bedclothes, and when the air strikes them they fall ill and die and they do not understand that the cause can be any other.

. . . they say that outside of the oaks, pines and cedars which there are in the forest in quantity, that the most notable tree which they have is the maguey, for the many benefits which they have from it, such as making cloths with which they dress themselves, leaves and aloes for stewing black honey, and another which they drink when half cooked, and of it before cooking they make *pulque;* when the pulpy leaves whence all this comes are dried, it serves as firewood, and if a shoot which comes forth in the middle is allowed to grow, it serves as a beam, they make shoes, *alpargates,* and the said juice is very healing for new and old wounds, and of great power, and the points of the leaves, because they are very hard and sharp, serve as nails for many things; likewise they have another tree in this town which they call *amaquapite* which is the tree of the paper used by the natives, which they get from the bark of the said tree, boiled, and afterward they wash it and pound it with stone clubs, on boards, and thus they make it.

. . . they say that the fruit trees of Castile do not grow in this town, except the lime and the orange, and that very little, because it does not grow, and although they have tried to plant the quince, pomegranate, peach, pear and apple, and that there have only grown the guava-trees, and aguacates, and the *cacahualsuchal,* which is a tree like the *calan,* of which they make bouquets to present, and *yolosuchil* which is a heart-shaped flower which smells sweet, and trees of *yzquisuchil* which are little white flowers, very little ones which smell sweet, and others which have white flowers, red ones and yellow ones, which smell sweet, which they call *calosuche,* which in Spanish means flower of the crow; it is like the rose-bay of Spain.

. . . that the garden seeds with which they ordinarily have sustained themselves and are sustaining themselves, are: corn, beans, chile, yams, and potatoes and *chian,* which is a very small grain like mustard, of which they make a gruel, and calabashes and *guahucoyeite,* which is wild amaranth, and another fruit which they call *chayotes* which are like the prickly hulls of chestnuts, except that they are larger and entirely edible; there grow also cabbages, lettuce, beets, onions, garlic, parsley, coriander, beans, chick-peas, except that they do not grow except in the garden of the church.

. . . they said they have a plant which is called *tamalcoco* and the root of which, drunk in wine, is good for the urine, taken with other herbs, they have another herb which is called *quahuchichiguale* the branch of which is good for them when they have fevers, given it to drink; they have also another herb which is called *hipatle,* the bark of which is good to give to drink to one who is spitting blood; they have another herb which is called *matlassuchil,* the root of which is good when given to drink for spotted fever; they likewise have another herb which is called *tlatlalote* of which the roots are very small, drunk when one has a chill, before they have fever, in a little wine or water, they sweat with it and vomit it again and then they are bled; they have another herb which is called *tlalancacitlapili* whose root is also good for the urine; they have likewise another plant which is called *tlalchichiplatli* whose root is good when given to drink for indigestion; they have likewise another plant which is called *tlatlaveapatli* the root of which drunk with *matlassuchil* and others is good for the spotted fever; many other herbs with other names are for the same purposes.

. . . they say that they have only seen that there are small lions, and wolves and coyotes which are like foxes and *ocotochite* which they say are like foxes and tigers they have not seen, and that the said animals do no harm except to the little dogs, and that of the animals of Spain there are none, except pigs and dogs, although they already had small dogs before and there are many fowls of the country, and domestic and wild cocks, and black pheasants in the forest, and that the fowls of Castile came from Spain, and that the manner of raising them is as in Castile, the ones as well as the others, except that those of the country are very tedious to raise because they are more delicate.

. . . they say that there are no salt pits in this town nor in its district, and that they furnish themselves with salt from the city of Mexico and from Chiautla and Piastla, which are thirteen or fourteen leagues from this town, and they lack nothing of the things to eat, except cows and sheep.

. . . the houses of this town are of stone and mud, and others of mud brick, small and square, and of bad appearance in the dwelling, because the rooms are opposed one to another, and all are covered with flat roofs whitewashed with lime, for there is much of it in this town and its district; there is *tezontle* which is a red stone which is ground for mortar to make it very strong, even though they do not use it except for large buildings and churches.

. . . their principal industries, which they had formerly, were paper and lime, and that they paid tribute in stuffs that they made, and that now all have horses and bring fruit from one place to another, and paper, lime, and other merchandise which they carry on some market-days for others, from which they live, and that at present they pay the tribute in corn and money, accordingly as they are appraised.

. . . there is no hospital for Spaniards nor any other seminary, except a hospital for the Indians which the town itself built to cure its sick.[2]

A study of sixteenth-century archive materials on Tepoztlán reveals that some of the pre-Hispanic industries mentioned in the above document, such as the manufacture of paper and cotton cloth, lasted for some time after the Conquest. In fact, the evidence suggests that rather than decline, the native industries may have expanded for a short time in response to the market provided by the Spaniards. Thus, a document dated March 2, 1551, containing a report on local conditions and submitted by an agent of the Marquesado del Valle reads as follows, ". . . the said Indians collect much chile, beans, corn, cotton, melons and *xicamas*. . . . Also, they have and make a great deal of paper, all of which they sell at excessive prices, dealing with Spaniards and with other Indian merchandise dealers." [3] Two other references indicate the continuation of the paper industry after the Conquest. One is found in the work of the great naturalist, Francisco Hernández, who visited Tepoztlán about 1575 and reported that Tepoztlán swarmed with workmen making paper.[4]

The other is a document dated February 4, 1591, which reports Tepoztecan complaints to the authorities to the effect that the cattle were damaging the trees from which they made paper.[5] This is the latest reference to papermaking in Tepoztlán that we found.

Cotton growing, which is mentioned in many documents during the sixteenth

---

[2] *Relación*, pp. 243-48.

[3] *Hospital de Jesús*, Leg. 289, Exp. 100.

[4] Francisco Hernández, *Historia de las Plantas de Nueva España*, I (México, D.F.: Imprenta Universitaria), 249. In discussing the *amaquahuitl* (paper tree), he writes as follows:

"Nace en los montes de Tepoztlán, donde se mira hormiguear de obreros que fabrican de este árbol un papel no muy a propósito para escribir o trazar líneas, aunque no deja pasar la tinta a su través, pero propio para envolturas y muy adecuado y útil entre estos indios occidentales para celebrar las fiestas de los dioses, confeccionar las vestiduras sagradas, y para adornos funerarios. Se cortan solo las ramas truesas de los arboles, para dejar que los renuevos se endurezcan; se maceran con agua y se dejan remojar durante la noche en los arroyos o rios. Al día siguiente, se les arrance la corteza, y después de limpiarla de la cuticula exterior, se extiende a golpes con una piedra plana pero surcada de algunas estrías, y que se sujeta con una vara de mimbre sin pulir doblada en circulo a manera de mango. Cede aquella madera flexible; se corta luego en trozos que, golpeados de nueve con otra piedra mas plana, se unen facilmente entre sí y se alisan; se dividen por ultimo en hojas de dos palmos de largo y palmo y medio aproximadamente de ancho, que imitan nuestra papel mas grueso y corriente, pero son más compactas y más blancas, aunque muy inferiores a nuestro papel más terso."

Tepoztlán was probably one of the most important sources of paper for the Aztecs. This opinion is given by Hans Lens and Federico Gómez de Orozco in their study, *La Industria Papelera de México* (México: Editorial Cultura, 1940). They point out that Tepoztlán was one of the 26 towns which, according to the Codex Mendocino, paid in taxes 16,000 *resmas* of paper annually to Moctezuma.

[5] *Indios*, Vol. 5, Exp. 181.

century, persisted in Tepoztlán almost until the Revolution. A reference to cotton growing in Tepoztlán is found as late as 1890 in one of the best early geographies of the state of Morelos.[6] Furthermore, some of my older informants remember having seen cotton plants grown in the late eighties and were able to give detailed descriptions of the plants and the way in which they were used.[7] Weaving went out at about the time cotton did.[8]

Another pre-Hispanic industry which has now practically disappeared is that of pulque making. According to old legends, pulque was invented in or near Tepoztlán, and Tepoztecans were famous for their celebrations and debauchery. In the ancient Codex Magliabecchiano manuscript at Florence there is a reference to Tepoztlán, as follows:

They celebrated another feast called Pilauana, which means intoxication in children, because during the said feast the boys would dance with the girls and they would mutually give each other drink until they became intoxicated . . . these Indians being already nine to ten years old.[9]

Referring to the figure of Tepoztecatl or Ometochtli it says:

This is the figure of a great debauch that a village which calls itself Tepuztlán had as a rite, and when an Indian died from intoxication, the others in the village had a great dance bearing hatchets, made of copper in their hands. This village is near Yautepec, a dependence of the Marquesado del Valle.[10]

The importance of the maguey plant in pre-Hispanic Tepoztlán can further be judged by Hernández' description of its uses.

It furnished the people with fire and fence wood, with gutters, tiles and thatching material, paper, and fibres from which shoes and cloth are made. They gather nails and needles from it, as well as fruits, wine, honey, sugar and vinegar.[11]

Other references to the Tepoztecan economy during the sixteenth century deal primarily with taxation and the operation of the *repartimiento* system. As one of the four villas of the Marquesado del Valle, Tepoztlán was an important source of labor supply for the neighboring haciendas. There are frequent references to Tepoztecan men being called upon to labor in the haciendas. During the latter part of the sixteenth century, Tepoztecans were assessed at the rate of four per

[6] Alfonso Luis Velasco, *Geografía y Estadística*, Bk. VIII.

[7] Cotton (*itchkatl* in Náhuatl) was planted on the edges of the cornfields so that it would not cut down corn production. The cotton seeds were toasted and eaten. Only the poorest families planted cotton and wove it into cloth. The cotton plant was opened and the cotton picked and then beaten to make it fluffy in preparation for spinning. Cotton cloth in Tepoztlán was called *tlazoptli*. Náhuatl terms used to describe the various processes are as follows:

> *itchawitepitl*—to beat the cotton with sticks.
> *tlapochina*—to loosen the cotton before spinning.
> *matzawa*—to spin thread.

[8] Redfield reported two looms in Tepoztlán in 1926-27.

[9] Miguel Salinas, "La Sierra de Tepoztlán," *Memorias y Revista de la Sociedad Científica*, Vol. XXXVIII, Nos. 9 and 10 (July, 1920).

[10] *Ibid.*

[11] This is an abstract of Hernández given by J. J. Valentine, in his article on "Mexican Paper," *Proceedings of the American Antiquarian Society*, N.S., I (1880–81), 69.

cent of the total number of taxpaying inhabitants of the town at the last census. That is, they were to send four men each week for every one hundred taxpayers.[12] In 1590 they were assessed sixty-three Indians to be given as follows:

"To the Ingenio de Amanelco, 37 Indians; to the Marquesado, 7; to Guastepeque, 10; to Guequepan, 5; to Contador Cassano, 5. . . ." [13] All of these localities were within the present state of Morelos.

Tepoztecans repeatedly complained against excessive demands for labor. A document dated June 20, 1590, reads as follows:

. . . the *maceguales* of the village of Tepuztlán have explained to me how they are vexed by the governor and principals of the above mentioned village, who demand, against every reason, 224 Indians, which are sent to different places. In behalf of their own interests and being tired of so many annoyances they beg me that they be assessed at the rate of four out of every hundred. . . .[14]

Tepoztecans were also sent to work in the mines, a practice against which they complained bitterly.

The nobles and prominents have complained that it was very hard for them to send the 14 Indians that had to work in the Taxco mines because these mines were too far away and it took six days to make the round trip. They ask that instead they be sent to the sugar plantation of the Marqués del Valle which is nearer and that in their place 14 Indians from Yautepec which is closer to the mines be sent there.[15]

The document goes on to say that the Corregidor of Cuernavaca investigated the complaint, found it just, and

. . . ordered the division of labor in the mines between the villas of Tepuztlan and Yautepec. 14 Indians from Tepuztlan were to go to the mines during six months in a year, beginning on Jan. 1, 1591. The other six months, the 14 Indians were to be sent from Yautepec. The six months that the Tepuztecans did not go to the mines they were to work in the sugar fields of the Marqués del Valle.[16]

Despite all the Tepoztecan protests, we find that as late as 1699 they were still sending some men to the mines of Taxco and complaining about it. In 1695 a royal decree had been passed reducing the number to four men a year. However, the local authorities did not advise the inhabitants of the order, but instead levied a special tax on the pretext that those who paid the tax would not have to go to Taxco. The tax was, of course, pocketed by the officials.[17]

It appears that in addition to the regular yearly assessment, Tepoztecans were also called upon to work on haciendas in emergencies. Thus when a neighboring *hacendado*, Diego Cavallero, who had rented a plantation from Cortés, ran short of Negro slaves during harvest of the sugar cane, Tepoztlán was ordered to supply

---

[12] *Indios*, Vol. 4, Exp. 911.

[13] *Ibid.*

[14] *Ibid.*, Exp. 728.

[15] *Ibid.*, Exp. 127.

[16] *Ibid.* See also Vol. 6, Exp. 417. This document tells of Tepoztecan deaths in the Taxco mines as a result of which they were henceforth to work only on nearby sugar plantations.

[17] See *Hospital de Jesús*, Leg. 312, Exp. 9.

"400 common Indians . . . to be taken to said Diego Cavallero . . . for what remains of this year and the coming year of 1600 only. . . ." [18]

What these frequent demands upon Tepoztecan labor supply did to the local economy can only be conjectured. It seems probable that it acted as a disruptive factor and may have contributed to the breakdown of local industries.

Indian complaints to the crown against mistreatment in the mines sometimes led to action in their behalf. A document of 1603 tells of an order from the Audiencia Real which suspended the sending of Indians from Tepoztlán to Cuautla because of "the grievances and mistreatment which his lordship learned were being inflicted upon the Indians." [19]

In addition to work on haciendas and in mines, Tepoztecans were also required to work on construction projects in Cuernavaca, the construction of the church in Tepoztlán, and as domestic servants for the *principales* of the village. According to the law, Tepoztecans were to receive payment for such work, but judging from the many Tepoztecan complaints against failure to be paid, the law was not always followed. This and other points can be seen from the following excerpts which suggest, among other things, that the church and the hacienda owners worked hand in hand in the exploitation of Indian labor.

The Count of Curuños, by order of His Excellency Martín López de Guana, orders in turn to the *alcalde* of Tepuztlan, D. Lorenzo Juárez de Mendoza, the following:

. . . . That the Indians and residents of Tepuztlan have complained to him, that the governor and some of the well-known persons of the villa oblige them to send Indians to work for their household and do personal things. They added that unnecessary numbers of people were compelled to go to work in the repairing being done in the Church of Santo Domingo [barrio of Tepoztlán]. They assured that less people could do the work and added that most of the ones who were asked to work in the Church were sent instead to the sugar plantations of D. Bernardino del Castillo Tlaltenango, where excesses were committed with them. They ask that not so many people should be sent to work because, due to the high mortality rate of the previous year, there are now very few people left in the town. . . . [20]

Large numbers of Tepoztecans worked on construction projects in Cuernavaca for Cortés. The following reference is one of many of this type in my possession:

It is hereby made known to the Corregidor of the Villa of Cuernavaca, that the governor and *regidores* of the villa of Tepoztlán, and 555 commoners worked for a month and a half in burning limekilns to prepare lime for use in the repair of houses of the Marqués del Valle, each Indian working two days; in addition 879 artisans, carpenters, bricklayers and lime makers worked, some working eight days, others ten and twelve days and longer depending upon the hurry of the job . . . and that they were never paid for their work and the said *maceguales* were aggrieved. . . . [21]

---

[18] Archivo General de la Nación, México, General de Parte V, 64v-65, quoted in Zavala, *Fuentes para la Historia*, Bk. I, pp. 308-09. This document also refers to an order of the King requiring the *hacendado* to buy Negro slaves to replace the Indians.

[19] *Ibid.*, Bk. V, pp. 94-95.

[20] *Indios*, Vol. 2, Exp. 103.

[21] *Ibid.*, Vol. 4, Exp. 410.

This complaint was investigated and it was determined that "the 1,800 *peones* who were occupied deserve one-half *real* each, and the 90 *oficiales* (artisans) one and a half *reales* each." [22] However, five months had elapsed since the first complaint and the Tepoztecans had not yet been paid.

In addition to levies on Tepoztecan manpower by the *repartimiento* system, Tepoztlán was also subject to taxation. In the years before the Conquest, Tepoztlán paid tribute to Moctezuma in the form of cotton mantles, cloth, paper, and corn. It is difficult to determine the amount of tribute paid in each item because our main source of information, the *Matrícula de Tributos,* lists Tepoztlán along with 25 other towns which apparently constituted a single administrative unit under Moctezuma. However, some idea of the kind of tributes collected can be seen from this document.

The tribute of the province of Huaxtepec of which Tepoztlán formed a part is given in the Codex Mendocino as follows: [23]

Clothing

400 bundles of loin cloths
400 bundles of women's clothing
1,400 bundles of large mantles of "twisted" cloth
8,000 bundles of rich little mantles
46 warriors' costumes with shields (6 being fine pieces)

Food

4 large wooden cribs (1 each of maize, beans, *chian,* and *huauhtli*)

Other Goods

2,000 polished pottery dishes of various colors
8,000 reams of native paper.[24]

In the early years after the Conquest, Cortés apparently followed the Aztec policy of collecting taxes in produce. However, shortly after the Marquesado del Valle was established we find Tepoztecans complaining against making payments in kind and asking that they be allowed to pay in currency. These data are especially important, for they suggest that by the latter half of the sixteenth century Tepoztlán was already beginning to function as a money economy.

---

[22] *Ibid.,* Exp. 962.

[23] The tribute list as given is taken from R. H. Barlow, "The Extent of the Empire of the Culhua Mexica," *Ibero-Americana,* XXVIII (1949), 81. I cannot agree with Barlow when he decides to consider Tepoztlán as belonging to the administrative district of Chalco rather than Huaxtepec. (*Ibid.,* p. 74.) This is admittedly a guess on his part, since Tepoztlán also appears in the list of villages belonging to Huaxtepec. There is fairly conclusive evidence from other sources to show that Tepoztlán belonged to Huaxtepec. The *Relación* specifically deals with this point, as do other early sixteenth-century documents from the *Archivo de Indios* and the *Hospital de Jesús.* Nevertheless, this matter reflects the marginal position of Tepoztlán to the three native administrative districts prior to the Spanish Conquest, namely, Chalco, Cuernavaca, and Huaxtepec. This appears clearly from an examination of these districts as shown by Barlow's maps of the Empire of the Culhua Mexica, printed in the work cited.

[24] Lens and Gómez de Orozco, *La Industria Papelera,* suggest that most of the paper came from Tepoztlán.

One of the reasons some Tepoztecans preferred money payments over payments in kind was that there were landless individuals who had to purchase corn at exorbitant prices to pay their taxes. This is seen in the following document addressed to the *corregidor* of Cuernavaca by the Audiencia:

. . . . The *maceguales* of the village of Tepuztlan have reported to me that many of them, due to the lack of arable land, do not work the ten *brazos* of seed [land] which belongs to the community, and by agreement with the governor and *alcaldes* they pay each year in money the value of 10 *almudes* of corn because they cannot pay in kind, which causes them a great deal of harm, because the price of grain changes from one year to another, and the valuation is made by the governor and mayors, who to profit themselves do this without regard to the common hurt; and that the hurt is so great that they can afford it no longer; and they requested that the tax in corn be changed to money, since they have no lands; and that each Indian be allowed to pay 2 *reales de plata* yearly as is done in other places where there is no corn harvest. . . .[25]

Later documents indicate that this was allowed, and that taxes were collected in both goods and money. In 1552 an agent of the Marqués del Valle, who visited Tepoztlán to investigate complaints against high taxes, reported back that it would be in the interest of both the Marqués and the Crown if Tepoztecans were forced to pay in cotton cloth as they had done earlier under Moctezuma. He reports that Tepoztecans were taking advantage of the great scarcity of cotton cloth and were charging exorbitant prices for it.[26]

In 1567 Tepoztlán was taxed by the Audiencia Real of New Spain "each year 2,718 pesos and one *tomín* of common gold . . . and in addition 1,327½ fanegas of corn to be paid at harvest time." [27] In 1569 they were taxed 2,655 pesos and 1,327 fanegas of corn.[28] According to one document the Marqués del Valle obtained 2,418 fanegas of corn from the Tepoztecan harvest of 1567 and 1568, and 1,095 fanegas from the harvest of 1569.[29] He then sold this corn at the price of "cinco tomines de Tepuzque la fanega," to one Miguel Rodríguez de Acevedo, who had rented the nearby "ingenio de Taltenango" from Cortés for a period of nine years beginning in 1567.[30]

A document of 1580 gives us a clearer picture of the taxation system in the village and municipio.[31] Taxes were collected for three purposes: as payment to the Crown; to help support the local officials of the municipio; and to support the church and the village fiestas. The over-all rate of taxation for heads of families was one fanega of corn per taxpayer, and the rate for Indian women, widowed or single, was one *tomín* each. A total of 1,460 fanegas of corn was collected from Tepoztlán and the surrounding six villages. A fanega was the equivalent of 48 *cuartillos*.[32] This item

[25] *Indios*, Vol. 4. Exp. 565.
[26] *Hospital de Jesús*, Leg. 289, Exp. 100.
[27] Francisco del Paso y Troncoso, ed. *Epistolario de Nueva España*, XI (Mexico: 1505–1818), 27.
[28] *Ibid.*
[29] It appears that Cortés took this corn as part payment of the assessment.
[30] *Ibid.*, p. 36.
[31] *Indios*, Vol. 1, Exp. 252. This document is given in its entirety in Appendix C, p. 455.
[32] This means that corn sold for three centavos per *cuartillo* in 1579.

is important as one of the very few instances of corn production figures for Tepoztlán during the sixteenth century. The 1,460 fanegas of corn collected would be the present-day equivalent of about 730 *cargas,* or approximately 3,759 bushels.[33]

Each fanega of corn was worth one and one-half pesos. This corn was collected at the rate of one fanega per head of family. In addition, there were 63 women, widowed or single, located in the outlying towns, who paid one *tomín* each; and 250 women, widowed or single, located in Tepoztlán proper, who paid .86 *tomín* each.

The community treasury received 498 pesos and 6 *tomines,* which went to the Crown for taxes. This sum was raised by taking the 40 pesos and 4 *tomines* paid by the single or widowed Indian women, adding to it the proceeds from the sale of enough corn to equal 2 *tomines* per taxpayer for the six small villages, and selling 253 additional fanegas of corn from the amount taken from Tepoztlán proper. To the municipio went 372 fanegas for payment to local officials and clergy; 60 fanegas went to pay officials of outlying villages; and 649 fanegas were left to the towns for festivals, church expenses, and visiting priests.

The document takes up each of the outlying villages: Santiago, San Juan, Santa Catalina, and San Andrés, and explains what has been paid and how it is to be divided and used. Using this as a basis I have inferred certain figures which were not given and have arrived at estimates for each village and for the municipio as a whole.

I have assumed five as the average size of a family. This is somewhat higher than figures used by other scholars. Mendizábal[34] used 3.2 in his population estimates, and more recently Cook and Simpson used 4.[35] However, the total population derived from my figures is not unduly high because I did not count the children of widows or widowers. Were I to follow the procedure of Cook and Simpson I would have to add the 313 Indian women, widowed or single, to the 1,460 taxpayers giving a total of 1,773 taxpayers, which would make for a total population of 7,392 as compared to my estimate of 7,613.

Table 16 shows the corn collected and sold and the population estimates. All figures for the outlying villages except those under "Corn Collected" were given in the document. However, in the case of Tepoztlán proper, only the figures under "Indian Women" and "Men Taxpayers" were given in the document.

To illustrate how the figures for Table 16 were derived from the document, we will use the village of Santiago as an illustration. The village had to contribute 20 pesos and 3 *tomines* to the community treasury. This amount was to be collected from 15 Indian women, widowed or single, at the rate of one *tomín* each. The other

---

[33] For colonial weights and measures, see Manuel Carrera S. Tampa, "The Evolution of Weights and Measures in New Spain," *Hispanic American Historical Review,* Vol. 29, No. I (Feb., 1949), pp. 12-24.

[34] Miguel Othón de Mendizábal, "La Demografía Mexicana," *Obras Completas,* Bk. III (1946), pp. 309-35.

[35] Cook and Simpson, "The Population of Central Mexico," *Ibero-Americana,* Vol. XXXI (1948), p. 5.

18½ pesos were to be collected from 74 taxpayers at the rate of two *tomines* each. These 148 *tomines* were secured by selling 12½ fanegas of corn at 1½ pesos a fanega; and after selling this amount there were 61½ fanegas left. All these figures were given in the document. To get the figures for the total population, we multiplied 74 x 5 (the figure I assumed as the average size of a family) which equals

TABLE 16.   First Distribution of Corn, 1580.

Village	Indian Women (Widowed or Single)	Men Tax-Payers or Heads of Families	Total Population	Corn (Fanegas)			Total Paid to Community Treasury	
				Collected	Sold	Held	Pesos	*Tomines*
Santiago	15	74	385	74	12½	61½	20	3
Santa María Magdalena	16	93	481	93	15½	77½	25	2
Santo Domingo	8	45	233	45	7½	37½	12	3
San Juan	6	34	176	34	6	28	9	2
Santa Catalina	8	46	238	46	8	38	12	4
San Andrés	10	45	235	45	7½	37½	12	4
Tepoztlán	250	1,123	5,865	1,123	253	801	406	3
Total	313	1,460	7,613	1,460	310	1,081	498	6

370, and to this we added the 15 Indian women to arrive at the total population of 385.

Following is the list of officials and the amount of corn which they received. (See Table 17.) This list includes only the officials of Tepoztlán proper; all of the 372 fanegas of corn, which was divided among them, came from the 801 fanegas which they had left after the first distribution shown in Table 16. Of the 82 people listed in Table 17 only five were not officials, namely, Doña María Cortés and four "Sons of ex-prominents." This leaves 77 officials for Tepoztlán proper.

In the last section of the document the viceroy directs the final distribution of the corn that remains. This is shown in Table 18. The document also indicates an additional three officials for each of the outlying towns. This brings the total number of persons supported at least partially by taxation to 85, and the total number of officials to eighty. Here then, we see that Tepoztlán supported a much larger bureaucracy in 1580 than in 1943. This will be considered in more detail later. In this last section of the document the amount of corn left for the real needs of the villages is also indicated. This corn was used to pay for feasts, priests who visited the town, celebrations, and so forth.

TEPOZTECAN ECONOMY DURING THE DÍAZ REGIME

One of the curious and unfortunate aspects of the historical record for Tepoztlán is the wide gap in our information between the end of the sixteenth century and the latter part of the nineteenth century. We know little of what happened in the

TABLE 17. Distribution of Corn to Officials, 1580.

Officials		Corn (Fanegas)	
Title	Number	Amount to Each	Total
Governor	1	30	30
Alcaldes	2	10	20
Regidores	6	6	36
Mayordomos	2	6;	12
Escribientes	2	6	12
Church *fiscal*	1	10	10
Singers of the church	20	2	40
Alguaciles of the fields	6	5	30
The great *alguacil* of the capital	1	6	6
Daughter of Don Hipólito *cacique*, Doña María Cortés	1	12	12
Sons of ex-prominents	4	5	20
Tequitlatos of the capital	10	4	40
Tequitlatos of barrio of Atenco	8	4	32
Tequitlatos of barrio of Teycapan	10	4	40
Tequitlatos of barrio of Olac	5	4	20
Alguacil of barrio of Pochitlán	1	4	4
Tequitlatos of barrio of Pochitlán	2	4	8
Total	82		372

village during this two-hundred-year period, our data being limited to some references to epidemics in the early nineteenth century, the foundation of schools about 1820, the loss of church lands after 1857, and the participation of Tepoztecans in

TABLE 18. Final Distribution of Corn, 1580.

Villages	Corn (Fanegas)		
	On Hand After First Payments	Final Payments	On Hand After Final Payments
Santiago	61½	15	46½
Santa María Magdalena	77½	15	62½
Santo Domingo	37½	7	30½
San Juan	28	7½	20½
Santa Catalina	38	7½	30½
San Andrés	37½	7½	30
Tepoztlán	801	372	429
Total	1,081	431½	649½

the "War of the Plateros" in the sixties. However, it is possible to reconstruct some aspects of the economic life of the village during the later part of the Díaz regime on the basis of informants who lived through that period and have vivid memories of what happened. Some data are also contained in regional geographies of the area published in the late nineties.

The impressions of life in Tepoztlán during the Díaz regime given to us by informants vary considerably. Some informants, particularly those who come from leading families, paint a picture of peace and prosperity similar to that recorded by Redfield. Other informants, primarily those who were poor and landless, give a picture of suffering and exploitation both by the surrounding haciendas and the local *caciques*. Let us examine two samples of informants' versions of life in the village at the turn of the century. The first version is that of a poor *tlacololero*, age 54, who is landless, who worked as a *peón* on many haciendas prior to the Revolution, and who has since held minor positions in the local government.

There was much more hunger about 1900 than at present. The majority of the population was very poor. The presidents of the municipio, in agreement with the *caciques*, forbade the sowing of *tlacolol* and so the poor had no way of helping themselves. This prohibition was due to the fact that if the poor planted *tlacolol*, the rich or *caciques* would not have *peones* during the rainy season to seed their lands.

The poor did not plant because they owned no lands. On the other hand, the *caciques* had much land. Among the *caciques* there were the following persons: Vicente Ortega, Pedro Ortega, Pedro Demesa, Demetrio Rojas, Donaciano Navarrete, Pedro Lara, Vicente Zúñiga, José María Martínez, Valentín Ortiz, Pedro Quiros, and Mariano Patiño—practically all of them belonged to the barrio of La Santísima.

The wealthy hired oxen and *peones* but there was always an excess of people. They paid the oxen driver 25 centavos a day, and the *peones* 18 centavos a day.

Corn sold at 3 centavos per *cuartillo*, but since work was scarce there was hardly anything to eat, and often it was necessary to subsist on grass, mushroom fungus, and *quelites*. During the months of January and February hunger increased, and then the poor had to go to one of the rich and offer to work during the rainy season; and if he were accepted, he asked his future "boss," for an advance of a *tercio de maíz*, for example, which would be deducted from the wages he would later earn. The deduction was made on the basis of 50 per cent of the daily wage; they amortized half the debt, and the other half was paid in cash to the *peón*. The very poor, pressed by necessity, were forced to pawn their sons, for a sum which varied between 5 and 10 pesos. The *empeñados* (pawned children) worked in the house of the *rico* carrying water, wood, guarding the cattle, and performing other domestic duties.

Domestic servants earned a salary of 1½ pesos a month, and had to grind corn, wash, and cook.

When some poor man did not want to pay the debt he had contracted with his *patrón*, the latter went to the municipal authorities and they placed the debtor in jail as *insolvente*.

The debt which oppressed the poor families was so heavy a burden that one never stopped paying, and debts were passed from father to sons.

The salaries of *peones* began to rise as a result of the competition offered to the wealthy of Tepoztlán by the haciendas. The haciendas sought many laborers and offered better salaries. The rich were not able to prohibit the *peones* from leaving for the haciendas as they had done in the case of *tlacolol;* they were thus obliged, much against their will, to raise salaries. Here is an approximate comparison of the salaries in those days.

Wages

Caciques	Haciendas
18 centavos	2 *reales y medio* or 3 *reales* or 37 centavos
3 *reales*	1 *tostón*
1 *tostón*	5 *reales* or 62 centavos
1 *tostón*	5 *reales y medio*
5 *reales*	6 *reales* or 75 centavos

It was customary to beat the *peones* who worked on the haciendas. The men charged with recruiting labor for the haciendas were known as *capitanes*. They always carried a "chicote de cuero crudo," about two meters in length; the foreman had a sheaf of long machetes. Both officials were responsible for beating the *peones*. They did not permit interruptions—when a *peón* tried to rest awhile he was given a lashing.

The *peones* did not protest when the overseers beat them. All were humiliated or cowed, for if they dared protest they were drafted into the army as common soldiers.

When the Revolution finally approached, they first began to show manifestations of discontent against the primitive regime of the haciendas. Thus, for example, I participated in a collective protest which occurred against one of the overseers. I was working at the hacienda of Temixco, whose owners and high ranking employees were all *gachupines* (Spaniards). The routine of work was as follows: work began at 5:00 A.M. and ended at 6:00 P.M.; at noon there was an hour to eat. All the Tepoztecans had to eat cold tortillas which were sent all the way from Tepoztlán. Once they decided to light a small fire to warm the tortillas. They used some twigs to hold the tortillas over the fire. It happened to be the custom to call these twigs "*gachupines*." The one-fourth hour they were allowed for breakfast was not long enough, and so one of the foremen arrived on horseback in front of the group of Tepoztecans around the fire and ordered them to stand and get to work, for the others were already at work. Tepoztecans explained why they were delayed, but the overseer did not listen and urged his horse onto the fire and the meal. Then the Tepoztecans picked up some stones and ran him off. Later they got up and went to the cashier to ask for their pay, for they no longer wanted to work on the hacienda. Then the *patrón* arrived and when he learned of what had transpired, he decided the workers were right, and he beat the overseer and stripped him of his authority. As a result of this incident the workers were convinced that the time had come to demand energetically the end of these abuses.

When the revolutionary uprisings finally began, the overseers and labor recruiters became more and more fearful and hesitated to mistreat anyone.

As to political freedom in the village, there was absolutely none; the *cacique,* Vicente Ortega, was the one who ruled, and all who rebelled he ordered imprisoned, banished, or sent to the army.

The *caciques* named the municipal authorities among themselves; they had no free elections such as there are now.[36]

Other informants gave more emphasis to the positive aspects of life under the Díaz regime. It should be noted that when an informant was told the versions of

---

[36] This informant worked in the following haciendas: Atlihuayan, San Carlos, San Gaspar, Temixco, and Cinconcuac; in Temixco they gave him a blow with a cudgel which knocked him out for quite a while; and in the other haciendas he was frequently beaten.

other informants, he usually agreed that many of the abuses mentioned had existed.

The second version is a summary and condensation of the account of an informant, age 67, who is a member of a small landholding family and who was very active in village politics during the Revolution and in the early twenties. He was also active in the religious life of the village and is a man of more than average ability and intelligence.

Life was good in the time of Porfirio Díaz. Everything was cheap. Corn sold for three centavos per *cuartillo*. A cup of alcohol cost one centavo; a kilo of sugar, ten centavos; a pack of cigarettes, three centavos; a meter of cloth, only fifteen centavos. It is true that wages were low. The daily wage was 25 centavos but was rising during the years immediately preceding the Revolution and had gone up to fifty centavos. The thing that was truly scarce was work. And so during the difficult times from January to May and from August to September, the stronger among us went to work on the sugar plantations of Oacalco, San Carlos, Atlihuayan, San Vicente, Temixco, and others of the many that were in the state of Morelos. The owners of these plantations were *gachupines,* and they mistreated the Indians, kicking and insulting them. These plantations also robbed the nearby villages of their lands. This is what happened to Tepoztlán. We lost some of our best lands.

The rich here had their lands and produced good crops, but the poor had no land. The poor ate chile and salt and some beans. Meat was had once a month at best. Animals were slaughtered in the local slaughterhouse only once every four days, but even at this rate all the meat could not be sold. Milk was used by only the rich. Most of the villagers lived on pure tortilla, squash seeds, and acacia pods. Clothing was almost entirely of cotton, and huaraches were made of crude leather. Huaraches were made in Tepoztlán, as were sombreros. There were surrounding plantations which at that time were more isolated from the cities than now. There were three tanning shops in the village and there was a saddlery shop which made harnesses, saddles, machete sheaths, and pistols, items which were used by the local *cacique* families.

The local government was in the hands of *caciques.* Vicente Ortega held power for many years, with the support of the state authorities among whom he had ties of *compadrazgo.* There were no political parties or opposition groups allowed. Ortega was good and kind to those who were good and was bad to those who were bad. Those were the times of order and respect for authority. Punishments were severe. Anyone who opposed his rule might be sent to prison in Quintana Roo. This happened a few times. A vigorous village guard made the rounds each night. Everyone was to be off the streets after dark, but in any case even a woman walking alone in the streets would be safe. Stealing was rare as was other crime, for the people feared the severe punishments.

Ortega looked out for the welfare of the villagers. When there was a shortage of corn he always knew where to get it and did. It is true that sometimes he sold it at rather high prices, but it was better to have it than not at all. He was also good, for when someone had a death in the family he would lend him money. He had many *peones* work his lands and paid them 18 centavos a day. He demanded that his *peones* work for him all through the agricultural season. If they arrived late at work he would scold them and oblige them to catch up with those who had arrived early. Sometimes he might go as far as to beat them.

The construction of the railroad by the Wells Fargo Company at the turn of the century led to bitter anti-American sentiment. Vicente Ortega, the leading *cacique* in the village, was accused of personally pocketing the funds received by the local government from the railroad for the privilege of cutting a road through the municipio lines. After repeated complaints to the state authorities, an investigation was held and Ortega resigned his position and was succeeded by a triumvirate of three other Tepoztecans.

It should be noted that there was much more public work done in the village during the Díaz regime than later. The present municipal building and park were constructed at that time. The leading streets in the village were lighted by *farolas,* and some of the funds obtained from the railroad was used to pipe water into the village. It was at this time also that Tepoztlán started its local museum, and its newspapers were published in Aztec and Spanish. This was indeed a time of cultural florescence for the village, even though it was limited to the better-to-do families.

In the preceding pages I have attempted to reconstruct some aspects of Tepoztecan economics before the Conquest, in the early colonial period, and during the later part of the Díaz regime. In summary it can be said that the pre-Hispanic economy was a varied one, for in addition to corn production, there were a number of important local industries such as cotton growing, weaving, the manufacture of paper, and the intensive use of the maguey plant for a variety of purposes. While there is no way of knowing the relative importance of each of these industries, it is interesting to note that corn and beans constituted only a relatively small part of the semi-annual tribute paid to Moctezuma by the district of which Tepoztlán formed a part.

After the Conquest we find that most of Tepoztecan taxes were paid in corn or its money equivalent. These data suggest that the Conquest had the effect of making Tepoztlán more and more dependent upon its corn, for the other industries soon disappeared. It would also seem probable that a greater land area was planted in corn after the Conquest in order to meet the new conditions, and that corn production probably increased as a consequence of the introduction of plow agriculture. This, in turn, has resulted in progressive exhaustion of Tepoztecan lands, so that at present the lands on which plow culture is practiced are among the least productive in the municipio and their corn yields compare unfavorably with the communal hillside lands on which hoe culture is practiced.

Our historical survey also shows that the Conquest was a disruptive influence on local industries, and also led to a marked decline in population. (See p. 29.) It also suggests that the land problem in Tepoztlán dates back at least to the mid-sixteenth century, at which time there were already landless people in Tepoztlán. Another point established by the documents is that Tepoztlán very early became subject to a money economy, with all that this implies for the development of a commercial spirit.

The essential facts which emerge from several informants' accounts of the Díaz regime are as follows: (1) a large portion of the population was landless and not permitted to utilize the communal lands; (2) most of these landless people worked on nearby sugar plantations; (3) the economic and political life of the village was dominated by the *caciques* or political bosses imposed by the state government; (4) prices were low and the cost of living much cheaper than at present; and (5) class differences were much more marked than at present.

division of labor: 5

BY SEX

The division of labor according to sexes is clearly delineated. Men are expected to support their families by doing all the work in the fields; by caring for the cattle, horses, oxen, and mules; by making charcoal and cutting wood; and by carrying on all the large transactions in buying and selling. In addition, most of the specialized occupations, such as carpentry, masonry, and shoemaking, are done by men. An important function of the father of the family is to train his sons in the work of men. When a Tepoztecan man is at home, his activities consist of providing the household with wood and water, making or repairing furniture or work tools, making repairs on the house, and picking fruit. Men also shell corn when shelling has to be done on a large scale. Politics and local government, as well as the organization and management of religious and secular fiestas, are also in the hands of the men.

Women's work centers about the care of the family and the house. They cook, clean, wash, iron clothes, do the daily marketing, shell the corn for daily consumption, and care for the children. Mothers train their daughters in women's work and supervise them closely until their marriage. Many women raise chickens, turkeys, and pigs; and some grow fruit, vegetables, and flowers to supplement the family income. Women do a great deal of buying and selling on a small scale, and they control the family purse. Tepoztecan women are not expected to work in the fields, and Tepoztecans of both sexes look down upon the women of the neighboring villages who do agricultural work, carry heavy loads of firewood or corn on tump lines, wear men's hats, and generally appear rougher and coarser than do the women of Tepoztlán.

In general, women's work is less rigidly defined than men's. Many women, especially widows, will do men's work without social censure. In contrast, men almost never do women's work and the few who do are objects of ridicule and are viewed as queer. Men carefully avoid housework of any kind or taking care of small children. Men build a fire and warm their food without compunction only in the fields where there are no women to do it for them. When a wife is ill or otherwise incapacitated, the husband will seek out the assistance of a female relative or, even though poor, may hire a servant. Occasionally one hears of a widower or bachelor who cooks and sweeps the house, but never of a man who washes or irons or grinds corn to make tortillas.

Women who have no one to support them may hire themselves out as domestic servants, laundresses, or seamstresses, or may become merchants or itinerant peddlers. The only profession which an educated woman can practice in the village is that of schoolteacher. As yet there is no demand for nurses, secretaries, or other skilled female workers. However, the lack of rigidity in the definition of women's occupations is reflected in the fact that on two occasions in the recent past a woman has held the job of secretary of the local government, a post traditionally filled by a man. Women are also members of religious *hermandades* as well as of the school committee. As a rule, however, women play only a minor part in public activities.

The more recent technological improvements represented by the increased use of the sewing machine, the commercial corn mills, the road, and the bus service have affected the work of women rather than men. The sewing machine and the corn mills save women many long hours of work. Previously women spent from four to six hours a day grinding corn by hand, often rising at four in the morning to prepare breakfast. The time now saved is used in various ways, such as getting more sleep, sewing, knitting, going to church, or visiting more often. In many cases the added leisure has been turned toward gainful pursuits, such as gardening, and raising chickens and pigs for sale. Not being so tied to the *metate,* women are able to leave the house more freely and undertake more extensive commercial activities. The improved communication offered by the road and bus has enabled some women to become merchants who go regularly to sell their produce in the Cuernavaca market.

BY AGE

Age is an important but not a rigid determinant in the division of labor. There are no organizations by age groupings in Tepoztlán which carry out assigned tasks. Most skills are learned within the family, beginning at an early age. However, in cases where a skill is learned outside of the family, apprenticeship begins in the late teens. The age at which men vote, begin guard duty, and do public collective labor, as well as enter the army, is determined by local or national law. By custom, men are not eligible for public office nor do they take part in political life until after marriage. Old people continue to work as long as they are physically able, and death is preferred to an incapacitated old age.

Children learn to work slowly and, with few exceptions, the belief that heavy labor will weaken a growing child governs the amount of work parents expect from their offspring. Boys are more carefully guarded in this respect than girls, since their labor in later life is considered harder and more important. At about the time they enter school, about age five, both boys and girls begin to do simple tasks in the house. As they get a little older they are generally glad to run errands near by, carry a small can of water or corn dough, or chase the chickens from the garden.

At the age of six, many children are sent alone to the corn mill or to the plaza to buy small articles. At seven, they may be required to take care of a younger brother or sister after school hours. Some differentiation between sexes in connection with work begins at about age six, when boys protest doing a girl's work and mothers tend to avoid assigning such tasks. But most small boys continue to do tasks for their mother at home for several years and are expected to obey her orders. At about age six, boys occasionally accompany their fathers to the fields. They look forward to this, and the first trip is an important occasion in their lives. Small boys are not expected to work in the fields but may help in weeding, watching the animals and tools, gathering wood for the fire, and in running errands. From about eight years of age, many boys regularly carry the noon meal to their father in the fields and are required to help with the weeding and cultivation.

As boys get older, their principal work is to pasture the animals and to guard them from being lost or stolen. This work is usually done alone but sometimes two brothers or cousins of about the same age go together. The boys are required to rise early, take the animals to pasture before school, and bring them home after school. Boys are frequently kept out of school to watch the animals or do some other work. From about ten years of age, boys join their fathers and brothers in the field daily to learn the work of a farmer. By the time a boy is fifteen he generally can drive a plow and go through all the necessary steps in planting and harvesting. Most boys enjoy this work and are eager to become farmers. At home, boys of fifteen or so usually haul water, water the plants, take care of large animals, provide firewood, pick fruit, and help shell corn.

Girls generally begin to help their mothers in a serious way at about age seven by taking care of younger children, sweeping, washing dishes, picking up the *petates,* putting away things, and feeding the chickens. Most girls are eager to learn to cook, grind corn, and make tortillas; they begin to learn at age five or six by imitating their mothers. By the time a girl is nine she is generally quite skillful at these tasks and can also cook beans, rice, and prepare coffee. At ten years of age, most girls are expected to wash and mend their own clothes and those of the baby of the family. A girl of thirteen frequently can do all the work of a woman except wash and iron large articles and cook more complicated dishes; this she begins to do at fifteen. Few girls are able to cut out and sew clothing before marriage, although it is one of the necessary skills.

BY SEASON

The seasonal division of labor follows quite closely the succession of wet and dry seasons. In plow culture, the agricultural cycle begins with the coming of the first rains, generally in May. In hoe culture, the preparation of the land begins in the dry season between January and February. In September and October the plum harvest engages most families, and then in December the corn harvest begins.

After the harvest many Tepoztecans leave for the haciendas, returning to the village and their families only once a week. Those who prefer to remain at home spend their time in making charcoal, cutting wood, making rope, or taking up one of the many part-time occupations available.

BY OCCUPATION

Tepoztlán is a community of peasants, merchants, and artisans, but it is essentially agricultural, and over ninety per cent of the gainfully employed are farmers. The occupation of farming has high status in the village, and the young men look forward to being farmers. Farming is not the sole occupation, but is combined in various ways with other gainful activities.

There are at least twenty-six non-agricultural occupations in Tepoztlán, with a total of 273 individuals engaged in them. The largest groups include storekeepers (20), teachers (21), masons (25), bakers (23), *curanderos* and midwives (28), and ropemakers (42). The next largest group consists of butchers (15), barbers (15), corn merchants (13), charcoal makers (13), tile and brickmakers (12), and employees of the bus line (17). In addition there are shoemakers (5), carpenters (9), ironworkers (3), *chirimiteros* [1] (6), *huehuechiques* [2] (2), fireworks makers (6), mask makers (6), *mágicos* (1), silver workers (2), millers (3), druggists (2), chauffeurs (6), and plumbers (2). (See Table 19.)

It should be noted that 186 individuals, or 68 per cent of the 273 engaged in the above occupations, own their own milpas. This incidence of land-ownership is nearly twice the incidence of land-ownership in the village as a whole, and indicates that the artisans and those with special occupations tend to be in a better economic position. Most of the artisans and merchants fall into the middle economic group of the village.[3]

Fifty-three of the 273 individuals engaged in these occupations are women, who are found in only six of the twenty-six occupations and are distributed as follows: storekeepers (5), teachers (10), butchers (4), bakers (2), *curanderos* and midwives (23), corn merchants (9). It can be seen that women predominate in teaching, curing, and as corn merchants. However, in the latter they are the smaller operators. Also, the few men who engage in curing enjoy greater prestige than the women in this field.

The occupations listed above represent a peculiar mixture of the old and new. Some, like the *chirimiteros, huehuechiques, curanderos,* masons, mask makers, charcoal makers, and ropemakers, probably had their counterpart in pre-Hispanic days. Others, such as storekeepers, shoemakers, and carpenters, have probably existed in the village since the colonial period. Still others, such as the teachers, bakers,

---

[1] The men who play the traditional music on the chapel roofs at fiestas in celebration of the saints. They use a primitive wind instrument called the *chirimía*.

[2] The men who know the traditional Náhuatl words and ritual in the ceremonies which form part of the fiestas for the saints.

[3] See Chapter 9, "Wealth Differences and Levels of Living," p. 173.

TABLE 19. Occupations, 1926 and 1944.

Occupations	Total in 1926 (Redfield)	1944					
		Total	Men	Women	No. Owning Milpas	No. Working in Milpas	No. with Additional Occupations
Storekeepers	5	20	15	5	15	6	4
Teachers	2	21	11	10	12	4	..
Butchers	3	15	11	4	9	7	1
Shoemakers	2	5	5	..	2	3	1
Carpenters	3	9	9	..	7	8	2
Masons	4	25	25	..	18	24	5
Ironworkers	2	3	3	..	3	3	1
Bakers	6	23	21	2	11	18	2
Barbers	5	15	15	..	11	14	4
Curanderos and midwives	23	28	5	23	14	4	1
Chirimiteros	3	6	6	..	6	6	3
Huehuechiques	2	2	2	..	2	2	1
Fireworks makers	2	6	6	..	5	6	1
Mask makers	3	6	6	..	5	6	4
Mágicos	2	1	..	..	..	..	..
Corn merchants	2	13	4	9	9	2	..
Silver workers	..	2	2	..	1	1	..
Ropemakers	..	42	42	..	39	41	9
Charcoal makers	..	13	13	..	9	9	2
Millers	..	3	3	..	3	1	..
Tile and brickmakers	..	12	12	..	9	12	..
Druggists	..	2	2	..	..	..	..
Chauffeurs	..	6	6	..	3	..	..
Plumbers	..	2	2	..	2	..	..
Bus line employees	..	17	17	..	12	11	..
Candlemakers[a]							
Total[b]	69	273	220	53	186	160	23

[a] Redfield did not give figures for the occupation of candlemaker. In 1949 there was only one candlemaker, who had a limited local trade. Most of the candles used in the village are made in Cuernavaca. Upon the death of the now aged candlemaker, this occupation will probably disappear in Tepoztlán.

[b] These totals, except Redfield's column, have been corrected for duplications of occupations. Twenty-three individuals have more than one profession so that the same individual may appear as ropemaker, charcoal maker, etc. Because we lacked the necessary data on overlapping of the occupations listed by Redfield, we could not arrive at an accurate number of individuals, although it was most certainly less than 69.

millers, barbers, druggists, chauffeurs, and bus employees, are more clearly modern, and most of them date from the time of the construction of the road in 1936.

One of the most important trends in the village during the past twenty years has been an expansion in the number of occupations and an increase in specialization. There are two kinds of specialists in the village, full-time and part-time. Among the latter are (1) specialists who divide their time between two or more occupations, and (2) specialists who divide their time between their specialty and farming. Still another distinction can be made within both of the above categories, for there are employers and employees within the specialties. Thus, a part-time carpenter may employ two assistants during the busy season in his trade. In this connection it should be noted that the numbers of occupations shown in Table 19 refer to both artisans and their day laborers.

The changes in occupation and specialization can best be appreciated by a comparison of our data with that given by Redfield for 1926. A complete comparison is not always possible because some of the occupations in Tepoztlán are new and others, though mentioned by Redfield, were not given in numbers. Table 19 lists the occupations and numbers of persons employed in 1926 as compared with 1944. Also included are the number who belong to families with milpas in *ejido*, private holdings or *tlacolol*, to indicate those who have other sources of income. Finally, I have listed the number who work in their fields, in addition to their trade, to determine the degree of specialization.

An examination of Table 19 indicates at once the magnitude of the changes in occupations. Considering first only those occupations for which there is comparable data, we find that there has been an increase from 69 to 187 individuals who work in the various occupations. This represents an increase of 161 per cent as compared with a population increase during this period of approximately 45 per cent.[4] Comparing the number of individuals engaged in special occupations in 1926 with the number today, we find an increase from 69 to 273. This represents an increase of over 290 per cent.

The difference between these two figures is in a sense a measure of the degree of acculturation and the rise in the standard of living. The sharp rise in the number of storekeepers, teachers, butchers, bakers, and masons bears out this statement. In contrast to the small number of stores (five), which existed in Redfield's time, all of which were in the plaza, there are now twenty stores, ten in the plaza and ten distributed among the barrios. The spread of stores to the barrios reflects the general tendency in the village, whereby the outlying barrios are becoming incorporated into the life of the center.

The stores have not only increased in number; they also carry a much wider variety of goods than twenty years ago. Formerly one had to go to Yautepec or Cuernavaca to buy sombreros, cloth, or pants. Now these items and many others are available in the village. The increase in the number of bakers from six to twenty-four attests to the widespread use of bread as a supplement to the tortilla. (See Fig. 17.) Even the poorest family looks forward to eating rolls at least a few times during the week. The figures on the increase of shoemakers from two to five do not adequately reveal the increase in the number of individuals who own shoes. According to the census of 1940, more than three hundred wore shoes daily. However, shoes are given little wear and are used primarily on Sundays and days of fiesta.

---

[4] This estimate is conservative, for as has already been indicated, there must have been fewer than 69 individuals with special occupations in 1926.

The increase in the number of butchers (Fig. 18) parallels the greater consumption of meat in the village. An analysis of the municipio records indicates that the consumption of meat from 1931 to 1941 rose more than 130 per cent while the population increase was approximately 30 per cent. There are four meat stores, but meat is also sold in the open marketplace. There are no refrigeration facilities; the meat is hung on a line in the open air.

The number of teachers given in Table 19 refers to those Tepoztecans who are employed as teachers either in Tepoztlán or in other villages. Those now teaching

Fig. 17. A local bakery.

in Tepoztlán number fourteen in contrast with two teachers in 1926. There are now two schools, one in the center and the other in the barrio of Los Reyes.[5] The registration in the former at the present time is 611 and in the latter 61. Thus, from the "few score" children reported by Redfield in 1926 there is now a total registration of 672.[6]

Two other items in Table 19 deserve comment: the increase in barbers from five to fifteen and in corn merchants from two to thirteen. The former is another index of acculturation. Most men now visit the barber on an average of once a month. In the family budgets we have studied, the cost of haircuts for the male members of the household amounts to a sizeable sum during the year. There are three barber shops in the center, with modern barber chairs and equipment, and one each in the outlying barrios of San Sebastián and Los Reyes. The equipment

[5] The school in Los Reyes was built in 1931 through the initiative of the inhabitants of the small barrios.

[6] The average monthly attendance was 430.

of the remaining ten consists of comb, shears, and scissors, and the barber usually performs in his yard under a *ciruela* tree. Barbering is still an occasional occupation. Even in the center shops there are no fixed hours, and they are normally open only on Sundays and Wednesdays.

Of the fourteen corn merchants in the village, four buy corn on a large scale; the

Fig. 18. Meat display in the market.

others buy up small quantities which they take to Cuernavaca twice a week. Two factors have been responsible for the increase in corn merchants. Most important was the expansion of the land base by the *ejido* grants and the privilege of using the communal *tlacolol* lands. Twenty years ago there was a greater relative number of landless *peones* than today, and the village had to import large quantities of corn for its own consumption. Today the village sells about 1,000 *cargas* of corn out of a total production of about 14,000 *cargas*.[7] The new needs of the people, the higher standard of living, and the sharp rise in prices in the last few years, demand a larger amount of ready cash than formerly and force many families to sell their corn.

Referring again to Table 19, we see that there has also been an increase in the number of *curanderos, chirimiteros,* and fireworks makers. These are the specialists which Redfield characterized as the *tontos* in contrast to the *correctos,* who were the storekeepers, merchants, etc. Today no such distinction exists in the village.

---

[7] One *carga* is about 213 pounds.

Of the *curanderos,* four are new and have learned their specialty within the last ten years. Of the two *chirimiteros* referred to by Redfield, one died a short time ago and the other still practices; four have learned their skill within the last six years. The two *huehuechiques* are the same ones of twenty years ago; there have been no new recruits. Of the two fireworks makers of twenty years ago, one has died; the other five are all new in the trade. The three mask makers of Redfield's time are still working, but in addition two sons and a cousin have learned the trade.

At this point we may ask what the prospects are for the survival of these folk specialists in the face of the changes which are taking place in the village. The prospects for the survival of the occupations of mask makers and fireworks makers are very good. The former is dependent primarily upon the Carnaval and the latter upon the barrio fiestas, neither of which shows the slightest signs of dying out. On the contrary, the former has grown in importance and has become an occasion of great spending, while the latter continues unabated and has the active support of the young men, many of whom are comparatively sophisticated.

The prospects for the survival of the *chirimiteros* are not quite as good because their function is gradually being taken over by the modern secular musicians. This tendency can be seen in the center barrios, where, as in Redfield's time, culture changes appeared first in the village. In the last barrio fiesta of San Miguel, in place of the primitive *chirimía,* a fifteen-piece band played from the chapel roof throughout the night. The profession that seems certain to become extinct is that of the *huehuechique,* for this occupation depends on the knowledge and use of Náhuatl, which is rapidly disappearing in the village.[8] An important change in connection with the occupations of *chirimitero* and *huehuechique* is that these specialists are now paid in money; formerly they were compensated with food and drink, another indication of the increasing importance of money.

Prediction in the case of the *curanderos* is more difficult. Most Tepoztecans are not ready to give up their *curanderos.* But they have reached the stage where they are willing to consider the doctor as an alternative, especially in the case of serious illness. Many Tepoztecans now visit private doctors and the Public Health Clinic in Cuernavaca. Certainly the hold of the *curanderos* has become much weaker; they are no longer as busy as formerly, and their income on the whole is very small. There are only two *curanderos* in the village who have great prestige and good income.

This raises the question of the relative desirability of the survival of old institutions in the face of general trends toward modernization. While this problem will be discussed later, it can be pointed out here that a sharp distinction must be made between the social effects of such old institutions as the Carnaval and barrio fiestas on the one hand and the *curandero* on the other. The fiestas, especially the Carnaval, provide much needed diversion for all age groups and tend to unify the village.

---

[8] During the time that this was being written, one of the two *huehuechiques* died, and no new recruit has appeared to take his place.

The *curanderos,* on the other hand, are prejudicial to the health of the people and are a definite impediment to the realization of national health programs. In view of our brief example, no blanket statements can be made; each institution must be examined in the light of its social function in the community.

The new occupations in Tepoztlán consist of the millers, chauffeurs, bus line

Fig. 19. A corn mill.

employees, tile and brickmakers, and druggists.[9] In all there are 41 individuals who work in these occupations. All the men who work for the bus cooperatives are members or sons of members of the cooperatives. Such membership is a prerequisite for employment. Tile and brickmaking are technically not new occupations, since these trades were practiced on a small scale prior to the Revolution. During the years of the Revolution and the hard times which immediately followed, the trade lapsed. In 1934 it was revived and now is growing steadily. The tile and brick-makers produce only for the needs of the village.

[9] The ropemakers and charcoal makers listed in Table 19 are occupations of long standing and were mentioned by Redfield, although an accurate comparison of the expansion in these occupations cannot be given here because Redfield did not state the number in 1926.

The successful establishment of corn mills in Tepoztlán (Fig. 19) is important as an example of the process by which a modern technological trait becomes incorporated into a "folk culture." The first mill was set up in 1925 by a non-Tepoztecan. The response of the village was so feeble that he left after two years. Redfield lived in the village during this first attempt and explained some of the obstacles.

There are three reasons why the mill has only a limited use: to many the slight cost is prohibitive; husbands assert that the flavor of *tortillas* made of mill-ground *nixtamal* is inferior; and, finally, to bring her maize regularly to the mill to the neglect of her *metate* lowers a woman in her neighbors' eyes.

To these reasons our informants added another: the strongest objections to the mill came not from the women but from the men, who viewed with great distrust the prospects of their wives having some leisure. The men believe firmly that the more occupied a woman is, the less are the possibilities of infidelity.

Shortly after Redfield left the village, a Tepoztecan opened another mill with great success. This success was due to a campaign of a group of women who saw the advantages which the mill would bring. Two years later another mill opened, and by 1942 there were four in the village. Today there is not a woman who does not regularly patronize the mills. A male informant described the success of the mill as "the revolution of the women against the authority of the men."

Having discussed the increase in the old occupations and the addition of new ones, we can now consider the question of specialization. It is here that we find one of the most important developments. Twenty years ago all of the so-called specialists were also farmers who closed their shops and went into the fields during the seasons of planting and harvesting. Today, considering all of the occupations, new and old, we find that of 220 men, 60 no longer work as farmers. The occupations in which we find the largest percentage of full-time specialists are as follows: storekeepers, chauffeurs, and bus line employees, teachers, butchers, shoemakers, millers, plumbers, druggists, barbers, and corn merchants.

It is interesting to note that generally the full-time specialists are in the "new" occupations, while the part-time specialists are in the occupations dating from the colonial and pre-Hispanic periods.

COLLECTIVE LABOR

Collective labor,[10] known as the *cuatequitl,* is in all probability an ancient tradition in Tepoztlán. At present it takes a number of forms, the village *cuatequitl,* the barrio *cuatequitl,* the *cuatequitl* of neighbors, and, on rare occasions, an inter-village *cuatequitl.* The village *cuatequitl* is a compulsory form of collective labor organized by the village authorities for public works such as improving the roads, constructing public buildings, or doing other work which, in theory, will benefit the village as a whole. Each able-bodied man between ages twenty-one and fifty can

---

[10] Family labor has already been treated in Chapter 3, "Status Distinctions and Family Organization," p. 61.

be called upon for service to the community. Failure to respond to such a call is punishable by a fine or jail sentence. However, a man can pay the daily wage of a substitute if desired. When the task is a relatively small one and more men are called up than are needed for the actual work, some are asked to contribute food or drink instead of labor.

The better-to-do families generally do not participate in the village *cuatequitl*, since they consider such work beneath their dignity and prefer to pay for substitutes. The main source of labor for the village *cuatequitl* are the poor who cannot afford substitutes or fines. The men from the smaller and poorer barrios have the reputation of being the most industrious and reliable workers for the *cuatequitl*. This is related to the fact that they have little political influence and have greater fear of the authorities.

The village *cuatequitl* is organized in terms of the eight *demarcaciones* or wards into which the village is divided. The *ayudante* or representative of each *demarcación* is ordered to announce a *cuatequitl* in his ward, and specific men are designated to appear at a given time and place. The attendance of the men is checked by the *ayudante* from his list.[11] Sometimes, when men are needed at short notice, more direct means are used to assure successful recruitment.

In a recent boundary dispute with the municipio of Tejalpa, the authorities posted aides at all the roads and paths leading out of the village to intercept the men as they went to their fields early in the morning. In this way 600 men were recruited in one day, and they were set to work to cut through the forest overgrowth which covered the disputed boundary line. In this case, since it was a municipio boundary, men from the other villages were also recruited. Other instances of inter-village *cuatequitl* have occurred in the repair of bridges which are used in common.

In recent years there have been very few village *cuatequitls* of major importance. In 1934 some work was done to improve the market place. The last important village *cuatequitl* was organized in 1926–27 while Redfield was in the village.[12] At this time, under the initiative of the local political faction known as the Bolsheviki, communal washbasins were constructed. (See Fig. 20.) During the twenties, political feelings ran so high and cleavages were so marked that members of the opposition group refused to work in *cuatequitls* organized by those in power. Fines were out of the question at the time because authority could not be enforced.

During the early thirties, when political schisms were still strong, there occurred an unusual type of voluntary village *cuatequitl* for the construction of the road to Cuernavaca. Led by two enterprising non-Tepoztecan schoolteachers and with the backing of the colony of Tepoztecans in Mexico City, the villagers decided to build a road to Cuernavaca. The two political factions, the Bolsheviki and the Frater-

---

[11] Some men will work until the check-off and then slip away.

[12] Before the Revolution, when there was more money in the local treasury and when the local government was in the hands of *caciques* whose tenure was quite stable, there were many more *cuatequitls* than now.

nales, refused to work side by side, and each organized separate shifts, one beginning at Tepoztlán and working toward Cuernavaca, the other working from Cuernavaca toward Tepoztlán.

Although the village *cuatequitl* is intended as a means of aiding the village as a whole, there are many obstacles to its successful operation, and it is gradually declining. Perhaps the fundamental difficulty is the inherent individualism of Tepoztecans, the suspiciousness and critical attitude toward the local government, and the paucity of local funds. The village *cuatequitl* has been traditionally associated in the minds of the villagers as a coercive rather than a voluntary institution. This may

Fig. 20. The communal washbasins.

be the result of having lived under an authoritarian system in which the local government had been imposed for years. Since the local government, generally the *síndico* or the president, has the power to designate the citizens who are to work in the *cuatequitl,* there is ample opportunity for favoritism and vengeance against political opponents or personal enemies.

It may be significant in this connection that children in their games will often say, "Unless you do this I will give you your *cuatequitl,*" suggesting that the *cuatequitl* is viewed as a punishment. It should also be noted that historically the existence of a native institution for collective labor was a distinct aid to the Spanish conquerors in their organization and control of the labor supply.

The second type of *cuatequitl* is the barrio *cuatequitl.* This is the collective working of the lands of the barrio saints. Barrio members are expected to cooperate in the preparation of the land, planting, cultivating, and harvesting of the crops from the saints' field. The sale of the produce goes for the upkeep of the local chapel. In contrast to the village *cuatequitl,* participation in the barrio *cuatequitl* is entirely voluntary. The barrio *mayordomo* goes through the barrio announcing at each house the time of the *cuatequitl.* While there are no fines or penalties for nonparticipation, there is strong social pressure as well as fear that the saint may be offended by failure to work for his upkeep. Still, in recent years there has been increasing difficulty in obtaining barrio cooperation. Now three of the seven barrios rent out the land and use the rental for the expenses of the chapel.

The barrio *cuatequitl* cleans the churchyard and repairs the chapel. Barrio differences in this connection are interesting. Although the smaller barrios of San Pedro, San Sebastián, and Los Reyes are the most reliable workers on the village *cuatequitl,* they appear to be the most neglectful in the upkeep of their respective chapels, indicating perhaps that Catholicism has less of a hold in these barrios. Indeed, it was in the barrio of San Sebastián that a Protestant sect won over about fifteen families. The barrio of Santa Cruz, also very poor, is known for its superior care and great devotion to its chapel. The larger barrios, too, keep their chapels in repair.

The third occasion for the *cuatequitl* is that of a group of neighbors within the barrio who may agree among themselves to repair the street or to build a water tank or some other local improvement. This *cuatequitl* generally involves fewer people and still occurs quite frequently. During our visit to the village four new water founts were built in this way. The *cuatequitl* of the barrio and of neighbors would seem to be a natural mechanism for a great deal of cooperative endeavor on a purely voluntary basis. But the poor quality of human relations in the village, and the fear to take the initiative in any venture, keep cooperative undertakings at a minimum. Yet the fact that there exists a tradition of cooperative forms of labor has occasionally led to truly heroic and dramatic undertakings. The most recent example of this was the construction of the road to Cuernavaca.

One of the features that characterize all occasions of collective labor is the free use of drink. It would seem that Tepoztecans need the stimulus of drink to enable them to work together successfully. The implications of this for the analysis of the Tepoztecan character will be discussed later.

WAGE LABOR

Although wage labor is an old practice in Tepoztlán, labor is not viewed impersonally as a commodity that can be bought and sold on the market. The relationship between employer and employee is a very personal one; and as a rule, a man will not work for someone he does not like. Tepoztecans are almost as particular about choosing the men they work with as they are in choosing drinking companions. This attitude of independence has become much more marked since the Revolution, for Tepoztecans now have alternatives not available then. The democratic ideology of the Mexican Revolution has influenced Tepoztecans, who are jealous of their new freedom. The harsh treatment received by Tepoztecan laborers on the haciendas and sometimes even in the village before the Revolution would be unbearable today.

It is the custom for the employer to seek out laborers, rather than vice versa. In fact, most Tepoztecans consider it humiliating to ask for a job, and ordinarily a man would rather go hungry than go about the village asking for work. Also, some of the younger men are sensitive about asking for their wages, and often the mother will collect the wages for her sons.

When a farmer needs a hired hand he will usually try to get a relative, frequently an uncle or nephew; or he will ask his neighbor or *compadre*. If no one is available within this rather close and intimate circle he may seek no further. As a result, we sometimes find the curious situation whereby some individuals complain of a labor shortage while others may have no work.

The peak wage labor season is from May to August when corn is being planted and cultivated, and from December to January for the harvest. During these periods there is sometimes a real labor shortage which leads to some mutual labor exchanges. It is estimated that a few hundred Tepoztecans work as day laborers during the busy season. At the most there are about four months of wage labor during the year. The landless may work as *peones* during the entire period or they may work part-time in *tlacolol*. The small landowners will also work as *peones* to get some extra cash. Thus some are employers of labor for a short time and are then, in turn, wage laborers for someone else.

Wages have gone up considerably in Tepoztlán during the past twenty years and are much higher than in other villages like Tzintzuntzan, Mitla, or Chan Kom. The reason is the proximity to large urban centers and the haciendas which pay relatively high wages to attract labor. But the rise in wages has not kept up with the rise in prices of many basic commodities.

land tenure: 6

THREE TYPES of land tenure are found in Tepoztlán: communal land holdings, *ejido* holdings, and private holdings. Communal lands comprise approximately eighty per cent of the land of the municipio and include four of the five land types, *texcal*, monte, *cerros*, and *terrenos cerriles*. These lands have belonged traditionally to the municipio and have been under its control. Any member of the municipio enjoys the right to use these lands, and they are not divided into plots.

Ejido lands constitute somewhat less than five per cent of the land within the municipio and consist primarily of arable land for plow agriculture. *Ejido* lands are communally owned by the municipio but are under the control of locally elected *ejido* authorities, rather than the regular municipal authorities. *Ejido* holdings differ from other communal holdings in that they are divided into small plots and assigned to individuals in accord with the rules of eligibility established by the National Ejido Program. *Ejido* and private holdings are practically identical, except that the former cannot be sold. However, *ejido* plots may remain in the same family for many years and may be passed down from father to sons if the need for the land can be satisfactorily proved. Private holdings consist mostly of the land used for plow agriculture and constitute about sixteen per cent of all the land in the municipio. Private holdings are held in free simple, and ownership must be proved by legal title.

It is important to remember that in Tepoztlán all three types of landholdings are worked individually rather than collectively. The only exception relates to the working of church lands. Here we find a curious combination of what is technically private ownership with a collective form of labor. Each of the seven barrios "owns" a plot of land which is worked collectively by the members of the barrio for the support of the barrio chapel. The land, however, is registered in the name of a trusted barrio member because of the law against the church ownership of land. This type of collective working of land is an old pattern. Before the Revolution of 1857 each of the twenty saints in the large central church of the village had its plot of land which its particular devotees worked collectively. The similarity between this system and that of the pre-Conquest days is noteworthy, and it is possible that the same lands which were worked for the Aztec priesthood were later worked for the Catholic Church.

COMMUNAL LANDS

The communal lands represent one of the oldest forms of landholding and have shown a remarkable stability through the years. The system of communal landholding has remained practically intact through both the Aztec and Spanish Conquests. Indeed, the similarity between the policy of the Spanish and Aztec conquerors of Tepoztlán toward the system of communal landholdings is noteworthy.

When Tepoztecans asked the Spaniards for legal title to their lands in the early sixteenth century, they were able to present maps showing the boundaries of their lands which they had held under Moctezuma. These ancient "titles" were used by the Spaniards as a basis for determining the limits of the land grants.[1] The present limits of the municipio are therefore almost identical with those of pre-Hispanic days. Because most Tepoztecan lands were ill suited for either sugar or rice plantations, and because of the policy both of the Crown and of the Marqués del Valle, who conquered Tepoztlán in 1521, to alter only those native institutions which constituted a direct threat to the conquerors, the Marqués was not interested in Tepoztecan lands as such. Rather, he wanted taxes in the form of produce and later in money, and he wanted the labor of Tepoztecans to work his mines and haciendas.

Tepoztlán received its first land titles from the Viceroy Don Antonio de Mendoza in a grant dated May 20, 1548. This grant consisted of two *sitios de ganado mayor;* its next grant under Don Louis de Velasco, dated February 6, 1555, was for four *sitios de ganado menor* and eight *caballerías de tierra*.[2] These land grants gave Tepoztecans legal title to lands which they had traditionally worked and claimed.

The titles for the communal holdings of the municipio are considered very precious, and responsibility for their safekeeping is entrusted to the *síndico* of the municipal local government in Tepoztlán. These titles are used primarily in boundary disputes, which have been going on with neighboring municipios for the past four hundred years. From historical documents we learn that less than one hundred years after the Conquest the land titles had already been lost. The loss and recovery of the land titles has occurred again and again in the history of the municipio.

According to local tradition, the titles to the municipal lands fell into the hands of the Hacienda de San Gaspar during the middle of the last century. Tepoztecans were prohibited from using their own forest resources, which the hacienda used for wood fuel. The Tepoztecans carried on an extended feud with this hacienda, and the agents were killed on sight in the village. Apparently the hacienda was

---

[1] In these early land grants, the land was described as follows ". . . la mayor parte de tierra infructífera por los muchos cerros y lomas ásperas, barrancas y montes intransitables." These early documents also establish the fact that the village of Tepoztlán was the administrative seat of the municipio. The surrounding villages are listed as *pagos*. See *Ramo de Tierras,* Vol. 67 (1591), Exp. 11, Foja 12; and Vol. 3501 (1745), Exp. 1, Cuaderno 4. The ancient boundaries are also given in the *Relación*.

[2] *Ibid.*

agreeable to settling the issue and offered to sell the land titles back to Tepoztlán. A wealthy Tepoztecan, Vicente Gómez, offered to lend the money to the municipio for the purchase of the titles. This man later became a leading *cacique* in the village and controlled the local government. In an attempt to recover his loan, he levied heavy taxes on each sack of charcoal produced by Tepoztecans. A group of villagers finally assassinated him.

The land titles were again lost between 1900 and 1905 when a local priest sold to an outsider the land titles and other important documents kept in the archives of the convent.[3] A few years later the village had to buy them back at a high price. This occurred again in 1925 when the municipio paid 800 pesos to buy back its land titles from a non-Tepoztecan woman into whose hands they had fallen.

Judging from the early documents, there was little change in the system of communal landholdings during the entire colonial period. The only references of significance show that as early as 1567 Cortés had rented some Tepoztecan lands to the operator of his Hacienda of Tlaltenango and also to some Tepoztecans. Presumably Cortés was using communal lands for this purpose. The first great change in the system of landholdings occurred after the Revolution of 1857 when most of the communal lands held by the church were taken over by some of the leading families of the village as private property. After this time Tepoztecans could petition the local authorities for title to some of the communal lands.

One occasion for a fairly large distribution of communal lands to individual Tepoztecans occurred in the late 1890's as a result of an attempt of the Hacienda of Oacalco to grab some of the Tepoztecan lands. To present a stronger legal claim, the local authorities encouraged Tepoztecans to file claims for individual plots of land in the area which was being threatened, so that individual court actions could be lodged against the hacienda if the lands were taken. The private owners of the said lands backed up their newly acquired claims by force of arms, and managed to keep the lands for Tepoztlán. However, despite the Reform Laws of 1857, most of the communal lands of Tepoztlán remained intact and were not converted into private property.

Although the municipio of Tepoztlán held on to most of its communal lands, these lands were under the control of the local *caciques* and, therefore, were not always available to the landless Tepoztecans. Before the Revolution of 1910–20, the *caciques,* with the support of state and federal authorities, prohibited the villagers from using the communal lands in order to assure a cheap labor supply for themselves. One of the most important effects of the Revolution upon Tepoztlán was that the communal lands of the municipio became open to all Tepoztecans.

Another important change in the status of the communal lands occurred shortly after the Revolution as a result of the National Ejido Program. On April 24, 1921, a group of Tepoztecans, led by members of the colony of Tepoztecans in Mexico

---

[3] Manuel Miranda y Marrón, "Una Excursión a Tepoztlán," *Société Scientifique,* Bk. 23 (1905–06), pp. 22-23.

City, appealed for *ejido* lands for the landless families in the village. The petition for *ejidos* asked that the lands of the neighboring Hacienda of Oacalco, which had taken Tepoztecan lands in the eighteenth and early nineteenth centuries, be restored.

After almost ten years of petitioning and investigations, the request was finally granted, and by a presidential order of November 24, 1929, Tepoztlán received in restitution 2,100 hectares of land from the Hacienda of Oacalco. Of these 2,100 hectares of land, 200 were unirrigated land cultivable only during the rainy season, 500 were forest lands, and 1,400 were scrub forest lands suitable for mixed grazing.[4] This meant that there were only 200 hectares of cultivable land available for distribution in individual *ejido* plots. In addition to these lands, there have recently been other so-called *ejido* grants. In 1937 and again in 1940, the Departamento Agrario created *ejidos* out of portions of the communal lands and allotted these lands to individual Tepoztecan families.

The working out of the Agrarian Reform Laws and of the *ejido* program in Tepoztlán has not been without difficulties. It has led to a conflict between municipal and *ejido* authorities. In the past the communal lands were under the jurisdiction of the local municipal authorities. However, the presidential order of November 24, 1929, gave Tepoztlán the lands it had lost and included a clause which stipulated that in the future the communal lands, as well as the lands granted to the municipio as *ejidos,* were to be under the jurisdiction and administration of *ejido* authorities.

This order violated an old and well-established tradition which had received legal expression in the laws of the state of Morelos, whereby control of all communal lands was vested in the municipal government. Shortly after the presidential decree was passed, conflicts between the newly created *ejido* authorities and the municipal authorities broke out. The municipal authorities insisted in their right to control the communal lands, and when the *ejidatarios* refused to recognize this authority, they were jailed. The sending of federal troops to the village was threatened, to straighten out the confusion. Legally and technically the point of view of the Departamento Agrario won out, thereby weakening local authority.

One of the results of the change in authority is that the very scanty income of the municipio has been further reduced. It may be noted that this trend from local to national authority over communal lands began in 1926, when the Forestry Department took over responsibility for controlling and preserving the forest resources of the nation. Since that date, Tepoztecans who want to cut or burn wood for charcoal must, in theory, obtain the permission of the forestry authorities and pay the tax set by them. However, as we shall see later, in practice there are many violations; and at the time of this writing there is a flagrant disregard of any authority whatsoever in the making of charcoal.

Another conflict resulting from the *ejido* program in Tepoztlán is that between the *tlacololeros,* who have traditionally depended upon the communal lands for hillside agriculture, and the newly created *ejidatarios*. These two have come to be

---

[4] Most Tepoztecans think of this land as part of the communal holdings; only the arable portion is called *ejido*.

separate interest groups, with the *ejidatarios* taking over, for private use, lands which have traditionally been worked by *tlacololeros*. The latter viewed with alarm this encroachment by the *ejido* authorities and formed an organization to defend their interests. This group is known as *comuneros,* in distinction to the *ejidatarios,* and has received official recognition as such by the Departamento Agrario. Each of these groups has become a political faction of weight in the village.

In theory any individual from any one of the eight villages of the municipio has the right to use the communal lands anywhere in the municipio, provided he obtains the permission of the municipal authorities, or, as at the present time, the forestry and *ejido* authorities. But in practice each of the eight villages has come to consider certain lands, generally those nearest the village, as its own. Thus, moral boundaries have developed and are today recognized by all concerned. For example, the people of the little village of Santo Domingo jealously guard "their monte" from use by other villagers, but especially from the inhabitants of San Juan, who depend heavily upon woodcutting to earn a living. Similarly, although all *texcal* lands are technically communal property, the villagers of Gabriel Mariaca have prevented Tepoztecans from opening *tlacolol* in "their *texcal*."

In recent years, conflicts over the use of communal lands have set village against village within the municipio and have seriously weakened municipal bonds. The increasing exploitation of communal resources for commercial rather than for subsistence purposes, which was encouraged by the railroad and the highway, made for competition which did not exist before. This led to a demand of the outlying villages for sole rights of control of adjoining communal lands. In effect the villages were demanding that the moral boundaries be accepted as legal boundaries, thereby interpreting the communal lands as village rather than municipio lands.

One of the first serious difficulties between the villages of the municipio began in the early twenties when the village of San Juan—taking advantage of the proximity of the railroad which ran through the village, and because of its very limited agricultural resources—began to develop the charcoal industry on a commercial scale and to export large quantities of charcoal to Mexico City. In 1926 the villagers of San Juan organized a forestry cooperative to meet the requirements of the national forestry law of the same year. The authorities of Tepoztlán at once challenged the right of the inhabitants of San Juan to exploit municipal resources for the exclusive benefit of a single village. The people of San Juan disregarded the prohibitions of the local authorities and appealed their case directly to the national government. The dispute was bitter and led to some violence. It was finally settled by the intervention of federal authorities, who ruled in favor of the municipio.

In March, 1930, the village of Tepoztlán then organized another cooperative— this time in the name of the municipio and theoretically open to all, but actually controlled by Tepoztecans—and continued to produce charcoal on a large scale. Government files for the next five years are full of complaints from the surrounding villages of the municipio to the effect that the Forestry Cooperative was not truly a municipal organization, but was dominated by the village of Tepoztlán in the interests of a small clique within that village. The schisms created by this cooperative within the village and the municipio will be treated later in this study.

These facts indicate the strong individualism of the villagers, and the interesting way in which new contacts with the outside and production for the market have disrupted the earlier stability of the municipio. As long as production of charcoal was primarily for household use, there seemed to be no conflict between collective ownership and individual exploitation of the resources. As a matter of fact, the communal lands have been one of the few unifying factors in the life of the municipio and have brought the villagers together to defend their lands in the face of threats from the outside. However, with commercial exploitation of the limited communal resources, competition became intense, and the concept of communal land ownership by the municipio was attacked.

PRIVATE HOLDINGS

As we have indicated earlier, private landholdings include most of the lands for plow agriculture; that is, most of the level lands. The only other privately owned lands are the house sites in the village, most of which include some ground for a garden and for some corn plantings. The history of private landholdings is not very clear. Certainly we know that private holdings have existed at least since the time of the Conquest. Whether or not it existed in Tepoztlán before the Conquest cannot be determined, but, judging from the data for other parts of Mexico, it is probable that private holdings coexisted with other holdings. Much of the land that is now privately owned, approximately one hundred hectares of the most productive lands of the municipio, once belonged to the church. This land was divided into private holdings after the Revolution of 1857. Most of the landowners now have some document to prove title; but there are still many individuals who work plots of land which have been passed down from family to family without any written proof of ownership.

The ownership of land is one of the basic aspirations of Tepoztecan peasants, and land-ownership is perhaps their most important single criterion of wealth. The value put on land-ownership is reflected, in part, by the fact that farmers, artisans, and merchants invest in land whenever they have the necessary capital and the opportunity. But there is no concentration of land-ownership in the hands of a few. There are several reasons for this. Few people in Tepoztlán will sell tillable land, and when they do they prefer to sell to close relatives. On the whole there is little land turnover. Tepoztecans with sufficient capital to purchase large quantities of land do not do so, because they seek more profitable kinds of investments, generally in cattle. The high cost of labor and the low and uneven yields in plow agriculture make corn production for commercial purposes unprofitable.

DISTRIBUTION OF PRIVATE HOLDINGS

According to our findings, only 36 per cent or 311 of the 853 families in the village own private land. Thus, in a village where the family ideal is to own a plot of land, we find that 64 per cent of the families own no private land. The distribution of privately owned land is shown in Table 20.

TABLE 20.   Distribution of Privately Owned Land by Family Units and House Sites, 1944.

Barrio	House Sites	Family Units	Families Owning Land		Families With Two Members Owning Land	Families With Three Members Owning Land	Families Not Owning Land	Families Not Owning Land Who Live With Landowners
			No.	Per Cent				
San Miguel	163	214	83	38.3	12	1	131	21
La Santísima	139	185	62	33.5	6	..	123	17
Santo Domingo	174	223	61	27.4	..	..	162	21
Santa Cruz (large)	67	82	44	53.6	5	..	38	10
Los Reyes	37	49	30	61.2	1	..	19	3
San Sebastián	34	42	11	26.2	1	..	31	3
Santa Cruz (small)	29	36	10	26.1	..	..	26	3
San Pedro	19	22	10	41.4	..	..	12	3
Tepoztlán	662	853	311	36.4	25	1	542	81

On the whole, the smaller barrios have a larger proportion of landowners. The outstanding exception is San Sebastián, by far the poorest barrio in the village. It should be noted that Los Reyes, one of the smaller barrios, has an extremely high percentage of landowners and is known as one of the richer barrios. On the other hand, Santa Cruz (large), which shows a high percentage of landowners, is known as one of the poorer barrios. Similarly, the large barrios which here show a low percentage of landowners have some of the wealthiest families in the village. In other words, the distribution of land-ownership is not in itself an accurate index of barrio wealth. Our data, however, do show that the largest number of landless families are in the center barrios.

The small number of families in which two or more members own land points to the lack of concentration of land-ownership along family lines, and also reflects the inheritance pattern of not dividing the property until the father's death. The fact that 81 families without land live on the same house site with families who own land tends to modify to some degree the picture of landlessness, for most of these 81 families are married sons living with their fathers and working for them.

SIZE OF PRIVATE HOLDINGS

The striking thing about landholdings is their extremely small size. This can be seen from Table 21,[5] which shows that 90.6 per cent of all private holdings are less

---

[5] Private holdings here refer to what Tepoztecans call *propriedad rústica* which is outside of the village, as over against *propriedad urbana* which is located within the village. The latter refers to house sites, some of which have small areas devoted to corn.

than nine hectares in size, and 68.4 per cent are less than four hectares. The two largest holdings are only between twenty-five and twenty-nine hectares. A man with fifteen or more hectares is considered a large landowner; only 3.3 per cent of holdings are of this size. The smallest holdings, of which there are many, are as low as two *cuartillos* (one-fifth of a hectare) in size.

TABLE 21. Size of Privately Owned Landholdings.

Size of Holdings (Hectares)	Number of Owners	Per Cent of Owners
0–1	109	36.2
1–4	97	32.2
5–9	67	22.2
10–14	18	5.9
15–19	4	1.3
20–24	4	1.3
25–29	2	.7

The distribution of privately owned land by size of plot and by barrio is shown in Table 22. It is evident from this table that there is a higher proportion of the small holdings (less than one hectare) in the smaller barrios. This is significant in view of the fact that we have seen in Table 20 that there was a larger proportion of land-owners in the smaller barrios. For example, although 53.6 per cent of the families of Santa Cruz (large) were landowners, 54.5 per cent of them had holdings of less than one hectare. On the other hand, in the larger barrio of San Miguel, in which 38.3 per cent of its families were landowners, only 18.07 per cent owned holdings of less than one hectare. Furthermore, while Santa Cruz (large) has no landowners with more than nine hectares, San Miguel has eight such landowners.

The greatest extremes in size of holdings are found in the large barrios, with the single exception of Los Reyes, one of the smaller barrios.[6] We have already seen that Los Reyes is also unusual in that it has the highest percentage of landowners. In general, these figures show that there is considerable range in the size of holdings by barrios.

The size of cornfields is small, because holdings are generally in small parcels located in different places. I have never seen a cornfield in Tepoztlán larger than 35 *cuartillos*, or three and one-half hectares. Although a few of the larger operators plant as much as one hundred *cuartillos* of corn, or approximately ten hectares of land, this would be divided among a number of small parcels. Operators of these larger plots own at least two teams of oxen and have enough capital for hired labor.

EJIDO *HOLDINGS*

Two hundred and sixty-seven families, or 31 per cent of all families, hold *ejido* grants. It is interesting that most of the cases of two members of a single family

---

[6] The case of Santa Cruz (small) presents a somewhat special problem; it adjoins the barrio of Santo Domingo and is not literally a separate barrio, for it owes allegiance to Santa Cruz (large).

TABLE 22. Distribution of Privately Owned Land by Size of Plot, 1944.

| Barrio | Hectares of Land | | | | | | | | | | | | | | No. of Plots |
| | 0-1 | | 1-4 | | 5-9 | | 10-14 | | 15-19 | | 20-24 | | 25-29 | | |
	No.	Per Cent	No.	Per Cent	No.	Per Cent	No.	Per Cent	No.	Per Cent	No.	Per Cent	No.	Per Cent	
San Miguel	15	18.07	32	38.55	28	33.73	6	7.23	..	..	2	2.41	..	..	83
La Santísima	23	37.09	15	24.20	17	27.43	6	9.68	7	1.61	..	..	1	1.64	68
Santo Domingo	21	34.42	27	44.26	10	16.40	2	3.27	..	..	..	..	..	..	61
Santa Cruz (large)	24	54.54	14	31.84	6	13.64	..	..	..	..	2	6.66	..	..	44
Los Reyes	13	43.33	9	30.00	3	10.00	1	3.33	2	6.66	..	..	..	..	30
San Sebastián	5	45.45	3	27.27	3	27.27	..	..	..	..	..	..	..	..	11
San Pedro	4	40.00	4	40.00	2	20.00	..	..	..	..	..	..	..	..	10
Santa Cruz (small)	4	40.00	3	30.00	1	10.00	..	..	1	10.00	..	..	1	10.00	10
Tepoztlán	109	35.00	107	34.40	70	22.50	15	4.82	10	3.21	4	1.28	2	0.64	317

having an *ejido* grant occurred in the larger barrios, which have controlled the local *ejido* organization from the start of the program. Again, we find a substantial number of families who do not have an *ejido* parcel living with a family who has one.

DISTRIBUTION OF *Ejido* HOLDINGS

The distribution of *ejido* parcels by barrio, shown in Table 23, seems to have been equitable; those barrios which had the smallest percentage of landowners show the largest percentage of *ejido* grants.

TABLE 23. Distribution of *Ejido* Parcels by Families and House Sites, 1944.

Barrio	No. of Family Units	No. of House Sites	Families Holding *Ejido* No.	Families Holding *Ejido* Per Cent	Families With Two Members Holding *Ejido*	Families Without *Ejido*	Families Without *Ejido* Living With *Ejido* Holders
San Miguel	214	163	61	28.4	3	153	15
La Santísima	185	139	39	21.0	1	146	14
Santo Domingo	223	174	99	44.3	6	124	19
Santa Cruz (large)	82	67	24	29.2	..	58	5
Los Reyes	49	37	11	22.4	..	38	2
San Sebastián	42	34	15	40.4	1	27	2
Santa Cruz (small)	36	29	10	27.7	..	26	3
San Pedro	22	19	8	36.3	..	14	1
Tepoztlán	853	662	267	31.30	11	586	61

SIZE OF *Ejido* HOLDINGS

The size of *ejido* parcels is shown in Table 24. *Ejido* holdings are also small; all are less than three hectares in size. Also, the larger barrios have the greatest number of larger holdings. If we compare the average size of *ejido* holdings with the average of the entire state of Morelos, we find that Tepoztlán holdings are somewhat smaller; the average *ejido* parcel in crop land, for the state as a whole, is four hectares.

PRIVATE AND EJIDO *HOLDINGS*

In the foregoing we have discussed private landholdings and *ejido* holdings separately. But there is some overlapping, since many holders of private land also have *ejidos*. Of the 267 families holding *ejidos*, 109 families also hold private land, and the remaining 158 have only *ejidos*. The way in which private and *ejido* holdings are distributed by barrio is shown in Table 25. It will be seen that 384 families neither own private land nor hold *ejido*. This reveals the land poverty of the village, as far as plow culture is concerned. The large number of landless people and the small size of landholdings result from shortage of tillable land, rather than from concentration of land-ownership in the hands of a few individuals.

TABLE 24. Distribution of *Ejidos* by Size of Plot, 1944.

Barrio	Hectares						Total
	0–1		1–2		2–3		
	No. of *Ejido* Plots	Percentage of *Ejido* Plots	No. of *Ejido* Plots	Percentage of *Ejido* Plots	No. of *Ejido* Plots	Percentage of *Ejido* Plots	
San Miguel	17	27.87	37	60.66	7	11.47	61
La Santísima	6	15.38	33	84.62	..	..	39
Santo Domingo	37	39.21	60	58.82	2	1.97	99
Santa Cruz (large)	10	41.67	12	50.00	2	8.33	24
Los Reyes	5	45.45	6	54.55	..	..	11
San Sebastián	9	60.00	6	40.00	..	..	15
San Pedro	3	37.50	5	62.50	..	..	8
Santa Cruz (small)	3	30.00	7	70.00	..	..	10
Tepoztlán	90	33.70	166	62.17	11	4.49	267

TABLE 25. Distribution of Privately Owned Lands and *Ejido* Parcels by Families, 1944.

Barrio	Total No. of Families	No. of Families Who Own Private Land	No. of Families Who Hold *Ejidos*	No. of Families Who Own Private Land and Hold *Ejidos*	No. of Families Who Have Neither Private nor *Ejido* Land
San Miguel	214	59	37	24	94
La Santísima	185	46	23	16	100
Santo Domingo	223	24	62	37	100
Santa Cruz (large)	82	29	9	15	29
Los Reyes	49	23	4	7	15
San Sebastián	42	9	13	2	18
Santa Cruz (small)	36	9	9	1	17
San Pedro	22	3	1	7	11
Tepoztlán	853	202	158	109	384

RENTAL OF LAND

Land is rented both on a cash and corn basis, depending upon the owner's choice. Rental agreements may be made on a verbal or a written basis. In 1947, a twelve-*cuartillo* plot of fair land rented for about 50 centavos a *cuartillo*, the value in corn would be about 150 to 200 pesos. Widows, who regularly rent out their land, generally ask for payment in corn. Despite the land shortage in Tepoztlán, more land is sometimes available for rent than there are people to rent it. This is primarily due to the lack of capital. Many families own no oxen, and very few can afford to pay for the rental of oxen in addition to the rental of land. And there is always the risk of a poor crop. In cases of crop failure, renters are supposed to make good, but many simply break their contracts. This leads to quarrels but rarely to legal action.

A man who pays his rent despite crop failure earns the reputation of being *muy honrado* (very honorable) and is sought as a renter.

There is no sharecropping as such in Tepoztlán. When rental is in corn, there is a fixed quantity of corn agreed upon in advance, rather than a percentage of the crop. The landowner, therefore, takes little risk.

LAND VALUES

The price of most agricultural lands, that is, the lands which Tepoztecans classify as second and third class, has increased more slowly than other lands, as can be seen in Table 26. During and immediately after the Revolution of 1910-20, land prices fell sharply. Many sold their land at any price in order to stave off starvation, and land parcels changed hands for a small quantity of corn. Since 1920, land prices have been rising steadily. This rise was accentuated by the new road which, with the influx of tourists who have sought land for summer homes, has made for a phenomenal rise in the price of house sites in the village. Distance from the road and from the central plaza, and proximity to one of the twenty-six water fountains, are the most important factors affecting the price of land.

TABLE 26. Land Prices From 1901 to 1944.

Year	Cost of House Sites (in Pesos)		Cost of Arable Land per Hectare (in Pesos)	
	10 to 500 Meters From Water Fountains	500 or More Meters From Water Fountains	Poorest Land	Best Land
1901–1910	60	40	40	60
1911–1920	30	15	10	20
1921–1926	40	25	25	100
1927–1930	70	50	60	150
1931–1935	100	75	120	200
1936–1940	175	125	200	400
1941	300	250	350	450
1942	500	300	400	500
1943	1,000	400	450	800
1944	2,000	1,000	500	1,000

The change in the Tepoztecan attitudes toward selling land to outsiders is one of the most interesting of all changes in the village. Until about 1942, Tepoztecans were very reluctant to sell their land to outsiders. A leading Mexican banker who wanted to build his home in the village had to negotiate for over a year before he could succeed in buying a modest-sized, idle plot of land whose Tepoztecan owner had been residing in Mexico City for many years. Similarly, one of my assistants had to wait for months before she was able to find a plot of land, and then she could only buy one at a considerable distance from the center.

When I returned to the village three years later, a change had occurred; Tepoztecans were looking for land buyers. In the summer of 1947, I was approached by three individuals who wanted to sell me a house plot. However, the high price paid by the Mexican banker and a few other early comers gave Tepoztecans an exaggerated notion of the value of their land. House sites which were worth about 100 to 200 pesos in 1927 now would not be sold for less than 10,000 pesos. This has made a few people wealthy, especially those who were fortunate enough to have house sites fronting the new road.

THE LAND PROBLEM

The land problem in Tepoztlán is not a recent phenomenon. It was at least as severe in the twenties, before the *ejido* grants, and it was certainly more acute before the Revolution. Twenty years ago, the 158 families who now have *ejidos* were landless *peones*. Thus, the *ejido* program in Tepoztlán has had at least two beneficial effects. It has reduced the number of landless families, and it has helped some families, who had insufficient land, to increase their holdings. But the *ejido* program has by no means solved the land problem, for 384 families still remain landless and have little prospect of becoming landowners. Although the *ejido* program brought new and more modern agricultural techniques, there is still not a single tractor in Tepoztlán.

It is apparent that our findings on land-ownership in Tepoztlán differ from those in Redfield's earlier study. Redfield did not mention the existence of a land problem or land shortage in Tepoztlán. Although Redfield gives no clear-cut statement on the matter of land-ownership, and treats the entire subject rather incidentally, there is an implication that each family in Tepoztlán owned its own land. Redfield writes, "Most families have at least a small milpa in which the men are active during the seasons of sowing and harvesting." [7] We have shown that in 1944, 64 per cent of the families owned no private land, and there is no reason to believe that the land situation was any better in 1926. Redfield's use of the term "milpa" is perhaps responsible for what appears to be a sharp difference in our findings. He did not distinguish between a privately owned milpa and a milpa of communally owned land. A Tepoztecan speaks of "my milpa" in referring to rented land, communal land, or private land. Unless the investigator probed further, he might well get the impression that all Tepoztecans were landowners.

Redfield conveyed this impression in another connection. In discussing private lands he wrote,

Characteristically each *sitio* has an appendant milpa which may be located as much as a mile away from the *sitio:* but the two are usually taxed and inherited together. These tracts are not infrequently sold, but most of them have been in the same family for many generations.[8]

This quotation raises a number of questions. First, Tepoztecans distinguish be-

[7] Redfield, *Tepoztlán*, p. 145.
[8] *Ibid*, p. 61.

tween *sitios urbanos* (urban house sites) and *predios rústicos* (rural parcels), and they are listed separately in the property register. Furthermore, a Tepoztecan who owns only an urban house site is not considered a landowner. This, despite the fact that some *sitios* have sufficient land to plant a patch of corn. Traditionally, the house site milpas are used principally for fresh corn. In 1944, however, less than 20 per cent of all house sites were planted in corn, a lower figure no doubt than that prevailing in 1926; as the population is increasing, the house sites are getting smaller because they are usually divided up for purposes of inheritance.

Second, Redfield's statement concerning the "appendant milpa" may refer to an old pattern which has not existed in the village since long before the Revolution of 1910, and I could find only a vague tradition of it remembered by a few older informants. After some investigation of this point I could not find a single example of a house site in the village with an "appendant milpa." The inheritance pattern that prevails today and that, as far as I was able to determine, has prevailed for a long time would rule out the situation of each house site having an "appendant milpa." It is common practice for the father to divide the inheritance, so that the house site goes to one child and the milpa to another.

It is possible that the conception of Tepoztecans as a landed peasantry was taken up from Redfield by Stuart Chase, who described Tepoztlán as a village with economic security. This is especially ironical in view of the fact that Tepoztlán was in the heart of Zapata country and was one of the first villages in Morelos to join the Revolution which, in this region, was essentially a bitter struggle for the land.

It has become traditional among historians, economists, and sociologists, in writing on the history of the agrarian problem in Mexico, to distinguish between two fundamental types of social and economic organization: the so-called free village and the hacienda. The free village represents the older Indian form of organization, and the hacienda represents the Spanish form. Much of Mexican history has been described as a struggle between these two ways of life. One of the best statements on this situation is the following:

The stage is set. On the one hand is the institution of private property, already present in its incipient forms in pre-Conquest days, but now, with the importation of the *encomienda,* the *peonía,* and *caballería,* fortified, strengthened, and ready to develop in stature and power until soon it stands full grown as the classic type of landed estate—the hacienda. On the other hand is the landholding, communal village rooted deep in age-old custom and tradition and now given life and legal support in the reorganized native pueblo and in the scores of new villages soon to be founded on the Indian model. From this point of view the history of Mexico is, in its most fundamental aspects the drama of the struggle between feudalism and the free village, between the individual private estate and the collective, communal holding-in fine, between the hacienda and the *ejido.* For almost four hundred years it is the hacienda which wins. The victories of the villages are only temporary triumphs; slowly but surely the *ejido* is pushed back and back until by the turn of the twentieth century only in the mountain fastness and in a few other isolated areas does it still exist. Finally, and at long last, the tide turns, a new chapter is opened and the *ejido* comes into its own or at least, so it would appear.[9]

There can be little quarrel with this summary of the basic process. I think, however, it is useful to recognize that between the isolated mountain villages, which held on to their own lands and were largely free of hacienda influence, and the landless villages, which were literally swallowed up by the hacienda itself, there was a middle type of village like Tepoztlán, which was marginal to the hacienda area and which maintained most of its communal lands in spite of the impact of the hacienda economy. Tepoztlán lost approximately 2,500 hectares of its 25,000 hectares to the neighboring haciendas. Although Tepoztecan economy was not basically changed by the haciendas, they came to be an important source of added income to Tepoztecans. Tepoztlán was a convenient source of labor supply for many haciendas in the state of Morelos, and Tepoztecans were recruited in large numbers.

In the formulation of Mexican history as a struggle between the hacienda and the free village, there has been an understandable tendency to blacken the former and idealize the latter. It is sometimes assumed that the free villages were organized on a democratic basis and that peasants who lived in these villages automatically had access to the communal lands. As we have seen in the case of Tepoztlán, this was not so. Tepoztlán, before the Revolution of 1910, was a highly stratified society in which the well-to-do *caciques* held political power and prevented the peasants, most of whom were landless peons, from utilizing their own communal lands. We do not know to what extent this situation existed in other regions, and this is a point which deserves investigation.

Another aspect of the tendency to idealize the free village has been the assumption that collective forms of land tenure are accompanied by cooperativeness and a form of collectivism in the economic organization of agriculture. As a matter of fact, Tepoztecans, like most Mexican peasants, are a highly individualistic group of farmers, and there is a minimum of cooperativeness or collectivization in the system of agriculture. The existence of collective forms of land tenure, in the face of this individualism, has been responsible for much bickering between the villages. The coming of the railroad and the subsequent increase in production for the market under a competitive system has further weakened the role of the communal lands as a unifying force.

What light does the Tepoztecan material throw on the working out of the *ejido* program? I think it shows that any evaluation of the *ejido* program in Mexico must carefully distinguish between its effects upon villages which had been landless and those which had retained their communal lands. In villages which had lost their lands, the *ejido* program was obviously a great boon. However, among villages which had retained their communal lands, while the *ejido* helped, it also created new problems.

---

[9] Simpson, *The Ejido*, p. 15.

The *ejido* program in Tepoztlán has meant that 267 families, who were formerly landless, now have some land. However, the size of landholdings is too small to support Tepoztecan peasants according to their own standards. That the *ejido* has not really solved the land problem is of course due in part to the small amount of land that could be distributed, for Tepoztlán is surrounded on three sides by municipios which have their own communal lands. The *ejido* program has also had disruptive effects in the village in that it has created two distinct interest groups, the *ejidatarios* and the *tlacololeros*. Furthermore, taking the control of the communal lands away from the local municipal authorities has eliminated a source of municipal revenue, and thereby weakened local government and initiative. At the same time, it has increased centralism and made the municipio even more dependent upon the outside.

The deforestation occurring in the municipio and the refusal of Tepoztecans to abide by the regulation of the forestry department point up an important problem of more than local scope. Much has been written about the superstitious and backward Mexican peasant who opposes progress and sticks to his ancient way of life. Too frequently the specific reasons which lead to resistance to change are not sufficiently understood.

The case of Tepoztlán is typical. The livelihood of hundreds of Tepoztecan families depends upon hillside hoe culture and charcoal burning, two activities which by their very nature destroy forest resources and bring about soil erosion. Many Tepoztecans are aware that the forest resources are their greatest wealth and that failure to conserve them may lead to eventual ruin. But they are caught on the horns of the dilemma of a rapidly rising population and limited natural resources. It is no less than absurd to expect peasants to abide by rules which would deprive them of their food supply. In the light of the Tepoztecan material, it would seem essential that national programs of forest and soil conservation be carefully synchronized with other programs which will give the people alternative sources of income, if they are to give up hillside hoe culture and charcoal burning.

agricultural systems: 7

Two CONTRASTING types of agriculture, representing different historical and technological levels, exist side by side in Tepoztlán. One is the primitive pre-Hispanic cutting and burning system of hoe culture; the other is the more modern post-Hispanic agriculture which uses plow and oxen. The differences between hoe culture (*tlacolol*)[1] and plow culture are not limited merely to the use of different tools; each system has far-reaching social and economic implications.

In Tepoztlán, plow culture and *tlacolol* have been known since the Spanish Conquest. In *tlacolol* the land used is the steep slopes of the *cerros* (Fig. 21) and

Fig. 21. Land used in hoe culture is steep, rocky, and wooded.

---

[1] This type of agriculture has been variously referred to in the literature as milpa agriculture, fire argiculture, slashing and burning, cutting and burning, etc. The use of the term "milpa agriculture," which was applied originally by O. F. Cook in his study of the Mayan area—"Milpa Agriculture, a Tropical System," *Smithsonian Institution Annual Report,* 1919—has established an unfortunate tradition, for the word "milpa" in Mexico refers to any cornfield whether in hoe culture or plow culture.

Fig. 22. Land used in plow culture, in the broad valley bottom of the municipio.

the rocky wooded area of the volcanic *texcal;* [2] in plow culture the land is less sloping, less rocky, relatively treeless, and includes the broad valley bottom in the southern part of the municipio. *Tlacolol* is practiced on communally owned land and necessitates a great deal of time and labor but very little capital. Plow culture is practiced on privately owned land [3] and requires relatively little time and labor but considerable capital. In the former, there is a dependence almost exclusively upon family labor; in the latter, there is a greater dependence upon hired labor. In *tlacolol,* the yields are much greater per *cuartillo* of seed planted than in plow culture, but the amount of corn planted by each family is relatively little and never reaches the amount planted by a few of the larger operators in plow culture. In *tlacolol,* rotation

[2] Tepoztecans use the word *cerros* to refer both to the spectacular, butte-like rock outcropping which surrounds the village and to the steep slopes covered with scrub forest. *Texcal* refers to land covered with the relatively recent volcanic flow which supports a thorny scrub forest with a predominating flora of copal gum, mimosa-like legumes, a true "sweet potato," and silk cotton trees. *Texcal* covers a strip of land approximately two kilometers wide on the western limits of the municipio, and constitutes about ten per cent of the total land area of the municipio.

[3] Lands recovered from the Hacienda of Oacalco by the municipio in 1930 represent an exception to the rule. Here we find communally owned lands divided into *ejido* plots and worked with plow and oxen.

Fig. 23. Tepoztecans, returning home from work.

is practiced by necessity, for the fields cease to produce after the first few years; in plow culture, the same fields may be planted year after year until the soil is completely exhausted.

Tlacolol is essentially geared to production for subsistence, while plow culture is better geared to production for the market. It is significant that most families who work *tlacolol* are landless and that *tlacolol* has traditionally been viewed as the last resort of the poor. However, farmers who own small plots of land may also work some *tlacolol* to supplement their meager income. Indeed, in the past few years a new trend is occurring in the village because of inflation. Tepoztecans who own considerable private land now rent it out or let it rest, and themselves work in *tlacolol.* This is resented by most *tlacololeros,* who believe that the communal lands should serve the landless. The attitude of the *tlacololeros* is better understood in the light of the fact that the communal lands are becoming exhausted and can no longer support the present-day population.

Other differences between *tlacolol* and plow culture include the cycles of work, the tools, the type of corn, the work techniques, and even the terminology. Generally speaking, the tools and techniques used in *tlacolol* are still known by their Náhuatl names, whereas in plow culture Spanish names prevail. Still another difference results from the location of the lands involved. (See Fig. 22.) With few exceptions the privately owned land used for plow culture is much closer to the village than the *tlacolol* land. *Tlacololeros* generally rise at 4:00 A.M., travel about two to three hours to reach their fields, and return home a few hours later than plow culture farmers. The building of the road directly through the privately owned lands has made this contrast sharper. It is not uncommon for some Tepoztecan farmers to take the bus to their milpa. *Tlacololeros,* however, always walk or go by burro. (See Fig. 23.)

PLOW CULTURE

The basic tools of production in plow culture are the ax, plow, machete, and iron hoe. Two types of plows are used: the *arado criollo* (wooden plow) and the *arado polco* (steel plow). The wooden plow (Fig. 24) was introduced by the Spaniards shortly after the Conquest; the first steel plow (Fig. 25) came into the village toward the latter part of the nineteenth century after the railroad had been built through the upper portion of the municipio. Before the Revolution of 1910-20 the steel plow was used only by a few families, and, as late as 1926-27, Redfield reported only a few steel plows.[4] However, by the early thirties plows became more widely used, and in 1943 most farmers used steel plows in addition to wooden plows, each being used for different operations. In 1943, approximately 213 families owned their plows. This number represented only 48 per cent of the families in the village who owned land. In other words, 52 per cent of the landowners lacked one of the basic tools for plow culture.

The wooden plows are made locally by several men who specialize in this work, and the cost of the wooden plow is comparatively inexpensive. However, the prices of both the steel and wooden plow have increased in recent years, so that now considerable capital is needed to purchase a steel plow. (See Table 27.)

TABLE 27. Cost of Plows, in Pesos.

Year	Wooden Plow	Steel Plow
1926	3.00	—
1935	5.50	14.00
1940	7.50	18.00
1942	—	30.00
1944	12.00	40.00

The precise date of the introduction of oxen to Tepoztlán is not known, but they have been used in the village since long before the Revolution. (See Fig. 26.) Most

---

[4] "The ground is prepared with a wooden plow. For new-broken or very strong earth there are a few steel plowshares." Redfield, *Tepoztlán,* p. 122.

of the oxen were killed during the Revolution; and in the early twenties, mules and donkeys were used and are still used by some of the poorer families. Tepoztecans buy most of their oxen in the nearby state of Guerrero and in the southern part of the state of Morelos. By 1944 there were 179 oxen teams in the village. (See Table 28.)

It can be seen from this table that only 57 per cent of the landowners owned oxen. In general, those barrios which have a higher percentage of larger land-holdings show a higher number of families owning plows and oxen. In Tepoztlán it is considered uneconomical for a farmer with only a few hectares to own oxen. Furthermore, the high cost of oxen makes it impossible for most Tepoztecans to own any, and teams may be rented by the day or the season. (See Table 29.)

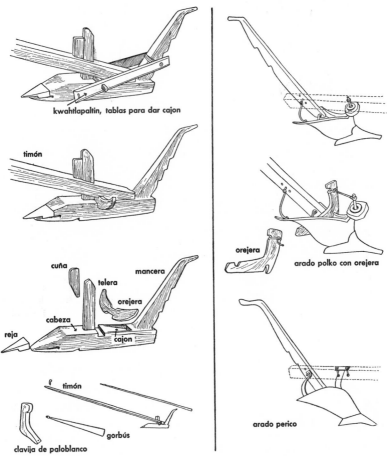

Fig. 24. The wooden plow.

Fig. 25. The steel plow.

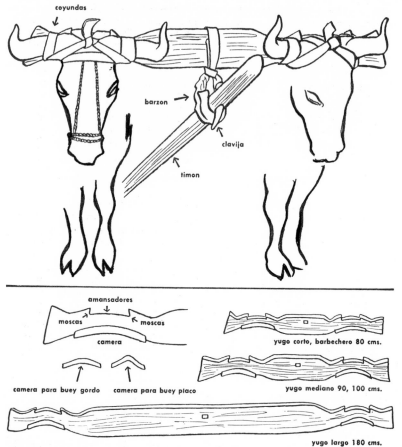

Fig. 26. Oxen and yoke.

The cost of oxen quoted in Table 29 refers to that paid in Guerrero. The cost in Tepoztlán was then considerably higher; today there is relatively little local buy-ing and selling of oxen. For a long time, trips to Guerrero were considered dangerous, and the few who made such trips did so at considerable risk—and profit.

When oxen are rented for three months, the renter must assume full responsi-bility and agree to give the animals good care. In case they are injured, the renter must pay full damages. A man who rents oxen enjoys the privilege of using them for custom work. From June to August, it is estimated that a team of oxen will work seventy-eight days. The small variation in rental price, when paid in corn, must be considered in the light of changes in corn prices from 1926 to 1944, an increase from twelve centavos per *cuartillo* [5] to sixty centavos.

---

[5] A *cuartillo* is equal to two liters in Tepoztlán.

TABLE 28. Distribution of Ownership of Plows, Oxen, and Land, 1944.

Barrio	Families Owning Plows	Families Owning Oxen	Families Owning Land
San Miguel	48	44	83
Santo Domingo	70	50	61
La Santísima	36	32	62
Santa Cruz (large)	14	14	44
Los Reyes	23	21	30
San Sebastián	8	6	11
Santa Cruz (small)	8	6	10
San Pedro	6	6	10
Tepoztlán	213	179	311

TABLE 29. Cost of Oxen, Rental of Oxen, and Wages.

Year	Cost of Oxen[a]	Rental of Oxen per Day (With Driver)	Rental of Oxen per Three Months		Wages of *Peón* per Day
			In Corn[b]	In Pesos	
1926–30	60.00	1.50	6	40.00	.50
1936	70.00	2.50	8	75.00	1.00
1940	100.00	3.25	8	125.00	1.25
1942	125.00	4.00	7	150.00	1.50
1943	200.00	5.00	7	150.00	1.50–2.00
1944 (April)	400.00	6.00	7	170.00	2.50–3.00
1944 (July)	400.00	7.50–10.00	7	200.00	3.00–3.50

[a] Cost in Guerrero.
[b] By 100 *cuartillos*.

WORK CYCLE AND PRODUCTION TECHNIQUES

The work cycle of plow culture in Tepoztlán is in four stages: preparation of the land, planting, cultivation, and harvest.

Preparation of Land: In discussing the preparation of the land, we must distinguish between breaking new land, or land that has been idle for a number of years, and preparing land that was under cultivation the year before. In the former case the process is referred to as the *barbecho* (breaking of new land); in the latter as *los tres arados* (the three plowings). The system of plowing used in each case differs considerably. Some Tepoztecans begin their first *barbecho* in the dry or slack season, generally in March. However, at this time the earth is parched and hard, and plowing is difficult and slow. For this reason, farmers prefer to break new land during the rainy season, generally in August, in preparation for the following year. If the weeds are tall and strong they are cut with a machete, piled up to dry, and are burned.[6] It takes a man about three days to clear a heavily

---

[6] The most stubborn weeds are known as *zacate chino*. These have deep roots, and if the field is heavily weeded it is necessary to plow in January and again in March. The older men say that this weed came in after the Revolution.

weeded field of one hectare. Whenever possible the weeds are plowed under to improve the fertility of the soil. The steel plow is used in the *barbecho,* and the land is plowed in one continuous furrow to make a concentric rectangular form.

If the field is large, it may be divided into two or three parts, each of which is plowed in the same fashion. The land is always plowed at right angles to the direction in which the rows of corn are to be planted, so that the rows can be kept straight. Tepoztecans pride themselves on having straight rows of corn, and farmers will compete with one another to see who can plow the straightest. One man with a single team of oxen can plow on an average of about two *cuartillos* a day. If time permits, two *barbechos* will be given; the second is always done soon after the first rains, toward the end of May or early in June.

In the case of *los tres arados* which is used in preparing a field that has been in cultivation the previous year,[7] the steel plow is also used, and the plowing follows the old corn beds and furrows. The plow is placed just to the right of the old cornstalks, and the earth is turned to the right. This is called the *primer arado* (first plowing). When the oxen reach the end of the furrow they are turned, and the same process is followed on the adjoining corn bed, so that a new mound of earth is formed where the furrow was before. This is called the *segundo arado* (second plowing). In both the first and second plowing a short yoke is used, and the oxen walk in the furrows on either side of the corn bed. The plow driver walks to the left of the bed, holds the plow with his right hand, and directs the oxen with his left. The *tercer arado* (third plowing) goes through the center of the corn bed. The third plowing forms part of the process of planting.

Planting: This generally begins a few days after the ground has been plowed, preferably when the earth is humid. But it is important to note that in Tepoztlán there is a great deal of leeway in the time of planting. A few days or even a few weeks make very little difference in the net results. Corn can be planted any time between June 1 and July 25 with a fairly good chance of getting a crop. Tepoztecans, therefore, follow no rigid work cycle. Of approximately four hundred farmers who may plant corn with plow and oxen in any one year, no more than a third begin their work immediately after the first rains. The reasons for this are varied. Many own neither land nor oxen and may be delayed in making arrangements for renting, in preparing their tools, plows, and yokes; others may still be busy selling wood and charcoal; still others may be delayed by illness or death in the family. It is a common sight in Tepoztlán to see corn at various stages of growth during the rainy season.

The selection of seed for planting is generally done soon after the harvest in January, when the finest ears of corn are set aside to be shelled later in May or June, just before planting. Three types of corn are used in plow culture, *ancho*

---

[7] Some use the *barbecho* on land that has been cultivated the year before, and then follow with *los tres arados*. This gives a better yield but involves at least three additional days of work for a plot of twenty *cuartillos* or approximately two hectares. Only the best farmers, about ten per cent, do this.

blanco, pepitillo blanco, and *semilla azul.*[8] *Ancho blanco* is the most widely used corn; *pepitillo* is used only in the heavier clay soils. *Semilla azul* is used for replanting cornfields which have not germinated, because it ripens faster and catches up with the earlier plantings.

A large number of Tepoztecans still follow the custom of having the seed blessed by the priest on the day of San Isidro, May fifteenth. Generally the women take the corn to the church. Each woman selects about ten of the finest ears of corn, as well as some of her best beans and squash. She may also take along some copal and a censer. As many as two hundred women may attend this blessing. As they burn the incense in the church, the priest comes out and blesses the seed with holy water. The ears of corn which have been blessed are to be placed in the milpas to rot and must not be burned, or the seed will not grow.

The ancient custom of addressing the seed in Náhuatl, before planting, is still remembered by most men over age fifty. Many informants recall that their grandfathers spoke to the corn in a short formal ritual, before planting. The ceremony in the fields was often accompanied by great emotion and even weeping. One of these speeches translated from the Náhuatl follows:

"My beloved body and strength, go and bear the cold and the storm of the seasons; all is for us." [9]

Today a similar ritual is still followed by a relatively small number of Tepoztecans, except that the recitations include references to God and are said in Spanish. The following are examples of present-day blessings:

God bless you. I bury you and if you return while I still live the satisfaction will be mine; if not then my descendants.

In the name of God I am going to plant this seed. I implore Thee to bless my work.

Bless your sainted name God Our Father who is the first one to care for us. From here you go out and from where you go out God wishes you to return. For I am going to throw you into the field and you will remain only with the blessing of God. And may God free you so that we all will have something.

In planting corn, two men and one team of oxen are the minimum requirement. More than one team is rarely employed on a single field. However, two or three men may be used if the owner has a large family or can afford to hire *peones.* In planting on land that has been newly broken, the plow is always pulled at right angles to the existing furrows. One man, the oxen driver, leads the oxen while another man follows and drops four seeds in the furrow for each plant at a space of about a pace apart. The seed is dropped in front of the left toe, and the dirt is pushed over the seeds with the right foot. In planting the first few seeds, some Tepoztecans still follow the old custom of making the sign of the cross with their hand as they drop the seeds. Older men believe that planting one day after the

---

[8] See Appendix A, p. 449.

[9] "Notlashocuyo yocatsin xomohuicatetsi quexquish cequistli tonalli huan yeecatl timoschicalhuitiul topampa."

appearance of the new moon brings a better harvest. The rows of corn are 80 or 90 cm. apart, depending upon the fertility of the field. Yokes are therefore two standard sizes.

Some farmers mix their corn seed with beans: *frijol chino, pepita,* and *frijol colorado.* When this is done, no special number of seed is used. After the first cultivation, *frijol negro* or *bayo* may be planted between the corn hills.

In planting a field that has been prepared by the *dos arados* rather than by the *barbecho,* the plow is directed right through the middle of the old corn beds, and this is known as the *tercer arado,* completing the three plowings involved in the preparation and planting. Both in the newly broken ground and in the land that has been in cultivation the preceding year, the *arado criollo* (wooden plow) is used in planting, and a piece of wood is inserted which acts as a double mouldboard and throws the earth to both sides. The amount of corn that is planted per day depends upon the type of corn and the speed of the oxen and driver. On the average, two men working with a team of oxen can plant eight to ten *cuartillos* of *maíz ancho* per day, and about five to six *cuartillos* of *maíz pepitillo.*

First Cultivation: Two or three cultivations are generally given to cornfields; these cultivations are known as *el primer mano* or *el primer beneficio, el segundo mano,* and *el tercer mano.*

The first cultivation of the corn is generally done twenty days after the planting when the corn shoots are still very small.[10] Again the steel plow and the short yoke is used, and the oxen walk between the furrows on either side of the corn bed. The plow is pulled to the right of the row of young corn, so that the earth is turned away from the corn. The driver walks to the left of the row and holds the plow with his right hand. Two *peones* are used in addition to the driver. The *peones* follow the plow, staying on the left side of the row of corn; they bend over the corn and with their hands they carefully push the earth around the young plants. The two *peones* work simultaneously about twenty feet apart and by-pass each other when they reach a section that has already been cultivated. The first cultivation of a plot of ten to twelve *cuartillos,* using two *peones,* takes on an average of two days.

Tepoztecans have an ingenious way of fighting ants which threaten the young corn. When the young shoots are about to appear, they take the leaves of a tree called *yamatl* (of the *amate* family), chop up the leaves, and sprinkle them over the rows of corn, and especially on ant nests. The ants prefer this leaf to corn, and Tepoztecans claim it makes them thin and eventually kills them. The leaf contains a white, milky substance so strong that it will peel the skin off a man's hand. Another tree whose leaves are used for the same purpose is *yoyohtli.*

Second Cultivation: The second cultivation begins about twenty days after the first cultivation is completed, generally in the last week of July. The process is very

---

[10] In fields which have gathered much water, Tepoztecans may plow in the furrows about eight days after planting, to spread the water. Such plowing is called *sobernal.*

much the same except that the plowing is deeper, and the steel plow is pulled to the left of the row of corn, and the earth is turned to the right toward the plant. This work is generally done with one team of oxen, the driver, and only one helper who follows the plow and sees that the plants are not bruised or injured. This second cultivation involves less work than the first because the corn is taller and stronger,

Fig. 27. Mouldboard plow.

and less care is needed in piling earth around the plants. An average of ten *cuartillos* of corn can be cultivated in this manner in two days.

Third Cultivation: Twenty days later the third and final cultivation begins. This time the wooden plow is used with a wide yoke for the oxen who walk two rows apart. The plow is directed between the two rows of corn, and a board is placed in the plow so that the earth is turned on both sides, thereby piling up the soil on the two rows of corn at once. (See Fig. 27.) Only one team, one driver, and one helper are needed for the third cultivation and eight to ten *cuartillos* of corn can be done per day.

After the third cultivation the corn plants in the first and last two rows of the milpa are hilled by hand with the *coa*. This hilling also serves as a symbol that the cultivation is over and is looked upon as a decoration or adornment of the work of cultivation. However, it probably also serves to strengthen the outside rows against the wind, and Tepoztecans believe that it protects the inside of the milpa.

In the more fertile lands which are in the hotter and lower portions of the municipio, it is customary to hill all the plants because the corn grows so fast that a third cultivation with oxen would damage the tall plants. The hilling of each plant requires much more labor, and therefore necessitates more capital when *peones* are hired for the job. In areas within the municipio such as Calamatlán, where this hilling is done, the process is referred to as *una tierra y medio cajón*, that is, one cultivation followed by hilling. The hilling is believed to safeguard the tall plants against the winds.

The termination of cultivation is known as the *acabada* and is celebrated by a fiesta in the fields and at home. This generally occurs toward mid-August. Immediately after the last hilling, some Tepoztecans walk around the milpa and recite a speech. The following is a typical speech.

Now I have fulfilled my obligation of attending and cultivating you as you deserve. Now if you do not want to produce, that is your responsibility. For my part I now retire.

A wooden cross is sometimes put in the center of the milpa after the last row is cultivated and prayers and religious songs are said by the owner. Fireworks are set off and bread and cheese, tequila and *ponche* are served to the workers and others present. The oxen are decorated with flowers, generally dahlias, tulips, and banana leaves, and a picture of San Isidro. After celebrating in the milpa the oxen are driven home, where there is more food and drink for the *peones,* the family, and any *compadres* and friends who may be invited. Tamales, rice, tortilla, *mole verde,* and drinks of *ponche* are plentiful, and firecrackers are set off in the patio.

The last cultivation and its celebration are generally over by late August. There follows a long period during which relatively little is done in the cornfields. During this time the farmers harvest their *ciruela* crops, which ripen in early September.

Toward the end of September the fresh corn is ready in the fields, and families turn out to the milpas to roast corn and to drink *ponche*. On September 28, the day of Saint Miguel, the farmers carry a cross made of *pericón*, which has been blessed by the priest, and they place it on the four sides of the milpa to protect it against strong winds which often blow at this time. It is an old belief that if the winds blow strong and the corn is damaged it is because the dancers who represent El Tepozteco at the fiesta on September 8 did not perform properly. While this explanation is widely known, few still believe it. Another old idea is that the wind is caused by the angels spreading their wings.

During October the weeding of the milpa with machete is done wherever necessary. A milpa of ten or twelve *cuartillos* can generally be done by a man in one or two days. After that there is a long period when no work in the milpa is done. During this time farmers continue to pick their *ciruelas,* look after their animals, cut wood, and do other tasks around the house.

Harvest: The harvest generally consists of two stages. The first is stripping the cornstalks of their leaves. This process is known as the *zacateo* and begins in early November. The leaves are bundled and transported to the house, where they are used for fodder. Stripping a cornfield of ten or twelve *cuartillos* takes six days of work. Sometimes men will compete to see who can strip two rows in the shortest time. The *zacate* is tied into bundles or *gavillas*. Twelve *gavillas* make up one *manojo* and twelve *manojos* make up one *carga*. These *cargas* of *zacate* are transported home on horse or mule. The transporting of the *zacate* produced on a field of ten to twelve *cuartillos* takes three days of work, using two mules and making two trips a day.

The harvest of the corn itself begins in early December.[11] It takes about five days of work to pick the corn on a field of one hectare. A good worker can pick approximately two *cargas* of corn a day. The corn, like the *zacate,* is transported by mule and it takes about the same time, that is, three days. It is customary to celebrate the harvest by serving *ponche* to the helpers and to the men who are hired to transport the corn. During the harvest the wives may help in stripping the leaves off the ears of corn. These leaves are known as *totomaskli* and are used in making tamales. Widows often ask for permission to gather corn leaves to sell.

The *cuatequitl* or unpaid cooperative labor system referred to earlier is reserved exclusively for the planting, cultivation, and harvesting of the land owned by the barrio for the support of its chapel, and working the barrio land is the only occasion for unpaid collective labor in agriculture. There are cases of labor exchange between relatives, but this is viewed as very different from *cuatequitl.* I should like to emphasize this point, for Tepoztecan farming is highly individualistic and in this sense quite similar to our own farming.

There is some time pressure in harvesting, in those cases in which many privately owned plots are encircled by a single fence or stone wall. The farmer who has completed his harvest is entitled to allow his animals to graze, and this endangers the corn on those fields not yet harvested. To avoid this danger and the many quarrels resulting from it, the farmers within a single enclosure generally come to some agreement to have their plots harvested within a specified time, which agreement is registered with the local authorities. Although this situation would seem to call for cooperative harvesting, each family, with the aid of hired labor, harvests its own field.

In the first few days of January most farmers begin to store the corn in the storage bins that are of two types, the *zincolotes* and the *ahuatlapiles*. The corn is generally stored without being shelled so that it will better resist the corn worms which are a great problem to Tepoztecans. Sometimes a considerable portion of the harvest is eaten or spoiled by these worms. It is customary in many families to leave the corn on the cob until April or May; prior to that, they shell only what they need.

---

[11] Formerly stripping and harvesting were begun after the appearance of the full moon.

The harvesting of corn, like all other operations in agriculture, is done on an individual family basis, with hired help if necessary. There is a minimum of labor exchange and cooperation. Our findings differ from those of Redfield. Redfield writes:

The men always work in groups; the owner of the field has asked them to help him—it it is *cuatequitl*—and then when their fields are ripe he will help them harvest. These are social occasions. Each group has *la muleta,* "the little mule"—a bottle of alcohol hidden under a pile of corn. The preparation of their dinner is also done cooperatively at the house of the owner of the field, and this is a social occasion for the women. They carry the dinner to the fields for the men. The owner of the fields supplies the food and drink. But there the cooperative harvesting ends, for the removal of the grain is done separately in each individual house, each member of the family taking a hand.[12]

This account refers to a type of cooperation which does not now exist in Tepoztlán, and our informants did not remember its having existed in 1926 or even before the Revolution of 1910. Corn is shelled by both men and women. Women generally shell corn by hand in small quantities for daily use in the house and for small-scale trade. Large-scale shelling by the *carga* is generally done by the men who use an *elotero,* which is made of dry corncobs bound together in the form of a flat disc, over which the corn to be shelled is rubbed. Some use the black volcanic rock from the *texcal* for shelling. However, the corn selected for seed is shelled by hand by the men. Women of the two upper barrios of San Pedro and Los Reyes frequently shell corn on a large scale, whereas in the larger, center barrios, large-scale shelling is considered a man's work. In many cases *peones* are hired for this job. The shelled corn is stored in sacks, for the most part, although there are still a few of the old *cuescomatl.* (See Fig. 28.) Many families put the skeleton of a dog's head or a piece of *ocote* wood and lime in the sacks or the *cuescomatl* to protect the corn against spoilage. Formerly when *cuescomatls* were made, the priest would be called to bless them. There is a belief that when a death occurs, the corn in the house or on the house site will be more subject to the ravages of insects.

The loss of stored corn from insects is one of the serious problems faced by Tepoztecans. Many farmers complain that they lose a few *cargas* a year in this fashion. It is rare to find corn that lasts through to August without being seriously damaged by corn worms. Tepoztecans have still received little help with this problem from Mexican agronomists.

An old tradition persists in the village to the effect that the boa constrictor was formerly used to prevent stealing of corn from the cornfields and the granary. It is said that the snake was fed salt and *tequesquite* by the owner of the field, and that thereafter the snake would frighten all strangers by climbing up the cornstalk and making a whistling noise. These snakes were apparently tame and did not harm the owner, but would attack strangers. There seems to have been some

---

[12] Redfield, *Tepoztlán,* pp. 126-27.

Fig. 28. The *cuescomatl* for storing corn.

magical qualities associated with the boa constrictor, for it was believed that a man who had tamed one would always have a good yield in his milpa, and that the seed would not be subject to insects.

YIELD

The yield of corn varies a great deal from field to field and from year to year on the same field. Table 30 shows something of this range for specific fields of varying size.

TABLE 30. Estimates of Corn Yields in Plow Culture, 1944.

Size of Milpa (Amount of Seed Planted in *Cuartillos*)	Yield in Ears of Corn by *Carga*	Yield in Shelled Corn by *Carga*
14.0	30.0	20.0
22.0	34.0	23.0
8.0	15.0	10.0
6.0	7.5	5.0
7.5	13.5	9.0
10.0	7.5	5.0
12.0	9.0	6.0

Judging from these figures, we would get an average production of 9.6 *cargas* of shelled corn a hectare. However, it is possible to arrive at a much more useful estimate if we follow Tepoztecan classifications: First-class land will produce on an average of two *cargas* of ears of corn for every *cuartillo* of seed planted; second-class land will produce on an average of one *carga* for each *cuartillo* of seed; and third-class land will produce about one-half a *carga*. Thus productivity of the best land is about four times that of the poorest land.

Most Tepoztecans do not use fertilizer in their fields. They are apparently aware of its benefits but, because of the shortage of manure and the expense of commercial fertilizer, are unable to use it.

A few Tepoztecan farmers have attempted to divert seasonal streams, which come down from the mountain forests to their fields, to capture some of the rich humus of the forest, and the results have been spectacular. Portions of fields which received this humus more than tripled their production. There are unfortunately few such streams, and even if all were diverted in this fashion, they would help only a few farmers.

PRODUCTION TIME AND COST

An analysis of production time in plow culture is extremely difficult, because Tepoztecan peasants keep no records and because of the large number of variables to be considered. The following account, based upon careful observation of a few cases and extended interviews with many farmers, is presented with an awareness of some shortcomings on our part.

There is considerable range in the amount of man-days of work that goes into the clearing, planting, cultivation, and harvest of a cornfield. The most important variables are the nature of the terrain, the quality of the soil, the speed of the oxen and the workers, the type of seed used, etc. Judging from our data, the total number of man-days of work needed for the production of one hectare of corn ranges from about 35 to 65 days, depending upon the variables previously mentioned.

If we were to consider 50 man-days of work as an average we would not be far wrong. Actually, however, there are only about 35 days spent working a field of one hectare by any one man. Most men work as day laborers in the fields of others, so that on the average a man puts in about 50 work days in plow culture from the beginning of June to the end of December. However, this estimate does not include many days spent by the farmer in guarding his field against cattle and trespassers.

In Table 31 we present a study of the time spent in the production of corn in a milpa of ten *cuartillos*. In this case we have participated in and carefully observed each of the operations listed. In addition we have obtained estimates of production time from many informants, and some of these are given in Table 32.

It will be seen from these tables that the greatest amount of time is spent in cultivating and harvesting the corn. The preparation of the fields and the planting take relatively little time. The fact that farmers spend a relatively small part of the year at their major occupation gives them a great deal of time for other economic activities, as well as enforced leisure.

TABLE 31. Time Spent in Production of Corn in Plow Culture on Sample Plot, 1944.

	Plot of Ten *Cuartillos*		
Operation	No. of Workers	No. of Days Worked	No. of Man-Days
Clearing of land (*limpio*)	1	3.0	3.0
Plowing (*barbecho*)	1	5.0	5.0
Plowing (*surcado*)	1	1.4	1.4
Seeding (*siembra*)	2	1.4	1.4
First cultivation (*primer mano*)	2	3.0	6.0
Second cultivation (*segundo mano*)	2	2.0	4.0
Third cultivation and hilling (*cajón o despacho*)	2	1.0	2.0
Weeding (*solada*)	1	2.0	2.0
Stripping cornstalks (*zacateo*)	1	6.0	6.0
Tying leaves in bundles (*juntado*)	1	1.0	1.0
Transport leaves (*acarreo*)	1	3.0	3.0
Corn picking (*pizca*)	1	5.0	5.0
Corn transport (*acarreo mazorca*)	1	3.0	3.0
Corn shelling (*desgranado*)	1	5.0	5.0
Total			47.8

PEONS

The question of estimating costs of production is difficult because Tepoztecans, like most Mexican peasants, do not keep accounts of their expenses, and more important, do not estimate their own labor in terms of its monetary value. They are, however, quite familiar with the value of a day's work in money, since they all hire labor at one time or another, or themselves work for a wage. Tepoztecan farmers are also apt to speak of "time lost" when they are called upon to serve on village guard duty, or if they have to go to court over some legal matter.

Despite the fact that labor time is not so evaluated locally, we have assigned money value to the labor of the farmer-operator to arrive at some notion of relative production costs. In estimating total production costs we have considered the prevailing daily wage of hired labor and the cost of hiring oxen as the two most important items of cost. Our estimates, although approximations, illustrate the wide range in production costs for a single hectare of corn, and the relative cost of each operation. Variations in production costs are due to such factors as differences in

Table 32. Estimate of Time Spent in Production of Corn in Plow Culture in Four Sample Plots, 1944.

Operation	Plot I (12 *Cuartillos*)		Plot II (10 *Cuartillos*)		Plot III (10 *Cuartillos*)		Plot IV (10 *Cuartillos*)	
	No. of Workers	No. of Man-Days	No. of Workers	No. of Man-Days	No. of Workers	No. of Man-Days	No. of Workers	No. of Man-Days
Clearing of land	1	4.0	1	6.0	1	3	2	2
Plowing	1	6.0	1	4.0	1	4	2	2
Total		10.0		10.0		7		4
Plowing	1	2.0	1	1.5	1	2	1	1
Seeding	1	2.0	1	1.5	1	2	2	2
Total		4.0		3.0		4		3
First cultivation	2	8.0	2	4.0	2	6	2	2
Second cultivation	1	4.0	2	8.0	1	3	2	2
Third cultivation	1	1.5	1	2.0	1	1	1	1
Weeding	1	3.0	4	4.0	1	1	2	2
Total		16.5		18.0		11		7
Stripping cornstalks	12	12.0	10	10.0	1	5	4	4
Tying leaves in bundles	1	1.0	1	1.0	1	1	1	1
Transport of leaves	1	6.0	1	6.0	1	4	6	6
Corn picking	4	8.0	7	7.0	7	7	4	4
Corn transport	1	3.0	1	6.0	1	3	4	4
Corn shelling	1	6.0	1	7.0	1	3	1	3
Total		36.0		37.0		23		22
Total		66.5		68.0		45		36

slope of field, quality of soil, rockiness of terrain, amount and stubbornness of the weeds, speed of the oxen and workers, and distance from the village.

We have gathered production cost estimates from twenty-five farmers and found considerable variation among them. In Table 33 we present three cases to illustrate the variation of cost of each operation and the range of total costs.

TABLE 33. Estimated Cost of Production of Corn in Plow Culture in Three Sample Plots, 1944.

Operation	Plot I (12 *Cuartillos*) Value in Pesos	Plot II (12 *Cuartillos*) Value in Pesos	Plot III (12 *Cuartillos*) Cost of Hired Labor	Plot III Value of Own Labor	Plot III Total Value
Clearing of land	8.00	7.50	3.00		3.00
Plowing	30.00	15.00		10.00	10.00
Total	38.00	22.50			13.00
Plowing	10.00	8.00		5.00	5.00
Seeding	4.00	4.00	4.00		4.00
Cost of seed	3.60	4.80		3.00	3.00
Total	17.60	16.80			12.00
First cultivation	36.00	16.00	4.00	10.00	14.00
Second cultivation	28.00	12.00	4.00	10.00	14.00
Third cultivation	7.00	7.50	2.00	5.00	7.00
Weeding	6.00	2.50	4.00		4.00
Total	77.00	38.00			39.00
Stripping cornstalks	24.00	15.00		8.00	8.00
Tying of leaves	2.00	3.00			
Transport of leaves	18.00	6.00		12.00	12.00
Corn picking	16.00	12.50	8.00		8.00
Corn transport	9.00	9.00		8.00	8.00
Corn shelling	12.00	10.00		11.50	11.50
Food and drink for peons	10.00	12.00			12.00
Total	91.00	67.50			59.50
Total cost	223.60	144.80			123.50
Amount and value of corn	7 *cargas* 210.00	6 *cargas* 182.00	5 *cargas*		125.00
Amount and value of fodder	12 *cargas* 48.00	12 *cargas* 36.00	8 *cargas*		32.00
Net profit	34.40	73.20			33.50

The production costs in these cases vary as much as 100 pesos and range from 123.50 to 223.60 pesos. The most expensive and most extended operation is harvesting. Harvesting is generally done under a certain amount of pressure, because of the need to be through when others in the same enclosure let in their animals to pasture. For this reason, many farmers hire several peons at this time, involving an outlay of cash. At least one peon is often hired during the plowing and seeding and the first cultivation. Farmers not owning oxen and plows must rent them.

The cost of production does not always have relation to the amount of corn produced, because some fields require more work than others. In the specific cases given in Table 33 the larger production was offset by higher costs (about 32 pesos per *carga* in Plot I) and conversely, the plot which required least outlay in cash or labor yielded the least corn (about 24 pesos per *carga* in Plots II and III). Differences in cash value of the corn produced are due to the changes in market price. Those who are forced to sell immediately after the harvest receive lower prices than those who hold on.

HOE CULTURE

The land used for *tlacolol* (hoe culture) is of two distinct types, located in different areas of the municipio. One type is known as *texcal*, which is covered with black volcanic rock and a semi-deciduous scrub forest in which the leaves fall and rot during the dry season and make a rich but thin topsoil in little pockets among the rocks. The other type of land is known as *cerros*, and refers to the mountainsides. Most of the *cerros* used for *tlacolol* are of lime rockbeds with many rock outcroppings and scrub forests, but of a somewhat different nature than in the *texcal*. Both types of land are at some distance from Tepoztlán, so that the farmers who work this land must spend approximately two hours each way in going and returning from work.

The use of the communal lands for *tlacolol* is a fairly recent phenomenon in spite of the fact that Tepoztlán has had its communal lands since pre-Conquest times. Before the Revolution of 1910-20 during the Díaz regime, the well-to-do *caciques* who controlled the political life of the municipio forcibly prohibited the use of the communal lands for *tlacolol*. As we have indicated earlier, their primary motive was to assure themselves of a labor supply for their own lands. One of the principal changes in the economic life of the village brought about by the Revolution was to deprive the *caciques* of their power and to return to the people the right to use their communal lands. But in the years immediately following the Revolution, that is between 1920 and 1927, relatively few individuals became *tlacololeros*. The population of the village was still small and there was a relative abundance of rentable land because of the absence of many families from the village.

In 1927 the municipio lost control of the *tlacolol* lands, which passed to the jurisdiction of the forestry department. At this time Tepoztecans lost their right to work *tlacolol* because the forestry department, as part of its national program of conservation and prevention of soil erosion, forbade the indiscriminate cutting and burning of trees—an integral part of the process of preparing *tlacolol* land for cultivation. With the rapid increase of population in the thirties, the shortage of land became acute and the need for the *tlacolol* land urgent. Many individuals began to open *tlacolol* plots illegally and were fined.

In 1938 a group of Tepoztecans organized themselves to fight for the privilege of working the communal lands. A delegation of 200 men went to the local authorities in Cuernavaca and explained that they had no other way of earning a living. They stated that they would open *tlacolol* even if it meant violence and arrest. Following this demonstration the *tlacololeros* were allowed to work without government interference, and the number of *tlacololeros* increased.

The fact that *tlacolol* land is now available to Tepoztecans is of paramount importance in the life of the community and has served two purposes. First, it has been a source of land for the landless. Together with the *ejido* land recovered from the Hacienda of Oacalco, it has reduced the number of peons and has broadened the agricultural base of the society. It has thereby reduced the sharp social and economic class distinctions which existed in the village before the Revolution.

NUMBER OF *Tlacololeros*

In 1944 there were 189 families, or 20.9 per cent of all the families in the village, in which one or more members worked *tlacolol* land. The distribution of these families by barrio and the extent to which the same families also carried on plow culture is shown in Table 34.

TABLE 34. Distribution of *Tlacololeros* by Barrio, 1944.

Barrio	No. of Families	No. of *Tlacololeros*	No. Who Have *Tlacolol* Only	No. Who Own Private Land Only	No. Who Hold *Ejido* Only	No. Who Hold *Ejido* and Own Private Land
San Miguel	214	45	23	10	8	4
La Santísima	185	34	24	4	5	1
Santo Domingo	223	26	10	5	6	5
Santa Cruz (large)	82	42	14	15	5	8
Los Reyes	49	12	9	1	1	1
San Sebastián	42	21	10	2	8	1
Santa Cruz (small)	36	2	1	1	0	0
San Pedro	22	7	5	1	1	0
Tepoztlán	853	189	96	39	34	20

It should be noted that while over fifty per cent of the *tlacololeros* are in the three larger barrios of San Miguel, La Santísima, and Santo Domingo, they constitute only a very small percentage of the total number of families in these barrios. On the other hand, in the smaller barrios the *tlacololeros* constitute a much larger percentage. Thus, in San Sebastián approximately fifty per cent of the families are *tlacololeros*. This concentration of the *tlacololeros* in the smaller barrios tends to set these barrios off as the poorest and most backward in the village.

It will also be seen from Table 34 that 96 families, or 50.7 per cent of all *tlacololeros,* depended solely upon *tlacolol;* that is, they had no private land or *ejido;* 39 *tlacololeros* owned private parcels; 34 held *ejidos;* and 20 had both private land and *ejido*. Most of the families who either owned private land or held *ejido* or both and who also worked *tlacolol* had turned to *tlacolol* because their holdings were too small to support their families. But there is a trend among even the better-to-do families to turn back to *tlacolol;* for example, twelve of the twenty families who owned private land, held an *ejido* grant, and worked *tlacolol,* were among the large landowners.

SIZE OF CLEARINGS

Most *tlacolol* clearings are small, averaging between eight and twelve *cuartillos* of seed. The largest *tlacolol* operator in the village plants only thirty-five *cuartillos*. As we shall see, the great amount of labor necessary for clearing *tlacolol* land is the most important limiting factor in the size of clearings used. A related factor, however, is the growing shortage of land which has sufficiently grown back into forest after earlier clearings. Furthermore, *tlacolol* is definitely viewed as subsistence agriculture, and any man who cleared inordinately large areas, even if he could, would incur the wrath of the other villagers.

TOOLS OF PRODUCTION

Plow and oxen are ruled out in *tlacolol* because of the nature of the terrain. In *texcal* the large volcanic rocks lie around helter skelter, so that it is difficult for a man even to walk. Similarly the steep slopes of the *cerros,* and the lime outcroppings make the plow and oxen impractical. In both types of *tlacolol,* the tools used are the *coa, tlalache, caxala, azadón,* and machete. (See Fig. 29.) They are homemade except for the iron tips in the hoe and machete, which are bought. Thus, in contrast to farmers in plow culture, most *tlacololeros* own their own tools. The cost of the *tlalache* and the *coa* are shown in Table 35.

TABLE 35. Cost of *Tlalache* and *Coa,* Tools Used in *Tlacolol.*

Year	Cost in Pesos	
	Tlalache	*Coa*
1926	1.50	1.25
1935	2.25	1.75
1940	3.00	2.25
1944	5.50	3.25

WORK CYCLE AND PRODUCTION TECHNIQUES

Preparation of Land: Work in *tlacolol* begins in January. The trees are cut with an ax, and the bush is cleared with a machete, extremely difficult and time-consuming work. It takes approximately 40 to 50 days for a man to clear enough land for the planting of 12 *cuartillos* of corn. The trees and brush dry out and are burned in April, and the ashes are left to "fertilize" the soil. Burning is generally done in a single day with two or three men working together. If the materials are not all burned, the group will return and work another day. Enclosures of rocks and brush are then built around the clearing to keep out stray animals that usually graze in these areas. Most *tlacolol* clearings are used two years in succession, and the work of clearing is considerably reduced the second year, although it generally takes 10 to 15 days to clear the milpa of weeds the second year.

Planting: Planting in *tlacolol* begins in May, before the rains. This planting of the corn "dry," as Tepoztecans say, eliminates the danger of rodents getting at it. The corn used in *tlacolol* is a very hardy variety which sends roots out in all directions and which penetrates the rocky terrain. In planting, the *caxala* or *coa* are used.

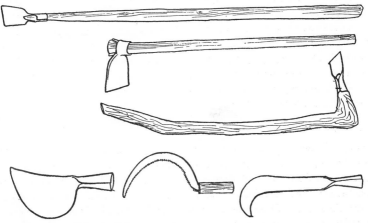

Fig. 29. Tools used in *tlacolol*.

A small hole about four to six inches deep is made wherever there is enough soil, and seeds are dropped in. Every interstitial space among the rocks is used. There are therefore no orderly rows in the planting. Beans and squash may be planted with the corn. A good worker can plant about one-half to three-quarters of a *cuartillo* a day; at this rate it would take about twenty man-days to plant the equivalent of one hectare of corn in *tlacolol*.

Cultivation: Unlike plow culture, there is no cultivation in *tlacolol,* nor is the corn hilled. There is generally at least one weeding which is done about forty days after planting, when the corn is about two feet tall. Weeding is of two kinds. In one kind, the weeds are pulled out by hand, and this process is known as the *tlamaltequa*. This is the preferred process, and it is believed that yields are higher if it is done this way. However, this is difficult and time-consuming. One man can weed about three *cuartillos* per day in *tlacolol* of *texcal* and considerably less in *tlacolol* of *cerro*. If there is some delay on the part of the farmer and if the weeds have grown very tall by the time weeding is begun, the machete is used. (See Fig. 30.)

After the weeding, the milpa is left alone except for occasional visits to check the enclosures. Sometimes night visits will be made and firecrackers will be set

Fig. 30. Weeding with machetes in *tlacolol* of *cerros*.

off at intervals all night to frighten away the rodents who have been getting after the corn. It is believed that a good fireworks session will keep them away for as long as two weeks.

Harvest: The harvest procedures are very similar to that of plow culture, except that most *tlacololeros* do not transport the fodder because the distances are too long, and it is considered uneconomical. Also most *tlacololeros* are poor and do not own a horse or burro and must hire them.

YIELD

Corn yields in newly cleared *tlacolol* fields are high, much higher than yields in plow culture. A normal yield on a newly cleared plot of *tlacolol* is about two *cargas* for each *cuartillo* of corn planted, and even three *cargas* are not unusual. But the yields decrease very markedly the second year, and most milpas are then abandoned for a new clearing because of the exhaustion of the slight top humus. The yields in *tlacolol* of *texcal* are somewhat higher than those in the *cerros*.

PRODUCTION TIME AND COST

An estimation of the time required in the production of corn in *tlacolol* must take into consideration both the *texcal* and the *cerro* plantings because of the variations within each. Table 36 compares the approximate number of man-days spent on each operation in both types of *tlacolol*.

TABLE 36. Estimated Time Spent in Production of Corn in *Tlacolol*, 1944.

| | Man-Days Spent in *Tlacolol* Clearing | |
Operation	*Texcal* (10 *Cuartillos*)	*Cerro* (7 *Cuartillos*)
Clearing with machete and ax	40	21
Fencing with poles	12	20
Burning	8	1
Seeding with *caxala*	12	7
Reseeding	4	2
Weeding by hand	30	40
Repairing fence	—	40
	12	8
Transporting corn	10	15
Shelling corn (15 *cargas*)	15	7
Total	143	161

Despite the fact that our sample from the *cerro tlacolol* is a smaller plot, it took thirty-eight days to work it. Taking into consideration differences in the size of both plots, the most obvious difference in production time is in clearing and fencing the land. Due to the rougher terrain, clearing and burning in *texcal* are more difficult and time-consuming than in *cerros*. On the other hand, because of the greater threat from grazing cattle, the building and repairing of fences are more time-consuming in the *cerros*.

Estimated costs of production based upon the same two plots clearly demonstrate the wide range in costs which prevails in Tepoztlán. (See Table 37.)

TABLE 37. Estimated Cost of Production of Corn in *Tlacolol*, 1944.

Operation	Pesos Spent in *Tlacolol* Clearing					
	Texcal (10 *Cuartillos*)			*Cerro* (7 *Cuartillos*)		
	Hired Labor	Own Labor	Total	Hired Labor	Own Labor	Total
Clearing with machete and ax		60.00	60.00		31.50	31.50
Fencing with poles		18.00	18.00	17.50	17.50	35.00
Burning		12.00	12.00		1.50	1.50
Seeding with *caxala*		18.00	18.00		10.50	10.50
Reseeding		3.00	3.00		3.00	3.00
Seed			3.00			2.10
Seed for reseeding			.40			.20
Weeding by hand		54.00	54.00	21.00	60.00	81.00
Repairing fence					39.00	39.00
Harvesting		18.00	18.00		12.00	12.00
Transporting corn	15.00		15.00	22.50		22.50
Shelling corn		22.50	22.50		13.50	13.50
Total	15.00	205.50	223.90	61.00	188.50	251.80
Amount and value of corn produced	15 *cargas* at 30.00 each		450.00	9 *cargas* at 30.00 each		270.00
Total cost and value			223.90			251.80
Net profit			226.10			18.20

The lower yields and higher costs of producing corn in the *cerro tlacolol* as compared with the *texcal tlacolol* make the *cerro* less economical to work, and it is also more time-consuming. But since the families who work *tlacolol* are for the most part subsistence farmers, our comparisons of the relative profits involved in each type are strictly for purposes of analysis.

PLOW AND HOE CULTURE COMPARED

Now that we have examined both plow and hoe culture, as they are carried on in Tepoztlán, let us compare the two systems in some of their more important characteristics. We have seen that there are more families engaged in plow culture than in *tlacolol*, and that there is overlapping in that some families participate in both systems. The distribution of the families who work private holdings, *ejido* holdings, and *tlacolol* is approximately as follows: 36 per cent of all families operate private land; 31 per cent operate *ejido* parcels; and 20.9 per cent operate *tlacolol*. Since both *ejido* and private parcels employ plow culture, it is evident that the *tlacololeros* constitute by far the smallest group. Hoe culture is secondary in importance to plow culture from the point of view of the number of families engaged in each. This is seen even more clearly when we recall that all but 96 of the *tlacololero* families had an *ejido* parcel, a private milpa, or both. However, *tlacolol* is still very important in the total economy of the village.

One of the most striking differences between the two systems is the much greater amount of time necessary in hoe culture. It will be seen from Table 38 that it takes approximately two-thirds more man-days to produce one hectare of corn in *tlacolol* than it does in plow culture. As we have seen, the single job of weeding by hand takes more time than all three cultivations with plow. The great difference in the total time spent in preparation of the land is also noteworthy. The somewhat longer time period for harvesting and transport is due to the greater distances of *tlacolol* fields from the village and the larger relative production of the *tlacolol* milpas. It should be noted that fencing the *tlacolol*, which is so time-consuming, has to be repeated each time a new *tlacolol* is opened—in contrast with the permanent stone fences of private milpas and *ejidos*.

TABLE 38. Comparison of Time Spent in Production of Corn in Plow and Hoe Culture.

Operation	Man-Days Spent on Plot of One Hectare	
	Plow Culture	Hoe Culture (*Texcal*)
Preparation of the land	8.0	60
Planting	2.8	16
Cultivation	14.0	30
Harvest	15.0	12
Transporting corn	3.0	10
Shelling Corn	5.0	15
Total	47.8	143

In addition to the differences in the actual time spent there is a corresponding difference in the nature of the work. Tepoztecans who have worked in both types consider work in *tlacolol* infinitely more exhausting than work in plow culture. The *tlacololeros* are in a sense perpetual pioneers who are always making new clearings in the forest. Also, weeding by hand is very difficult and leaves welts for days on the hands of the toughest *tlacololero*. It is said in the village that a *tlacololero* is known by his hands.

Another very important point is the difference in time pressure demanded by each system of agriculture. On the whole there is much less time pressure in *tlacolol*. A man can clear his land anytime between January and April. He can work for a few days at clearing, spend a few days doing some other job, and then return to clearing. After planting there is also considerable leeway before the first and only weeding. This is not the case in plow culture. Although there is considerable leeway in the time of planting, once planting has been done, the cultivations must follow soon after at regular intervals or the yields will be cut appreciably. Furthermore, there is need to take advantage of dry days when the oxen can get into the field.

The differences between the work cycles of the two systems are shown in Chart 2.

CHART 2. Comparison of Work Cycles in Plow and Hoe Culture, 1944.

PLOW CULTURE	MONTH	HOE CULTURE
No work in fields.	JANUARY	Clear land with machete and ax.
	FEBRUARY	
	MARCH	No work.
	APRIL	
Clearing land, plowing and seeding.	MAY	Burning brush. Fencing, seeding.
	JUNE	
First cultivation. Second cultivation. Third cultivation.	JULY	Reseeding.
	AUGUST	Weeding.
Visits to field.	SEPTEMBER	
Weeding.	OCTOBER	Visits to field.
Stripping corn stalks.	NOVEMBER	
Harvesting and transporting corn.	DECEMBER	Harvesting and transporting corn.

It will be seen that the agricultural year begins at different times in each case. The *tlacololeros* begin work very soon after the harvest and work through the larger part of the dry season, while the farmers of plow culture let their land rest, except for a relatively few farmers who plow new land in January or March. The fact that different farm families in the same village are engaged in different activities during the same season of the year adds to the complexity of village life. Here again, the picture of homogeneity in activities which is so often associated with so-called folk cultures has to be modified. Most *tlacololeros* are through planting before planting begins in plow culture, and many accept work as peons in plow culture. However, during late July and early August the peak labor season for plow culture finds *tlacololeros* busy in their own fields. Similarly, harvest comes at the same time in both systems and it is at this time that there is a labor shortage in the village. Many Tepoztecans have described this overlapping of work cycles as a conflict of interests between *tlacololeros* and milpa owners, for the latter are unable to get sufficient hired help.

A comparison of the yields of the two types of agriculture reveals that hoe culture yields are equal to the best yields in plow culture and are generally about twice as high as the average yields of plow culture. These larger yields make hoe culture quite attractive. One might ask therefore why more people do not work *tlacolol*. There are a number of reasons. First, the difficulty of the work discourages many, and the fact that *tlacolol* has traditionally been viewed as work for the poor is also undoubtedly a factor. Second, many families who have worked as peons have no corn at the harvest and have to seek some cash income regularly to support their families. In other words, even in the case of *tlacolol* which takes so little capital a man must have corn to support his family if he is to spend the long periods of time necessary for clearing the scrub forest. Third, and by far the most important consideration, is the limited amount of *tlacolol* land; a shortage which is being felt more and more as the number of *tlacololeros* has increased. The *tlacolol* system of cutting and burning, by its very nature, demands large reserve areas; it takes about ten years for cleared land to grow back into scrub forest and be worth clearing again. If all the villagers were to open *tlacolol* clearings in a single year, there would be no possibility of planting in new clearings again for at least ten years.

The costs of hoe culture in terms of the value of man-days are much higher than in plow culture, but by the same token little hired labor is used. *Tlacolol* is practical only for people with a lot of time and little capital. It is much too inefficient a system for production for the market on a large scale. As we have seen in Table 37, there is considerable range in costs even in hoe culture. Most of this range in the cases cited is due to the difference between the two types of terrain used in hoe culture, that is, *cerro tlacolol* and *texcal tlacolol*. In the *cerro,* fencing is a much more time-consuming operation because there is more danger of cattle getting into the fields, but cattle rarely get into the *texcal*.

This brings us to one of the crucial problems in Tepoztlán, namely, the rapid increase of population with no accompanying increase in resources or improvement in production techniques. On the contrary, the increase in the number of *tlacololeros* represents a return to a more primitive type of production in an effort to escape the devastating effects of a money economy during a period of inflation. We have already noted the sharp rise in the cost of renting or buying a team of oxen as well as other tools of plow culture, and we have also noted that only about one-third of all landowners have their own oxen teams. Labor costs have also gone up, and indeed the wages paid to day laborers in Tepoztlán are considerably higher than in other parts of Mexico, perhaps because of the proximity of Tepoztlán to large urban centers. In any case these costs are beyond the capacity of many Tepoztecans, and they turn to *tlacolol*. *Tlacolol* has eased for many the shock of the rapid rise in prices. Although it is helping to resolve the immediate problem, it by no means offers a satisfactory solution. In fact, it increases the problems to be faced.

Were Tepoztlán a primitive culture with the usual high birth rate and high death rate, and stable and small population, the technique of *tlacolol,* though wasteful and inefficient, might be workable. But in the face of an ever-increasing population and higher standards of living, the primitive techniques of *tlacolol* no longer seem to be feasible. The necessity of clearing new plots of land every third year, the rapid depletion of the land and its forest resources, and the consequent danger of erosion are problems which will soon have to be reckoned with.

local industry and trade: 8

LIVESTOCK

There is relatively little livestock in Tepoztlán and most of it is of poor quality. The Revolution of 1910–20 saw the destruction of practically all domestic animals in Tepoztlán, and present herds have been slowly and painfully acquired since then.[1] Tepoztecans, because of their experience during the Revolution, still view investment in cattle as precarious, and they invest only as a steppingstone to the acquisition of land or as a secondary source of investment. It should be noted, however, that cattle raising was never an important industry in Tepoztlán and never became well integrated in the local economy. Topographical conditions and climate in the municipio are not conducive to large-scale stock raising. The land is steep, rocky, and forested; the little level land is used for agriculture. During the dry season, which begins in December, pasture becomes progressively scarce and by March the cattle are excessively thin. In these months, herds are generally reduced by fifteen to twenty per cent.

The care given to cattle is minimal. For the most part, cattle graze on the communal lands and in the cornfields after the harvest. Only milk cows, plow-oxen, and pack mules and horses are given fodder, such as hay or sesame plants, poor corn, and sugar cane stalks brought by Tepoztecans who work on near-by haciendas. Occasionally they are given salt to keep them "tame," and almost any disease or sign of ill health is treated with a mixture of vinegar, lemon, and *sal de nitro*. Hoof and mouth disease is treated with applications of iodine to the affected parts, a cure which Tepoztecans claim gives excellent results.

Care of animals in Tepoztlán consists mostly of guarding them against the danger of being lost or stolen. A great deal of time is spent in watching livestock, irrespective of whether the family owns only one or two animals or a herd of thirty or forty. Cattle stealing is frequent and is one of the hazards of cattle raising. Some families have lost over twenty-five head of cattle in a few years. It is said

---

[1] Only a few families managed to escape with their animals to southern Guerrero.

that cattle stealing increases markedly before important fiestas, particularly before the Carnaval in February, the fiesta of Ixcatepec in April, the celebration of the national holidays in August, and All Saints' Day on November first. Cattle thieves are shot on sight, and each year a few are killed.

It is estimated that the families who own considerable cattle spend approximately 140 days during the year in caring for them. A rough estimate of the distribution of the time, based on interviews with a few cattle owners, follows:

Month	Days Spent Guarding Cattle
January	8
February	8
March	8
April	12
May	12
June	4
July	4
August	15
September	30
October	31
November	4
December	4
Total	140

Although cattle and other livestock are an important supplementary source of income, animal ownership is on a small scale and is limited to a relatively small proportion of families. Table 39 presents the distribution of cattle, oxen, horses, mules, donkeys, and hogs among families in each of the barrios.

It can be seen that only 179, or 21 per cent, of the families own cattle. Well over 50 per cent of these families own between one and three cows; about 40 per cent own four to ten cows. The largest herd in 1943 was a little over seventy head, although estimates obtained in 1947 showed much larger herds, with the two wealthiest cattlemen having about 150 head each. There are only about a dozen men in the village who might be said to raise cattle on a large scale, and only six of these have herds of over fifty.

The ownership of oxen is limited to 177, or 20 per cent of the families. Of these, only two families own more than one team of oxen. The low percentage of families owning a team of oxen indicates the limited extent to which Tepoztecan farmers own one of the basic means of production.

The distribution of horses, donkeys, and mules owned by families in the proportions of 28 per cent, 11 per cent, and 14 per cent, respectively, reflects the local evaluation of work animals. Mules are more popular than donkeys, and horses are valued more highly than either. Riding horses as against work horses are considered

TABLE 39. Distribution of Livestock Among Families by Barrio in 1943.

Barrio	Total Families	Families	Cattle	Families	Oxen	Families	Horses	Families	Donkeys	Families	Mules	Families	Hogs
San Miguel	214	56	386	43	43	47	64	17	24	31	39	23	52
Santo Domingo	223	48	224	51	51	72	92	20	33	27	36	114	270
La Santísima	185	43	316	32	32	59	75	17	25	42	63	126	305
Santa Cruz (large)	82	11	38	14	14	23	30	11	17	3	5	7	13
Santa Cruz (small)	36	6	47	6	6	10	10	1	1	6	8	13	27
Los Reyes	49	8	24	21	21	20	25	18	23	11	19	36	90
San Sebastián	42	4	6	4	6	13	16	8	11	3	4	16	31
San Pedro	22	3	13	6	6	0	0	0	0	0	0	1	4
Tepoztlán	853	179	1,054	177	179	244	312	92	134	123	174	336	792

a luxury. The prestige associated with horse ownership goes back to the colonial period when only leading men of the village were allowed to ride a horse.[2]

Ownership of horses, mules, or donkeys is on a small scale; most families have only one animal. The largest number of work animals owned by a single family is six horses and four mules.

Hogs are more widely distributed among the villagers. About forty per cent of the families of Tepoztlán own at least one hog, and many own two or three. The smaller outlay of capital and the lower gains involved in the purchase and sale of hogs limits hog-ownership to the poorer families. It is interesting to note that a very small proportion of the families in the barrio of San Miguel own hogs despite the fact that this barrio has a large proportion of poor families. This may be attributed to the fact that the road runs through this barrio, and the passing buses and automobiles have killed off too many of the hogs to make hog-raising profitable or safe.

Most of the animals used for food are slaughtered in the village. There is practically no trade in cattle or hogs outside of the municipio. There is also relatively little buying and selling of cattle and oxen within the village, since most of them are traditionally purchased in the state of Guerrero where prices are lower. Some men make it a practice to go to Guerrero to buy cattle for resale in Tepoztlán at a nice profit, but this is done on a small scale and only intermittently. Several of the better-to-do farmers became prosperous by doing this during the turbulent years after the Revolution when few dared to leave the village.

It is estimated that a team of oxen work on an average of ninety days a year. Since most families do not own their own oxen, the oxen owners do a good deal of custom work. In 1947 an oxen owner charged 16 pesos per day, that is 4 pesos for the driver and 12 pesos for the team. The income from renting a team of oxen for a ninety-day period would therefore be 1,080 pesos, less about 120 pesos for the cost of feed. When oxen are rented by the season, the charge is generally only 200 pesos, but the renter has the obligation of feeding and caring for the animals and assumes all responsibility in case of accident or death. Plow-oxen are also rented in exchange for corn, generally for six *cargas* of corn, worth about 300 pesos in 1947.

Mules and donkeys are considered to yield an even greater income than plow-oxen, for they can be rented for a greater variety of jobs and for longer periods. Mules are used primarily for transporting charcoal, wood, corn, and beans. The rental for two mules was 14 pesos a day in 1947. The income from a team of mules would therefore be close to 500 pesos over a ninety-day period.

Hogs are bought, fattened, and sold by many families, but the profit is kept low because of the local custom of fattening hogs with good corn, which is expensive. A young pig costs about 30 pesos and after a year of fattening can be sold to a butcher for 225 pesos. The cost of food per day runs to about 50 centavos, or 182½

---

[2] For documents on this point see *Indios,* Vol. 4, Exp. 398.

pesos per year. Adding to this the cost of the pig, we have an expense of 212½ pesos. If the pig is sold for 225, there is a profit of only 12½ pesos after a year's work.

Raising pigs would seem to be more profitable, but the risk is also greater. A year-old breeder pig costs about 150 pesos, and feed for a year runs to 182½—a total expense of 332½ pesos. An average litter of eight, sold at 30 pesos each, gives an income of 240 pesos, providing there are no losses. This income can be obtained for three or four years in succession and then the pig can be fattened and sold for 250 to 300 pesos.

The price of livestock, like that of most other items, has increased greatly since the turn of the century. The sharpest increase has occurred since 1940. (See Table 40.)

TABLE 40. Price of Work Animals in Pesos, 1901–1944.

Years	Plow Oxen	Mules	Horses	Donkeys
1901–1910	40	60	35	15
1911–1920	35	30	25	15
1921–1925	50	100	40	20
1926–1930	60	125	50	25
1931–1935	65	125	60	25
1936	70	150	70	30
1937	75	170	75	30
1938	80	175	75	30
1939	85	180	80	30
1940	100	180	85	30
1941	110	200	100	35
1942	125	200	125	35
1943	200	200	125	50
June, 1944	400	300	200	75

Milk is sold locally by less than a dozen families. The local market consists of a small but increasing group of schoolteachers and Mexican tourists. Most of the milk produced is converted into cheese and sold in the village. It is estimated that a cow produces an average of two liters of milk daily during a period of seven months a year. At current prices of 45 centavos a liter, this would give an annual income of 159 pesos plus about 50 pesos for the value of the calf.

Cattle owners will often pay the priest to say a Mass for the protection of the cattle, and are expected to contribute generously to religious fiestas. When a cow or ox is sold, it is customary for the seller to use a portion of the money to light a candle to El Señor de Ixcatepec. When there are *jaripeos* and bullfights, the larger operators generally contribute bulls and money for *ponche* and fireworks.

Most cattle owners have an image of San Antonio, the patron saint of cattle, in their homes. Horseshoes are believed to bring good luck and are seen on the walls of many houses, especially in the homes of livestock owners.

To keep cattle from wandering away, it was customary for the owner to cut off hair from the ear of the cow or ox and bury it under the hearth. This was done with cattle brought in from Guerrero in the belief that the animal would forget its past home.

Milk products are used for medicinal purposes. Whey, cheese, and butter are used for skin rashes, and cheese is used as a poultice for snake bites. Some families use, as a purgative, milk in which a cow's tail has been soaked. Pig's fat is commonly used as a salve for inflammations.

CHARCOAL

The production of charcoal by the burning of oak and other woods is one of the most important sources of income for many Tepoztecan families, but primarily for the poor. Charcoal production demands very little capital and few tools; it utilizes the communal forest resources; it serves as a convenient source of income for the landless peasants and as a supplementary source of income for those engaged in agriculture. As a rule, charcoal production is carried on as a part-time activity by farmers during the slack season. But in the smaller barrios of San Pedro, Los Reyes, and San Sebastián, about fifteen individuals engage in charcoal production as a full-time occupation.

Charcoal production has risen and fallen at different times in recent Tepoztecan history. Charcoal production on a large scale began shortly after the Revolution, when Tepoztecans returned to the village from their enforced exile. Desperately poor and with all their animals killed off, they eagerly turned to charcoal as salvation. This development was encouraged and organized by a provisional president of the municipio, Jesús Monroy, who was imposed by the state authorities in 1919 shortly after peace was established in the village. Monroy called a meeting of Tepoztecans and organized workers into brigades of charcoal burners. As a result, a large portion of the forests of Tepoztlán was practically denuded, and there arose in the village a cleavage between those who wished to conserve the forest resources and those who cut the trees for charcoal.

During the late twenties, Tepoztlán organized a forestry cooperative, the first in the state of Morelos, and large-scale production began again. Conflict ensued and the cooperative ceased to exist in 1937. Since that time, charcoal production has continued on an individual basis. Data on charcoal production in the municipio are available for the years 1934–42. (See Table 41.) During this period 3,921,518 pounds of charcoal were produced. These figures are in all probability lower than the actual amount, for much charcoal is produced secretly in violation of federal forestry regulations.

The tools used in charcoal production are an ax, a shovel, a pickax, and a machete. Charcoal workers generally leave the village for the mountains in the early morning, going alone or in groups of two or three friends or relatives. It is not customary to hire workers in this occupation, because most workers want to come home at the end of the day, and charcoal burning necessitates staying out for a few days at a time. To make charcoal, oak and sometimes pine trees are felled, cut up into logs a few feet long, and piled upright to form a charcoal oven or kiln. (See Fig. 31.) The kiln is then covered with earth on all sides, except for a small opening which is left for a draft of air to enter, so that the fire can be kept

Fig. 31. A charcoal kiln.

smouldering. The kiln is then lighted and allowed to smoulder for anywhere from 24 to 48 hours, depending upon the size of the wood pile. The worker must continuously be on the watch to prevent too much air from fanning the fire, and thus burning the wood rather than producing charcoal. So it is necessary for the charcoal burner to sleep out in the forest for one, two, or three nights.

The following estimate of the production time, cost, and yield was obtained from a charcoal burner, and gives us some insight into the economics of this

TABLE 41. Charcoal Production, 1934–1942.[a]

Years	Vegetable Carbon (in Kilos)
1934	1,209,430
1935	137,400
1936	264,500
1937	955,060
1938	475,400
1939	426,570
1940	—
1941	221,119
1942	232,039
Total	3,921,518

[a] The sharp decline after 1934 reflects the falling off in production following the killing of the forestry cooperative leader, Juan Hidalgo. Slowly production increased until 1937, when the cooperative was disbanded. Since that time there has been a marked diminution in production.

occupation. The informant worked for ten days: three days in felling trees and cutting up the wood, one day in collecting the wood at one spot, one day in making the kiln, four days and nights in watching the kiln, and one day in taking off the dirt and putting the charcoal into sacks. The yield was 18 sacks or 9 *cargas* of charcoal. Each *carga* sold at 13 pesos, yielding 117 pesos. From this sum the informant had to pay 2 pesos a *carga* for transportation to Cuernavaca and 1½ pesos a *carga* for tax, totaling 31½ pesos, leaving him 85½ pesos for ten days' work. Since daily wages in agriculture at the time were about 4½ pesos, the income from charcoal is considered good in Tepoztlán. But charcoal burning is thought of as dirty work, and it ranks very low in prestige, being identified as a last occupational resort of the poor. Nevertheless, some well-to-do families in the outlying barrios spend part of their time in burning charcoal.

Until 1947, most of the charcoal in Tepoztlán was transported by burro to Yautepec. Since that time the bus line has agreed to transport charcoal, so that much of it now goes to Cuernavaca. The price of transport in 1948 was 2 pesos a *carga*. Occasionally a truck from Mexico City or Cuernavaca comes into Tepoztlán to transport charcoal.

CIRUELAS—HOG PLUMS

The *ciruela* is now an important cash crop in Tepoztlán, and according to informants it was introduced into Tepoztlán in 1865. There was little interest until it was discovered that the *ciruela* was pleasant to eat, and more trees were planted.

The *ciruela* can be easily propagated by cuttings. All that is necessary is to prepare a hole some 30 x 30 cms. wide and about 70 cms. deep and to place in it a branch from the mother tree—a branch 2 to 3 meters long and 5 to 10 cms. in diameter. The hole is then filled with soil and tightly packed. Cuttings may be made at any time of the year with good results. The only precaution necessary is to see that the cuttings are not disturbed while they are rooting, lest the young roots be broken. The trees begin producing in from 3 to 4 years, and production increases as the trees grow. Trees grow to a huge size. (See Fig. 32.)

Ciruelas first became a cash crop in Tepoztlán about 1901, or shortly after the railroad was built through the municipio. But transporting the *ciruelas,* by mule to the railroad and then by rail to Mexico City, incurred great expense and delay. Irregular train schedules often caused the fruit to spoil. After the highway was built, merchants from Mexico City and Cuernavaca sent their trucks to Tepoztlán during harvest, and the cash crop value of the *ciruelas,* transported in this way, increased. They are packed in wooden boxes known as *guacales*. Each *guacal* contains about nine gross of *ciruelas*. The price of a *guacal* in October, 1943, was six pesos. It is estimated that Tepoztlán exports about 7,000 *guacales* a year, a total crop value of about 42,000 pesos.

Prices are fixed by merchants from Cuernavaca and Mexico City. The merchants get together and decide among themselves what they will pay per gross for the fruit. Mexico City is the principal market.

A survey of the numbers of *ciruela* trees in the village by barrio is shown in Table 42.

TABLE 42. Estimate of Number of *Ciruela* Trees, Average Yield, and Value of Harvest, 1944.

Barrio	No. of Trees	Average Yield per Tree in *Guacales*	No. of *Guacales*	Crop Value in Pesos
San Pedro	86	4	344	2,064
San Sebastián	127	4	508	3,048
Los Reyes	377	4	1,508	9,048
Santa Cruz (small)	153	4	612	3,672
Santa Cruz (large)	139	4	556	3,336
San Miguel	411	4	1,644	9,864
Santo Domingo	633	4	2,532	15,192
La Santísima	595	4	2,380	14,280
Tepoztlán	2,521			60,504

There has been a notable increase in the price of *ciruelas* since 1926, as can be seen from Table 43.

TABLE 43. *Ciruela* Prices, 1926–1943.

Year	Price per Gross, in Pesos [a]	
	Commercially Ripened	Tree Ripened [b]
1926	.12	
1927	.12	
1928	.13	
1929	.14	
1930	.15	
1931	.17	
1932	.20	
1933	.20	
1934	.23	
1935	.25	
1936	.25	
1937	.20	.30
1938	.20	.35
1939	.30	.40
1940	.30	.50
1941	.40	.60
1942	.50	.70
1943	.60	.80

[a] The average of the prices recorded during the harvest season for each year. Prices are highest at the beginning of the harvest and in the middle of August; they decline as the production increases until the end of the harvest, about the middle of November.
[b] Until 1937, nearly all tree-ripened *ciruelas* were used for home consumption and for hogs.

Fig. 32. Picking hog plums.

ROPEMAKING

Ropemaking, like charcoal burning, is limited to the smaller upper barrios of the village, and is concentrated in the barrio of San Sebastián where ten families engage in this occupation during the dry slack season. All of these families are in the lower economic level of the village, so ropemaking is also an occupation of the poor.

According to local tradition, ropemaking was introduced into the village about 1883 by a man from Ajuchitlán who came to live in the barrio of San Sebastián.[3] It is interesting that in all the years since then, there has been little spread of rope-making to other parts of the village, and there has been little change in the techniques employed, except that the ropes have become much longer. In 1890 ropes only 12 varas long were made. Now Tepoztecans make ropes 24 and 30 varas long.

Ropemaking is a family affair; it takes two or three persons for the major operation, twisting. Most of the *ixtle* fiber is obtained from the maguey plants which grow on the *cerros* of the communal lands. But only about half of the families who make rope gather their own *ixtle* fiber; the others buy it.

The maguey plant is beaten with a special tool which breaks up the plant so that the fibers can be extracted. The fiber is then soaked overnight. The fiber is spun on a simple spinning device and is then ready for the rope twisting process. This is done on a rather complicated homemade device shown in Fig. 33.

[3] Although we have no evidence as to whether ropemaking as it is now known existed in pre-Hispanic Tepoztlán, it is probable that some type of cordage was known and used in connection with weaving.

Until a few years ago, ropemaking was done only in response to specific orders from individual buyers, and each producer took great pride in his product. In the last few years, however, some producers have been competing with one another, and profits have been reduced. (See Table 44.)

TABLE 44. Estimated Cost of Production of Rope, 20 Varas Long.

April, 1944	*Pesos*
Cost of 3 lbs. of *ixtle* fiber	3.75
Preparation of fiber	1.00
Cost of twisting	.70
Cost of spinning	1.50
Labor cost in rope twisting	.50
Total production cost	7.45
Sale price of rope	8.00
Profit	.55

Since all the labor is done by members of the family, there would be a daily income of 3.70 pesos plus .55 for profit above cost.

CIRCULATION AND DISTRIBUTION OF GOODS

The circulation of goods in Tepoztlán is carried on by means of the local market, stores, itinerant merchants, inter-village trade, the sale and purchase of goods in

Fig. 33. Ropemaking.

Cuernavaca and other large towns, and the exchange and barter of goods between families in the village. Changes in the means of communication within the last twenty years have made some of these factors more important than others. In general, the effect of the road to Tepoztlán has been to weaken the local market, to increase the importance of stores and trade relations with Cuernavaca, to decrease the extent of inter-village trade within the municipio, and to abolish completely earlier trade relations with other villages of the region.

The market days in Tepoztlán are Wednesday and Sunday. As in Redfield's time, vendors from the satellite villages and from more distant localities gather in the central plaza where they offer their wares. Merchants from Cuernavaca, Toluca, and Mexico City may be seen occasionally. Some come by foot in the old tradition, others by bus, and others with their own cars.

The old tradition, as reported by Redfield, whereby each of the seven villages of the municipio had its customary place in the market, is still remembered and followed. But it is only on a rare occasion that vendors from all the villages are present on the same market day. During the greater part of the year, vendors from only two or three of the villages come. (See Fig. 34.) By comparison with a market in an Oaxacan town of equal size, the Tepoztecan market is indeed

Fig. 34. Woman selling lime.

"raquítico," as the Tepoztecans would say. Furthermore, the quality of the local fruits and other goods is poor and, unlike other Mexican villages, little care is given to display. There is also little variety of goods, and it is difficult to predict what will be available from one market day to another. In short, the market at Tepoztlán shows symptoms of decline.

In addition to the market days, there are permanent stores in the plaza. As has been indicated earlier, their number has increased and they have spread to the outlying barrios. The stores sell most of the daily household necessities and have a fairly stable clientele. Most sales are in small quantities because of the Tepoztecan custom of running to the store once or twice a day. But Tepoztecans are going to Cuernavaca more and more, and are making larger purchases; this has been a blow to local tradesmen who cannot compete with the Cuernavaca stores and market.

Itinerant merchants who peddle through the village streets come with a wide variety of goods, such as blankets, *petates,* palm-bottomed chairs, sweets, and clothing. In recent years these merchants have introduced selling on the installment plan, and make collections on their rounds.

Goods are also circulated by barter between families, although this is declining. Corn may be exchanged for eggs or other food. Corn is still used as payment for wages or for the services of *curanderos,* especially when small sums are involved.

Most Tepoztecan produce is sold outside the village, primarily in Cuernavaca. It is estimated that Tepoztecans sell approximately 1,000 *cargas* of corn per year. Many poor people complain that they have to go to Cuernavaca to purchase corn because none is available locally. Other Tepoztecan cash crops, charcoal and *ciruelas,* are also sold outside the village; charcoal goes to Yautepec and Cuernavaca, and *ciruelas* go to Cuernavaca and Mexico City.

Before the Revolution, Tepoztecans' trade relations spread over a wide area ranging from southern Jojutla, Guerrero, Ozumba in the Federal District, Puebla, Xochimilco, and Mexico City. Indigo was sold to Puebla, which, in turn, supplied dried fish. Merchants made frequent trips to Mexico City by foot, and the following account from an informant, aged 67, gives some idea of the role of the merchant and middleman in Tepoztlán before the Revolution.

My father was a farmer, a butcher, and a tradesman. He worked his fields and slaughtered pigs which he sold to the neighboring villages of the municipio, but especially in San Andrés and Gabriel Mariaca. Later he would go to the southern part of the state of Morelos to buy up fruit and send it to Mexico City where he would live for a portion of the year to sell the fruit. He would leave Tepoztlán in April or May. He returned here in early June to plant and remained here in June, July, August, and September. At the end of September he returned to Mexico City until November. After All Saints' Day he would return for the harvest.

My father went to Mexico City on foot, and the trip took all day. We would leave the village about 6:00 A.M., arrive at Xochimilco at 5:00 or 5:30 P.M. The route was as follows: first to San Juan, then to a rancho called Oshokiah, in the mountains; from Oshokiah to

San Pablo Ozozapec. Here we stopped to have lunch and then continued to San Salvador, then down to San Andrés Agueyuc, then to San Lorenzo, then to Xochimilco. By 5:30 P.M., we were generally at the place in Xochimilco when the canoes left. If there were no canoes we walked all night. We generally arrived in Mexico City the following morning and took our fruit to the market.

Some inter-village trade still occurs at the time of fiestas and village *ferias*. However, Tepoztecan trading contacts seem to have become limited for the most part to Cuernavaca. Yautepec, at one time the key market for much of Tepoztecan produce, has now faded in comparison with the role of Cuernavaca.

The circulation of goods and money in Tepoztlán is generally small, but it varies considerably with the seasonal cycles. It is lowest during the months of May, June, July, and August, which is a period of scarcity. The most rapid circulation of goods and the greatest volume of money transactions occur after the plum harvest in September and October, and again after the corn and bean harvest in December and January. Money from plums is generally used to buy new clothing for the family.

Perhaps the most important single occasion for spending during the year is at the Carnaval, which comes in February after the harvest. I have estimated that approximately 50,000 pesos are spent by the villagers for the Carnaval. It is an occasion for buying new clothes, but the largest expense is for the elaborate costumes of the Chinelo dancers. A costume in 1947 cost as much as 800 pesos, and there were 45 dancers from the three competing barrios. Of course most of the costumes are used from year to year, but there is always the expense of repairing and improving them. Some people rent the costumes. The food expense is also great; musicians from each of the competing barrios are fed by the leading families in the barrio. In addition, most families entertain on this day.

The tourist trade has brought some income to Tepoztlán, especially to storekeepers, vendors of soft drinks, and the owners of the two tourist houses, but most of the money spent by these Tepoztecans goes to Cuernavaca.

The other important occasions for spending in Tepoztlán are the barrio fiestas, the gifts for *compadres* at baptisms, the expenses of the groom in weddings, and the expenses for the wakes and funerals.

There are a few corn merchants in the village who speculate in corn by buying in small quantities throughout the year to sell at higher prices during June to September. Speculation in corn is apparently an old practice in the village, for as early as 1579 we find complaints of Tepoztecans against price fixing by local politicians. Some of the corn merchants will make loans on the future corn crop and will be paid back in corn at the time of harvest.

CREDIT, LOANS, AND INTEREST

There are no organized credit facilities in Tepoztlán. Although a few hundred Tepoztecans have had *ejido* parcels since 1930, no *ejido* credit has come to the village. It is said that an effort had been made at one time to obtain such credit but

Tepoztecans withdrew the petition because they feared that it would be necessary for the *ejido* authorities to investigate the belongings of each of the families for whom the credit was designed.

There are a few money lenders in the village who make loans at an interest rate of ten and twelve per cent a month. The money lenders are extremely cautious about making loans and are careful in choosing a good risk. The leading money lender in the village, a wealthy peasant, explained that he generally requires the borrower to come back about three times on the pretext that there is a shortage of funds. He assumes that any Tepoztecan who will put himself in the humiliating position of asking for a loan three times must have real need and appears to be a good risk. Money loans are made by oral or written agreement, but in most cases some property is necessary as security. The practice of pawning property as security for a loan is common. Usually land, oxen, or *ciruela* trees are pawned, but smaller items such as an iron, or even a woman's *rebozo,* may be pawned for small loans from neighbors. During our stay in the village, neighbors often came with small items of property which they offered before asking for a loan.

When a man cannot repay a loan, although he may be bound by a written agreement which is filed in the municipio, it is rare that the creditor takes legal action. In fact, not a single case could be remembered. Instead, the borrower must relinquish his pawned property, or get another loan from a second party to repay the first one. All such transactions are viewed essentially as affairs between two individuals or families in which the coercive action of the law is rarely sought.

Borrowing money is generally limited to emergency situations when money is needed for food, doctors, medicines, or clothing. Borrowing may also occur to pay for a wedding feast or a funeral. But there is little borrowing for investment in capital goods or for starting a business. Loans are generally for small sums of 100 or 200 pesos. Larger loans are almost prohibitive because of the high rate of interest. While borrowing is not infrequent, it is viewed as an act of desperation rather than as a matter of everyday business. The idea of borrowing money from the bank in Cuernavaca is entirely foreign to the thinking of most Tepoztecans.

wealth differences and levels of living: 9

THE FIRST step we took in the study of wealth differences in Tepoztlán was to determine how wealth was defined by the villagers. Invariably, *los ricos* (the wealthy) were described as "those who own much land and cattle." Private land-ownership (in contrast to *ejido* holdings) was considered the most important single form of wealth. In all, twelve items were most frequently mentioned by informants as forms of wealth in the village. These were *ejido* plots, privately owned land, teams of oxen, plows, cattle, burros, mules, horses, hogs, sewing machines, urban property (that is, the ownership of more than one house site and house in the village), and plum trees. These items have this in common—they are all means of production and a source of income.

To rank the families according to their wealth, we devised a point scale using one point for every 100 pesos of value.[1] Points were assigned to each of the items in accordance with the approximate sale value, the approximate production value, or both. Thus, one hectare of *ejido* land was assigned 3.6 points because the average annual production of one hectare of *ejido* land in Tepoztlán as of June, 1944, had a market value of 360 pesos. One hectare of privately owned land was assigned 7.2 points, which represented both the value of production and the sale value.

The items of the scale, and the assigned points for each item are given as follows:

1 hectare *ejido*	3.6
1 hectare private land	7.2
1 team of oxen	7.2
1 plow	.7
1 cow	3.1
1 donkey	1.5
1 mule	3.0
1 horse	2.5
1 hog	1.5
1 sewing machine	3.5
1 urban site and house	7.5
1 plum tree	1.0
1 non-farm occupation	1.0 [a]

[a] For every 100 pesos earned annually.

---

[1] This scale does not measure income.

A score was obtained for a given family by adding the number of points which were obtained for each item. For example, if a family owned 4 hectares of land (the minimum size of holding considered necessary by Tepoztecans for a "decent living" for a family of five), 1 plow, 1 team of oxen, 1 horse, 1 cow, 2 hogs, 2 plum trees, and 1 sewing machine, it would receive a score of 47 points. Since this is a very modest list, even according to Tepoztecan standards, a score of 40 to 50 points may be taken to represent approximately the minimum in property ownership necessary for a self-sufficient farm family. The distribution of scores is presented in Table 45.

TABLE 45. Frequency Distribution of Tepoztecan Families on Economic Point Scale.

Score	No. of Families	Per Cent of Total	Sub-Group	Per Cent of Total	Main Group	Per Cent of Total
400–407	1	.11				
220–253	3	.35				
200–219	2	.23				
190–199	1	.11	B	1.5		
180–189	1	.11				
170–179	3	.35				
160–169	2	.23			III	4.4
150–159	3	.35				
140–149	3	.35				
130–139	5	.58				
120–129	4	.46	A	2.9		
110–119	4	.46				
100–109	6	.70				
90–99	16	1.87				
80–89	18	2.11				
70–79	17	1.99				
60–69	20	2.34		13.9	II	13.9
50–59	28	3.28				
40–49	20	2.34				
30–39	74	8.67				
20–29	111	13.00	C	21.6		
10–19	206	24.15			I	81.5
1–9	213	24.02	B	49.2		
0	92	10.78	A	10.7		

The most significant features in this frequency distribution are (1) the extremely wide range of wealth differences from zero to over 400 points; (2) the great majority clustering around the lower end of the scale, indicating widespread poverty (note that 81 per cent of the families have scores below what we have tentatively designated as a minimum for decent subsistence); (3) the 92 families having a zero score; and (4) the manner in which, from the distribution of the scores, the families fall into distinct economic groups. Eighty-one per cent of the families are in the lowest group (point score 0–39); 13.9 per cent are in the middle group

(40–99); and 4.4 per cent are in the upper group (100–407.4). The lowest group can be broken down into three subgroups: those with 0 score, from 1–19 and 20–39, which we shall call I-A, I-B, and I-C, respectively. The middle group will be referred to as II. The upper group will be III–A (100–159) and III–B (160 and over).

To test the validity of our groupings, we asked ten informants to name the ten wealthiest families in the village. All those named were in our top group. Another way in which we checked our scale was to present names selected from each of the economic levels of the scale and ask informants to rank them according to their wealth. Again we found a very high correlation.

What are the characteristics of each of these economic groups? First let us consider the families with zero scores. For the most part they are either young married men, most of whom live with their parents, who also have low scores; or they are widows or old men, many of whom live alone. One-third of this group are women who manage to earn a living by small-scale trade and by doing odd jobs.

Groups I-A and I-B, which consist of 511 families with scores 0-19, contain 97 per cent of the landless people in the village. Three hundred and fifty-four, or 70 per cent, of the families in this group have zero scores for land. How do these landless people live? Approximately one-third depend upon *tlacolol,* but all depend upon a variety of activities which together provide a meager income. Many burn charcoal, sell wood, work as peons, are small traders, or have some other part-time occupation. They have some measure of security in that most of them own their houses and house sites or will inherit them. About one-third have hogs. Less than one-third own a mule, horse, or donkey.

The 119 families in Group II include most of the artisans and merchants as well as better-to-do farmers. The former are the most acculturated group in the village. They are the ones who wear ready-made clothes, send their children out of Tepoztlán to high school, and generally have a higher standard of living.

Group III consists of 38 families, all of whom have high scores on land, cattle, or both. About one-half of these families have inherited their land from wealthy relatives who before the Revolution were *caciques* and dominated the village. The other half have worked their way up to their present position.

We might ask whether there is any relationship between position on this scale and standard of living. Do the wealthiest people have the highest standard of living? On the whole, the people in Group III consume more meat, milk, eggs, and bread, and they generally live in better constructed and better furnished houses, some of which have running water. But they are not the ones who go in for modern dress or any ostentatious spending for comforts or luxuries. They are a hard-working people and not a leisure class. One of the distinguishing characteristics of this group is that they generally have hired men all year around, but, with the exception of two men, they work side by side with their peons.

What is the relationship between wealth and the adoption of new traits? The Mexican Census of 1940 included three interesting items which provide us with some data on acculturation in relation to standard of living. The questions were: Do you eat bread (as against tortillas)? Do you wear shoes (as against going barefoot or wearing huaraches)? Do you sleep on a bed or a cot (as against sleeping on the ground or on a *tepexco*, a raised frame upon which the *petate* is placed)?

From a special tabulation of the census of Tepoztlán, we were able to correlate the responses to these questions with the family position on the economic scale. The results are shown in Table 46.

TABLE 46. Distribution of Acculturated Habits by Economic Groups.

Group	Per Cent Who Eat Bread	Per Cent Who Wear Shoes	Per Cent Who Sleep on Beds or Cots
I-A and I-B	23.20	6.46	14.12
I-C	32.30	6.78	23.18
II	50.82	12.06	30.71
III-A	41.55	7.14	21.42
III-B	57.69	5.12	16.66
Total	41.11	7 51	21.22

It is clear that eating bread correlates positively with economic position. Thus, 23 per cent of the people in Groups I-A and I-B, as compared with 57 per cent of the people in Group III-B, ate bread. Furthermore, we know from our observation that the wealthier people do eat bread more often and in greater quantities; bread is still a luxury in this village.

Wearing shoes and sleeping in beds do not correlate with wealth, but rather with age. That is, the older people, rich or poor, prefer to use huaraches or go barefoot, and to sleep on the traditional *petate* or on a *tepexco*. We have here a nice example of the factor of selectivity in the adoption of new traits. Families who do not use shoes or beds will often buy sewing machines.

It should be noted that a larger percentage of Group II have adopted new traits, even though their economic resources are less than those of Group III. Table 47 shows the frequency distribution of the age of heads of families by economic categories.

TABLE 47. Age Distribution of Heads of Families by Economic Group.

| Group | Years of Age | | | | |
	Less Than 29	30–49	50–69	70–99	Total
I-A	31	31	18	12	92
I-B	63	194	132	30	419
I-C	6	88	77	14	185
II	3	46	52	18	119
III-A	0	9	15	1	25
III-B	0	1	11	1	13
Total	103	369	305	76	853

It is apparent that there are no younger people in the upper group and very few in the middle group. The bulk of the younger people are at the low end of the scale. Conversely, the wealthiest are of an advanced age, mostly between fifty and sixty-nine. Forty-one per cent of the heads of families in Group I are over age fifty; 59 per cent are in Group II; and 74 per cent are in Group III. But while most of the wealthy are of advanced age, not all the old people are wealthy. The fact that 41 per cent of those in Group I are older people shows that vertical mobility is quite limited. The practice of not dividing up the property until the death of the parents often results in married sons, with as many as five children, being entirely landless and without a house of their own.

There are no institutionalized barriers to vertical mobility in Tepoztlán. No single group has a monopoly of the means of production or the sources of wealth. No single group controls sufficient capital or labor to achieve wealth by its use or exploitation. The rate of capital accumulation is very slow because of the limited natural resources, the poor technology, and the low productivity, since the family is the basic productive unit. Nevertheless, there is a trend toward the concentration of wealth, especially in land. The upper economic group, though constituting only four per cent of all the families, owns approximately twenty-five per cent of the land, including some of the best land. Cattle ownership shows a similar trend.

It should be emphasized that there were no younger men as heads of families in the upper economic group. And the majority of the young men now in Groups I and II have little prospect of ever achieving the top position. In this sense there is little upward mobility possible in Tepoztlán. In keeping with this situation, we find that most Tepoztecans are convinced of the impossibility of becoming wealthy, and accordingly do not organize their lives around the goal of wealth. Rather, they are concerned with the day-to-day problems of subsistence. It is primarily among the families of Group II that we find higher aspirations, and it is from this group that there is some upward mobility.

Though the upper group is small, it is important to note that more people qualify for the upper group now than would have been the case before the Revolution, indicating that there has been increased upward movement since that time. Indeed, the shape of the social and economic pyramid has changed considerably. Before the Revolution the distribution of wealth was more concentrated in the hands of a few at the top of the pyramid, and the majority of Tepoztecans were day laborers for the local *caciques* and haciendas. One of the effects of the Revolution was to broaden the land base, enlarge the class of small landowners or *ejidatarios,* and at the same time increase the size of the upper group. It must also be noted that at least half of the families in the upper group worked their way up and are not members of the old *cacique* families. The wealthy are largely a new group who have taken advantage of the greater economic and political liberties since the Revolution. In fact, some of them were Zapatistas who had fought against the old regime.

Some of the newly rich got their start during the hectic days of the Revolution when they were able to buy land at low prices from hungry and half-starved villagers. The chaotic conditions during the Revolution, and the burning of the local archives and property registers, enabled some families to obtain land by devious methods. When the *caciques* fled the village, their lands were cultivated by the poorer families who remained. For the most part, however, these lands were returned to the owners or their heirs when they came back after peace had been established. In some poor families in which the head of the family was killed in the Revolution, the widows lost their land because they could show no legal title and were too poor to fight the cases in the courts.

Perhaps the most important ways in which families have obtained their wealth since the Revolution are through hard work, thrift, and self-denial over many years, and through the purchase and sale of cattle. Cattle trips to Guerrero and southern Morelos immediately after the Revolution were dangerous, and only those with courage, initiative, and a little capital went. In regard to self-denial, it is a common saying in Tepoztlán that the rich are the most miserly and thrifty. The terms *codo* (stingy) and *miserable* are often applied to the rich by their poorer neighbors. It should also be noted that in practically all cases of better-to-do families, the wife has been a hard worker and a good manager and has played a crucial part in aiding the family.

Movement down the economic ladder is occasioned by a number of factors. The fact that property is divided more or less equally among all the children makes it difficult for the same family to maintain its high position from one generation to another, although the sons of such families have an obvious advantage over the sons of landless families. But there are also other factors. Illness, lack of thrift, or poor management may result in a rapid loss of resources. Well-to-do families are also subject to some pressure from the community to participate in the fiesta life, and some of the wealthier families spend more heavily on costumes for the Carnaval and accept the job of barrio *mayordomo,* which always entails expenses. But as a rule it is the families of the middle group that go in for this type of spending.

HOUSING AND HOUSE FURNISHINGS

The houses of Tepoztlán are essentially of three types, the primitive *jacal,* the adobe house, and the more substantial dwellings found in the center of the village. The *jacal* and the adobe house are basically Indian, and the houses in the center show more of the Spanish influence.

The *jacal* is the poorest type of house in Tepoztlán and is considered primitive and extremely undesirable by the majority of the population. (See Fig. 35.) It is a flimsy structure of cornstalks or *otate* (Mexican bamboo), with thatched roof and earthen floor that give insufficient protection against cold, wind, and rain. The roof is apt to be gabled, in contrast with the one-sided sloping roof that is common in the village. The *jacal* is relatively infrequent in Tepoztlán and makes up less than 5 per cent of all dwellings; it is almost entirely limited to the smaller, outlying barrios, particularly in the upper part of the village. The *jacal* is far more

Fig. 35. A *jacal,* with thatched roof.

numerous in the surrounding villages of the municipio and, according to the Mexican Housing Census of 1939, it makes up 38.7 per cent of all dwellings in the Central Mesa region in which Tepoztlán is located.[2] The per cent for Mexico is 44.9, while in some southern states the per cent is sixty-five. Thus, the small proportion of *jacales* in Tepoztlán points to a comparatively high standard of housing in this village.

The great majority of Tepoztecan families (approximately 90 per cent) are housed in adobe, tile-roofed houses (Fig. 36), which sometimes have brick floors but more usually have earthen floors. These houses are more solid than the *jacal* and provide better protection from the elements. They consist of one or more rectangular rooms, each of which generally has only one opening, a doorway. Some of the more recently built adobe houses now have wooden-shuttered window openings as well. The door of each room opens onto the yard or porch, rather than being connected directly with other rooms in the interior of the house. Many families add a kitchen in the form of a lean-to with a tile-roof, and additional sleeping rooms are frequently constructed as families grow larger. The addition of a roofed porch across the front length of the house is an important improvement,

---

[2] Whetten, *Rural Mexico,* p. 287.

Fig. 36. Adobe house, with separate kitchen.

since it increases living space and may be used as kitchen, sleeping room, work room, and for storage. The porch usually consists of an extension of the house roof supported by columns of adobe brick. There may be a low wall connecting the columns, and the porch may be enclosed by Mexican bamboo.

One of the common characteristics of the *jacal* and adobe house in Tepoztlán is that they are detached type dwellings, generally built within a patio or yard and set off from the street by a low stone wall or terrace. This is especially true in the smaller barrios where there is more space.

In sharp contrast with the *jacal* and adobe houses are the few but striking homes of former *caciques* or of wealthier families of the center barrios. (See Fig. 37.) These houses invariably show marked Spanish or modern urban influence, and several of them border on elegance. They are large and imposing, and surrounded by an outer wall, built flush with the street, in which glass-paned windows and small balconies of iron grillwork are set. The roofs are of tile and slope from the street side inward, so that the outer wall is higher than the inner one and makes the house appear tall. Sometimes a high stone or plastered wall shields the house from the street and opens into the patio by means of a massive wooden door, or *zaguán*. Other houses have more elegant exteriors of one or more arches and col-

Fig. 37. *Cacique* homes.

umns. The rooms of the house are grouped in a rectangle or U-shape and open onto a wide *corredor,* which generally runs the inside length and sides of the house, enclosing the patio. These houses are constructed of brick or stone, covered with plaster, and whitewashed inside and out. A good number of these houses are now in disrepair. Not infrequently the families living in them are the impoverished sons or widows of formerly wealthy men.

While only the poorest live in *jacales,* it is by no means true that the wealthiest live in the finest houses. Families of every category of wealth live in simple adobe houses. A few of the richest men, who represent the conservative older generation, continue to live in relatively unimproved houses.

There is a distinct tendency for newly rich families to build their homes with simple exteriors, even though the interior may have a degree of elegance and the family can well afford a more imposing looking house. This is done to avoid getting the reputation of being wealthy and to avoid the envy and malice of others. The violence and destruction wreaked against the homes of the wealthy during the Revolution are well remembered, and a few informants made specific reference to the fear of such a recurrence in explaining why they had built their new homes with such plain exteriors.

The great majority of houses in Tepoztlán have no running water or sanitary facilities of any kind. Water is carried in tin cans from the closest public fountain;

and although this is the traditional and common practice, it is now considered a real hardship by more and more families. The quantity of water consumed by a family is usually determined by the amount of labor it can devote to water-carrying, and many families limit their use of water for bathing, for plants and animals, and for laundry. Use of the public laundry, generally considered undesirable, is made of necessity by many. The few families with water piped into their patios invariably have flourishing flower, fruit, and vegetable gardens. These families are very much envied, and not infrequently their water pipes are deliberately stuffed or damaged by less fortunate neighbors.

The benefits of toilets are not as generally recognized, and only one private home and the two tourist houses have toilets that can be flushed. The new schoolhouse, however, has toilets and showers, and the younger generation is becoming accustomed to their use. The schoolteachers, the students who have been away to boarding schools, and the not insignificant number of Tepoztecans who have spent time in Mexico City are also familiar with the use of toilets and will undoubtedly be among the first to install them in their dwellings in the future. Some already have constructed screens around their latrines in their yards or orchards to afford some privacy.

Bathing facilities for women and children generally consist of a clay or tin basin at home; the men and older boys bathe in the river. Many women bathe and wash their hair when they do their laundry in a stream or at the public washing place.

No Tepoztecan house has any means of heating other than the kitchen fire. This, however, gives little heat and is extinguished as soon as cooking is completed, to save fuel. In the winter months the family generally retires earlier to keep warm, but since most families have a minimum number of blankets, there is probably some suffering during the night due to cold. Except for early morning, the days are warm all the year round.

There are various means of lighting the house after dark, the most common and inexpensive being candles. Some homes have kerosene lamps and a few of the houses and stores in the center have Coleman gasoline lamps. One Tepoztecan house—that of the prosperous curer, Don Chucho—has electricity which is operated by a privately owned generator. There is talk of installing electricity in the plaza and in the church and chapels near the center, and it is probably only a matter of time before this is done.

Differences in house furnishings are even more striking than differences in house types, and there is an unending variety of combinations of new and old or modern and primitive household items. It is not at all unusual to find under one roof a battery-operated radio, a pre-Hispanic hearth as the only means of cooking, a hand mill for grinding coffee, and the Indian stone *metate* for grinding corn. Modern equipment for cooking, serving, sleeping, lighting, and so forth, is with few exceptions greatly esteemed; and in the majority of families only lack of money prevents its purchase. Among the youth, the more educated, and the large middle economic group, there is a strong desire to live better and to invest in household comforts. On the other hand, many of the older generation, even those with means, scorn innovations and prefer to live the way they have always lived, investing what surplus they have in land and cattle. The use of modern household equipment correlates more with age and education than with wealth. On the whole, we find modern equipment more frequently in the homes of families with a medium income. In the homes of the better-to-do there is almost always a greater quantity of household goods, whether primitive or modern.

Kitchen in
poor home.

Fig. 38.

Kitchen in
well-to-do home.

Wealthier families generally own enough plates, pots, glasses, spoons, chairs, etc., to be able to serve fiesta meals to a large number of people without having to borrow, as do so many other Tepoztecan families.

The four features mentioned by Redfield as being inevitably present in the Tepoztecan kitchen of 1926-27 are still found, though with some modifications.[3] (Fig. 38 illustrates the contrast between kitchens in a well-to-do and a poor home.) These features are the hearth, the griddle, the grinding stone, and the pot. Today

[3] Redfield, *Tepoztlán*, p. 35.

almost every house has a hearth made of three stones set in a triangle, or of stones plastered in the shape of a horseshoe, to support the griddle. It is no longer always located on the floor, but is frequently raised to almost table height by means of a cement platform. The use of platforms has been stimulated by the cultural missions that have visited the village and demonstrated to the more interested and enterprising women some ways of improving their homes. The *brasero,* a raised clay stove with two or three charcoal-burning iron grates on top, is generally still found only in better-to-do homes and is used sparingly or only for preparing fiesta meals. The *comal* (griddle), which in Redfield's time was always clay, is now frequently iron, and many families own one of each type. Though the *comal* is still an indispensable utensil in every home, the increasing consumption of bread, especially for breakfast and supper, makes it somewhat less used than formerly. The same is true of the *metate* (grinding stone), since almost all women now have their corn ground at the mill. But every home has one or more *metates* for regrinding mill-ground corn and for emergencies. *Metates* are also used for coffee and for large quantities of chile for fiestas. Despite the commercial mills, no Tepoztecan woman would set up housekeeping without her own *metate.* Finally, the *olla,* mentioned by Redfield, is the clay pot in which the maize for tortillas is cooked. To this utensil must be added the pot for beans, another for coffee, and another for meat. Most families have one large pot to retain the water in which maize has been soaked and cooked, and the water needed to moisten the woman's hands as she makes tortillas. This water, which contains some nourishment, is then fed to the pigs.

The remaining house furnishings are relatively few; they consist mainly of sleeping equipment, religious articles, and various containers for storage. For sleeping there are three kinds of beds: the *petate* or straw mat placed on the floor; the *tepexco,* a raised bed of bamboo sticks tied together and placed on a wooden frame or on two sawhorses; and a brass or iron bedstead with metal springs over which a *petate,* rather than a mattress, is generally placed. The great majority of the population sleep either on the floor or on the *tepexco,* and only 19.29 per cent sleep on a bed or cot.[4] The proportion of those who sleep on a bed or cot for Mexico as a whole is far greater (61.1 per cent), and even for communities of 10,000 or less inhabitants it is 53.4 per cent.[5]

The majority of Tepoztecans sleep on the floor because they lack the funds to buy beds, but most of the older generation, regardless of their economic status, sleep that way by preference. Many an acculturated family has sought without success to accustom the old mother or grandmother to sleeping on a bed. Some old people are afraid of falling off during the night, others say that to sleep off the ground is to be more subject to *los aires* (evil winds). One old woman told her grandchildren that it is better to sleep on the floor because it is closer to mother

---

[4] This figure was derived from a special tabulation of census data for Tepoztlán taken from the Mexican Census of 1940.

[5] Whetten, *Rural Mexico,* p. 291.

earth. Most of the younger people of the village view beds as a desirable luxury. Pillows, mattresses, pillowcases, sheets, and bedspreads are found in only a few Tepoztecan homes. A wool serape is all the bedding known to the majority of the population.

Sleeping arrangements vary somewhat from family to family, but the most widespread custom is for the parents to share their *petate* with the children of about two to six years of age who sleep between them. This is also true when a bed is used. The nursing baby sleeps on the other side, next to the mother. Cradles are used only during the day. Older children sleep apart, the girls sharing one *petate* and the boys another. In homes with more than one room the parents and small children sleep in one room and the older children in the other; in few homes are there enough rooms to permit the separation of older brothers and sisters. Sometimes parents are embarrassed to lie down together in the presence of their children, and the mother sleeps with the daughters while the father sleeps with the sons.

Most homes have a makeshift altar in the main room of the house. This is usually a table on which are placed candles, flowers, incense burners, and images of saints. These images are highly prized and occupy a prominent place in the home. Some families have large images of Jesus, Mary, or one of the saints, which have been in the family for many generations. Religious pictures are hung on the wall over the table, and frequently there are tissue paper decorations arranged around the table. (See Fig. 39.)

Wooden boxes and one or two wooden chests are used for storage of clothing, blankets, and other personal property. Extra clothing in regular use is hung on

Fig. 39. A domestic altar.

nails and now, not infrequently, on wood or wire clothes hangers purchased in Cuernavaca. Clothes closets are used only in a very few well-to-do homes in the center of the village. Food, except corn and beans, does not present a storage problem, since it is purchased in small quantities for immediate consumption. A few cans, bottles, jars, and baskets usually suffice to take care of current food. But the more modern or acculturated the family, the greater the number of storage facilities.

The family supply of corn presents the most important storage problem. For this purpose separate structures resembling corncribs are built in the family patio. Redfield describes these as follows:

The storehouse (S. *troje*) is practically always present, and is usually placed immediately in front of the dwelling. It occurs in three forms, all of which are probably of entirely pre-Columbian design. The *ohuatlapil* (N. *ohuatlapilli*) is most common. This is circular, about six feet high and of varying diameter; it is made of vertical cornstalks bound together with rope. It contains maize on the cob (S. *mazorca*). Also made to contain *mazorca* is the *cincolote* (N. *zincolohtli*). This is square, of poles laid horizontally, one pair upon another at right angles to the first until the structure is raised tall enough to contain the maize to be stored. The *cuezcomate* (N. *cuezcomatl*) is a vasiform granary, plastered inside and out with clay. In it is kept shelled corn.[6]

The *cuescomatl* is now a rarity in Tepoztlán, since most of them have been dismantled or allowed to fall in ruin. They are considered very primitive in appearance, and the few families who still own them are not keeping them in good repair and obviously do not take pride in them, although some of them are over a hundred years old. Now shelled corn is stored inside the house in large sacks made of *petates* sewn together, in large baskets, or in burlap bags.

The sewing machine has, as Redfield put it, "become a part of the general Tepoztecan material culture; it is found in all parts of the village and in houses otherwise Indian in character." At present there are 215 sewing machines in Tepoztlán, owned by 25.3 per cent of the families. This is a relatively high proportion in comparison with other rural areas. The average distribution in rural areas throughout Mexico is 15.6 per 100 families; the average for both rural and urban areas in the nation is 22.5 per cent.

Although sewing machines are apt to be found in the poorest homes, as well as in well-to-do homes, there is a high correlation between degree of wealth and ownership of sewing machines. We find such ownership in 76 per cent of Group III, 39 per cent of Group I–C, and 10 per cent of Groups I–A and I–B. It is interesting to note that among Groups I–A and I–B there is a considerable number of families who own no property except a sewing machine. The few wealthy families who do not have their own machines either have little need for one or have all their clothing made by a local seamstress. The 215 machines in Tepoztlán service many more than that number of families, since it is customary to lend or rent machines to relatives and neighbors, and most machines are in continuous use. Indeed, it may be said that one of the secondary but not unimportant effects of the sewing machine

---

[6] Redfield, *Tepoztlán*, pp. 33-34.

is to provide women with an excuse for visiting each other, and that it has extended their social life.

There are less than a dozen battery-operated radios in the village, and most of them have been purchased since 1944. There are also about 44 spring-driven phonographs.

DIET

As in rural Mexico as a whole, the basic diet of the people of Tepoztlán consists of corn, beans, and chile. Squash, which was reported by Redfield to be an important element in the food complex of Tepoztlán, is not part of the regular daily diet and is eaten only a few months of the year. The proportion of corn, beans, and chile in the diet varies sharply from family to family and depends upon the season, income, and food habits of the family. The consumption of corn, which is the major food staple, ranges from 10 per cent to as much as 70 per cent of the family diet. In general, the poorer the family, the higher the proportion of corn, beans, and chile in the diet.

Yellow corn is most commonly used in Tepoztlán, but blue and white corn is also locally grown and used. Corn is most frequently eaten in the form of tortillas and occasionally in the form of *atole* (gruel). Tamales made of corn dough are eaten at certain fiestas; corn *pozole* and corn *pinole* are known but are not characteristic foods in this village. The preparation of the corn dough or *nixtamal* with lime is the same in Tepoztlán as in other parts of Mexico. There is a wide variety of beans in Tepoztlán, but the most commonly eaten are red kidney beans cooked with lard, chile, and sometimes tomato and onion. Green chile, ground with onion and tomato, is prepared daily as a sauce to be eaten with tortilla and whatever other foods are served. *Chile pasilla,* a large dried red chile, is more expensive and is generally reserved for use in the fiesta *mole* sauce.

The basic diet is supplemented by many other foods which are either locally cultivated, gathered wild, or purchased in the stores and market place. Among the foods used in Tepoztlán are the following:

zapote	beans	honey
banana	avocado	spices
orange	hog plum	herbs
lemon, lime	*chirimoya*	beef
grapefruit	*mameys*	pork
chayote	papaya	chicken
manzanillos	mango	turkey
tomato	squash	milk
sugar cane	peanuts	eggs
pitos	coffee	cheese
acacia seeds	prickly pear	clotted cream

The fields, forests, and mountain sides provide many free foods the year round. There are several varieties of wild edible greens, which are important in that they provide food elements which the Tepoztecan diet would otherwise lack, since there is little cultivation of leafy green vegetables. But it is impossible to determine to what extent wild greens are consumed, because they are considered very poor fare, and Tepoztecans do not readily admit eating them. During times of scarcity a large number of families eat wild greens in quantity several times a week, and the chronically poor eat them regularly throughout the year. During the Revolution many families escaped starvation by subsisting almost entirely on wild plants. The names of most of these plants are native Indian terms, and are as follows:

quintoniles	*papalo*
verdolaga	*chipiles*
tesquite	*tequesquite*
pipisacos	*quelites*

Violets boiled with *tequesquite* are also eaten. The herbs are well-known spices, and medicinal grasses or leaves are used to make a variety of teas.

Additional fruits and vegetables are brought in by traveling merchants or are purchased in the large market in Cuernavaca. However, most of these are expensive and only the few well-to-do families of Tepoztlán can afford to purchase them more or less regularly. Foods not locally produced and commonly purchased in the stores of Tepoztlán, Yautepec, Cuernavaca, or Mexico City are bread,[7] sugar, salt, rice, certain types of chile and beans, noodles, and dried codfish. Chocolate is also purchased but is considered a luxury. Foods which are slowly becoming more popular but which are still purchased by a small minority are evaporated and powdered milk, canned sardines, tomato herring, or other fish.

The eating of white bread made of wheat flour is of particular interest in Mexico, since it is a relatively new trait and one which has been taken to indicate the degree of acculturation of individuals and groups. In Tepoztlán, bread is considered a very desirable food; and often the social and economic status of a family is judged in terms of the amount of bread that it consumes. From the Mexican Census of 1940, which included a question designed to estimate the number of persons who eat bread fairly regularly, we learned that over 31 per cent of the population of Tepoztlán eat bread. At present there is scarcely a family that does not eat some bread during the week or month, though it may be but once or twice. It is especially favored as a food for very small children, and even the poorest family seeks to provide a piece of bread daily for its youngest child. There is no indication, however, that bread will eventually displace the tortilla; at most, bread consumption among well-to-do families may represent about 10 per cent of the total food expenditure.

There is, of course, much variation in the actual consumption of food. Except among the wealthier families, irregularity in diet is characteristic throughout the year, and few families maintain a uniformly good diet from day to day even according to local standards. The type and quantity of food consumed is determined by the season, the fiesta calendar, and, most of all, the amount of cash on hand. "When

---

[7] Bread is baked locally, but wheat flour is purchased outside.

we have money we eat, when we don't, we don't" is an oft-heard statement. The leanest part of the year for the majority are the three or four months preceding the harvest. During this time, many families are reduced to minimum quantities of tortilla, beans, and chile as steady fare or even merely *tortilla con sal* (with salt).

Before fiestas many families pull in their belts and eat less in order to sell their corn, beans, eggs, and chickens to get cash for new clothing, for the fiesta meal, and for spending money. The best eating occurs just after the harvest, and on fiesta days when *mole* made with chicken or turkey and rice and beans is served. Other irregularities of consumption are due to the seasonal availability of fruits and vegetables. Also, if the family trees produce poor *ciruelas,* papayas, or wormy mangos, it means that the family goes without these foods. The locally grown oranges, grapefruits, and lemons are normally inferior in quality and quantity.

Meat consumption rises during the dry winter months when pasture is scarce and cattle are slaughtered. Eggs are generally eaten only by men, especially during the planting season when work is most intense. Chicken and turkey are delicacies which are reserved for fiestas, weddings, baptisms, and birthdays. With the exception of the wedding feast, which is socially obligatory and served by rich and poor alike, many families must forego serving fiesta meals, sometimes for years on end, and partake of them only when invited by other families. Game is not eaten extensively, and the few men who hunt do so only when there is no other work, mostly during the dry season.

The correlation between diet and wealth is a positive one, in that the wealthier a family is the better it tends to eat. Its meals are larger and contain more variety throughout the year. But differences in the diet of the rich and poor consist principally in differences in the amount of food eaten, and in the relative frequency with which a family can afford to eat the more desirable of the locally known food types. There are no class differences in food quality, in food types, or in ways of preparing dishes. The better-to-do have no special recipes, no unusual ways of cooking, no exotic foods which are unknown to the poor.

Many of the wealthier families, because of custom and habits of thrift, do not always eat the newer foods, such as bread or canned fish, nor do they necessarily indulge in luxuries like milk, eggs, chicken, sweets, fruits not locally produced, or out-of-season foods except for fiestas. In fact, it is commonly said in Tepoztlán that the rich are too miserly to eat any better than the poor. Whatever the reason, there is an underlying homogeneity in type of foods eaten; and if all families were equal financially, there would be much more uniformity in diet than at present. It is not wealth, but education or degree of acculturation, which is beginning to create real differences in diet.

Tepoztecan families normally eat three meals a day, although many remember eating only twice a day before and during the Revolution, because of poverty. It is seldom that the entire family eats together, and often there are no fixed hours for meals. The father and older sons eat together in the morning before they go to the fields and in the evening when they return. If the field is at a great distance, the

men carry their breakfast with them, to be warmed and eaten later. (See Fig. 40.)
They may eat once again at noon and have their dinner when they arrive home, at
any time from 5:00 to 9:00 P.M.

When they eat at home they are usually served first and receive preferential treatment. The women and children who remain at home eat breakfast at 7:00 or 8:00
A.M., dinner at about 1:00 P.M., and supper at dusk. Younger children are generally
fed before the mother and the older daughter sit down to eat. In most homes the

Fig. 40. Men eating in the fields.

members of the family sit on low chairs or stools, or the women and children sit
on the floor. Very few families use a table except during a fiesta meal, and then it is
only for the men and guests. Likewise, knives and forks are generally reserved for
fiesta times only. The mother serves, handing each person his food in a bowl or
wrapped in a tortilla. Spoons may be used, but food is usually eaten with the tortilla
as a spoon.

For most people, breakfast consists of black coffee and tortilla. Some take milk
in their coffee and eat bread instead of tortilla; some eat toasted meat or warmed-
over beans. During hard times, poorer families drink tea made from cinnamon or
local herbs instead of coffee. It should be remembered that coffee drinking is a
relatively new phenomenon among the poor; in the late nineteenth century only
the *caciques* could afford it. Today, tea drinking is associated with poverty or illness, for many of the teas are used to cure stomach-ache, colds, sore throats, etc.[8]

---

[8] In many families it is customary for the father to begin the day with a drink of alcohol.
Similarly, when the peasants return from the fields at night, they generally take a drink of
alcohol to counteract *los aires* and to avoid taking cold.

Dinner, the most substantial meal, is eaten in the middle of the day whenever possible. It may consist of beans, tortilla, and chile. A good dinner, according to the Tepoztecan view, should include meat cooked with some vegetables, a bowl of rice or noodles cooked in broth, and the inevitable beans, tortilla, and chile. Coffee may or may not be taken at the end of dinner. Supper generally consists of coffee and tortillas or bread, with perhaps a piece of cheese.

Variety is provided by changing the type of meat or by using fish and by varying the vegetables. Fruit, peanuts, sugar cane, candies, cookies, and other sweets are eaten between meals and are generally not regarded as food to be included in a meal. The taste for sweets is developing among the children, particularly school children, and they are becoming more demanding of their parents in this respect.

To get a better notion of the quantities of food consumed, as well as of the variety, we will examine a typical weekly food budget of a well-to-do family and of a poor family. (See Tables 48 and 49.) The prosperous family selected is in the upper economic group and is one of the more respected, educated families in the village. At the time of our study, the family consisted of the parents and an adult son and daughter. Both the son and daughter had received considerably more education than is common, and both had lived in Mexico City with relatives.

The other family is one of the poorest in the village. The father is a *tlacololero* and works alone to support his wife and seven young children. An older daughter left home to work as a servant in Cuernavaca, but she contributes nothing to the family. The ages of the children at home range from an infant-in-arms to fifteen years. Both families were observed during the summer months before the harvest in the year 1944. The slight differences in some of the prices were due to local fluctuations; the smaller quantities purchased by the poor family sometimes resulted in higher costs. The weekly budgets represent a summary of daily expenditures directly observed or estimated by our field workers.

A comparison of the weekly food budgets reveals that, although Family I has fewer mouths to feed, it spends three times more on food and consumes consistently more of every food item, with the exception of corn, green chile, lard, and salt. Its weekly diet provides greater variety, more sources of protein and more of the highly prized "luxury" foods. The corn-beans-chile-complex mentioned earlier makes up only 13 per cent of the diet of Family I and 46.9 per cent of that of Family II. Taken alone, corn represents 34 per cent of the food expenditure of the poor family and 9 per cent of that of the well-to-do family.[9] Despite this, the latter consumes only 2½ *cuartillos* less corn a week. If we consider those food items which are consumed daily or in the greatest quantities weekly by the poor family, we find that corn, beans, green chile, lard, wild greens, coffee, sugar, salt, and green tomatoes make up 83 per cent of the expenditure of this family. These foods may be said to be the real core of their diet. The same foods take up only 22 per cent of the expenditure of the other family.

---

[9] During certain times of the year some Tepoztecan families live on a diet which consists of from 50 to 70 per cent corn.

TABLE 48. Typical Weekly Food Budget, 1944.

Food	Family I (Well-to-do, 4 Adults)		Family II (Poor, 2 Adults, 7 Children)	
	Quantity	Cost in Pesos	Quantity	Cost in Pesos
Corn	10½ *cuartillos*	2.94	13 *cuartillos*	3.64
Beans	1¾ *cuartillos*	1.12	1½ *cuartillos*	1.02
Lard	¼ *cuartillo*	1.00	¼ *cuartillo*	1.00
Green chile	½ *cuartillo*	.25	Over ½ *cuartillo*	.35
Lime (for tortillas)		.10		.05
Coffee	¼ *cuartillo*	.25	⅛ *cuartillo*	.35
Sugar	2 kilos	.90	⅓ kilo	.35
Salt	About ½ kilo	.20	½ kilo	.35
Tomatoes (green)		.50		.35
Tomatoes (red)	1 *cuartillo*	.60		
Eggs	1⅓ dozen	2.80		
Milk	10½ liters	6.30		
Meat	1½ kilos	3.00	⅙ kilo	.20
Bread		4.20		.15
Rice	1 kilo	.50	About ½ kilo	.20
Noodles		.70		.20
Cheese	1 kilo	1.80	¼ kilo	.45
Vegetables		1.75		.45
Fruits and sweets		3.00	Peanuts and acacia seeds	.05
Wild greens			3 times a week	1.50
Total		31.91	Total	10.66

TABLE 49. Fiesta Meals.

Family I[a]		Family II[b]	
Occasion	Cost of Food	Occasion	Cost of Food
June:		June:	
Son's Saint's Day	25.00	Barrio Fiesta	6.35
August:		Mother's Saint's Day	1.05
Barrio Fiesta	15.00		
October:		November:	
Daughter's Saint's Day	20.00	Day of the Dead	5.00
November:			
Day of the Dead	25.00	February:	
December:			
Christmas			
The Posadas	70.00	Eldest Daughter's Saint's Day	31.25
February:			
Fiesta of La Candelaria	30.00		
Total	185.00	Total	43.65

[a] The fiesta meals of this family always include the traditional appropriate dishes and an abundance of sweets, fruit, and drink.

[b] The fiesta meals of this family generally consist of extra meat. This year, for the first time, the family had a birthday celebration for a child. It was for the purpose of inviting her godparents, who are also her employers. Three chickens were served with *mole* sauce and rice. There was also pulque, lemonade, and fruit on this occasion.

Unfortunately, we were not equipped to analyze family diets in terms of nutrition or caloric values, nor to determine the presence of vitamins, minerals, and other food elements. In our comparison of the two weekly diets presented here, we can only point to some of the quantitative aspects involved. These tend to parallel and support the more detailed data gathered by Beals and Hatcher in their study of the diet of Cherán.[10] The "wealthy" diet in Cherán is higher in vitamins A, B$_1$, and B$_2$ and protein and calory intake but lower in vitamin C than the "poor" diet. The latter was deficient in vitamins B$_1$ and B$_2$ and low in proteins and calories; vitamin C intake was higher because of the greater use of chile.

In Tepoztlán, we find that the wealthier family spends twelve times as much on the important protein foods—meat, eggs, and cheese—and that they also consume a larger quantity of beans, which is another source of protein. The high consumption of milk, in contrast to the complete absence of milk in the diet of the poor family, is important as a nutritional difference. The greater weekly consumption of sugar, fruits, and sweets would also result in higher calory intake for the wealthier family. Although the poor diet includes somewhat more chile, which is a good source of vitamin C, the better diet includes some vitamin C because of greater fruit consumption. The reliance of the poor family on wild greens, absent in the diet of the wealthier family, is an important source of minerals and vitamins.

The consumption of bread provides another strong contrast in the diet of our rich and poor families. The rich spend 28 times more on bread, or 13 per cent of the total weekly food expenditure. This item, which, in addition to its nutritional aspects, is an important indicator of social and economic status in Tepoztlán, represents an expenditure of 1.4 per cent for the poor family. The basic homogeniety of the Tepoztecan diet is deceptive in terms of nutrition and, in all probability, in terms of the simple satisfaction of hunger as well. It is not insignificant that all the children in the poorer family are small, thin, pale, and listless, while the two grown children in the wealthier family appear well nourished and well developed.

Diet is also affected by fluctuations in the cost of food. During the year there are seasonal changes, prices generally being higher in the months before the harvest, beginning with May, and dropping after the harvest. It is in the pre-harvest period when most families keenly feel a shortage of cash. But more important than seasonal variations in food costs is the fact that prices have risen sharply and steadily from 1926 to the present. This rise, more than any other factor, has tended to maintain the traditional or conservative diet in Tepoztlán and to hold back the definite trend toward new foods and greater variety. For instance, although the consumption of bread is viewed as desirable and has increased considerably (the number of bakers rose from 6 to 24 between 1926 and 1944), it is still a luxury for a large proportion of the population. The price has more than doubled in the past four years and is still rising. We find a strong correlation between the degree of wealth

---

[10] Ralph L. Beals and Evelyn Hatcher, "The Diet of a Tarascan Village," *América Indígena*, Vol. 3, No. 4 (October, 1943), pp. 298–301.

and bread consumption, indicating that the economic factor is an important one. The following percentages show this correlation:

Economic Group	Per Cent Who Eat Bread
I-A and I-B	23.20
I-C	32.30
II	50.82
III-A	41.55
III-B	57.69
Tepoztlán	31.18

The consumption of meat has also risen considerably. In the same period, from 1926 to 1944, the number of butchers increased from three to fifteen. From an analysis of the municipio records which, for purposes of taxation, show the number and kind of animals slaughtered, we can arrive at a fairly accurate quantitative estimate of the increase in meat consumption.[11] Comparing 1931 and 1933 with 1941 and 1943, we find the following:

Animals	1931 and 1933	1941 and 1943
Hogs	289	640
Oxen	93	277
Cows	29	225
Yearling calves	94	130
Steers	173	264

Assigning approximate meat weights to the above animals, we find a total of 80,035 kilos for 1931 and 1933, as compared with 190,250 kilos for 1941 and 1943. Since practically no meat is sold outside the village, we can conclude that the consumption of meat during those years rose more than 130 per cent, while the population increase was approximately 30 per cent. As in the case of bread, and based chiefly on our observation and data on budgets and diets, the consumption of meat is directly affected by family income and prevailing prices.

We have figures to show the rise in price of corn, beans, sugar, lard, salt, meat, and rice from 1926 to 1944. They are shown in Table 50.

In a period of eighteen years, the price of corn, beans, and meat has risen 400 per cent; lard and salt, 500 per cent; and sugar and rice, 300 per cent. In 1948, the prices were a great deal higher. For example, corn sold for 70 centavos a *cuartillo* in the local market. Unfortunately, we have no comparable data on family income, nor can we show how the rise in price has affected the gross consumption of the basic staples. But we have already noted in the budget studies that poverty tends to limit diet to the staples and to restrict sharply the purchase of new or varied foods.

---

[11] Many individuals do not report all animals killed, to evade the tax. These figures are, therefore, an underestimate.

TABLE 50. Some Basic Food Prices, 1926–1944.

Year	Price in Pesos						
	Corn (*Cuartillo*)	Beans (*Cuartillo*)	Sugar (Kilo)	Lard (Kilo)	Salt (Kilo)	Beef (Kilo)	Rice (*Cuartillo*)
1926	.07	.16	.32	.80	.10	.50	.32
1927	.07	.16	.32	.80	.10	.50	.32
1928	.07	.16	.32	.80	.10	.50	.32
1929	.08	.16	.32	.90	.10	.50	.32
1930	.08	.17	.32	.90	.10	.55	.32
1931	.08	.20	.32	.90	.10	.50	.32
1932	.08	.20	.32	.90	.10	.50	.35
1933	.08	.20	.32	1.00	.10	.50	.35
1934	.09	.22	.32	1.00	.10	.50	.35
1935	.09	.22	.35	1.25	.12	.55	.35
1936	.09	.25	.35	1.50	.14	.60	.40
1937	.10	.25	.40	2.00	.18	.60	.40
1938	.10	.28	.40	3.00	.20	.60	.40
1939	.11	.30	.40	3.00	.20	.80	.50
1940	.15	.30	.40	3.50	.20	.90	.50
1941	.15	.35	.45	4.00	.22	1.20	.80
1942	.18	.40	.50	4.00	.24	1.20	1.00
1943	.20	.50	.55	4.00	.30	1.80	1.00
1944	.28	.60	.65	4.00	.50	2.00	1.00

To understand the buying pattern and the relation between income and food expenditure, we kept a daily record of the income and expenditures of one family for a period of twenty-six days. This family consists of the parents, three grown sons who work in the fields, a grown daughter who works at home, a ten-year-old boy still in school, and a five-year-old grandson—six adults and two children in all. The family is poor and landless, having only *tlacolol*. When not working on *tlacolol*, the sons hire out as peons, and the father devotes himself to politics and other non-income producing activities.

Our record was kept from July 20 to August 14, 1948, when there was a lull in work on *tlacolol*. During this period the sons worked as peons, giving the family a much needed source of cash. However, food prices are particularly high at this time of the year, and despite the comparatively good income, the family was hard pressed. The family had no savings and several debts. A record of seven of the twenty-six days follows:

July 20	
6 *cuartillos* corn	4.20
1½ *cuartillos* corn for animals	1.05
Lard	.15
Beans	.30
Kerosene	.20
Total	5.90
Source of funds:	
Borrowed cash	

July 21

6 *cuartillos* corn	4.20
1 *cuartillo* corn for animals	1.05
¼ kilo sugar	.23
Coffee	.10
1 box matches	.10
Total	5.68

Source of funds:
Borrowed cash

July 22

5 *cuartillos* corn	3.50
1 *cuartillo* corn for animals	.20
Tomatoes (red)	.15
Salt	.05
Garlic	.05
Onions	.10
Cinnamon	.05
¼ kilo sugar	.23
Dry *guajes*	.25
Drinking alcohol for parents	.45
Hay for mule	1.00
Kerosene	.10
Milling corn	.22
Firewood	.20
Total	6.55

Source of funds:

Sale of 12 *cuartillos* corn (advance payment sons' wages as peons)	8.40	
Cash for same	4.00	
Total	12.40	

July 23

6 *cuartillos* corn	4.20
1 *cuartillo* corn for animals	.70
½ kilo salt	.15
Chile	.15
¼ kilo sugar	.23
Drinking alcohol for parents	.15
Milling corn	.18
Hay for mule	1.30
Repaid debt to employer	20.00
Repaid debt to neighbor	5.00
Repaid old debt of father	8.00
Total	40.06

Source of funds:

Sale of 1½ *cuartillo* corn	1.05	
Beans (gift of married daughter)	.20	
Wages of two sons for six days' work	48.00	
Total	49.25	

July 24
6 *cuartillos* corn	4.20
2 *cuartillos* corn for animals	1.40
1 *puño* beans	.50
Tomatoes (green)	.20
Chile	.10
¼ kilo sugar	.23
Milling corn	.20
Kerosene	.20
Total	7.03

Source of funds:
Sale of 4 *cuartillos* corn	2.80	
Wages for one son's work	6.00	
Total	8.80	

July 25
7½ *cuartillos* corn	4.55
1½ *puños* beans	.75
Lard	.20
Chile	.20
1 *cuartillo* corn for animals	.70
Tomatoes (red)	.15
¼ kilo sugar	.23
Kerosene	.15
Milling corn	.16
Total	7.09

Source of funds:
None

July 26
7½ *cuartillos* corn	4.55
1 *cuartillo* corn for animals	.70
Cheese	1.00
Lard	.50
Noodles	.50
½ kilo sugar	.46
½ *cuartillo* beans	.40
Tomatoes (green)	.40
1½ *decilitros* rice	1.50
Drinking alcohol for parents	.30
Laundry soap	.50
Chili, onions, tomatoes	3.00
Total	13.81
Huaraches and bus fare to Cuernavaca	10.50

Source of funds:
Wages for two sons' work	20.00	
Sale of plant to tourist	7.50	
Total	27.50	

July 27
7½ *cuartillos* corn	4.55
1 *cuartillo* corn for animals	.70
Beans	.50
Lard	.40
Chicharrón (pig's skin fried in lard)	.50
Cheese	.20

¼ kilo sugar	.23
Bread	.20
Coffee	.10
Drinking alcohol for parents	.30
Milling corn	.32
Total	8.00
Source of funds:	
None	

The amount earned by this family for the week was 97.95 pesos in cash and corn. The outgo was 48.60 for food, 33.00 to repay debts, and 24.03 for non-food items, leaving a deficit of 7.68. The hand-to-mouth, day-to-day existence, involving borrowing, receiving wages in advance, and buying food and necessities to last one day or so, is readily apparent from this record. Although approximately 50 per cent of the income is spent on food, the diet is monotonous and sparse, and conforms with our previous description of the diet of a poor family. During these seven days, the family ate no meat, no milk, no eggs, and no fruit. Wild greens were eaten in large quantities approximately every other day, but they have not been included in the record since they were gathered by the family and involved no expense. Corn makes up 69.8 per cent of the food expenditure and is eaten in large quantities.

The irregularity of food consumption, depending upon the amount of cash on hand, is more apparent from a study of our full record. For example, in the week of August 4 to 11, three and one-half kilos of meat were purchased, but during the rest of the month almost no meat was bought. Also, when there is money or corn, the family eats 7½ *cuartillos* of corn, but when money is lacking, consumption goes down to three *cuartillos*. When there is no money, the mule is taken to pasture to save buying hay, and the turkeys and chickens are sold or left to fend for themselves. To save money, the mother and daughter sometimes grind corn on the *metate* instead of at the mill.

Tepoztecans are very food conscious, as might be expected in view of the food situation we have described, and they show a keen interest in the eating habits of their relatives and neighbors. There is much gossip and criticism, often contradictory in nature, concerning the type of foods eaten by others and the amount spent on food. For example, the poor say, "The rich do not eat well because they are too stingy," or the poor are frankly envious of those who "eat better because they are rich." The better-to-do scornfully characterize the poor as eating only tortillas and salt, and those in the larger barrios contend that families in the small barrios of San Pedro and Los Reyes eat only two meals a day because they are "backward." Older or more conservative individuals criticize "modern" families for being presumptuous and unthrifty in eating too well, and the latter in turn accuse the former of ignorance concerning proper eating. Much of the talk about food reflects the changing standards of diet and the importance of food habits for social status. The interest in food and the critical attitude toward the eating habits of others may be a carry-over of the behavior which we have noted among children in the home.

Children tend to be preoccupied with food. Food was a recurrent theme in all the psychological tests, and boys particularly seem to think and talk about food a good deal. In the written themes, boys and girls invariably mentioned that they liked their parents because they provided them with food and other necessities, that they liked certain relatives because they gave them good things to eat, and that they liked fiestas because then they could eat *mole*. Many said that the worst thing that had ever happened to them was when their mothers did not have money to make *mole* or some other favorite dish. Boys wrote that they wanted to marry someone who was a good cook, and the thing they liked best about their mothers was that they cooked well. Thematic apperception stories also contained a good deal about food.

Boys, more than girls, tend to be fussy about food, although they like the food that makes up the family daily fare and do not refuse to eat it. They are sensitive about the order in which they are served, the size of their portion, the way in which the food is cooked, and the manner in which it is given to them. Eldest sons or favorite sons easily become angry and sometimes throw down their food, plate and all, or refuse to eat. In this they follow the pattern of their fathers who do the same thing when they are angry.

Girls may cry quietly or throw their food to the animals if they are not pleased with what they are given, but most often they suppress their feelings. The tendency of mothers to serve larger portions and choicer food to their favorite child is a source of quarrels and resentment. Many mothers give more food to the younger children because "the others are already big and the little ones need it more." On the other hand, grown sons who work are given more food than children still in school. Some children complain that their mothers do not cook well, and we know of a few cases in which the mother neglects to prepare meals from time to time. Food is also withheld as a punishment. Taking food without permission is called stealing and is punished. Despite this, children frequently steal food, and some mothers say that they cannot leave even a bit of sugar without it disappearing. Children also now commonly beg for food or for centavos to buy candy or fruit.

Tepoztecans tend to be secretive about food. Women do not discuss with each other what their families are going to eat that day nor what they bought at the market. Market baskets are generally kept carefully covered from prying eyes. There is also some fear of food sorcery, and, except for fiesta meals, Tepoztecans prefer to eat within the safety of their own homes. One family, in which the young son attends school daily in Cuernavaca, complained that he must eat cold, stiff tortillas and cold beans for lunch. When asked why he doesn't eat at one of the many inexpensive restaurants the mother answered that it would be dangerous because someone might "put something in his food." Persons who have known enemies will generally not accept food from anyone outside their own household.

Tepoztecans, like most other Mexicans, believe that food can be classified into two types, hot and cold (which has no relationship to temperature), and that under certain conditions only one or the other type should be eaten. In general, cold foods are believed to cause diarrhea and to be less easily digested than hot foods, and are not given to very small children, to the ill, or to women who have just given birth. Illnesses are also classified as hot and cold types, and it is believed that only hot foods should be eaten with certain illnesses and cold foods with others.

Foods may be neutralized and made less dangerous by mixing certain hot foods with cold foods. For example, milk is not given to new mothers because it is "cold," but it may be taken in coffee, which is "hot." *Atoles* made of corn, a highly recommended food for the ill, have their cold qualities removed by adding brown sugar and cinnamon. *Mole* is cold but may safely be eaten if served with alcoholic drinks. The green tomato, which is eaten almost daily in Tepoztlán, is made harmless by being cooked with beef or served as a sauce with onion and chile, both of which are hot. Hot herbs such as *tequesquite* and *epazote* are often used to neutralize a cold food. Despite this elaboration, Tepoztecans, unlike the Maya, do not preoccupy themselves with this classification of food and do not follow any set rules of eating. Nor is there always agreement about what the rules are or how a food, particularly a new food, is to be classified. The following list of hot and cold foods is based on data from several informants and include only those foods on which there is substantial agreement.

Cold Foods

milk	papaya	*quintoniles*
eggs	*granadas*	*papalo*
cheese	lettuce	lima beans
cream	radish	*verdolaga*
jitomate	corn-on-the-cob	white sugar
rice	avocado	bread
noodles	banana (*macho* and	apple
potatoes	*manzana* type)	pear
all beans except black	green chile	fish
lentils	quince	frog
mole verde	carrot	pigeon
mole colorado	prickly pear	deer
atoles made of corn	*nopal*	rabbit
peanuts	*chayote*	boar
jicama	lemon	squirrel
white *zapote*	lime	chicken
chick peas	*pipisacos*	veal
watermelons	*chilacayote*	pork
peaches	*chipiles*	
guayava	*quelites*	

Hot Foods

black beans	*epazote*	wine
chile pasilla	banana (*guines*)	*tequila*
coffee	melon	pulque

beef (bull or ox)	*chirimoya*	onion
cinnamon	honey	ice
orange	squash	ices
plums	garlic	ice cream
black *zapote*	*mamey*	oil
brown sugar	alcohol	all fats
tequesquite	acacia seeds	

CLOTHING

The old-style clothing is essentially Spanish in origin, with some admixture and adaptations from pre-Hispanic times. The old-style costume for women consists of a long dark-colored skirt (*enaguas de encima*), a white underskirt, (*enaguas de dentro*), a collarless undershirt (*camisa*), and a high-necked blouse (*blusa* or *saco*). The costume includes a half-apron (*delantal*) and a sash (*cenidor*). The *rebozo* is also invariably worn. About three or four generations ago women still wore the dress of pre-Conquest times. This consisted of a *huipil,* or blouse, which was a large square of cloth worn poncho-like, by slipping it over the head through a slit in the center. It was worn in such a way that two corners fell over the shoulders, and the front and back corners were tucked into the skirt. The *huipil* differs markedly from the prudish high-necked, long-sleeved *blusa* which displaced it, in that it was very loose covering and freely revealed the breasts. The ancient skirt (*cueitl*) was a rectangular cloth which was wrapped around the lower part of the body and held in place with a sash.

The old-style clothing for men consists of white cloth pants (*calzones*), long white cloth underdrawers, a white collarless undershirt (*camisa*), a white collarless overshirt, and a white cotton jacket. Leather huaraches and a straw sombrero complete the costume. (See Fig. 41.) The large, Zapata-type sombreros have given way to smaller-brimmed hats, since the advent of the bus and increased travel. The serape is an important article of clothing and is used for warmth and for protection against rain. The *gabán* is a poncho-like wool blanket and is now considered more old-fashioned than the serape.

The pre-Conquest clothing worn by men differed considerably from that in the post-Conquest period, but has nevertheless had more influence on later styles than pre-Conquest women's dress.

The ancient costume of the male Aztecs, although modified according to the social position of the wearer, was composed of three principal garments, the *maxtlatl,* a belt or loincloth with the ends hanging down in front like an apron; the *tilmahtli,* a woven cape worn over the shoulders and knotted in front; and the *cactli,* sandals of leather or woven of *maguey* fiber. Of these three, the first has entirely disappeared, the second influenced the form and use of the modern *sarape,* while the third remains little changed today.[12]

Children's old-style clothes were reproductions of adult clothing and were worn almost as soon as a child began to walk. (See Fig. 42.)

[12] Redfield, *Tepoztlán,* p. 42.

Fig. 41. Old-style clothing for men.

The new type of dress existed among the wealthier and more citified Tepoztecans in the 1920's but has, during the past twenty years, spread among the rest of the population. For women, the new-style dress (Fig. 43) consists of a one-piece dress (*vestido*), a full-length slip (*combinación*), underdrawers, a long apron (*babero*), and perhaps shoes and stockings. Some of the younger women now use a brassière (*portabusto*), though these, as well as underdrawers, are often dispensed with after marriage. The *rebozo* is also commonly worn, but sweaters, jackets, and even coats are now coming into use. Girls wear one-piece dresses, underdrawers, and occasionally an underslip. The dresses vary in length from below the calves up to the knees.

Modern male dress consists of ready-made pants, a collared and buttoned shirt, and a collared jacket. (See Fig. 44.) Huaraches, now usually made of rubber soles, are still commonly worn, but shoes are worn daily by some, and on holidays and on trips to the city by many. The sombrero is sometimes replaced by a narrow-brimmed felt hat, but only the most citified men in Tepoztlán wear neckties. Modern dress for boys may be overalls or pants and a buttoned shirt. Occasionally a small boy may be seen in a blouse and short pants. Straw hats are universally worn by boys. The *gabán* and serape are now often replaced by a sweater or jacket, and many boys wear shoes.

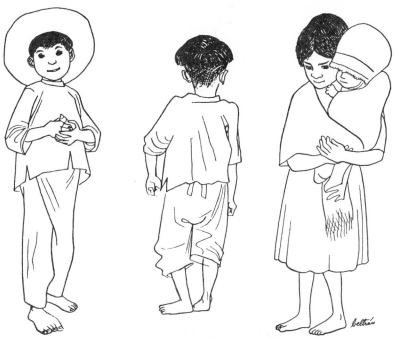

Fig. 42. Tepoztecan children's dress.

Older women wear the old-style costume, and younger women wear the new style, indicating as might be expected that age is a primary factor. An analysis of data in the 1940 census shows a clear-cut difference between the dress of women over forty and under forty.

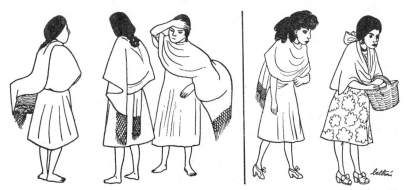

Fig. 43. Old and new styles in women's dress.

Fig. 44. Modern dress for men.

No girl under age 9 and only seven girls under age 19 wore long skirts.[13] The small percentage of women over 40 who wear dresses are women of wealthier or more citified families.

Women under 40:	Long skirts 10.5%	Dresses 89.8%
Women over 40:	Long skirts 87.5%	Dresses 12.4%

Age is also a factor among men in the wearing of new- and old-style clothing. An analysis of those wearing *pantalones* and those wearing *calzones* shows that the *pantalones* are worn primarily by men under 40, but that *calzones* are more popular among the male population as a whole.

Men under 40:	*Pantalones* 44%	*Calzones* 56%
Men over 40:	*Pantalones* 11%	*Calzones* 89%

In the age group from 1 to 9, the majority of boys wear *calzones*. However, half the boys from age 10 to 19 wear *pantalones,* and the other half, *calzones*.

Occupation is another important factor in determining the type of clothing worn by men. Farmers prefer the old-style dress because, they say, it is better adapted to work in the fields. (See Fig. 45.) *Calzones* are cooler, afford better protection, and are more economical. Huaraches, too, are half the price of shoes and last four times as long. The merchants, artisans, and teachers of the center make up the bulk

[13] In 1948, long skirts were not to be seen among this age group.

Fig. 45. A Tepoztecan farmer.

of those who wear modern dress. (See Fig. 46.) These men have frequent contact with the city, and shoes and dark trousers are more practical for their mode of life.

In comparing men and women, we note some interesting differences in the trend of styles. Seventy per cent of the women, as compared with 38 per cent of the men, use the new style of clothing; the old styles are disappearing among the women but not among the men. We also find that 14 per cent of the women, as compared with only 5.4 per cent of the men, wear shoes daily. Of course, it should be remembered that the only alternative a woman has to wearing shoes is to go barefoot, whereas men may and do wear huaraches. Nevertheless, in terms of departing from tradition, the wearing of shoes by women is significant. In general, women are less conservative than men in dress and have a stronger drive to be citified and to dress according to the prevailing fashions.

The wearing of modern clothing is related to barrio residence. This is more true of men than of women, as Table 51 indicates.

TABLE 51. Percentage of Men and Women Who Wear Modern Dress.

Barrio	Dresses	*Pantalones*	Shoes (Daily)
Santo Domingo	68.8	37.4	18.5
La Santísima	74.0	52.0	26.0
San Miguel	70.6	46.2	25.9
Santa Cruz	65.1	21.3	3.9
Los Reyes	70.0	17.5	1.7
San Sebastián	63.2	16.6	2.0
San Pedro	65.8	8.8	0.0

The use of dresses is almost equally distributed throughout the village, with the smaller barrios showing slightly less. In contrast, there is a sharp drop in the use of *pantalones* by men in the smaller barrios. Similarly, there are fewer people in these barrios who use shoes daily. The explanation lies principally in the fact that these barrios consist almost entirely of farmers.

Wealth and economic status is only a limited determining factor in style of clothing worn. Before the Revolution, style differences between the upper and lower economic groups were sharper. At present, although clothing is becoming more and more important as an indicator of social status, it is not necessarily an indicator of wealth. The middle economic group, which we have already noted as being the most acculturated group in Tepoztlán, tends to wear modern dress and shoes more frequently than the upper economic group. This was clearly seen in Table 46, p. 176, which attempts to correlate the wearing of shoes with the economic grouping.

The wearing of shoes relates more to the factors of age and occupation than to wealth. The lowest percentage of those wearing shoes is found among the wealthiest, Group III-B, primarily because they are all of the older generation. The largest percentage of those wearing shoes is found in Group II, which contains most of the merchants, artisans, students, and teachers.

The type and quality of clothing worn by children also depend upon age, degree

Fig. 46. A Tepoztecan artisan.

of acculturation of the family, barrio residence, and, to a greater degree than among adults, upon the family's economic status. Other factors affecting children's dress are school attendance and favoritism at home.

The younger a child is, the less effort and money is expended on his clothing and the less significance his clothing has in revealing economic status. In most families, pre-school children are not as well dressed as children who go to school. The only exception to this is the young favorite child of a better-to-do family. A favorite son may be given a little *gabán* as early as three years of age, but most boys do not receive *gabanes* until they begin to go out into the fields. A favorite girl may be given a little *rebozo* as soon as she asks for one, but generally girls receive a *rebozo* at about eight or nine. In very poor families a girl might not be given a *rebozo* until eleven or thereabouts. A favorite girl may receive a pair of gold earrings or a pair of holiday shoes at the age of two or three. Most girls do not receive these before they are fifteen; boys are given huaraches when they begin to work in the fields. Sweaters are worn by children of better-to-do families only.

Parents tend to keep their school children's clothing cleaner and in better repair. Many also make some attempt to keep children dressed in the prevailing styles for their age group. This usually means shorter, better-fitting dresses for the girls, jackets and ready-made pants for boys. (See Fig. 47.) There is also a definite trend among families with enough means to buy children's shoes for special events and school fiestas. The school now places some pressure upon parents to provide shoes for their children by forbidding the latter to join public school parades if they are barefoot. Differences in the clothing of the children of the rich and poor and of the more conservative and acculturated are becoming more marked and school children are becoming aware of the social distinctions involved. Their responses to the thematic apperception cards show school children to be particularly sensitive to clothing and to make appearance a significant aspect of their stories.

The quantity of clothing owned varies considerably from individual to individual. Even within the same family there is some variation. In general, youths and adolescent girls have the most and finest clothing, and the very young and very old have the least. In the poorest families each member may have only one dress or suit of clothing, but this is not common in Tepoztlán. Most women have at least two cotton dresses for daily wear and one rayon dress for fiestas; most men own at least four shirts, four *calzones,* and one or two pairs of huaraches. The children of the poor tend to have less than this minimum and frequently do not have special clothing for fiestas. In contrast, the middle and upper economic groups have many clothes, and among a few families there is evidence of extravagance in dress.

DIVERSION

Fiestas, both religious and secular, continue to be the main source of diversion for all groups in Tepoztlán. Every year the church calendar provides at least sixty-two important fiestas for Tepoztecans to celebrate, either as participants or observers. Not a month passes without a fiesta, and in some months there are five.

Fig. 47. Modern dress of Tepoztecan youth.

No one attends all fiestas, but all attend some. Widows and older women are known to be *muy fiestera* and habitually attend as many fiestas as possible. The very poor tend to participate in the fiestas of other barrios and other villages, whereas the well-to-do are more careful to attend the religious services held in the central church. Children especially like to attend fiestas and beg to accompany their mothers or aunts. The sharp drop in school attendance during certain fiesta times is a chronic complaint of the school. Tepoztecans also frequent the fairs of Chalma, Jiutepec, Tepalzingo, Tlayacapan, and Mazatepec. Some go to buy or sell, but others go purely for diversion.

The establishment and increasing popularity of many national and patriotic holidays are making for a new type of diversion in the village. These occasions differ from the traditional fiestas, in that they are organized by the school staff and are carried out by the children. They consist of plays, dances, recitations, speeches in explanation of the holidays, and singing of national songs. Parades of school children are also becoming familiar events during the year. These celebrations are liked and well attended, and are becoming more and more a significant part of local life. Other contributions of the school to local entertainment are occasional dances and *kermeses,* at which food and drinks are sold and games played to raise money for various school needs. These activities are enjoyed by the young people, but attendance is generally small because of the resistance of the older generation to modern ballroom dancing; they look upon it as immoral, even when supervised. The school organizes occasional excursions for the children, but since these involve some expense many parents do not permit their children to participate. A literary and dramatic group was once organized in the school, but it was short lived because of local criticism and gossip.

Perhaps the next most common form of diversion is to go to Cuernavaca on one pretext or other. On Sundays, groups of young men take the bus to Cuernavaca where they spend the day walking about, playing pool, drinking in the *cantinas,* and visiting with prostitutes. Other men go to Cuernavaca for secret rendezvous with widows or married women from Tepoztlán. Women and girls go to Cuernavaca to buy or sell things at the market and to look at the store windows. A few of the more citified girls go to Cuernavaca to attend the movies and to buy the latest fashion magazines. Although it is impossible to estimate the effect of the pressure of this small but sophisticated tourist center on Tepoztlán, it is certain that it plays a strong role in providing a source of diversion and temporary personal freedom.

Sports as a form of popular diversion are limited. The traditional cockfights are all but gone and the *jaripeo* (rustic rodeo), although still liked, is declining because of the lack of skill and interest on the part of young men. Hunting is seldom indulged in as a sport, and even less so as a source of food supply. Those who are hard pressed to earn a living find it more profitable to spend the slack seasons working as peons for others. Singing and serenading at night is still popular among young men and is a source of pleasure for most villagers.

Organized sports or games were first introduced in Tepoztlán in 1922 as a consequence of a national campaign by the Minister of Education. Baseball, soccer, basketball, and volleyball were taught by the school and had immediate appeal among the youth. From the first, soccer was most popular. In 1929 a sports club of 22 soccer players, all from the three center barrios, was organized. The popularity of the game developed slowly until 1930, when the number of enthusiasts increased sharply because of the efforts of a new school director. Between 1934 and 1936, at the time that the road was being built, there were as many as 15 soccer teams. Even the religious barrio of Santa Cruz had its team. This enthusiasm lasted for about three years. In 1939 no soccer team existed and the interest in the sport lapsed for a few years.

There are now five teams, four in the large, center barrios and one in the small barrio of Los Reyes. The teams play against each other with the traditional barrio spirit of competition. They also play against teams from Cuernavaca and other nearby towns. There is no athletic field in the village, and the center teams play in the large yard of the Cathedral while the Los Reyes team rents a field. The scarcity of level land makes it impossible to use any of the communal land, and the young men are thinking of buying a plot of land for an athletic field. The only equipment bought by the team is the ball. About half of the players own special soccer shoes; the other half play barefoot or in huaraches.[14]

The teams usually play to an audience of small boys. Adults are disinterested in games or actively disapprove of them, and parents do not permit their daughters to attend. When teams from other villages play, only a few girls from the center barrios come to watch. The skill and triumphs of the players are appreciated by a handful of people; there are no fans and there is no community spirit in connection with this sport.

In 1947, when a Cultural Mission was in Tepoztlán, there was an attempt made to stimulate wider interest in games by organizing an inter-village competition and appointing committees of *madrinas* or godmothers for each team. The *madrinas* came dressed in white and bearing flowers for each team, but the audiences remained as small as ever.

The advantages of the cooperative action involved in team playing, and the unifying effect of a strong common interest, are experienced only by the actual members of the teams. Small as this group is, their experience in cooperation is of some significance in so highly individualistic a village as Tepoztlán.

Recreational activities in Tepoztlán were further diversified with the opening of a billiard room in 1935. This was another point of conflict between the older people and the younger men of the village. The poolroom was quickly characterized as a breeding place of drunkenness and bad habits. But despite their objections, pool became popular among the boys of all the barrios. When boys began to stay out of school to play, parents forced the local administration to ban poolrooms from admitting boys under eighteen years of age. There are now two poolrooms, one with

---

[14] A professional soccer player from Mexico City admired the skill of young Tepoztecans in kicking the hard ball with their bare toes.

two tables and the other with three. Gambling has not developed to any marked degree, and consists of small occasional bets. Despite the pessimistic evaluations of the older people there is no evidence that the presence of the poolrooms has encouraged vice or has helped to develop any new bad habits. Rather it seems to have provided a harmless and much needed diversion for the young men.

Shortly after the road was built, a man from Mexico City attempted to establish a cabaret in Tepoztlán providing "hostesses," dancing, and drinking. The boys and young men responded with vigor, using such desperate methods as stealing from their parents or selling chickens to raise the necessary money. The adults were aroused and drove out the owner and his staff and have managed to prevent any such new establishments. At the present time there are two *cantinas* for drinking purposes only. Before 1926 the men of the village drank punch, pure alcohol, and *mezcal*. Since the road there has been an increase in beer and *tequila* drinking, and the "Cuba Libre" has been introduced.

Tepoztecans have always been strong drinkers, but there are fewer habitual drunkards here than in some of the surrounding villages. From 1935 to 1938 there was more drinking than there is today because alcohol was much cheaper. Within the last few years, alcohol has risen in price from 40 centavos to 5 pesos per liter. The prohibitive cost of alcohol has been responsible, in part, for the return to the use of pulque. In 1942 a *pulquería* was opened in the plaza. "Soft" drinks such as Coca-Cola, lemonade, and other carbonated drinks are also sold in the village.

In 1939, moving pictures were shown for the first time. Movie equipment was installed in the school and there were nightly performances. After one month the entrepreneur moved out because of the small attendance. Since then, there have been two or three other unsuccessful attempts. To most Tepoztecans the admission charge of 30 to 50 centavos is prohibitive.

From time to time a puppet show reaches Tepoztlán and runs for about a week. This, together with several school plays each year, comprises the theatrical entertainment. In 1943, there were no radios in Tepoztlán; their costliness and the absence of electricity ruled them out.[15] However, there are 44 victrolas in the village. Thirty of these belong to families in the three larger barrios and the others are distributed in each of the smaller ones.

In the past two years the church has endeavored to take a more active part in providing leisure-time activities for Tepoztecans. The Acción Católica has been greatly strengthened and its membership extended. Different age groups within it have separate meetings and elect officers. The activities include singing, presenting religious pageants and plays, attending funerals, celebrating saints' days, and receiving instruction in various subjects, both religious and secular. It also provides religious reading matter and organizes religious pilgrimages. Money-raising activities continue throughout the year through collections, *kermeses,* and even public dances, although the Acción has forbidden its female members to dance. Once or

---

[15] In 1948, several families owned battery-operated radios and some people were regular listeners to dramatic and humorous programs originating in Mexico City.

twice a year the Acción invites members from other villages and provides them with a banquet and special religious services.

From the point of view of its effects upon the social structure and levels of living, recent trends in entertainment have tended to make for greater differences among the various economic groups. The new forms of diversion invariably involve an expenditure of money for dues, equipment, bus fare, shoes, clothing, and appropriate food. Thus, the very poor cannot join organizations like the sports club or Acción Católica, or go to Cuernavaca or to the movies, or celebrate birthdays with invited guests. The diversions which they can most easily afford are the fiestas and fairs and they rarely partake of others. It is the middle and upper economic groups which participate most actively in the newer type of diversions.

FAMILY BUDGETS

Having considered several separate aspects of levels of living in Tepoztlán we can now turn to a comparison and analysis of a few specific family budgets as a whole.[16] How much do families actually spend on food, clothing, health, recreation, and religious activities? How does a poor family compare with a rich family on the various items? What proportion of the expenditures are for subsistence, self-improvement, or economic investment?

We have estimated the approximate annual expenditures of seven families on each of the following items: food; basic household necessities; house upkeep, repair, and tax; clothing; education; health; religion and fiestas; diversion; investments; and miscellaneous. We will present again the two families for which we have already considered food expenditures.[17] It will be recalled that Family I is in the upper economic group and is made up of the parents and two adult children. Family II is one of the poorest families in the village and includes the parents and seven children. Table 52 presents a summary of the annual expenditures of each family.

---

[16] The study of family budgets in a community like Tepoztlán is beset with many difficulties. Illiteracy is high and most Tepoztecan families are not in the habit of keeping accounts of expenditures or income. In addition, there are attitudes of reserve and even suspicion concerning this type of investigation, so that intensive budget studies can be done only where rapport is excellent. Also, as we have seen earlier, there is much seasonal variation in diet and expenditures, and the prices of many items vary a great deal during the year, so that many adjustments have to be made in arriving at an accurate annual budget. To study income and expenditure for a few weeks and then assume a weekly average and multiply by 52 would not yield accurate results in the case of Tepoztlán. Ideally the investigator should live with a family for at least a year and keep a daily account of income and expenditures for the family. In practice this is not always feasible. It seriously limits the range of data that the anthropologist can get and is very time consuming; only a few families could be studied in this manner by a single investigator. In getting the budgets presented here, a combination of the intensive and extensive approaches was used. Detailed schedules were drawn up, and daily records were kept for a few families for periods ranging from two to eight weeks. In addition, budgets were reconstructed for the preceding year by questioning of family members. In general the data on expenditures were much more satisfactory than those on incomes. Also, we found repeatedly that income was below expenditures, a common phenomenon in budget studies of low income families in rural areas in the United States.

[17] See "Diet," p. 187.

TABLE 52. Comparison of Annual Expenditures of Two Families.

Item	Family I		Family II	
	Pesos	Percentage	Pesos	Percentage
Food:				
Daily	1,686.88	28.6	564.20	56.5
Fiestas	180.00	3.1	43.65	4.3
Alcohol	—[a]	—[a]	25.00	2.5
Basic household necessities	303.28	5.2	120.64	12.1
House upkeep, repair, and tax	1,165.00	19.7	2.00	.2
Clothing	412.50	7.0	79.15	7.9
Education:				
School supplies	0	0	4.24	.4
Newspapers, magazines	26.00	.4	0	0
Health	180.00	3.0	8.24	.8
Religion and fiestas	46.80	.8	32.05	3.2
Diversion	64.80	1.1	21.80	2.0
Investments:		27.8		7.2
Purchase of animals	670.00		68.00	
Feed for animals	972.24		4.20	
Miscellaneous:	179.40	3.0	25.50	2.5
Total	5,886.90		998.67	

[a] Undetermined.

Family II spends only one-sixth as much as Family I. The way in which the money is apportioned among the various items reveals some significant differences in the level of living of these two families.

FOOD

The annual regular food expenditures were estimated from the weekly expenditure already presented (see p. 192). Family I spends almost three times more on food than Family II, but this annual expenditure represents only 29 per cent of its total expenditure, whereas that of Family II represents 56 per cent of its total.

The proportion spent by both families for fiesta meals is almost equal, being 3 per cent for Family I and 4 per cent for Family II. This is a disproportionately heavy burden for the poorer family, which normally does not spend so much on fiesta meals.[18]

---

[18] See p. 192 for fiesta meals included under irregular food expenditures.

It is to be noted that the birthday of the father was not celebrated in either family, despite the fact that it is traditionally the most important birthday. It is quite common for men past youth to forego birthday celebrations as an economy measure.

Expenditure for alcohol is an almost inevitable item in every Tepoztecan household. It was impossible to estimate this item in Family I since the family was reticent to discuss it. The father has, in recent years, begun to drink heavily, and during periods of drunkenness, has wasted considerable family funds. A conservative estimate of his expenditures on alcohol would be at least four times that of Family II. It is interesting to note that the daughter in Family I also likes to drink wine and beer with her more sophisticated friends. This is a custom she learned while in Mexico City; in Tepoztlán she and her friends indulge only in great secrecy.

In Family II only the father drinks. When he has money he drinks about 10 centavos worth of alcohol each morning.

BASIC HOUSEHOLD NECESSITIES

The articles included and the cost of each for both families are as follows:

	Family I (Pesos)	Family II (Pesos)
Soap	62.40	26.00
Charcoal	57.00	—
Wood	18.00	54.60
Kerosene	18.72	10.92
Cigarettes	43.68	7.80
Candles	43.68	18.72
Matches	7.80	2.60
Laundress	52.00	—
Total	303.28	120.64

The better-to-do family uses more soap, bathes and changes clothes more often, uses labor-saving charcoal, and has better lighting in the home. The father and son each smoke about three times more cigarettes than the father of the poor family, and the mother of the first family has the aid of a hired woman for the laundry. However, expenditures for household necessities for Family I is 5 per cent of the total, whereas for Family II it is 12 per cent.

HOUSE UPKEEP, REPAIR, AND TAX

This item provides a sharp contrast between the two families. The better-to-do family spent 1,165 pesos, or 19 per cent of its total expenditures, on improving its house; the poor family spent nothing but the 2 pesos for house tax. Family I regularly paints, whitewashes, and repairs its house; Family II has not done anything to improve its house in the past five years. The former has continually added rooms and out-buildings to the original house; the latter has lived in the same one-room house since marriage. It is one of the hopes of this family to add a room or porch, so that the older children may sleep separately from the parents and young children.

It is interesting to note that the tax for the improved house is little higher than that of the poor house. The expenditures for both families are summarized as follows:

	Family I (Pesos)	Family II (Pesos)
Roofing and remodeling three rooms	980	—
Painting one room	30	—
Whitewashing porch	20	—
New henhouse	100	—
New corncrib	30	—
House tax	5	2
Total	1,165	2

CLOTHING

Clothing takes approximately the same proportion of the total annual expenditures for both families—7 per cent for Family I and 7.9 per cent for Family II. An examination of the type and amount of clothing purchased reveals some interesting differences.

Family I	Pesos	Family II	Pesos
Entire family: cloth for making clothing	138.00	Entire family: cloth for making clothing	53.45
Father: 2 prs. huaraches at 11	22.00	Father: 1 pr. huaraches	5.00
2 sombreros	11.50	2 sombreros	5.50
		1 *gabán*	11.00
Son: 1 pr. huaraches	11.00	First son: 2 sombreros	1.65
1 pr. shoes	22.00	Second son: 1 sombrero	.90
2 sombreros	12.50	Third son: 1 sombrero	.65
1 felt hat	18.00	Infant son: cotton booties	1.00
Mother: 2 prs. shoes	20.50		
Daughter: 2 prs. shoes at 15	30.00		
2 prs. shoes at 20	40.00		
1 pr. shoes	27.00		
3 prs. stockings at 10	30.00		
2 prs. stockings at 15	30.00		
Total	412.50	Total	79.15

The cloth purchased for Family I was used to make men's shirts and pants, women's blouses and dresses, and underclothing for both. Every member of this family still has a good supply of clothing from the previous year. The cloth for Family II was used to make shirts and *calzones* for the father and first three sons. One daughter received a new dress this year because she took part in a religious program. The mother received a dress as a Mother's Day gift from the daughter who works, and the second daughter received a worn dress from the same girl. The younger daughters have worn hand-me-down dresses ever since they were born. The infant wears old clothing given by the mother's sister. All the members of this family except the father and the working daughter always go barefoot.

Shoes represent an important expenditure in Family I, particularly for the daughter, who spent more on shoes than Family II did to clothe the entire family. In the former family, the expenditure for the children exceeds that for the parents; in the latter family, the largest expenditure is for the father. There is an appreciable difference in the quality of the clothing worn by both families.

EDUCATION

The low proportion of money spent on educational materials by both families is notable. Family I no longer has children in school, but it spends a regular amount of money on newspapers and magazines which the daughter buys for the new dress styles.[19] Family II sent only two children to school in 1944.

HEALTH

In 1944, Family I had more illness than Family II. The daughter was seriously ill with typhus and required a doctor from Cuernavaca. Approximately 100 pesos were spent to cure her. The family also contributed 80 pesos to cure the ailing grandmother. Family II had no serious illness; all colds, intestinal upsets, and infections were treated with home remedies. The mother gave birth to a baby during this year and was attended by a midwife. She received fourteen massages, and the cost of these plus the delivery was 8.24 pesos.

RELIGION AND FIESTAS

Included under religious expenditures are taxes or contributions and money spent for flowers, candles, and incense. They are as follows:

Family I	Pesos	Family II	Pesos
August—Barrio fiesta	5.00	August—Fiesta of barrio of Santa Cruz	.50
		September—Fiesta of Tepozteco	.25
November—Candles for Day of the Dead	24.00	Fiesta of barrio of San Miguel	.50
March—Carnaval	10.00	November—Candles for Day of the Dead	8.00
		Flowers	.20
April—Semana Santa	3.00		
Church contributions at 40 centavos per month	4.80	December—Fiesta of Our Lady of Guadalupe	.25
		January—Fiesta of Santa María of Tepoztlán	.50
		Fiesta of Gabriel Mariaca	.10
		Candles	1.00
		Flowers	.25
		Incense	.10
		February—Day of Candelaria	.25
		Constitution Day	.50

---

[19] It should be noted, however, that this family has spent a relatively large amount on education in the past, since both the children received advanced schooling.

Family I (Cont.)		Pesos	Family II (Cont.)		Pesos
			March—Carnaval		6.00
			Fiesta of Chalma		.50
			Fiesta of Tlayacapan		.75
			Candles		.40
			April—Fiesta of Mazatepec		2.00
			Saturday of Glory		.50
			May—Fiesta of barrio of Santa Cruz		.50
			Fiesta of Ixcatepec		1.00
			June—Fiesta of barrio of La Santísima		
			Music		3.00
			Fireworks		1.00
			Bullfight		1.00
			Tax		1.75
			Candles		1.00
			Flowers		.25
	Total	46.80		Total	32.05

There is a striking difference in the religious activity of the two families. Family I gives larger contributions but to a minimum number of fiestas; only a small regular contribution of 10 centavos is made to the church every Sunday. This family does not attend or contribute to the fiestas of other barrios or villages. The religious expenditures are only .8 per cent of the total family expenditures. Fiesta celebrations are generally in the form of a special fiesta meal for the family and visitors.

In contrast, the poor family makes smaller contributions but attends about four times as many fiestas, including fiestas of other barrios and villages and those of the central church. However, this family does not generally attend church on Sunday and makes no contribution there. This family bears out the local pattern in which poor families in desperate economic circumstances eagerly support as many different fiestas as possible in the hope of obtaining the blessing and indulgence of one of the saints. A more generalized support of the central church is apparently too indirect and impersonal a way to achieve this. The religious expenditure of this family constitutes 3.2 per cent of its total annual expenditure, or proportionately four times that of Family I.

DIVERSION

Diversion other than that provided by the fiestas was as follows:

Family I		Pesos	Family II		Pesos
Movies in Cuernavaca			Fair of Jiutepec		1.00
(including bus fare)		64.80	Bus fare to visit daughter who		
			works in Cuernavaca		20.00
			Two tops and marbles for boys		.80
	Total	64.80		Total	21.80

These expenditures constitute 1 per cent and 2 per cent of total annual expenditures for Family I and Family II, respectively.

INVESTMENTS

The most common form of investment among rich and poor in Tepoztlán is the purchase of animals. In 1944, the investments of both families were as follows:

Family I	Pesos	Family II	Pesos
Purchase of cattle and other animals	670.00	Purchase of four pigs during year for 58. (Two died and two were	
Animal feed	972.24	sold for 52, resulting in a loss of 6.)	58.00
		Purchase of two chickens	10.00
		Feed for chickens for two months	4.20
Total	1,642.24	Total	72.20

The above expenditures constitute 28 per cent of the total expenditures of Family I, and 7 per cent of those of Family II.

MISCELLANEOUS

	Family I (Pesos)	Family II (Pesos)
Plow	25.00	
5 Plow-scrapers	12.50	
Dishes, *comal,* clay pots	48.00	10.25
Barbershop:		
Father and son	20.40	Father 15.25
Daughter	8.50	
Stamps	25.00	
Gifts by daughter to friends	40.00	
Total	179.40	Total 25.50

The expenditures for miscellaneous items are 3 per cent of the total expenditures for both families.

SPENDING PATTERNS

The spending patterns, indicated in the annual expenditures of these two families, can be taken as typical for the socio-economic levels which they represent. Family I, like other acculturated families in the middle and upper groups, spends relatively large proportions of its income on items connected with comfort and health, such as food, household articles, house repair, doctors, and medicines. Expenditures for clothing, birthdays, and other fiestas celebrated within the home are also comparatively large, sometimes reaching the point of conspicuous consumption. Families of this type usually spend more than other families to educate their children. Expenditures for diversion and contributions to the church and other religious activities are proportionately small. Economic investments, which represent the largest and most important expenditure among the majority of well-to-do Tepoztecan families, is, in this acculturated family, little more than one-fourth of all expenditures.

Family II, like most poor families in Tepoztlán and, indeed, everywhere else, spends most of its income on food and basic necessities. Economic investment is at a minimum. One of the striking characteristics of the expenditure of poorer families in Tepoztlán is the relatively large proportion spent on religious fiestas. In the case of Family II, more was spent on religious contributions than house upkeep, or education, or health, or diversion.

local government and politics: 10

THE MUNICIPIO OF TEPOZTLÁN is one of twenty-seven municipios of the state of Morelos. It is governed by the State Constitution of November 20, 1930, which abolished the older political divisions known as districts and established "free municipios," each with local governments to be elected by popular vote. The village of Tepoztlán is the seat of the municipal government and as such is the most important administrative and political center of the municipio.

Tepoztlán, like Mexico as a whole, has had a long and complicated political history which antedates the Spanish Conquest by many centuries. As has been noted before, Tepoztlán had experienced a number of conquests before the coming of the Spaniards and had a long history of living under political domination and an authoritarian system. The more than three hundred years of Spanish rule during the colonial period continued this tradition. In fact, Mexican independence from Spain brought very little political change for the village, and it continued to live under an authoritarian and imposed regime up to the Revolution of 1910–20.

Since 1910 political life in the village has been unusually intense, dramatic, and not without its tragic aspects. Because of its proximity to both the state and national capitals it has been particularly subject to outside political influences and has reflected state and national political trends. Almost every political current of national importance has had some repercussions in the village. The village participated in the struggle against the Huerta Uprising, and later against the Cristeros.

In the thirties the village had a Communist cell and was strongly pro-Cárdenas. Later it was in favor of Almazán and there was even talk of armed uprising when he was defeated. The Sinarquistas were also active in the village, though quite unsuccessful. And during World War II the villagers were decidedly pro-axis and anti-gringo. More recently the campaign against hoof and mouth disease again fanned anti-American sentiment, because of the widespread belief that American pressure was responsible for the killing of diseased animals. In all of this, Tepoztlán reflected national tendencies.

Local government in Tepoztlán shows many of the characteristics and problems familiar to students of Latin America, and of Mexico in particular, and presents a sorry picture. Inefficiency, irresponsibility of officials, dishonesty and graft, lack of local funds for public improvements, betrayal by leaders, widespread suspicion of the government and its motives, lack of village unity, and apathy are among the salient traits.

LOCAL GOVERNMENT

The local government is known as the *ayuntamiento* and consists of the following officers: president, *síndico procurador, regidor de hacienda,* secretary of the *ayuntamiento,* treasurer, police chief, sub-police chief, *juez menor,* secretary to the *juez menor,* and porter. In addition there are eight *ayudantes,* each representing one of the *demarcaciones* of the village. The president, *síndico, regidor,* and *juez menor* are elected by popular vote for a two-year period.[1] The other officials are appointed by the president in agreement with the *síndico* and *regidor.*

The duties of the major officials are determined by state law. The way in which the officials function depends upon their personalities. A meek president will serve only as a figurehead and allow the *síndico* and secretary to run the government. An aggressive president may in turn take over the functions of the other officials. The president is the executive officer and as such is the official representative of the village in dealings with the outside. His signature is necessary for most correspondence and official acts. He sets the fines for infractions of the law; in addition, the inhabitants often bring their private difficulties and family quarrels to him.

The *síndico* is charged with responsibility for protecting the communal resources of the municipio, that is, the lands, forests, and water resources. It is he who guards the titles to these resources. He has authority to use the local police to apprehend anyone suspected of immoderate or illegal use of communal resources. The *síndico,* together with the president, inspects the accounts of the municipio. In addition, he is responsible for the inspection of cattle before they are slaughtered to determine that they are not diseased. He must inspect the cattle brands to be sure that the cattle have not been stolen. Furthermore, he is the sub-agent of the Ministerio Público, and in this capacity acts as an attorney general, responsible for investigating all violations of the laws of the state.

The *regidor* is responsible for the financial operations of the municipio, and the treasurer serves as his assistant.

By far the greatest number of tasks falls to the secretary of the *ayuntamiento.* He is generally the most literate of the officials, and the present officeholder is a competent typist. He opens and closes the government offices six days a week, signs all correspondence, attends all public functions, maintains the records of the municipio, advises the other officers of the state law, keeps the president informed of all complaints, and attends to all complaints and requests for certifications.

The chief of police is directly responsible to the president and the entire *ayun-*

---

[1] There have also been other changes in the number of government employees. The present government organization follows the requirements of the State Constitution of 1930. From 1910–30 the state of Morelos was under military rule.

tamiento. He organizes the nightly village watch and makes arrests when necessary.

During the dry season the government offices are generally open between 9:00 A.M. to 1:00 P.M. and between 4:00 P.M. and 7:00 P.M. During the agricultural season the hours are much more irregular, and oftentimes the officials close the offices and go to their fields to plant or cultivate. The same thing happens during the harvest.

The salaries paid to officials are extremely low, even by Tepoztecan standards. They are paid a daily rate in pesos as follows:

President	3.00
Síndico	2.00
Regidor	2.00
Secretary	2.50
Treasurer	2.50
Chief of police	2.00
Assistant to chief	1.75
Porter	1.50
Judge	1.00
Secretary to judge	1.50

These low salaries are one of the factors which encourage graft on the part of the officials.

The village officials are mostly from the larger barrios of San Miguel, La Santísima, and Santo Domingo. A review of the officeholders since 1920 showed that not a single president was from San Pedro, Los Reyes, or San Sebastián. The reasons given for this are as follows: (1) the smaller barrios have traditionally been viewed as the more backward barrios and without political power; (2) residents of the small barrios say that only dishonest people seek the presidency, that they have connections with politicians in Cuernavaca, and that they have some funds for propaganda. Most of the presidents and officials between 1920 and 1943 could read and write, and included individuals who were highly acculturated and little acculturated. In 1943 all the officials wore huaraches while at work, but all could read and write.

The sources of income of the municipio are varied and are shown in the following budget for the year 1943: [2]

	Income
	(Pesos)
Traveling merchants [3]	50
Public diversions (movies) [4]	20
Slaughter of animals	2,500
Service for water	300

---

[2] These data were copied from local records and are official estimates of budget income. Generally the income is about 1,000 pesos below these estimates.

[3] The very small income obtained from traveling merchants reflects the decadence of the local market and the paucity of merchants from other areas.

[4] The municipio receives a ten per cent tax on the gross receipts from movies. The small

	Income (Cont.)
	(Pesos)
Certificates and copies	200
Charge for entries in the civil register	50
Exemption of publication of acts of the civil register [5]	700
Corral de consejo	50
Tax on cattle	300
Commercial and industrial register	200
Registration of cattle brands	200
Registration of private documents	400
Miscellaneous authorizations	50
Tax on use of the market and plaza	500
Burial permits	300
Taxes on use of communal resources	800
Payments in lieu of public service and non-specified income	1,000
Ten per cent tax on commercial and industrial enterprises	200
Income from the state	150
Income from the state and federal governments as specified by particular laws	500
Fines imposed for infractions of laws	230
Products from sale of *Bienes Mostrencos y Hallasgos de Tesoro Ocultos*	200
Gifts to the municipio	200
Total	9,200

It can be seen that almost fifty per cent of the income of the municipio is derived from four sources: the slaughter of animals, the payment of residents in lieu of working twelve days a year in public service, the exemption of publication of acts in the civil register, and taxes from the use of communal resources.

The income of the municipio over a twelve-year period from 1931 to 1943 (data for 1936 were not available) is shown as follows:

Year	Income
	(Pesos) [a]
1931	4,360.74
1932	2,586.35
1933	4,855.91

[a] The figures for 1931 are for ten months, and those for 1932 are for six months. All others are for a twelve-month period.

___

income from this source indicates how rarely movies or other public entertainment comes to the village.

[5] According to state law, marriages and other acts recorded in the register should be officially announced by posted notices in the *ayuntamiento* and in the official government bulletin. But Tepoztecans shun this kind of publicity and by paying a special fee can avoid it. The same thing occurs in relation to the reading of the marriage banns by the priest. By special payment this also can be avoided.

Year	Income (Pesos)
1934	4,011.80
1935	3,742.60
1936	—
1937	5,162.49
1938	4,795.75
1939	6,494.70
1940	7,088.58
1941	6,467.74
1942	7,617.03
1943	7,568.99

Since the salaries of the officials amounted to over seven thousand pesos per year (during the forties), it is obvious that there was little money left over for public improvements. This is one of the demoralizing factors in local government and also one of the reasons that the Tepoztecans generally look to the federal government for help. Each president who enters office promises to do something for his pueblo. But he soon learns that there are no funds, not to mention the other difficulties. To make matters worse, many villagers are convinced that the local government officials, especially the president, *síndico, regidor,* and secretary, are dishonest and have a large income from illegal dealings. But this does not deny the fact that the official income is much too meager for any significant public works program with local funds.

It will be noted that the municipio has practically no income from land taxes. Most of the taxes on land goes to the state government. The state government collected over sixty thousand pesos in taxes in the twelve years between 1931 and 1943 for which data are available.[6] During this entire period the only state funds which went back to the village were for the salary of the state tax collector who was paid on a pro rata basis.

The taxes which go to the federal government are considerably smaller than those which go to the state. Federal taxes taken out of Tepoztlán are shown in the following:

Year	Pesos
1938	2,529.86
1939	2,455.04
1940	—
1941	3,118.99
1942	3,794.55
1943	3,568.77

The routine business of the local government consists primarily of issuing permits for various types of activities. The most frequent requests include the following:

Permits for fiestas, religious and secular
Permits for slaughter of animals

---

[6] These data were obtained from the official state tax records in Cuernavaca.

Permits to utilize municipal resources: to cut wood, pasture
  animals, and gather stones
Requests for certifications of birth, death, and marriage
Requests to register brands on cattle
Requests for marriage licenses
Permits to repair streets
Requests for *ejido* plots
Permits to pipe water to a house from the main line
Permits to dynamite rock

In addition to these routine functions, the local government, through the office of the *juez menor,* hears many complaints and quarrels. Complaints are usually first presented to the president, and he attempts to resolve the difficulty without recourse to the judge. The complaints most frequently heard by the president are given in the order of their frequency of occurrence.

Quarrels between neighbors about family matters
Litigations between neighbors over property matters
Quarrels due to drunkenness
Quarrels between neighbors over animals
Quarrels between husbands and wives
Quarrels because of damages caused by animals
Cases involving accusations of stealing of animals
Cases involving assault
Cases involving calumny
Charges of immorality
Fraud
Infanticide

When the quarrel cannot be settled by the president, it is passed on to the local judge, and occasionally Tepoztecans are jailed. An analysis of the records of the local justice for 1920, 1927, 1935, 1941, 1942, and 1943 revealed the types and frequency of cases shown in Table 53.

The thing to be noted about these data is the relatively high incidence of crime. An analysis of the relative frequency of each type of case shows that five offenses—robbery, lesions and blows, injuries and threats, calumny or defamation, and damages—account for 73 per cent of the 808 cases recorded. It must be remembered that these data are only for reported cases. A large number of cases never reach the judge.

POLITICAL HISTORY

As has been noted earlier, recent archaeological work in Tepoztlán shows a continued occupation of some sites since the Archaic period.[7] This would place the age of these sites at about the time of Christ. The early ceramic horizons show eastern and southern influences, and the later horizons show northern influences from

---

[7] Muller, *Chimalacatlan,* p. 55. See also Appendix B, p. 453.

TABLE 53. Criminal Offenses, During Six Selected Years.

Criminal Offense	1920	1927	1935	1941	1942	1943	Total
Robbery	9	20	11	14	18	14	86
Homicide	3	2	1	2	2	..	10
Lesions and blows	17	44	38	39	20	34	192
Fraud	2	3	..	1	1	3	10
Rape (or elopement)	2	2	2	2	3	2	13
Injuries and threats	3	31	45	26	40	55	200
Breaking into a house	3	16	13	6	9	10	57
Abuse of authority	..	1	..	1	1	2	5
Trespass	..	3	..	7	5	2	17
Calumny or defamation	..	8	12	13	10	17	60
Damages	..	17	12	11	8	12	60
Plunder or spoilation	1	3	5	4	..	8	21
Adultery	1	6	2	2	2	1	14
Seduction	2	5	3	3	..	..	13
Violation (sexual)	..	5	1	1	..	..	7
Arson	..	2	1	..	..	1	4
Assault	..	..	3	1	2	5	11
Abandonment	..	2	4	9	3	..	18
Scandal	..	2	..	..	..	..	2
Aggression	..	1	1	..	2	..	4
Helping a criminal	..	1	..	..	..	..	1
Falsification of documents	..	1	..	..	..	..	1
Bigamy	..	..	..	1	..	..	1
Kidnapping	..	..	..	1	..	..	1
Total	43	175	154	144	126	166	808

Teotihuacán and also from Cholula. This agrees in a general way with the historical reconstructions based on the early chroniclers for this area. Wigberto Jiménez Moreno has suggested [8] that Tepoztlán was probably one of the places settled by the earliest Nahua invaders who entered the Morelos region from Guerrero and the southeast, perhaps in the seventh century, after having come from the north. According to Orozco y Berra, the early Toltecs passed through Cuauhnahuac or Cuernavaca in VIII Acatl or 603 A.D.[9] However, more recent historians place the earliest recorded invasion of the present region of Morelos in the tenth century.

Mixcoatl, the founder of the Toltec Empire, invaded the valley of Mexico about 900 A.D. and the valley of Morelos in 902 A.D.[10] Mixcoatl led a Nahua horde which came into contact with the Mazahua-Otomies with whom they mixed. According to Jiménez Moreno, Mixcoatl had a son by a Tepoztecan woman. This son, Ce Acatl Topiltzin, was born in the year 935 A.D. by the Mixteco calendar, or 947 A.D. by the Nahua calendar, the same year that his father, Mixcoatl, was assassinated by paternal relatives who were Chichimeca. Jiménez Moreno identifies Topiltzin as

---

[8] In personal communications to the writer.

[9] Manuel Orozco y Berra, *Historia Antigua de la Conquista de México,* 3 (Mexico City, 1880), 24.

[10] Florencia Muller, *La Historia Vieja del Estado de Morelos.* (Unpublished thesis, p. 151.) See also, Alberto Ruz Lhuillier, *Guía Arqueológica de Tula* (Mexico, 1945), p. 12. Introduction by Wigberto Jiménez Moreno.

the legendary hero, Tepoztecatl, who fought against Zochicalco and then adopted the worship of the god Quetzalcoatl. Topiltzin then went north to avenge the death of his father. It was he who transferred the Toltec capital from Colhuacan to Tula.[11] The Toltecs held power until 1168 when their ruler Huemac was defeated. But Toltec groups continued on, and not until their defeat by the Chichimecas in 1246 was the Toltec empire smashed.[12] In 1296 the conquest of the valley of Morelos by the Chichimecas began.

From the fall of the Toltec Empire until 1437 we have no references to Tepoztlán. In historical references to the first Aztec domination of the valley of Morelos by Acamapichtli in 1375, Cuauhnahuac, Mazatepec, Xochitepec, Zacatepec, Xiutepec, and Chiautla are mentioned as conquered towns, but not Tepoztlán.[13] Since Tepoztlán was still an independent seigniory at the time, this seems significant. Oaxtepec which continued to be inhabited by Xochimilca was also not conquered.[14] Again in 1386 when the peoples of what is now Morelos joined against the Matla-zincas, Tepoztlán is not mentioned. Similarly, in the second Aztec invasion of the valley of Morelos by Huitzilhuitl, there is no reference to Tepoztlán in the list of conquered tribes.[15] The first notice of the Aztec domination of Tepoztlán is in 1437 when Moctezuma Ilhuicamina took Oaxtepec, Yautepec, Tepoztlán, Yecapixtla, and Totolapa.[16]

The Codex Aubin-Goupil tells that in 1487 new "kings" were installed in Cuauhnahuac, Tepoztlán, Huaxtepec, and Xilotepec.[17] Finally, the glyphs on the ruined temple just above the village shows the name of Ahuitztol, an Aztec war chief, who ruled about 1502.[18]

From the above data it appears that by the time of the Spanish Conquest, Tepoztlán had been subject to Aztec domination for less than one hundred years.[19] It was

---

[11] Muller, *La Historia Vieja*, p. 155; and Jiménez Moreno in Lhuillier's *Guía Arquelógica*, p. 14.

[12] Jiménez Moreno, in Lhuillier's *Guía Arquelógica*, p. 14.

[13] Muller, *La Historia Vieja*, p. 168.

[14] Fernando de Alva Ixtlixochitl, *Obras Históricas*, I (Mexico, 1891), 141.

[15] Muller, *La Historia Vieja*, p. 167.

[16] *Ibid*, p. 168; see also Redfield, *Tepoztlán*, p. 23.

[17] Redfield, *Tepoztlán*, p. 24. He bases this on Edward Seler's statement in his article, "Die Tempelpyramide von Tepoztlán," *Globus*, LXXIII, No. 8 (Feb., 1898), 123-29.

[18] *Ibid.*

[19] Redfield, probably following Plancarte, identified the Tepoztecans at the time of the Conquest as members of the Tlahuica, one of the seven tribes which invaded the valley of Mexico and Morelos. The other tribes were the Xochimilca, Chalca, Tepaneca, Acolhua, Tlax-calteca, and Azteca. Redfield wrote, "Tepoztlán was a *pueblo* of the Tlahuica, one of the last Náhuatl speaking tribes that made up the last immigration south to the plateau region before the coming of the Spaniards." *Ibid.*, p. 23. This would make Tepoztecans relatively recent residents of Morelos and does not agree with other data. It should be noted that the Dominican Padre Durán lists Tepoztlán as one of the Xochimilca tribes and he places the Xochimilca as the first Nahua group to enter the valley of Mexico and later spill over into Morelos. (Fray Diego Durán, *Historia de las Indias de Nueva España y las Islas de Tierra Firme*, I (Mexico, 1867), 9-11.) According to Durán the Xochimilcas entered the valley of Mexico a few hundred years before the Tlahuicas. This identification of Tepoztlán with the Xochimilcas would perhaps be more consistent with the tradition of the constant warfare between Tepoztlán and Cuernavaca, since the latter was clearly of Tlahuica affiliation.

probably a semi-autonomous seigniory and occupied a position on a par with Cuernavaca, Yautepec, Xiutepec, Yecapixtla and Hauxtepec. However, under the later Moctezuma, Tepoztlán was for administrative purposes part of the district of Huaxtepec.

Tepoztlán submitted to the conquering troops of Cortés in 1521. Cortés passed through Tepoztlán on his way to Cuernavaca from Yautepec. He set fire to half the town because some Yautepec chieftains who were seeking refuge in the town would not give themselves up. Cortés and his troops stayed in Tepoztlán for only a day. Bernal Díaz del Castillo wrote of this, "There we found many pretty women and much loot." [20] Later, by decree of June 6, 1529, Tepoztlán was one of the four villas granted to Cortés and became part of the Marquesado del Valle de Oaxaca. When Cortés decided to make Cuernavaca the capital of his large estate, Tepoztlán became subject to the corregidor of Cuernavaca. The Spanish Conquest resulted in a marked change in the relative status of the former towns of this area, with Cuernavaca overshadowing Tepoztlán. This change probably began earlier, immediately after the Aztec conquest of Cuernavaca.

Information on political life and local government during the colonial period is scant. We know that the Spanish administrative machinery was set up in Tepoztlán very soon after the Conquest, probably about 1535, and that Tepoztlán was subject to the corregidor of Cuernavaca and the entire administrative machinery of the *audiencia* and the *repartimiento* system. In government as in other aspects of the culture, we find the tendency for the village to change slowly and in one way or another to modify rather than discard its pre-Conquest institutions. In documents of 1551,[21] the earliest one available for Tepoztlán, the major officials enumerated are the *gobernador,* three *alcaldes,* two *principales, tequitlatos,* and *calpisques.* The latter three terms undoubtedly refer to officials who held some office in the pre-Conquest administrative organization of the village. The *tequitlatos* were probably those who supervised field work; and the *calpisques* were the tax collectors.

The next significant document is for 1575,[22] eight years after the Crown had taken over the Marquesado del Valle, including Tepoztlán. This document gives the more important officials and the salaries paid to them in pesos, as follows:

1	*gobernador*	50
2	*alcaldes*	30
6	*regidores*	55
2	*mayordomos*	20

Here we find a total of eleven officials receiving 155 pesos annually. In addition, a maximum of fifty persons were employed as church singers, cooks, gardeners, laborers, and stone cutters, at a rate of two pesos each, totaling one hundred pesos a year.

[20] Bernal Díaz del Castillo, *The Conquest of New Spain,* as quoted in Redfield, *Tepoztlán,* p. 26.
[21] *Hospital de Jesús,* Leg. 289, No. 100.
[22] *Indios,* Vol. 1, Exp. 31.

Another document written four years later gives the fullest account we have of the officials and the political organization of the village.[23] This document lists the same officials as the one of 1575, but in addition lists many others, including the church officials. The document reveals clearly the integration of church and state, and is interesting in that it reveals the existence of a remarkably large government bureaucracy, certainly when compared with present conditions in the village.

From the latter part of the sixteenth century until the nineteenth century we have little data on political history in Tepoztlán. Before the Revolution, from about 1880 to 1910, Tepoztlán was governed by local *caciques* who held power with the aid and support of the Díaz regime. Older informants remember back to the time of the *cacique* Felipe Gómez, who was the president of the municipio for a number of years beginning about 1880. Tradition has it that Gómez was dictatorial. He sold wood from the communal lands to the neighboring haciendas and pocketed the money. He prevented the Tepoztecans from opening *tlacolol* and from producing charcoal for sale. Those who protested were recruited into the army or sent to the penitentiary, Quintana Roo. Finally the villagers rose against him and he was murdered in his house, which was in the center of the village where the new school now stands.

Gómez was followed by Vicente Ortega, a famous *cacique* who was in office from about 1887 to 1910. It was during his regime that the Wells Fargo Company built the Mexico City–Cuernavaca Railroad which runs through the municipio. The coming of the railroad led to much internal tension in the village; it was opposed by Tepoztecans who accused Ortega and the government in power of selling out to the gringos. It is said that Ortega received one peso for each tree cut down by the railroad workers, and that much of the income enriched him. However, it must be noted that this money was also utilized for public improvements in the village. The water pipeline was put in in 1902, the Palacio Municipal was built a few years earlier, the market place was improved, and oil lamps were set up on the main street to provide night lighting.

During the Ortega regime, in 1893, there was a small and abortive attempt to overthrow him. The story of this incident is told in the autobiography of one of my informants and is here paraphased.

In 1893 a man by the name of Canuto Neri, of the state of Guerrero, headed a small armed uprising against the Díaz government. A Tepoztecan, Roberto Ibarra, sympathized with the movement and sought to enlist support for it in the village. He managed to recruit twenty men who met secretly and Ibarra was made a colonel. Three nights later they started the rebellion by shooting off their guns in the plaza and crying "Death to Vicente Ortega." However, Ortega was not frightened. He armed his servants and waited for the rebels to come for him. But the insurrectionists were frightened and went home. Colonel Ibarra, however, left for the town of Tlayacapan to see his *compadre* Quiroz, who was also in the plan for the uprising and had the rank of general. Ibarra related

---

[23] *Ibid.,* Exp. 252. See Chapter 4, "Economics: General Aspect and Historical Background," p. 92, for the officials listed in this document.

what had happened and Quiroz asked many questions, getting the names of each of the rebels. Then Quiroz felt a sudden pride in being able to tell the government, so he called Yautepec and asked them to send troops saying, "Come here quickly for here is the *pájaro de cuenta* (culprit)." Meanwhile Quiroz entertained Colonel Ibarra and had his wife serve a meal. Two hours later the troops arrived and surrounded the house. Quiroz then said, "Compadre, we are besieged. When you came in someone must have seen you and informed the government." Then Ibarra gave himself up.

Ortega voluntarily retired from public life and was followed by a triumvirate consisting of Demetrio Rojas, José Donaciano Navarrette, and Don Pedro Mesa. This group took over the responsibility for the administration of the communal resources and were most unpopular because of their refusal to permit Tepoztecans the use of the communal lands.

The first serious threat to the dominant position of the *caciques* in the village occurred in 1909, just on the eve of the Revolution. The occasion was the contest for state governor. The Díaz candidate Escandón was opposed by Patricio Leyva. The village divided and a Comité Liberal Tepozteco was formed with Leyva as its candidate. The leaders of the pro-Leyva group were Refugio Sánchez, Esequiel Labastida, and Bernabel Labastida, all of whom were later to become Zapatistas. The slogan of Leyva was "Down with Porfirio Díaz." Demetrio Rojas imprisoned Bernabel Labastida and had him sent to Quintana Roo on what informants say were trumped-up charges of robbery. In addition, they had the support of two Tepoztecans who had been living in Mexico City since 1901, Tranquilino Hernández of the barrio of Santo Domingo, and Carlos Ortiz Rojas of La Santísima. The men were members of the Typographical Union of Mexico City and had helped found the Confederación Regional de Obreros Mexicanos, known as CROM, one of the first Mexican labor organizations. These two Tepoztecans later played an important role in the political life of the village during the twenties.

Escandón won the governorship, and apparently the Díaz regime was in. But suddenly in 1910 the Revolution broke out in the north and it was not long before it started up in Morelos. It should be noted in this connection that Tepoztlán was one of the first places in the state of Morelos to join the Revolution.

Few villages in Mexico have suffered more than Tepoztlán during the Revolution. In February, 1911, more than a year before Zapata's call for revolt in Morelos, Tepoztlán was liberated from the rule of the local *caciques* and the Díaz days were over. The village was the scene of repeated invasions, first by rebel troops and then by government forces. From the start the villagers' sympathies were with the rebels. The promise of land was a great appeal, but for a time the Tepoztecans attempted to continue their normal routines and remain neutral in the impending struggles. This was impossible, since neither the Zapatistas nor the Federales would have it that way.

The Zapatistas recruited soldiers and demanded services from the villagers, just as did the Carrancistas later on. The difference, however, was that most of the villagers helped the former voluntarily but were forced to help the latter. As a rule the Zapatista forces rarely were stationed in the village for more than a few days at a time since they were guerrilla fighters.

The Federales, on the other hand, set up troops whenever they could hold the village. Tepoztecans suffered at the hands of both the rebels and the government forces. Cattle were killed off, corn was requisitioned, women raped. Most informants attribute to the Carrancistas the greatest brutalities. Because of the pro-rebel sympathies of Tepoztecans, the government forces on a number of occasions carried off hundreds of Tepoztecan men and women as hostages to Cuernavaca and Mexico City. Tepoztecans were suspected of secretly helping the Zapatista forces, and by removing the women to Cuernavaca the government prevented them from making tortillas for the rebels. Moreover, the village was partially burned by Federales in 1912, 1913, and 1914.

By 1915 the village was in the hands of the Carrancistas, but then the Zapatista counter-offensive began and Tepoztlán again changed hands. During 1914, 1915, and 1916 the villagers fled to the *cerros* and lived there for as long as six months at a time. The men would sometimes steal back to the village to pick up some fruit or supplies and to bury their dead.

During 1916 Tepoztlán suffered a severe typhoid epidemic, thought to have been brought by the Carrancista troops. It was not until 1918 that the fighting was definitely over.

The history of the Revolution in Tepoztlán demonstrates a fundamental lack of unity among the people. Within the first few months after the revolt began, some of the ablest Tepoztecan rebel leaders had killed off one another and the village was left with no leadership. Only a handful of Tepoztecans understood the ideals of the Zapata movement and were motivated by them. Most Tepoztecans, though attracted by the promises that they would be given the lands of the neighboring haciendas, joined the conflict only when it was absolutely necessary in terms of self-defense. Were it not for the terrible abuses of the Federales it is probable that most Tepoztecans would have remained neutral.

In getting accounts of the Revolution from informants we found that many, particularly the women, had only the vaguest notion of what the Revolution was about. The following excerpts paraphrased from the life stories of informants give some of the details of life during the difficult days of the Revolution:

At first I gave little attention to the beginning of the Revolution. I saw soldiers, Federales, in the Palacio Municipal. They seemed alarmed and on the alert. They wore black hats with pompoms. I asked my father what this all meant and he told me the Revolution was coming. And so it came to pass. In February or March of 1911 Gabriel Tepepa and Lucio Moreno, the latter from the village of Gabriel Mariaca, entered the village at the head of troops. There was no battle. All I heard were cries, "Viva Madero," "Viva la Virgen de Gaudalupe." Then the people in my barrio were alarmed and little groups began to form to ask what was happening. I learned that the Revolution had begun and that they had burned the documents in the municipal archives. They looked for the *caciques* but could not find them, for they had heard the attack on the Palacio and had fled. The revolutionaries then broke into the *cacique* houses and ransacked them. Lucio

Moreno and Tepepa were here only one day; they just passed through. They were guerrilla fighters and left for the *cerros*. Although the *cacique* families had fled there were no demonstrations in the village. Everyone remained silent.

The trouble really began when my uncle, the brother of my mother, Bernabel Labastida of the barrio of San Miguel, entered the village a short while after Moreno. He found Moreno in power here. Moreno had established his headquarters behind the *cerro* Chicuasemac. Labastida had returned to take vengeance upon the *caciques* who had sent him to Quintana Roo. When he found that they had gone he sought out the brother of one of them, a Cresenciano Guzmán, and executed him. He also killed Jesús Mora.

At this time the greater part of the villagers was behind the rebels. Many joined up with them. The rebels put guards at three points—Chalchi, Huilotepec, and Celotzin, all dominating *cerros*. It was the duty of the *pacíficos* to take turns at watching. Two men were put at each of the three points. They were to signal the approach of troops by setting off an explosion. The rebels had 50-calibre Remingtons, 44-calibre rifles, and a few U. S. Winchesters. Some had their own *escopetas de pistón* in which they had to pack powder for each shot. Some had 38-calibre pistols.

The first attack came in Gabriel Mariaca about April when Patricio Leyva tried to enter the village at the head of Federal troops. He was met by his old friend Labastida, who now opposed him. Leyva and his troops got into the church. The battle lasted all afternoon. Meanwhile the villagers went up to the top of Chalchi to watch the battle. It was obvious that they sympathized with the rebels, for they wore red serapes as if to indicate that they wanted blood. The Federales retreated during the night.

Labastida had his headquarters on the site of Tlatlocapan just above the barrio of San Pedro on the outskirts of the village. On May 11 he imprisoned José Gómez and planned to have him executed. The Gómez family complained to Lucio Moreno. Moreno came to see Labastida with the idea of assassinating him because of the excesses he was committing. The two leaders met and shot one another. Thus both leaders of the Revolution in Tepoztlán were killed within the first few months. Teófolo Martínez was named head of both groups of troops. But Martínez was not a Tepoztecan and he fell out with Refugio Sánchez, another Tepoztecan leader. Martínez wanted to elope with the daughter of Refugio and when Refugio protested he was arrested by Martínez. Tepoztecans came to his aid and killed Martínez.

About ninety per cent of the troops defending the village were Tepoztecans. In all there were about 200 armed men. But when the battles began the *pacíficos* were expected to help. The *ayudantes* from each of the *demarcaciones* of the village collected tortillas twice a day in large sacks and carried them to the soldiers. Most women gave the tortillas voluntarily. Only the families of the *caciques* were against the rebels. Many women went to the church to pray for the rebels. The rebel generals ordered the citizens to cut poles, light them, and group together in large numbers on the *cerros* to give the enemy the impression of a large army.

In 1912 Federal troops took the village and set up their headquarters in the church. In March of this year the Zapatistas attacked.

In 1914 and 1915 there were people in the village under the control of the Zapatistas. At the end of 1914 most of the people left for the *cerros*. In 1915 and also in 1916 there was much planting. But in September, 1916, almost all of the population left for the *cerros*.

In March, 1916, the Carrancistas came and we escaped. We went to Jiutepec, my father and I. I feared they might get us. Some took up arms to defend themselves. We heard some women say that the Carrancistas were not molesting the *pacíficos* so we went back to Santa Catarina to learn more about true conditions. We heard that all we had to do was to show a white flag. We did, with our three animals. At about the place of the present kilometer 16 on the road, we were stopped. They wanted to take our animals but we pleaded and they let us go. When we got back to the village we found that a couple were living in our house. The man was a sub-lieutenant of the Carrancistas. This helped us very much for at that time the Carrancistas were compelling the people to work as forced laborers.

Formerly, in the time of Zapatismo we had paper money and lots of bills but we couldn't buy anything. Prices were high. A small piece of soap cost 60, 70 pesos. A plate of soup cost three pesos. Silver was scarce. In 1912 and 1913 there was still some silver but by 1914 and 1915 paper money ruined confidence and prices soared. But in 1916 with the Carrancistas there was a great change. Money was recognized by the government and prices went down. In 1914-15 there was a commercial blockade of Morelos and that is why prices went up.

The Carrancistas paid well at first for any work done, and trade again flourished in the village. For a while the blockade was over. But by June the situation again changed. General Marino and Timoteo Sánchez were among those who broke the Carrancista line and put up their headquarters in nearby Tlayacapan. And the Zapatistas began their successful counter-offensive. In August, 1916, the Zapatistas took over the village, but left after one day.

From March to early July of 1916 things were bad in the village. Julio Quiroz was the president and he tyrannized all the Zapatistas. Jesús de Mesa was the secretary. There was a great typhoid epidemic. They buried about ten a day. Our business [making coffins] increased. We thought the Carrancistas brought the epidemic. On August 16 the Zapatistas killed many Carrancistas and the local government fled.

After the successful Zapatista attack of August, Tepoztecans went to the Carrancista governor of the state of Morelos, General Dionesio Carrión, to ask for guarantees for the village because the Carrancista soldiers who came in after a successful attack were killing peaceful citizens.

Gabriel Rojas was appointed as president of the municipio, and my father was secretary for a while. But then the Zapatistas attacked and now they remained in the Chalchi Cerro while the Carrancista troops occupied the Cerro del Tepozteco and Cuaiyolwalotzin. Now the village was caught in the crossfire of the battle. The Carrancistas kept using artillery against the Zapatistas who held their fire.

We fled to the Cerro de Cematzin on the side of the Zapatistas. We were there two days. The Carrancistas climbed Chalchi and began to fire on the *pacíficos*. Again we fled to a cave. We had no tortillas. We feared the Carrancistas were encircling us. We fled to the Cerro de Barriga del Plata, then to the Cerro de Algodonar. Now it was dark and we entered the *texcal* area towards Amatlán. We ate some green corn and I became ill with fever. We ate only *guayavas* and *calabazas* that we found. Since the situation looked very bad we decided we might better go to Cuernavaca. (During this time my mother was in the village with the other children.) We entered Cuernavaca at night. My father carried me half of the way.

In February of 1917 the Carrancistas left the village and the Tepoztecans began to return from the *cerros* and nearby villages where they were dispersed. We were left without animals and in complete poverty.

By 1919 the state of Morelos began to be pacified. The state governor appointed Jesús Monroy, a non-Tepoztecan and a military man, to serve as president of the municipio of Tepoztlán. Monroy called meetings of the populace and advised them that the time of civil war and recriminations was over and they must now attempt to normalize their lives and rebuild village life. But work was scarce because of the destruction of the neighboring haciendas during the war years. Monroy therefore organized the Tepoztecans into brigades, gave them axes, and paid them a daily wage for cutting down the forests and making charcoal which he sold. At first Tepoztecans cooperated but soon this led to bitter resentment, for the communal forest resources were being depleted and this was the only wealth the village had. Indeed, the political history of the village for the next twenty years centered on the issue of the preservation of the communal resources. On the whole the ex-Zapatistas led the group favoring the conservation of this resource, while the sons of the former *caciques* led the group in favor of the continued exploitation of these resources.

To understand the political developments in the village we must turn briefly to Mexico City where an organization called Colonia Tepozteco was formed. This was an organization of Tepoztecans who had left the village before or during the Revolution. The organizers were Don José Donaciano Rojas, Mariano Rojas, Jesús Conde, and Pablo García. The aims of the organization were to be purely cultural and non-political. They were to work for the elimination of illiteracy, the preservation of the native Náhuatl, the development of a broad civic interest among Tepoztecans, and finally, "To take a direct interest, moral and practical, in the designation of the local authorities of the pueblo, so as to realize the aspiration of the Colonia." [24]

The first important act of the Colonia was to get the governor of the state of Morelos to substitute a Tepoztecan, José Oliveros, then living in Mexico City, as the president of the municipio. But the Colonia did nothing to stop the large-scale production of charcoal. This led to a split within the ranks of the Colonia as well as among the villagers. Carlos Ortiz and Tranquilino Hernández, members of the Colonia, began to form an opposition group. These men were socialistically minded and urged upon the Colonia Tepozteco that they concentrate their efforts on the economic problems of the village. As a first step they demanded the preservation of the communal forest resources. When the Colonia turned down their plan, Ortiz and Hernández resigned and accused the organization of attempting to re-establish the old social system based upon *cacique* rule.

Meanwhile, in early 1922 a group of Tepoztecans led by Dimas Martínez of the barrio of La Santísima organized a group of about thirteen Tepoztecans. They pro-

[24] Redfield, *Tepoztlán*, p. 210.

tested to the president of the local government against the continued depletion of the forest resources. When the president paid no attention to their demands they went directly to the governor of the state, José G. Parres. Parres had himself been a revolutionary and a sympathizer of Zapata. He advised them to form a peasant organization. Upon this advice, and with the prompting of Carlos Ortiz and Tranquilino Hernández of Mexico City, they formed the Unión de Campesinos Tepoztecos. The Unión began to organize the peasants in the smaller and poorer barrios of the village, Santa Cruz, San Sebastián, and San Pedro.[25] When they gained some strength they openly joined the CROM and thereafter were called "Bolsheviki" by their political opponents in the village. The village was now clearly divided into two factions, the Bolsheviki vs. the Centrales. The former was led primarily by ex-Zapatistas, the latter by the sons of the ex-*caciques*. The main slogans of the Bolsheviki were "Conserve the Communal Resources" and "Stop the Exploitation of the Forests."

The Bolsheviki now openly used the red and black flag of the CROM as their emblem and began to organize demonstrations in the village. They went as a group to the office of the president to protest the continued depletion of the forests. The president jailed the leaders for a few days and then sent them on to Cuernavaca. An informant, a leader in the Bolsheviki, described the incident as follows:

We marched to Cuernavaca in perfect formation holding aloft the red and black flag which was our emblem. As we entered Cuernavaca we shouted in unison, "Arriba los huarachudos!" "Abajo los caciques!" [Up with the wearers of huaraches! Down with the *caciques*!] "Abajo los aristócratas! Arriba la CROM." [Down with the aristocrats. Up with the CROM.] This yelling of slogans continued until we reached the palace of the governor where we were jailed on charges of sedition for having raised the red and black flag in the municipal building. After some days we were released from jail through the efforts in Mexico City of Ortiz and Hernández. At once we bought cloth to make a new flag. Then we formed a column and marched back to Tepoztlán. At the entrance of the village near the Cerro del Tesoro, we were joined by about a hundred sympathizers and we all marched through the streets of the village shouting our slogans. In this fashion we passed by the offices of the presidency and insulted the president. But he only shut the door. Soon our demonstration was over. The next day we accompanied the delegate from the CROM, who had been with us, to the railroad at El Parque. In his farewell address he advised us strongly against violence.

Encouraged by their release from Cuernavaca and the attitude of the governor, the Unión de Campesinos Tepoztecos grew in numbers and influence and soon succeeded in having the acting president deposed and one of their own men installed. But no sooner was their own man in office when the Centrales organized a delegation to the governor and returned with new instructions deposing the Bolsheviki president. This struggle went on all through 1922 and 1923, during which time nine local governments fell.

---

[25] The Bolsheviki, like the church, used the barrio rather than the *demarcación* as the unit for their organization.

In 1923 the national presidential campaign for Calles began and the Unión, under the guidance of Ortiz and Hernández, backed Calles. But the revolt of Huerta against Obregón occurred at this time, and Ortiz and Hernández came to Tepoztlán to organize the village against Huerta. The Hernández brothers of Tepoztlán, ex-Zapatistas, joined the troops of Don Genova de la O, head of operations in the state of Morelos for the Obregón forces. Ortiz obtained about fifty 30-30 rifles for the Hernández brothers and other active members of the Unión who were anti-Huerta. The Huerta revolt was put down and the Unión became stronger in the village.

In 1924, 1925, 1926, and 1927, the Unión succeeded in having its slate of candidates elected to the local government. It was during the term of office of Rafael Gutiérrez that the Bolsheviki revived the village *cuatequitl,* which had not functioned since the pre-Revolution days, and built the public washing places, improved the market places, and paved many streets.

In the latter part of 1926 the Cristeros entered Tepoztlán but were repulsed by Tepoztecans who were organized by the Hernández brothers. This increased the prestige of the Bolsheviki in the village, but their domination was not to last long. Toward the latter part of 1927 the Centrales became active politically and were armed by the newly appointed head of operations for the state of Morelos, Juan Domínguez. Now both village factions had arms. In December of 1927 the Hernández brothers of Tepoztlán declared themselves in rebellion against the local authorities. At this point some of the Bolsheviki members of the local government fled to Mexico City.

The Centrales, led by Juan Hidalgo, now organized armed defense corps known as the Defensa Social and the village was again in the throes of a minor civil war. The Hernández brothers and their followers had many sympathizers in the village. They killed Valentín Ortiz, whom they considered a *cacique* and therefore an enemy.

In February of 1928 on the day of the Carnaval, the Hernández brothers entered the village masked as *chinelos* and carrying arms under their robes. The corps of the Defensa Social, who were on guard and armed, were taken completely by surprise. The rebels disrobed and opened fire, seeking to kill the leaders of the opposition. But in the struggle many innocent men, women, and children were killed. The casualties at the end of that day were twenty-two dead and about twenty-four wounded. With this massacre the Unión de Campesinos Tepoztecos came to an end. Carlos Ortiz and Tranquilino Hernández kept out of the state of Morelos for a long while, and within a few years three of the Hernández brothers were tracked down and shot by government forces. The remaining two were shot by relatives of the victims of the massacre of 1928.

In 1929, under the leadership of Luis Quiroz, the Unión made a come-back in the form of a new organization known as the Fraternales. A meeting of about forty Tepoztecans was held in the school and an organization called the Unión Fraternal de Campesinos Tepoztecos was formed. Its slogan was "Union, Justice, and Civilization." It had two major projects: first, the building of a road to join the village to Cuernavaca, and second, the preservation of the forests. The road building project tended to unite the village temporarily although opposition to the idea was not lacking, especially from owners of mules who feared the road would hurt their business. But the Fraternales were less successful in their attempt to preserve the forests.

In 1930, Tepoztecans organized the Cooperativa Forestal Central de Tepoztlán for the purpose of producing charcoal. The story of this cooperative deserves to be told in detail, because it reflects so clearly the schisms and conflicting interests in the village. The story given here was obtained from leaders of the cooperative and leaders of the opposition group, the Fraternales. In addition, documents and reports concerning the cooperative were obtained from the Departamento Forestal in Mexico City.

Tepoztecans and inhabitants of the other villages of the municipio of Tepoztlán had traditionally relied upon the forest resources for their firewood and charcoal, and a handful of Tepoztecans had specialized in the making of charcoal which was sold locally. The forest resources constituted an important part of the subsistence economy. While the sale of wood outside of the village occurred, for example to the Hacienda of Oacalco, it was never on a large scale. For such enterprises Tepoztecans were required to obtain a permit from the municipal authorities for 50 centavos a week.

In the early twenties the village of San Juan, taking advantage of its proximity to the railroad which runs through the village, and because of its limited agricultural resources, began to develop the charcoal industry on a commercial scale and exported large quantities of charcoal to Mexico City. In 1926 the villagers organized a forestry cooperative to meet the requirements of the national forestry law of 1926.[26] This was the first cooperative in the state of Morelos.

The authorities of Tepoztlán challenged the right of the village of San Juan to cut large numbers of trees from forests which were municipal rather than village property, and the residents of San Juan were prohibited from cutting trees. But they appealed their case directly to the national authorities, maintaining that the mountains in question were village property. The dispute was bitter and accompanied by some violence. It was finally settled by the intervention of federal authorities who ruled that the municipio had legal title to the land in question. In March, 1930, Tepoztlán organized its own cooperative to which the villagers of San Juan were admitted.

Juan Hidalgo, a poor young man from the central barrio of Santo Domingo, became president of the cooperative. Under his leadership the cooperative grew and prospered. In a short while it had over five hundred members, ninety-five per cent

---

[26] This was Mexico's first serious attempt to legislate for the conservation of its forest resources. The law took control of forest resources out of the hands of local municipal authorities and provided that permission from the forestry authorities was necessary before any trees could be cut.

of whom were Tepoztecans. The cooperative was organized according to a plan suggested by the authorities in Cuernavaca. It had a directive body consisting of a president, secretary, and treasurer. The cooperative bought the charcoal from its members at the price of thirty-five pesos a *tonelado*. But it deducted eight per cent for handling expenses, including payment of the tax to the forestry department, a salary for the secretary, and for office equipment.

The cooperative became a powerful force in the village, and entered into politics. Its president, Juan Hidalgo, was elected president of the municipio in 1933 and 1934. In this capacity, Hidalgo was able to use the funds of the cooperative for public works and thereby gained much popularity. Under Hidalgo's leadership the cooperative sponsored the repair of the municipal building, the construction of the few public toilets in the courthouse, the construction of a school in the barrio of Los Reyes, and one in the outlying villages of San Juan, Santiago, and Ocotitlán.

Juan Hidalgo became wealthy and powerful. An informant, sympathetic to Hidalgo, explained how this happened.

In spite of the fact that Hidalgo began very poor he earned much money. He controlled the funds of the cooperative and made many loans to his friends and *compadres* in the village. He had in his hands the credit of the village, for anyone who needed a loan had to come to him. This way he became very powerful. In his hands was the economic fate of many. He could make them or break them.

Hidalgo had many enemies, especially the leaders of the former cooperative of the village of San Juan. In 1935 he was shot and killed. Informants blamed the killing on residents of San Juan. In the village itself the cooperative was fought by the Fraternales. But the prospects of an immediate income could not be resisted by the Tepoztecans, and the cooperative won out in the early years. After Hidalgo's death, however, the cooperative began to decline. The succeeding president was accused of financial irregularities and fled the village for his life. An investigator from the Departamento Agrario confirmed the accusation and charged all the officials with negligence. The major burden of blame fell on the president; and since he had fled, nothing could be done.

After the death of Hidalgo, the candidate of the Fraternales was elected president, and many difficulties were placed in the path of the cooperative. The president denounced the cooperative to the federal forest authorities for excessive and illegal cutting of trees. The authorities investigated and fined the cooperative and finally in 1937, the cooperative went into bankruptcy and was dissolved.

The political history of the village since the middle thirties is given in the following account, written for me by an informant who has been close to the local government throughout this period. His account gives the reader something of the local flavor of politics, with its buying of votes "by dint of a few glasses of pulque," the drunkenness and petty thievery of officials, and the bitterness between local political factions. His use of the term "Bolsheviki" in referring to the Fraternales reflects the identification of the two in the minds of many Tepoztecans.

ADMINISTRATION OF 1935–36

In 1934 the candidates came up for the state elections. There were three contenders, Francisco Alvarez, J. Guadalupe Pineda, and Refugio Bustamante. Most Tepoztecans were Alvaristas. Pineda ranked second, and Bustamante, with less than thirty followers, ranked third. But since Bustamante was the official candidate, he became the governor of the state. As a result, the members of the town council had to be Bustamantistas. The few Bustamantistas and the Pinedistas joined forces and elected Leonardo Sánchez and Carlos Labastida, Bustamantistas; and Marcos Flores, who represented the *ejido* faction in the village. The townspeople were their unyielding enemies, and the most scandalous days in Tepoztecan politics followed. The new council took office on January 1, 1935. The opposition party began to criticize the members of the council. One member of the opposition was Jesús Conde. When the municipal president learned that this Conde was criticizing the council, he waited for an opportunity to attack him.

Once when Conde was in a drunken state he struck a certain Angel Hernández with his pistol. The municipal president sent his chief of police to apprehend Conde and put him in the public jail. On the following day, when they brought him out to question him about his crime, Conde's anger had not lessened, and in the very council chamber he stated that it was a well-known and notorious fact that the incumbent council was a nullity. As the municipal president also continued to be angry, the matter went to the department head of the Ministerio Público. The matter even reached the ears of the governor of the state at that time.

On March 23, 1935, at about eleven o'clock in the morning, an envoy arrived at the municipal presidency stating that the president of the republic, General Lázaro Cárdenas, was approaching the town on account of the matter of the monument, "El Tepozteco." The council sent messengers from one place to another proposing a reception, conferring with the band, some of whose members were not in town. That day the president reached the town by rail and returned by truck to Cuernavaca, via a road which had been laid out and built by some citizens of the town about 1930. Among the persons making up the reception committee was Jesús Conde, who brought up among other problems that of the highway of Cuernavaca. On the first of April, 1935, work on the highway began, with the help of Cárdenas.

About the middle of April, there were elections to select deputies to the state legislature. The candidates for this district were Daniel Ramos Mendoza and the alternate, Juan Hidalgo, ex-municipal president of this town. As the council took its seat first, the people of the candidate for alternate deputy counted on plenty of enemies. On election day, as was usual, the people were milling around in the central streets from early in the morning, awaiting the time of the recount to deposit the votes bought by dint of a few glasses of pulque [27] and some barbecued meat. After midday, their spirits began to rise as a result of the pulque. The municipal president sent the police to pacify the turbulent ones. The police were received with blows and stones. The voters, heated by alcohol and by the anger they felt toward the council, saw that it was a propitious occasion to revenge themselves somehow upon their political rivals, and throwing themselves upon the police they succeeded in taking away their weapons. Some of the troublemakers were arrested. They succeeded in sending a lawyer, who insulted the municipal president in the council chamber and achieved, by shouts and insults, the liberation of the troublemakers.

---

[27] Tepoztecans generally do not drink pulque.

During these months, the municipal president and the councilmen ruled that the sellers of pork should slaughter the animals in the municipal slaughterhouse. The meat dealers accepted, but little by little they began to make difficulties, disobeying the orders of the municipal authority. The butchers were quite right because the little shed built by the council did not meet their needs. The council forgot the projects it had laid out, and because of the reduced state of the municipal exchequer, and the very few people who would help the council in any undertaking, it resigned itself to completing the paving of a few streets in the town.

Among the people upon whom the council counted were the Bolsheviki, who from the beginning adhered to the Bustamantistas. That group controlled what was then the National Revolutionary Party which at that time owned good office equipment which passed on to the municipal president. But in the month of May, without explanation, the Bolsheviki elements quarrelled with the municipal president, and in vengeance took back all the furniture from his office, leaving the clerks there with only two or three rickety chairs. Finding the office without furniture, they went to the Cooperative Forestry Association, at that time in enemy hands, to ask for a half dozen chairs. As a result of this quarrel the municipal president was completely abandoned, without friends; there remained only a few Bolsheviki who were loyal to the president's office.

On the twenty-fourth of June, Juan Hidalgo, the victorious alternate candidate for local deputy, celebrated his saint's day. This gentleman was in the market place completely drunk. At about seven-thirty in the evening when the employees had just left the municipal offices, loud detonations were heard in front of the Town Hall, where there was a party of federal troops. Those who had attacked the Town Hall divided into two groups, some went toward the federal troops and some went toward Juan Hidalgo's house where they proceeded to drag him from his home by force and take him to be murdered on the edge of town. It was learned afterward that the municipal president at that time had come to an agreement with the attackers, according to investigations made afterward which were never brought to light.

About that time the local comptroller (*regidor de hacienda*), Carlos Labastida, was very fond of alcoholic beverages. He used to go behind the Town Hall with his bottles of liquor and offer drinks to the federal troops. The commanding officer of the detachment became aware of this and succeeded in having the aforesaid functionary relieved of his position. They called up the alternate, who was then Pablo Gómez, a completely ignorant person. About the month of October, when the completion of the highway was almost at hand, the council began to organize the work for the inauguration of the highway by creating its governing board.

One Sunday, while the comptroller was presiding over a meeting concerning the work of organizing the inauguration, the same group, which had come to attack them before, entered the town again, going as far as the meeting place and threatening the comptroller. They made all those present shout "Long live the Virgin of Guadalupe!"—which they all shouted with a single voice, to avoid being beaten or murdered by the opposition. Among the bandits was one from this place who was nicknamed Juan the Drum,[28] who fell into the hands of the municipal president, as will be seen later.

The ninth of January, 1936, was the day of the inauguration of the highway; attending were the governor of the state and the secretary of communications and public works,

---

[28] John the Liar.

representing the president of Mexico. The ceremony progressed in a humble manner, with a simple meal being served to the guests in the parlors of the *ayuntamiento*, paid for by the state government with some help from the township. It was nearing the time of Carnaval when the municipal president was drinking with a few friends, some of whom were already drunk. One of them lived in the barrio of La Santísima, and the municipal president was on the alert, carrying a good pistol which the governor of the state had sent him. It was about eight in the evening. They came near the corner of La Santísima, when there appeared a suspicious looking person wrapped in a serape. The municipal president threw himself upon him without saying a word, and succeeded in knocking him down. The man was carrying a rifle concealed in his serape. They turned a flashlight on him and were able to recognize that he was the so-called Juan the Drum. At the moment in which he was recognized, he made a supreme effort to flee and succeeded in slipping away, and as he took flight the municipal president made use of his pistol and hit the man. The man was brought to the Town Hall and later was taken to Cuernavaca. He died on the way.

Politics was still at its apogee, and the council continued to be the target of every criticism. Someone of the opposite party proposed that the council be deposed. One day the people began to riot in the public gardens, as if it were an election day. There was a table and a number of people around it, taking part as if they were electing a candidate. The municipal president and the rest of the *regidores* had noticed it, and began to spread the alarm to his adherents, all Bolsheviki, so that he should not be alone. The people were awaiting the arrival of a representative of the League of Agrarian Communities,[20] and as soon as he arrived, they set out en masse toward the municipal president's office to request by main force that he should resign. But they did not succeed. The municipal president pointed out to them that there was among them no representative of the state government to declare legal that which they requested. The people attached to the municipal president found themselves only spectators, since no one came up with a solution, and they left the municipal president to defend himself.

Soon afterward, the municipal president came down with a venereal disease. A house of prostitution had opened in Tepoztlán some months before, and the president had gone there almost daily. As his illness pursued its course he was obliged to go to Mexico City to have it attended to. He began by taking a furlough of seventy days from his office, leaving in his place the comptroller. At this time the acting comptroller was a teacher who was not from the town but who was in with the municipal president for reasons which were not clear. Taking advantage of the president's absence, the opposing politicians plotted to get rid of him without fulfilling the legal requirements. When he returned from Mexico City he found that instead of the comptroller officiating, the alternate municipal president was in office. The municipal president protested, pointing out that it was contrary to the law, and after a great deal of excitement he again took charge.

The time for seeking new candidates for the municipal presidency arrived. Fortino Guzmán was the candidate for the League of Agrarian Communities, and Rafael Gutiérrez for the Fraternales. Rafael Gutiérrez also was of the party of the council. The council was fighting desperately to get a successor from its own party. They were conferring every moment with the deputies and in some cases even the governor himself, who told them that victory was assured.

---

[20] This organization worked with the Centrales against the Bolsheviki and the Fraternales.

The day of the elections and days before, the council had sent messages to the municipal councils so that they should try to spread propaganda as much as possible in favor of their candidate. That election day, in spite of the fact that the League had spread a lot of propaganda, the candidate Rafael Gutiérrez won. The case was completely certain, and the council was congratulating itself.

Before the installation of Rafael Gutiérrez on the first of January, 1937, the computing body had already extended him his credentials. It was the twenty-fourth of December, when after the employees at the municipal president's office had gone home leaving everything in its place, it was noted upon opening the office the next day that one of the doors was wide open and that a typewriter was missing. Later it was learned that someone of the opposite party had entered the president's office and removed the typewriter. Now the installation was only two or three days off. The candidate Rafael Gutiérrez went to the municipal president's office to register his credentials which the computing body had given him.

Then, one afternoon about five o'clock, there appeared a group of men led by Pedro Flores, to present to the municipal president an official publication in which the state Congress declared that the municipal president was Fortino Guzmán! (He had availed himself of the help of some friends in the city of Cuernavaca who were close to the state Congress.) When the municipal president learned this he immediately informed Rafael Gutiérrez who told him what had happened and immediately yielded, pointing out that if superior authority declared it so, there was no help for it. The municipal president and the rest of the *regidores* immediately left for Cuernavaca to interview the governor of the state, but he answered them that he had nothing to do with the matter since the state Congress had declared it so. They came back completely downcast, and that was the end of this administration of 1935–36.

ADMINISTRATION OF 1939–40

Before January 1, 1939, Donaciano Linares was elected municipal president to officiate in the period 1939–40 with Serafín Velásquez and Rafael Gutiérrez. The candidates Donaciano Linares and Serafín Velásquez belonged to the then famous League of Agrarian Communities, and Rafael Gutiérrez belonged to the Fraternales. The new municipal president bought himself a black suit for the installation. The day of the installation there were people of the two political parties, the council having been made up in the following form: President, Donaciano Linares; Attorney General, Serafín Velásquez; and (*regidor*), Rafael Gutiérrez.

The municipal president had in his service his brother as chief of police. Since both were rather fond of drink, there were occasions when they fought with each other in public. Once when the municipal president was drunk, he had a few silver pesos in his pockets, and went to the market and began to drink toasts, at the same time striking his pockets to make his money jingle to show how much he had. On another occasion, there was a woman in the market whom he disliked considerably, and when he recognized her he began to insult her with vile words until he grew tired of it. In the Town Hall there were quarrels even among the *regidores,* especially with the comptroller who was not of their party. The comptroller did not allow himself to be insulted and constantly threatened the municipal president with sending word to the governor of the state.

Since this municipal president was one of the most politically minded men in town, during his administration he dedicated himself to giving banquets to influential people, among them the governor of the state, the local deputies, and the federal deputies. He was helped by some friends of his backed up by the employees. The comptroller, who scarcely liked to drink at all, occasionally took the president home when the latter was too drunk to walk.

The attorney general, who was charged with listing all the animals that were slaughtered in the municipal slaughterhouse, was known to let some stolen animals pass, from which he received a share of the profit. Other people said that these were mere calumnies, but the real truth was never known, namely, that he stayed simply to help at the slaughtering time and to take some pieces of meat or a bucket of blood which he used for food.

The municipal president, in turn, was sometimes known to be playing a bad game, that is, if some person had some problems he sold favors, charging a few pesos. There was a concrete case. A young man tried to rape a girl one evening. The members of the family immediately went to the Town Hall to ask for help from the police. The young man was caught and taken to the municipal jail. The next day the members of his family succeeded in bribing the municipal president with 20 pesos. The municipal president there told the boy to say that he was very sick at his stomach. The boy did so, and since the municipal president could not pronounce judgment then, he tried to have the girl's family desist from their claim and threatened to fine them. They withdrew very calmly, without knowing they had been deceived. Various cases of this kind were seen during this administration, sometimes by agreement with the attorney general but almost never with the comptroller, because the latter had occupied posts of this nature before, and did not wish it to turn out badly again.

There were times when this municipal president went to see one or another of the business men who had unsettled accounts with the municipal treasury. He would order beer or something else and say, "Charge this up to your contribution." Then he would tell the municipal treasurer that he owed money in such and such a tavern. The same thing happened with the butchers; he would go and ask for a kilo or two of meat and charge it to the account of the butcher's license to slaughter cattle in the municipal slaughterhouse. When the butchers were killing beef cattle he willingly assisted them, so that they would give him a piece of meat.

Once when the neighboring people of Tejalpa had violated the boundaries and were trying to invade the lands of this township, the matter reached the ears of the council, who immediately proceeded to call a meeting of all the citizens. With the support of the guard, which existed in the town, they marched toward the place where the aforesaid violation had occurred. When they got there, the people from here, who numbered about 150 armed men, with the municipal president at their head, threw themselves upon the men from Tejalpa; and an engineer, commissioned by the Department of Agriculture, was disarmed and taken prisoner to this place. The rest of the men from Tejalpa were put in the public prison. The engineer tried to protest, but his protests had no effect.

Several months after his installation as president, Donaciano Linares bought a little car; no one knew how. He began to drive it in the evenings on the highway, sometimes having an accident, hitting an animal or another car. But since he was the municipal president hardly anyone protested. During his administration the budget improved a little, a typewriter was bought. But he carried it off to his house about two days before the installation of the succeeding council. The same thing happened with a wall clock which was bought in this period. He tried to take it away, but he did not succeed because the other councillors prevented him.

During this administration there were some efforts to complete the highway between Tepoztlán and Yautepec. After many attempts the administration succeeded in getting the state government to send a few men to work. They completed a small stretch of road. At the end of the administration, the municipal president began to work in politics, with the aim of leaving some friend or relative of his as his successor. He even began to inform the towns in the township of the official slate, and he was quite involved because he was leaving his stepfather as the future attorney general. This slate was victorious, as may be easily understood, since there was no opposition candidate. The municipal president organized a dance for the installation, as a symbol of his satisfaction with his administrative effort, although almost nothing was done during his term, except the paving of a few streets.

ADMINISTRATION OF 1941–42

On the eighth of December, 1940, the victory was won by the only candidate for the municipal presidency, with the other councillors whose names were as follows: President, Fulgencio Campos; Attorney General, Saturnino Córdova; and Comptroller, Fortino Lara. To complete the installation, a lively dance was organized in the market place at eight in the evening on December thirty-first, and at ten the following morning the transferring of the municipal powers was accomplished. Shortly after the installation the municipal president called together all the councillors and employees of the township, and when they were all together he spoke to them, pointing out the errors that the previous council had committed, with relation to the frequent drinking sprees of the municipal president and all the employees. He proposed that if any one of them wanted to take a few drinks, he should ask permission the day before, so that his place might be taken by someone else. In this way, it would at least be known that an employee was not staying away because he had some other job to do. All the employees and councillors accepted the proposal.

The council began to work and make efforts for the introduction of electrical power into the town,[30] making trips to Mexico City to interview the chiefs of the Secretariat of National Economy. Engineers were sent to the town to make studies to be submitted for the consideration of the high chiefs of this secretariat. A few months after the installation of the municipal president, his aspirations for improvements in the town fell to earth. Before becoming president, Fulgencio Campos had many illusions about the council having plenty of funds which might be used to improve the economic situation of the inhabitants. He soon lost heart, seeing that the municipal treasury was not receiving the money that he had imagined it would. He had also been saying that the previous presidents had done nothing for their people because they did not want to, and that they became presidents in order to get drunk and to commit misdemeanors.

Saturnino Córdova was functioning as attorney general and under-secretary of the Ministerio Público, and he was not at all qualified, for he could hardly sign his name. The municipal president proposed that it would be preferable that Córdova might better occupy the post of comptroller, changing with Fortino Lara so that the latter might become attorney general. Córdova was not opposed to this and in an act of council the change of commissions was recorded.

This council had many difficulties with the Commissariat of the Ejidos, because the

---

[30] In 1947, the date of my last visit to the village, Tepoztlán still had no electricity.

latter had control of the forests. The municipal president maintained that the commissariat should not have authority in matters of forestry. There was a certain amount of hatred between them, though not declared. The council was seeking funds to meet the outstanding expenses which were incurred within the municipal administration. Seeing that there were no sources of revenue, the council voted to call together on a certain day all the charcoal makers and to ask them for their cooperation; that is, that they should give one day's work to cut down trees and cut them into logs, so that they might make charcoal kilns for the benefit of the council, and that the profits from those kilns would go into the municipal treasury.

All agreed to accept and to meet on the appointed day in the appointed place to cut the trees. The charcoal makers only cut about ten trees, which yielded little money for the council's purposes. There was nothing to do about it but give in, because only enough money came of it to pay the person who watched over the furnace when it was burning. The municipal president despaired more than ever, because he saw that the money coming into the municipal treasury was barely enough to pay the few miserable salaries of the township employees. Not even the police could afford three men to keep watch over the peace.

The municipal president did not give up. He wanted to follow faithfully what he had promised. He began to work to improve the public market, soliciting federal aid. When it came to the ears of the dwellers in the town that there was a question of building the market, some of them immediately went to the municipal president's office; they made it clear that if such a market were to be completed, their properties in that vicinity must be respected. The municipal president demanded documentation to substantiate the true ownership of the small pieces of land which were within the property belonging to the township. Most of them presented their documents, and they reached a settlement that it would be preferable to pick the property by lot, in agreement with the owners. And, together with the council, they would finish the rooms which would be used for trade. As was said before, all this reached the stage of study but nothing more was ever done.

About the month of August of the second year of his administration, Fulgencio Campos admitted that he was failing in his intention to bring about some improvement for the town. He decided to play his last card and pave the public gardens. This time he interviewed not the civil authorities but the military. It happened at the time that federal workers were within the township breaking stone for the highway. Campos interviewed the chief of the military zone and set forth all the reasons for his aspirations and his desire to leave some work for his people. The military chief agreed that a few of the trucks which were being used to carry stone for the highway should be left at the municipal president's office so that they might be utilized in the paving of the public gardens. The trucks arrived right away, and the council tried to raise funds to pay for the sand and cement. The council agreed that the work should be completed after the end of the rainy season, that is, about the month of October, so that the rains would not slow up the work of the paving.

The day of the national celebrations, that is, the sixteenth of September, the comptroller, Saturnino Córdova, who was commissioned to list the animals at the slaughterhouse, got drunk with some friends. Most of his acquaintances were men in the meat business.

On the seventeenth it was learned that Córdova had disappeared and could not be found anywhere. About five in the afternoon a woman reported a corpse in a ravine near the municipal slaughterhouse. The authorities took the corpse to the Town Hall for identification, because birds of prey had already mutilated the face and part of the body. The investigations began, and finally it was known that Córdova had been murdered inside the slaughterhouse and his body thrown into the ravine.

At that time there was also an investigation going on in the office of the undersecretary of the Ministerio Público for cattle stealing. It was discovered that the lost animals had been slaughtered in the municipal slaughterhouse, and that the animals had been stolen by the same persons who had murdered Córdova because he was trying to discover the thieves. The council aided Córdova's family with burial and what was necessary to settle a few other expenses. The council proceeded to call the alternate for the comptroller's office, to take charge of the post which Córdova had been filling.

In a short time the cement necessary for the paving of the public gardens was bought. Only half of the job could be done, and this only with the councillors giving a part of their pay. An additional sum of fifty pesos, which had been given by a woman toward the pipe line for drinking water, also went into the paving of the public gardens and the fixing of benches. The president, on leaving his post, got into a suit over this fifty pesos; the people said he had stolen it.

ADMINISTRATION OF 1943–44

On the first of January, 1943, the only candidates who had taken part in the elections of the first Sunday in December were inaugurated: Municipal President, Emilio Martínez; Comptroller, Benito Vargas; and Attorney General, Carlos Quiroz. In the first council meeting they decided to increase the taxes of the township for the purpose of town improvements. All those who take office as presidents are always eager to improve their town. The council in agreement with the Commissariat of the Ejidos, who had some funds for the development of the forests, took those funds and bought the necessary cement and sand to finish the paving of the public gardens. And the work was finished in a few weeks.

There came a fiesta at which people drank too much, and as this municipal president, Emilio Martínez, had many friends, who were constantly inviting him to have a drink, he drank all that day. When evening came and it was getting dark, he was completely drunk. Upon getting into the bus he met another man who was also far gone, and they started a commotion. They went from words to blows and from blows to kicks. When Martínez saw the other man stretched out, he began to kick him until his relatives and the police intervened. Of course, the man was taken to jail, and although he had received the blows from Martínez, he was fined five pesos.

Martínez had a son who was completing his military service. In a short time stories began to circulate to the effect that young Mexican men were going to be sent to war, which was then at its height. Undoubtedly they hinted this to Martínez. According to the story they tell, he organized a band of bad fellows, and on the Sunday when his son was en route to the barracks this band attacked the vehicle in which he was riding. Martínez claimed that his son had been kidnapped by bandits, but the matter did not end there. The state governor gave orders to the chief of the judicial police, and one day when Martínez was in the city he was apprehended and taken to the state penitentiary at the disposition of the governor of the state. As soon as the other members of the council learned that Martínez was being held in prison, they called the comptroller, as was provided in the law, to take the office of municipal president for seventy days. The comptroller accepted gladly because from the beginning he had wanted to be president. In a few days Martínez was freed, and when he returned to the president's office, the comptroller was forced to resign. The alternate comptroller, Froylan García, was called up to take the office.

The attorney general for some reason or other began to quarrel with Martínez, gradually drawing away from him even in the negotiations which involved both their offices. It reached the point where the attorney general undertook obligations without informing the municipal president. This deepened the rift still more. The attorney general began to hurl charges at Martínez availing himself of the support of some citizens who were his adherents.

When this reached the ears of the state government, Martínez and the other councillor were called on for explanations, but it turned out that they could not prove the charges they were making. On the contrary, the attorney general and his supporters suffered a call from the government to appear. It did not end there.

At that time citizens were taking stone out of the quarry, and the attorney general alleged that the president was charging for the extraction of the stone and keeping the money. Because of this the split became even deeper, until finally the attorney general hardly ever went to the municipal president, but contented himself with carrying on his affairs in the lower tribunal. He tried to win the friendship of the comptroller so that there would be a majority against the municipal president, but as there were occasions when there were things which were damaging to the comptroller, he could not come to terms with the attorney general but continued faithful to the municipal president. Those two councillors, together with a few enthusiastic citizens, tried to form a committee to bring about the construction of a school in the town. They could get together only a small fund because at that time the president of Mexico had already ordered the construction of the present school, through the diligence of Angel Bocanegra. That was the end of the labors of the committee formed by the council and other citizens; they had succeeded in getting together barely 250 pesos which have remained in the power of the comptroller up to the present time.

When the dry season arrived, and drinking water began to be scarce everywhere, the council decided to improve or level the piping which brought water to the town. The council succeeded in getting together many people who willingly lent themselves to improving the pipe line. They asked for help from a man who was the manager of the Bank of Mexico, who collaborated by buying some pipes which the council needed. As the attorney general saw that he had not succeeded in discrediting the president, he decided to complain to the office of the attorney general of the state, so that the president would be judged for all the crimes which, according to the attorney general, he had committed. After trying every means to harm the municipal president without success, the attorney general presented his resignation. It was accepted right away, and the alternate for the position was called immediately. The people of the town had grumbled about the outgoing attorney general because, when he was sitting in judgment on a case, he almost always used vulgar words to call attention to the delinquents.

The council, which was about to finish its term, began to think about its successor. Each member tried to leave a friend in office, using every means possible so that he might remain. The municipal president held conferences with some friends of his in the town and in the other towns. Again the town was divided into three parties; some belonged to the party of the council and its candidates, others were led by Vicente Campos, and others by Federico Campos, aided by the Fraternales. The municipal president took up this problem with the governor of the state, with the deputy for the district, and with the president of the political party, but nothing was gained. After the legal elections, all the candidates came out null and void. The state government intervened in the matter and appointed the municipal council. This council, made up of completely different persons, was to take office on the first of January like a legally elected council.

ADMINISTRATION OF 1945–46

On the first of January, 1945, the appointed municipal council was installed, consisting of J. Guadalupe Ortega, Miguel Ríos, and Fortino Guzmán, in place of all the candidates who had set out to occupy the municipal offices. This council was pledged to send out within ninety days the summons for new elections to form the council which was to officiate during this same period. On the first of April, the candidates who were supported by the Fraternales—that is, Federico Campos as president, Domingo G. Alvarado as *regidor de hacienda,* and Juan Z. Rodríguez as attorney general—were installed. After having taken office, they proceeded to notify all the important people to take notice, also other friends whom they had in Mexico City.

Before coming to power, Federico Campos had counted on some adherents, among whom were some persons of moderate culture. But since he did not listen to their counsel he achieved nothing but hatred. These persons had proposed that he should improve the water system, a matter of great importance to the town. After the labors of experts, and efforts on all sides, Campos succeeded in getting the governor to sign a contract with the Secretariat of Health and Social Work to complete the work which was so much desired.

At the same time, the matter of obtaining electricity was discussed in an interview with the secretary of national economy, who ordered that additional studies should be made concerning the matter. Later they had an interview with the president of Mexico, who gave orders to the secretary of national economy. After all the efforts made in the different departments, the federal election of new officers gravely harmed the works completed. Since there was a complete change in the government, they declared that all the work was useless because it was necessary to have new studies made by the new officials.

With this, Campos lost heart completely, and he limited himself to expediting the matters in his office. Furthermore, since the other villages of the township knew that Campos was trying to improve the villages, others approached him for aid in the matter of bringing drinking water to their people. When the municipal president, or rather the council, saw that the villages were also interested, they tried to unite in order to bring about an adequate water system for all, and on one occasion they interviewed the authorities of another township which had a sufficient water supply to make additional outlets possible. The negotiations were successful, but this township was a considerable distance away, and much capital was required to purchase the materials needed to bring in the water. When the estimates were made, the sum was fantastic in relation to the economic possibilities of the villages.

This council also tried to improve the town by aiding in the literacy campaign. Since the adults, who did not know how to read or write, refused to study, the council visited all the villages of the township and named the sub-committees, just as an extension of the committee of four hundred working in the municipal seat. Campos tried to raise funds to pay the teachers at the literacy centers. When people refused to contribute or to attend classes, he acted in accordance with the law and punished those who did not comply.

But as there are always people who try to interfere with the work of the individual in charge, these people got together and complained to the government of the state. They declared that they were being charged large sums, and that the money was being taken by the municipal president for himself. In view of this, Campos was suspended and called before the governor of the state, to render an account of the funds collected. The governor of the state later realized that these charges were merely calumnies with which the people were trying to discredit the municipal president.

This council did not work in harmony with the Commissariat of the Ejidos, since they were of opposing parties. Because of this, the Commissariat of the Ejidos tried to usurp some properties of the township, such as the textile workshops, which are almost on the edge of the town. It was on this account that Campos, seeing that this was wrong, tried to oppose them. He also opposed them in the matter of the communal forests, which, though owned by the town, were being managed by the Commissariat of the Ejidos.

During this administration they also held the inauguration of the school which had been built by the request of Angel Bocanegra. Of course, there had to be high personages present, among them the president himself. The council tried to get together some funds for the inauguration, proceeding immediately to print coupons for sale to the citizens. The governor of the state learned of this and, as the state government had taken on itself the matter of the inauguration, he ordered that the funds which had been collected in the town should be refunded to each of the contributors.

On one occasion when the governor was to speak on the matter of the inauguration, the municipal president was not to be found in the town, and this was sufficient reason for the governor to become very angry. Speaking with the enemies of the council, he declared to them that they were authorized to impeach Campos and all the other members of the council and to set others in their places, who would know how to take care of the administration of a town. Some people wished to do this, but others decided that it was preferable that Campos should continue.

On the day of the inauguration of the school, Campos pinned a medal on Angel Bocanegra, calling him "favorite son of this town," and he also pinned another medal on the governor. When this council finished its term, it also tried to elect its candidate for the municipal presidency. He was an intimate friend, but he could not win because of being from another township.

SUMMARY

The above account gives some insight into the behavior of politicians and touches upon some of the salient aspects of political life in the village. (See Fig. 48.) These might be summarized briefly as follows:

(1) According to the law of the state of Morelos, municipios are to be free and autonomous political and administrative units. In practice we have seen that this is not the case. Rather, the municipio appears to be no more than an administrative dependency of the governor. It is he who resolves conflicts and makes most of the important decisions for the municipio, including the determination of who shall be the successful candidate. The incident cited above, whereby the president arranges with the opposition group in Tepoztlán to depose the president because the latter did not happen to be in the village when the governor made an unexpected call, is indicative of his arbitrary action.

Fig. 48. A political rally for state governor.

(2) The practice of buying votes is a well-established custom in the village. Because of this, only candidates with some financial resources can hope to be successful.

(3) Political parties as such exist only in name. Instead there are poorly organized and undisciplined political factions whose members are united more by personal ties of friendship or kinship than by common political ideology. During the twenties and thirties the Bolsheviki and Fraternales attempted to introduce some ideological bases for politics but with the disappearance of these organizations the older personalism prevailed. Informants active in one or another of the political factions could not tell us with any precision how many members they had. At best the reply would be, "We are many," or "We have most of the village with us." From time to time the official party of the government in power sends directions to the village to form a local section of the party, be it the Partido Nacional Revolucionario, the Partido de la Revolución Mexicana, or the present-day Partido Revolucionario Institucional. This is generally done but the Tepoztecans think in terms of a particular man rather than the party he represents.

(4) Tepoztecans are as a rule very critical of the motives of the municipal and state government, and only less so of the federal government. Nevertheless, they

become quite enthusiastic participants in the election campaigns. Much of this is stimulated by visiting politicians who are skillful in making promises which Tepoztecans no longer even expect to be fulfilled. As a result they generally favor the opposition candidate as a matter of principle.

(5) The Colonia Tepozteco plays a major role in the political life of the village and tends to direct politics toward the right; some, however, proclaim their adherence to the principles of the Mexican Revolution. The Colonia keeps in close touch with the villlage and advises the village leaders on all important undertakings and offers legal and financial aid when the occasion arises.

(6) Finally, the accounts show the division within the municipio government itself. It is a rare administration in which the three major officials, the president, the *síndico,* and the *regidor* work harmoniously. There are also administrative difficulties between the municipal authorities and the federal and state authorities, particularly between the president and the Commissariat of the Ejidos.

religion: 11

AT THE TIME of the Spanish Conquest Tepoztlán had been under the domination and influence of the Aztecs for about one hundred years, and had absorbed much of Aztec culture. Tepoztecans paid homage to Aztec gods and practiced the Aztec rites of human sacrifice. But before the conquest by the armies of Tenochtitlán, Tepoztecans worshipped the more benign gods of the Toltecs which did not involve human sacrifice. As late as 1580, Tepoztecans still conserved the memory of this pre-Aztec period. This is learned from the oft-cited *Relación de Tepuztlan* of 1580, containing the following passage on Tepoztecan religion:

That anciently they made offerings to their gods, of paper, quail, wild pigeons and copal, until the Mexicans came; then they observed their customs. When they went to war they cut through the heart [of prisoners] and offered them to their gods; they [the prisoners] belonged to those who had captured them. When it began to thunder and they wanted rain they bought two or three small children, took them to a high peak, and when it began to rain and thunder they tore out the heart and the blood was offered to the rains so that it would rain much; for this purpose they would first keep the bought children for thirty or forty days; in the case of an adult, on the day he was sacrificed they dressed him very well and they led him singing and dancing unto where the idol stood and there, having invited many neighboring villagers, since it was a great fiesta, they drank and slit open his breast and tore out the heart and the blood and offered him to the gods; and they threw the body down below and later they cut up the body and offered pieces of it to the warriors.[1]

Here we find a description of a typical Aztec ceremony very similar to the description by Sahagún. This indicates that the rain god, Tlaloc, and the war god, Huitzilopochtli, were worshipped in Tepoztlán before the Conquest. To the first, children were sacrificed; to the second, adults.

But Tepoztlán also had its own special cult of Ometochtli (Two Rabbits), the god of pulque (Fig. 49) whose fame extended throughout the Aztec empire. Indeed, Tepoztlán was a very important religious center during this time. A sixteenth century Dominican chronicler tells us that Ometochtli was a

---

[1] *Relación*, p. 241.

Fig. 49. Ancient god of pulque.

... famous idol celebrated by this entire kingdom and visited by the foreigners who made pilgrimages to it and offerings which they carried from the kingdom of Chiapas and Guatemala.[2]

The discovery of pulque, the popular intoxicating drink of the Aztecs, is attributed by legend to El Tepozteco, a Tepoztecan culture hero who was later worshipped as a god. In certain seasons of the year the cult of Ometochtli had all the characteristics of a collective orgy, celebrated in a feast called Pilhuana, at which children were intoxicated. The Codex Magliabecchiano of Florence describes it as follows:

This is the figure of a great god of intoxication that a town which is called Tepoztlán had as its rite; when a drunken Indian died the others of the town made a great feast carrying copper axes with which they cut the wood.[3]

THE COLONIAL PERIOD

The story of the conversion of Tepoztecans to Catholicism is still conserved in village legend, and the following version was given us by a conservative and aged

[2] M. F. Agustín Dávila y Padilla, *Historia de la Fundación y Discurso de la Provincia de Santiago de México*, 2nd ed. (Brussels, 1625), p. 617.

[3] *Estado de Morelos. Estudios Histórico—Económico—Fiscales Sobre los Estados de la República* (México, Secretaría de Hacienda), II (1939), 42.

informant who was an ardent supporter of the church and claimed to be a descendant of Martín Cortés who had lived in Tepoztlán.

When the sons of the Sun [referring to the Spaniards] arrived at the place today known as Vera Cruz, some of the worshippers of Ometochtli began to waiver because the conquerors bore the Catholic religion. . . . The king and *cacique,* Tepoztecatl, an intelligent and astute man, naturally realized at once that it was the true belief. He began to weaken morally and he abandoned his subjects because he knew their beliefs were false. Then the sub-kings of Cuernavaca, Xiotepec, Yautepec, Tlayacupec, and Tlalmanalac demanded of King Tepoztecatl that he follow his former beliefs. But Tepoztecatl did not know what to tell them to convince them that the idol which they venerated was false. And he thus became an enemy of the others and they said they were going to fight him as a traitor. Now this King Tepoztecatl, learning their plans to fight, ordered his Tepoztecan subjects to place advance guards to await the enemy.

Finally the Spaniards reached Tenochtitlán and then the Tepoztecans secretly went there to learn about the new faith. Tepoztecatl was baptized there and they named him Natividad because this was on the eighth of September, and when he returned to Tepoztlán he was already a Christian. But the priest had advised him to convert his subjects amiably and with affection, that they should treat one another as brothers and that they should respect the fifth commandment of the Decalogue. This he did. He talked to all of them of the good and the bad and ordered his advance guard to suspend the bloody quarrel. When his adversaries learned of the order they came right in to where he was, not to fight but to learn about the new faith. It was at this point that there began the celebrated polemic between Tepoztecatl and his enemies. [This polemic is still conserved today and is recited, with its many variants, in the Náhuatl language during the fiesta of the eighth of September. It is called the Oration of Tepozteco.] The visitors were satisfied and asked forgiveness of Tepoztecatl. The King Natividad, formerly Tepoztecatl, gave them a warm embrace and they reciprocated and each returned to his own tribe. Natividad was highly pleased and satisfied in having complied with the task the missionaries of Tenochtitlán had given him.

Natividad continued to teach all that he had learned to the natives of his own town, and when he thought they were ready to be baptized he returned to Tenochtitlán to inform the priests. He came accompanied by Dominican priests and on the following day gave their promise there on the spot of Oxibolta where today there is a stone cross mounted on a column of masonry like a historic monument. Tepoztecatl worked hard to help convert the natives. When he died he was interred in a special place called Tlaulahu and they placed a monument there. A cross was also placed at the site of Tlallacualayan where the first Mass was said.

From the above account we see that Christianity was brought to Tepoztlán with little difficulty. The alliance of Tepoztecatl with the Spaniards, whose strength aroused the awe of the natives and their leaders, facilitated a peaceful conversion. The polytheism of the ancient religions permitted a relatively easy shift from the old gods to the new, who had demonstrated their superiority by the victories of the Spaniards. But many pre-Hispanic religious elements were carried over to the new religion.

The figure of Tepoztecatl, as both El Tepozteco and Natividad, permanently fused old Aztec concepts with those of the Catholic Church. His figure is also confused with the god, Ometochtli, so that today he is known as El Tepozteco, god of the wind and son of the Virgin Mary. For Tepoztecans the Catholic Trinity is viewed as a combination of three distinct gods, and the cross is a magical symbol which has no relation to the death of Jesus. Tepoztecans continue to fear omens, evil spirits, and *los aires*. When they are in dire need of rain they pray to El Tepozteco for aid.

The growth of Catholicism and the church in Tepoztlán was rapid. When the first mass baptisms of the Tepoztecans occurred, no priests resided permanently in Tepoztlán, but a few years later the natives began to petition for the construction of a church in the town, since they did not want to be dependent upon the services of the priests from Yautepec or Oaxtepec. We do not know the exact date of the construction of the first church in Tepoztlán. However, in the *Relación* of 1580 we are told that the church had already been established:

There is in this village a monastery of Dominican friars with three friars who administer the sacraments and that at the beginning they did not have any priest in this town and that they came from Yautepec and Guaxtepeque to baptize and confess the people, and that in the time of the Viceroy Luis de Velasco they asked for priests since many had died without confession and without baptism and so it was ordered that a monastery be built and the village did so at its own cost.[4]

Since the Viceroy Luis de Velasco was in office from 1550 to 1564, it must be supposed that the construction of the Tepoztecan church began during that time.

The Dominicans in Tepoztlán, while occupied in carrying out the administrative measures of the viceroy and in arousing in the natives respect for the Spanish authorities, also attempted to extirpate all pre-Hispanic cults. The Dominicans were especially vigorous in their attacks upon the native priests whom they regarded as witches, and upon the ancient idols which were instruments of the devil. One of their first objectives was to destroy the great image of Ometochtli, situated at the top of a mountain overlooking the village.[5]

Father F. Domingo de la Anunciación ordered the idol hurled over the cliff to show the natives that it could be smashed, hoping thus to destroy their faith in the power of the god. Despite the great height from which the idol fell, it remained intact. However, with the aid of prayers, exorcisms, and large hammers, the priests managed to break the stone.

According to our informants, when the idol fell it made a terrible noise which put fear into the spectators. When it did not break, alarm spread among the Indians and many would have defended their god had it not been for the presence of Spanish soldiers. After the destruction of the image, Tepoztecans lived in fear of the vengeance of the god. Tradition has it that Ometochtli ran through the streets at night crying and bemoaning the fate of the Tepoztecans at the hands of the con-

[4] *Relación*, p. 245.
[5] Remains of the temple and the stairway still exist in Tepoztlán, and attract many tourists.

queror. His words were not threats but sad laments, "Oh, my sons, they have taken you out of my hands and I cannot help you. . . . Oh, you poor things, that I see you outside of my palace and my abode."

The Indians heard his voice, and in fear went to Father Domingo de la Anunciación, saying that as a true father he should help his sons. He told them it was the work of the devil who, having lost, was now trying to frighten them away from the road of salvation. The Father advised the Indians to make the sign of the cross when they again heard the voice and thus to dispatch the devil.[6] The priests then placed large wooden crosses at every pathway leading to the village to keep out the god. The natives no longer reported hearing Ometochtli, but they continued to believe that he comes to the village when some calamity threatens.

The fight to eliminate aboriginal beliefs and practices continued. In an account of a Dominican priest in the late sixteenth century we learn of another incident:

The demon was well entrenched in Tepoztlán, recognized by various kings and aided by great deceit and as a haughty man he very much resented his fall. This town had had great idols and the fame of its doctors was due to the fact that the demon had taught them the virtue of herbs so that they could deceive the rest of the people and even today despite the great care of the priests there still are found survivals of their communication with the demon as happened in my presence during this year of 1592 in the month of May.[7]

The incident referred to was as follows: The governor of Tepoztlán dedicated himself to the production of lime, burning the stone in a temporary oven; usually two days after the stone was burned, the lime was ready for use. But then it happened that despite all the burning and the passing of many days, the required lime was not produced. The governor, "who was an Indian of good understanding," suspected that it was due to some type of sorcery and he complained to the Dominicans, pointing out an Indian as the possible author of the sorcery. The Dominicans took this matter very seriously. They called in the accused, frightened him, and forced him to confess to the deed, saying that his father had given him an oration written on paper with which he could conjure at will the forces of the demon. The Dominicans immediately tried to exorcise the kiln and the stones, calling the villagers around so that they could be duly impressed by the power of the Virgin of the Rosary, to whom an invocation was made during the rites.

On the following day the rock was burned and the lime was produced. The Indian who was accused of witchcraft was punished, leaving the natives as amazed by his powers as a witch, as by the superior power of the priests. The Dominican author of this account observed that the demon had good reason to cry for having been displaced from among people over whom he had had such great influence. Even after seventy years of having been baptized into another faith, they still had pacts with him.

Slowly the Dominicans, like other religious orders in Spanish America, gathered

---

[6] Dávila y Padilla, *Historia*, pp. 617-18.

[7] *Ibid.*

the natives into religious associations which facilitated the administrative and political functions of the colony.

Cofradías (brotherhoods) and *gremios* (societies) were organized under the auspices and protection of a saint. A *mayordomo* and other officials were chosen from among the *principales* and loyal supporters of the Crown. The system of *cofradías* had the following functions: (1) it facilitated formation of other organizations, such as cults of particular saints; (2) it simplified the collection of religious taxes; (3) it supplemented local police and helped seek out delinquents, escaped slaves, and others; (4) it aided in the collection of tribute; and (5) it provided extra companies of troops in times of emergency.

The church, united as it was with the state, became very strong. Church personnel were numerous and were paid from public funds. High public officials were obliged to preside over all religious processions and ceremonies. Religious fiestas, which greatly increased church income and stimulated local trade, became very numerous during the colonial period.

THE EPOCH OF INDEPENDENCE TO THE FALL OF THE DÍAZ REGIME

The first years of Mexican independence from Spain passed almost unnoticed in Tepoztlán, where life changed very little. The church, aided by the guarantees of the plan of Iguala, continued to be united with the new state without any major changes in its organization. As a matter of fact, after being liberated from the colonial tribute, Tepoztecans were subject to an even greater tribute by the church in the form of the forced collection of the *diezmo*, a tax whereby Tepoztecans had to pay one-tenth of their produce to the church.

The first great change in the religious life of Tepoztlán occurred during the reform period of Juárez, when church and state were separated and church property confiscated. Until this time the church in Tepoztlán, as in most of Mexico, was the institution that stood for the status quo. After Juárez, the church became an aggressive force struggling against the state and became involved in the so-called Wars of the Reform, fighting against the liberal orientation of the Mexican government. While we have little specific data for Tepoztlán on this point, it may be assumed that the village was also affected and that some Tepoztecans worked through church associations against the government while others participated in the liberal ranks of the victorious party of Benito Juárez. Later, during the struggle against the Emperor Maximilian, who was blessed by the Pope and had the aid of the church, we know that liberalism had penetrated into Tepoztlán, for one of Tepoztecan's sons, General Prisciliano Rodríguez, organized a column of Tepoztecans and fought heroically against invading French troops. The church had indeed lost much of its old power.

The economic revolution brought about by the amortization of the wealth of the church produced a new oligarchy which, under President Díaz, again delivered itself into the arms of the church. In Tepoztlán the new upper class, the *caciques,* united the church and state and supported the church as a strong conservative force. During this period the church recuperated much of its former glory and once more, pompous religious fiestas were celebrated in the village. The church, the *caciques,* and the merchants all benefited by the increase in religious activity. Attendance at fiestas was very large and public officials were present. As some of our informants said, "Formerly, the people participated in religious fiestas much more than today because they believed attendance was compulsory. No one dared to miss church after they had been visited by an official and told to attend."

Not only did the public attend religious ceremonies but they spent much money on fireworks, candles, music, flowers, and so forth. An informant compared present religious participation with that during the Díaz regime as follows:

In the religious ceremonies it was common to have large processions which consisted in carrying the saints through the streets and all believers followed with their candles and prayers. Today we no longer burn artificial *fuegos* as formerly. Today the citizens no longer sacrifice as much to make a good barrio fiesta. Formerly they had as many as three or four bands of dancers. Today only a few barrios send a band of dancers to the fiestas.

During the Díaz period, religious taxes were collected as they had been in colonial times, that is, by the *huehuechiques,* who went from house to house asking for the contribution. Today this custom is almost gone; *huehuechiques* function only in the barrios of Santa Cruz and San Sebastián.

Participation in fiestas was claimed as a public service by the local government. The president ordered citizens to do certain tasks or play certain roles on pain of fine or other punishment. For example, we were told of one president:

He commissioned eight or ten men to go to the mountains of Acaloqua and Calencuahiuchuy, both distant from Tepoztlán, to cut palms for the celebration of Palm Sunday since these palms could not be obtained from nearby areas. The men were not paid for the work, which was considered very difficult. The *caciques* received the best palms so that they might march in the procession.

The president also named commissions to collect flowers and adorn the temple. On Holy Thursday the president appointed men to play the role of the Jews. These men had to provide themselves with special suits and a long cape and mask. They had to rise at 2:00 A.M. to collect the images for the procession. This role had been very unpopular during the colonial period, not only for what it symbolized but because the villagers shouted insults and even spat at them. However, later the symbolism was forgotten, and the "Jews" were invited into the homes of those who had the images to be collected and were given *champurrado* and *semita* to eat.

Despite the Constitution of 1857 which specifically imposed separation of state and church, there was much fusion of the two at the time of Díaz. In Tepoztlán the president and councilmen attended Mass and the *rosario* in a body on January first, and after receiving the blessings of God held the first session of the year. On Ash Wednesday again all the local officials, the judges, and their employees received the ashes together in a special place set aside in the church. The apportionment of the ashes was done in a hierarchal order for the entire population, first the high functionaries, next the *caciques* and their wives, then the assistant functionaries, and finally the townsmen. In another distribution, ashes were given to those from neighboring villages, then to individuals from more distant villages, and finally to all latecomers.

Despite the increased importance of the church at this time some Tepoztecans, without giving up their faith, had developed a critical attitude toward the church. While most remained passive and docile, by the time the Revolution began many Tepoztecans were ready to join the struggle against the church and state.

THE REVOLUTION

The coming of the Mexican Revolution severely disrupted the religious life of Tepoztlán. The priest and the *caciques,* the strongest supporters of the church, fled for their lives and religious activity came to a standstill. The church and chapels were abandoned, the ancient monastery became troop headquarters and stables, and soldiers camped in the churchyard. Church and municipal archives were reduced to ashes, the sacred communion cups disappeared, cloaks were taken from the holy images to cover the wounded. For weeks at a time the local population had to live in the hills to avoid being killed. As an informant put it, "Who could think of religion in those days?"

After many bitter years peace was slowly established, and "since man cannot live without religion, for it makes him bad," once again the people began to think of the church.

In 1920, when the fighting was about over, an incident occurred which greatly stimulated religious life. At that time there was a drought in Tepoztlán and the surrounding area and the crops were severely threatened. In the same year, according to our informants, El Tepozteco returned to Tepoztlán. He appeared to a peasant from Yautepec who was on his way to Tepoztlán. The mythical figure no longer wore his ancient dress but was dressed as a humble peasant in white shirt and *calzones* and broad-brimmed Zapatista sombrero, and with a handkerchief tied around his neck in typical local fashion.

El Tepozteco spoke to the peasant, saying, "Go and tell my village that I am very angry because they have my mother (the Virgin of Natividad) naked and that is why I have not wanted it to rain. They must buy her a crown and a tunic of silk and satin and then I will send abundant rain."

Then he mysteriously disappeared and the man from Yautepec hurried to Tepoztlán to tell what had happened. When the news had spread through the village, some of the *mayordomos* of the old *cofradías* took it upon themselves to collect money to buy the clothing and adornment for the Virgin. A few days later, according to Tepoztecans, it began to rain and the crops were saved.

With the help of this incident the more pious people sought to re-establish the church and return to their former religious practices. The village priest, Padre Pedro

Rojas, still resided in Mexico City and refused to return for fear of attack by the revolutionaries. During his absence some of his functions were carried on by *rezanderos,* laymen who knew from memory a great number of prayers for different occasions, such as for a dying man, a difficult delivery, the reappearance of lost or stolen articles, good crops, avoiding arguments in the family, keeping the husband from drinking too much, and so on. The *rezanderos* were kept busy in those difficult days and earned a comfortable income.

In the absence of the regular priest, a young priest was sent to the village in 1919. He energetically set about to put the church in order. He appointed new *mayordomos* of the *cofradías,* a new leader of the Asociación de la Divina Providencia, and a church *cantor.* But Tepoztecans seemed to have forgotten Catholic practices during the Revolution, and hardly anyone went to confession or Mass—despite the exhortations and threats of the Father.

The only practice the villagers still conscientiously clung to was baptism, and they were eager to baptize the children born during the Revolution. To get the people to attend church once more, the priest refused to baptize any child until the godparents were confessed. But Tepoztecans had forgotten the prayers and the formalities of confession and were afraid and embarrassed to appear before the priest. As a result, they were unwilling to become godparents. Parents were then forced to ask the few *rezanderos* who had kept their connections with the church to be the *padrinos* of their children. These men eventually monopolized the godparentage of the village and even came to charge for this service. One *rezandero* had about one hundred godchildren. Needless to say, the *rezanderos* were unable and unwilling to fulfill their obligations as godfathers, and scarcely recognized their godchildren. The parents considered the original godparent of their choice as the true godparent, rather than the *padrinos rezanderos* who were forced upon them.

When the village was more peaceful the regular priest returned with some of the *cacique* families, and religious life became normal once again—but without its former splendor. Fiestas were again celebrated, the popular Carnaval again held. The ban against baptism without confession was lifted and anyone might serve as godparent.

But the new tranquillity was soon to be shattered, this time by the Catholic Church which feared restraining measures of the post-revolutionary government. The church adopted a policy of non-cooperation and active resistance. On July 31, 1926, the archbishop of Mexico ordered all priests to leave the churches and to cease public religious services. Faithful Catholics were called upon to withdraw their children from the public schools to protect them from "socialist teaching." Priests were instructed to give Mass and to administer the sacraments in a clandestine manner.

In Tepoztlán these church orders resulted in the priest's once again leaving for Mexico City, and religious activity waned. The most important prayers and ceremonies were conducted secretly by one of the more able *rezanderos,* Don Francisco

Cortés Sedano, who had been selected by the priest for this purpose. The priest wrote frequent letters to Sedano, giving instructions and sending church literature for his use. The giving of Mass was a special problem since it required the presence of an ordained priest. In a letter to Cortés Sedano the priest offered a solution:

One thing appears essential to me and that is that since it is not possible to celebrate Holy Mass with solemnity and the attendance of the faithful in person they might be told to congregate in their respective chapels at a convenient hour and there unite themselves in spirit with the priest who will celebrate it in the name of the contributors. This may be done for the days of the Holy Jubilee and for fiestas of each village and barrio. Propose this to the people concerned, for I believe the pious ones will be entirely satisfied. Please say ahead of time who have accepted this proposition so that I may fulfill their wishes on the days they designate. They may be certain that I will carry out this obligation. The charge now is five pesos, as an aid to the priests. But those who cannot give it all at once can give as much as they are able. You are charged with sending it and if they wish I will send a receipt by return mail.

The priest also made suggestions as to which books or pamphlets should be read to the congregation. For example, in a letter dated January 30, 1929, two and one-half years after he had left Tepoztlán, the priest urged Cortés Sedano to use the following pamphlets: "Prisoner of Love," "A Visit to the Altar," "My Vote for Christ the King," "One Year More," "Where Are You Going, My Son?" and others. These tracts, written in great numbers and printed in secret presses, played an important role in the church program; some were simply of a religious nature but others, such as "My Vote for Christ the King," incited armed uprising against the government.

Cortés Sedano, as the priest's representative in the village, bore the burden of the struggle. He collected money for the church, distributed the many "subversive" leaflets exhorting Catholics to join the fight against the government and gain supporters among the faithful. He was also in contact with the Cristero movement which was then opposing the government with arms in the states of Jalisco, Guanajuato, and Michoacan. His attempts to arouse similar action in Tepoztlán failed. Pro-government forces—the CROM, the Fraternales, and the Bolsheviki were stronger in the village at that time and resisted the Cristero movement. A band of Cristeros once attempted to take over Tepoztlán with arms, but the village was defended by former Zapatistas, and the Cristeros were dispersed. After this incident Francisco Cortés Sedano was imprisoned as an agent of the Cristeros and the church. He was apprehended by ten federal soldiers and placed in the local jail under the supervision of José Rivera, then president of the municipio. A group of Cortés Sedano's supporters brought the prisoner tequila, salt, and lemons to comfort him.

One woman had the temerity to scold José Rivera soundly for arresting anyone on Good Friday and for offending the Lord by working on that day, an act only a Pilate would do. Her words amused the villagers and for the rest of his life the president was called "José Pilato." Cortés Sedano feared for his life but the Zapatistas did not shoot him. The morning after the battle with the Cristeros, Cortés Sedano was removed to the Cuernavaca prison and two days later was released by the governor with a warning. Cortés Sedano returned to the village and continued his religious work but abandoned the Cristero movement.

ORGANIZATION OF THE CHURCH TODAY

The church of Tepoztlán is an integral part of the structure of the Roman Catholic Church and is under the jurisdiction of a hierarchy of authorities, most of whom are outside of the municipio. Most of the characteristics of the local church are similar to Catholic churches everywhere, but a few are unique, if not to Tepoztlán, then to Mexico. For example, the Catholic Church is a highly centralized, authoritarian organization in which officials and prelates are appointed by their superiors and in which all policy is laid down by those in high positions. But in Tepoztlán, as in other Mexican villages, there is a democratic element in the election of *mayordomos* and a marked freedom in the conduct of all secular aspects of religious affairs, such as the maintenance of the barrio chapels, the celebrations of fiestas, and the collection of money for these fiestas.

Added to this type of local autonomy is the fact that the church in Tepoztlán is not a dynamic, militant organization and interferes only minimally in the private lives of the villagers. In general it is tolerant toward practices of magic, sorcery, and paganism, and toward drunkenness. Even the few Protestants have been left to go their own way. This situation is, in part, due to the passivity or disinterest of the local priest, who is himself a native Tepoztecan and tolerant of local traditions.

The arrival of a group of nuns in 1945 injected an aggressive religious attitude in the local church, for these women have actively applied pressure upon the villagers to live more Catholic lives. They have established a school to compete with the public school; they urge parents to attend services, to confess, and to have their children baptized, confirmed, and instructed in doctrine. They make frequent visits to homes, seek out those living in free union or married only by civil law and exhort them to have church marriages, and finally, they have attempted to convert several Protestants.

The complex organization of the church includes seven levels of ecclesiastic hierarchy. (See Chart 3.) The first and highest in the nation is the archbishop of Mexico. He maintains connections with Tepoztlán through the medium of circulars, pastorals, and general orders. Few if any Tepoztecans have ever seen him. Next is the bishop of Cuernavaca who is in charge of the churches in the state of Morelos. He visits Tepoztlán about once every five years, but has been seen occasionally by Tepoztecans when in Cuernavaca.

On the third level in the hierarchy is the local priest, the main figure in the central church of Tepoztlán (see Fig. 50), and the highest spiritual authority in the municipio. The fact that he is a native of Tepoztlán has facilitated his work there. Tepoztecans feel more comfortable with this priest than with all of his "foreign" predecessors, and are less inclined to complain and criticize him. His lack of mysticism and religious fervor and his attitude of detachment suits them well. However, being a native son has diminished somewhat the aura of respect which generally surrounds a village priest and has encouraged some Tepoztecans to make direct appeals to him to lower his fees and to settle family conflicts and personal problems. He has also been drawn into some small conflicts, a result of which was his being denounced to the archbishop of Mexico City by a group of Tepoztecans.

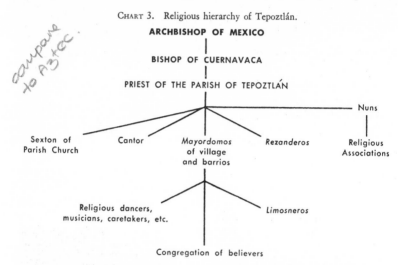

CHART 3. Religious hierarchy of Tepoztlán.

ARCHBISHOP OF MEXICO

BISHOP OF CUERNAVACA

PRIEST OF THE PARISH OF TEPOZTLÁN

Nuns

Sexton of Parish Church — Cantor — Mayordomos of village and barrios — Rezanderos — Religious Associations

Religious dancers, musicians, caretakers, etc. — Limosneros

Congregation of believers

In the fourth place are the Monjas Carmelitas, the aforementioned nuns, who, although a recent addition, are to reside permanently in the village. These nuns are all outsiders and are treated with great respect by Tepoztecans. In addition to their other activities, the nuns have assumed the direction of some of the religious associations, particularly the *Juventud de Acción Católica*. They have greatly extended the activities and increased the membership of these associations and by their work have brought about a religious revival in Tepoztlán.

On the fifth level of the hierarchy are various lay functionaries of the church. These are: (1) The sacristan or sexton hired by the priest as his personal aid and caretaker of the church building. Specifically, the duties of the sacristan are to help the priest dress for ceremonial occasions, to memorize several prayers in Latin in order to assist at Mass, to care for the altar and the sacred vessels, to clean the temple, and to keep a record of the priest's religious program. At the time of this study the sacristan was a young unmarried man of twenty of an acculturated family in the barrio of Santo Domingo. He was paid a wage of from three to five pesos a day and more on certain fiesta days when there is an excess of work.

(2) The cantor or church singer is an assistant to the sacristan but is selected by the priest and responsible to him. He is expected to play the organ and sing religious songs in Spanish and Latin. He participates in the singing during Mass

Fig. 50. The central church.

and in leading the hymns and *Te Deums*. He is paid one peso for each Mass and fifty centavos for each *Te Deum*.

(3) The *rezanderos* are men who make a vocation of religion by memorizing many prayers and hiring themselves out to intone these prayers for others on special occasions. For example, if someone loses a horse or cow and wishes to ask San Pedro to help him find the animal he will pay one or two pesos to a *rezandero* to go to the chapel in the barrio of San Pedro and recite the appropriate prayer.

Although the *rezandero* is not recognized by the church as a functionary he is thought of as such by the populace. Some *rezanderos* play an important role in local religious life and enjoy certain prestige. The more skilled have a large repertory of prayers and deliver them with the impressive skill of a priest. It is interesting to note that the two most important *rezanderos*, both of whom were our informants, were also political leaders; one in the Cristero movement, the other in the opposing leftist group. The latter, incidentally, became the first Protestant in Tepoztlán. At present there are approximately ten *rezanderos* in the village and the majority of these live in the barrio of Santo Domingo.

(4) The members and respective officers of the religious associations are a type of lay church functionaries. Many of these associations were founded in colonial times and had a long history of ups and downs. They suffered misfortunes during the struggle for independence and during the Reform and the Revolution but were always reorganized in times of peace. Some of these associations are national and international in character, such as the Asociación Guadalupana, the Apostolado de la Oración, and the Acción Católica; others are essentially local and lack external ties. We shall describe the more important of these organizations.

a) The Asociación de la Vela Perpetua, the objective of which is to give homage to the *Santísimo Sacramento* by permanently maintaining a lighted candle on the altar. The Asociación consists of thirty-one women who identify themselves by wearing a medal suspended on a white ribbon. Each member dedicates one day a month to keeping vigil at the altar. Membership is limited to the maximum number of days in a month and this society is considered honorific and select. In the days of Díaz only the wives of *caciques* were members. The organization has a president, secretary, and treasurer; apart from its routine religious activity, this society serves no other social function.

b) Asociación del Apostolado de la Oración celebrates the first Friday of each month. Although men may join, the present membership consists of twenty-five to thirty women. The distinguishing mark is a medal worn on a red ribbon. It is interesting to note that although this organization has different levels of membership to stimulate the mystic devotion of its members, in Tepoztlán the members fulfill only the rituals of the first order without aspiring to the superior orders.

c) Asociación Guadalupana celebrates the twelfth day of each month in honor of the Virgin of Guadalupe. Membership is made up of thirty women.

d) The Cofradía de la Virgen del Carmen is a sisterhood of about thirty women who celebrate the sixteenth day of each month. The scapulary of the Virgen del

Carmen is used widely in the village because of the numerous virtues attributed to it. It is useful to frighten away devils and other fear-inspiring beings. It also saves lives by deflecting bullets or machetes. If carried at the time of death, it insures the possibility of "dying well" and the certainty that the Virgen del Carmen will soon remove the soul from purgatory. For these reasons approximately three hundred men, women, and children customarily carry this scapulary.

e) Sagrado Corazón de Jesús celebrates Mass on the first Friday of each month in homage to the Sacred Heart of Jesus. Again membership consists of thirty women. This association is considered most powerful because its members are "the best women in the village." The present president is the priest's sister.

f) Asociación de la Adoración Nocturna is made up exclusively of men. The forty members are obliged to confess each month and keep vigil all night of the first Saturday of each month, praying and giving praise to the Holy One. On the following Sunday each member takes communion. However, this society scarcely functions because the majority of the members refuse to fulfill the requirement of confession.

g) Acción Católica de Jóvenes Mexicanos consists of two sections, one for each of the sexes. There are about eighty youths and thirty girls in the organization. The members work to arouse the religious spirit of the people, to organize fiestas to raise funds, and to attract the youth to join. Under the stimulation of the nuns this organization has become extremely active. For the first time, young Tepoztecans have manifested a militant Catholicism of a modern type and have become interested in understanding the religious dogma and in recruiting new members. It is also the only religious association which has a sense of solidarity and imposes mutual obligations upon its members. Members visit each other when ill, celebrate each other's birthdays, and attend weddings and funerals.

h) Vanguardia is an association for children from seven to fourteen years of age. They are required to attend Mass, to confess, and to take communion every Sunday. Membership varies considerably during the year.

Other associations which function only once or twice a year also exist. Some of these are the Hermandád de las Ánimas which celebrates All Saints' Day on November first, the Sociedád de la Virgen de la Natividad which is in charge of preparations for the fiesta of the patron of the village on September eighth. Before the Revolution there was an Asociación de Caridad called San Vicente de Paul which distributed food and clothing to the poor. The society disappeared during the Revolution and was never reorganized.

(5) The *mayordomos,* religious leaders of the barrios, are important functionaries in connection with religious fiestas. They decide how the fiesta is to be celebrated, whether or not to have Mass sung, or to have a sermon, or to invite additional priests, and so on. They arrange for all these services, for the band of musicians, for fireworks, and for whatever else they decide to have. They frequently must spend their own funds to produce a successful fiesta. They also generally serve *mole* and tamales and *ponche* to large numbers of people.

In addition to barrio *mayordomos* there are *mayordomos* of the chapels of the seven surrounding villages. Occasionally the people of these villages select someone in Tepoztlán to be their *mayordomo,* as did Ixcatepec in electing a young man from the barrio of San Pedro in Tepoztlán.

There are also several *mayordomos* of an inferior category who are in charge of certain images. Thus, for example, in the barrio of Santa Cruz there is a *mayordomo* to care for the Virgen del Rosario situated in the barrio chapel.

The *mayordomos* have several assistants whom we include on the sixth level of religious functionaries. The *limosneros* are permanent functionaries who collect the taxes from house to house. These men, attired in their clean Sunday clothes and carrying a plate on which is a spray of Bougainvillaea or some other red flowers, visit every house asking for contributions, such as "A *limosna* for the image of the *Divino Rostro* whose day is to be celebrated on Sunday." One type of *limosnero* of special interest is the *huehuechique,* who can say Catholic prayers in Náhuatl and who collects money for the New Year. At one time there were many *huehuechiques* but now there is only one in the barrio of Santa Cruz.

Among those who assist the *mayordomos* and who animate the barrio fiestas are the musicians. When there is not enough money to hire a professional band from Cuernavaca or Mexico City, the *mayordomos* will hire local musicians. Other assistants clean the local chapel and repair the masonry. The *danzantes* who dance in honor of the barrio saint are also temporary functionaries. It is the task of the *mayordomo* to organize dance groups and to persuade parents to permit their children to participate. Still another temporary functionary is the *mayordomo* in charge of organizing religious peregrinations to other parts of Mexico.

CHART 4. Organization of the church.

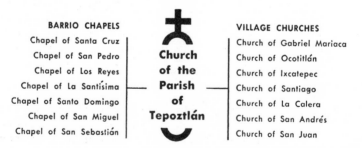

BARRIO CHAPELS		VILLAGE CHURCHES
Chapel of Santa Cruz		Church of Gabriel Mariaca
Chapel of San Pedro	Church	Church of Ocotitlán
Chapel of Los Reyes	of the	Church of Ixcatepec
Chapel of La Santísima	Parish	Church of Santiago
Chapel of Santo Domingo	of	Church of La Calera
Chapel of San Miguel	Tepoztlán	Church of San Andrés
Chapel of San Sebastián		Church of San Juan

On the seventh level of the religious hierarchy are the faithful members of the church. It is from among the more pious of these that a regular congregation and members of the religious associations are drawn; almost everyone in the village, however, participates at some time in religious activities, in barrio fiestas, and in the *cuatequitl del santo,* which is the collective working of the milpas dedicated to the support of particular saints.

All Tepoztecans, whether pious or not, contribute money to the church; indeed, the church of Tepoztlán is entirely self-supporting and does not require subsidies from the church of Mexico. Rather, it makes substantial contributions to the national church of Mexico.

The church of Tepoztlán includes the seven villages of the municipio and controls fourteen village and barrio chapels. This is illustrated in Chart 4.

Summarizing the total personnel of the church of the municipio of Tepoztlán we find the following:

Functionary	Number
Priest of the parish	1
Sexton	1
Cantor	1
Mayordomos of the barrios	7
Mayordomos of the villages	7
Monjas Carmelitas	8
Rezanderos	10
Limosneros	42
Mayordomos of the images	28
Mayordomos of peregrinations	15
Functionaries in charge of cleaning the chapels and the temple	37
Total	157

CHURCH FINANCES

As has been pointed out earlier, the church in Tepoztlán not only supports itself but also sends contributions to the bishop in Cuernavaca. It is difficult to do more than approximate the annual income of the church because of variation in contributions from year to year. Records of church income were not available to us and probably were not kept. However, we have more or less accurate data on the most important sources of income. In the following pages we will present a conservative estimate of this income.

BAPTISMS, MARRIAGES, AND FUNERALS

Our data indicate an average of 273 live births in the municipio over a six-year period. There are two classes of baptism, one a simple type at three pesos and the other with the ringing of the bells at four pesos. Assuming that the number of baptisms is about equally divided between these two types, we get a total annual income from baptisms of 956 pesos.

The charge for the *sacamisa* (the Mass said for a mother forty days after the birth of a child) is two pesos if said from the *cancel* and one peso if said from the altar. Again assuming about an equal number of each type, we have a yearly income of 408 pesos.

The priest charges twelve pesos for a simple marriage ceremony and twenty to twenty-five pesos for a more elaborate wedding. It is difficult to determine exactly how many weddings are simple and how many are elaborate. It is our impression that most church weddings in Tepoztlán are of the second type, that is, *con ceremonia*. Judging from the marriage statistics, there is an average of about twenty-five church weddings a year. Assuming that twelve are of the elaborate type and thirteen of the simple type, we get an income of 426 pesos a year.

Another source of income is from the ceremonies at death and burial. The simple benediction for a dead child costs five pesos; benediction with *vigilias* costs thirty pesos; for going to the home of the deceased and praying, and then saying a Mass in the church and later at the cemetery, the cost is forty pesos.

The number of deaths in the municipio over a six-year period was 101, one-fourth of which was infant mortality. From this data we can calculate the church income. There is considerable variation in the costs of funerals. Often the rich will take only the simplest ceremony, while the poor will go into debt for an elaborate funeral. We can assume that about 60 per cent of the adult deaths yielded an income of at least 30 pesos to the church and the rest yielded about 40 pesos. We therefore get the following:

25 Benedictions for infants at 5 pesos each	125
46 Benedictions and Masses for adults at 30 pesos each	1,380
30 Benedictions and Masses for adults at 40 pesos each	1,200
Total	2,705

GENERAL MASSES

Here we can consider the Mass said in memory of the dead once a year; those paid by the religious associations in the village; and Masses said on Sundays and fiesta days.

It is customary to have a Mass said on the anniversary of the death of a close relative for at least two years, and some continue for much longer. Thus, given 101 deaths a year we can assume that at least eighty per cent will have Masses said the first year, sixty per cent the second year, and thirty per cent the third year. This would mean 180 Masses a year. These Masses have three prices: simple Mass for 2 pesos, a sung Mass for 11 pesos, and a Mass with a sermon for 40 pesos. The priest encourages the people to have Mass said for their dead and points out that the more elaborate the ceremony, the better the dead will fare in purgatory. Even the poor try to have the most elaborate Mass. Still, we will assume that at least 50 per cent of the Masses for the dead are simple, about 25 per cent are sung, and 25 per cent include a sermon. This yields the following income:

90 Masses at 2 pesos each	180
45 Masses at 11 pesos each	495
45 Masses at 40 pesos each	1,800
Total	2,475

In addition, we must add the money collected by the priest on the Days of the Dead when he says Mass for the dead as a whole, but mentions in particular the names of those who pay a three-peso fee. Informants believe he receives about 400 pesos from such Masses, giving a total of 2,875 pesos as income from Masses for the dead.

The ten religious associations in the village are each obliged to pay for 12 Masses a year in honor of the particular patron saint of the association. Their Masses are always sung and followed by a sermon and should cost 40 pesos, but the priest gives them a special price and charges only 25 pesos. The income from 120 Masses is, therefore, 3,000 pesos a year. On Sundays and holy days the priest says two Masses which are free of charge. However, those who assist Mass are expected to make some contribution. Assuming that an average of 150 persons assist weekly at each of the two Masses and that each contributes ten centavos, we get a weekly income of 30 pesos. If we add eight days for special holy days to the 52 Sundays, we get 60 days with an income of 30 pesos daily, or 1,800 pesos a year. In addition, approximately 100 persons attend church daily and contribute about 10 centavos each, making an annual total of 3,650 pesos. In summary then, we find a total of 11,325 pesos received from Masses, as follows:

Masses for the dead		2,875
Masses for the religious associations		3,000
Masses on Sundays and holy days		1,800
Daily Masses		3,650
	Total	11,325

FIESTAS

The priest charges 75 pesos for officiating at each barrio fiesta and at the village fiestas. For this price he says three Masses and a sermon. With seven barrios and seven villages he has an income of 1,575 pesos a year.

OTHER SOURCES

The priest charges 20 centavos for praying the *evangelios* and 20 centavos for singing the responses. In addition he has occasional income from extraordinary requests for prayers or Masses. Informants who aided us with this study of church income estimate about 300 pesos as a minimum from these sources. In summary we find the total church income as follows:

Income from baptisms		956
Income from *sacamisas*		408
Income from marriages		426
Income from ritual for the dead		2,705
Income from Masses		11,325
Income from barrio and village fiestas		1,575
Income from other sources		300
	Total	17,695

CHURCH EXPENSES

The only expense of the priest, apart from his own living expenses, is the salary of the sacristan which is approximately 1,200 pesos a year. The salary of the church singer is paid by the churchgoers. The ceremonial clothing and ceremonial objects are not replaced often, and when the occasion arises, special collections are made for this purpose.

THE ANNUAL CYCLE OF RELIGIOUS FIESTAS

The religious fiestas in which Tepoztecans participate are of four types: (1) the barrio fiestas in which each barrio celebrates its patron saint; (2) the village-wide fiestas which celebrate the holy days in the central church; (3) the fiestas of other surrounding villages of the municipio; and (4) the fiestas of villages and towns outside the municipio. In all, there are a total of 63 named fiestas in which Tepoztecans participate. Of these, 27 are village-wide fiestas, 12 are barrio fiestas (some barrios celebrate two separate days), 7 are fiestas of surrounding villages within the municipio, and 7 are fiestas of villages outside the municipio.

Of the village-wide fiestas, the most important are the Carnaval, Ash Wednesday, the fiestas of Holy Week, the fiestas for El Tepozteco and María on September 8, the blessing of the *pericón* on September 28, the Days of the Dead, and the Days of the Posadas.

It is difficult to estimate accurately the total number of days during the year devoted to the fiestas. Some of the 63 fiestas last three or four days, and a conservative total estimate would be about 100 days. It would be quite erroneous, however, to conclude that most Tepoztecans spend approximately a third of the year in fiestas. Most fiestas are attended by only a small portion of the population. Certainly less than five per cent of the populace attend the 14 fiestas of the surrounding villages and other towns. And less than ten per cent of the villagers attend the fiestas of barrios other than their own. And there are probably only about a half-dozen village-wide fiestas during the year in which the village as a whole participates. Much time is also consumed in preparations which may begin two to four weeks before the celebration of the fiesta.

Barrio fiestas follow a more or less definite pattern. The religious ceremonial which takes place within the barrio chapel is generally celebrated with three Masses given by the priest. The first Mass is called *preparación;* the second, *función;* and the third, *consumir.* The first two are conducted *sin vinar* (without taking wine), but in the third, the priest takes the sacred wine. In the afternoon the priest conducts the *exposición del Santísimo,* some church music is played and sung, and finally a *rosario* is prayed. If the barrio has insufficient funds, some parts of the ceremonial are dispensed with.

The secular aspects of barrio fiestas overshadow the religious aspects in popularity and attendance. These festivities generally consist of a display of fireworks, both day and night, which have been arranged on a *castillo* or wooden framework. The *castillo,* in the shape of a bull, is most often used. Entertainment may also be supplied by a *jaripeo,* which is a type of rodeo devoted to a display of roping and mounting bulls. Music may be supplied by a band of hired musicians, and some fiestas include groups of religious dancers. Finally, all in the barrio, except the poorest families, prepare a meal of *mole* and other festal dishes and entertain visitors from other barrios or villages. Those who participate in a fiesta, dress in their best clothing, often purchasing new clothing for this annual occasion.

Barrio fiestas and some village-wide fiestas are supported by popular subscriptions which are more in the nature of voluntary taxes. The *mayordomo* of each fiesta collects the money in a ceremony called the *Moxotlaloyan y Cerapah* at the place where the money for candles for the church is paid. A similar payment is made for the *castillo,* either at the same time or, in some cases, in a separate ceremony called the *castillopah.* This ceremony is usually held one day after the fiesta so as to collect the *limosna* a year in advance. The amount paid is generally fifty centavos, or one peso, according to how much had been promised to the *santo* the year before. The people, who had been reminded earlier of the coming payment by the *huehuechique* or *limosnero,* convene at the *mayordomo's* house to leave their money. Upon payment, each receives a portion or two, according to the amount contributed, of *mole verde,* tamales, and a drink called *tepache.*[8] Contributions are carefully recorded and there have been few cases of misuse of these funds.

The calendar of religious fiestas is a typical Catholic calendar which includes moveable and fixed fiesta days. The dates upon which many of the fiestas fall are calculated from the key date, Ash Wednesday.[9]

RELIGIOUS PRACTICES AND BELIEFS

Just as the cycle of religious fiestas in Tepoztlán follows Catholic practice, with some local modifications, so does the individual Tepoztecan. Only a few persons, mostly women, in the village fulfill all the ritual and other obligations set by the priest and church. These people are looked upon by the rest as fanatics who are "always dressing the saints." The priest does not consider his flock to be "good Catholics." The older people maintain a respectful passivity toward most church activities, while the adult males and many older youths, although not irreligious, tend to scoff at the nuns, the Acción Católica and other "fanatics." Among these recalcitrants there is much more interest in the barrio fiestas and one or two of the nearby village fiestas than in the regular daily and weekly religious acts which are required of them. On the other hand, the nuns and the religious associations tend to emphasize the latter. The school, too, so far unsuccessfully, discourages attending fiestas because of the disastrous effects upon school attendance. Regular participation in church ritual is associated with becoming "more cultured." Those who go to boarding schools or who have occasion to live in Mexico City for some time

---

[8] This ceremony has been described in detail by Redfield, *Tepoztlán,* pp. 99-100.
[9] See Appendix D, "Fiesta Calendar of Tepoztlán," p. 458. For a more detailed description of the fiestas, see Redfield's chapter, "A Tepoztecan Book of Days," in *Tepoztlán,* pp. 83-132.

learn to attend Mass, to confess, and to take communion more often than is customary in the village.

Prayers for various occasions are memorized by Tepoztecans. The older generation learn them in Náhuatl, the younger in Spanish. The people do not know how to improvise prayers, and when their memory fails they prefer to keep silent, or merely cross themselves, or kiss a scapulary to invoke the protection of the appropriate saint. The obligatory morning prayers are seldom said with regularity. Some of the old people still say a prayer at noon when the bell of the municipal clock strikes; the men remove their hats and give thanks to God because they still have strength to work. When the evening church bell rings, the men are again supposed to take off their hats and the women to kneel to give thanks because the day has passed without mishap. We cannot estimate the number of people who fulfill the latter obligation, but in all the time we were in the village we never observed anyone kneeling in prayer outside the church. But men returning home from the fields lift their hats respectfully whenever they pass a cross, and on the bus from Tepoztlán to Cuernavaca all hats go up in unison each time a church is passed. Some Tepoztecans recite prayers on special occasions, such as planting corn, lighting a charcoal furnace, or pruning a tree.

As indicated earlier, most Tepoztecans do not feel strongly the need to attend Mass every Sunday or even on holy days. On the basis of our own observations and informants' estimates, it appears that, on the average, about two hundred, mostly women, attend church on Sundays. The 6:00 A.M. Mass is preferred; those who attend the 8:00 A.M. Mass risk being called lazy. Mass, like other public gatherings, is a welcome form of diversion. It is one of the opportunities for sweethearts to see one another; young people are said to attend not out of devotion but to flirt. Everyone puts on his best clothes for Mass. The older men wear huaraches, white *calzones,* and shirts; the youths wear trousers and modern shirts, and many wear jackets. The women use *rebozos* to cover their heads. Upon entering the church, the women cross themselves with holy water and take seats up toward the front. The men generally do not cross themselves and remain in the rear. Some of the youths stand at one side of the nave, leaning against the pillars so as to be able to see the girls during the service. The children sit with their mothers and sisters. Five- and ten-centavo pieces are dropped into the plate passed by the sacristan.

After Mass the young men are the first to leave. They remain at the church door, talking, joking, and laughing quietly among themselves, until the girls appear. The older men are the next to leave the church, and then the women. Most of the men go off to drink, while the women go home in little groups of relatives.

Tepoztecans do not rigorously observe Sunday or other holy days as days of rest. During planting and harvesting, everyone works in the fields, and the storekeepers in the center who profit by the week-end tourist trade always work on Sundays and holidays. Informants say, "It is no sin to work on Sunday when it is done out of necessity." Some of the very old people believe that he who works on Sunday ruins himself economically for the rest of the week.

Tepoztecans do not like to confess; the majority do so only once a year. Not giving much importance to sin, Tepoztecans do not regard confession as necessary. Most men consider confession important only when one is about to die but "with the pangs of death, who's going to remember to confess properly?" Women, particularly married women, are less reluctant to confess, and about fifty women are known to take communion and confess quite often. Through the Acción Católica the number of young people of both sexes who do this has increased. Perhaps the most important deterrent to confession, especially among the older people, is that the priest may exact from the confessor the recitation of certain prayers which most people cannot say accurately. Fearing a scolding from the priest, they prefer to avoid the situation. There is no such difficulty with communion. "We would all take communion more often if we didn't have to confess; that we always avoid."

In general, the Tepoztecan feels obliged to contribute to the church and does so by paying *limosnas*. There is a belief that he who refuses to give alms will find that no one receives his soul in heaven and that therefore he must go to hell. He who always gives alms finds that when he dies and his soul goes to heaven, "the Saint to whom he has given alms comes to receive the soul and intercedes with God to allow him to enter, and so he gets to heaven." Thus, when a Tepoztecan lights a candle to some saint or deposits a coin or two in the box, he considers himself deserving of the protection of that saint.

Tithes, which were obligatory and were collected by the government for the church before the Revolution, no longer exist. The local priest, however, hires a *limosnero* at harvest time to go about the fields, riding on a mule, to collect contributions from the farmers. As a rule, each farmer gives about twelve ears of corn, so that the priest collects a good amount for his stores.

Religious beliefs in Tepoztlán reflect Tepoztecan social character and world view. The profoundly practical nature of Tepoztecans precludes religious fantasy, mysticism, and any preoccupation with metaphysics; they seek from religion concrete solutions to problems of daily life and go about it in as direct a manner as their religion permits. Their religious world, like the world in which they live, is full of hostile forces and punishing figures which must be propitiated to secure good will and protection. The act of propitiation is direct and simple, consisting of giving something or doing something which is known to please a particular saint, such as lighting a candle, giving a few coins, offering flowers, burning incense, reciting a special prayer, or performing a certain dance; these offerings incur an obligation on the part of the recipient to favor the donor.

As in most mestizo communities in Mexico and Central America, Tepoztecan religious beliefs represent a fusion of Catholic and pagan elements. The people's concept of God is vague at best; the one characteristic which is clear to Tepoztecans is that he is a punishing God who acts in ways hostile to men. Most misfortunes are ascribed to him; good fortune rarely.

The Holy Trinity is viewed as consisting of three distinct gods. One is God the Father, who is usually pictured with a long, white beard and a large ball in his hand, "that one is the Lord of the World." The second is "the one who died for us, the one who was crucified." The third is "the Holy Ghost or the Holy Dove," who is frequently depicted with the symbol of a dove to which Tepoztecans give divine attributes.

El Tepozteco occupies a special place in Tepoztecan religion and is unique to this community. The process by which he was deified and confused with Catholic figures was paralleled in localities all through Mexico during the colonial period. He continues to play an important role in Tepoztlán, is constantly evoked, and is one of the few legendary figures in the village. He is described to the children in the following manner:

Tepozteco cannot be known; his house is on the hill near El Parque. There he has his *comal,* his *metate,* and everything which he needs in his house, but he himself does not appear. He always lives far off among the clouds. When they don't give him a good celebration on the eighth of September he sends a great wind; when the celebration is a good one then he does nothing, he is content. Tepozteco is a god who is lovable and cruel. He has only one punishment for the village—he takes away the water. He makes *los aires* and they cause illness. He has a mother who is in the church. We say a Mass for his mother. His mother is named *Tonantzin* and also *Natividad.*

Legends about El Tepozteco continually spring up. The most recent of these was told in the early days of World War II, after Mexico declared war on the Axis and obligatory military service was established:

In those days of worry and confusion, a conscript was walking the streets of Cuernavaca. He was crying because he had been called to the army. Suddenly at the corner he saw a boy, dressed like a peasant. The boy asked the youth why he was crying. "Why shouldn't I cry, for I must be a soldier, and they have ordered me to the war to defend the United States, and I must leave my old parents. If it were to fight for my country it would be bad enough but to fight for the gringos. . . ." Then the boy said, "Go in peace. Your tears are not in vain. Neither you nor other young Mexicans will have to go to fight for a foreign government. You will learn to be a soldier, but you will never leave the country. Go to the village of Tepoztlán and take an offering to my mother, the Virgen de la Natividad." Then the boy disappeared mysteriously.

The soldier was very impressed by what had happened. He told his parents and they decided to go to Tepoztlán with an offering. After that they began to tell the people of that village what had happened, and everyone understood that El Tepozteco had spoken again. El Tepozteco kept his word, for none of the conscripts went to fight for the United States.

Tepoztecans do not distinguish clearly between those misfortunes which might be considered punishments of God, or the work of the devil. Tepoztecans believe firmly in the devil, who is generally called *el pingo,* and to whom is attributed many of the evils which befall them. The powers of the devil, however, are relatively few; he cannot cause drought but he can cause harm to a person, making him an idiot or carrying him off bodily. The devil always appears dressed as a Mexican horseman or as "a tall gentleman, dressed in black like respectable people, with a suit of fine cloth." He is almost always met on lonely roads or in the woods during the night. To combat his evil influence, Tepoztecans recite a prayer to some saint, especially to St. Michael and St. Gabriel. When a Tepoztecan brings an offering to St. Michael he considers it necessary to light a candle to the devil as well, even though it be a small candle, so that he will not be angered.

Despite four hundred years of Catholicism, most Tepoztecans do not yet have a clear concept of the Catholic heaven and hell. According to Aztec religion the equivalent of heaven was a pleasant place where dead warriors and women who died in childbirth went to live. The existence of hell as a place for expiating sins committed in life was totally unknown. There was only Mictlán, the region of the dead, where souls continued to live the same life as they had on earth. Tepoztecans have no concept of eternal punishment. Hell is a form of purgatory to which only the greatest sinners are sentenced. Ordinary people do not fear hell, for "the temperate ones, those who believe in God, those who have done some good," go to heaven. The threat of hell is chiefly used to control the conduct of children; adults are not generally concerned with life after death.

Tepoztecans view heaven simply as a place of glory, "that is, a place where one has no necessities." Although hell may be described as "a place where there is a lot of fire and where sinners are burned," Tepoztecans do not actually view hell this way. To them going to hell means being condemned to wander over the earth at night, dragging chains until the period of punishment and suffering is over and the soul is admitted to heaven. Many accounts of such punishment are told in the village. The following is typical:

A woman who was a witch didn't leave her property well distributed, nor any written directions about it. Her children did not know what belonged to each and wanted to give the younger brother only a small share. He didn't agree to this, and it would have been better if he had, for after that every night at a late hour the children heard chains dragging and the sound of weeping. The sounds stopped at the door of their house and then began again. The brother consulted several people, and they advised him to confess and tell the priest what he had heard. He did this, and the priest told him to wait a day, and he would tell him where he would find his mother. The next day the priest said he could not locate his mother, but that he should go to where they sent the bones from the butcher's. He did so, and at midnight he found his mother tied to a post with a strong chain. When she saw him, she began to cry and told him that if he did not wish to see her in this state, he should accept the small share. The son was convinced and took his portion of the inheritance and after that they never again heard the noise, and the mother ceased to suffer.

All accounts include the dragging of chains by the soul and the scene at the slaughterhouse. The soul is released from suffering by some of the living who make up for the sins of the dead.

The saints are viewed as intermediaries with God, and Tepoztecans devote themselves to cultivating their favor. The saints are endowed with personal qualities, and their images are worshipped directly as divine beings rather than as mere symbols of living saints. This is evident when, in times of drought, the saints of each of the barrios, as well as of some of the villages, are appealed to for rain. All the images are shut up in the parish church and are taken out in procession only in the afternoon when the sun is high, so that the images will feel the heat and notice the people's discomfort and sadness.

The saints with greater punishing powers are most assiduously worshipped. Saint Peter, of the barrio of San Pedro, is one of these. If there are not enough dancers at his feast day, he brings illness and misfortune to those who did not participate. Saint Peter, whose image is accompanied by a lion, is said to use this animal to frighten children into dancing for him and sometimes to appear to a father who has refused to permit his children to dance. It is also believed that if a person does not accept the office of *mayordomo* of the barrio of San Pedro, the lion will be sent to frighten him.

In their view of the saints, Tepoztecans reveal a tendency toward polytheism. This is indicated in the distinct attitudes toward the different images of the same saint. For example, the various local figures of Christ do not all have equal powers and are not all worshipped with equal fervor. The Christ of Ixcatepec is considered "very miraculous" and is called upon when there is great misfortune, such as extreme drought. He is rendered special homage by taking children, dressed in white tunics and wearing a crown of thorns and little thorn crosses on their backs, to the chapel of Ixcatepec to do penance.

The conception of the soul will be discussed in Chapter 19, "Old Age and Death." Here it should be noted that Tepoztecans distinguish between the body, the soul, and the spirit in the following way: "The body serves us for all our needs, to satisfy our necessities," and "The soul is that which gives life to the body and which will be punished in the other life according to our sins."

When a sin is committed, "The body is not at fault, it is the soul which rules." The spirit guards the body and soul from all that is bad, it is the Guardian Angel, "like a dove, like a pigeon, but invisible." The spirit is the companion of the soul and gives it strength. "That is why when a person is not brave, he has little spirit."

The question of sin does not overly concern Tepoztecans. Sin is inevitable, for "we are all sinners." It comes as "malice" enters a person and as innocence leaves, it comes with knowledge of life, with sexuality, with loss of virginity or purity. Malice can be delayed by keeping children in ignorance, but sooner or later they will become sinners. However, sinners are differentiated according to the degree of their sin, so that there are good sinners and bad sinners.

Sins, too, vary in degree. To the Tepoztecan, lying, adultery, and failure to attend Mass, to take communion, to confess, or to celebrate feast days are without importance as sins. The Ten Commandments and other fundamental rules of conduct imposed by the Catholic Church do not control the behavior of the Tepoztecan. For him the most important sins are stealing, killing, and practicing witchcraft. These acts are also differentiated in degree of gravity.

In the case of theft there is a wide range of permissible stealing which is not considered sinful. Thus, it is no sin to steal the roof tiles, or the hearthstones, or the religious images of a temporarily abandoned house; "that is not a sin, that was abandoned, and it would be worse if it were lost." When someone's pig is run down by an automobile on the highway, the neighbors quickly come with knives and cut away the best portions of meat; this is no sin "since it is the custom of the people." But if one steals the growing corn, or corn after the harvest, or money —"that is really a great sin." Who does the stealing and from whom he steals also determine the degree of the sin. When cattle are stolen from a fellow villager it is a serious matter, cattle stolen by an outsider even more so, but cattle stolen by a Tepoztecan from a non-Tepoztecan is an act of minor importance. Thus, a young man whose father had died, and whose mother had lost most of their property to lawyers, supported himself by stealing cattle in places distant from Tepoztlán. He would go away for several weeks and return with cattle which he sold in the village or used in the fields. He is generally respected and considered *honrado*, although his actions are well known. "Since the poor fellow lost his inheritance, he sometimes goes out of Tepoztlán to struggle with the cattle of others."

While we were in the village, a highly respected person, prominent in state politics, was accused of having stolen a Zebu bull from a national experimental farm. The townspeople were impressed by his astuteness and did not take the attitude that he had done anything sinful or reprehensible.

In regard to killing, Tepoztecans also distinguish between excusable and inexcusable murders. If "one is like an assassin who kills in cold blood and for mere pleasure," it is a sin. But if one kills for some purpose, it is another matter. To kill a mortal enemy without warning is not a sin since the killer "only got ahead of the dead man" and took advantage of his carelessness. The shooting of a thief or suspected thief on sight is another type of justified killing.

Sorcery and witchcraft of any kind are great sins. Those who practice these "devil's arts" are certain to be punished after death, but they are left unmolested while they live and may be consulted by fellow villagers for cures or for advice in bewitching others.

Adultery is considered a sin only for women, but here again certain cases are excused. For example, "When a man demands good food at home and doesn't give the money to buy it, then he is forcing his wife to look for other men," and since he is the cause of the adultery or if he permits it, it is not a serious matter.

Calumny, criticism, and gossip are special sins of women, but drunkenness on the part of men is not considered a sin.

Other beliefs held by Tepoztecans which are of interest are those of *Naguales, los aires*, omens, healers, witches, and sorcerers.

The *Nagual* is a person who has the power to change into an animal, such as a dog or pig. This ancient belief is widely known in Tepoztlán but is considered to be dying out. Informants alluded to *Naguales* as beings of the past, as no longer existing, or, at least, no longer wishing to show themselves. To become a *Nagual*, one must make a pact with the devil and learn certain prayers which allow a man to turn into an animal. Other prayers take away the powers of a *Nagual* and make him revert to human form. *Naguales* have the power to enter houses, even when doors are closed, can steal anything, and can quietly carry off girls by putting them into a deep sleep. To prevent thefts by *Naguales* a cross is marked on the bottom of *metates* which then become too heavy for the *Nagual* to lift. Some *Naguales* will steal girls for a sum of money. *Naguales* cannot be wounded by a knife or a gun, and it is impossible to hit them or throw stones at them because of a secret power which defends them. Some people believe that El Tepozteco can turn himself into a *Nagual* and that he is their chief.

Los aires are mysterious forces, variously thought of as winds, spirits, or little people who may cause sores, pimples, paralysis, and other illnesses. They are found in stream beds, ravines, in stagnant pools, and atop the highest hills. Tepoztecans are careful to avoid *los aires* and not to offend them. Some old women still say certain Náhuatl phrases asking permission of *los aires* to take water from the stream. Those who must pass by stagnant water after bathing in a *temascal* must drop some of the leaves, with which they dried themselves, into the pool in order to avoid headaches, earaches, or watering of the eyes. To get rid of these afflictions one must be cleansed with salt and yarrow leaves which are afterward thrown into the middle of the street. Sometimes when a person eats beside a stream or near a ravine, he will be attacked by *los aires* and will have a headache and fever. The illness is treated by cleansing the person with herbs, which are then thrown into the stream or ravine. If the sick person continues to have fever and dreams of canes, water, or food, it means that *los aires* struck him very hard and must be fed. *Mole*, tamales, and fruit are prepared, and a special loaf of bread in the shape of a doll is ordered from the baker. The doll is decorated in red, and the meal, adorned with red crepe paper, is carried to the suspected stream and left there.[10]

Los aires are also believed to take refuge in anthills, and one who disturbs an anthill may suffer grave injury. For this reason no Tepoztecan dares open an anthill to remove the queen ant, despite the fact that the local variety of ants is very voracious and can destroy an entire cornfield. When a farmer discovers an anthill in his field he will place food, such as mango leaves, around the hole, so that the ants will not eat the corn. The farmers sometimes place poisonous leaves at an anthill, but the ants soon learn not to eat them. Some of the more advanced farmers use chemical products including D.D.T. to kill the ants but even the most educated will not open an anthill.

Informants relate that not long ago a man, not of Tepoztlán, used to sell ant dung as fertilizer. He collected the material from anthills, but after six months of this work he fell ill, became badly crippled, and died. The same thing happened to the uncle of one of our informants; after opening an anthill he spent eight years in bed, crippled and inflamed from the effects of *los aires*.

Belief in good and bad omens continues in Tepoztlán. These beliefs are innu-

---

[10] In Redfield's account a real doll, with red cheeks and decorated with colored yarn, is used. The bread doll is more closely reminiscent of the dough images offered in propitiation in pre-Hispanic times.

merable and not unlike many reported in other studies of rural Mexican communities. Omens are seen in the cry of the opossum, the entry of a bat into the house, the howling of a dog at midnight, the rainbow, the death of a snake within the house, the songs of certain birds, an egg laid without a shell, an egg with a double yolk, and many more such phenomena. When an evil omen appears in a home, the entire family feels threatened, not knowing upon whom misfortune will fall, and for a time everyone takes extra precautions against accident. Sometimes a favorite saint is appealed to or a powerful *curandero* is sought out, but more often the family does nothing, and the sense of apprehension soon wears off.

Evil supernatural forces can be made to act or can be counteracted by sorcerers and witches who receive their power from the devil. Witches are thought to be most active on Tuesdays and Fridays, and some people take extra precautions to hide soiled clothing or not to accept gifts of food on those days. Several old women, particularly those who know a great deal of herbal lore, are thought to be witches. Aggressive or bold women may also be suspected, particularly women who are able to dominate their husbands. Such women are often thought to have bewitched their husbands with *toloache,* a local herb. It is interesting to note that some of the young girls who have studied outside the village, and who live by urban standards, are also suspected of being witches by a large portion of the population. One such girl married a boy in the barrio of Los Reyes and was accused of being a witch by her mother-in-law on the ground that she refused to behave like a good daughter-in-law and continued to see her former school friends.

Sorcery is used in courtship by unsuccessful suitors. The leg of a beetle is introduced into a drink to arouse the passions of an indifferent girl, or a powder made from skulls may be thrown on the palm of a woman's right hand or on her head, or into her food or drink. Foods which spoil too quickly are often believed to contain some powder meant for sorcery. A young Tepoztecan schoolteacher who received a gift of apples from a pupil was very much alarmed when she noted that the fruit rotted the very next day, and she suspected the child's family of trying to bewitch her. The most feared type of sorcery is that in which an image of the victim is fashioned out of his soiled clothing and pierced with a pin in the region of the heart or head to bring about his illness or death. To be doubly certain of success, the doll may be thrown into an anthill, so that *los aires* will also attack him.

Almost any unusual illness, but particularly swelling of the head or joints, may be attributed to sorcery by the local *curanderos.* A bewitched person usually leaves the village in the belief that he is no longer safe there and can be cured only away from the sorcerer. In such cases, Tepoztecans generally consult *curanderos* of wide repute in Yautepec or other towns and may spend several hundred pesos to undergo a cure. However, mild symptoms of sorcery or illness due to supernatural elements may be treated within the village by use of prayer, holy water, local herbs, ritual "cleansing," and by consulting certain local healers who go into a trance and converse with spirits to get a diagnosis and prescribe a cure.[11]

---

[11] This may be an element of African culture introduced into Tepoztlán by Negro slaves.

healer

The most celebrated healer in Tepoztlán is one Rosalino Vargas, known as Don Rosas. He is believed to be a powerful sorcerer and is feared by many of the villagers. Some people claim to have seen him riding through the town at midnight wearing a long black cape, with sparks issuing forth from his eyes and mouth. Don Rosas, who often uses the fear he inspires to his own advantage, has several enemies, at least three of whom made attempts to murder him in recent years. Don Rosas is wealthy and has a flourishing practice. He has seven female assistants; there is much gossip to the effect that these women are his paramours who sleep with him in turns, one for each day in the week. Don Rosas' loyal clientele insist that the seven women help him treat the sick and perform a series of mysterious devotions which he practices nearly every night.

The technique employed by Don Rosas on his patients contains an interesting combination of Catholic, pagan, and possibly African elements. He does not deal directly with a patient but gets information concerning the nature of the illness through an assistant who questions the patient. After the conference the patient is taken to a room which resembles a chapel in that it has an altar and images of saints. The patient is seated on a chair close to a heavy curtain behind which sits Don Rosas. The visitor is given an image of a saint to hold while the *curandero* prays and goes into a trance. When he is "as if dead" an assistant wafts incense smoke toward him and he begins to speak, as though from a deep sleep, telling what illness the patient is suffering from. Whether or not a cure is possible is determined by a glass of water which has been placed among the images near the incense burner. If the water turns white there is hope for a cure, if black there is none. If a remedy is possible, Don Rosas then points out the necessary steps to protect the individual and his family from the enemy who is provoking the symptoms.

The patient must drink a sweet-sour tasting liquid, prepared by Don Rosas and stirred with a metal cross. The patient then pays two pesos for the cure but first must "cleanse" himself with the bills in the parts of his body which give him pain, and leave the money on the altar. Before leaving, the patient is given additional medicines to take each night and is generally advised to "cleanse" himself with very hot herb applications. More medicine is given as needed without charge and the patient is advised that the medicine must never be placed on the ground since it would lose its potency. Some patients need several consultations, all of which are conducted in the same manner, before they feel well again.

evil eye

The traditional remedies for evil eye and *espanto* (fright) involve a combination of folk beliefs, ancient herbal lore, and Catholic practice. A child is believed to be the victim of the evil eye if he comes home crying and very much disturbed. An egg is broken into a glass and if a long eye-shaped spot appears on the yolk, the person who put the eye upon the child is a man; if the spot is round, it is a woman. The child's clothes are changed and he is "cleansed" with a soiled kerchief or shirt if the guilty person was male, and with an apron or *rebozo* if a female. Some children are cured by being "cleansed" on their foreheads, with the tongue making the form of a cross.

Espanto or fright, an illness which leaves children sad and pale, is cured by women who can "lay the shadow" that afflicts them. These *curanderos* keep a supply of powdered cedar, palm, and blessed laurel which they throw on the forehead, breast, wrists, palms of the hand, nape of the neck, and into the nostrils of the sick child. While this is being done the woman prays the Credo, and at the end holds the child's head and cries out that the shadow should withdraw and that the child no longer need be frightened. Some cure *espanto* by having the priest pray the gospel over the child in the presence of the child's godparent of the same sex.

part 2: **THE PEOPLE**_____

the quality
of inter-personal relations: 12

TEPOZTECANS are not an easy people to get to know; they are not an outgoing or expressive people. Most inter-personal relations are characterized by reserve, constriction, and carefully guarded behavior. Spontaneous or informal behavior is limited to the most intimate relationships and rarely occurs in public. Tepoztecans do not like to attract attention by word or deed, and self-control is learned early. In the presence of adults, children are expected to be unobtrusive.[1] In large public gatherings of adults and children, there is a minimum of noise. A family whose quarrels or boisterousness can be heard by passers-by soon earns a poor reputation.

In the street, most faces are somber and quiet; smiles, brief and appropriate; hearty laughter, rare. Women and girls are expected to walk with eyes downcast and those who smile freely may be suspected of being flippant and flirtatious. Adolescent girls, in particular, must have good facial control, for even a glance of interest may be taken as a sign of encouragement by some hopeful male. To smile unnecessarily at other people's infants is to be suspected of the evil eye, and most children do not learn to smile at strangers or visitors until they attend school.

Correct behavior is important at all times, at home, with friends, with relatives, and in public. Only in the case of old people and men who are drunk are deviations from customary reserve tolerated. Nevertheless, men recovering from drunkenness are apt to worry over having committed some improper act, such as behaving disrespectfully to a *compadre*. For this reason, men are careful about choosing drinking companions; individuals in a respect-relation, such as father and son, uncle and nephew, and *compadres,* must never drink together.

There are no fiestas in Tepoztlán which are openly bacchanalian in character, or in which women as well as men become drunk and promiscuous as in some other parts of Mexico. Even at the Carnaval, when Tepoztecans behave with relative freedom, the leading participants are disguised in masks and costumes, and whatever love-making takes place is done secretly.

---

[1] Only during the recreation hour in school do children make a great deal of noise and play wildly. The play pattern in school is in sharp contrast with that at home and is clearly out of keeping with the older culture pattern.

The quality of constriction is also reflected in artistic expression and creativeness, both of which are limited. There are practically no handicrafts, no pottery, no weaving, no basketmaking. Although sewing, knitting, crocheting, and embroidery are becoming more widespread as a result of the influence of the cultural missions, the patterns used are purchased in Cuernavaca stores or copied from style magazines, and this work can hardly be called creative.

Music and the dance are very poorly developed. There are no traditional dances for men and women. The only traditional step used is the *brinco,* literally "the jump," which is a short jumping or skipping step done repeatedly without variation, to the accompaniment of a simple and monotonous melody played over and over. Only men are permitted to dance this step, and they do so singly or arm in arm with others, around the plaza in a large circle.

Modern social dancing has been learned by some of the more acculturated young people, and dances are held about once a week in the plaza under the uncertain light of a Coleman gasoline lamp. Social dancing has not become popular; most parents still refuse to permit their daughters to attend these dances, and boys have difficulty finding partners. By and large, the dancing lacks skill and grace and the dances seem dreary affairs. The school teaches a few traditional dances from other parts of Mexico, and these are occasionally performed in public by the school children. Most children, however, do not participate or have occasion to use these dances later. In short, the dance is not an important part of Tepoztecan life.

Musical expression consists primarily of singing typical regional songs to the accompaniment of the guitar. The local manner of singing is characterized by loudness and shouting, with little variation of style. These songs are sung exclusively by unmarried youths. Groups of boys or girls may serenade a friend or relative at dawn with the *mañanita,* or birthday songs, which are popular throughout Mexico. Perhaps the best singing occurs in the church where a selected choir of women and children sing under the direction of the *cantor.* New types of songs are being introduced by the school but are sung only by children; popular songs of the city, heard on the radio, are sung by girls in the privacy of their homes.

There are a number of bands of musicians who perform at local fiestas, dances, and at the more elegant weddings, baptisms, and funerals. These bands have a broader repertory than the singers, and play well-known music of Mexico and other nations. In musical skill, however, they compare unfavorably with the village guitar players and with musicians in other parts of Mexico and Latin America.

There is very little storytelling, and unlike villages in Spain, there is no rich lore of proverbs or sayings. Also, mothers generally do not sing to their children.

The clothing of the villagers is somewhat drab. The bright colors found in some parts of Mexico—the red skirts of Cherán, the red seed necklaces of the Tarascan women, the flamboyant serapes and *rebozos* of the south, the colorful pottery of Puebla and Oaxaca—are missing in Tepoztlán. Bright colors, particularly in clothing, are not in accord with Tepoztecan ideas of propriety, and only young girls are now beginning to wear them. Older women wear dull colored dresses, shawls, and skirts; men use black and grey serapes; pottery is invariably of un-adorned clay. Although *rebozos* of many colors and patterns are easily available in Cuernavaca, there is hardly a Tepoztecan woman or girl who wears anything but a dark blue, brown, grey, or black *rebozo*. The desire to be inconspicuous and less easily identifiable is one of the underlying reasons for this choice. There is also a belief that it is dangerous to wear bright colors, because the rainbow is attracted to them and will follow them.

There is a marked quality of detachment in inter-personal relations in Tepoztlán. Although living side by side, Tepoztecans communicate little of their innermost thoughts, aspirations, fears, likes, and dislikes and, for the most part, remain strangers to one another.[2] While a man may know a great deal about most of his neighbors in a small barrio, and about some in other barrios, and may know them as so-called whole persons, that is, in their various roles as parents, neighbors, godparents, *mayordomos,* or farmers, what is known are the relatively superficial aspects of personality only. Tepoztecans are a practical people concerned with ex-ternal behavior, and they judge others by actions rather than by attitudes, ideas, or inner life.

When a Tepoztecan is asked to describe the personality of another, the most frequently used terms for positive traits are "hard worker," "serious," "manly," "intelligent," "honorable," "good person," and "good humored." The most com-monly pointed out negative traits are "liar," "foolish," "stingy," "drunkard," "talkative," "coward," "crazy," "bad tempered," and "miserable." Traits which imply knowledge about the internal life and quality of an individual, such as "warm" or "cold," "imaginative" or "unimaginative," "sensitive" or "hard," "sympathetic" or "unsympathetic," etc., are significantly absent.

Like many peasant peoples, Tepoztecans are not introspective. They have little insight in understanding their own character and even less of others. There is little interest in or need for self-revelation, mutual confidences, confession, or lengthy conversation; imaginativeness, fantasy life, originality, initiative, and individuality are either undeveloped or suppressed. Always, the emphasis is upon conformity to traditional ways.[3]

The general restraint and constriction which characterize most inter-personal relations are also seen in the relations between the sexes and in the prevailing atti-

---

[2] Sol Tax has called attention to the impersonality of relations between traders in the Guatemalan highlands. See his "World View and Social Relations in Guatemala," *American Anthropologist,* 43 (1941), pp. 22-42.

[3] I should like to call attention to some of the implications of the above for the traditional distinction made by many sociologists between folk and urban society in terms of primary and secondary relationships. This distinction assumes that in the folk society, which is a small society, most relations are of a face-to-face type and therefore of an intimate nature, in contrast to the impersonal and superficial relationships in the city. The point is that, within the category of primary relationships, the range in the quality of these relationships may be so great as to require finer distinctions. Certainly, for purposes of cultural and psychological analysis, the folk-urban dichotomy is inadequate in that it lumps together societies which are very different. See also Chapter 21, "Summary and Conclusions," p. 433.

tudes toward sex and sexuality. Most of the attitudes toward sex are negative and prudish and, at least superficially, in accord with Catholic tradition.

Women have a negative attitude toward bearing children. They try to keep the number of pregnancies to a minimum by long nursing and by abstaining from sexual intercourse. Pregnancy is commonly described as "being ill with child," and pregnant women are embarrassed by their condition and make every attempt to conceal it. There is an absence of sexual play between husbands and wives; many women refer to the sex act as "the abuse by the man," and the genitals are generally considered ugly or dirty. There is a widespread belief among adolescent girls that sexual intercourse is painful. Open courtship is not sanctioned, and girls are severely punished for having any relations with boys. The existence of the double standard and the greater personal freedom of boys and men tend to encourage male sexuality. Romantic love, as we conceive it, is practically unknown; romantic attachments are relatively superficial and easily made and broken. Courtship is an intriguing, exciting pastime but it is always cautious, seldom impulsive or passionate.

It cannot be said, however, that Tepoztecans are puritanical, nor are they burdened with feelings of guilt or concepts of sexuality as something sinful.[4] Rather, Tepoztecans place greater value upon sexual restraint than upon sexual activity; just as they do not encourage emotional expressiveness, so do they not encourage active sexuality. Adult sexual activity is discouraged, not so much for reasons of morality but for practical reasons of safety. Parents fear that a young son may make an undesirable attachment with a widow or a dangerous attachment with a married woman, or he may be bewitched by a jealous sweetheart; they fear even more strongly that their daughter will lose her good reputation and the chance of a respectable marriage. Women are generally reluctant to have sexual relations, because of unwanted pregnancies; men discourage sexuality in their wives for fear of being humiliated by the wife's unfaithfulness; wives fear the loss of income and the poor treatment which inevitably attend their husband's extramarital alliances.

While there is much gossip, there is no ostracism or public denouncement or persecution of those who are guilty of sexual indiscretion. The couple living in free union is unmolested, the promiscuous widow maintains her usual relations with neighbors and kin, the illegitimate child is given a similar if not entirely equal position in his mother's household and may receive aid and inheritance

---

[4] The relative absence of guilt feelings can also be seen in the reactions to stealing and drinking. Drinking is not considered bad in itself, but may be criticized because it takes a man away from his work and takes money which may be sorely needed for other purposes. Stealing is quite frequent and may be severely punished, but it is detection rather than the act itself which is disturbing. In case histories, informants frequently refer to little stealing episodes without any manifestation of remorse or guilt, but emphasize how ashamed they were when discovered. Men do not appear to have guilt in promiscuous sexual relations with women or in deceiving young girls. Rather, they are proud of these feats and consider any conquest to their credit. There is also practically no sense of moral responsibility toward children born out of wedlock.

from his father. A man who fathers children with many women is placed under no social pressure to support his offspring or to marry the mother of any of them. Even in the case of a daughter's elopement, an act made worse by its rebellious flouting of parental authority, forgiveness is usually forthcoming after a lapse of time.

Sexuality is discouraged from childhood on; sex is a taboo subject within the home. Infant sexuality, masturbation, and sexual play among children, as well as curiosity concerning the bodily functions, is forbidden and punished. It is one of the more important obligations of the parent to keep their children "innocent," or, as they say, "to keep their eyes from being opened." The separation of the sexes for work and play begins from about age seven to ten and is strictly enforced at puberty. Coeducation in the school violated this basic attitude and was bitterly opposed by parents. Girls are unprepared for menstruation, which comes as a shock to most of them; girls will rarely confide in their mothers about menstruation or other intimate subjects.

In most inter-personal situations, Tepoztecans do not express affection in a demonstrative fashion and generally avoid bodily contact. Perhaps the major exception to this occurs in the mother-child relationship during the nursing period, when the child is held, fondled, and sometimes kissed. In courtship there is an increasing amount of demonstrativeness and physical contact, but kissing is still not customary.

Tepoztecans learned the Spanish custom of kissing the hand of the priest and of parents and godparents, but it never came easily to them and is now disappearing. The shaking of hands in greeting and departure and the typical Mexican double embrace are not generally practised in Tepoztlán and occur only among politicians and some of the more citified families. When Tepoztecans are drunk, this restraint is frequently relaxed, and male companions will walk arm in arm, and men may hug and even kiss their children and wives in the privacy of their homes.

It must be apparent from the preceding pages that Tepoztecans are not, on the whole, a very affectionate people and that means of expressing affection are limited. Normally, the Tepoztecan shows his affection for his children by hard work, good habits, and by providing them with the necessities of life; the child expresses his affection for his parents by obedience, respect, and diligence. Other inter-personal relations reveal good will or affection in so far as they fulfill the required reciprocal behavior. If these formal or practical qualities exist between people, Tepoztecans consider that they have a satisfactory relation with each other, and little else is demanded.

Between parents and children there is now a noticeable tendency, particularly among the younger generation, to express affection and to seek it in terms of greater demonstration of personal interest in each other, in their wants and needs and general welfare over and above life's bare necessities. This interest may be expressed by greater giving of food, clothing, toys, sweets, gifts, and now, by a willingness to make sacrifices for an education. Tepoztecans, particularly men, often express affection most easily toward their dogs and other favorite animals.

The limited expression of affection in Tepoztlán is part of a larger pattern whereby what might be called the positive emotions—love, tenderness, kindness, sympathy, generosity, and joy—are less easily expressed and not as well developed as the negative ones, such as anger, hate, irritability, fear, jealousy, and envy. One of our informants with more insight than most Tepoztecans succinctly described the lack of warmth and positive emotion by saying, "Somos muy secos," that is, "We are dry." This is related to their general world view and their conception of human beings, both of which tend to stimulate negative emotional responses.

There is a readiness to view people as potentially dangerous, and the most characteristic initial reaction to others is suspicion and distrust. Lack of trust is not only present among non-relatives but also exists within families and affects the relations of husbands and wives, parents and children, and brothers and sisters. This is not a neurotic distrust, but one rooted in the hard realities of Tepoztecan social and economic life, in patterns of child-training, and in a long history of conquest, colonial status, and internal and external political and economic exploitation. In Tepoztlán, the motives of everyone are suspected, from the highest public officials of the nation, to the local priest, and even to close relatives. It is assumed that anyone in a position of power will use it to his own advantage at the expense of others. Honest government or leadership is considered an impossibility; altruism is not understood. The frank, direct person, if he exists anywhere in Tepoztlán, is considered naive or the greatest rogue of all, so powerful or shameless as to have no need to conceal his deeds or thoughts. An individual who is obliging without cost to those who seek his aid is understood to have some as yet unrevealed plan for capitalizing on his position.

Friendships, as defined in terms of mutual trust, loyalty, aid, and affection directed toward one individual are few in Tepoztlán, and are avoided rather than sought. Friendship as such is not a Tepoztecan ideal and is not institutionalized in the form of a best friend or in any other way. Cases of lifelong friendships are rare and are almost always limited to the more acculturated families. Friends are viewed by adults as potential enemies, as a source of trouble, and as a waste of time. Traditionally women and girls are not supposed to have any friends whatsoever. While one may have friendly relations with individuals in Tepoztlán, these relations are segmented in that each is limited to one or two purposes. With one individual, there may be a work exchange relationship; with another, a borrowing relationship; and with others, a drinking relationship.

An exception to this is a type of friendship among men and youths known as the *cuate,* which means "twins." [5] These are more in the nature of close alliances made between two or more individuals of the same age group for a more generalized companionship. The *cuate* is depended upon for loyalty and defense in time of trouble, for political support, and for companionship in drinking, in

---

[5] The *cuate* is not traditional in Tepoztlán, having been introduced by soldiers from outside during the Revolution.

romantic undertakings, and in fiestas. The *cuate* is not expected to aid in domestic or economic difficulties, although he may do so. The *cuate* relationship is frequently stabilized and formalized after marriage by being turned into a *compadre* relationship at the birth of a *cuate's* child. In this way, a comparatively intimate alliance is short lived and gives way to a more formal respect-relationship.

There is a great deal of hostility in inter-personal relations in Tepoztlán. But much of this hostility is suppressed, or expressed indirectly in the form of malicious gossip, stealing, secretive destruction of property, ridicule, deprecation and envy, and sorcery.

A particularly interesting example of the Tepoztecan attitude that aggression in inter-personal relations should not be expressed directly is the widespread use of *indirectas,* which are criticisms indirectly expressed. These take various forms such as criticism by allusion, self-deprecation, use of the diminutive in a cutting way, and belittlement. Whenever these are used, it is immediately understood that insult is intended. For example, one man addressing another who had boasted of being the undisputed head of his household, said, "I don't rule in my house but everything is in order. Others say they are very manly, but if they only knew enough to look around they would find their wife with another man."

The following conversation between two women further illustrates the *indirecta.* The first woman is a prosperous storekeeper who is very pious but whose children have turned out "bad," according to other villagers. Recently, one of her daughters was almost dragged off by her sweetheart, but she managed to escape leaving him holding her *rebozo.* The second woman in this conversation is the wife of a prosperous farmer and is known to be ambitious to educate her children. Three of them have scholarships and are studying at a public school to become schoolteachers.

The first woman said, "I will educate my daughters but not for four years like other people so that they can come here and get jobs as little teachers."

The second woman answered, "The rich can send their children to the best schools. We are poor and cannot afford it. I hope God helps you in all you desire."

First woman, continuing, "And I won't let my daughter work like some because it is dangerous for a girl to be away from her parents."

Thereupon the second woman said, "As much as people guard their daughters I notice that they elope or have their *rebozos* taken from them. Some people swallow saints and defecate devils."

Other examples of common *indirectas* are: "They are a little rich and now have a little calf, but before, they knew how to steal." "They say they eat very well, but I notice that they are as skinny as I." Another type of *indirecta* is the generalization meant to apply to someone present. For example, a young schoolteacher who took pride in wearing stylish clothing appeared one day in a new-style skirt. She joined a group of other teachers, whereupon one of them said loudly that she heartily disliked the new styles and would not wear one of them for anything. The young girl turned pale and immediately left the group.

A man who believes himself to be the butt of an *indirecta* will also usually leave the group, but sometimes the statements are so obvious and crude that he interprets them as a challenge to fight. However, rarely does a fight occur as a result of such a situation; rather, the insulted person waits for an opportunity to harm the other secretly, and he, in turn, spends many an uneasy hour not knowing what to expect.

Gossip is unrelenting and harsh in Tepoztlán, especially when directed against an individual or family with whom there is a grievance. Facts about people are unconsciously or maliciously distorted, and gossip sometimes leads to tragedy. Relatives and neighbors are quick to believe the worst, and motives are always under question. A woman who puts on her best dress and takes a bus to Cuernavaca is said to be going to meet a lover. A girl who leaves town to work or study is going "to throw away a baby." A man who has gained weight and wears better clothing than before, for no known reason, must have been stealing. A wife who dominates her husband must have bewitched him.

There is a readiness to inform on others and to carry complaints to the head of the family. Neighbors and relatives are quick to let parents know that their daughter has been seen talking or walking with a boy, or that their child has been throwing stones. Claims for even slight damages are readily made. For example, a widow selling squash in the market place made a row and demanded payment when someone's two-year-old son knocked over a squash and caused the stem to fall off.

Successful persons are popular targets of criticism, envy, and malicious gossip. A new calf or cow may come home with a deep slash from someone's machete. Some unknown enemy may stone another's dog or drive away his chickens or pigs. Tourists, government representatives, or other outsiders, whether from another country, state, or village, are favorite targets for private ridicule which is often carping and picayune. Their way of dress, their speech, their manners are all fair game, and any mishap they suffer or error they make gives special delight. Most of the humor in jokes, stories, and conversation is in the form of ridicule of some person or group. At the Carnaval it is the custom for some of the masked dancers to caricature and criticize public figures, much to the glee of the villagers.

Even the priest is not above criticism. At one period in the history of the village there was so much criticism of successive priests sent in from the outside that the archbishop decided to punish the village by threatening to withhold a priest for seven years. However, a Tepoztecan who had studied for the priesthood agreed to take the job and retained it successfully for many years. Nicknames are common and also tend to expose personal weaknesses, sometimes to an embarrassing degree. In addition to personal nicknames, there are also nicknames for each of the barrios and villages within the municipio.

The most feared, but perhaps least common, form of indirect aggression is sorcery. Fear of sorcery is not omnipresent. It occurs only when a person has reason to expect it as the result of having injured or insulted another or of having become wealthy or otherwise outstanding. Young men and women are also apt to be bewitched as a result of romantic entanglements, and some mothers express anxiety over this and warn their children to be careful. Chronic illness and most deaths accompanied by swelling of the head or other parts of the body are frequently attributed to sorcery.

This situation makes for an oppressive atmosphere, particularly for those individuals who are striving to improve themselves or who, for one reason or another, deviate from strict conformity. It is most true for the more educated or acculturated minority and for a few of the well-to-do. Many of these people give evidence of neuroticism and display the type of tension and discomfiture so often noted among marginal groups who live within two cultures, not wholly accepting or being wholly accepted by either. We have had occasion to observe some of these people who moved to Mexico City, subsequent to our acquaintance with them, and we were astonished to note the transformation which they invariably underwent. Their faces had become less impassive; they had gained weight; they looked happier and more relaxed; they laughed more and behaved with far less formality.

One girl who went to the United States with us described herself as feeling that a great weight had been lifted off her shoulders from the time she left Tepoztlán. She no longer had to worry about gossip, criticism, sorcery, secrecy, and felt more free to express herself as she wished. Of course, this sensation is common among all people who shift from a small rural town to a large city, but in Tepoztecans we noted more striking physiological, psychological, and personality changes.

The sanctions against the overt expression of aggression in inter-personal relations sometimes give rise to an interesting type of disease locally known as *muina,* an illness caused by anger, in which aggression is apparently turned inward against the self. The symptoms of *muina* are loss of appetite, inability to take food, vomiting, loss of weight, and very often death. *Muina* is a fairly common condition and occurs among members of both sexes, primarily among adults but sometimes even among children. It may be caused by insult, humiliation, bad luck, or any other frustration which arouses anger. People with *muina* are not supposed to eat certain foods lest they become seriously ill. The dangerous foods include pork, eggs, milk, bananas, avocados, *chirimoya,* and most "hot" foods.[6]

There are also situations in which the direct expression of aggression is sanctioned, and other occasions in which it is expressed despite community sanctions against it.

Aggression is sometimes expressed directly in the beating of children, wife, or younger sisters or brothers. Men also beat their animals in moments of anger, although generally they are careful not to injure them. Attitudes toward wife-beating and child-beating have been changing in the direction of disapproval. In extreme cases of cruelty, the guilty party may be denounced to the authorities and punished. Most cases of wife-beating now occur only when the men are drunk.

---

[6] It is interesting to note that most of the foods to be avoided contain considerable fat or oil. This suggests the possibility that the emotional disturbance causes liver disorder which makes the patient extremely sensitive to fat and unable to digest it.

In anger Tepoztecans frequently throw stones at an offending person or animal. If a man is not pleased with his food he may throw it to the ground. Some women throw household objects in a fit of temper. Small children express rage in temper tantrums; and fighting among children, particularly boys, sometimes occurs in the absence of adults. Assault and murder also occur from time to time.

Fighting or attack is rarely the result of a direct challenge but may occur if two enemies meet when drunk or when one is ambushed by another. There is no tradition of giving warning or a "sporting chance"; rather, the victim is generally taken unaware, preferably under cover of darkness. A man may be beaten, shot, or fiercely slashed with a machete. Often the aggressor hits and runs without pausing to ascertain the condition of the victim. Several men, principally *políticos,* bear scars from such attacks. Men in positions of wealth, power, or authority habitually carry a gun for protection and prefer not to venture out at night. The authorities generally are unable to apprehend the culprit, who flees the village for a time.

Viewed historically, revolutions, civil wars, and political upheavals have offered a major outlet for direct aggression. It must be noted, however, that militarism and the glorification of the soldier are not Tepoztecan ideals. The history of the Revolution of 1910-20 in Tepoztlán reveals much bickering and feuds and a great deal of killing for reasons of envy and the seeking of power. Tepoztecan generals and other leaders were killed by jealous rivals within their own ranks as much as in battle.

How do Tepoztecans seek security in this environment? Security is sought first and foremost through the economic independence, of the biological family. Work, industry, and thrift, for the purpose of accumulating property in land and animals, are the highest, most enduring values in Tepoztlán. To be able to provide the family with food, clothing, and shelter is the only real assurance against want or interference. To many, hard work becomes an end in itself. So long as a man devotes his time and powers to work, he feels secure and blameless; he judges his worth by the amount of his labors, rather than by what he produces. Thus, Tepoztecans frequently say that all is well even though they eat only *tortilla con sal.*

The absolute emphasis upon the need to work and the brutalizing, isolating nature of the farmer's work have far-reaching effects on his personality and his relations with others. One of these effects is to make him an individualist with faith in his own power alone and with reluctance to seek or give economic aid, to borrow or lend, or to cooperate with others in public and private enterprises.

On the other hand, economic independence and individualism do not preclude certain loyalties, identifications, and reciprocities with others, but rather make these imperative for survival. Loyalty and cooperation within the biological family is a necessary adjunct to individual independence. Without a family to back him up, the individual stands unprotected and isolated, a prey to every form of aggression, exploitation, and humiliation known in Tepoztlán. The fate of lone widows and of orphaned or fatherless children is generally a sad one, even when the extended family offers help. Although the role of the extended family in protecting the individual is becoming more and more limited, it still offers a relative degree of security, especially in times of serious trouble.

In a more vague way, there is also a certain amount of security felt within the barrio and within the village as a whole in comparison to the world outside. The consciousness of Tepoztecans of being in a position of relative power and superiority over the rest of the municipio has made for local pride and a feeling of unity which also foster a sense of individual security. In contrast, the population of the surrounding villages suffers from a chronic feeling of injustice and exploitation at the hands of the village of Tepoztlán.

Tepoztecans also seek security through privacy. The withdrawal and personal detachment noted earlier, as well as a fear of intimacy, are characteristic of a majority of Tepoztecans. The man who speaks little, keeps his affairs to himself, and maintains some distance between himself and others has less chance of creating enemies or of being criticized or envied. A man does not generally discuss his plans to buy or sell or take a trip, except with persons who are directly concerned. A woman does not customarily tell a neighbor or even a relative that she is going to have a baby or make a new dress or prepare something special for dinner.

If an accident occurs to another's property, few hasten to inform the owner, who may not discover it until it is a total loss. In one case, a widow's pig was killed by a bus. Although it was known that she was the owner, no one told her about the accident. By the time she learned of it, most of the meat had been cut away by nearby residents, and she was left with only the head and tail.

There is greater readiness to commiserate in another's misfortune than to take joy in his success, resulting in a more widespread sharing of bad news than good. There is an almost secretive attitude toward good fortune, and boasting is at a minimum. People in Tepoztlán do not ordinarily advise each other where a good purchase or sale is to be made, how an animal can be cured, or in what ways a crop may be improved. Articles and market baskets carried through the streets are kept carefully covered from prying eyes. Although matters of illness and health are often a topic of conversation, there is reluctance to recommend a good remedy or *curandero*. In general, there is an absence of altruism, generosity, charity, and the spirit of sharing. Doing favors for others is rare and creates suspicion. Favors are generally associated with people *de cultura* who, it is said, do favors to get favors.

When young people or children show kindness or pity to outsiders they are frequently "corrected" by their mothers. Children are scolded for giving things to their friends or for being trusting and generous in lending articles to persons outside the family. Children or others who expect sympathy and help are called fools and are derided. It is attitudes such as these which daily reinforce the Tepoztecan's harsh view of life and throw him upon his own resources.

Security is sought through respect and the extension of respect-relationships. By respect, Tepoztecans mean an appreciation or recognition of high status as demonstrated by the use of the respectful *Vd.*, by the avoidance of intimacy or undue familiarity, joking, and discussions of sex or other subjects of intimate nature. A person in a respect status has certain powers, authority, and privileges and at the same time may not be insulted, criticized, or attacked. Respect status may stem from superior social and economic position, advanced age, education, or political power. Respect status may also stem from a specific, formal respect-relationship established between two individuals, such as that between parents and children, in-laws, and *compadres*. All inter-personal relations fall into three respect categories, that of reciprocal respect in which both parties address each other in *Vd.*, that of superior-subordinate respect-relations in which one party is addressed in *Vd.* and the other in the familiar *tú,* and the intimate relation in which both parties address each other in *tú.*

The *Vd.-Vd.* relation of mutual respect is perhaps the safest and therefore the ideal relationship in Tepoztlán. It implies recognition of equality of status, and each party is guaranteed respectful behavior and the fulfillment of certain formal obligations by the other. It involves no further intimacy or personal compromise and emphasizes mutual reserve and constraint, which well suits the Tepoztecan temperament. This relationship is however the least frequent in Tepoztlán, being limited to *compadres, consuegros* (the respective parents of married couples), and adults who are strangers to one another. Very rarely, a husband and wife may maintain an *Vd.-Vd.* relationship indicating the highest degree of mutual respect.

Some of the more ambitious younger people in the village now seek to establish an *Vd.-Vd.* relationship between themselves and older people on the basis of superior education or professional standing. Thus, a young man or woman who is a teacher desires to be addressed respectfully rather than familiarly by the parents of his pupils, partly to maintain authority and partly to obtain recognition of personal achievement. In this sense there is a present trend to extend the number of *Vd.-Vd.* relationships and to approach more nearly the situation which occurs in the cities.

The *Vd.-tú* relationship establishes a clear-cut status differentiation in terms of superordinate-subordinate. For the person in the dominant position, this is the most satisfying and preferred relationship. With the exception of the possibility of insubordination or hostility on the part of the submissive individual, this respect status is a very secure one. Age and relative social position are the essential determinants in the use of *Vd.-tú.* All children are addressed in *tú,* and all persons use *Vd.* when speaking to someone older than themselves. Thus, one is in an *Vd.-tú* relationship with parents, grandparents, aunts, uncles, older brothers and sisters, cousins, and all older non-relatives.

The respect of children for parents and older relatives is traditionally expressed by kissing their hands in greeting and each evening when the church bell rings. This practice is dying out and only rarely occurs in the presence of a stranger. In many families there is also resistance to addressing older brothers and sisters in *Vd.* and to giving them the respect and obedience that should accompany it. The number of cases in which children address parents in the familiar form is rapidly increasing. In the recent past, when there was a greater age differential between husbands and wives, a young wife often addressed her older husband in *Vd.,* while he used *tú* to her.

The *Vd.-tú* relationship may also exist between employer and employee, particularly if the latter is younger and is well known to the employer. However, if an employer addresses an older employee in the familiar form, it is a sign of lack of respect and is taken to be an insult. When both persons are of the same age and are not strangers, they address each other in the familiar form.

In pre-Revolutionary days it was customary for wealthy *caciques* to address the rest of the population as *tú,* regardless of age, and to be addressed as *Vd.* Today, wealth plays a minimal role in the *Vd.-tú* relationship, in part because of the absence of sharp class differences, in part because of the humble origins of many of the present well-to-do. The memory of the deep hostility and fierce vengeance of the subordinate population toward the *caciques* is also a deterrent in taking advantage of higher economic status.

Men holding political office or political ambitions are generally careful to avoid the *Vd.-tú* relationship with other adults for fear of offending. They prefer the *Vd.-Vd.* relationship, for they seek many *compadres,* or the *tú-tú* relationship in which they acknowledge friendship or acquaintance with most people of their own age group. However, local officials tend to speak condescendingly in the *Vd.-tú* relationship to more humble Tepoztecans, as well as to people from outlying villages, regardless of their age. This attitude of arrogance on the part of the officials and respect for the authorities on the part of the general population is carried over from pre-Revolutionary days, as is the notion that to speak to the local president in the familiar *tú* adds to an individual's importance. However, within Tepoztlán proper, officials no longer dare to express superiority of status to the majority of the adult inhabitants. Only the priest and nuns maintain an *Vd.-tú* relationship with the rest of the population.

The *tú-tú* relationship is an intimate one and is used between husband and wife, sweethearts, and children. It is also used between two people of the same sex and of approximately the same age. However, in Tepoztlán this *tú-tú* relationship does not always imply intimacy, but rather the possibility of intimacy. Thus, it is from the same age group that the *cuates,* drinking companions, singing companions, and so on, are drawn; but for the rest, the *tú-tú* relationship may be almost as reserved and formal as *Vd.-Vd.* In this, Tepoztlán and other rural villages differ from the city where the use of *tú-tú* is reserved for only the most intimate friends, all others of the same age being addressed as *Vd.*

At least among the school children and older students there is a tendency toward urban usage of *tú* and *Vd.,* that is, the custom of having fewer but more intimate *tú* relationships and a greater number of *Vd.* relationships. Traditionally in Tepoztlán, although members of the same sex and age group continue to call each other *tú,* there is a marked withdrawal from intimate relations as they get older and particularly after marriage. The *tú-tú* relationship is undoubtedly a potentially dangerous one to continue, because of the equality of status and the possibility of familiarity, joking, ridicule, insult, or attack. Although the *Vd.-Vd* relationship also implies equality of status, it is by no means the same psychologically, since both parties extend reciprocal respect.

In the light of the individualism of Tepoztecans, a great deal of competition in inter-personal relations might be supposed. But this is not the case. Tepoztlán is not a competitive society.[7] Accordingly, a lack of strong drive and ambition for self-improvement and a lack of initiative and originality are notable. Most adults tend to be self-satisfied if they have enough food and clothing from harvest to harvest. Among the young people, too, there is a general acceptance of the way of life: young men wish to be farmers as their fathers are, and most young girls continue to work at home and serve their elders. The rewards they seek are not impossible of achievement: occasional new clothes, shoes, a sweetheart, freedom to attend fiestas, and ultimately to marry, with some parental help.

Most married adults find sufficient reward in their growing children, who by their obedience and labor little by little lighten the burden of the parents and give some promise of protection for their parents' old age. (See Fig. 51.) There is almost no pressure upon the parents by the children in the form of demands for material comforts or for independence. Even parents who do not provide minimum necessities for health and comfort, or who are lazy or who drink, do not lose their authoritative position or their right to respect. Few Tepoztecan parents feel inadequate or a failure for not providing well or advancing economically. Insubordination on the part of the children would have a far more shaking effect than chronic poverty upon parental esteem.

There is a relative absence of concern for the future. Only the minority, who recognize education as an important source of security, save in advance for the education of a son or daughter. It is among these families that self-denial in the present, in order to gain future reward, is encountered—a familiar pattern among the urban middle class. The rest of the population exercise general thrift, but it can best be characterized as spending when there is money and pulling in their belts when there is none. The absence of saving "for a rainy day" or for a "nest egg" is striking.

Young people planning marriage do not save in anticipation of their many needs; they marry at short notice, as soon as there is money to pay for the wedding, the money being supplied by the boy's parents from the sale of an animal, by borrowing, or sometimes by the boy's going to work for a few months until the money is raised. Again, when a child is expected, there is no saving in anticipation of its

[7] Though competition occurs in Tepoztlán it is generally between groups rather than between individuals and, for the most part, is limited to social rather than economic activities in which prestige rather than material gain is at stake.

It is interesting to note that in recent years the introduction of certain forms of competition has had disastrous effects. The violence, murder, and bitterness which have grown out of the new competitive enterprise, such as the two bus lines, and the inter-village competition in the communal forest resources for the commercial production of charcoal, suggest that Tepoztecans were quite unprepared for such innovations.

Fig. 51. A Tepoztecan husband and wife.

birth, but rather greater application to the task of earning money after its arrival. The lack of foresight forces individuals into many distasteful borrowing situations and creates indebtedness among a people who abhor it.

There is comparatively little anxiety or sense of frustration in connection with personal success or self-development. What anxiety there is, stems from fear of a hostile environment and from the poor quality of inter-personal relations. Exceptions to this are found primarily among the more educated and acculturated group, particularly among the youth who have been to school outside of the village. It is among these individuals that we find greater dissatisfaction, ambition, desire for self-development, and fear of personal failure. These are also the people who show signs of maladjustment in the village.

Of special interest, for the understanding of the relative absence of frustration or anxiety, is the tendency to shift personal responsibility to others or to impersonal forces and to explain non-conformity in terms of magical or other supernatural forces, which are believed to control the individual. The illness or death of a child may thus be attributed by the mother to the "evil eye" or to *espanto,* rather than to her own negligence. Illness of a child after weaning will be attributed to jealousy rather than to the brusque change in diet or poor maternal care. A young girl who breaks all the rules and goes after a boy may be said to have been bewitched. A man who is dominated by his wife is said to have been drugged.

This shifting of responsibility is also expressed in other situations. In the short formal speech made by the parents to their future son-in-law, they remind him that the decision to marry their daughter is his own, and that he must not blame them if she turns out bad. Parents sometimes express a certain amount of relief when a son or daughter leaves home to work or to marry, for they no longer feel responsibility for his or her behavior. It is also not uncommon for parents to comfort themselves with the same thought at the death of a child.

Other traits, such as fatalism, stoicism in the face of misfortune, passivity, acceptance of things as they are, and a general readiness to expect the worst, tend to lift from the individual the burden of personal responsibility for his fate, and perhaps help to explain the relative absence of guilt or self-blame. Even in the face of gross injustice, in which the individual is protected by law, there may be little or no self-defense.

For example, a man who has been cheated out of a piece of property by a wealthier or more educated person may put up little fight on the ground that he will surely lose against the greater power of the other. A widow whose daughter was raped by a wealthy man did not press charges because, she said, "There is no justice for the poor and defenseless."

This attitude is even more striking in regard to injustices against society as a whole or against village interests. Stealing public funds, misleading or mishandling citizens by officials, or immoral behavior on the part of a person in power usually go unpunished and often uncriticized in public, although there may be much private resentment. The absence of strong public opinion, which generally controls the behavior of public figures, is directly related to many of the characteristics described previously.

Is the social character of Tepoztlán unique to Tepoztlán, or is it typical of other rural Mexican communities? A definitive answer must wait until we have seen more culture and personality studies than are now available. Indeed, the study of inter-personal relations in rural Mexico and other parts of Central America is still in its infancy.[8] Nevertheless, some of the existing monographs give us considerable insight and make some comparisons possible.

George Foster, in his monograph on the Tarascan village of Tzintzuntzan, writes as follows about the people:

> The collectivistic aspects of rural and Indian Mexican life have been stressed in many studies of Mexico, and much recent Government planning, such as the development of the *ejidos,* has been predicated on the assumption that this is a dominant characteristic of rural peoples. In Tzintzuntzan one is struck, not with the collectivistic but rather with the strong tradition of individualistic attitudes. . . .[9]
>
> Self-criticism is an unknown virtue—if such it is—and failure is always due to elements beyond one's control; the weather, bad luck, the unscrupulousness of other persons, but never is it the fault of the individual himself. . . .[10]
>
> Mistrust, suspicion, and fear are the common reactions to new persons or situations. One tends to jump to conclusions, to suspect the worst rather than the best about both old friends and new. In any new social relationship it is assumed that the other person is trying to get the better of one. . . .[11]
>
> . . . the possibility of material success is so limited by ecological and economic factors that few persons can ever expect to get far ahead . . . the wealth goal is difficult and almost impossible of attainment; hence, the stimulus of a reasonable chance of success is lacking. Since one's own life is so much a series of frustrations one takes pleasure in noting the difficulties of neighbors, even though . . . it is a case of biting off the nose to spite the face. Consciously or unconsciously the average Tzintzuntenyo realizes that in a material way he probably never will advance far. Hence, he envies, criticizes, and abuses his rare neighbor who does so, meanwhile further neglecting his own work.[12]

All of this applies accurately to Tepoztlán.

Elsie Clews Parsons, in her monograph on the Zapotecan town of Mitla, gives us a summary of Mitla character in a discussion of what traits are Indian and what are Spanish. Again we find many similarities in Tepoztlán. She writes,

> Psychological analysis I cannot attempt, as this study is cultural rather than psychological, but on occasion I have referred to psychological attitudes which have appeared to me

---

[8] There are very few studies of Mexican national character. The Mexican philosopher, Samuel Ramos, has made a pioneer effort in his *El Perfil del Hombre y la Cultura en México,* Mexico, 1938. Ramos believes that feelings of inferiority are the basic traits of the Mexican character. Findings in Tepoztlán do not bear this out.

[9] Foster, *Empire's Children,* p. 287.

[10] *Ibid.,* pp. 287-88.

[11] *Ibid.,* p. 288.

[12] *Ibid.,* p. 289.

to partake of Indian rather than of European character: the attitude of secretiveness as a protection from ridicule or criticism or interference, the impulse to escape from a situation you do not like rather than to resist it or to reform it; wearing opposition down by repetition or nagging or, as we say, not knowing how to take no for an answer; non-competitiveness and a lack of personal aggressiveness; desire for social peace and unity, and conviction of the need of town solidarity; repugnance to physical contacts; unwillingness to give offense or make an enemy, which includes reticence about other people's affairs and unwillingness to take responsibility for anything which is not personally pressing; unwillingness to entertain anger, animosity, or revengefulness, emotions which will make you sick or lead to enmities (as the Hopi put it, "a man with a warm heart is an angry man and one to be avoided"); fear of making enemies, no manifestation of sexual interest whatsoever; and, finally, taking much more interest in how people behave than in how they feel or think. . . . Condemnation falls on one who is *egoísto,* self-seeking and competitive, on the *ambicioso,* the grasping or greedy, and most of all on the *envidioso,* the envious man who fails to act in ways enabling all "the sons of the town" to have equal opportunities as well as equal obligations. *Muy miserable* is the one possessed of these traits of competitiveness, greed, and envy whether he or she be president or member of a prestigeful family or the mother of San Pedro or the baker who cheats the Holy Child of his loaf. The opposite of the *hombre miserable* is the *hombre honrado* who lives and lets live, is liberal and welcoming, *cariñoso,* who is *humilde,* neither quarrelsome nor cantankerous, who is *buena gente.* The terms are Spanish, but the evaluation, I think, is characteristically Indian. . . . It is based on a person's conduct, not on his opinions or on his emotional reactions except as expressed in conduct. In this community where there are no refinements in sex relations, no arts, few handicrafts and these giving no range in design, few or no games, no song, little story-telling, and getting drunk is almost the only diversion, where speech is guarded, and personal intercourse is standardized as family or *compadre* relationships, it is only what you do in conformity with others that matters, not what you think or feel or imagine. Whether or not you believe in the saints is a matter of indifference as long as you hold the two *mayordomías* that are expected of you. Except in connection with official position you are not called upon to go to church nor need you partake of any of the sacraments; it makes no difference if you call yourself a Protestant as long as you work on the new curacy when you are called upon, or with the other officials pay calls of respect upon the *cura,* or if solicited function properly as a godparent. . . . You may believe in any form of government you like, providing you do your work in the *tequio* and fill your term of service in the municipality. If you express opinions you run the risk of being called *un hablador,* a talker, which is an uncomplimentary epithet, and your opinions are not considered. A talker may be accounted a rebel, *un revoltioso,* a very objectionable type. If your relations with the opposite sex are conventional, either in or out of marriage, they are nobody's concern, unless a wife or parent complains to the president; but should you seek companionship with one of the opposite sex in any open way, you would be talked about and ridiculed, ridicule or humor turning ever on incongruities of behavior. . . . Whatever your age as long as you live in the household of your parents or kindred you are subject to the head of the household, you are *en su poder,* and your personal predilections or attitudes are negligible, at least theoretically. None of these conditions is favorable for the development of independent or self-expressive character. I have found individuality among my acquaintances—less among the women than among the men, for the life of the women is much more uniform than that of the men—but the range for personal expression, and opportunities for the development of personality are certainly more restricted than in mestizo society.[13]

The similarities of both the above accounts with our account of Tepoztlán suggest that our findings may be typical of wide areas in Mexico, certainly in the central highland area. Moreover, our data show many similarities to the recent findings of Redfield in his revisit to Chan Kom, Yucatan.[14]

Finally, let us read the description of a more isolated group in the Cuchumatanes highlands of Guatemala, the people of Santa Eulalia, as described by Oliver La Farge. He writes:

Like the Hopis, these Indians are at once peaceful and quarrelsome; dreading open warfare and overt action, they bicker endlessly. One feels that long living too close together, plus the effects of a religion of fears and much belief in bad magic, has produced a condition of exasperation expressed in gossip, fear, and ill-will. Yet, individually, the ordinary man is friendly with outsiders whom he meets casually. The instant one begins to impinge upon the Indian's life, to settle within his zone, one receives the full force of his suspicious speculations. As friends, they are loyal, thoughtful, trustworthy, generous, and tend to become dependent. As enemies, they are quiet, underhanded, meek, and interminably patient. They hate the Ladinos with a great and consuming hatred and almost never show it. They are rather rough with each other and overbearing when in power, and their hospitality is distinctly restrained, save towards their friends. They have a great reputation for dishonesty, but their thievishness does not extend to those they like, and, on the whole, they are as honest as anybody else; in this they have been somewhat debauched, inevitably, by their inferior caste position. They are a quiet people, although easily amused, and under their surface quietness goes on an intense, internal, repressed life which is indescribable. . . .[15]

Their external life is drab, their lot is hard, they are a conquered people, and occasional bouts of drunkenness do them good. When they drink they become jovial and tend to treat Ladinos as equals; then they become morose, dance, and lament the dead. Finally, they fall into a coma. Afterwards they sober themselves and return to work, unlike the Ladinos, who, once started, are likely to continue for a week or more.[16]

It will be seen that the people of Santa Eulalia are quite different from Tepoztecans, although some of the traits mentioned above also apply to Tepoztecans. Comparisons are in fact difficult because of the absence of a Ladino-Indian caste or class dichotomy in Tepoztlán.

[13] Elsie Clews Parsons, *Mitla, Town of Souls* (Chicago: University of Chicago Press, 1936), pp. 480-83.

[14] Redfield, *The Village That Chose Progress, Chan Kom Revisited* (Chicago: University of Chicago Press, 1950).

[15] Oliver La Farge, *Santa Eulalia, The Religion of a Cuchumatan Indian Town* (Chicago: University of Chicago Press, 1947), p. 6.

[16] *Ibid.*, p. 7.

the people as seen from their rorschach tests: 13

by Theodora M. Abel and Renata A. Calabresi

IN OUR ANALYSIS [1] of the Rorschach protocols we have attempted to find out what the people of Tepoztlán are like. We have compared the records of children, adolescents, and adults, to investigate changes that take place in personality structure and dynamics as the maturing processes unfold. We have also attempted to obtain from the projective material some conception of what it means to be a boy or girl, a man or woman in this Mexican community. Our emphasis has been on intergroup comparisons, where the groups to be compared vary in sex and chronological age.

It is true that there are limitations in the effectiveness of interpreting material from a cultural group with which we are but slightly familiar and to which we have not been directly exposed. But enough work has been done by various investigators to verify Rorschach's initial premise that the fundamental dynamics and structure of a personality in any culture can be ascertained.[2] What the psychologist has to be aware of in the interpretation of a personality-in-culture, are such pitfalls as labeling records in terms of standards of normalcy and psychopathy, and in terms of behavior, using subjects in the United States, particularly the urban and the more sophisticated and educated groups as criteria.[3]

CONDITIONS OF TESTING AND SUBJECTS CHOSEN

The Rorschach tests were given in Spanish by Ruth M. Lewis [4] over a four-month period in 1943–44, as one part of a broad ethnographic and historical study of the village. The selection of subjects for the test was determined by the objectives of

[1] This chapter was written by Dr. Theodora M. Abel and Dr. Renata A. Calabresi prior to their reading of an earlier chapter on the people. However, they had seen three short published articles of mine, one of which dealt with inter-personal relations. In addition, they had read an early version of one of my family studies.

[2] E. Oberholzer, "Rorschach's Experiment and the Alorese," *The People of Alor* by Cora Du Bois, Chap. XXII. (Minneapolis: University of Minnesota Press, 1944.)

[3] Theodora M. Abel, "Rorschach Test in the Study of Cultures," *Rorschach Research Exchange and Journal of Projective Techniques,* XII (1948), 1-15.

[4] This section, "Conditions of Testing and Subjects Chosen," was written by Ruth and Oscar Lewis.

the broader research program, and the testing was done on a family basis as part of the intensive family case studies. Twenty-one families, representative of the socio-economic and barrio differences in Tepoztlán, were selected for the testing program, and each member of the selected families was given the Rorschach.

As part of the project, seven student assistants were assigned to live with seven of the selected families. The testing was begun in these seven families only after the field worker had established good rapport. In each case the assistant who lived with the family prepared the way for the testing. The tester was then invited to meet the family and spent some time with each in friendly visits. The parents were tested in the home, but most of the children were tested in the school.

There was relatively little resistance to the testing, partly because of the slow, indirect way in which each family was approached, and partly because of Tepoztecan passivity, particularly toward city people or those in positions of authority. Very few Tepoztecans asked questions about the test; they seemed content to accept the tester's statement that a series of ink-blots were to be looked at, and that they were to tell the tester what the ink-blots made them think of. In the few cases in which questions were asked, the ink-blots were explained as a test of the imagination.

The cooperation of the children was gained, first, by testing the parents and winning their confidence, and, second, by testing the children in descending order of age. It was also found effective to ask the mother to arrange the appointments, so that it was she who told the child when to take the test. Small gifts of toys and sweets also helped. Rapport was far better with the children tested at home in familiar surroundings and with family members near-by, than with those tested in the school.

Testing in the school had many disadvantages. The school in rural Mexico does not enjoy the same prestige as in the United States, and is often subjected to criticism and interference by conservative elements in the community. Our school testing program, which included a battery of psychological tests and collections of drawings and written themes, attracted a good deal of attention and gave the anti-school group a pretext for criticism.

In Tepoztlán it is assumed that when two people are alone together they are up to no good. Since it is necessary for the child and the tester to be alone during the administration of the Rorschach test, the removal of the children from the classroom, one by one, came in for particular protest. To make matters worse, a local *curandero* considered the doctor on our staff as a possible competitor and circulated pornographic pictures which he said were the pictures that our tester was showing to the children. When the tests were given in the home no such difficulties arose.

The children did not enjoy being the center of attention in the testing situation. They were shy, ill at ease, and unaccustomed to taking tests involving much talking, and they soon became weary with the effort of expressing themselves. There is a general feeling in the village that it is not good for a person to study or think too much, and the many questions were *molestia* (a bother). One mother objected to the continuation of a test on the grounds that *se calienta la cabeza,* that is, the child's head would get too hot from thinking so much!

SUBJECTS CHOSEN

The total population whose records could be used in the study was one hundred and six. Six records were discarded since the subjects failed to give any responses or gave responses not related to the stimulus material. The subjects ranged in age from five to seventy-four years, fifty-nine were males and forty-seven were females. No attempt was made to secure an equal number of subjects at different age levels by sex, but we did obtain a small but fair sampling of children and adults at various age levels. The subjects were divided into five chronological age categories with the idea of comparing them: young children, children just before puberty, adolescents, younger adults, and older adults. This selection was somewhat arbitrary, since we had in mind the accepted age range of children, adolescents, and younger and older adults in American Society.[5]

Groups used for comparison in this study were as follows:

		C. A. Range	Females	Males
A	Older adults	47-74[6]	12	9
B	Younger adults	20-39	9	12
C	Adolescents	13-19	15	10
D	Children just before puberty	9-12	12	13
E	Young children	5-8	4	10

RESULTS: THE GROUP AS A WHOLE

The intellectual approach of Tepoztecans to the world around them appears to be concrete rather than abstract (D larger than W, see Table 54). They stick predominantly to the actual world in which they live, a world of everyday occurrences (D responses and no preponderance of phantasies over responsiveness to stimulation from the world around). Their movement (M) and color (Sum C) responses are fairly equally balanced except in the case of the older males, who give preponderantly color responses. A small deviant group (14 cases out of 106), ten of whom belong to one family, have a more exaggerated mode of responding to the cards. They are determined and try to do their best, as do the rest of the population, but when a job is too hard for them they resort to a fragmentary type of Rorschach response, breaking down the situation into minute and repetitive items (seeing countless parts of animals and plant details).[7] Aside from this minority group of fussy individuals, who would be called obsessive-compulsive in the United States, the majority of tested Tepoztecans do not give up a task, nor do they resort to unrealistic aloofness with flights into phantasy.

---

[5] Although many girls between the ages of thirteen and nineteen are married in Tepoztlán, they usually do not maintain their own homes nor take on the full responsibilities of adulthood until they are older, so that their place in the adolescent group is not without justification.

[6] Two females and five males in this group were fifty-five years of age or older.

[7] In a subsequent study on family groups, this family will be discussed in detail.

TABLE 54. Number of Subjects in Each Subgroup Who Made a Score in Various Rorschach Categories of Response Which Was at the Approximate Median or Exceeded It For the Whole Group.

Subgroup	Sex	C. A.	R	W	W%	D	M	FM	F%	C	c	C'	A%	H	Obj	Anat	N
A_1 9	F	40–74	5	4	5	3	1	2	7[a]	4	5	2	2	6[a]	9[a]	2	5
A_2 12	M	40–68	6	8[a]	8[a]	3	2	3	4	9[a]	7[a]	5	1	4	4	9[a]	4
B_1 12	F	20–39	4	5	8[a]	5	4	4	6	3	7[a]	3	6	3	3	2	4
B_2 9	M	20–39	6[a]	2	4	6[a]	3	4	4	5	5	5	3	5	5	5	5
C_1 10	F	13–19	4	3	6[a]	4	2	2	7[a]	4	2	0	3	5	6	5	4
C_2 15	M	13–19	9[a]	7	7	6	5	8	5	7	11[a]	2	7	9[a]	10[a]	2	10[a]
D_1 12	F	9–12	9[a]	2	3	6	4	5	10[a]	5	2	1	6	8[a]	8[a]	1	9[a]
D_2 13	M	9–12	10[a]	4	5	9[a]	2	5	10	4	3	0	9[a]	4	7	0	7
F_1 4	F	5–8	3[a]	1	3[a]	1	0	0	4[a]	1	0	0	3[a]	2	1	0	2
F_2 10	M	5–8	4	3	6[a]	3	0	2	9[a]	4	1	2	5	4	3	0	6[a]
Approximate median for whole group			15	7	30	12	2	5	50	2	1	1	60	2	1	1	2

[a] Sixty per cent or more of the subjects.

Tepoztecan interests seem to be predominantly centered around those animals found in their surroundings, nature, and inanimate objects which are part of their material culture. The records suggest that Tepoztecans have a strong tendency to avoid close contact with people, and are limited in their social outlook. Each individual appears to act pretty much as a lone wolf, with little understanding of cooperative enterprise. Human movement responses do not envisage two people doing anything together, except in rare instances where two people are described as holding something. Nor do Tepoztecans express open hostility; human and animal movement are not expressed in aggressive terms, such as fighting, pulling, pushing. There is rather an atmosphere of caution and reserve; movement of animals and people is expressed in terms of holding, looking, staring, as well as the more passive or indifferent descriptions of sitting and standing. The exception to this passive trend is in the subgroup of young boys between nine and twelve years of age, who sometimes describe animals as jumping, running, and climbing.

The people of Tepoztlán seem to have good mental control (F+ and F%), and show themselves capable of attending to tasks that have to be performed in the world around them. They do not live in the clouds, yet they are not merely rigid or inflexible. They are capable of being impulsive (using color-form responses), and their phantasy life (as expressed in human movement responses) is not entirely repressed. In general, the pure-form response is high (the median is around 50 per cent), but rarely goes up to a rigid extreme of 75 per cent. All of these modes of response are revealed in modified ways at the different age levels.

RESULTS COMPARED WITH THOSE OF OTHER INVESTIGATORS

In studies carried on in the United States and Europe both among the white, Negro, and some North American Indian populations, and among individuals of average and superior intelligence, with more or less educational opportunities and favorable socio-economic backgrounds, the usual number of responses to the ink-blots ranges from twenty to forty.[8] Only a few of our subjects gave as many responses as this. The median number of responses for our young adult males (Group B_2) is 23, for the adolescent boys it is 19.6 (Group C_2). For the children between nine and twelve years of age (Groups D, female, and D_2, male), this median is 24.5 for the girls and 22.0 for the boys. For the other groups, the medians are lower: 15 responses for the older women (A_1), 14.5 for the older males (A_2); 12.2 for the younger adult women (B_1), 14.0 for the adolescent girls (C_1); 12.2 for the four little girls (E_1) and 16 for the little boys (E_2).

Comparison of our results with those found by Billig, Gillin, and Davidson in their study of the Ladinos and Indians in Guatemala shows our adult male groups to be somewhat more productive than the Guatemalan groups.[9] Among our adults

---

[8] B. Klopfer and D. M. Kelly, *The Rorschach Technique* (Yonkers, N. Y.: World Book Co., 1942), pp. 207–08.

[9] O. Billig, John Gillin, and W. Davidson, "Aspects of Personality and Culture in a Guatemalan Community," *Journal of Personality,* 16 (1947), 153–78; (1948), 328–68.

(Groups A and B, C. A. 20–74), 15 out of 42, or roughly one-third, give 20 or more responses to the cards, and among our younger subjects (Groups C and D, C. A. 9–19), 28 out of 50 give 20 or more responses to the cards. Only one out of 25 Indian males (C. A. 20–78) in the Guatemalan village of San Luis Jilotepeque, gives 20 or more responses; and out of 25 Ladino males of equivalent chronological age, only three give 20 or more answers. The adolescent groups in the Guatemalan study are very small (five Indians and five Ladinos with C. A. 10–19). Two of the five in each group give a great many responses, as did a few of our subjects. The other three in each group give less than 20 answers.

Kaplan has found adult males (ages 20–40), among Navajo and Sioux Indians, Spanish-Americans, and Mormons in the South West of the United States, who produce, on the average, between 19 and 22 responses, which approximates what we have found in our B_2, C_2, D_1, and D_2 groups.[10] The females tested in Tepoztlán gave fewer responses than the males, but there is no reported material on the productivity of the females in these other Indian groups with which our results can be compared. Among the Berens River, Salteaux Indians in Canada, Hallowell found both males and females giving between 20 and 30 answers to the cards, but he did not report differences between the sexes as to number of responses.[11] These Salteaux Indians appear to be somewhat more productive and more imaginative than the people of Tepoztlán, living more freely in their phantasy world (high M frequency). We can say, however, that the Tepoztecans appear to be more productive than the Guatemalan Ladinos and Indians. This greater responsiveness of Tepoztecans can again be seen by the extreme infrequency with which they rejected cards, as compared with the Indians and Ladinos in the Guatemalan study. Fifty-six per cent of the adult Ladinos and 60 per cent of the Indians rejected at least one card. Among all our population (adults and children, out of 106 only 15 (14 per cent) rejected one card or more; ten of these rejected one or two cards, and five rejected three or four cards.[12]

In some ways our Tepoztecan adults are closer to the Ladinos than the Indians, in quality of response. This is seen in the extent to which they were able to show some degree of expansiveness in their imaginative and emotional modes of functioning (as measured by the human movement and color responses to the cards). Among the Guatemalan Indians, 80 per cent gave no M responses, 56 per cent no color; among the Ladinos, 46 per cent did not perceive human movement in the cards, and 43 per cent perceived no color. In Tepoztlán among our adult A and B groups, 43 per cent gave no human movement and 42 per cent no color. Thus, we can say that the Ladino and the Tepoztecan adults appear less rigid, and possibly better endowed intellectually than do the Guatemalan Indians. Also they show

---

[10] B. Kaplan, a study in process at Harvard University, Department of Human Relations.

[11] A. I. Hallowell, "Acculturation Processes and Personality Changes as Indicated by the Rorschach Technique," *Rorschach Research Exchange and Journal of Projective Techniques*, VI (1942), 42–50.

[12] The cards most frequently rejected were IV, VI, IX, those most usually rejected in Rorschach testing.

greater ability or willingness to reveal their phantasy life (M) and feelings (C) than do the Guatemalan Indians. Since there are not two cultural groups with different status positions living side by side in Tepoztlán as in San Jilotepeque, our adult groups are freer than the other Indian group to move in a world of their own, and do not have to withdraw from or resist the assumed feelings of superiority of a mestizo group.

On the other hand Tepoztecans do not live in as lively a phantasy world as do the Berens River, Salteaux Indians investigated by Hallowell. Among 58 adults (men and women sixteen years of age or over), the average number of M responses was 3.9; but in Tepoztlán, among our adolescents and adults (subgroups A, B, C), only 17 out of 67 gave more than one M response. The Tepoztecan group as a whole was not spontaneous in the use of creative imagination nor in living in a phantasy world. They are living much closer to a concrete and realistic world than were the Salteaux Indians, and did not allow themselves the kind of freedom in which their phantasies are encouraged or left uninhibited.

INTER-GROUP COMPARISONS

In the following discussion when we speak of a characteristic in which a subgroup shows a definite high or low trend we shall mean something specific statistically. By high trend we shall mean that over 60 per cent of a subgroup gives a score at or higher than a rough median for the whole Tepoztecan group. For example, we found out how many cases in a subgroup gave fifteen or more responses to the blots, how many gave seven or more whole answers, two or more human movement answers, 50 per cent or more pure form. On the other hand, if less than 40 per cent of a subgroup had a score at or below the whole group median, we have taken this to indicate a low trend in a particular scoring category. (See Tables 54 and 55.)

The older adults (subgroups A_1 female, and A_2 male) are characterized by a low frequency of large detail responses (D), low frequencies of human and animal movement (M and FM) and low percentage frequency of animal content responses. The older adults, men and women, appear to have low energy drives (FM); their imaginative life is to some degree restricted, but they also seem to have not too conventional attitudes toward problems of everyday living (low A% and D). The deviant position of these older men and women, however, is not the same. The men move from a more conventional and everyday way of life to a more highly uncontrolled and explosive emotional one; the older women, although still functioning in a very concrete and controlled way, become rigid, pedantic, and fussy in adapting to their life situations. The older males are high in giving crude whole answers, while the older women are varied in number of whole answers and in number of small detail. In their manner of approach to the cards, the women do not show the rather poorly controlled, unreflective, and uncritical intellectual approach that is characteristic of the older men.

Along with the crude approach of these older males goes a low pure-form fre-

TABLE 55. Summary of Table 54 Showing the Rorschach Categories in Which Each Subgroup Was High in Frequency (60 Per Cent of the Subgroup) or Low in Frequency (40 Per Cent of the Group).

Subgroup	A_1	A_2	B_1	B_2	C_1	C_2	D_1	D_2	F_1	F_2
High Frequency (60 per cent of the subgroup exceeded rough median for group as a whole)	F% H Obj	W W% C c Anat	W% C	R D	W% F% Obj	R c H Obj N	R F% H Obj N	R D F% A%	R W% F H	F%
Low Frequency (40 per cent of the group did not reach the rough median for group as a whole)	D M FM C' A% Anat	D M FM F% A% H Obj N	R FM C C' H Obj Anat N	W M A%	R W D M FM C C' c N	M F% A% Anat	W W% M C' c Anat	W W% M FM C C' c H N	W D M FM C C' c Obj Anat	R W D M FM C C' c H Obj Anat

quency (F%) and a high color and shading frequency of the more impetuous type (C, CF, FC-, c, C'), indicating impulsiveness in behavior with weak control over emotional outbursts, thoughts, and ideas. The older males also give a high frequency of anatomy answers with low frequencies for human, object, plant, and nature content, as well as a high percentage of animal responses. They show some self-consciousness and preoccupation with sexual functioning, by the number of anatomy responses given. These men seem to be overwhelmed by circumstances they cannot handle and are forced to react to them with impulsivity, and with some depression, anxiety, and helplessness. If we found such protocols among subjects living in the United States, as we have found in Tepoztlán,[13] we should consider them to be records of individuals traumatized in some way, perhaps from excessive alcohol or from a severe and overwhelming emotional experience.

In comparing the protocols of the older men with those of the older women in Tepoztlán, we should say that the women are working hard to be in control, perhaps dominating the men. This pattern is seen among the older women by their strict intellectual control over their impulses and phantasies (high F%), and by their interest in people and in concrete objects (high frequencies for human and object content). They are low in the anxiety-ridden anatomy answers characteristic of the men; seven of the nine women perceive no anatomy while nine out of twelve older men interpret the blots as anatomy at least once. The women appear to be functioning well in a concrete and realistic manner, although it is rather limited and rigid. They are organized in their routine activities and have control over their impulses. They seem efficient, determined, and can assume considerable responsibili-

[13] For a sampling of the protocols taken in Tepoztlán, see Appendix E, p. 463.

ties in their affairs, but they do not show any warmth toward people or desire to cooperate with them through friendliness or in give and take.

Among the males and females in the next younger group (C. A. 20-39), we find a somewhat different picture from that of the older groups. The women are low in a great variety of factors: in number of responses, in animal movement, in use of bright and achromatic color, and low in variety of content (human, object, plant, nature, and anatomy). They are also less productive than the males, less rigid than the older females, and show a less clear-cut channeling of their interests than the older women; they do not show any high trend in giving specific types of content, such as human and object. They seem to be playing what may be a more passive or perhaps more adaptive role than do the older women; that is, adaptive in the sense of accepting domination on the part of males more readily. They do have some tendency to be timid and cautious, or at least to be more subdued in emotional responsiveness (seven give small c responses), and they apparently do not reveal the obstinacy or ability to express and enforce their wishes and desires as much as the older women. We might say that they seem to be more or less at peace with themselves and more accepting of their role in society than any other female group.

The males in this age group (C. A. 20-39) appear to be in a dominant position. They are quite productive on the Rorschach test (high R), quite concrete and realistic in their approach to situations (high D), characteristics contrary to those found in the older males. On the other hand, they have a tendency to show the characteristics of the older males; at least five of the nine men showed the impulsivity, the anxiety, bodily precoccupation, and depressive features revealed in the records of the older men. But they are in control over these impulses and do not reveal the disorganization shown by the older men. They are, it would seem, able to run the show, make decisions in their families, have their authority respected or at least not directly opposed, as must be the case in the relationships between the older males and females. Nevertheless we see some of the characteristics of the older males beginning to appear in the younger men.

The predominant pattern for the adolescent girls (C. A. 13-19) is that of low productivity (number of responses), low energy drives (FM), and high intellectual control over phantasies and impulses (low human movement and color responses and high form percentage frequency). They give but few animal responses but a fairly high number of object answers, suggesting a removal from the more childish world of interest. They have more of the pattern of the older women (C. A. over 40), exercise a rigid control over impulses, and pay attention to the concrete but necessary objects in the world around them. In general these adolescent girls look as though they are not having much fun and as if they have been trained and pushed beyond their years to fit into an adult female pattern. But their way of adjustment is less flexible than that of the young adult women (higher F% and lower Fc).

In contrast the adolescent boys (C. A. 13-19) do not have rigid intellectual control over phantasies and feelings (low F%) as do the adolescent girls. They are more expansive in responding to the world around them than are the girls (eight of the fifteen boys gave two or more color responses). They gave a high frequency of shading responses (c) which are associated with nature answers, such as rain clouds, waterfalls, water in a pool, sky. The objects that they see in the blots are not those of daily use (pots, pans, flower-pots) as perceived by the women, but things like a gun, a hinge, or a box. This suggests that these boys are exploring the world around them, are interested in girls (giving human but no anatomy answers), and in doing things they want to do. But at the same time they feel anxious about their sexual phantasies and perhaps about their more direct sexual activities (shading responses and seeing such :xual symbols as waterfalls, rain, etc.).

It looks as though these boys had been handled much more permissively than the girls, allowed to have their own way much more, given greater sexual freedom, and had not been pinned down to responsibilities beyond their years. But even though they enjoy more freedom, these boys are conflicted over the role they are expected or able to play in society. If they have been raised by women who have the characteristic pattern of the women in our older adult group, who appear dominant and in control, and by the older men who appear disorganized and ill-controlled emotionally, we can surmise that these adolescent boys are more deeply under the control of women and influenced by them.

The Rorschach records suggest that the girls are held down, and that they are expected to refrain from sexual activity, to do their duty, and to work—patterns of behavior that are not expected from the boys. They want to behave like males, be free and dominant, but they cannot quite make the grade. They are concerned over their sexual phantasies, and they are not repressed like girls, but they do not have any steady and secure influence to help them overcome their feelings of anxiety; the older men are too disorganized to help the boys in this, and the older women are too dominant and rigid.

As we have said before, it is the young adult males (C. A. 20-40) who appear the best adjusted and able to handle themselves. We hypothecate that the better performance of the young adult men, as compared with that of adolescent boys and older men, may be due to the fact that they are expected by the Tepoztecan society to play the leading role, work, raise families, and have recreation. For a time they succeed in following this pattern, but later on they break down and become less well integrated and less dominant. The older women take over and run the show, while the older men tend to lose control and become impulsive and less well organized.

In several respects, the prepubertal boys and girls (C. A. 9-12) are more alike than are the two sexes above this age level. Both groups are high in productivity (fifteen or more responses per person, for nine out of twelve girls and ten out of thirteen boys), a characteristic which has been found true only of males at the older age, Groups B_2 and C_2. Groups D_1 and D_2 have a high-form percentage (ten out of twelve for the girls, ten out of thirteen for the boys). Both sexes are low in human movement, color, and shading responses, exhibiting a rigid (high F%) but determined approach (high R) to situations without allowing themselves freedom for enjoyment (C) or creative phantasy (M).

The boys are high in animal content and fairly high in giving large detail answers, revealing interest in the usual and everyday events of the world and doing what would be expected of children of this age in various cultures. But they do not all exhibit the spontaneity (FM) we should expect to find in young children. They exhibit none of the anxiety and self-consciousness (c) and preoccupation with the body (Anat) shown by older males. They give a picture of children who are expected to behave a certain way—not to give way to temper tantrums, not to show too much of their feelings—but who are not forced to have interests beyond their years (only high content is the animal).

The girls are also expected to behave in a certain correct way and not give vent to their feelings, but it also looks as though they were being pushed to take interest in matters beyond their years. They are low in animal content and high in human and object content as are the older women. This kind of interest we should not expect to find in young girls in any culture, rather they would be expected to see animals frequently in the blots as do boys. It looks then as if their childhood was being taken away from them and that they were expected to act like adults and suppress their more natural impulses and interests for their age level. Not only are they pushed by adults, but they have succeeded in pushing themselves in this direction; they show no signs of revolt or worry about what they are forced to do. This push of theirs is further seen by the fact that seven of these twelve girls give seven or more small detail responses (dd), suggestive of fussiness, while only one boy gives this many responses of this kind.

We suggest that both boys and girls are being driven in some ways and have not been reared in a warm and accepting atmosphere, but rather in a neutral one emotionally. We can see from the records of these children and the adults that their attitudes toward each other are not those of friendliness, but rather of duty and getting things done.

We cannot say a great deal about the little children (C. A. 5-8) especially the little girls, since there were only four records that could be used; three were discarded because no answers were given or none relating to the blots. A few of the children are quite productive and show a high frequency of response. Nearly all of them give a high percentage frequency of pure-form answers, but with children as young as this it would be hard to conclude the extent to which this mode of response indicates rigid intellectual control. This high frequency of pure form may be due to inability to elicit from the children statements about their percepts in terms of movement and color. We may say, however, that some of the little boys show spontaneity by giving color responses, while both boys and girls show some interest in the world around by not limiting themselves to the more stereotyped animal answers. Boys and girls in this group do not seem to be as differentiated as they are in the C. A. 9-12 group.

Although we have very little evidence from these records, we suggest that these children do not seem to be crushed by adults and allowed no chance to enjoy themselves. We hypothecate that they are being accepted in a matter of fact and detached manner.

CONCLUSIONS

On the basis of the Rorschach data we may say that sex differentiations become well marked among the prepubertal boys and girls (C. A. 9-12). The girls appear to be living or forced to live in a world where they are expected to have grown-up interests and to carry on adult activities. They seem to be able to control their impulses well. The prepubertal boys, in general, have the same pattern in the Rorschach as do the girls, having a controlled and efficient way of life without showing warmth or getting close to people. But their records are more spontaneous than are those of the girls of the same age level, and they take an interest in the kind of activities related to children rather than to adults.

In her adolescent years (C. A. 13-19) the girl in Tepoztlán does not expand and enjoy herself. Her sex life is suppressed. She appears more rigid and controlled than at any other age level. The adolescent boy in Tepoztlán does not seem to be hemmed in by the discipline imposed on the adolescent girl. He is productive and fairly spontaneous, and his range of interests and activities seems to be broader. It looks as though his sexual life was less inhibited than that of the adolescent girl. But still the adolescent youth reveals anxiety about his sexual needs and satisfactions.

In her younger adult years (C. A. 20-39) the Tepoztecan woman is less tense in her efforts to conform and do her duty than is the adolescent girl. But even so she shows little signs of liveliness and warmth. We surmise that she accepts her role in life and does not make demands or bids for sympathy and understanding. She has learned to be the kind of person she is expected to be, a controlled and efficient individual who takes care of the material needs of everyday living, and who does not express emotional needs nor give out any love and affection. It is suggested that she has somehow learned to get more satisfaction from activities and enterprises related to the daily routine rather than from her sexual activity. To the woman of Tepoztlán sex is not to be enjoyed or cultivated but to be suppressed or considered a duty.

We have the impression from the Rorschach protocols that when the male in Tepoztlán reaches adulthood (C. A. 20–39), he feels fairly secure in his role in society and especially in his sexual role. But from the records, it looks as though the fully adult males in Tepoztlán can rely on themselves, be efficient, productive, and derive satisfaction from life only when they feel secure in their sexual role. The anxiety experienced in their adolescence is never entirely removed. We see in the younger adult males, signs that point to the impulsive, undisciplined behavior that is the characteristic pattern of the older males. But nevertheless these younger adults are able to handle their impulses and anxieties. We suggest that they are running the show and playing the role of masters of the society.

As she grows older (C. A. 40 +), the strict discipline which has been impressed on the female from childhood in Tepoztlán becomes her strength; it would appear that she realizes she can control and manipulate the world about her. She is undisturbed by daydreams, sexual urges, and emotional needs. The older woman has somehow discovered that she can now run the show and does so. We suggest that the older men do not accept this role on the part of women, and that they become the ones in conflict.

What seems to happen to the male as he matures (C. A. 40 +) is that, for physical and psychological reasons, he becomes sexually impotent. We surmise that he is losing mastery over his world and becomes impulsive as well as conflicted.

About Tepoztecan society as a whole we may say that friendliness and cooperative enterprise are not among their characteristics. These people seem rather to be uncooperative and rigid, and are trained to do their duty and to work hard in their daily tasks. The people of Tepoztlán are realistic. They live and struggle in a concrete world in which phantasy living has been reduced to a minimum or even excluded. They exist together but do not act cooperatively. No doubt they work for a common aim, keeping alive and maintaining the family unit, but each one must do his tasks with reserve and with little feeling for others.

In conclusion we may say that the outstanding feature of the Rorschach records in Tepoztlán is the indication of the opposite course taken by the life cycle of the men and women. Women appear to be initiated early in their role in life, and are consistently expected to avoid sex as a source of pleasure. They follow a well-defined line of development, with conscious control over their feelings and impulses, but in later years they assume the dominant role in society. Men experience more discontinuity and inconsistency in behavior; they are likely to be more exuberant than women but also more anxious and insecure. As they grow older they lose their dominant position, and the older adults appear disturbed, impulsive, and anxious. They seem to be losing the grip on society that the older women are taking over.

inter-personal relations within the family: 14

HUSBANDS AND WIVES

According to the ideal culture patterns for husband-wife relations in Tepoztlán, the husband is an authoritarian, patriarchal figure who is head and master of the household and enjoys the highest status in the family. His prerogatives are to receive the obedience and respect of his wife and children, as well as their services. It is the husband who makes all important decisions and plans for the entire family. He is responsible for the support of the family and for the behavior of each member. The wife is expected to be submissive, faithful, devoted, and respectful toward her husband. She should seek his advice and obtain his permission before undertaking any but the most minor activities. A wife should be industrious and frugal and should manage to save money no matter how small her husband's income. A good wife is not critical, curious, or jealous of her husband's activities outside the home.

The ideal patterns for the expected roles of husbands and wives are, in large measure, a social fiction. Although in most homes there is an outward compliance to the ideal pattern, with the wife apparently submissive and serving, there are actually few homes in which the husband is the dominant figure he seeks to be, or in which he truly controls his family. Most marriages show some conflict over the question of authority and the respective roles of the spouses. The most placid marriages are those which take a middle course, in which the wife does little to challenge the authority of the husband and in which the husband is not too overbearing toward his wife. On the other hand, conflict is most acute in those families in which the woman is openly aggressive and actively attempts to dominate the husband, or in which the husband is so insecure that he becomes an over-violent and fear-inspiring figure.

Women's standards of behavior for their husbands and for themselves are influenced by their own needs and experiences and are not always consistent with the ideal roles. Older women tend to conform to the culturally set standards of female behavior more than younger women, but to a large extent women of all ages share the same attitudes. While women readily admit the superiority of men and tend to admire a man who is manly, they describe the "good" husband as one who is relatively passive and not too domineering. But they are as critical as men are of wives who answer back or resist their husbands, even though they do it themselves. Also, while women unanimously prefer a submissive daughter-in-law for themselves, they do not always advise their own daughters to yield to mothers-in-law. There is also a definite tendency to regard the completely submissive wife more as a fool than as an ideal. The fact that there is no feeling of inadequacy among women for not achieving the ideal of feminine behavior, and the fact that they feel pride rather than guilt in self-assertion, indicates that they no longer hold the cultural ideal as their own.

Women are, then, more in conflict with traditional ways than are men. Husbands generally find themselves in a defensive position in which they must conserve the old order of things in the home, to maintain their control over the family. Men show symptoms of anxiety and feelings of inadequacy because of their inability to fulfill their roles to their own satisfaction. Wives tend to reject certain aspects of their role, particularly those which interfere with their freedom of movement and economic activities. The strong preference women display toward work which takes them outside the home, and their feeling of deprivation when they cannot leave the home, are evidence of this. Perhaps related to this is the fact that pregnancy and bearing of children are viewed without enthusiasm by women. These attitudes of women are in sharp contrast to those of men. The reaction of women to the pressure to conform, is one of a sense of frustration and deprivation. The martyr-complex is widespread among married women, and in telling their life stories, women are often so overwhelmed by self-pity that they break down and cry. They dwell on the sadness of their lives and the faults of their husbands. It is, they say, a woman's unhappy lot to suffer at the hands of men. The hostility toward men is quite general, and women readily characterize all men as "very bad."

The question of authority in husband-wife relations is very much in the minds of men and women in Tepoztlán. There is an awareness, on the part of both, of the growing assertiveness of wives and the continual struggle of husbands to keep them under control. The changes within the village in the past twenty years or so have made this struggle more acute and have brought it into the open. There is a saying among men, "When the man relaxes, the woman takes over." Similarly, women say, "When we give in, the men impose." Even the most conventional women believe that there is a time to yield and a time to resist.

Basic to the conflict in the relations of husbands and wives is the discrepancy between the actual roles and the ideal roles in the organization of the family. Although the wife is subordinate to the husband, it is she who has the greatest responsibility for the planning, organizing, and operation of the household, and for the training and care of the children. The husband traditionally turns over all his earnings to his wife, and she holds the funds and controls much of the spending. In most homes, the husband will not interfere with the wife's handling of the money, so long as she gives him money when he wants it. The good wife is not supposed to refuse her husband's request for money and may receive a beating or scolding if she does. A wife will refuse her husband money when she suspects that it is for drink or for another woman.

Wives are in a position to do a great deal of secret spending, borrowing, and paying back, which gives them a considerable source of added independence. Wives are also free to sell small quantities of the family corn or their own chickens or eggs, and to use the cash whenever they see fit. Although wives are supposed to get the permission of their husbands before going to see a doctor or *curandero,* visiting, or buying and selling in quantity, the frequent absence of the husband from the house permits the wife to do many of these things without his knowledge.

A few men, in an effort to control family affairs, keep their earnings and dole out small daily sums to their wives. Such men are considered very undesirable as husbands. They are called *cuilchilete,* or men with very long penes, and are said to be miserly. Even in those cases where the husband holds the funds, the wife always has an immediate source of cash from selling corn. Some husbands attempt to secure independence by withholding part of their earnings. This leads to quarrels, however, because wives generally know the exact amount of a husband's earnings, and they feel justified in demanding all the money. The fact that the husband often spends the money on drink puts him at a further disadvantage; the wife may then accuse him of wasting it, of not caring whether his family eats, etc. Wives in such situations may complain to the mother-in-law, or in extreme cases to the priest or *padrino* of marriage, who will invariably advise the husband to relinquish all his earnings.

In contrast to the wife's central role within the home, the husband's actual participation in family and household affairs is minimal. His work, with the exception of hauling water and making occasional repairs in and around the house, is outside the home. The division of labor is clear-cut, and the husband, except in emergencies, never does anything in connection with the house or children. For the majority of men, the home is a place where they have their physical needs attended to. Men are away from home a good part of the day, and sometimes for several days at a time, depending upon their work and the season of the year.

The history of Tepoztlán has been such that men frequently were forced to leave the village for long periods, and it is interesting to speculate on the effect of this on family life. We know that many Tepoztecans had to work in the mines of distant Taxco and on faraway haciendas during the early sixteenth century. This pattern continued in modified form throughout the colonial period and until the Revolution. Before the Revolution, large numbers of men worked on the neighboring haciendas and returned to the village only once every two weeks. Even today, about 150 men work on the haciendas during four to six months of the dry season, returning home once a week. With the husband away, the wife was not only head of the family but also often had to find means of supporting herself and the children until his return.

Perhaps more important than a husband's absence from the home is his behavior and attitude when he is at home. Traditionally, husbands keep aloof from the petty details of the household. It is evidence of respect if the husband is not molested by his family with stories, complaints, or requests. He does not customarily inquire about the children or the events of the day when he arrives at home, nor does he expect an account from his wife. Unless he is told otherwise, the husband assumes that things are going the way he desires them. Actually, the husband learns only what the wife wishes to tell him or what he observes for himself. Since wives are held accountable for everything that happens at home, they tend to withhold information which might result in disapproval or punishment.

The husband avoids intimacy with members of his family to be respected by them. He expects them to demonstrate their respect by maintaining a proper social distance. His contacts with his children are brief and reserved. The Tepoztecan husband expects his wife to see that the children are quiet when he is at home, and it is her obligation to teach them to fear him. Men are generally not talkative at home and contribute little to family conversation, nor do they seek or expect their children to confide in them. When the husband is at home during the day, he sits apart from the rest of the family; at night he eats alone or with his grown sons and goes out or retires soon after. The loftiness of the husband's position in the home makes him remote from the family. He loses touch with the individual members and situations which he is endeavoring to control, and, inadvertently, he gives his wife and children the freedom he does not wish them to have.

In many homes, the husband's sense of security depends upon the extent to which his wife and children fear him. Some men are more violent than others and beat their wives at slight provocation. Suspicion of adultery is one of the major causes of beatings, but a wife may receive a beating for lesser offenses, such as not having a good meal ready, failure to have clean and well-ironed clothes for her husband, or selling too much corn without permission. A jealous wife, or one who questions her husband's activities or judgment, may also receive a beating. Wives are supposed to take their beatings without fighting back. Women may report their husbands to the local authorities for wife-beating, which is a recognized offense. But relatively few cases are reported, for going to such lengths may mean the separation of the couple. In many families, particularly among older couples, the role of the husband gradually comes to be little more than that of provider and punisher.

It is interesting to note that in written themes, in which school children were asked to tell what they liked best about each member of the family, they invariably wrote that they liked their father because he supported them. The comments of widows concerning the death of their husbands are all phrased in terms of economic loss. One widow, when asked how she felt at the death of her husband, said, with much feeling, that at the time she had wished that it had been her young son rather than her husband because in that case she would at least have been sure of her food. Although sentiment and grief over personal loss at the death of a husband undoubtedly is present in many cases, it is not required of wives to express this grief and it is considered perfectly natural for them to emphasize the economic loss.

More and more women are undertaking to contribute to the support of their families, even when the husband is a relatively good provider. Women traditionally raise a few chickens and pigs, and some now grow fruit trees, to earn money. Men recognize this type of activity as necessary. Some poor men blame their inability to get ahead on the fact that their wives are inept at earning or saving money, or that their wives refuse to raise chickens and pigs because they dirty up the patio and are too much trouble. One attitude, sometimes expressed among married women, is, "Why should I work? That is what I have a husband and sons for." However, many wives try to earn enough so as not to depend upon their husbands entirely for food and clothing, because "the men are too miserly to spend much on these things." The more capable women are able to earn enough to aid their husbands substantially. Without exception, every man who has been able to improve his economic situation since the Revolution has done so with the help of his wife, and in all the more prosperous homes the wives are known to be unusually capable and industrious.

Several fairly recent social and economic changes which have occurred in the village have affected the roles of women. Women have been more affected than men by such technological changes as the building of the road, the establishment of bus service to Cuernavaca, and the introduction of the corn mills. These changes have also affected the relations between husbands and wives. Women began to patronize the corn mills over the objections of their husbands, and the success of the mills was described by a male informant as the result of "the revolution of the women against the authority of the men." The corn mills have given women from four to six additional hours a day to devote to other activities. Since women are not so tied to the *metate* now, they are able to leave the house more freely and can undertake more extensive business activities.

An increasing number of more ambitious married women are now raising animals or growing fruit on a larger scale or are devoting more time to selling the family produce at the Tepoztlán and Cuernavaca markets. However, husbands tend to balk at the latter activity and do not easily give their wives permission to go to Cuernavaca, despite the fact that the extra earnings would be welcome. This type of work has, in the past, been carried on exclusively by widows or older unmarried women who "had no man to control them." Many of these women are known for their promiscuity, and they and their occupation have little status. In addition, men tend to associate going to Cuernavaca with going to meet a lover and do not permit their wives to go alone. Husbands also fear that people will say they can no longer support or control their wives if they go out to work. The fear of giving the wife more freedom, as well as the recognition of the threat to the man in his role as provider, outweighs the obvious economic advantages, and most men prevent their wives from earning as much as they might.

Another factor which has affected husband-wife relations is the increased independence of young couples, who now seek to set up separate households soon after marriage. In the past, when wives often lived for many years with their mothers-in-law and were subject to their authority, the husband had relatively little difficulty in controlling his wife. But the young wife now assumes earlier the full burden of running the household and requires a certain freedom and authority which has not been traditionally hers. Men, however, are still unprepared to permit their wives the freedom to carry out these new responsibilities and interpret many of their demands and activities as threats to the husband's authority.

The quality of husband-wife relations is perhaps most clearly revealed by the latent fear that husbands have of being bewitched or poisoned by their wives. Tepoztecan men believe that wives who have suffered beatings and harsh treatment may take revenge by resorting to sorcery. The most commonly feared sorcery is a potion made from an herb called *toloache,* which may be secretly put into a man's coffee or other drink.[1] This herb is supposed to make a man *tonto,* stupid or foolish and easily led. An overdose of *toloache* will make a man an idiot. The most important symptom to Tepoztecans is that the drugged man can no longer control his wife and becomes dominated by her. When a woman is known to dominate her husband and to have many lovers, she is suspected of having given her husband *toloache.* According to Tepoztecans, the man is unaware of his condition and can do nothing about it. His mother or some other close relative may attempt to cure him secretly by putting a counter-potion into his coffee. It is interesting to note that there is not a single case of *toloache* being given by men to women.

There is a readiness to explain all mildness and passivity in men, in relation to their wives, as a result of the man's having been drugged by *toloache* or bewitched by other means. For example, a man in the village continued to give his wife a regular sum of money, although she had left him and they had no children. His unprecedented solicitude was believed to have been the result of magic applied by the wife. There are about fifty recognized cases of *toloache* poisoning or bewitching in the village. The following cases were described by one of our male informants:

MAXIMO C.: He was a bachelor until age forty, at which time he married a widow, age fifty. Before his marriage he was a strong man, but after a while he became weak, thin, humble, and always kept his head down. That is why we believe she gave him something. She is the mother, the queen. She is all and he is her servant. She had had many men and had always lived with bachelors. She lured him and married him. Her first husband was a fool. He was a *capitán* for the hacienda and was away a lot. He came here every eight days and often found another man in the house. He permitted this. She had many men, and they all died. She gave some potion to all of these men to make them live with her. She died last year.

ANTONIO F.: He eloped with his first wife. He beat her often because she ran around. After twenty years of marriage, she gave him the stuff and he began to show the symptoms.

RICARDO V.: He was the boss in his home for about five years. Then she began to sleep with just anybody, and he began to show all the symptoms.

---

[1] *Toloache* is a well-known plant in Mexico and is said to contain a drug which, when given in large doses, will affect the brain.

FEDERICO P.: He ruled for about ten years. Then he beat his wife terrifically, but later he began to show all the signs, and now he says nothing.

CLAUDIO L.: He ruled in his house for about three years. His wife had wanted to marry someone else, but her parents forced her to marry him. She began to run around with other men. She has a son of twenty years and still runs around.

Our informant, a widower, remarked about himself, "I used to say to my wife, 'I rule in my home. If you butt into my business I will kill you.' I didn't weaken, so she never ruled. Sometimes I feared she might give me some of this stuff but, thank God, she never did."

Wives who "answer" their husbands and resist their authority sometimes earn the reputation of being witches, particularly if their mothers were suspected of being witches. A wife who continues to have female friends after marriage is sometimes said to be one of a group of witches. Girls with some education also are apt to be suspected, because they do not assume a submissive role after marriage. The following case illustrates this:

A girl living in one of the smaller barrios was recently married. This girl had attended normal school and had several friends who had been her classmates there. She is known to be unusually jolly, active, aggressive, and is very pretty. After marriage, she went to live in her mother-in-law's house and soon came into conflict with her. She was so impertinent and aggressive, both to her mother-in-law and her husband, that the former began to suspect her of being a witch. Her suspicions increased when she saw that her son did nothing to control the girl and continued to show affection for her. The mother-in-law began telling people that her daughter-in-law was a witch, because when she was scolded she kept looking into the person's eyes to try to get him under her power. She elaborated this by saying that one night she saw the devil jump in at the window and carry off the girl, and that the next morning the girl was found naked near the stream.

The mother-in-law's stories came to the ears of the girl, who laughingly told her friends that from now on she was going to act like a witch and frighten her mother-in-law. She invented a little technique whereby she covered her face with her outspread fingers and stared through them with big eyes whenever her mother-in-law or husband scolded her. People say that she has both of them in her power now because when she does that, they both become quiet and keep their heads down. The young wife continues to see her friends, who have now all become known as witches among the less "modern" portion of the population.

Information concerning the sexual relations between husbands and wives is rather difficult to obtain, because of the prevailing taboos. Even trusted informants were reluctant to discuss their intimate marital relations. This was especially true of the older generation. However, some of our younger informants gave us much material. We found that older women generally spoke more freely about sex than older men, once their confidence was gained. Widows, who have a reputation in Tepoztlán for being worldly, were among our best informants.

In sexual relations as in social relations in Tepoztlán, the husband is expected to take the initiative. It is the wife's duty to submit and the husband's prerogative to demand. It is believed that women have less *naturaleza,* that is, they are sexually weaker than men. Many women enter marriage with the belief that intercourse is painful. Husbands do not expect their wives to be sexually demanding or passionate, nor are these viewed as desirable traits in a wife. Husbands do not complain if their wives are not eager for or do not enjoy sexual intercourse. Frigidity is considered a source of security by the husband, for the assumption is that a frigid wife will not seek sexual contact elsewhere. A husband is more likely to suspect a wife who is passionate and may feel impelled to keep her under close surveillance. Women who are passionate and who "need" men are referred to as *loca* (crazy), and it is believed to be an abnormal condition frequently brought about by black magic. Some husbands deliberately refrain from arousing their wives sexually, because they do not want them to "get to like it too much."

One informant said he did not encourage his wife for fear that he would be unable to satisfy her when he was older. Another informant explained that he did not teach his wife what he knew about sexual techniques, because "that would be making a whore out of her." Few husbands give attention to the question of their wive's sexual satisfaction. In general, sexual play is a technique men reserve for the seduction of other women.

Much of the women's expressed attitudes toward sexual relations with their husbands dwell upon its negative aspects and reveal feelings of self-righteousness which border on martyrdom. Women speak of submitting to their husband's "abuse" because it is their obligation to do so. Most women emphasize their desire to avoid sexual intercourse for a long time after giving birth, in order to avoid pregnancy. They complain of the difficulty of keeping their husbands away from them at this time, and they put it in terms of the husband not caring sufficiently for the nursing infant.

In discussing the sexual relations of husband and wife, it is important to consider the fact that there is little privacy for couples even on the first night of marriage, and, as the family increases, there is less and less privacy. In view of the obligation of Tepoztecan parents to protect their children from learning the facts of life, the prevailing sleeping arrangements must act as a strong inhibiting factor. We were unable to find a single informant who would admit the possibility of a child hearing his parents at night. Also, there is a strong block among adults in recalling ever having heard their parents in sexual intercourse. Tepoztecans value privacy, and, as the children grow up, they make some attempt to put the older ones in a separate room or shelter. Occasionally a couple will creep into the *temascal* (sweathouse), or go into the patio for additional privacy.

Account after account from informants indicate that most couples spent their first night with the husband's parents or other relatives sleeping in the same room. Many brides, particularly in the past, who married at thirteen and fourteen years of age and who scarcely knew their husbands before marriage, were in complete ignorance of sexual intercourse and were reluctant and fearful at first.

According to our older informants some brides did not submit to their husbands and had to be forced to do so. In one case a thirteen-year-old girl fought off her husband for six nights. Several times she ran out of the house to evade him. He finally became embarrassed and tied her hands behind her and forced himself upon her. Another girl left her husband permanently, because he forced her to submit to him for the first time in a field. But these stories apply more to the older generation. The young people in Tepoztlán today have many more opportunities for premarital contacts with the opposite sex and are generally familiar with the details of sexual relations by the time they marry.

Tepoztecan men are, for the most part, suspicious and distrustful of their wives and believe that they are capable of being unfaithful to them at the first opportunity. Men are unanimous in the belief that women must be kept under strict surveillance and control. The adulterous activities of men reinforce this attitude toward women. "I see how easily other women fool their husbands, my wife can, too." To insure his wife's loyalty the husband seeks to isolate her from outsiders.

When the couple lives with the husband's family for several years, it is relatively easy to guard the wife, but when there is early separation from the parental home, the husband is deprived of an important source of security. It is common for husbands in this position to ask the cooperation of relatives, neighbors, and friends in watching over his wife when she is left alone. As a result of these spies, some husbands know, in any given day, exactly when their wives went out and returned, with whom they spoke, and for how long.

Wives are generally forbidden to have female friends and most women discontinue all friendships at the time of marriage. Husbands view such friends as potential arrangers or go-betweens for the wife and a lover. Men frequently drop their own friends after marriage or do not encourage them to visit for fear that some intimacy might develop between the wife and the friend. The majority of husbands are suspicious of any activities which take the wife away from home. During the first few years of marriage, most wives are not permitted to leave the house unaccompanied. In cases where young couples live alone, the wife will prefer to ask a neighbor or a relative to make purchases for her, rather than risk her husband's anger or the gossip of others by going to the market alone. Although some young wives now go out alone, they are considered suspect by others.

When a woman leaves the house she is expected to return in the shortest possible time; any delay on her part may earn her a sound scolding or beating. Gossiping with other women is discouraged and sometimes punished. Most husbands do not approve of their wives going to wash clothing at the public washing place for fear they will gossip and learn "bad things" from other women. However, the burdensome task of hauling water to do the washing at home serves to keep most husbands from banning the public washing place.

The suspiciousness and jealousy of some husbands is extreme. There are cases of wife-beating merely because the husband saw a man standing at the street corner near the house and suspected him of being his wife's lover. If a wife's work is not done by the time the husband comes home, or if the children and animals look neglected, he may suspect her of having spent time with a lover. In one case, a husband noticed that the family cat ate ravenously at night as though she had not been fed all day, and he accused his wife of having been out with someone. If a wife is unusually careful about her appearance before going out, or if she is reluctant to have sexual intercourse, her husband's suspicions may be aroused.

The following conversation, or rather monologue, overheard on the Tepoztlán bus illustrates the degree of suspiciousness of the Tepoztecan husband. One woman was telling another of her difficulties with her husband whenever she returned from a trip to Cuernavaca: "If I return annoyed, he says, 'You are annoyed to have to come back to me.' If I come back contented, it is worse. Then he says, 'Now you are happy. Now you are satisfied because you saw the one you wanted to see.' It seems that I have to have a face of wood when I enter my house."

Husbands generally become less suspicious after several years of marriage, if the behavior of the wife warrants it. However, as the children get older and can assist the mother at home, and as the needs of the growing family increase, women frequently wish to devote more time to earning money. For this they need freedom and must leave the house more often, and tension and suspicion in the husband are again awakened. Men are most secure when their wives are pregnant or have an infant to care for; then women keep to the house more and are unable to undertake outside activities. Having many children, one following close upon the other, is a source of security for the men.

Promiscuous sexual activity is considered a male prerogative in Tepoztlán, and men feel under pressure to have "affairs." Although male adultery is considered undesirable, it is also viewed as natural behavior and is widespread on the part of married men. Men make no secret of the fact that they have children by other women and often recognize these children as their own. There is no strong feeling or prejudice against illegitimate children; rather they are pitied, because "they don't have a father."

Illicit relations are usually with widows or unmarried women, but also frequently with other married women. Many men now go to Cuernavaca where they visit houses of prostitution, and venereal disease is becoming more common in Tepoztlán.

The "good" wife does not interfere with her husband's extra-marital affairs, but many wives express resentment, especially if money is involved. Some women will openly quarrel with their husbands because of jealousy and may refuse to give them money. This type of interference particularly enrages husbands and often results in a beating.

Drunkenness is not as common in Tepoztlán as in surrounding villages or other parts of Mexico and is more disapproved of. Most men drink a small amount of alcohol regularly in the evening, "to heat themselves" against the cold air of the fields, but extensive drinking is limited to Sundays, fiestas, or formal occasions. Most wives resent drunkenness, because of the probability of violence and the expenditure of money. But only the most aggressive wives try to break their husbands of the habit.

Drinking is an important emotional outlet for men. It is believed that drinking helps one to get over *muina,* and it is traditional for men to go out to drink after a quarrel at home. Sometimes the men come home drunk and aggressive; other times "because they lack judgment" they arrive full of affection and kiss and caress the members of the family. It is interesting that only under intoxication will husbands and fathers openly demonstrate their affection in this way. Repressed hostilities toward wife, mother, child, or others also frequently come out when a man has been drinking. Some husbands beat their wives only when drunk. Drinking to get courage to punish a wife, seduce a woman, or attack an enemy is also common. Men often give a particular shout or cry *"grita"* after drinking, to show that they feel brave.

Although women in Tepoztlán are not supposed to drink, a few women are known to drink regularly and have been seen in a drunken state. Drunken women often cry for hours at a time and are inconsolable. In contrast to men, they do not respond to intoxication with aggression or impulsiveness but with self-pity. Widows or abandoned wives, more than other women, tend to drink for comfort. A few modern young girls get together occasionally for drinking and smoking in secret, but they discontinue this after marriage.

PARENTS AND CHILDREN

The relations between parents and children in Tepoztlán are also conditioned by emphasis on respect and authority. Children are reared to respect and obey their elders and to submit to the will of their mother and father so long as they live under the parental roof. Not long ago, all children in Tepoztlán kissed the hands of their parents, grandparents, and godparents in greeting; now only a few families continue this custom, and children are embarrassed to do it in the presence of outsiders. In the smaller outlying villages in the municipio, hand-kissing is still a common practice.

From infancy on, children in Tepoztlán are encouraged to be quiet, passive, and unobtrusive; older children are required to be obedient, self-controlled, and helpful. There is great emphasis placed upon "good" behavior in children, and the possibility of a child "not turning out well" is one of the fears of Tepoztecan parents. It is feared that a child who is badly raised will not be a good worker and will get into trouble. Such a child reflects ill upon his parents and is a cause for shame.

The responsibility of child rearing is felt as a heavy burden, particularly by mothers. Upon the death of a small child, it is not uncommon for the mother to comfort herself with the statement, "It is better thus, for who knows if he would have turned out well."

While both parents are held responsible by society at large for the care and conduct of their children, within the home the major burden falls upon the mother. It is the mother who feeds, bathes, and clothes the children and cares for them when they are ill. It is she who is expected to train them in good habits and behavior and to see after their religious training. The father rules the children through the mother and holds her responsible for their behavior. As far as the children are concerned, family life revolves about the mother, and their contacts are primarily with her. It is to her that they turn for help, permission, information, protection, or affection. In matters involving small sums of money, children always go to the mother because the father does not hold or control family funds. Children beg the father for pennies when he is drunk; then he may have change in his pockets.

Children are supposed to make important requests directly to the father. However, the mother is often the mediator for the children, and most requests are made through her. If a son wishes to continue school or a daughter wants to go to a dance, they will almost always first discuss the matter with the mother; and if she sees fit, she will ask the father. Older children occasionally speak directly to the father, particularly if the mother refuses to do so. Many fathers also use the mother as the go-between in dealings with the children. If a father thinks his son is staying out too late or that his daughter is too free in her manner, he will often tell the mother to see that the children improve their behavior, rather than speak directly to them himself. In the same manner, if a child does not improve or if he commits an offense, it is sometimes the mother who receives the scolding or beating and not the child.

The father depends on the mother to maintain his position of respect in the home. It is one of her more important obligations to teach the children to fear the father's anger, to avoid offending him, and to demonstrate continually by her own behavior her respect for him. Children are also repeatedly warned by the grandmother, aunt, godmother, and other adults that the father must be respected. Respect for the father is also sought by emphasizing to the children the importance of family unity, and the dire fate of orphans. There is a good deal of talk about the family as a unit; and the individual who lives in a peaceful, hard working, united family group is considered fortunate.

Although mothers generally comply in building up the father as a feared and respected figure, they make little effort to place him on a pedestal, or to portray him to the children as an awe-inspiring personage. It is common for mothers to complain to their children about the husband and to point out his faults. When a man dies, there is little or no effort on the part of his wife to create an honored memory of him among the children. At best, a mother might tell her small children that their father had "no vices and was hard working," and that they had no cause to be ashamed of him. If a man had weaknesses, however, the mother generally does not overlook them, even after his death. Many of our case histories reveal the part the mother played in developing an uninspiring father-image. The following, for example, is not unusual:

"My mother told me that my father was a drunkard and a vagabond, a gambler interested in cockfights."

A youth of nineteen said, "My mother warns me not to do as my father did [see other women] or I will come to the same bad end."

Another widow told her two sons that their father was a *político,* and that they lost their inheritance because he wasted his time and money.

When the question of administering a Rorschach test to one husband came up, his wife laughed and, in the presence of her eight children, said that her husband was very ignorant and would not do well. "He doesn't even know how to read," she remarked.

In a few cases, when the mother has a true admiration for her husband, particularly if he is better educated, she will transfer this to her children. For example, the wife of the village secretary, who is widely respected for his fine hand and ability to type, has taught her children to look up to their father as a *sabio* (wise man). It is, however, more common for mothers to instill fear of the father rather than respect for his positive personal qualities.

It is interesting to compare our description of the role of the mother and father in Tepoztlán today with Sahagún's description of parental roles, as obtained from his Aztec informants shortly after the conquest. The role of the father was described as follows:

The father is the prime root and originator of the family. The quality of the father is to be diligent and careful, who, with his perseverance rules his house and sustains it. The good father raises and supports his children and gives them good training and doctrine, scolds them and gives them good advice and good examples and makes a treasure for them and guards it; keeps account of the expenditures of the house and rules his children's spending and foresees things in advance. The nature of the bad father is to be lazy, careless, idle, who cures no one, who out of laziness leaves undone that which he is obliged to do; and loses time to no purpose.[2]

This description might well apply to the present-day Tepoztecan concept of the role of the father, with two important exceptions: The Tepoztecan father is not expected to train or teach his children. The Tepoztecan father does not keep the family accounts, and he rules his children's spending in a limited way. The father, as described by Sahagún, is a more truly patriarchal figure than the present Tepoztecan father.

The mother's role was presented by Sahagún as follows:

The quality of the mother is to have children and to give them milk; the virtuous mother is vigilant, an active caretaker, solicitous, anxious. She raises her children, has continual care of them; she sees that they lack nothing, she is like a slave of all in her house, concerned with the needs of each; she is not careless with necessities of the house; she saves, is industrious and is a hard worker. The bad mother is foolish, dirty, stupid, sleepy, lazy, wasteful, improvident, careless of the house, allows things to be lost out of laziness or anger, doesn't cure those of the house; doesn't look out for household things; doesn't correct the errors of those of the house and for this reason every day gets worse. There are among such persons legitimate children and bastards.[3]

---

[2] Bernardino de Sahagún, *Historia General de las Cosas de Nueva España,* ed. Pedro Lobredo, III (Mexico, 1938), 11.

[3] *Ibid.*

Tepoztecans tend to view mothers in similar terms, but do not emphasize the mother as a slave of all in her house. Rather, in the hierarchal set-up, she serves her husband, but her daughters and younger sons work for her to whatever extent she may demand.

Sahagún's description of the good son and daughter, though limited, still applies today in Tepoztlán. He describes them as follows:

The son of good quality is obedient, humble, grateful, reverent, imitating his parents in custom and in body; he is similar to his father and mother. . . .

The daughter who is raised in her father's house has these good qualities; she is a true virgin, never having known a man; she is an obedient, modest, prudent, capable, genteel woman, honorable, respectful, well-raised, who knows the doctrine, taught by a careful, informed person.[4]

The only exception to be made for Tepoztecans is the attitude of reverence in the son. Reverence and awe on the part of the children toward their parents is not demanded and is notably absent. It is interesting to note that the daughter "who is raised in her father's house" is a true virgin. In Tepoztlán, it is believed that a girl who has no father to fear or to protect her is more likely to have lovers or to be attacked or carried off by boys.

There is a marked difference in the quality of mother-child and father-child relations in Tepoztlán. It is a stereotype that fathers are "harder" and mothers "softer" by nature. It is considered natural for the mother to feel closer to the children than the father. The mother who abandons her children is considered abnormal or *machorra* (like a man). It is more common for a man to desert his children and, although it is disapproved, it is not considered abnormal, for "that is the way men are." It is also taken for granted that children feel closer to the mother, and that they will be more disturbed at losing her. It is recognized, too, that the death of the mother is more disruptive to the household than the death of the father.

The relationship between father and child is one of respect and avoidance of intimacy. The unvarying role of the father results in consistent behavior toward him on the part of the children. They are always obedient, subdued, controlled, and inhibited in his presence and remain so well into adulthood. It is extremely rare to find a child who does not behave this way to his father, even though children frequently disobey their father's wishes, especially when he is not present.

Children are less consistent in their attitudes and behavior toward the mother and reflect her own varying behavior, which alternates between being protective and administering punishment, and being indulgent and strict, being authoritative and submissive, and serving and demanding service. The child's relationship with the mother is one of respect, yet it is marked by intimacy. Mothers often complain that the children are less obedient and less fearful of them than of the father, and this is attributed to the fact that the children take advantage of the mother's "softness." Children sometimes display signs of ambivalence toward the mother; expect-

---

[4] *Ibid.*, p. 12.

ing more from her, they show hostility when she fails them; receiving more from her, they feel dependent upon her. In general, the children are more emotionally involved with the mother than with the father. The word "mother" flung in anger during a quarrel is a strong insult and usually results in fighting and violence.

The father maintains his position of respect by being withdrawn from the children. Traditionally the Tepoztecan father does not carry infants except in emergencies, nor does he play with them. Children are sharply reprimanded for climbing on their father's lap or for grabbing his leg. Infants soon learn not to reach out to their fathers or expect much attention from them.

When four- or five-year-olds run to meet their father on his return from the fields, they are not permitted to jump on him but are taught to walk demurely at his side. As the child, particularly the son, gets older, the father becomes more receptive, but he does not permit physical contact, nor does he spend more time at home with the boy. The traditional way for a father to express his affection is to buy the child little gifts, give him pennies, or take him to the fields or to a fiesta. If the father is very pleased at the birth of a child, he will generally express his pleasure by purchasing as many protective amulets as he can afford.

The mother has more ways of demonstrating her affection for a child than has the father. She may kiss, fondle, or carry a nursing child as much as she wishes and may continue to do so until he is five. Generally, the mother avoids demonstrative affection for children after weaning. Because of the mother's position as server, dispenser of food, nurse, etc., she can express her affection by means of all of these. Giving more attention and pennies for sweets, serving larger portions of food, sewing more clothing, worrying over illness or accident, devoting more time to curing, and buying needed school supplies are all common means by which mothers express their affection for a child. Mothers also show their affection by not informing the father of the child's misdeeds or by intervening when the father is punishing the child. Such intervention and deception, although infuriating to the father, is viewed as "natural" in a mother.

A child is always punished for flouting the authority of his parents and for unwillingness to work. Behavior which does not involve these has a good chance of being indulged, particularly if backed up by a show of temper, tears, whining, begging, or demanding. If a child wants something badly enough he generally gets it. Even in families in which children are beaten with severity and worked hard, they may get whatever it is they want merely because they "want it."

Parents, despite their authoritativeness, can be intimidated by a strong-willed child. Although children in Tepoztlán show obedience early, they are not completely submissive. The ways in which they can express their own tastes and desires with impunity or reward has made for a certain development of the ego. Children sometimes display a self-centered, demanding attitude in connection with food, clothing, money to spend, going to school or fiestas, and, more recently, time for play. The variety we find in both punishment and indulgence stems from differences in interpretation as to when parental authority is or is not involved. For some, any manifestation of independence is taken to be disrespectful of the parent; for others, only disobedience to a direct command and a show of aggression toward the parents are cause for punishment. Also, the varying requirements for the assistance of children in the home, favoritism, and the different status of boys and girls and older and younger children make for variation in parental treatment.

Fear is the principal technique by which parents control their children. Fear of punishment is widespread, and parents who have successfully instilled this fear in their children are considered good parents. It is believed that too much kindness or softness spoils children and that they may grow up without knowing respect and fear.

There is a tradition of severe punishment in Tepoztlán. In the past, children were more repressed and were sometimes brutally punished for slight offenses. Tepoztecans recall such punishments as hanging a child in a net over a smoky fire of chile seeds to asphyxiate him partially and to make him ill for days.[5] Similarly if a child broke a dish, he might be punished by scraping his arms with a piece of the broken dish until he bled. It may be that these old practices had some magical aspects and were not done in a spirit of cruelty, but it is significant that they are interpreted as cruel today.

About forty years ago, children were painfully whipped at school and at home with *la disciplina,* a rope which had five, fingerlike extensions. This is no longer used. Not so long ago if a teacher or a neighbor accused a child of some misbehavior, the child was often beaten by his father in the presence of the accuser. Now, it is said, parents more often tend to find fault with the accuser than with the child. In the past, almost any adult could punish a child, but non-relatives no longer do this for fear of starting a family quarrel. Tepoztecans generally agree that punishment has become more lenient, and that there is more toleration of childish faults and whims, particularly among younger or more educated parents.

Our data show wide variations in the form of punishment and in the degree of severity. It is clear that children between the ages of five and twelve are frequently punished, but for children over twelve, physical punishment is reserved for the most serious offenses. The father generally inflicts the most severe punishments, but the mother punishes more often. In most families the father is more feared and more promptly obeyed, even though he may have punished his children only once or twice. Usually a rise in his voice will get quick response from his child. Mothers tend to punish their daughters more than their sons, but fathers punish their sons more than their daughters. Girls generally receive more punishment than boys and are made tractable at an earlier age.

Punishment usually does not begin until the child starts to walk, and it is limited to a slap on the hands or buttocks. Some mothers slap the hands of a nine-month-old baby if he touches a forbidden object, and others may spank a baby hard if he cries too much. However, punishment during infancy is not common. When toilet

---

[5] This practice is reminiscent of the Aztec form of punishing rebellious subjects by placing them in a room filled with fumes of burning chile seeds.

training begins, children are sometimes spanked. More occasion arises for spanking during and after weaning and after the birth of another sibling. Most parents believe it is important to punish a child when young, and some children receive their first severe beatings at three or four years of age.

For example, I saw a three-year-old boy beaten with a switch by his father. The boy had been annoying the father while he was cleaning beans. When the father scolded the boy sharply, he began to cry. Because the boy refused to stop crying, the father went over to a bush, tore off a long thin switch and beat him hard. The mother, who was also cleaning beans, paid no attention. The boy did not go to the mother, but ran off to the corral where he sobbed quietly for a long time. Beatings of this sort are rare before five years of age.

Fathers usually punish with a beating, using a stick or a rope. Mothers also sometimes do this, but more often they hit with their hands, or they may slap, pinch, kick, shake, or even throw a stone or two at the offending child. Sharp scolding, calling names, not being allowed to play, being put to work at something unpleasant, and being put out of the house and denied food are other ways of punishing.

In the themes entitled, "My Worst Punishment," written for us by children in the fourth, fifth, and sixth grades in school, we learned of several other types of punishment. One boy wrote that he was severely beaten with a rope and then tied up all night by his mother for having grumbled too much. Another was not allowed to lie down and go to sleep when he wanted to. Not being bought new clothes or not being taken to fiestas are considered severe punishments by girls, and both boys and girls mentioned that they did not like to be scolded or shamed before others. Occasionally a boy is punished by having to do work ordinarily done by girls, such as carrying corn to the mill. It is particularly embarrassing for an eleven- or twelve-year-old boy to stand in the long queue of women and girls to wait his turn at the mill. Girls who are incorrigible may not be permitted to leave the house for a week or two.

Both boys and girls are punished for disobedience, for breaking or losing things, for grumbling or rudeness, or for doing things without permission. Girls are more often punished for coming home late from school or from an errand, and for mistreating young brothers and sisters or other children. Punishment for these offenses is usually quite severe. Boys are more often punished in connection with their work of taking care of the animals; they are beaten for playing when they should be watching the animals, for losing animals, or for bringing them home late. Small boys often have difficulty in handling oxen and cows and may be punished for acts they could not avoid. Boys are also often punished at home and at school for absenting themselves from school to go swimming.

Physical punishment still occurs in the school, although there is a law forbidding it. It is much less severe than in the past and consists of slapping, pulling hair or ears, and hitting with a ruler. I saw one teacher instructing her third-grade class with a switch in her hand, which she occasionally used against the legs of some inattentive child. Beatings with a switch are relatively rare and are applied only to "bad" boys. Other punishments are keeping a child in during the recreation hour; reporting bad behavior to the parents; giving out tasks, such as sweeping the classroom or yard, working in the garden, or writing an assigned sentence one hundred times. One girl was locked up in the henhouse for hitting other children. Parents generally approve of physical punishment in the school, and some think the school is now too lenient. In the past, it was common practice for parents who could not control their children at home to ask the teacher to discipline them. Children who are punished in school rarely tell their parents about it for fear that they will be punished a second time at home. Causes for punishment in school are inattentiveness, not knowing the lesson, fighting, and disobedience.

Other methods are also used to instill fear in the child. It is common for parents, particularly mothers, to threaten to desert their children, playing on the children's fear of becoming orphans. One mother said that she can get obedience from her children by telling them that she will stop eating and die so that they will have to live with a cruel stepmother. Children are told that if they are naughty they will be carried off by a stranger who will make soap out of them. Any passer-by, and recently the *gringo,* is used to frighten children in this way. In Tepoztlán, where children have occasion to see many tourists and outsiders coming and going, the fear of strangers has worn off, but in the nearby smaller villages children run to hide when an unfamiliar person appears in the streets.

Many mothers and grandmothers tell children stories of owls and coyotes coming out at night to eat bad children and of bats and opossums that drink blood. Children who lie or disobey are told that they will turn into devils and burn in hell. They are told that badness is always punished in some unexpected way, such as being bitten by a mad dog, and that goodness is rewarded with good luck.

The sound of a child crying appears to be a particular source of irritation in adults, especially in men, and children are frequently frightened into silence by threats of punishment. The story of Cahuasohuanton, a spirit who listens outside the walls of the house and imitates the child crying, is told to frighten crying children into silence. The story, translated from the Náhuatl, goes as follows:

Once it happened that a child was crying a great deal, and his parents told him to lie down and go to sleep. He did not want to and sat near the hearth crying. His parents kept telling him to stop and then they fell asleep. After a while they awoke and heard a voice saying, "Cahuasohuanton yo ni concua," or "Cahuasohuanton has eaten him." The parents stood up and lighted a candle and there, near the hearth they saw the child dead, with his abdomen torn open and his intestines out and they knew that Cahuasohuanton had been there.

Cahuasohuanton is a very fear-inspiring figure and children invariably cease crying when told that he is coming.

Frightening children is sometimes done for the amusement of adults. One informant remembered being very frightened as a child when his favorite uncle, after having told some ghost stories, suddenly told the child to run because a ghost was chasing him. The boy ran terrified and screaming. In his haste he tripped over a stone and fell, causing much laughter among the grownups. Another boy of two is often deliberately frightened by his mother and relatives with worms, which make him scream in terror.

Lying and deception play an important part in parent-child relationships. Deception is used by parents and other adults as a technique in controlling children, and Tepoztecans would be at a loss without it in rearing their children. Mothers particularly tend to make and break promises easily and to trick their children into doing things. The use of little lies is so common as to be taken for granted, and children early become accustomed to it. The importance of deception in the relations between parents and children cannot be overemphasized, particularly in its effect upon the development of the character of Tepoztecans.

Deception of the parents on the part of Tepoztecan children becomes habitual at an early age. Lying is encouraged by the need to escape punishment, and punishable situations occur almost daily. Outright disobedience, which occurs often in the absence of the parents, must be covered up, as well as unavoidable but punishable acts, such as accidental losing or damaging of property or hurting a younger sibling. Children who are restricted as to when, where, and with whom they may play will lie to get more freedom. There is, of course, much deception concerning *novios* or sweethearts.

Parents view a child's lie primarily as a means of escaping difficult situations. There is little evidence of any moral indignation on their part, however. In punishing a child, the parents do not punish the lie as much as the misdeed the lie was meant to cover up. The child who lies is also viewed as an insubordinate child, and as such is resented by parents. Although children experience embarrassment when caught in a lie, there seems to be little guilt involved or shame in recounting the event to a third party.

The most important effect of the frequent use of deception is to cause mutual distrust between parents and children. Parents show a general distrust of their children and sometimes punish them for acts they deny having done, on the assumption that the children are lying. Much of parental behavior is rooted in the belief that a child tends to do wrong when he is not under the surveillance of an adult. Although fear is relied upon to control behavior, it is a form of remote control and as such is not entirely trustworthy.

Children's distrust of their parents is manifested primarily by withdrawal from the parents. Children generally do not confide private thoughts to their parents and gradually stop coming to them to seek information. The tendency of adults to give absurd or teasing answers further causes children to avoid asking questions. Questions on the part of children are generally not encouraged by parents and are frequently forbidden and punished. This is especially true of questions concerning sex and the body. The role of the parents in "keeping the eyes of the children closed" requires much use of deception, and children quickly learn not to ask questions about such matters nor to expect straightforward answers.

Attachment to people on the part of children often depends upon or results from the receiving of some material good. They will seek out or be loyal to whichever parent or relative gives them what they want when they want it. It is common for children to say, "I like him because he gives me good things." The psychological tests and themes written by children in the fourth, fifth, and sixth grades contain evidence of this. One boy wrote that he was very sad when his uncle died, because his uncle used to give him pennies. Another girl said, "I like my aunt best because she takes me to fiestas." Similarly, a mother, in discussing her children's attitudes toward their grandmother said, "Naturally, Delfina liked her grandmother more than the other children do, because her grandmother gave her more."

The father assumes an important role in the life of his son when the boy is old enough to go to the fields. Most boys enjoy working in the fields with their father and look forward with great anticipation to being permitted to join him. Fathers, too, are proud to take their young sons to the fields for the first time, and frequently show great patience in teaching them. But even when father and sons go to the fields together day after day, there is no lessening of the respect relations. The father maintains the role of teacher, and when he speaks it is to teach or advise his son. Boys generally do not speak much in the presence of their fathers. Talk about intimate subjects, telling jokes, or discussing women is strictly taboo, generally even after the sons are married.

Regardless of age or marital state, a son is under his father's authority as long as he lives and works with his father. The son receives no recompense other than his support and care and what spending money he can get from his mother or father. Some fathers are generous and permissive in their treatment of grown sons who do a man's work; others are not and continue to treat them as children. Comparatively few unmarried sons leave home to seek work elsewhere. Even boys who are very dissatisfied with their situation at home are reluctant to strike out for themselves. Among youths there is a certain apprehensiveness of the outside, a fear of falling ill among strangers, of having to do menial and laborious work, of not having the backing of a family in case of trouble, and of not being properly respected by others. The economic dependency of sons upon their parents, as well as a desire for a share of the inheritance, prevents most sons from leaving home. The dependence is mutual; fathers are eager to have their sons remain at home to help support the family, and temper their behavior accordingly. In most homes, grown sons who work enjoy the same service and care received by their father.

Although there is some feeling that a father should be a good example for his sons, there is no emphasis upon this. The father feels entitled to his son's respect regardless of his behavior. In this sense, the role of the Tepoztecan father is quite different from that of the father in the German family, for example. The German father generally seeks respect based upon awe and admiration; the Tepoztecan father is content with respect based upon fear and prerogative. Thus, in Tepoztlán, although most fathers forbid their sons to drink, this does not prevent the father from drinking in the presence of his sons. When a father gets drunk, it is the obligation of the sons to find him and help him home. Fathers may experience some shame, primarily because of the fear that they may not have behaved well while drunk.

The relations of a father with his daughters are not very different from his relations with his sons. Although fathers prefer to have sons to daughters, favoritism toward a daughter is not uncommon. As the son grows older and is able to work in the fields, his contacts with his father become more frequent, but those with the older daughter become more distant and formal. Physical contact between father and daughter is even more avoided, and kissing or embracing has strong incestuous connotations. Young girls are often extremely shy in the presence of their fathers, and married women have stated that they were embarrassed to be seen by their fathers when pregnant.

Fathers expect their daughters to avoid all contact with the opposite sex and to be virgins until marriage. Any trespass against this is taken to be a blow against his honor and that of the family, and incurs his most severe punishment. A father sometimes forces a wayward daughter to leave home or does not speak to her for several years. Girls are very fearful of their father's attitude in this, but nevertheless almost always have a secret sweetheart. Although Tepoztecans explain the father's wrath as jealousy, what is meant is jealousy of his respect status rather than jealousy of his daughter's lover. The lover is considered so lacking in respect for the father that he dares to flaunt the father's will. A rich man is doubly outraged and will often go to great expense and trouble to punish the boy.

Grown daughters may take over their mother's duties in serving the father, and sometimes strong ties of affection between father and daughter develop as a result. There are many cases of fathers favoring their eldest daughter and secretly providing her with gifts because of her devotion in serving him. This is particularly true of a widower whose eldest daughter fills the place of the deceased mother. Incest between father and daughter is not infrequently suspected in such a situation.

In one case, a widower lived alone with his nineteen-year-old daughter, who did all the work of a wife. The daughter had the reputation of being *loca* and having had many *novios* when younger. After the death of her mother, she no longer had *novios* and kept to the house. Her father dressed her well and gave her all the money she wanted, and people began to suspect them of having incestuous relations. A neighbor claimed to have seen them in the act of sexual intercourse and reported that the girl was pregnant. One day she saw the girl bury something in the corral and notified the authorities, who found that it was the fetus of a child. The girl was sentenced to prison for one year, but her father, who was prosperous, sold some animals and bought her freedom. His solicitude in bringing her food and in arranging for her release contrasted sharply with the traditional fury of the father at a wayward daughter, and was taken to be further evidence of their illicit relations.

Although it is believed that it is the duty of the children to take care of the father when he can no longer work, there is a widespread feeling that children cannot be relied on, and that death is preferable to a dependent old age.

Mothers, more than fathers, tend to demonstrate favoritism among their children, and favor boys over girls and small children over grown children. (See Fig. 52.) Mothers tend to be more indulgent and permissive toward their sons. From early childhood, boys are permitted more freedom of movement and expression and more leisure for play. Mothers punish boys less often and make fewer demands on

Fig. 52. Tepoztecan mother and sons.

them. Mothers assume a protective attitude toward the son working in the field and sometimes think that the father is expecting too much. However, only an occasional mother interferes on the boy's behalf.

It is common for a mother to favor the youngest child in the family, and she may continue to nurse him and sleep with him much longer than the usual period. The indulgence of the youngest child is often in sharp contrast with the treatment of other children in the family, but mothers commonly favor all children under five or thereabouts. They are given more food, choicer food, toys are bought for them, and they are taken along to fiestas and on visits and trips.

The oldest son also enjoys a favored position in many ways. He is more indulged than subsequent sons and receives more care and attention. His is often the only birthday among the children to be celebrated by a fiesta. A mother looks forward to the day her eldest son marries and brings a daughter-in-law to assist her. One mother proudly displayed a pillowcase she had embroidered with the words, "Sleep, my love" for her eighteen-year-old son. But mothers experience some difficulty in controlling the eldest son, who frequently imitates his father in demanding much service from the women in the family and in ordering his younger siblings about. The oldest son is expected to take the place of the father upon the latter's death, and to support his widowed mother and orphaned brothers and sisters. When this occurs, there is sometimes an extended struggle between the mother and the son for authority as head of the family. Widows who inherited their husband's property are in a better position to maintain authority and are usually careful to hold on to the property until death, for fear of losing all control of their sons. Propertyless widows, whose sons work as peons to support the family, usually permit the sons to rule over their brothers and sisters and over their mothers as well. Quarrels between mothers and sons arising out of the question of authority and inheritance are not infrequent; many mothers voice apprehension as to the treatment they may expect from their sons in their old age. There are several instances in which married sons do nothing to help support an old widowed mother or even mistreat her. On the other hand, there are several cases in the village in which an adult son, married or unmarried, continues to live with the mother and to work for her, sometimes well into his thirties, before receiving a share of his inheritance.

Many widows do not remarry because "the children get angry." Grown children tend to resent sharing the mother with a stranger and fear that they will be displaced. Eldest sons are known to be especially angered or "jealous," because they will no longer be the male head of the family. One widow said her eighteen-year-old son threatened to beat her if she remarried. Some women express a sense of shame in taking another husband after their children are grown. The presence of grown children also act as a deterrent to widows having lovers.

The relations of mothers and daughters are usually very close. Not only does the mother teach the girl the household skills she knows, but they work side by side in the home until the daughter's marriage. The daughter gradually assumes the mother's role in the home and generally identifies with her. The mother's attitude toward her work, toward bearing children, and toward men and marriage becomes the girl's attitude. In homes in which the mother is dissatisfied or unhappy with her husband, the daughters are apt to take a negative attitude toward men and marriage.

With few exceptions, mothers press their daughters into service as early as possible and use them for all types of errands and chores; indeed, the way in which Tepoztecan households function makes it almost impossible for the mother to get along without help. The custom of having daughters work in the home is deeply ingrained in Tepoztlán, although less so than in the smaller surrounding villages. Many mothers resent the fact that the school takes away the girls for the major part of the day. Mothers frequently absent their daughters from school or withdraw them permanently as soon as the husband permits. Girls under the age of thirteen usually prefer to be in school and may resist the mother's attempt to keep them home. However, the majority of girls leave school after the third grade, or at eleven years of age. An occasional mother identifies with the daughter and expresses her own ambitions for schooling by allowing the girl to complete the elementary school course.

When a girl is at home, she is at the complete disposal of her mother. The mother is in a position to exploit the daughter and frequently does, especially the eldest daughter. Many girls marry to escape the hard work at home, and some of our case histories reveal the resentment daughters sometimes hold in retrospect toward their mothers. The following was told by a woman forty years of age:

My mother was a widow. When I was nine we went to Tacubaya because it was the time of the Revolution. My mother borrowed three pesos and made *atole* and *tacos* and sold them. She did well the first year. Then she made meals for 190 factory workers. I made tortillas when I wasn't going to school. I went to school for four years and each morning I got up at 5:00 A.M. and ground corn, and made coffee for my mother, brothers, and sister. I never ate breakfast before school for lack of time. I also made the tortillas for the family for lunch and supper. My mother hired three women and a boy to help her at her work, and she made a lot of money. After four years she took us back to Tepoztlán because she didn't want us to grow up perverse. Then my three older brothers became teamsters and left the house at 4:00 or 5:00 A.M. every day. I had to get up at 1:00 A.M. to grind and make tortillas and *tacos* for them. After they left, I swept the patio and garden and fed the pigs and chickens. Then I made tortillas for my mother, grandmother, and sister. After breakfast I had to grind corn for the two or three pigs we always had and then again for the evening meal. I cut and sewed the clothes, washed and ironed, and did all the work of the house when I was fourteen. I also milked the cows. My mother was always a merchant. Since I was such a hard worker they began to ask for my hand but my mother and brothers did not want me to marry. I, poor thing, loved my mother and didn't understand how mean she was. She didn't love me because she made me work so hard when she had enough money to hire a maid. I took care of my mother, but when I was twenty I was fed up with it and eloped with my *novio*.

The mother is usually the daughter's chaperone when attending fiestas or when visiting. It is the mother's obligation to guard all grown daughters from having contact with boys. If she fails in this the mother will be subject to the father's anger. Many mothers complain that the necessity to "spy" on their daughters is a heavy burden. A mother who must leave her fifteen-year-old daughter at home with the little ones while she goes to the plaza is anxious over the possibility that the girl will speak to a boy in her absence. If the mother learns that her daughter has a *novio*, it is common for her to beat the girl without the father's knowledge and to keep the matter a secret. Although most mothers are harsh in their treatment of a daughter who becomes pregnant before marriage, they are less so than the fathers and tend to be more forgiving.

Respect-relations between mother and daughter require an avoidance of intimate subjects. Mothers do not customarily prepare their daughters for menstruation or discuss the body or any aspect of sexual relations. And girls do not inform their mothers when they first menstruate, nor do they seek information concerning pregnancy, birth, or marriage. If a girl becomes pregnant before marriage, she will consult a friend or *curandero* as to what to do. Even after marriage, the girl informs her mother-in-law rather than her mother of her pregnancy, and the mother takes an active role as adviser or assistant only if there is no mother-in-law to do so.

Mother-daughter relations are almost severed when the girl marries, particularly if the girl lives with her mother-in-law for several years. It is common for mothers to weep at a daughter's marriage because they are "losing her," and they miss her for a long time.

When a married daughter leaves her mother-in-law's home to live alone, close relations with her mother are generally resumed. Women do not expect financial assistance in their old age from their married daughters because it is "up to the son-in-law." But many married daughters help their mothers with money and corn without the knowledge of their husbands.

SIBLINGS

If the mother-child relationship is the strongest bond in Tepoztlán, that between siblings ranks next. Sibling solidarity is an ideal which parents try to instill in their children. "Take care of him, he is your brother" is often repeated. Nevertheless, sibling relations are often poor, especially in adulthood, and Tepoztecans themselves recognize the sharp gap between theory and practice. The ties between siblings are closest in childhood. Up to about age five or six, siblings are constant companions, and their relationship is but little affected by the differences in sex. Later, sex status becomes much more important, as the sister begins to identify with the mother and her work, and the brother with the father.

An older sister has a special role in caring for her younger siblings and often shows affection and devotion in bringing up the children. But some of the older daughters are rejecting this role in favor of continuing their education. Older brothers have a preferred status in the family and can demand respect and obedience from younger brothers and sisters. In the absence of the parents they take on the role of the father and may discipline their younger siblings. Even after marriage, younger siblings are expected to consult with the older brother about important decisions. But this pattern is rapidly disappearing.

The authority of older siblings over younger is tempered somewhat by the parents' insistence that the older sibling protect and even defer to the younger child. If a young child wants something belonging to an older brother or sister, the parents see to it that he receives it. If an older child is sitting in a chair wanted by a three-year-old, the older child is told to get up and give it to him. In one family a ten-year-old boy, who complained to his parents that his six-year-old brother woke up at night to steal his marbles, was told not to be selfish and to let the younger one have them. When two children quarrel, the older one is automatically blamed because "he is older and should know better," or both children are punished without the parents inquiring into the situation. It is significant that older children never appeal to their parents for justice, but younger ones always go to parents with complaints and tales about the others. Even when all the children are grown, this pattern of the younger telling tales continues. Children tell the parents when an older brother smokes, plays billiards, stays out of school to play, and so on. Parents frequently use younger children to spy on older ones and especially as chaperones for grown daughters.

The general pattern of male dominance is learned by boys from their fathers and is first put into practice in the boys' relationships with their sisters. As soon as a sister is old enough to do housework and chores, the brother begins to put demands upon her, just as the father does upon his wife. A sister is expected to serve her brothers by washing, ironing, and mending their clothes, by preparing and serving their food, and in other little ways. A brother may ask his sister to run errands or to take notes to a *novia*. But a sister will never have her brother act as an intermediary in her private affairs. On the contrary, sisters try to conceal their own relations with boys for fear of offending and angering their brothers. Brothers assume the role of protectors of their sisters' reputation and morality, and a brother may beat his sister if he finds her with a boy. But sisters do manage to get information about boys from their brothers.

Data on the sexual relations between brothers and sisters are very difficult to obtain since this is one of the strong taboo relations. But there is some evidence that sexual relations sometimes occur. Parents do not like to leave an adolescent daughter alone at home with grown brothers. In one case, a widow with two grown daughters and one grown son locked the girls in the house and required the son to sleep outside when she had to leave the house at night.

Siblings of the same sex tend to associate more than siblings of the opposite sex. Brothers work in the fields together, share confidences, and may have the same friends, particularly when there is no great age difference between them. This pattern is even stronger in the case of sisters. Grown brothers and sisters do not participate together in public affairs, do not have mutual friends, and are reserved toward one another in public.

This picture of sibling relations would not be complete without mention of the fact that in many families there are quarrels and resentments. Most of these result from favoritism on the part of the parents. Boys are generally favored over girls, the first-born son and the last born or *xoco* are favored over the other children. Favoritism may be expressed in the unequal distribution of food and clothing, the celebration of the birthdays of one child and not another, the greater attention given to the favored one when ill or injured, and a greater leniency in punishing. The resentment of the children to this treatment finds expression in surreptitious quarreling, fighting, irritability, unwillingness to share possessions, and an avoidance of one another.

After marriage there are a number of factors which further weaken the ties between siblings. Each sibling sets up an independent household and there are practically no institutionalized forms of cooperation between married brothers or sisters.

As we have seen earlier, there were only fourteen cases of married siblings living together on a single house site. Married sisters go off and soon identify their interests with those of their husbands. Since a married woman is under the authority of her husband, she is no longer free to visit her brothers at will. And while brothers are more free to visit with their married siblings, there are often strained relations between the in-laws.

The most frequent causes for friction between adult siblings is favoritism of the parents for a brother or sister. Favoritism may be shown by preference for the children of the favored son or daughter, by more frequent visiting, by economic aid, and by leaving a larger share of the inheritance. In most cases which we studied, grandparents showed favoritism to the children of their daughters rather than to those of sons.

Quarrels between siblings over inheritance are frequent, and often lead to permanent rifts in the family. The difficulty of dividing up the property equally, the tendency to give more to sons than daughters, more to an older son, or again to a favorite, leads to quarrels.

The following case, which is typical of many, illustrates some of the points made about sibling relations.

Anastasio, age 54, has one elder brother and three sisters, all of whom are married and reside within short distances of one another. At present Anastasio is on good terms with them but there had been a rift in the family for several years, with Anastasio on one side and his brother and sisters on the other. Before the death of his mother, Anastasio visited his brother and sisters more often, he and his brother helped each other with harvesting and often drank together. When Anastasio had an important decision to make, he would seek the advice of his siblings. They also occasionally borrowed tools or corn from each other, and their wives would use the same sewing machine and went together to the market to sell. Anastasio was never as intimate with his two older sisters. Of them he said, "We behave respectfully toward them. We joke a little but not much." One of these sisters visits only on the day of the annual fiesta, on Anastasio's birthday, and when he is ill; the other sister visits even less because her husband is jealous and violent and beats her if she goes out unnecessarily. Anastasio feels closer to his younger sister because he supported her after the death of their father. Anastasio passes her house almost every day when he goes for water, and he always greets her. There is mutual visiting between the two families when there is illness, and they help each other in little ways. Anastasio hires this sister's sons to work for him when he needs peons. However, this sister rarely visits Anastasio because her husband is retiring and unsociable.

After the death of their widowed mother, these brothers and sisters quarreled over the inheritance. Some time before her death, the mother had sold Anastasio her house and *sitio* at a nominal price to keep him from moving to Yautepec. At her death he received nothing, but his brother and sisters each inherited sums of money. Anastasio believed he had been unjustly cut out of the will, and his brother and sisters were disgruntled because their share was less than the house and *sitio* were worth. As Anastasio became more prosperous, his brother and sisters became more envious and vindictive. Later another quarrel arose over a small wooded plot of mountain land which their mother had left for the use of all her children.

One day Anastasio made a charcoal oven there to burn wood for charcoal. At once his brother and sisters interpreted this to mean that he was appropriating the land, and they all went together to denounce him. Anastasio was very much angered and said that he merely intended to burn charcoal there. His brother then demanded payment because Anastasio had cut wood without having given notice to him as elder brother. The quarrel lasted a long time and made for much bitterness and a complete break in relations. The elder brother began to spread gossip about Anastasio's wife having relations with another man. The gossip reached Anastasio's ears while he was drunk, and he attacked his wife in a rage and would have choked her to death had he not been stopped by his children. This incident, which Anastasio now attributes to his brother, has all but ruined Anastasio's marriage.

Bad feeling remained between the two brothers and between Anastasio and his sisters for a long time, but bit by bit Anastasio's bitterness subsided. He described his attitudes in these words: "We are not like animals. We quarrel a little but later we get along like brothers and sisters. To keep up grudges?—that no." There is little visiting among these families now, and Anastasio no longer asks for or accepts advice from his siblings, but he still feels obligated to inform his elder brother of events of importance, such as sending his daughter to a distant school and permitting another daughter to seek work in Mexico City. Anastasio also still sends meat to his elder brother when he slaughters a pig, and both families exchange *mole* at fiesta time. Anastasio's wife is again beginning to borrow corn from her brother-in-law when she cannot get it elsewhere, and recently when Anastasio fell from a tree and broke his hand, his brother and sister-in-law came to visit him and brought him food. Anastasio is considered "good" by his relatives, because he forgives those who cause him trouble.

COUSINS, UNCLES, AUNTS, AND OTHER RELATIVES

The relations between cousins are often close and show some of the qualities of sibling relations. Generally an individual will have one or two favorite cousins, usually a first cousin or *primo hermano*, with whom there may be regular visiting and the giving of mutual aid. But in time of emergency, aid can be counted on even from more distant cousins. There is one important difference between cousin and sibling relations, namely, the strong taboo against sexual relations between siblings is considerably weaker in the case of cousins. It is quite common for children who are cousins to play together, particularly when the cousins live on adjoining or nearby house sites, and in some cases a boy's first sexual experience will be with an older cousin. The Spanish refrain, "A la prima se la arrima," has some application to life in Tepoztlán.

The relations between uncles and nephews is more of a respect-relationship but it may also become quite intimate. An uncle is often a child's favorite and will frequently bring some gift for a nephew or niece. The fact that the uncle relationship has more of the respect quality makes it a more solid relationship than the sibling relationship. Work exchanges between uncles and nephews occur more often than between married siblings. But quarrels with uncles also occur, particularly over matters of inheritance. We have a number of cases where, upon a man's death, his brother will step in and claim a portion of the inheritance from the widow, especially when her children are still small.

IN-LAWS

Because of the predominance of patrilocal residence, the mother-in-law and daughter-in-law relationship is the most important of all in-law relations. When the young bride goes to live with her husband's family, she is expected to take the role of a grown daughter, addressing her husband's parents as mother and father and giving them the same respect and obedience she owes her own mother and father. Her work is assigned by the mother-in-law and generally consists of the most burdensome tasks, such as grinding corn, making tortillas, and washing and ironing the clothing of the entire family. In the past, when girls married at twelve or thirteen and were unskilled, it was the duty of the mother-in-law to teach them the work.

It is the obligation of the mother-in-law to chaperone her daughter-in-law and to see that she remains a faithful wife. To this end the daughter-in-law is expected to remain within the house most of the time and not to go out alone. There are many jokes told which depict the mother-in-law as the "policeman." When the daughter-in-law gives birth to a child, the mother-in-law has the major responsibility of caring for both of them; the quality of this care often depends upon whether or not the mother-in-law approves of her daughter-in-law. In cases in which the mother-in-law disapproves of the marriage, because the couple eloped or because the girl was pregnant before the marriage, or because she had a bad reputation, the young wives may be grossly neglected during and after childbirth.

Although many mothers-in-law and daughters-in-law manage to get along fairly well, the relationship is obviously a "charged" one and is generally recognized as such by Tepoztecans. Both women tend to approach their new relationship with apprehension. The young wife fears that she may not be able to please her mother-in-law, that too much work will be demanded of her, that she will feel like an outsider in a strange house. Many girls have grown up with the idea, learned from their mothers and other married women, that the daughter-in-law is merely the "slave" of the mother-in-law and suffers much at her hands. The mother-in-law, on the other hand, fears that her new daughter-in-law will be lazy and just another mouth to feed. If the girl comes from a better-to-do family, she may look down upon the way of life in her husband's home and cause uneasiness. It is for this reason that when marriages are arranged, the boy's parents seek a poor girl who will not be demanding or afraid to work.

In many cases the fears are justified and much quarreling occurs. The mother-in-law expects the younger woman to work as hard, if not harder, than she herself works. In fact, many women shift almost the entire burden of the household upon the daughter-in-law, so that they may take up business activity outside the home. The daughter-in-law, who may be seventeen or eighteen years of age, has been working hard from the age of thirteen in her own home under the instruction of her mother, and may have looked to marriage as an escape from work and supervision. When, after marriage, she finds herself working even harder for the family of her husband under the sharp, critical eye of her mother-in-law, the situation is one of jumping into the frying pan to be saved from the fire. The young wife today is more mature and more skilled than the child-wife of thirty years ago and no longer needs the mother-in-law's teaching and guidance.

Certain differences between the older and younger generation also affect mother-in-law and daughter-in-law relations. The mother-in-law, whose generation suffered the acute privation and misery of the Revolution and learned to live in the utmost economy, expects of her daughter-in-law a self-denial and economy for which the young woman is not always prepared. Often after marriage the young wife finds that she has fewer dresses and shoes, goes out much less to fiestas, to Cuernavaca, or to the movies. Many young women have learned to bathe three or four times a week and to change clothing whenever soiled, much to the annoyance of their mothers-in-law who must provide the soap and clothing.

In one case a mother-in-law scolded her daughter-in-law for this and said, "What difference is it to you if your dress is a little dirty. Is it for a lover that you are keeping yourself so clean?" Many young women have now become accustomed to using face powder, lipstick, cold cream, toothpaste, and fine soap, the use of which is considered distasteful and extravagant by the mother-in-law and discontinued after marriage. Many of the younger married women chafe over the restraints placed upon their personal movements, their friendships, and, of course, their right to go out unaccompanied. The slow but steady increase in the freedom of the younger women, particularly of those who have spent several years in school, makes the role of the daughter-in-law more difficult.

The way out of an unpleasant relationship for both the mother-in-law and the daughter-in-law is to separate their households. Usually the young couple move out, but occasionally the old couple or the widowed mother-in-law will move away. If no other dwelling is available, separate households may be established in the same house site, with each family cooking over its own fire and carrying on its economic affairs independently. Sometimes the wife is unable to persuade her husband to move away or to convince him that she is not at fault, and is forced to continue to live with her mother-in-law. Not infrequently, if the situation becomes too intolerable, the young wife will separate from her husband and return to the home of her parents. It is believed in the village that many marriages have been broken because the mother-in-law and daughter-in-law did not get on well together.

Father-in-law and daughter-in-law relations are generally similar to father-daughter relations, only more reserved. When the daughter-in-law lives in the same household, she serves the father-in-law under the direction of the mother-in-law; beyond that, contacts between the two are generally few because the men spend a good deal of time away from home. A few cases of incestuous relations between daughter-in-law and father-in-law have been reported. In each of these cases the father was a widower, and the indiscretion caused deep family rifts.

Because of patrilocal residence, relations between the wife's parents and their son-in-law depend more upon personal factors than upon formal obligations, except for the usual formal respect-relations which prevail between them. Relations may be amiable and even mutually helpful, but more generally are not close, almost to the point of avoidance. Some Tepoztecans recall that in the past the son-in-law was obliged to work for his father-in-law for two years by providing him with wood and water, as part of the bride price. Work now done by the son-in-law is voluntary and is usually limited to times when the father-in-law is ill or in need. If the mother-in-law is widowed and has property, her son-in-law may give her some aid regularly; if she is left alone with no means of support, the son-in-law may invite her to live in his home.

Tepoztecan men are generally wary of the mother-in-law as a meddlesome, trouble-making figure, and most sons-in-law prefer to keep the relationship a distant one. Despite this stereotype, and the fact that some mothers-in-law have been critical of the way the son-in-law treated her daughter, often to the extent of urging the girl to return home, it is more common to find the mother-in-law who insists that her daughter try to please her husband and bear up under domestic difficulties. Most fathers-in-law take the same attitude, unless their daughter is ill-treated by her husband. In such cases, the father-in-law may feel personally affronted, interpreting the son-in-law's behavior as being disrespectful to him.

Relations between sisters-in-law and brothers-in-law are not formalized and depend largely upon personal factors. Sisters-in-law, whether wives of two brothers, or the husband's wife and sister, may be friendly and mutually helpful or, just as frequently, suspicious and hostile. In some families the wives of brothers compete for the esteem of the mother-in-law and carry to her tales and gossip about each other. When the mother-in-law favors one sister-in-law over another, hostility between the two younger women usually results. Relations between sisters-in-law frequently depend upon how the brothers get along with each other; quarrels over inheritance involve the sisters-in-law as much as the siblings.

Brothers-in-law generally have less contact with each other than do sisters-in-law, since they tend to reside farther apart. Two sisters may live at opposite ends of the village after marriage and, like their husbands, see relatively little of one another. Even when brothers-in-law, particularly the husband and brother of the woman, live nearby or on the same house site, they tend to maintain their distance. Ill-feeling between brothers-in-law may arise over inheritance, or because of favoritism on the part of the parents-in-law, or because of a quarrel between the wife and her sibling. In a few cases, brothers-in-law have fairly close relations involving labor exchange, supplying each other with meat when they slaughter a pig, and drinking together.

The parents of the husband and wife are *consuegros* to one another. Theirs is a mutual respect-relation, with each addressing the other in *Vd*. There are no formal obligations between them. It is customarily understood that after a girl's marriage her parents relinquish their rights of control over her in favor of the husband and his parents. Ideally, the wife's parents maintain a certain distance in the affairs of their married daughter. For example, they are not supposed to give her gifts without the knowledge and consent of her husband or parents-in-law. Relations between *consuegros* hinge upon the fulfillment of their respective roles toward the married couple. In some cases parents are "jealous" of their children and interfere a good deal.

GODPARENTS, GODCHILDREN, AND CO-PARENTS

By the system of *compadrazgo*, two sets of relationships between non-relatives are established: one is that between spiritual godparents (*padrinos*) and their godchildren (*ahijados*), the other is between the parents and the godparents, a relationship known as *compadres*. Both the *padrino-ahijado* and the *compadre* relationship are among the most solid in Tepoztlán. They establish bonds which sometimes are stronger than ties of kinship. The general purpose of the godparents is to provide security for the godchild, by the selection of an additional set of parents who will act as guardians and sponsors of the godchild, care for him in emergencies, and adopt him if he is orphaned. The *compadre* system, in turn, by extending the bonds of kinship in a ceremonial way, enlarges the in-group. This system seems ideally suited for a society like Tepoztlán where the extended family is weak.

Social, economic, and political factors may enter into the operation of the *compadre* system. Poor families will seek better-to-do families as godparents for their children. Similarly, it is thought desirable to have *compadres* from the city, for it is assumed that a city family can be of greater help in time of need. But this also works to some disadvantage. We found a number of cases of godparents from Mexico City who have taken their godchildren as servants and paid them very low salaries, even according to Tepoztecan standards.

The more godchildren a man has, the more *compadres* and the wider the circle of persons who can be counted on for favors. For this reason, anyone who aspires to a position of leadership in the village must have many *compadres*. On the other hand, there is some feeling against the use of the *compadre* system in this fashion. Many families view the *compadre* system as a burden and try to limit their *compadre* relations to a few families, by asking the same set of godparents to serve for all their children.

The three most important types of godparents in Tepoztlán are those of baptism, confirmation, and marriage. In selecting godparents of baptism, individuals are sought who can be relied on to aid the child in times of emergency. Tepoztecans prefer to choose godparents and *compadres* who are neither neighbors nor relatives, so that intimacy and quarrels can be avoided. An analysis of the *compadres* of a few families from the smaller barrios showed that most of the godparents and *compadres* were from other barrios. A brother, sister, cousin, uncle, or aunt may serve as a godparent, but they are rarely called upon.

In the case of the first child of a newly married couple, the godparents of baptism are chosen by the parents of one of the spouses, usually by the husband's mother.

As the couple grow older, the husband may make the selection, and often friendship, rather than higher economic status, dictates the choice.

Godparents address their godchildren in the familiar *tú* and are addressed in turn by the respectful *Vd*. Traditionally, the godchild had to kiss the godparent's hand at each meeting, but this is no longer common. It is customary for the godparent to offer the child a few centavos upon meeting. But the obligations of the godparent are many. They must assist at the baptism, purchase the child's clothing for the occasion, and pay the fee to the priest. They also accompany the mother and child to the *sacamisa,* or first Mass, which should take place forty days after the birth of the child. If the infant dies they arrange for the wake, dress the child appropriately for burial, and contribute to the expenses of the musicians at the funeral. One of the obligations of the godparent is to urge their *compadres* to send the child to school. If the child learns bad habits or otherwise needs correction, the parents may call upon the godparents to scold the child.

The godparents of confirmation are generally selected by the godparents of baptism, and occasionally the latter may accept both roles. The godparents of marriage are also important figures. One of their functions is to act as mediators between the couple, in case of quarrels or separations.

One of the distinctive aspects of the *compadre* system in Tepoztlán, and in Mexico as a whole, is the way in which the godparent relationship has been extended far beyond the original Catholic forms. In most of Spain there are only two or three types of godparents, popularly those of baptism, communion, and confirmation. Not so in Tepoztlán. In addition to the types mentioned above, Tepoztecans also have the following: *padrino de miscoton,*[6] *padrino de medida o listón,*[7] *padrino de evangelio,*[8] *padrino de escapulario, padrino del niño Jesús,* and others. It would seem that Tepoztecans have utilized every possibility for extending the godparent relationship. This may be a reflection of their seeking security through the extension of ceremonial kinship, for in most of the above cases a *compadre* relationship is formed.

The godparent system has also been extended to secular activities. At soccer and basketball games in the village, each team has its godmother who dresses in white, carries flowers, and acts as the sponsor of the team, handing out the prizes to the winners. At social dances there are also godmothers who act as chaperones for the young people.

Compadres address each other with the respectful *Vd.* and avoid intimacies. They may not drink together, discusss sexual matters, or tell dirty jokes. It is a respect-relationship and in this lies its strength. *Compadres* will often exchange favors, and

---

[6] The term *miscoton* is Náhuatl and refers to a small sweater which the godparent places on the godchild as a protection against illness.

[7] The *medida o listón* refers to a small piece of ribbon which has been blessed by the priest and is placed on a sick child as a charm against evil.

[8] This godparent is also chosen for a child who is ill. A woman of the world is preferred, a woman with a "hard heart." By going to church and saying a prayer, she becomes the child's godmother.

borrowing between them is probably more frequent than between kin. Upon the death of a *compadre* one is supposed to contribute toward the funeral expenses. *Compadres* are invited to barrio fiestas and are always treated with special deference. In meeting, the general salutation is, "Good day, *compadre*. How is everything?"

pregnancy and birth: 15

In TEPOZTLÁN it is considered a sin for a married person not to want to have children and not to accept all those sent by God. It is said, with more or less conviction, that many children are desirable. The most frequently expressed attitude on the part of men and women concerning the advantages of raising a family is that children are a source of labor supply and security for the parents, particularly during old age. Boys are much preferred, because they are economically more productive. Although daughters aid the mother more directly than sons do, the large majority of women express strong preference for boys and favor their sons. Some younger more acculturated people occasionally express a desire to have children because it is "nice" or "less sad" not to be alone, and otherwise indicate that children are a source of emotional satisfaction. This is in contrast with most Tepoztecans, however, for whom the economic usefulness of children is the most obvious advantage in having them.

There is a notable difference in the expressed attitudes of men and women toward having children. Women for the most part "accept" children fatalistically as a burden to be endured. "Having children is our destiny and the will of God . . . it is the duty of every married woman to accept all that come." Another typical statement is the following: "There is no way out, I have a husband. If more children come, what can we do? We will endure it even though like pigs they come one after another." It is common for women to complain at having to bear many children which they believe to be a punishment of God. Women consider themselves fortunate if they do not conceive soon after marriage or after a previous birth. Most women do not want to have more than four children; those who have only one or two, or even none, are envied. Twins are considered a great misfortune.[1] A typical reaction to having twins is, "What, am I a pig to have them this way? It is a terrible punishment of God." Many women actively express interest in birth control. There is no doubt that if such information were available, and if permitted by their husbands, a large number of women would practice birth control. Abor-

---

[1] A similar attitude toward twins is reported in Chan Kom. Redfield and Villa Rojas, *Chan Kom—a Maya Village* (Washington, D.C.: Carnegie Institute, 1934), Publ. No. 448.

tion, although very secretive, is not uncommon, and it is said that many women take medicine to make themselves sterile.

In sharp contrast to women, men in Tepoztlán prefer large families and are outspoken in their desire to have many sons to help them. In many husband-wife relations there is an underlying struggle in which the wife tries to limit the number of pregnancies against the protests of her husband. If conception does not take place within a reasonable length of time, husbands may suspect their wives of taking medicine to prevent it. Failure to conceive may be sufficient cause for abandonment, and in the few cases in which women were known to have prayed for a child the motive almost always was to please the husband. Men show little interest in learning methods of birth control, and it is highly improbable that many husbands would practice it or permit their wives to.

The differences in the attitudes of men and women toward having children stem from several factors. Men often marry at a more mature age and when they feel ready for marriage, but girls marry quite young, and often as a result of pressure from their suitors or their parents or because of pregnancy. Men frequently marry for the purpose of raising a family; women, except when they are pregnant, usually marry for motives entirely unrelated to having children. Unlike women, who become more dependent upon their mother-in-law and husband at the birth of a child, men acquire a new independence and a more respected status as *padre de familia*. Becoming a mother does not in itself improve a woman's status, nor is there any perceptible change in the treatment of wives during pregnancy. As one informant put it, "A good husband will continue to be good when his wife is pregnant, and a bad one will continue to beat her."

The strict division of labor in Tepoztecan homes, in which the burden of the care of the children in sickness and in health falls upon the mother, is often given as an explanation of the different attitudes of men and women toward having children. "It makes no difference to the men how many children there are. It is the wife who has to see that there is enough for all."

Motherhood is not glorified in Tepoztlán. The prevailing prudishness toward sex, as well as the reciprocal respect-relations between parents and children, results in the avoidance of the subject. Most Tepoztecan girls grow up in an atmosphere in which negative attitudes of fear and shame toward motherhood, pregnancy, and even marriage have more opportunity of developing than positive ones. Despite the early assumption of the care of small children and household duties, there is an absence of positive psychological preparation in the training of young girls for the acceptance of motherhood. This is reenforced by the martyr-like attitude of their own mothers toward husbands and children.

PREGNANCY

The most common expression to describe pregnancy is "to become ill with child." Sterility (*yomitztili*) is thought to be due to "cold" in the womb,[2] and massages

---

[2] Sterility is also explained by "cold" in Chan Kom. *Ibid.* p. 181.

with warm oil of rosemary and violet are given to "heat" the womb. A woman who wishes to prevent conception takes "cold" medicines. A woman who wishes a child and cannot conceive may visit the Virgins of Chalma or Tlaltenango, who are believed to have special powers to grant the desire for children. There is a belief that if conception occurs during the full moon, the child will be strong, and married couples sometimes plan to have intercourse during this time.

The most common symptom of pregnancy is the cessation of menstruation. This is almost always true of a first pregnancy, but may not hold for subsequent pregnancies. Menstruation often does not occur for as long as one or two years after giving birth to a child. Since many women conceive during this period, they do not know that they are pregnant until they feel movement or other symptoms, such as nausea. Sometimes women do not become aware of pregnancy because they continue to menstruate for two or three months after conception. This condition is attributed to *los aires* or to weakness of the back.

When Tepoztecan girls married at a younger age than they do now, they were often ignorant of the signs of pregnancy. They would report the cessation of menstruation to the mother-in-law, who would explain its meaning. The girl's own mother would be advised, but the respect-relations and sense of shame between mother and daughter prevented much direct discussion. The young pregnant wife becomes dependent for advice and care upon her mother-in-law, who may keep the girl's mother informed if she wishes to do so. In later pregnancies, mothers and daughters are generally less inhibited in their behavior toward each other.

Pregnant women make every effort to conceal their condition by carefully covering themselves with their *rebozos*, both at home and in the street. When the pregnancy becomes very obvious, women keep to their homes and the more "careful" mothers remain seated as much as possible, so that their children will not take note of their condition. Women who are careless about concealing their condition are looked down upon. City women who walk in the street without *rebozos* to hide their pregnancy are regarded as particularly shameless. Once a city woman who did not wear a *rebozo* came to live in Tepoztlán during her pregnancy, but left shortly because no one would speak to her. Tepoztecans had ostracized her because she was "opening the eyes of their children." More recently Tepoztecans were aroused by the fact that one of the schoolteachers continued to attend school, although in an advanced stage of pregnancy. The school director was chastized, and the teacher was asked to resign.

When a woman knows she is pregnant she informs her mother-in-law, if residence is patrilocal, or her husband, and arrangements are made to hire a midwife. The cost of the midwife has risen, from about ten pesos in 1943 to about twenty pesos in 1948. Before the Revolution, midwives in Tepoztlán received as little as one and two pesos. The rise in price reflects the increasing urbanization of Tepoztlán, as well as the general rise in cost of living in recent years.[3]

---

[3] In Mitla, in the 1930's, midwives were paid 75 centavos for delivering a girl and one peso for a boy. See Parsons, *Mitla*, p. 78. In Tzintzuntzan, midwives received from 3 to 7 pesos in

Care during pregnancy consists principally of massages of the abdomen by the midwife. The general purpose of the massage is to make the birth easier and to determine the position of the fetus. Midwives say they can change the position of the fetus if necessary by means of massage. Faith in the importance of massage is widespread, and there are few who do not take massages regularly. Newly married women often begin to take massages during the second or third month, but others do not begin until they feel movement. Since there is an additional charge of fifty centavos (in 1943, the price ranged from twelve to twenty-five centavos) for each massage, there are many women who cannot afford to take them until the eighth or ninth month. Sometimes the husband will object to the number of massages his wife takes, and there may be quarrels. Massages are given every eight or fifteen days, depending upon when they are started and what the pregnant woman can afford. The patient lies down, with knees slightly bent, and the midwife gently massages the abdomen from right to left.[4] No oils or unguents are used.

Some say they can predict the sex of the baby by its position in the womb. If it is to one side, near the hip, it will be a boy; if it is in the middle, it will be a girl. If the fetus feels round, a girl is indicated; and if it feels elongated, it is a boy. If the mother looks sleepy and if her face is white, the child will be a boy, because boys are more "demanding" and make their mothers pale. If she is red-cheeked, the child will be a girl. However, some informants believe just the opposite and say that red cheeks indicate a boy because boys are more robust. If the mother becomes fatter all around, including the hips, it will be a girl; if she protrudes only in front, it will be a boy. It is also believed that a boy is born after nine months and a girl after eight months.

The midwife advises the pregnant woman concerning self-care. She is not to lift heavy objects but should continue to work because it makes the delivery easier. It is believed that a woman who is lazy and who sleeps often during pregnancy will have a difficult birth because the fetus adheres to the womb. Pregnant women should not urinate where an animal has just urinated because the rising steam may cause inflammation of the womb. Pregnant women are also advised not to bathe in the stream, since *los aires* may endanger the baby and cause it to be born with physical defects.[5] It is also said that bathing in the stream may cause the pregnant woman to fill up with water. Although pregnant women sometimes continue to use the stream to wash clothes, this also is considered unwise. Some say that pregnant women should not bathe more than once a week for fear of catching cold, but many women bathe every three days in warm or cold water, according to preference.

1945. In Cherán, in 1940, the cost of delivery was from 1½ to 2½ pesos. See Ralph L. Beals, *Cherán, A Sierra Tarascan Village,* Institute of Social Anthropology Publ. No. 2 (Washington, D.C.: Smithsonian Institution, 1946), p. 166.

[4] Foster describes the massage in Tzintzuntzan as "heavy pummeling" and attributes the many miscarriages to this.

[5] Redfield's informant said, "After three months she [the pregnant woman] goes to the *barranca* [stream] to bathe. She may do this many times before the birth." According to our data, although some women do it, this is generally regarded as undesirable.

There is a belief that if an eclipse occurs during a woman's pregnancy, the child will be born with some part of his body missing; that is, it will have been eaten by the moon. To prevent this the mother should wear a pair of scissors under her sash. An earthquake will also cause some physical defect in the child.

There are no diet restrictions for pregnant women. There is a widespread belief that the pregnant woman should satisfy any food whim, otherwise she may suffer a miscarriage or a premature birth, or the baby may be born with skin colorations. Many subsequent difficulties are assigned to the failure to satisfy food whims. It is the husband's obligation to provide his wife with the food she wishes. But women do not make frequent or unreasonable demands, particularly if their husbands are not "good" to them.

Women who are nauseated during the second and third months are treated with herbs which are said to decrease the water in the abdomen. Many women do not take this treatment because of the restriction in diet and movement that follows. They may not go out into the street for three days, they may not go to the fields or to the stream, they may not stand near a water jug.

There are no restrictions on sexual intercourse during pregnancy, and many continue to have intercourse up to the time of birth. No special positions are used in the last months to protect the fetus.

When there are signs of miscarriage, the midwife tries several remedies. The patient may be asked to recline on a *rebozo* or cloth and is then moved or jerked two or three times from one side to another by means of the cloth. Another remedy is to soak an old tortilla in water of *nixtamal* or vinegar and place it on the small of the back. A mixture of the following herbs is also used: *tlatlazcametl*,[6] *camotito de San Diego*,[7] and *muicle*.[8] To this some midwives add wine, chocolate, leaves of *Santa María* (*artemisa*),[9] and a gold earring to be boiled with the mixture. Miscarriages are not frequent, and when one occurs the woman is often blamed for bringing it about by carelessness.

Induced miscarriages are fairly common. But the frequent deaths in such cases deter most women, and it is said that women who try to "cure" themselves will have to account for their behavior on Judgment Day. Miscarriages are said to cause *paños* or brown discoloration of the skin, so that women who suffer from this are believed to have aborted frequently. To bring on delayed menstruation, many women drink *muicle*. Ground *chayotillos* with salt may be taken, or a tuber *aboyote* may be used. Another way is to use the same preparation which brings on labor. The ingredients are as follows: opossum tail (*tlacuache*), *pimienta gorda*, *sasalik*, and *tlatlatzcametl*. Sometimes women will bring about a miscarriage by deliberately lifting heavy objects. Many women, and particularly unmarried girls, secretly go to

---

[6] *Montanoa tomentosa*, a very well-known plant. See Maximiano Martínez, *Las Plantas Medicinales de México* (México, D. F.: México Ediciones Botas, 1939), p. 330.

[7] Unidentified.

[8] *Jacobinia spicigera, ibid.*

[9] Unidentified.

curanderos in other villages to "cure" themselves. However, the only approved method of limiting the number of pregnancies is to avoid intercourse as long as possible after the birth of a child.

BIRTH

When the baby is expected, a curtain is hung to screen the bed of the expectant mother, and delivery takes place behind this. Poorer families hang up a *petate*. When labor pains begin, the midwife is called. Occasionally the husband will assist the wife, but the majority of women are embarrassed by his presence and insist that he leave. One of the underlying beliefs throughout the delivery is that difficulty is due to "cold" and that "heat" must be applied. The patient lies on a *petate* on the floor, and the midwife massages the abdomen, the back, and the hips, with various heated oils and unguents. These may be oil of violet, white lily, rosemary or almonds, or *altea,* depending upon the midwife. The heat and the massage is to warm the infant, loosen it, and make it slip out more easily.

The patient is then given a mixture of *tlatlazcametl* with chocolate, sherry, and egg, to make the labor pains stronger, or *pimienta gorda* is boiled and given. The abdomen is massaged and rubbed all the while, and the mother is wrapped in a blanket to make her perspire. A *cenidor,* or sash, may be tightly bound around the waist at this time to keep the back from weakening and the bones from spreading and to prevent hemorrhage later. The patient may kneel at this stage, and the baby is delivered on the *petate* and wrapped by the midwife in a clean, warmed, old cloth. If it is a dry birth, the mother is given more *tlatlazcametl.* In cases of difficult or delayed births, the family, at the suggestion of the midwife, may buy a candle for the Virgen de Monserrat, the guardian of pregnant women. The patient measures four fingers on the candle, a mark is made at that point with a centavo, and the candle is put before the image. If delivery does not occur before the flame reaches the mark on the candle, the case is considered very grave.

Delayed births are sometimes attributed to the fact that the woman does not bear down at the proper time, and attempts are made to eject the child by provoking nausea and vomiting. This may be achieved by putting a chicken feather or the tail of an opossum into the woman's mouth.[10] The tail is sometimes cooked and given as a drink. The woman may also be given her husband's urine or the dirty soapy water in which he has washed his hands. It is believed that when a woman in labor breathes out or screams every time she feels pain, the child rises instead of descends. The mother is given something to bite on, usually her braid, and is told to keep her mouth closed. Even speaking is discouraged. It may be such practices, found in many parts of Mexico, which have led observers to describe Mexican Indian women as stoical during childbirth. In Tepoztlán, women frequently pray and scream when they suffer severe pains, and only the *más valientas* are quiet.

Difficult births and extended labor, sometimes over several days, are not uncom-

---

[10] In Tzintzuntzan, the woman's braid is forced down her throat.

mon. Without exception, our informants described labor dramatically, with emphasis upon the pain. "It is death to bear a baby" is a common sentiment. Some look back at labor with shuddering and expressions of horror, even fifteen years after the birth of their last child. Midwives report that many mothers are severely frightened during and after delivery and must be calmed by being heated with a smoky fire. *Pericón* or rosemary or laurel, or all three, are burned in an old clay pot, and the strong smelling smoke is directed underneath the blanket to heat the woman's lower parts.

After the child is born, the *cenidor* is tightened around the upper part of the abdomen to prevent the blood and the placenta from rising in the mother and possibly causing her death. If the afterbirth is slow in coming, it is a common custom to put salt and onion into the mother's hand so that she can smell them, and she is given some mint leaves to chew. Sometimes a very hot tortilla is placed on the right side of the abdomen and pressed down by the midwife. In very delayed cases some midwives insert their hands to try to pull out the afterbirth.

The afterbirth is buried under the hearth. It is believed that if it is left anywhere else, the baby's face will swell; if it is thrown into the corral, as some do, it may cause *daño;* if it is eaten by a dog, the mother will die. The umbilical cord is cut with a scissors about 4 or 5 fingers away from the child. The remaining cord is tied with a thread and burned with a few drops of wax from a tallow candle. The wax is applied every day until the cord drops off. The umbilical cord is generally kept inside the house and saved to be later used in the treatment of some eye diseases. Some sell the cord to *curanderos* for about twenty-five centavos each. Many believe that only the umbilical cord of the first child or the first son is effective. When a child is born in a caul, it is said he will be rich. The caul is carefully saved for good luck.

Only an occasional woman in Tepoztlán has her child delivered by a doctor. Somewhat more frequently he is called in after delivery if there is some difficulty. The high cost of calling a doctor from Cuernavaca [11] made it prohibitive for the great majority of the families. However, even those with money do not generally call a doctor, particularly a male doctor. The prudishness and suspiciousness of the women are a major inhibiting factor. Women who have used a doctor have become the target of much malicious gossip.

The following quotation from a woman of one of the large barrios is an example of the nature of the gossip, in this case concerning a local schoolteacher, "First she called a *curandero,* and her baby was born, and everything was fine. But she sent for a doctor just to have him feel her, to play with her because that is what she wanted. The midwife said that when the doctor arrived he uncovered the patient and put in his hand and after he played with her he sewed her up. Then he grabbed the baby by the belly and he had it hang that way as though it were his toy. He could have killed him! But that is what they wanted. As for me, for nothing in the

---

[11] Now there is a doctor in the village.

world would I let a man doctor take care of me. It is better that the child be born alone." This attitude, encouraged by the midwives, is very widespread, even among women who have lived outside the village or who have had more education.

POSTNATAL CARE

When the delivery is over, the mother is lifted onto a board and up to the bed or *tepexco,* if she uses either of these. If there is no one to lift her, she may get up herself without danger, for she is still "hot." She is wrapped in a sheet to prevent getting *mal aires.* The midwife binds the mother around the abdomen and tucks in a *muñeca,* a piece of rolled up cloth. The purpose of this *muñeca,* which is placed over the abdomen so as to bring pressure upon it, is to "fix the matrix." As far as we could ascertain, there is no magical or symbolic qualities connected with this *muñeca,* and there is little attempt to make it resemble a doll.[12] Clean cloths which are washed and replaced every day by the girl's mother or mother-in-law are placed between the patient's legs. Her soiled clothing is removed and she is given an old-fashioned *huipil* made from a large square cloth and slipped over her head. A skirt, made from a large cloth, is wrapped around her hips and legs. The mother is not bathed until the next day, for she is still "hot." After a bath of warm water she is dressed in clean clothing. The temporary *huipil* and skirt are then used as diapers for the baby. The mother is not completely bathed again until the first *temascal* or sweatbath.

The baby is wiped with clean old rags and is bound with a strip of cloth, doubled over the umbilicus and tied with a string. Some mothers prepare a belt for this purpose. The child is wrapped in warmed cloths, usually cut from his father's old shirt or pants. Some midwives drop lemon juice into the baby's eyes and give him a spoonful of castor oil as a purgative. The child is not washed until the following day because water will chill him.

The mother's diet for five days after the birth is poor and provides little nutrition. She is given cinnamon and water and a roll soon after the birth. If she has after-pains she is given honey and alcohol. At the next mealtime she eats toasted meat and tortilla, and for the next five days her diet consists of *atole,* cinnamon tea, and rolls. Some women take only cinnamon tea, tortilla, a small piece of cheese, and warm water during this period. Milk, coffee, and chocolate are thought dangerous when taken alone because they "chill" the ovaries, but some of the more modern women take a little coffee with milk. All food restrictions cease when the woman

---

[12]Redfield, *Tepoztlán,* pp. 136-37. Redfield states, "She [the midwife] makes a doll of rags and ties this against the patient's abdomen." According to Redfield, this doll is removed forty days later at the time of the *sacamisa* and "on that day the rag doll symbolizing the child in the womb is taken from its place on the mother's abdomen." Although we made repeated inquiries among women of all ages and degrees of sophistication we could find nothing which would justify this interpretation of the symbolism of the so-called doll. The "doll" is actually a wad of cloth placed under the binding or sash in order to bring more pressure upon the abdomen. Many women wear this "doll" for months after childbirth, or even after they are past childbearing age because they are more comfortable with it. It is of interest to note that the use of the "doll" in this way was not mentioned in the monographs on Tzintzuntzan, Cherán, Mitla, or Chan Kom.

is "clean," that is, when bleeding stops. This sometimes occurs in the first week but more often in the second. After delivery it is obligatory to give the midwife something to eat as an expression of appreciation, but it is up to the family to decide what is given. Generally the midwife is offered chocolate or coffee and bread. Sometimes wine and cigarettes are also given. During and after the delivery, the midwife is not restricted in any way as to the food she may eat.[13]

The mother's milk generally flows after one or two days, sometimes even before the birth. If the milk does not appear by the second day, some midwives give the mother an *atole* of sesame seed, chick peas, chocolate, and cinnamon. Others give *necuatole* or *atole de alegría* made of ground corn, *chile pasilla, epazote,* and brown sugar. Another remedy is the penis of an ox, cut up and cooked. Sometimes the *flor de pascua* is boiled and taken by the mother. A few midwives place the baby at the mother's breast to stimulate the flow of milk. Many babies are nursed at another woman's breast until the mother's milk comes. During the day the wet nurse, usually a relative or a friend, comes to the child's house every three or four hours to nurse him. At night the child is taken to the wet nurse once or twice by the father or grandmother. There is no charge for the services of the wet nurse, but often the child's family sends her some meat to nourish her during this time. Some families are afraid to take a young infant out because of *los aires,* and it is fed cinnamon and water until the mother's milk begins to flow.

It is a common belief that the first milk is harmful to the infant and should be discarded. It is squeezed out and either thrown to the ground (this is called *motlaltoka,* burying the first milk), or it is thrown over the roof (*monokia*) to prevent the mother's milk from going away. It is also thought that squeezing out the first milk hastens the flow of the true milk. If the mother has no milk, it is considered a calamity because the cost of a regular wet nurse is prohibitive, and many children die when put on a diet of cow's milk. Canned milk is now used safely, but the expense is a heavy burden for most families.

The amount of attention and care given to the new mother in Tepoztlán is striking. At no other time are women accorded so much service and time for rest. This care consists of a prolonged period in bed, freedom from household duties, taking sweatbaths, and abstention from sexual intercourse.

The prime motive underlying this postnatal care is to delay a new pregnancy as long as possible. It is believed that early resumption of sexual intercourse causes the back to weaken and the menstrual flow to begin, thus making conception more probable. Women say that extended rest from work and sexual intercourse can

---

[13] We could find nothing to support Redfield's statements that "The midwife is magician-priest rather than obstetrician; she eats the same food as her patient as long as their relation of intimacy is maintained during postnatal care . . . during the first week, the new mother and the midwife, who must eat the same food as her patient, observe food restrictions." *Ibid.,* pp. 134, 136. Our questions concerning this called forth the same response from informants in Mitla; that is, they laughed at the thought and denied that it occurred. It should be noted that Redfield's account of the above, as well as other aspects of pregnancy and birth, is based on the report of a single informant and probably represents an individual variation.

prevent the reappearance of menstruation for as long as two years. According to them, the ideal length of time to abstain is one year. Some women boast that they abstain for two years, and grandmothers say that in the old days women were not "molested" by their husbands for as much as three years, and that children were often born four and five years apart.

Today women complain that their husbands do not wait long enough and force their wives to resume intercourse after six months, some even sooner. Generally it is the husband who is blamed for the early resumption of intercourse, but it is recognized that some women are *calientes* and lack self-control. Such women are considered selfish because they are often *añeras,* women who have babies every year, and endanger the life of the child, who must be weaned too soon. *Añeras* are subject to much gossip, but they are relatively rare. Most women are glad to avoid sexual intercourse, which is frequently referred to as *abuso de hombre,* male abuse.

The following expresses the attitudes of many women, "My grandmother told me to guard myself from men for they are the danger. I don't protect myself from work. The thing I am afraid of is the man. My husband respects me and doesn't insist even when he is drunk. That is why I am never pregnant when I am raising little ones." The majority of husbands refuse to abstain as long as the wives wish them to, and many men use the threat of taking a sweetheart to get their wives to comply. The wife who is not jealous is fortunate, because then her husband can leave her alone for a long time. Those wives who are jealous "give in" to their husbands to keep them from going to other women and may resume intercourse in as little as two or three months. It is one of the obligations of the mother-in-law to warn her son not to "molest" his wife and to urge the daughter-in-law not to be jealous. However, it takes money to have a sweetheart or to go to prostitutes. More often the poor couple will resume intercourse sooner than others.

The extended rest of the new mother also allegedly prevents backaches, illness, and ugly skin discolorations (*paño*) on the mother's face and protects the baby's supply of milk. Thus, the good husband and father owes it to his wife and child not only to abstain from sexual relations, but also to hire a servant for two or three months. Many husbands are unable to do either. If a woman's skin remains clear of *paño* and wrinkles, it is said that "her husband has been good to her" and that "she knew how to take care of herself." When the couple lives with the husband's parents it is one of the more important obligations of the husband's mother to see that her daughter-in-law receives the proper postnatal care. Normally, a woman, who is married under both civil and religious law and who has had the blessings of both sets of parents, can expect to receive the required care. Because of the expense involved, a poor woman is not always certain of getting the maximum amount of rest and attention, but women of more means are always assured of it. Even among very poor families, if other conditions are favorable, women are well cared for after giving birth. This is not true for unmarried mothers, abandoned mothers, poor women without close relatives, women living in free unions or married only under civil law, mothers of very large families, and other special cases.

After the birth of the child, the mother is visited by the midwife every day for eight days, to be massaged and rebound. The massaging of the abdomen is considered important because it encourages the flow of blood and "cleanses" the mother internally. The appearance of clots of blood in the flow is taken to be evidence of the need for massaging. It is believed that if the mother does not receive massages, her abdomen will continue to protrude. The midwife also bathes the baby daily during her visits. The day after the birth of the child, close relatives usually come with jars of suitable food for the mother. A week or two later, aunts, uncles, and cousins may come bringing food for the mother and perhaps soap for the baby. In some families, because of ill feeling between in-laws, one side of the family may stay away. If the new mother has not been properly married or is not approved, she may receive no visits from her husband's or her own family. One young woman from a small outlying village, who had recently married into the village of Tepoztlán, received no visits from her husband's family at the birth of her first child; they regarded her as an outsider and disapproved of the marriage. Many women remain resentful for years at relatives who do not visit them at this time.

The mother is expected to stay in bed for from thirty to forty days. Those who cannot do this stay in bed for at least fifteen days; anything less is considered gross neglect. During this period the mother is urged to lie quietly on one side with her legs close together and her knees bent. Once or twice a day her husband or mother-in-law turns her over on her other side. Some women do not lift their heads at first but drink through a straw. During the first eight days, a new mother should remain behind the curtain because she is in a "delicate" state. She is not to be visited by anyone who has been to a wake or funeral because that visitor may carry a *mal humor* which causes "cancer" in menstruating women.

The *temascal*, which is still widely used even by those women who go to doctors, is usually given after eight days, though some midwives give it after fifteen days. (See Fig. 53.) Most women do not take their first *temascal* until after bleeding has stopped. Before the *temascal*, the mother, midwife, and other women of the house may also bathe and eat *clemole*—a dish made of chicken or beef, with the bone cooked in washed, ground chile *pasilla*—and a piece of *epazote*. The mother eats only the meat, for the chile sauce is "cold" and bad for her. She eats at this time to give her strength for the ordeal of the *temascal*, for some women faint or vomit from the extreme heat. Unmarried mothers sometimes do not use the *temascal* but bathe at home after twenty days in bed. A few younger women do not like the heat of the *temascal* and bathe in warm water in which some rosemary has been boiled. On the day of the *temascal*, the midwife, for the first and only time, must limit her diet to what the mother eats. A fire is made in the *temascal*, and a large can of hot water is placed there. Leaves of white *sapote* are placed on the floor, and a small bundle of these leaves are tied together to form a brush.

The mother is well wrapped and is traditionally carried to the *temascal* on the back of her husband. Although this is still done by many, the woman is now often carried on a board by two men. Some men find it embarrassing to carry their wives and hire someone to do it for them. Some of the younger women walk to the *temascal*. The new baby is also taken to the *temascal* with the mother and is briefly exposed to the steam, then carefully wrapped and taken home. Many modern women disapprove of giving infants and small children sweatbaths and believe that they cause navel hemorrhages and even death. A bunch of *sapote* leaves are

Fig. 53. A sweathouse.

placed between the mother's thighs to cover the genitals. Throughout the bath, the midwife is assisted by a female relative of the mother. The midwife rubs the mother's body with egg and alcohol, particularly on the face and back, for this mixture is thought to prevent *paño*.

The mother then lies down on the leaves, and spoonfuls of water are thrown into the fire to make it steam. The midwife rubs the mother with the brush of leaves. After this she asks for the *estropajo,* which is a brush of *ixtle* in the form of a basket, containing a piece of soap. This basket may be made in the shape of an animal and is presented by the baby's godmother. Some women do not like to be washed with the *estropajo* because it is too harsh for their skins, and they use something else. The midwife washes the mother's entire body except for the genitals, which the mother washes herself. Warm water is thrown over her to wash off the soap, and she is dried. She is rebound and wrapped in a sheet and carried back to bed. When she leaves, the other women of the house, friends, and neighbors may take advantage of the hot *temascal* to bathe. These baths are taken by the mother every eight days for as long as she stays in bed. Almost everyone takes at least two *temascales,* and many take the traditional four. After the first *temascal* the mother may eat a greater variety of food. Most women continue to avoid black coffee and chile for one month because they "irritate."

When the mother has taken her last *temascal* and gets out of bed, she is usually given a boiled mixture of many herbs (*paclaposon*),[14] which she drinks before meals twice a day until two quarts are consumed. Some also take this before entering the first *temascal* and for one day thereafter. If the woman does not feel well before entering the second *temascal,* she may be given the same mixture of herbs *potlatestli,* which are now toasted and ground rather than boiled. If bleeding has not stopped after two months, the woman is again given *paclaposon.* Strained honey is also used because it provokes more bleeding which, it is thought, brings the end of bleeding closer. A mixture of herbs similar to a mustard plaster (*vilma*) may also be placed on the back. Excessive bleeding is attributed to a weakening of the back.

After leaving her bed, the mother is supposed to sit quietly with knees doubled under and to avoid walking or moving about for as long as she can. If she must walk, she goes very slowly with her thighs close together. If this is the first child, the mother may keep this up for three months; others return to normal moving about, in from one to two months. Only the most unfortunate women, however, do heavy work, such as washing and ironing before three months. In the past, women frequently did not work for as long as six months and were considered too weak to carry the baby. The new mother is not supposed to leave the house before the *sacamisa* attended by the new mother and child, which generally takes place in forty days or after the fourth *temascal.* If the mother leaves the house before this time, the baby's godmother may refuse to attend the *sacamisa,* on the grounds that the mother is not taking proper care of herself.

COMPARISON WITH OTHER MEXICAN COMMUNITIES

Many of the practices and beliefs concerning pregnancy and birth found in Tepoztlán are widespread in rural Mexico and have been reported for at least Tarascan (Tzintzuntzan and Cherán), Mayan (Chan Kom), and Zapotecan (Mitla and the Isthmus of Tehuantepec) groups. The similarity, even in small details, is sometimes quite striking. For example, we find that in Tzintzuntzan and Mitla the satisfaction of food whims during pregnancy is important. In Tzintzuntzan and Cherán, pregnant women should not urinate where an animal has urinated, and in both these communities, as well as in Mitla and in Tehuantepec,[15] there is fear that an eclipse may deform the unborn child. In Tzintzuntzan and Tehuante-

---

[14] The following herbs are placed in several gallons of water and boiled for twenty-four hours, or until one quart of the liquid remains: *cacamotitl, coch-ḳoḳ-ḳoḳ, pulmonaria, bretonica* or *ojolote, sangrinaria, calriguala* or *cola de tlacuache, lengua de sejerba, nesḳtiḳshiwitl, tochaḳatl, sasaliḳ, tripa de judas* or *tzacili, tlacuawitl, mananchi, ijutch ḳatitl* or *algodoncillo, cascara de encino, flor de pudra* or *doradillo* or *siempre viva, saḳateḳomatl* or *ḳwateḳomate,* and *tletlematzitzia* or *barbolio.*

[15] Miguel Covarrubias, *Mexico South, the Isthmus of Tehauntepec* (New York: A. A. Knopf, 1946), p. 342.

pec, a metal object is also worn for protection during an eclipse. The use of herbs and other remedies to produce abortions is also reported for Tzintzuntzan, Cherán, Mitla, and Tehuantepec. In Chan Kom a partition is put up in the room before delivery. The use of prenatal and postnatal massage, and during delivery, is mentioned in the monographs on Tzintzuntzan, Cherán, Chan Kom, and Tehuantepec. In Mitla the flow of blood after birth is encouraged by an herbal preparation. The application of heat during a difficult delivery is mentioned in Tzintzuntzan, Cherán, and Chan Kom. Putting the mother on a blanket to hasten the birth occurs in Tzintzuntzan, Cherán, and Mitla; the inducement of vomiting for the same reason is practiced in Tzintzuntzan and Tehuantepec. In Cherán, Mitla, and Chan Kom certain drinks are given which probably result in vomiting, but this is not specifically stated by the authors.

The use of sweatbaths during confinement is common in Mitla, and small infants are also sometimes so bathed. Hot tallow is dropped on the umbilicus in Tzintzuntzan and Tehuantepec, and the umbilical cord is used as a remedy for sore eyes in Mitla. In Cherán lemon juice is dropped into the infant's eyes. Finally, the burying of the after-birth under the hearth is practiced in Tzintzuntzan, Cherán, and Chan Kom. In Mitla and Tehuantepec it is buried elsewhere. In Tehuantepec the mother is bound and a "doll" is placed over the abdomen, to prevent the "matrix from falling out of place."

A comparison of the period of postnatal confinement, which is so important in Tepoztlán, also shows some similarity. In Tzintzuntzan and Cherán, some share the widespread belief that women should not go out or resume work until after forty days. But a woman in Tzintzuntzan may sit up in bed after three days and often goes out after three weeks. In Cherán a mother stays in bed from eight to fifteen days and may leave the house after twenty days. In Mitla there is no set confinement period, but it is usually not longer than fifteen days. In Chan Kom, the mother "must stay in her hammock for a week, remain quiet for two weeks, and after three weeks she may go out into the street." [16] In Tehuantepec the midwife visits the mother in seven days, and the mother goes to *sacamisa* in forty days.

It is difficult to say to what extent these similarities are due to contacts between these groups before the Conquest, or to the common exposure to Spanish colonial influences. A full comparison of our material on Tepoztlán with that of the foregoing groups is not always easy or possible because of the unequal coverage and treatment of the material. For the same reason, it is difficult to compare the psychological significance of practices that appear similar.

---

[16] *Ibid.*, p. 183.

infancy and early childhood: 16

THERE IS MUCH variety in the treatment and care of infants and children in Tepoztlán because of individual differences and because of the presence of groups representing different cultural and economic levels. The most obvious contrasting practices in child care are those of the more acculturated families and those with only minimal contacts with the outside. The distinction between these two groups is not always clear-cut. Sometimes the mother represents one group and the father the other, reflecting the state of transition which pervades the village and complicates the discussion of customs in no small measure. Frequently there is no difference in customs as such, but rather in the practice of them.

INFANCY

At the birth of a child there is no celebration, and generally little fuss is made. When the first-born is a son, there are usually expressions of pleasure on the part of the father and relatives. But many mothers describe the arrival of their children as causing "neither joy nor argument," and frequently complain of their husband's indifference at the birth of a child. Men do, in fact, maintain an attitude of reserve but often respond to a new arrival by working harder. More modern men do not conceal pleasure at the birth of a child, and behave much the way new fathers do in our society. Gifts are not traditionally given to the child, although some of the more acculturated do this and invite friends in to drink and to eat *mole*.

It is believed that the first weeks of life are dangerous, for the infant is particularly susceptible to the "evil eye," "bad humors," and *los aires*. Non-relatives are not encouraged to see a newborn child, though the more modern families permit it after a few days. Babies sleep behind a curtain and are protected from "bad humors" with *ruda* and chile which are placed in the form of a cross beneath the pillow or mattress of the cradle, and by a few drops of iodine on their clothing. Some families hang a gallstone, taken from the gall bladder of a bull, around the child's wrist to protect him from the "evil eye." This is no longer done in some of the better educated families. After one month, a centavo may be hung on a string around the child's neck to protect him from whooping cough. Some tie on a little bag of chile seed as protection from other diseases. Babies in all families wear little caps for seven months to protect them from *los aires* or, as the more modern mothers say, from cold drafts.

Anyone coming in from the street must "cool" for awhile before going to see the baby because they may be "hot" and make the child ill. If the father of the child has committed adultery and then comes home "hot," he must be particularly careful to "cool," lest he give the child an eye inflammation. Sometimes jealous wives will accuse adulterous husbands of selfishness on the ground that they are endangering the infant's health. Children are rarely taken into the street during the first four months, or until their caps are removed, for fear of *los aires*. More modern families take their children out earlier.

Every child is believed to have a *tonal* or *sombra,* something akin to a guardian spirit which protects him from illness. A weak child has a weak *tonal;* a robust child has a powerful *tonal*. A child's illness is sometimes attributed to the fact that his *tonal* has left his body and must be called back if he is to be cured. In such cases of spirit-loss, a special *curandero* is called in to "lay the shadow." Incense is burned while the *curandero* cures the child.

Babies are usually baptized within the first week after birth. An infant who is expected to die is baptized on the same day, otherwise most parents prefer the third day. Children born out of wedlock or under abnormal circumstances may not be baptized until many months or even one or two years later. Godparents of baptism are selected before the birth of the child. While the couple is young, their parents, generally the husband's parents, select the godparents, who are usually though not necessarily a married couple. Later, the husband alone makes the selection. The husband's mother or some older woman in the family goes to the house of the prospective godfather and makes the formal request, "Would you be so kind as to take a child to be baptized?" If the answer is in the affirmative she thanks them and says that she will return to let them know when the baptism will be. Sometimes the person refuses the request, pleading that he is too old or ill or cannot undertake new obligations, in which case he may suggest the name of a relative.[1] When the grandmother making the request returns, she carries two branches of white flowers and two four-ounce candles. On the day of the baptism, the child, his father, and grandmother meet the godparents inside the church. The godmother holds the child during the baptism and pays the priest's fee, which is from five to ten pesos. At the door of the church the godparents distribute small coins to all the children who happen to be gathered there, and every one returns to his respective home. On the following day the child's family brings a gift usually consisting of bread, sugar, chocolate, and milk to the godparents.

---

[1] Theoretically, an invitation to become godparent is a high token of esteem and respect, and the acceptance of it creates a deep obligation. However, it is an honor which is frequently rejected. There are many stories of parents choosing a godfather for selfish motives. For example, many parents are said to seek a childless couple who have some property, in the hope that their child will inherit it at the death of the godparents.

The *sacamisa* is supposed to occur forty days after the baptism. It frequently takes place a week or two later because the godparents may not keep track of the time, or one of the families involved may lack the necessary funds for the ceremony. When the godparents are ready, they appear at the house of their godchild with a tray containing the baptismal clothes, a white silk gown, a set of underclothes, a long robe, a hat, a pair of socks, and perhaps a pair of shoes. Sometimes these clothes are not presented until the child is in church, where he is then dressed.

The next day at 5:00 A.M., the parents, parents-in-law, and godparents meet at the church. The child is carried by the father or grandmother since the mother is considered too weak. The priest prays over the mother and child and throws holy water on them. During the Mass the mother is seated and holds the child in one arm and a candle in her other hand. When the party leaves the church, each goes home without taking any more formal leave of one another than saying "hasta luego." At noon the godparents are visited by their *compadres* and some relatives of the latter, who bring a gift of *mole* with turkey, rice, macaroni, beans, a bottle of wine, and a package of cigarettes. They leave the gift and return home. Later in the afternoon, if the godparents wish, they may bring musicians and friends to their *compadres'* house for a celebration. The *compadres* are obliged to serve food and drinks to all who come, and the dancing which follows may continue until about 8:00 P.M. This celebration involves considerable expense, and most families are able to fulfill only a minimum of the obligations.

It is said that a boy who is not taken to *sacamisa* will be refused when he asks for the hand of a girl in marriage, and that a girl who is not taken to *sacamisa* will elope. Some of the younger women who leave their homes before the forty-day period of rest forfeit the right to *sacamisa*. In one case, an educated woman who no longer observed the forty-day period received a tray of clothing from her child's godmother at the time of *sacamisa* and was forced to refuse the gift. She returned it with a suitable gift of her own to placate the godmother. The baby's mother, in telling the story, added that the godmother knew very well that there would be no *sacamisa* and sent the clothing just to cause embarrassment.

Each child in Tepoztlán has godparents of baptism to insure a guardian for him in case of the death of either of the parents. It is the obligation of the godparents to inquire periodically about the welfare of their godchild and to see that the child is sent to school. Very few godparents in Tepoztlán take a more active interest in their godchildren. The godparents may not refuse to take in their orphaned godchildren, but many take them only temporarily until other arrangements can be made for them. Most orphaned children are cared for by relatives rather than godparents. There are stories of godparents abusing and exploiting their godchildren, as well as stories of kind and affectionate treatment.

The naming of children follows the Catholic custom of selecting a name from the list of saints' names on the day of birth. A *sobrenombre,* or an additional name, is selected either from the saints' list on the day of baptism or at will, depending upon the desire of the father or the godparents. The *sobrenombre* is the name by which the child is most frequently called. Many names are shortened for daily use, and nicknames are common for boys. The children take the surname of the father as their own. For example, when Juan Gómez marries Carlota Villamar, their son Francisco may sign his name as Francisco Gómez Villamar or just Francisco Gómez.[2]

The parents alone, or sometimes with the help of the grandparents, prepare the necessary clothing for the new baby. In former days, when a girl married at twelve or thirteen, the burden of preparation for the first child fell upon her mother-in-law or mother who usually made baby clothes out of old clothing. Although this is still true in the majority of cases, some more acculturated young wives prepare new baby clothes when they become pregnant for the first time. Later children are generally dressed in the used clothing of the first child. Used clothing is given away only to intimate relatives or to poor people who beg; to offer such clothing to friends or distant relatives would offend them.

Infants are dressed in cotton shirts and *pañales* or diapers of rags tied around the waist with a string. This string is often tied so tightly as to leave a deep red welt. The clothing of infants up to three months is generally warmed before being put on. Dresses are put on girls, and pants on boys, at about four months. Young infants are kept warm by a blanket; older ones, particularly in better-to-do families, by woolen sweaters. Girls' ears are pierced usually about one week after birth, but often later, by a competent female. Red, green, or black silk thread is drawn through the ears until earrings are provided.

Infants are expected to be kept fairly clean. Most babies up to one year are bathed every three days, but some young mothers bathe their first-born son every day, sometimes even twice a day if the infant is restless. They are bathed in warm water during the warmest part of the day. Most mothers are careful to keep the soap out of the baby's eyes, and babies seem to enjoy their baths. After the bath they are rubbed with alcohol to warm them or are dusted with talcum and are dressed in clean clothing.

Pañales are changed whenever soiled or only once a day, depending upon the mother. In general, first-born or favorite children are changed more often, as are the children of the more educated families. Other women tend to add dry cloths over the wet ones and make a complete change only when there is a bowel movement. The most *dejada* or careless mothers reuse soiled rags without washing them and may not clean the child for a long time after a bowel movement. For the most part, however, babies are kept clean and do not suffer unduly from rashes or skin irritations caused by diapers.

---

[2] It is interesting to note that as late as 1806, most people in Tepoztlán still followed the Indian custom of identifying people by the name of their house site, in Náhuatl. A census of the village taken at this date shows most of the names as names of house sites, with the first name in Spanish preceding it. The following are some examples of how the names appear in this census, Juan Isidro Tlatelpa, Mariano Eusebio Tecuapan, María Tomasa Tecuapan, María Victoriano Ayopac, María Luisa Tejoac, etc. Note that the surnames are in Náhuatl. These "surnames" were really the names of the house sites, or *sitios*.

Infants are traditionally swaddled in a sheet or cotton blanket with the arms bound tightly at their sides during nursing and sleeping. It is said that this is done to prevent the sleeping child from waking himself with a sudden movement of the hands which might cause *espanto*. Swaddling also serves to prevent the child from touching his genitals and from touching the mother's breast during nursing, "for the breast is not a toy." Swaddling, however, is viewed primarily as an important part of child training.

There is a widespread belief, particularly among the older women, that swaddling and binding the arms of the child will prevent him from "turning out bad" when he is older. Binding is an effort to make children more passive and quiet. Many families in the smaller barrios tie the sleeping child's wrists and ankles to keep him from moving under the swaddling blanket. This is done up to the time he walks, in order to train him to sleep quietly, for there is a belief that a quiet sleep is a good sleep. As girls get older, they are trained to sleep quietly and modestly, with their legs together.

It is believed that children who are bound will not touch things, will not be active or demanding, and will be less trouble to the mother. When an older child is mischievous or overactive, it is said that his mother did not bind his arms long enough. Also, when an older boy attempts to embrace a girl she might say, "What, didn't they bind you when you were a child?" Older women say it is more effective to keep a child bound for one year, but most women today do it until the child no longer permits it, or from six to nine months, depending upon how active the child is. More acculturated mothers often bind their children for only three months "out of pity," much to the annoyance of their mothers-in-law. One grandmother complained that she must always be watching her two-year-old grandson because he touches everything and wants to keep moving about. She blamed this on the fact that his mother swaddled him for only three months. A few women do not swaddle their infants at all. Old women frequently comment that infants and children are much more active today than they were a generation ago.

During the day, babies sleep in a shallow wooden cradle which hangs from the ceiling by a rope. The sleeping baby's face is covered with a *rebozo* or cloth to protect him from *los aires* and to keep out light and flies. The swaddled child is safer in the cradle, since swaddling prevents movements which might cause him to fall over the low sides. As the child gets older and more active he must be tied in or watched constantly because of the danger of falling out. Most cradles can be raised, to safeguard the child from animals wandering into the house, or lowered to prevent a high fall. Babies may be rocked to sleep in the cradle, but most of the time they fall asleep in the mother's arms while nursing and are then placed in the cradle.

Babies sleep with their mothers at night, on a *petate* on the floor or on a *tepezco*. If the mother is accustomed to sleeping in a bed, the child will be heavily wrapped at night to prevent wetting the mattress. Cases of mothers smothering babies during sleep are not rare, and usually the mother is blamed for carelessness. An unusual case occurred in which a mother smothered her first two infants. She was severely beaten by her husband and scolded by her mother-in-law and all her relatives. When she gave birth to a third child everyone warned her to sleep lightly and quietly so as not to hurt the child, and her husband said that if the same thing happened he would accuse her of murder. Now a few better-to-do and more acculturated families have their infants sleep in cribs for the first three months, as a precautionary measure.

Nursing is not considered a pleasurable activity by most Tepoztecan women. Not one of the many mothers we interviewed enjoyed nursing, and some expressed strong dislike for it. Some complained that it was painful, that nursing made them thin or ill, and that they could not go anywhere without the child. Nursing is looked upon as of the utmost importance to the child and to the mother, since it is believed by many that nursing delays conception. When nursing in the day-time the mother is usually seated, holding the child in her arms. During the first six months, mothers frequently lie down to nurse. Despite the expressed belief that it is improper for the baby to touch the mother's breasts, it is quite common to see babies doing so when they are no longer swaddled, with the mothers making no attempt to prevent this. Also, expressed attitudes to the contrary, mothers appear to enjoy caressing and playing with infants while they nurse. Nursing is best for mother and child during the first three months when the mother is well rested and has little work to do. As the infant gets older and is given over to a child nurse, so that the mother can resume her duties, she becomes more passive and distracted during nursing and may pay little attention to the baby. However, the baby is given the breast whenever he cries and is permitted to nurse as long as he wishes. The breast is used as a pacifier, and almost all nursing children are put to sleep this way. Until the child is weaned he is almost never denied the breast.

Solid foods are introduced to the child at varying ages. Some mothers do not give their children any solid food other than bread or tortillas until the end of the first year, or until the first two teeth have appeared. Most mothers give babies tastes of foods when they begin to grab for things, generally at about the age of six months. The most common foods given to nursing children are bread, tortilla, bean soup, rice, noodle soup, fruit, and coffee. A few better-to-do families of more education give small children eggs, *atole* cooked with milk, and soup cooked with meat.

Infants are not permitted to cry, and every effort is made to quiet them. There is an attitude that a crying child is hungry, neglected, or ill, and many husbands scold their wives and get angry when much crying occurs. Women are usually more careful to stop a child's crying when their husbands are at home. Infants are sometimes spanked or frightened to make them stop crying.

Children who cry a great deal are often described as greedy. It is said that they will be poor when they grow up because they are crying for bread. If a crying baby is not consoled by the breast, the leaf of the ḳoḳochiaton, or *dormidera*,[3] which

---

[3] *Numosa púdica.*

closes when touched, is sometimes placed under the child's pillow to make him stop crying and go to sleep. Sometimes the leaf of the *sapote blanco* may also be used. When a small child cries because he is *chincual*, or irritated in the rectum, the small berries of the *toheachichi* [4] are put into the rectum to stop the crying. If a child is restless and sleepless because of diarrhea, his abdomen and buttocks are rubbed with hot tallow, into which has been mixed the powdered flower of the *cempaxochitl*, and then wrapped in a hot cloth.

Children are, for the most part, not hurried in their development. A healthy child is expected to walk at about one year and to talk at about two years. If the child does not walk by that time, some parents rub his leg and calf muscles with earth warmed by the sun, to remove the "cold" from his legs. More acculturated women may help their children learn to walk by placing a sash under the arms for support or by putting a toy before them. Children are only mildly encouraged to speak, by repeating words to them. There is little correction of childlike errors in speech, such as substituting "y" for "r" or omitting "s," or misplacing syllables, so that errors persist until the child is five or six years of age. If a child cannot speak by the time he is three or four, a church key may be borrowed and turned in the child's mouth to "unlock" it. It is believed by many that the fingernails of a child should not be cut until he begins to speak, because the palate will fall and the child will be mute. To prevent children from scratching themselves with their long nails, some mothers put little mittens on their hands. When teeth are late in coming, the gums may be rubbed with a grasshopper's leg until the gums bleed. This is an old practice and is no longer known by many of the younger people. It is also believed that a child's hair should not be cut before one year, or the child will become ill.

Most mothers prefer a quiet child to an active one and do not encourage children to be independent. It is considered careless and neglectful to permit children to crawl on the floor or in the dirt, and few mothers put their infants down for more than a moment. This attitude is in part due to the fact that children who crawl are more troublesome and need watching, and in part because there is usually no clean, safe place in which a child may crawl. Inside the house or in the patio there is always danger from insects and animals. Women point out that infants who are allowed to crawl about unobserved almost always suffer from chronic diarrhea, worms, and intestinal diseases. Mothers who have no one to help them often put their small children into a large box while they do their work. In the past a busy mother tied her child to a stake and let him play on a *petate*, but this is no longer done.

All infants in Tepoztlán are carried almost every waking moment up to the time they begin to walk. Children are carried a great deal even after they can walk and not infrequently until they are three and four years old. In Tepoztlán, children are not cradled or slung in the *rebozo*, as in some parts of Mexico, but are held in

---

[4] *Solanum nigrum.*

the left arm with one end of the *rebozo* tightly tucked around the child's body and the other end brought around the mother's shoulders and also tucked under the child. This makes the child snug and takes some of his weight off the mother's arm. Tepoztecans regard carrying a child on the back as primitive and associate it with poverty, because a poor woman needs both hands free to work. Most children are quiet, passive, and content as long as they are being carried. The child's arms are free if he is past swaddling age, but his ability to move is relatively limited. Many mothers say that as long as there is someone to carry the child they prefer him to be carried, otherwise he gets dirty, touches things, and demands the mother's attention.

The majority of mothers have someone to assist them in taking care of their small children. The assistant may be an older child, a grandmother, a niece, the daughter of a neighbor, or a young girl hired for the purpose. Most often the assistant is an older brother or sister, who may also be a small child. The practice of giving over the infant, from the age of four months on, to a child-nurse is almost universal in Tepoztlán, and infants early come into contact with people other than the mother.

Under the best conditions, the infant is cared for by the oldest daughter, who may be thirteen years of age or over and who has had experience in the care of children. This sister often is an adequate mother substitute, and a close, affectionate relationship may develop between the girl and the infant. But frequently the infant is given over to the care of an eight- or nine-year-old, or one even younger, who sometimes resents the role of nurse. Sometimes children, particularly boys, run off into the street when they are told to take care of the baby. The child-nurse is expected to carry the baby about, usually in the patio and sometimes in the street. The baby may not be taken far away, in case he cries and wants to nurse. If the baby is hurt or becomes ill, the child-nurse is blamed and often punished.

For example, a seven-year-old girl was taking care of her seven-month-old brother while the mother went to the plaza. The baby awoke from sleep and began to cry. The little girl took him out in the street to divert him but neglected to cover him well. That night the baby had a fever, and six days later he died of pneumonia. The mother blamed the girl for the death of the baby but did not punish her because "she had only wanted to keep the baby from crying." But the little girl cried a great deal because of the things her mother had said to her. A large number of children, particularly girls, receive severe punishment because of accidents which occur while they are taking care of younger brothers and sisters.

A first-born or favorite child, or a child in a more acculturated family, often receives different treatment than other children. In addition to more solicitous, indulgent, and affectionate care, these children are unswaddled earlier, not carried as much after they can walk, and are permitted more freedom to walk and play where they wish. They are followed about by their grandmother, nurse, or even their father, or some other indulgent member of the family, and carefully watched. They are often allowed to play with many objects, usually forbidden; get dirty without being scolded; have more opportunities to exercise initiative; make choices; and develop their individuality. Such children also receives rattles, balls, dolls, wagons, etc., which the majority of small children in Tepoztlán do without. One of the wealthier families bought a toy automobile with pedals for a favorite grandchild, but large expenditures such as this are extremely rare. Even in poor families, there is indulgence toward the favorite child. In one very poor family, for example, the oldest daughter had no textbook for school because her mother had permitted the baby brother, a favorite child, to tear it up. This type of indulgence is unusual, because most Tepoztecan families are careful not to permit children to damage property.

There is little preoccupation with toilet training, and there is no conventional method or set time to accomplish it. There is almost no effort made to control urination during the first two years. If an infant tends to urinate too frequently, it is believed that the spleen is "cold" and should be warmed by an application of unguent of *altea* and hot tallow. Bathing the child in the *temascal* is another form of treatment.

Although expressions of disgust at having to clean up bowel movements are frequent, these do not appear to be related to any deep-seated repulsion. It is the rare mother who is persistent or methodical in training her children early in bowel control. Only two informants displayed any compulsion concerning toilet training and followed a rigid procedure with their children from the age of six months. It is the more acculturated mothers who give earlier and consistent attention to toilet training.

Most mothers take their children to the corral with them two or three times a day when the children are able to walk well. Before that time, children are scolded when they soil themselves and "are called 'little pig,' so that they will be ashamed." By the time children are sixteen months or two years of age, many mothers begin to spank them hard enough to make them cry for doing their "necessities" in the wrong place. At two, some children ask to have their pants removed and can go to the corral alone. Some are able to clean themselves with a stone or leaf or paper at this age. When a child is able to tie and untie his pants, usually by four or five, he is able to go independently. After age four, children are no longer permitted to accompany their mothers to the corral.

There is a tendency for mothers to be more lenient with boys, especially favorites, than with girls in toilet training, with the result that girls are trained earlier. They are spanked and scolded more consistently and harshly, and are required to be less demanding of assistance. Boys between the ages of two and five are occasionally seen playing in the patio naked from the waist down, but more "correct" people consider it very improper to permit boys to play without pants.

Infancy ends with weaning. A child who is nursed for less than two years is generally considered to be deprived. Most mothers nurse their infants until they know that they are again pregnant, which may not be until the fifth month after conception. It is a widespread belief that it is harmful to the child to nurse while the mother is pregnant, but many mothers do not wean the child until he shows definite symptoms of becoming ill. If weaning due to a new pregnancy occurs before two years, the mother and father are said to be inconsiderate of their infant. Weaning at one year sometimes occurs because the mother is ill or has insufficient milk. Although women frequently complain that they become thin and tired when they nurse, or that they receive painful bites, they rarely wean a child for these reasons. A few mothers regularly wean their children at eighteen months. Weaning may be delayed in the case of a favorite child, to avoid making him cry.

One mother, who suffered from sore nipples, decided to wean her three-year-old son while her husband was away. When her husband came home that night he became angry and said that if the boy cried, the mother would receive a beating. Many people believe that the longer a child is nursed, the stronger he will be. It is not uncommon for the youngest and last child to be nursed as long as he wishes, sometimes for four or five years. Some believe, however, that after two years of nursing, the child begins to drink the mother's blood "like a bat," and that nursing a child too long will make him stupid.

When the mother decides to wean the child she places a bitter substance (*sávila*) on the nipple, often in the child's presence, and tells him that her breast is sore and that he may no longer nurse. Some mothers wean *por derecho,* that is by binding the breasts and not permitting the child to see them again. But many do not bind the breasts for several days, and if the child cries or begs hard he is given the breast so that he "will not be angry" with the mother. If the child continues to nurse despite the *sávila,* a more bitter substance (*prodigiosa*) [5] is applied. Today, bicarbonate of soda, iodine, alcohol, etc., are also used. A child is considered difficult to wean if he continues to nurse despite the "medicines" applied. Crying, even if prolonged over eight days, is viewed as a normal part of weaning. In general, the younger the child the more difficult he is to wean. A delicate or sickly child may be treated more gently, by gradually reducing the number of nursings for eight or fifteen days before weaning is begun, but few women do this. Since so many children are nursed for at least two years, most of them are weaned in a few days. Few mothers consider weaning difficult.

Many women have a great deal of milk, and their breasts are painful during weaning. Some express the milk with their hands to relieve the pain, others cannot and must rely on binding. Hot alcohol is rubbed on the breasts and back, or heated tortillas are placed on the breasts, to ease the pain. Another technique is to heat the *tejolate* (pestle) and rub the breast with it. It is believed that nursing should not be resumed once the breasts are bound because the milk changes and acts as a purgative. When milk is expressed, it is generally buried in the earth in a place where the ants will not get to it so that the mother will have a good supply of milk for her next baby. Some women express the milk into a cloth and throw it over the roof for the same reason.

---

[5] *Coleosantus.*

Most families attempt to console the child during weaning. He generally receives more attention from his mother and continues to sleep with her. However, most mothers do not carry the child during weaning because of the pain in their breasts. The child is generally carried about by others in the family, is given little toys or goodies, and is taken visiting. The child starts to eat with the family, and this is often presented to him as a compensation for the loss of the mother's milk and usually serves to divert him. Occasionally, if a child is inconsolable and cries hard for a long time, particularly at night, the mother, or more usually the father, will lose patience and spank him hard and then frighten him into silence by telling him the coyote will come to eat him. Sometimes a child will be taken to sleep at his grandmother's house for a few nights.

Illness and death are frequent in children after weaning. Often the illness or death is attributed to indigestion or *ético* (tuberculosis?), in which the child wastes away. These are associated with the changed diet of the child at weaning, and it is highly probable that these children do not receive sufficient nourishment, or are given foods unsuited to the digestive systems of young children. Many women wean *con pura tortilla,* that is, with inadequate food substitutes. These children are shifted to the diet of the adult, which consists of tortilla, beans or bean soup, rice or noodles prepared with much lard or oil, and black coffee. In some families children of two are also permitted to eat chile and various local seeds which, whether toasted or raw, are difficult to digest. The best traditional method of feeding a weaned child is to give him an *atole* of ground corn cooked in milk, if the family can afford it, or in water, and sweetened with cinnamon and brown sugar. Many women say that children never become ill if given this food daily for one, two, or six months after weaning. Today better-to-do and more acculturated families wean with a daily diet of eggs, cereals, milk, soups made of chicken or meat, and vegetables and fruit, in addition to the traditional foods. Sometimes cooked meat and bread are given to a small child, even when the rest of the family cannot afford to eat them. This diet, however, is limited to very few children.

Chipilez, or jealousy, is an important childhood illness which begins when the mother of the child again becomes pregnant.[6] The world *chipil* (jealous) is derived from the Náhuatl *tzipitl* which means last or smallest one and refers to the jealousy of the youngest child toward the expected baby. It is believed that nursing children can tell from the taste of the pregnant mother's milk that a new child is coming, and the illness is due to the fact that they are now "carrying the weight of the baby," a euphemistic term for jealousy. Weaning is begun with the first display of symptoms. Children who are no longer being nursed but who still sleep with the mother are able to "sense" the coming of another child and may also become *chipil.* Young husbands are also subject to *chipilez* when their wives become pregnant for the first time. They also are "carrying the weight of the baby," since there is no other child to do so. The symptoms of *chipilez* are pain all over the

---

[6] This illness is well known in many parts of Mexico, including the large cities, but, to my knowledge, it has not been reported in anthropological literature.

body, diarrhea, loss of appetite and weight, pallor, and weakness. In fact, almost any symptom or illness during this time is called *chipilez*. It is said that husbands become sleepy and do not want to work. A husband can be cured by wearing a strip of his wife's skirt around his neck.

In the case of children, there is no known cure, and mothers try to comfort the child with more attention. Grandmothers often advise against too much kissing and embracing of the child when he is *chipil* because it "makes the burden heavier." Indeed, the greater attention required by the sick child makes more difficult his later adjustment to the withdrawal of the mother at the birth of the next baby. It is said by some that if a child is very *chipil,* the next baby will be of the opposite sex, and if the child is not very ill, the next baby will be of the same sex.

Sometimes a *chipil* child dies before the birth of the next child, and several families attribute as many as four or five deaths of children to *chipilez*. From the symptoms and number of deaths, and from the obvious relation to weaning, it is highly probable that many cases of *chipilez* are due to nutritional deficiencies or intestinal parasites. Most children and all husbands recover at the birth of the new baby, for, it is said, "Tlayish qua mak awa," (the weight is lifted).

EARLY CHILDHOOD

The transition from infancy to childhood is characterized by the breaking of the close ties between the mother and the youngest child. This process begins at weaning and generally culminates with the birth of the next sibling. As we have seen, in this interval of from two to four months, most children become *chipil,* losing their symptoms after the birth of the baby. Other children continue to be ill, sometimes for several months or even years. This illness reflects the widespread sibling rivalry which exists among children.

Children in Tepoztlán are not prepared for the arrival of a new sibling. When delivery is expected, the children of the house are sent to sleep with the grandmother or a relative or neighbor. When they return home the next morning they are told their parents have bought a new baby, and they are shown their new brother or sister. The initial reaction of the children may be one of pleasure, curiosity, or apprehension, the latter particularly on the part of the younger children. Older girls often express displeasure, and some even scold their mothers for buying a new child because the burden of raising it usually falls upon them. A girl of thirteen said to her mother after the birth of another child, "You cannot even buy us good food or shoes. Why did you buy another child?"

Jealousy and hostility on the part of the other children, particularly the younger ones, are so common as to be considered inevitable and normal. Children often call the baby names and, if not watched, may slap, pinch, or throw him on the ground. Small children, too, scold their mother for buying the infant and beg her to return him. A mother said that her four-year-old son used to stand at the gate and call to passers-by to take away his little sister. Jealous children are often regarded with amusement by adults, but striking the infant or mother in jealousy is quickly punished. Some parents try to assuage the children's resentment by placing fruit and candy under the infant's dress and saying that the baby brought gifts to his brothers and sisters. Affection shown by the grandmother, the father, and older brothers and sisters also serves to comfort younger children. Demonstrative affection from the mother is almost entirely absent after the new baby is born. In general, it is rare for a child over five to be held, hugged, or kissed, and by the time the child reaches ten this never occurs.

Temper tantrums, which rarely occur in the nursing child or even during weaning, are frequent in the next-to-the-youngest child, after the birth of a new sibling. These tantrums are distinctly associated with the coming of the other child and are attributed to jealousy. The child becomes irritable and hypersensitive, and any rebuff or show of indifference on the part of his elders is enough to cause a temper tantrum. The child throws himself to the ground in a rage, screaming and kicking and pulling his hair. Some children bang their heads on the ground, tear at their clothing, and hit or scratch themselves. Frequently children urinate *por muina,* or out of anger, during a temper tantrum. They also throw themselves on the offender and beat him.

The child usually gets what he wants, in order to quiet him, but if the father is at home he may receive a spanking. If the child has the tantrum because of an older brother or sister, he usually gets what he wants. As the baby of the family, the child has learned to get what he wants by crying; when he becomes next youngest to the baby he gets what he wants by temper tantrums. Children may have temper tantrums up to the time they go to school. If a child is *muy encaprichudo,* or very willful, demanding, or stubborn, his temper tantrums may not be tolerated, and he may be subject to beatings and punishments during this period.

The importance of the grandmother to the child who is displaced by a new sibling cannot be overemphasized. Sending the disturbed or unhappy child to live with the grandmother is a traditional, almost institutionalized, way of handling the problem. The grandmother represents an adequate mother-substitute and softens the abruptness of the child's separation from his mother. The stereotype of the grandmother who is constant, loving, patient, and solicitous toward her grandchildren, while not true of every grandmother, is true of many. The child who has a grandmother is considered fortunate. The child who is difficult to wean, who is *chipil,* or who has many temper tantrums, is sent to the grandmother to receive the attention and care he craves. First-born sons and favorite children, whom the parents are reluctant to punish, are most often the ones to go. Children may stay with the grandmother for a month or a year or, not infrequently, until they marry.

After the birth of a new sibling, the next youngest child no longer sleeps with the mother. Occasionally the youngest child sleeps with the mother for five or more years because there is no one to displace him. In one case, the youngest son, who was also his mother's favorite, slept with her until he was ten. In another family a girl of five who had slept with her father since she was weaned was so attached to him that she would sleep with no one else. Occasionally, too, we found a grown boy still sleeping with his grandmother or older sister, to whom he had been transferred at the birth of another child. In the only case we have of sexual intercourse between children, a girl of eight and a boy of six, the boy said he had learned it from his older sister with whom he shared a *petate* at night.

Enuresis is very common up to the age of five and is not infrequent in boys and girls of seven. It is not considered very much of a problem, but children are sometimes scolded and shamed for doing it. Some parents attempt to curb enuresis by insisting that the children urinate before going to sleep. Children are urged to go to the patio during the night, but parents do not get up to remind them or take them. Although urine tends to pulverize the straw of the *petate,* so that eventually it must be replaced, parents do not express annoyance or concern over this. The *petates* are washed in the morning or merely set in the sun to dry. Children up to the age of seven seldom sleep on a mattress, because of enuresis.

The transition from infancy to childhood is also characterized by less care concerning cleanliness. In general, the cleanest children in Tepoztlán are infants and school children. Children between the ages of two and six are often dirty and unkempt. In more acculturated families there is greater emphasis on cleanliness. Most children are bathed and have their clothing changed once a week, usually on Sunday. In a few families children may be bathed and changed every three or five days. These families also exhort their children to wash their face and hands before eating, but most children receive no training in this until they go to school. Poorer families, which are in the majority, do not wash and change clothes often, as a matter of economy; soap is expensive, and clothing, which is scrubbed on stones, tends to wear out more quickly with frequent washings. In the past, because of greater poverty, people washed and changed clothes once in fifteen days.

Children are bathed in warm water by the mother or older sister, up to the age of seven or eight. They stand for the bath, and their bodies and hair are scrubbed with soap and a pad of rough *ixtle.* The water is poured over their heads, and the soap gets in their eyes. Children do not appear to enjoy the bath as infants do and show much fear of the water. In families in which the children early acquire a sense of shame (usually the more acculturated families), boys of five may refuse to be bathed by their mothers and will accompany their elder brothers to the ravine. Girls exhibit shame earlier than boys, concerning nudity. I saw a ten-year-old boy, stark naked in the patio, being bathed by his grandmother. He seemed a little concerned about hiding his genitals but otherwise showed no embarrassment. This situation, which is unusual in the village, was explained by the fact that the boy was an only child and the favorite of his grandmother, who had bathed him from infancy.

Except during the bath, children are never seen without clothes. Boys who are not yet toilet trained sometimes go without pants, but this is very rare over age five. On the whole, nakedness or incomplete dress is associated with poverty, neglect, and immorality. One of the major reasons given for keeping children fully clothed is to prevent masturbation.

Masturbation is not tolerated at any age and is swiftly punished. Punishment consists of slapping the hands, beating, shaming, and frightening. One boy of five was severely beaten with a rope by his father without explanation because the latter saw the boy holding his penis. One woman threw stones at her eight-year-old daughter and called her names when she saw her examining her genitals while urinating. Children who show interest in their body are *viciosa* or *maliciosa* and are called names, such as *cochino* (pig) and *puerco* (hog). Parents who fail to correct their children are called *imoral* or *indecente*. Careful parents keep their children off the streets for fear that they might learn masturbation from their friends. Although occasionally an incorrigible boy may be seen to masturbate surreptitiously, with his hands in his pockets, it is rare to see a child touching his genitals. If masturbation occurs it is secretive.

Between the ages of two and five, children are free to devote themselves entirely to play. Small children are limited, for the most part, to playing in the patio or corral. The only time they are seen in the streets is when they are accompanied by some older member of the family. (See Fig. 54.) They play alone or more usually

Fig. 54. Mother and child.

with brothers and sisters or cousins or perhaps neighbors, whose ages range from five to ten. Older children are required by the parents to play with their younger brothers or sisters, so that it is rare for the latter to be shut out of play. The older children are also expected to keep the younger ones contented and are responsible for their safety. As during infancy, a cry or complaint to the parents on the part of the youngest child usually brings scoldings or punishment down upon the older children. Small children frequently receive rough treatment during play, both intentionally and unintentionally, and are sometimes bribed by the older children not to inform the parents. In a few cases the younger child is the object of much hostility and rivalry on the part of his older siblings, and is subject to surreptitious abuse. In one case a three-year-old girl was hit and mistreated so often by her brothers and sisters, that, to protect her, her parents had to send her to stay with her grandmother.

Small children begin, at first in a passive way, to join the games of the older children as soon as they are able to understand what to do. Often the two-, three-, or four-year-old plays the part of the baby and is merely carried about, put to sleep, or fed in play. It is when they play at house, school, *compadres,* fiesta, baptism, musician, funeral, and other games imitating adult behavior, that the small child begins to learn the customs of the culture. Girls of five often beg for a little corn to grind and make into tortillas, or for a *rebozo* in which to wrap a rag doll. Boys of five imitate older boys' games, such as spinning tops or playing marbles. Other toys are rarely made or bought for children of this age group, and generally only favored children receive them. The majority of children content themselves with playing with sticks, stones, leaves, flowers, corncobs, etc. Pencils, crayons, and writing paper are considered too valuable for children to play with, and preschool children have very little experience with these articles, to say nothing of books and pictures.

It is difficult to get information concerning sex play of children. Questions about sex play of children received a blanket denial from parents, who maintained that their children are innocent and know nothing of life. But it is clear from the life stories we have taken that children have notions about sex, and sex play does occur secretively, particularly in playing house and at being *novios*. Girls of ten frequently teach smaller boys what to do.

For the most part children between two and four years of age are kept at home if there is someone to take care of them, because they are often too heavy to carry long distances and cannot walk well over the hilly, stone-paved streets. At four or five years, girls and boys often accompany their mothers to the plaza and may carry the can of corn or *nixtamal*. Some mothers report that their children are extremely timid when they first begin to go visiting or marketing, and nervous habits such as chewing at their clothing begin at that time.

children of school age: 17

GOING TO SCHOOL is the next most important step in the life of a Tepoztecan child. The kindergarten, which was founded in 1935, accepted children between the ages of three and six until 1947, when the lowest admitting age was changed to four. (See Fig. 55.) But only a small percentage of children attended so early. (See Table 56.) Many parents do not approve of beginning school at an early age, for it will "heat the heads" of the little ones. Fear for the physical safety of the small child is another factor delaying enrollment. In one family a favorite, only son was kept at home until he was nine, so that he would be able to defend himself against the attacks of older children. In another, a boy of five was withdrawn from kindergarten because older children had been sticking him with cactus spines. The age of enrollment is decided by parents, despite the law for attendance at age six.

Fig. 55. The kindergarten.

TABLE 56. Enrollment in Central School, 1941-1948.

Year	1st Grade		2nd Grade		3rd Grade		4th Grade		5th Grade		6th Grade		Total		Total
	B	G	B	G	B	G	B	G	B	G	B	G	B	G	
1941	86	55	82	57	48	22	29	37	26	9	23	8	294	188	482
1942	77	69	76	44	53	26	33	34	21	11	14	6	274	190	464
1943	:	:	:	:	:	:	:	:	:	:	:	:	:	:	:
1944	89	80	78	68	64	56	56	38	31	19	13	19	331	280	611
1945	77	86	66	53	53	53	39	31	28	19	21	14	284	256	540
1946	83	68	72	72	74	61	50	52	35	24	30	20	344	297	641
1947	80	66	62	65	89	59	48	50	29	23	30	12	338	275	613
1948	99	68	61	68	93	63	65	63	44	34	26	19	388	315	703

Enrollment in Central Kindergarten, 1941-1948.[a]

Year	1st Grade		2nd Grade		3rd Grade		Total		Total
	B.	G.	B.	G.	B.	G.	B.	G.	
1941	17	18	26	21	18	25	61	64	125
1942	28	32	10	18	20	29	58	79	137
1943	:	:	:	:	:	:	:	:	:
1944	11	17	13	14	28	29	52	60	112
1945	12	4	10	16	16	21	38	41	79
1946	8	11	27	13	38	25	73	49	122
1947	13	15	11	8	21	15	45	38	83
1948	:	:	22	27	24	18	46	45	91

[a] The kindergarten is divided into three grades. The first is for the children of four years, the second for five-year-olds, and the third for six-year-olds.

In any one year, school enrollment is highest in the first and second grades and successively lower in the third, fourth, fifth, and sixth grades. As each class is promoted, the number of pupils declines.

For example, if we follow the class of 1941 from the second grade we find the following drop in enrollment:

Year	Grade	Enrollment		Total
		Boys	Girls	
1941	Second	82	57	139
1942	Third	53	26	79
1943	Fourth	—	—	—
1944	Fifth	31	19	50
1945	Sixth	21	14	35

Between the second and third grade, the drop in enrollment was over 40 per cent. Although the average decline is less than that, it is high enough to reflect the negative attitude of parents toward education. The ability to read and write on a simple level satisfies the standards of most mothers and fathers.

Despite this widespread attitude, total school enrollment has increased steadily. There has been an increase of more than 50 per cent in school attendance between 1941 and 1948. In 1941, approximately 49 per cent of the children between age six and fifteen were enrolled in school. A greater proportion of boys (56 per cent) of this age group than girls (41 per cent) went to school. In the other six years for which we have figures, the enrollment of girls is consistently less than boys in each age group.

According to the teaching staff of the central school (see Fig. 56), the most serious problem is attendance. Absence from school is extremely high during all the important fiestas and in the months of June and July, when there is a great deal of work in the fields. Truancy among boys in the third and fourth grades is also high. Only a minority of the parents feel obligated to give school priority over such activities as helping at home or in the field, and this minority is generally in the middle economic group. The wealthy, who own many animals, and the poor, who "have nothing," depend more upon their children's labor. The school staff is helpless in putting pressure on those parents who keep their children home from school, and must depend upon the local officials whose policy it is to do nothing to incur the anger of the voters unnecessarily.

Tardiness is also a serious problem since parents, in general, are not time conscious, and often keep a child at home until he has completed his chores. This situation has been met by ringing the church bell each morning and afternoon, and by arranging a competition for punctuality among the classes.

In the kindergarten and first grade, the fearfulness and crying of the children are problems. Each year, at the beginning of the term, five to eight children cry chronically and must be sent home. The first-grade teacher observed that the children who had attended kindergarten before entering her class showed much

Fig. 56. The central school, seen from inside the patio.

less fear of strangers than did older children entering the first grade without previous school experience. This attests to the importance of the socializing role of the school in Tepoztlán. Children in the two lowest groups, as well as in the second grade, are frequently too timid to ask to be taken to the toilet, with unfortunate results. In the second grade, for the most part, teachers note that the children are more self-confident and more mischievous. They still cry readily but for such reasons as not being able to do the work, being assigned to another group, or being sent to the blackboard.

In the third and fourth grades, teachers note that the children tend to be less respectful and more disobedient. But at the same time they seem to be more afraid of their parents than before and often, for fear of being scolded, fail to take home messages from school, asking for contributions, a new notebook, or a costume for a school function.

The pupils in the fifth and sixth grades are described as being the "most obedient and respectful and the most studious." These two grades usually have the best attendance records.

It is interesting to note that in the third and fourth grades, among the boys and girls of from nine to twelve years of age, there is voluntary segregation according to sex. In the lower grades boys and girls play freely together, and in the two upper grades there is much courtship.

The influence of the school has been profound, not only for those who attend classes but for the village as a whole. This is especially true in recent years. Although schools have existed in the village for about a century, they formerly affected only a small percentage of better-to-do families. It was the great expansion of education after the Revolution that made the school a more significant factor in local life.

For most Tepoztecan children, the school is not only a source of learning the usual academic skills but also of learning new ways of living. The children are taught to wash their hands before meals, to brush their teeth, to wear clean clothing, to use handkerchiefs, to cover up coughs and sneezes, and to be punctual. They acquire new knowledge of germs, vitamins, diet, dress, social participation, and cooperation. On a different level the school teaches respect and love for the mother, and children are encouraged to make or buy a gift on Mother's Day. Through Children's Day, for which the parents and teachers collect money to buy goodies and take the children into the fields for a picnic, consideration for the needs of children is engendered. The school also encourages the celebration of family birthdays, with felicitations and small gifts.

The extent to which these teachings are practiced in daily life is difficult to determine, but they appear to be minimal. This does not mean that they are rejected; on the contrary they are generally taken to be desirable and are supplying new standards and goals. So far as we can determine, new practices are not introduced at home because of the resistance of parents to spending money on such articles as toothpaste, toothbrushes, and handkerchiefs. Some mothers complain that their children, particularly the daughters, become too fussy about being clean and refuse to go out in even slightly soiled clothing.

There is a growing tendency for young married couples, who have become independent of their parents, to practice what they have learned at school as soon as they are financially able. The young people who have attended school outside the village are more immediately and permanently affected by the school experience. Sometimes the difference in way of life between the parents and son or daughter who has been educated outside is extreme, and is reminiscent of the contrast between immigrant parents and their children born and reared in a different land.

In Tepoztlán, however, the educated person who returns to the village and lives in poverty usually reverts to the old ways.

Going to school has a different significance for girls than for boys. Girls tend to associate going to school with freedom and pleasurable activity. Being away from home and the surveillance of the mother for six hours a day and having the opportunity to play with children of the same age, to form friendships with other girls, and to meet boys, are some of the advantages school offers to girls. (Fig. 57.) They tend to feel deprived at having to leave school, and many cry and express resentment when forced to do so. Boys, on the other hand, tend to associate school with

Fig. 57. Going to school frees many girls from heavy chores.

confinement, and generally do not resist staying home from school to work. From the third grade on, many of them often play truant (*pintar venado*) to go swimming, to play games, or to go to a nearby town. Most boys look forward to the time when they will withdraw from school permanently to become farmers.

Most Tepoztecan mothers are accustomed to putting children to work as soon as they are physically able, and to keep them at home, available to do tasks as they arise. The amount of work to be done at home by boys and girls of school age varies from family to family, and frequently depends upon the degree of control the mother has over her children. Parents traditionally punish young recalcitrants severely, so that by the time they are ready to assume regular tasks there is no question of obedience. Play has always been, and still is, viewed by most parents as a possible source of danger and a waste of time. Attendance at school has caused parents to modify their view of children as a source of labor and has disrupted the traditional division of labor within the home. It has thrown a heavier burden of work on the mother, who depended upon her children for assistance, and on the father, who now must do some of the minor chores traditionally done by boys.

School has not only helped to reduce the amount of daily work done by children, but has postponed for many the age at which they work to contribute to their own support. Going to school has taken children out of the limited sphere of parental influence and has awakened new desires. One immediate and obvious effect of school has been the great increase in the desire of children to meet friends and to play after school. They are no longer always content to return home and remain within the patio walls, at the beck and call of their mother. In many families there is a constant tug of war between parents and children over how much time is to be given to play. Children are more difficult to control, and some parents find it necessary to withdraw their children from school or to punish them frequently. In the past, by the time a child reached nine or ten years of age he seldom required a beating; he had learned to obey. Today, obedience from a child of school age, particularly a boy, is maintained by the parents with continued application of "a strong hand."

In general, boys have more freedom to play than girls. But even when boys still too young to go to the fields with their father are not required to work at home, it is thought highly desirable for them to play at home with brothers and sisters. More "careful" parents try to keep their young sons off the streets, to protect them from learning "malice" from other boys, who are invariably described as "bad companions." But, as we have indicated, it is difficult for the mother to control sons, in the absence of the father. Boys from the age of six to ten frequently are seen playing in the street.

With few exceptions, girls are much more under the control of their mothers than boys are. Girls play in snatches between errands and chores, and as they grow older, less and less time for play is available. The burden of household work usually falls on the eldest daughter, although in most families all girls over ten are pressed into continual service. There is a particularly sharp, consistent drop in the enrollment of girls in school after the fourth grade, and approximately half of the school girls between ages ten and eleven are withdrawn from school to help with the younger children at home. (See Fig. 58.) Under special circumstances—such as the death of either parent, the birth of a new sibling, or the inability of the mother to take care of many school children or many grown sons unassisted—a girl may be permanently withdrawn from school before the age of ten. By the time a girl is twelve or thirteen she is considered too mature to attend school because of the possibility of involvements with boys, and she is generally kept at home. A very small percentage of girls attend school until the sixth grade. They are usually, though not necessarily, from middle-group or better-to-do families and often continue their schooling to become teachers or dressmakers. These girls are almost the only girls in the village who enjoy daily leisure and have some personal freedom.

Children of school age play a wide variety of games, some of which are learned and played at school, but most games are learned from older children. In the latter group are some games which have in all probability been played for hundreds of years, and others were taught in the schools before and just after the Revolution. Most of the games played in Tepoztlán are well known in other parts of Mexico and Latin America.

A comparison of some of the old and new games reveals significant contrasts and is suggestive of the type of influence being exerted by the school. The older games are characterized by quiet play, relatively little physical exertion, little or no

Fig. 58. Child nurses.

physical skill or individual competition (except for marbles and tops), and loosely organized play groups. These games also reflect, to a striking degree, the customs, religion, and temperament of the people. Most of the older games involve running and tagging, singing, responding, and imitating adult life. Choosing between alternatives and receiving punishment in the form of work tasks are also common features.

In contrast, the games taught at school are those in which teamwork, competition, scoring, definite goals, loyalty, leadership, sportsmanship, and physical exertion have an important place. This is especially true of games organized for boys and older girls. These games are popular among the young people and are played with enthusiasm.[1]

The range of activities of boys and girls varies widely insofar as work, school, and play are concerned, and can best be appreciated by describing some cases. The following brief accounts of three boys and three girls represent both the extreme and the middle-of-the-road type. The extreme of more work than play, and almost no schooling, is perhaps the most widespread situation in Tepoztlán.

---

[1] See Appendix F, p. 491, for list of games most commonly played in school and at home by Tepoztecan children.

ELEUTERIA V.: Eleuteria is sixteen years old and the oldest child in the family. Her mother is a widow who supports her children by teaching school. Eleuteria had to take care of five younger brothers and sisters from the time she was seven and one-half years of age. She attended school for one and one-half years until she was nine. During this time she helped her mother cook, sweep, carry water, and make tortillas. Before going to school in the morning she cleaned the house and on her return she took care of her sisters and brothers. She liked school but she was always tired, and when her mother suggested that she stay home all the time Eleuteria was glad to. She then did all the work of the house. She bathed and dressed the children, washed and ironed their clothing, and did all the cooking. At that time she was still young enough to be afraid to lift the hot *comal* off the fire. She also ground the corn and coffee. Eleuteria envied the girls in the neighborhood who could play, and sometimes she tied her youngest brother to her back with her *rebozo* in order to join their games. She did this in the greatest secrecy because if her mother had known, she would have been severely punished. Her mother often scolded or beat Eleuteria for not doing her work well or for letting anything happen to the smaller children. Eleuteria frequently scolded and hit her brothers and sisters to get them to obey her. When her younger sister was able to help at home, Eleuteria went to work at a corn mill for sixty centavos a day. She used this money to buy herself clothing and sometimes little toys or goodies for her younger brothers and sisters. She always cleaned the house before going to work in the morning and did the heavy washing and ironing at night.

FELICITA Z.: Felicita is fifteen years old. She lives with her mother, stepfather, three older brothers, and three younger half-brothers and sisters. Felicita was enrolled in school at the age of seven and attended irregularly until she was ten. Her mother kept her home at the slightest pretext, and Felicita learned very little. When she was ten, another child was born, and Felicita was withdrawn from school. Felicita cried when she was taken out of school, not because she liked to study but because she could no longer see her friends or play at school. She went about her work sullenly and took little interest in it. Everyone considered her lazy and bad tempered, and her younger brothers and sisters were afraid of her. Her mother complained that she had to shout and scold, or hit the girl, to get her to do her work. Once her mother threw a stone at Felicita and bruised her badly because she had played deaf when she was called. Felicita refused to go on errands for her grandmother or aunt who lived nearby unless they gave her five centavos in payment. When Felicita was ten she once expressed fear (to the investigator who knew her then) of becoming fifteen, because then she would have to do heavier work. Now at fifteen she still goes about her work unwillingly but is much less sullen and resentful. She takes more interest in her appearance and is happier because she has nicer clothes. Whenever her mother promises to buy something for her, she does her work with a will.

CARMEN G.: Carmen, age seventeen, is the youngest daughter in a well-to-do family. She lives with her parents and older brother. She has two older sisters, both of whom have had an advanced education and are now married. Carmen attended school from kindergarten to the sixth grade and was absent only when ill. She never did any work at home during this time because her older sisters helped her mother. Carmen had many friends and spent all her time playing with them, either at her home or theirs. At the age of twelve, Carmen was sent to Mexico City where she lived with her mother's sister and attended a secondary school. She studied dressmaking and learned to do fine work. After she had completed her course she began to earn a comparatively good salary and wanted to continue living in the city. But her parents did not think it proper for a single girl to live away from home and insisted that she return. Her two sisters had married, and her mother needed help. At sixteen, Carmen returned discontentedly because there was no market for her expensive work in the village. It soon became evident that Carmen was not going to be of much assistance at home. When she was asked to do any work in the kitchen she developed a backache or a headache and had to lie down. If she was sent to the plaza to buy anything, she returned with inferior articles for which she had paid too much. After a while one of the married sisters took over the family marketing, and Carmen now spends most of the day making dresses and blouses for herself or going for walks with some of her friends, all girls who have been educated outside of the village. She gives frequent parties and dances at home for her friends of both sexes and attends the public dances in the plaza. Her parents disapprove of her parties, but they permit her to have her own way. Most people in the village, except some of the younger ones, disapprove of her.

Albino R.: Albino is thirteen years old and is the youngest child. He lives with his parents and older brother. An older sister is married and lives away. His father works on a hacienda and comes home every eight days. His brother works as a laborer in Tepoztlán. The family is landless and poor. Neither Albino nor his brother and sister went to school for more than two years, and all are practically illiterate. His mother kept Albino and his sister at home to do errands. Albino, from the age of eight, had to take his brother's horse to and from the pasture. Albino was always at the beck and call of his mother, and if he wandered too far or played too much he received a sound beating. When he was ten the family acquired a burro, and the boy was withdrawn from school in order to guard the burro and the horse in the pasture. From age ten to thirteen, Albino did nothing but this work and ran errands for his mother. Since the family is landless, the boy never had an opportunity to learn to farm. When he is fifteen he will be hired out as a day laborer.

Juan R.: Juan is fifteen and has lived with his widowed grandmother from the time he was weaned. His mother, stepfather, and married uncle live on the same *sitio*. Juan entered school at eight and attended irregularly until he was twelve years old. During this time he took his grandmother's cows to and from pasture and sometimes accompanied his uncle to the fields in order to learn to farm. He also carried water and helped his grandmother gather wood, though sometimes he was disobedient and refused to do anything. After school hours, he played in the street with his friends or joined a baseball or basketball game in the school yard. As he grew older he began to stand at street corners with older boys. He frequently stayed away from school to go swimming and did not come home until late. His teachers twice complained about his behavior in school. His grandmother was afraid "something bad would happen to him," and in order to make him more "serious" took him out of school and put him to work full time in the fields with his uncle. She attributed his behavior to the fact that he did not have a father to fear. Juan was sorry to leave his friends but was happy to go to work with his uncle and soon forgot about school. He worked hard and gave all his money to his grandmother. He occasionally went out with his friends in the evening but was usually tired and went to bed early. By the time he was fifteen, his grandmother had saved enough money for him to buy a burro. After that he became "very serious" and always brought her all the wood and water she needed and worked like a man in the fields. Juan is very contented and looks forward to the time he will receive the land which his grandmother has promised him as an inheritance.

HIGINIO F.: Higinio is fifteen and lives with his parents and five younger brothers and sisters. His father is a former schoolteacher, merchant, and bus driver. At present his father is an official of one of the local bus companies. Higinio had been sickly as a child, and it was early decided that he was better suited to the life of a student than to that of a farmer. He was enrolled in kindergarten at the age of five and, except for one year which he lost because of illness, he attended regularly until he completed the sixth grade. During the time he went to school his father did not permit him to play in the street or to have friends. If he was found playing marbles with other boys, as he frequently was, or if he delayed too long in running an errand, he was severely scolded or spanked by his father. Higinio was required to take care of his youngest brother after school hours. Higinio has never gone to the fields and knows nothing of taking care of animals or farming. Nor has he ever gone to the hills to gather firewood, and only occasionally is he asked to carry water. Higinio attended religious classes at the church for many years. He reads a good deal at home, and his parents have encouraged this by buying him a book from time to time. When Higinio was thirteen, he entered a secondary school in Cuernavaca since he could ride on the bus every day without charge. His parents hope to be able to have him educated to be a lawyer.

adolescence,
courtship, and marriage: 18

THE PERIOD between childhood and adulthood is relatively ill-defined in Tepoztlán and unmarked by special occasion or ceremony. In the recent past, this interim was brief or non-existent for girls. Until about age twelve, girls were called *niña* or *sisigwa,* and from twelve to fourteen they were called *señorita* or *ichpokame.* But because of early marriage most girls passed directly from *niña* to *señora. Señoritas* who did not marry soon were *solteras* or *ichpokath.* At the present time in Tepoztlán, girls are *niñas* until about age fifteen and are *señoritas* between about fifteen and twenty. Though girls over twenty are still *señoritas* they are viewed as *solteras.* Both the period of childhood and marriageability have been lengthened by several years. A majority of the parents withdraw their daughters from school at about twelve, the age at which girls were married a generation ago. This practice extends the interim period rather than childhood, because girls of twelve and over conduct themselves more like *señoritas* than like *niñas.*

The situation was and is quite different for boys, who, unlike girls, were not hurried into adulthood by early marriage. In the past, as well as now, boys are called *muchachos* or *piltontle* from about age seven to seventeen or eighteen. There is no native term to differentiate any periods within this wide age range. After seventeen or eighteen, boys are called *jóvenes, muchachos,* or *telpokath.* This period varies considerably in length, since there is no set or recommended age for marriage for boys. Compared with girls, the change in age status of boys occurs later, more gradually, and with less strain. Today the development of boys is even slower because the assumption of full-time adult work, which for many in the past took place at about ten years of age, now generally occurs at fifteen. Childhood, or the period of play and education, has thus been lengthened, and boys may go to school as late as fourteen years of age without incurring criticism.

ADOLESCENCE

The intermediate period between childhood and adulthood begins to have the characteristics of adolescence, as we know it, and some of the better educated people in Tepoztlán now use this term. There are, however, several fundamental differences to be kept in mind. In Tepoztlán, adolescents generally work for their parents and do not attend school. Thus, rather than becoming more of an economic burden at this time, they are a decided economic asset to the family. The dependence of the parents upon the children becomes clearer during adolescence, and as a result the young people tend to have a more secure position in the family. The strongly authoritarian family and other factors have tended to produce passive, dependent youths rather than youths noted for initiative, ambition, drive, and independence.

In contrast with our own society, there is in Tepoztlán, with the outstanding exception of courtship and elopement, a notable absence of open "revolt" against the authority and example of parents or against local tradition. A very small percentage of the youths are willing or able to strike out on new paths or leave home to seek more profitable work elsewhere, and those who do, invariably have the support and backing of their parents. There is no pattern of running away from home "to seek one's fortune," although it may occur among boys when home conditions are unbearable.

The only evidences of a sharp break with tradition come from the small group of boys and girls who have studied outside the village and returned imbued with new customs and ideas. A small minority, they are nevertheless extremely important, since they serve as models for the youth of the village. Although few village youths imitate the style of dress and of manners of their educated neighbors, many undoubtedly would if they could. There is among the young people a vague desire for self-improvement and a more enjoyable, comfortable life. This wish finds immediate expression in a desire for better clothing, shoes, beds, and so on. *Señoritas* particularly want attractive dresses, jewelry, cold cream, fine soap, and talcum. The more sophisticated now use cosmetics, nail polish, and hair curlers, attend public dances, and have friends of their own. Some few even drink and smoke in great secrecy. Boys want free time and money for the new sports and to go to Cuernavaca occasionally. Almost all young people would like to travel, go to the city, attend movies, and have some money to spend.

These aspirations sometimes engender conflict with the parents, but in most cases the young people do not express their desires. Nevertheless, we heard parents complain that the young people are becoming more difficult to control.

In terms of behavior and experience, the period of adolescence has different, almost contrasting, significance for boys and girls. For girls, it brings added confinement, personal restrictions, chaperonage, the conflict and fear as well as the excitement of secret courtship, the discovery of which often brings shame and harsh punishment. Girls also assume at this time a greater burden of not entirely desirable work, with few rewards. Boys, on the other hand, have greater freedom than before and receive more respectful treatment at home. They do work which they generally enjoy and which brings many rewards. Youths have an increasing number of diversions in which most of them are free to indulge, and courtship is a source of satisfaction and sense of achievement. In view of these differences, a discussion of adolescence should consider the adolescent girl and boy separately.

THE ADOLESCENT GIRL

Although a girl becomes a *señorita* at fifteen, adolescence may be said to begin at twelve or thirteen. At this age girls are withdrawn from school to stay at home and work with the mother. They are expected to give up friends and habits of play and to devote themselves to caring for younger siblings and doing household chores. Some girls of this age are reluctant to discontinue their former activities and receive a good deal of punishment before they resign themselves to it.

At a girl's fifteenth birthday, her parents prepare her for marriage by presenting her with a pair of shoes for holidays, a bright colored dress and apron, and perhaps a pair of silver or gold earrings. Even very poor parents make an effort to give their daughter new clothing to attract a husband. Girls are very pleased by this and pay much attention to their appearance. They generally look better groomed than either *niñas* or married women. Despite the new clothes and other finery, some girls are reluctant to become *señoritas* because they have even less freedom and are expected to do more work at home. They must now do everything that a married woman does, wash and iron the heavier clothes, as well as the badly soiled ones, sew, grind corn, make larger tortillas, grind coffee, cook all the food eaten by the family, learn to make *mole* and prepare fiesta dishes, and also sometimes go for water. In addition the girls are given almost entire care of their younger brothers and sisters. The girls are held responsible if the children are hurt, become ill, or are naughty. Usually the older girls are permitted to punish their charges lightly and to send them on errands, but they do not have full authority, even when the mother is not at home. In general the elder girls are expected to defer to the younger ones and to be protective and compliant. If a younger brother or sister complains to the mother about the older girl, she may be punished.

The contrast between the girls who stay at home and those who continue going to school is striking. The educated girl usually does very little housework, assisting only with the lighter tasks. She has more leisure time, more friends, and is generally less restricted by her parents. Even if she does no professional work after completion of school, she automatically enjoys a higher status than do her less educated peers. These girls tend to marry late because of the difficulty of finding a suitable husband. Girls who continue to go to school until fifteen years of age or longer are a particular source of apprehension to their parents. As a precaution, and at much expenditure of time and money, girls who attend school out of town are taken to and from school by one of the parents or an elder brother on week-ends or holidays.

After menstruation occurs, the mother becomes more strict in her surveillance of her daughter. The most emphatic restriction and discipline are applied to the adolescent girl in her relations with boys. She is warned over and over that the worst thing she could do is speak to a boy or pay attention to anything he might say to her. She is told that boys are dangerous and often the cause of disgrace, and that only crazy or "bad" girls have anything to do with them before marriage. Girls are warned not to bring shame to the parents and they are threatened with severe punishment. Girls are so guarded that a delay in returning from an errand may be cause for a sharp scolding or slap. Ideally, the girl is not supposed to leave the house unaccompanied, though expediency frequently demands that she does.

The responsibility of guarding the chastity and reputation of one or more daughters of marriageable age is often felt to be a burden by the mother. One mother said that she wished her fifteen-year-old daughter would marry soon because it was inconvenient to "spy" on her all the time.

For most girls, the appearance of the first menses is a traumatic experience. Many fear it signifies that they are no longer virgins, others that they have an internal lesion and will bleed to death. Most girls associate it with something shameful, dirty, and even punishable, and keep it secret from parents and sisters. A very much frightened girl sometimes seeks reassurance by confiding in her grandmother or in a friend. Girls who are still in school at an age when there is interest in such matters generally learn some of the facts of menstruation from other girls. There is a tendency for more educated girls to feel less guilt and be less secretive about menstruation both in school and at home, but almost all girls express shame and disgust in connection with it.

When girls married before puberty, it was widely believed that menstruation was caused by sexual intercourse. When marriages began to take place after puberty, this belief broke down and is no longer held by most people, but it still persists among some. For example, an uncle, who accidentally became aware that his fifteen-year-old niece was menstruating, denounced the girl as not being a virgin and scolded her mother for not guarding her.

The grandmother, or the mother when she learns of it, gives the girl advice on proper care during menstruation. Most warn against bathing or washing the feet or eating "cold" foods, such as pork, avocado, beans, and lemon, since these are believed to stop the flow. Menstruation is expected to last three days, and the flow is generally sparse, requiring only the wearing of an extra pair of underdrawers. If the flow is longer than three or four days, there is some concern over it, and herb medicines are usually taken.

The adjustment of the adolescent girl to her situation at home varies considerably. In large part it depends upon the girl's relations with the mother, since it is with her that there is most contact. The close relationship of the adolescent girl with her mother is recent in Tepoztlán, for child marriage and patrilocal residence in past years effectively severed the mother-daughter tie. The young daughter-in-law was looked upon as the main source of assistance for the mother. Now it is the grown daughter who partially fills this role. Her work is obligatory, "Why then do we rear children except to help us?" The mother of a grown girl is considered fortunate because "now she has someone to work for her."

Many of the attitudes of the mother-in-law toward the daughter-in-law have been carried over to the daughter. There is a tendency for mothers to "retire" from most of the heavy household duties and to shift the major burden of the household upon the daughters, assuming the role of director rather than partner. Many mothers are critical, demanding, and querulous with their daughters and scold them at little provocation. Mothers also tend to spend a good part of the time in gossiping with neighbors or visitors, going to the plaza, and visiting relatives. Some take jobs or start up small businesses and are away from home much of the day.

The pleasanter or more rewarding aspects of an adolescent girl's life are the new clothes and little luxuries her parents see fit to buy for her, trips to the plaza or mill, and attendance at church and fiestas. The majority of girls are permitted only a minimum of these. Rewards in terms of higher status, increased respect or authority, or expressions of appreciation or praise are generally absent. Courtship provides a great deal of excitement but also is a source of worry and fear.

THE ADOLESCENT BOY

It is at the beginning of adolescence that boys begin to work seriously at farming, which is the most important and most respected work in the village. The improved status of boys, their larger share of food, clothing, and spending money, and their increasing authority over younger brothers and sisters, all stem from this. Boys of thirteen and fourteen, who may still be in school, begin to chafe under the confinement, authority, and "childishness" of school, and long to do farming and partake in its rewards. This coincides with the wishes of most parents, for boys of this age generally spend their days working under the supervision of their fathers. Boys who are orphans or whose family owns no land may work with an uncle or brother-in-law during the learning period and later work as hired hands for others. Boys in very poor families sometimes work at simpler tasks for wages several years before adolescence, but this is no longer common.

The work relations of father and son are generally smoother than that of mother and daughter. The more authoritarian, reserved figure of the father usually inspires the son to complete obedience. Fathers also tend to be more patient and less hurried in teaching their sons, and the work is done side by side, with the father usually taking the heavier burden.

Interest and participation in sports and other "modern" diversions are becoming characteristic of adolescent boys and older youths in Tepoztlán. Although recreational activities are still quite limited in Tepoztlán, especially when compared with the United States, there is much resistance to them on the part of the older generation. Not only is play generally viewed as a small child's activity exclusively but, even for children, it is often thought of as being a waste of time and having a strong element of danger. In the case of sports for boys of thirteen to twenty or more years of age, it is considered harmful and unnecessary. Parents believe that sports consume the precious energy needed in the milpas; they say that the ax, machete, and team of oxen provide all the exercise a farmer can endure. Mothers complain that their sons get overheated and are particularly liable to *los aires*. Older men tend to dislike the new sports because they are successfully pushing out the older diversions, such as *jaripeos* and cockfights.[1]

---

[1] For a discussion of new sports and forms of diversion for young people, see Chapter 9, "Wealth Differences and Levels of Living," p. 208.

COURTSHIP

Courtship before marriage is relatively new in Tepoztlán. Before the Revolution most marriages were arranged by the parents, with or without the consent of the children. Girls married at a very early age, leaving little opportunity for courtship. From the life stories of informants now in their fifties, we learn that in some cases young people did not know each other before marriage and met for the first time at the wedding ceremony in the church. Parents frequently had to threaten their young daughters with physical punishment to get them to consent to the marriage. The following excerpt from the life story of a woman, now a widow of sixty, is quite typical:

I was eleven years old when a boy came from Gabriel Mariaca to ask for my hand. He came with his parents and a jar of silver money. But my grandmother became angry and told them I was still a child, and she didn't want to see me going about carrying babies yet. When I was twelve my mother took me home again. Then a boy of sixteen came to ask for me, and my mother said yes. She told me that she wanted me to marry before something bad happened to me. I did not want to marry, especially because I did not know who the boy was. My mother said that if I did not say yes to the priest in the church she would throw me down from the top of the church. I was afraid and did what my mother told me.

Often young people knew each other, at least by sight, but contacts were few, brief, and secretive. Being *novios* at that time meant only that the parents had made arrangements for the marriage, and the date had been set. *Novios* were not permitted to be alone together at any time before marriage. In a few better-to-do and literate families, *novios* would court secretly by exchanging love letters.

Today courtship before marriage is common. Parents lament the changing of the old ways and are concerned over the fact that boys and girls have many opportunities to become acquainted with one another, particularly at school. Indeed, it is unusual for a girl over thirteen or a boy over fifteen not to have a *novio*. The local priest has recognized this and has stated in doctrinal classes that having a *novio* is not a sin, and the girls need no longer mention it at confession. But, he added, it is a sin to be *novios* for more than six months before marriage. It is common for girls to have an initial sense of guilt in accepting their first *novio*, but this is only a fleeting reaction, and girls are much more conscious of fear than guilt.

There is much secrecy surrounding courtship. A girl who is found to have a *novio* is severely punished by her parents. She may be beaten, denied food, not given new clothing, and not permitted to leave the house alone for a long time thereafter. There is a great readiness among the older generation, particularly among relatives, to inform a girl's parents if they see her talking or walking with a boy, and *novios* take extra precautions not to be seen by them.

Courtship is usually initiated by the boy. Fear of refusal is very strong, and he plans his conquest carefully and proceeds slowly. The timidity of boys in approaching a girl for the first time is the subject of much joking among girls. Drinking to bolster up their courage is common among boys setting out to court a girl. A boy may admire a girl from a distance for several weeks or months without declaring himself, or he will try to get her attention by staring hard at her (*echar el ojo castigado*).[2] (See Fig. 59.) If she notices it and smiles, he is encouraged to proceed

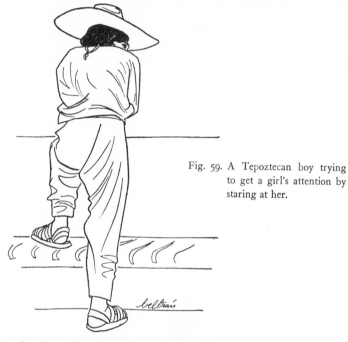

Fig. 59. A Tepoztecan boy trying to get a girl's attention by staring at her.

with the courting. Some few do not approach a girl themselves but do so through a go-between. Boys whose attentions are refused have been known to get drunk for days because of the humiliation. Occasionally a boy who is spurned will revenge himself by attacking the girl with the help of friends. A boy who has received encouragement from a girl in the form of smiles and direct glances and is subsequently rejected by her is especially outraged and feels justified in forcing himself upon her. Girls do not experience the tension and fear of rejection involved in initiating courtship, but they do fear revenge and must be very guarded in their manner with boys. The occasional girl who smiles directly at a boy, or gives him meaningful glances, has almost always set her heart upon him and is quite ready to accept him as a *novio*. Encouragement as open as this is usually successful, for it is a rare boy or man in Tepoztlán who would resist an easy conquest.

The first step in courting is to send the girl a letter declaring love. Occasionally, before writing, a youth may approach a girl in the street and detain her (*atajarla*)

---

[2] Other expressions used to describe a boy's flirting are *echar vidrio* and *están dandole un gallo la novia*.

and say, "*Señorita,* may I accompany you for a moment?" If the girl consents, he will at once propose that they be *novios,* and he then will begin to send her love letters. This approach is recent and is limited to those with more education or contact with the outside, or to those with courage enough to face a possible refusal or scolding from the girl. The writing of love letters is no longer limited to a few but has become widespread with increasing literacy. Young people who are unable to write well ask a friend with more education to do it for them. Girls and boys who have been to secondary school are particularly sought out as letter writers, and they derive a great deal of prestige in this way. The letters are written in flowery style and are usually copied out of a book of etiquette. A typical letter is the following:

Adored Señorita:

The impulses of my heart are such that they encourage even the most cautious man to commit indiscretion which sooner or later he will regret. Perhaps this will not happen to me in taking the liberty of writing this letter. My feelings are such that I am taking the liberty in order to ascertain my coming fate, pending the day when you honor me with your affirmative or negative response.

My soul is carried to the extreme in manifesting in exaggerated phrases, which are lacking in substance and sound, the love that you inspire. But do not think that because of this I do not feel a true passion for your incomparable beauty and goodness. The proof is that, despite the fear that my petition will be denied, I tremulously write this declaration and anxiously await the result, hoping that my love will be requited.

Favor me, Señorita, and attend my entreaty; and if, unutterable words, you feel a little sympathy toward one so audacious as to love you tenderly, communicate with me quickly and in all sincerity.

With all the sentiment which invades the heart of your respectful and constant adorer.

Your devoted servant,

A boy may send two or three such letters anonymously before he has the courage to affix his name. If a favorable reply is received, the boy arranges for a meeting. Any answer but an outright refusal is taken to be favorable; when a girl asks for time to think it over, a boy considers her his *novia.* It is a common sight to see a young boy loitering at a street corner for hours, waiting for an opportunity to get a glimpse of his *novia* or to say a few words to her. (See Fig. 60.) This "cornering" a girl (*esquiniar la muchacha*) is a regular courting practice in Tepoztlán. At night boys often gather at a corner to play the guitar and serenade a nearby *novia* of one of the group. A typical song is as follows:

> I come to greet you
> With this serenade of love.
> May you have no trouble,
> My charming angel.
>
> Your laughter or your fear
> Will tell me of your feelings.
> I am your faithful lover
> And adore you always.

There are enough flowers in my heart
To make a bouquet for you.
I shall be happy and you will have no trouble
When you enjoy my love.

Novios continue to write letters to one another because of the difficulty of getting together. There is, of course, much secrecy involved in the sending of letters. Many *novios* have a secret place to leave letters, or they may be delivered by a trusted friend or by a child hired for the purpose. Sometimes *novios* deliver letters to one another in passing. Some widows and girls are known to hire themselves for the purpose of delivering messages for lovers, to patch up quarrels, or

Fig. 60. A boy waiting hopefully at the plaza for a glimpse of his *novia*.

to convince a girl to become someone's *novia*. These women are known as *alcahuetes*. Another term for them is *corre-ve-y-dile* (run-see-and-tell). Both of these are insulting terms, and such go-betweens are strongly disapproved of; they are also suspected of knowing sorcery especially appropriate for *novios*.

Meetings between *novios* may take place at the fountain (Fig. 61), in the corral of the girl's house after dark, or in a deserted spot in the daytime, always with much apprehension about being discovered. If they are *novios* for the first time, acquaintanceship generally develops slowly. *Novios* generally caress and embrace but rarely kiss. Kissing is a modern innovation in courtship, and only the more sophisticated *novios* do so. Kissing is traditionally associated with religious worship,

Fig. 61. Courtship at the fountain.

kissing the saints and kissing the priest's hands. One girl, when asked whether she
ever kissed her *novio,* said, "What, is he a saint that I should kiss him?" Sexual
relations between *novios* occurs frequently but not, as believed by parents, inevitably. Among young people who are *novios* for the first time, sexual relations
may not occur until after one or even two years, or the pair may eventually separate
over the question. Among more mature *novios,* platonic relations are a rarity.
Ideally, both the boy and the girl are expected to be virgins at marriage, but it is
safe to say that most boys and some girls have sexual relations before marriage.

Young boys and girls often seek out older companions to learn from them the
art of courtship. Girls at school and in the Juventud Católica discuss their *novios,*
read each others' love letters, tell of experiences, and even tell off-color jokes and
stories. Boys entering their teens loiter among older boys at every opportunity.
The following excerpt from the story of one of our informants (now age forty) is a
typical experience:

When I was about fourteen, I managed to join up with some boys of eighteen and twenty.
They began to say, "How many *novias* have you?" I answered, "None." "How stupid!
Haven't you noticed the girl nearby who likes you?" They began to teach me how to
speak to *novias.*
Once a girl of about seventeen who lived near my house said to me, "I see you go out a

lot." I answered, "No." "Well," she said, "if I were a man I would have three *novias* at a time." "But I can't support a woman," I answered. "Well, let her support you," she said. I consulted my friends and told them of the conversation. They urged me on. Once I got up enough courage to tell the girl I loved her. I already had sexual desires, but I didn't know how to act or talk. I don't recall the year, but it was in 1915 or 1916 when one day in June I told her I liked her. On the day before the barrio fiesta, on August 5, she said to me, "Where have you been that I haven't seen you?" I asked to meet her and said I wanted to talk to her. She agreed to meet me that night. I threw little stones in the darkness to tell her I could come out. She told me to meet her behind the house. The night was pitch black, and there was a little drizzle. I began to make little noises to tell her where I was. I moved the little twigs. When she arrived I got the chills. She stopped about three feet in front of me and said, "Well, here I am, what did you want to talk about?" I didn't know what to say so I said, "Do you or don't you want to marry me?" "But I am older than you, perhaps your folks won't want you to." We were about two feet apart. "Come closer," I said, and I grabbed her and drew her under my serape. And then I got more chills. "What's the matter with you?" she said. "Do you have malaria?" Finally, I said, "Let us lie down here." She said no, and I said yes. It was yes, no, yes, no, until finally at about 3:00 A.M. we heard the *chirimía*, and since her father was to get up soon, she left and nothing happened. The next day, I saw her and she laughed at me. I told my friends what happened. They called me a fool and said, "Why did you just talk and talk instead of grab her and throw her down?" I never got beyond the *novio* stage. I never really got her. She had a serious lover who wanted to marry her. Once he asked me not to continue talking to her, and he threatened me. He was twenty, and I was fifteen, and I was very thin. Soon after that I bought a knife and always carried it with me for protection.

Being *novios* does not always mean that a boy and girl will marry. In the past, when a girl accepted a *novio* she usually expected him to become her husband. Today it is common to have several *novios* before marriage, and some girls and boys have several *novios* simultaneously, a practice which is considered dishonorable. A girl who has many *novios* is called *loca,* and a boy who has many *novias* is called *muy enamorado.* Boys often court girls for the purpose of having sexual relations and then abandon them.

Many young men resort to love magic when they have difficulty in courting a girl. The most common procedure is to use a powder made of crushed human skull bones. This powder is to be placed in the girl's right hand, in her hair, or in a sweet drink. Once this is done, it is believed the girl will begin to love the boy and miss him. Some men in Tepoztlán, and in other parts of Mexico, believe that the leg of a beetle placed in a girl's soda drink will get her very *loca* and make her desire sexual relations. Care is taken not to use too large a dose. The following story was told to illustrate what can happen when an overdose is given.

A youth of twenty-four liked a girl very much and decided to "corner" her and speak to her, but she insulted him. This happened three times. He still wanted her. A friend advised him to get some magical skull powder and put it into a drink for her. He did this but gave her too large a dose. Then the girl began to feel so much desire for him that she went to his house alone. The boy's parents refused to let her stay, and she became *loca* and a street woman. The authorities jailed her. Later a man took pity on her, married her, and "cured" her.

The use of sorcery for revenge is very much feared by those who have jilted or humiliated a *novio*. Young women are believed to take the picture of the former lover and stick pins in the head or breast or other part of his body, depending upon where she wishes to harm him. Often chronic illnesses in young men are attributed to some girl's black magic.

MARRIAGE

The traditional and most respectable form of arranging a marriage is the *petición de mano,* or asking for the hand of the girl.[3] This is done by the boy's father and his godfather of baptism. If the boy's father is dead, the mother may act as substitute; if the boy is an orphan, his godfather may go alone or with one of the boy's relatives, preferably the uncle. Formerly the parents chose a wife for their son and generally asked for his approval. Nowadays the procedure is reversed, with the boy indicating the desired girl to his father, and asking him to make the formal request for her hand. Most often the boy and girl are *novios* secretly before they inform their parents of a desire to marry. If so, the girl may ascertain her parents' attitude toward the marriage before a formal request is made. Sometimes the boy may first write a formal proposal of marriage to the girl's parents and only after getting a favorable reply will he ask his father to begin negotiations. When the boy's father and godfather appear at the girl's home, her parents, even though they plan to accept the offer, ask for a stay of a few weeks (*pedir un plazo*), as a matter of form, and the men are asked to return at the end of that time.

In cases where the boy and girl are not *novios* and where the matter was not prearranged, there is the humiliating possibility of the marriage request being refused. But, to avoid offending, direct refusals are rarely made. Various excuses may be given, and a long stay may be requested to consider the matter. A request for a stay of one year is generally taken to mean a negative reply, and few

[3] The only account of marriage customs which I have been able to locate in the historical documents dealing with Tepoztlán is found in the *Relación,* pp. 241-42, and is presumably a description of pre-Hispanic customs, as told to the Spanish officials by the natives. This account, though sketchy, suggests the existence of class differences in marriage customs and suggests patrilocal residence. It also reveals an example of the underlying similarity between native symbolism and Catholic ritual in parts of the marriage ceremony. The pertinent excerpt is as follows: ". . . and thus when a nobleman married he sent for the woman who was carried on a litter decorated with arches of flowers at midday, if she were from the upper class; but in the case of the daughter of a commoner, she was carried on the back [of someone] and they carried before her a burning torch of pine, one for her and one for her betrothed, and upon arriving at the house of the betrothed they took her into a small room, where there was a stone of the kind upon which they place the *olla* [for heating] and they commanded her to give them something as a sign that she was mistress of the house, and this done they allowed them to be there for four days, without one going to the other, and finally they took them out and washed them and dressed them and made a knot with the stuff of his garment and her *huipil,* and when this knot was made the marriage was completed. . . ."

Tepoztecan boys will wait that long. If the decision is favorable, the girl's parents may question the boy about his willingness to undertake the obligation of supporting a wife, and they may warn him that their daughter is young and inexperienced. They suggest that if he is unwilling to endure the girl's faults this is the time to say so, and the entire matter will be dropped. The boy is also warned that he must not blame his wife's parents or abandon his wife if he is dissatisfied with her after the marriage. At the same time the girl is advised that her life will be very different in the home of her husband and his parents. She is told that she must change her character and her ways. She must try to please her husband and his parents and work hard. She must learn to obey them and always ask her husband's permission to leave the house. She is warned not to be jealous or to heed gossip about her husband's affairs. If both the boy and girl agree to this, a date for the marriage is set.

One of the underlying principles in marriage arrangements in the past was the compensation of the bride's family for the loss of a working member. There was a formal bride price known as the *chichitomin,* which means payment for the mother's milk, that is, the milk used in raising the child. The *chichitomin* was paid in silver pesos, and the price varied from a few pesos to twenty-five or thirty. Many old people in the village still remember the payment of the bride price. It was also customary for the young man to bring wood and carry water for his future in-laws for a period of one or two years. In addition there was the custom known as the *puesto de flores,* whereby the boy's mother had to bring flowers and candles for the *santo* of the girl every eight days for a month before the marriage. The boy's parents were also expected to bring gifts of chocolate, bread, and wine each Sunday from the time of the *petición de mano* until the date of the marriage. Today the *puesto de flores* is rarely practiced, and no one now works for the father-in-law. But the boy's mother is still expected to bring gifts during the interval of the marriage negotiations.

When either set of parents refuses to give permission for the marriage, or if the couple have reason to believe that their parents will object in any way, the boy and girl will usually elope. Sometimes if a couple is seen together they will elope immediately, rather than have the girl punished by her parents. Elopements, which are known as *raptos,* consist of going away together and living as man and wife for a few days in the home of a well-disposed aunt or uncle or friend of the boy. Sometimes the boy brings the girl to his own home directly, or after a day or two. The girl is kept hidden until her parents stop looking for her, then the boy's father and godfather may visit the girl's parents and ask for their permission for the marriage. The elopement in most cases is for the purpose of breaking down resistance to the marriage, and often the girl's parents will accept it as a *fait accompli* and will agree to the marriage, in which case they may take the girl home and go through the proper procedure. But the girl's parents frequently remain angry and will not speak to either the boy or the girl for several years. If they get married, the parents may refuse to attend the marriage. In some cases the girl's parents may bring legal charges against the boy and try to get the girl home. If they are adamant and threatening, the boy may, in revenge, refuse to marry the girl and send her home where she will be severely beaten.

Raptos have existed as far back as informants can remember, but there is evidence that the number have increased considerably since the Revolution. During 1942 and 1943, approximately fifty per cent of all marriages began as elopements. This is symptomatic of the breakdown of parental authority and the increasing independence of young people. In the majority of cases after elopement, the respective *padrinos* of the boy and girl will intercede and bring pressure upon the couple to marry. Most elopements end in marriage. Of the thirty elopements in the village during 1942 and 1943 all but three ended in marriage. In these three cases the girls were orphans, with no one to intercede in their behalf.

IN THE CHURCH

To be well married in Tepoztlán is to be married in church. Because civil marriage is now compulsory by law, most couples marry by both laws. Approximately 75 per cent of 133 marriages in the village between 1941 and 1946 were by both laws.

On the day the couple obtain their civil marriage certificate,[4] they appear before the priest with two character witnesses for the *presentación*. The priest writes down the name, age, and civil status of the boy and the girl and then begins to question each of the character witnesses. He asks the boy's witness if the boy has other *novias*, or other commitments, or whether he has children with another woman. Then the girl's witnesses are asked similar questions. The priest then turns to the boy and girl and asks each in turn whether they want to marry of their own free will, or whether they are being forced to marry. On the following three Sundays the priest reads the marriage banns in the church and if there are no protests, the couple are married on the fourth Sunday. Because of the Tepoztecan sense of shame and reticence to publicize private affairs, protests during the time of the reading of the banns are rare, even when some jilted lover or an unwed mother may have good cause.

On the evening before the wedding, the boy's parents traditionally send a basket of bread, chocolate, some bottles of wine, and a turkey prepared with the necessary condiments to the home of the girl. They also send along the wedding dress, with its accessories, shoes, stockings, and flowers. That evening the girl is taken to the home of the godparents of marriage, where she spends the night. The godparents give her marital advice at this time, and again the emphasis is upon her need to obey and conform to all of her husband's wishes.

In the early morning the godmother helps the girl wash and dress. Church weddings require the bride to be dressed in a white dress, shoes, and stockings. A dress with a train, *la cola,* and a veil is desirable. (See Fig. 62.) Widows who

---

[4] For a discussion of civil marriage, see Chapter 3, "Status Distinctions and Family Organization," p. 73.

remarry, or girls who have eloped and are pregnant at the time of marriage, wear a colored dress. The man may be married in simple *calzones* and huaraches and straw sombrero or in dark woolen store pants, poplin shirt, a cream colored linen jacket, fancy leather boots, and a felt hat, depending upon his resources. The man may wear his wedding clothes on later occasions but the woman's dress and veil

Fig. 62. A wedding party on the church steps.

are carefully put away and guarded throughout life. Many women are buried in their wedding dress, but others cut the dress short and wear it at fiestas.

The marriage vows, the placing of the ring, and the giving of the thirteen coins (*arrastomines*) take place at the church door. Most church weddings are held early Sunday morning. Traditionally, the godfather accompanies the bride to the church door where she is "delivered" to the groom. In some recent weddings the girl no longer sleeps at the godfather's house and instead is accompanied to the church by her own father and meets the groom and godfather at the church door. The ceremony of the wedding follows the traditional Catholic ritual. The ring is generally put on at the church door, and then the couple enter for the Mass.[5]

---

[5] Some writers have called marriage at the church door a Spanish custom. It is interesting to note that this custom is found in Chaucer in fourteenth-century England; see John M. Manly, *Canterbury Tales by Geoffrey Chaucer* (New York: Henry Holt, 1928), p. 279.

Some Tepoztecans now have borrowed the customs of the city by having separate godparents for the giving of the hands (*padrino de mano*) and another pair of godparents for the nuptial Mass (*velación*), but most couples still follow the older custom of having only one set of godparents. In a few cases of highly acculturated families, the bride has a car waiting at the entrance of the church and the couple ride off for their honeymoon. Some informants expressed the opinion that the time is not far off when this custom will be widespread in Tepoztlán.

After the ceremony it is customary for the couple and the friends and relatives to return to the home of the *padrinos* where refreshments are served, and where the couple again receive marital advice from the godparents. At about noon the couple go to the groom's house. In the old days, it was usual for the couple to carry burning incense over the threshold, and I have seen this tradition carried out on two occasions. A dinner is given with *mole poblano* as the main dish. Many drinks are served, with beer taking the place of *ponche* in the more acculturated homes. After the festivities are over, the guests go home and the couple remain. Most couples do not sleep alone the first or subsequent nights because of crowded living conditions.

Church weddings are becoming increasingly costly, ranging from 300 to 1,000 pesos. Young people of both sexes look forward to having a fine church wedding. If the boy's parents approve of the girl, they will make a fine wedding, even if it means selling their animals or pawning their house. As one informant put it, "I exchanged my cows for a daughter-in-law." If parents are not willing or able to provide a suitable wedding, their son sometimes works and saves to do so himself. Saving for a wedding is much more common than saving to buy a team of oxen, a house, or something which will improve the boy's economic situation. The majority of Tepoztecan couples begin married life with little except their clothing and the satisfaction of having had a nice wedding.

BY FREE UNION

When a man and woman live together as husband and wife without either civil or church marriage, it is referred to as a free union (*unión libre*). The more acculturated Tepoztecans no longer regard this as a form of marriage. But there are many couples who have been living in free union for many years, and they are regarded as husband and wife by all concerned. The children of such marriages, if the parents record their birth in the local registry, have equal rights with other children in cases of legal disputes concerning property. During the days of the Revolution, when priests were unavailable and life was precarious, many people joined in free unions. But the existence of *uniones libres* cannot be explained simply as a phenomenon of the Revolution. Of the fifteen per cent of the couples living in free union in the village in 1940, about half of them were fairly young people, indicating that this type of marriage is not entirely going out.

An analysis of the free unions in the village reveals that the great number were second marriages for one or both of the spouses. In most cases the previous spouse was still living, and remarriage by church or civil law was ruled out. Many widows with children prefer free unions, to be free to leave if the stepfather abuses her children. Some women promise their dying husbands not to remarry, to protect the children. Some of the most stable marriages in the village are cases of free unions. Most of the younger people living in free unions are cases of *raptos*.

Every few years, on the day of the barrio fiesta, the priest visits each barrio to marry all those living in free union. Sometimes there are many couples who, followed by their children, line up to be married. The nuns in the village have been campaigning since 1945 to have all free unions legalized.

old age and death: 19

In Tepoztlán a person is thought to be old when he can no longer do his customary work because of physical weakness or when he is obviously gray, wrinkled, and bent with age.[1] This is equally true of women. The menopause is not taken as a sign of old age; women generally welcome it because they will no longer be able to bear children. There is no custom of retiring to a life of rest and leisure; everyone works as long as he is able. (See Fig. 63.) The habit of useful activity keeps old people from becoming a burden to their children or a "social problem." Children are expected to care for old parents and the majority do, but many old people prefer to live alone, even at a miserable subsistence level.[2]

Old age as such is not feared, but dependence upon others and inability to work are generally very much feared. (See Fig. 64.) A "useless" old age is considered a sad thing, and many would prefer death. Chronic or lingering illness is not a serious problem because old people continue to work until their illness becomes acute, and death quickly follows. There are relatively few individuals who are bedridden or severely disabled because of their advanced years.

Old age is traditionally the time when a Tepoztecan receives greatest respect and consideration. Men over fifty are not required to do guard duty, and old people are permitted greater freedom of speech and behavior. They may get drunk, insult others, use sexual terms, laugh and cry, and even urinate in public without censure, although younger people may find it embarrassing. On the whole, however, old people are as restrained in behavior as other adults.

It appears to be the consensus that less and less respect for old people is being shown. It is pointed out that many children now address their grandparents in the familiar tú and that some of the old customs of greeting elders, such as the kissing of the hand, have fallen into disuse. In addition to the disappearance of outward signs of respect, there are more sources of conflict between the older and younger

[1] Approximately fifteen per cent of the population of Tepoztlán is over age fifty. Tepoztlán has a higher proportion of old people than does rural Mexico as a whole. At the time of this study, the oldest person in the village was ninety-nine.

[2] Of the forty-five individuals who live alone, the majority are over sixty years of age.

Fig. 63. Widows carrying firewood.

generations because of recent social and economic changes. Also, the facts that old people do not usually take an active part in community life, that a large number of the aged are poverty stricken, and that their speech, dress, and manners are now viewed as old-fashioned has somewhat diminished their respect status. Despite the nostalgia of the older folk for the "good old days," however, they are treated with relative respect, and the grandparent-grandchild relations are often of an affectionate nature.

Fig. 64. Tepoztecans worry about facing a dependent old age.

The situation of the aged varies considerably from family to family. The owner-ship of property, particularly of the kind which can be rented out and which pro-duces an income with little or no work, is the best assurance for a secure old age. It is for this reason that parents generally do not divide their property among the children until after death. Delayed inheritance also gives them continued control over their children; if a married son lives with his parents well into their old age they are indeed fortunate, for he works the land, and the daughter-in-law does most of the work of the household. But most old people own only their house and *sitio*, with perhaps a few fruit trees and a pig, and can be self-supporting only by hiring themselves out to others, or by carrying on a business.

A large proportion of old women, especially widows, support themselves by wash-ing and ironing clothes, by selling tortillas, by raising a few pigs and chickens for sale, by buying small amounts of fruit and garden produce to sell in other villages, or as midwives and *curanderas*. There are fewer non-strenuous, gainful activities for old men, particularly for those who have learned no skill other than farming. Those who have no children or relatives to whom they can turn for regular or occasional aid are in a difficult position. Occasionally an aged person finds it neces-sary to support not only himself but an orphaned grandchild or a disabled, un-married son or daughter. But the majority of Tepoztecan old people are at least partially aided by a son or daughter, a nephew, or grandchild. Cases of neglect, indifference, and even cruelty occur, but are few.

To illustrate the range of situations of the aged we have briefly described the manner of living of all the old people in one of the smaller barrios. They are as follows:

MARGARITA C., *age 72, widow for twelve years:* Lives with half-blind bachelor son of thirty-two whom she must support. He is able to carry wood and water and to plant a little corn in the corral. The mother raises pigs and chickens on a small scale and buys up corn and beans which she sells in Cuernavaca. She works very hard and receives no aid from her other children or relatives. One daughter is also a widow and depends upon her sons for support. Another daughter is married, lives in Mexico City, and rarely visits Tepoztlán.

RICARDO C., *age 64, and wife, Petra B., age 69:* Two married sons and one married daughter have families and live in different barrios. All are poor. Ricardo continues to plant his small milpa, and his wife buys local products which she sells in Cuernavaca. She has always done this, even when her children were small, because her husband never earned enough to support them. They receive no help from their children or relatives.

PEDRO F., *age 64, and wife, María C., age 60:* Live with two married sons who support them. Pedro was a charcoal maker until recently but can no longer work so hard. He makes ropes and feed bags of *ixtle,* and his wife works in the kitchen with her daughters-in-law. The sons treat their parents well, and all eat and live equally.

EUSTAQUIA L., *age 69, widow for many years:* Lives with her unmarried son of forty-seven. They are not poor and have no financial problem. She owns some land and a team of oxen which she rents out. She also has some cattle which her son takes care of. The son owns some property too and has money which he earned in the United States, but he works for his mother, and she is the head of the household. He must have her permission before he can sell anything, and he still asks for her permission when he wants to go anywhere, such as Mexico City.

JUANA G., *age 72, widow for eight years:* Has no children, but is in good health and works hard as a laundress and servant. She lives alone in her own house; she has no land but owns two or three *ciruela* trees and raises a few pigs and chickens. Her closest relatives, nephews, live in Mexico City and visit her about once a month, often bringing her clothing. This woman is considered to be unfortunate because she must carry her own wood and water and must depend upon neighbors if she gets ill. But she wears decent clothing and is respected.

JUAN M., *age 72, and wife, María G., age 59:* Live in their own house. They had two children who died. They own no land, and since the husband is lame and ill he cannot work as a peon. They support themselves by making rope and by selling fruit from their garden and twelve *ciruela* trees. The wife takes in laundry occasionally and raises a few chickens. She has no relatives, and the husband never receives any aid from his.

Death is viewed as natural and inevitable, and apparently inspires no undue fear or preoccupation. Old people readily speak of death and frequently use the expressions, "when I am dead," or "when I am underground," in conversation. There is no attempt to protect children from the facts of death. Children of all ages attend wakes, view the corpses, participate in funeral processions and at burials. Little emotion is expressed about death or the dead, although close relatives of the recent dead may shed brief tears if the subject is discussed. Grief is restrained but varies somewhat according to the age and status of the deceased.

The death of an old person or an infant causes relatively little disturbance, that of a parent or adult who is still in full vigor, or of a grown son or daughter, much more so. Reactions to the death of a husband or wife depend upon the quality of the marital relationship but, again, is rarely demonstrative. Suicide is uncommon, and in no case has anyone ever killed himself because of the death of a loved one.

At death, Tepoztecans are concerned with the release of the soul from the body and with its journey to heaven. It is said that under certain circumstances it is difficult for a person to give himself up to death, and the agony of dying is prolonged. Witches and some *curanderos* are said to die "very badly," that is, slowly, losing consciousness and fainting without being able to give up their soul, because they need time to repent all the evil things they have done. Prostitutes also suffer a difficult death, "because they supported themselves with their own bodies. These women see terrible visions and figures which threaten to drag them off, and in their agony they scratch at the bedclothes and at their own faces and hands." Often children "cannot die until they receive a benediction from their parents or godparents." Also a father or mother "cannot die if their children cry too much." In such cases the children are taken away, to hasten death. When death comes, the soul leaves the body and may be seen as a figure, resembling the deceased, leaving the house, and Tepoztecans say, ". . . this is his soul which walks without touching the ground and without showing its face although it wears no hat. It is very white, like foam, and disappears when it touches something."

It is believed that when a person is about to die "his eyes go up and become whitish, his nose sharpens, his hands get cold and still, and his body becomes loose." At these signs, the dying person is taken from the bed and placed on a *petate* on the floor in a corner. He is covered with a sheet, his clothing is removed, and he is dressed in clean clothes. After death he is placed on a table and covered with a sheet, so that "those of little spirit" will not be made ill at the sight of the corpse. A newspaper is spread on the *petate,* and a cross of sand and lime is fashioned on the newspaper.[3] Flowers are placed above the cross, and a candle, which burns day and night for nine days, is placed at the head of the *petate.* If the deceased is a man, his sombrero and huaraches are laid next to the candle; if a woman, her *rebozo* is placed there. The clothing of the dead person is washed and ironed and placed at the head of the *petate.* A *rezandero* is hired by the bereaved family to come to the house to pray twice a day, at noon and in the evening, for nine days. The women of the house are required to be present and to kneel in prayer.

---

[3] A similar custom is reported for Mitla. See Parsons, *Mitla,* p. 141.

A wake is held day and night, and friends, relatives, and *compadres* come to keep vigil. The family serves coffee, alcohol, bread, and cigarettes, the cost of which is a burden to the poor. Some of the visitors leave a few coins to help pay the expenses, but the majority do not. The more kindly disposed, close relatives may voluntarily offer financial or other assistance, and most godparents fulfill their obligation to provide a coffin, burial clothing, and perhaps music at the death of a godchild.

During the wake men and women pray together, but after each prayer the men separate to drink and play cards in order to keep awake. On the following day a few of the men go to the cemetery to dig the grave. The deceased is placed in a coffin and carried to the cemetery, with mourners preceding and following the coffin. Some funerals, particularly those of important persons or members of the Acción Católica, enter the church before proceeding to the burial place. After burial, a cross with the name and date of death is placed on the grave. On the *novena*, or ninth day, the ceremony of the raising of the cross takes place at a night wake similar to the one held on the day of death. This time, however, an offering of tamales, *mole verde*, oranges, chocolate, cooked chicken, and bread is placed on the house altar for the deceased. The offering is left there for twelve hours, each hour corresponding to one month of the year, so that the deceased will have food for the entire year.

For the ceremony of the raising of the cross, two boys and girls, who are non-relatives, are selected by the kin of the deceased to act as *padrinos*. The children carry flowers and, accompanied by the *rezandero*, walk toward the *petate* on which is the cross of lime and sand. The *padrinos* stand on either side of the cross, while the *rezandero* recites special prayers. Meanwhile, the children take small brooms, which must be new, and sweep the sand and lime together, gather it on a tray, and later take it to the grave. The clothing which had been left on the *petate* is now also raised. As each article is picked up, the *padrinos* recite the following prayer: "Rise up, soul of Christ, awake if you are asleep. God is looking for you to accompany you to heaven." After the cross and the clothing have been raised, the prayer hymns (*alabadas*) are sung in honor of the dead.

It is also customary to ring the barrio chapel bells the day after the death. If a special fee is paid, the bells of the central church will be rung, and the priest will perform a benediction for the deceased.

One year after the death, another wake may be held and a special Mass arranged. In some families, members visit the grave with flowers.

A child's funeral is somewhat different. Tepoztecans adhere to the Catholic belief that the soul of a child goes directly to heaven, and the funeral is therefore supposed to be an occasion of rejoicing. Gay music is played at the wake and at the funeral procession. The *novena* and prayers for the soul of the deceased are unnecessary in the case of children and are not held, and the burial clothing and decorations must be befitting to an *angelito*. If the dead child is a boy he is dressed like San José, if a girl, like the Virgen de Guadalupe. Both wear socks and cardboard sandals lined with gold paper. The hands and feet are tied with a ribbon when the body is laid out, and untied at the grave. When the child is dying, a palm to offer to God is placed in his hands; and after death, flowers are added. A crown of paper flowers is placed on the head, and the face is covered with a veil. Both of these are removed at the grave. A small painted gourd is placed beside the body, to provide the soul with water on its journey to heaven. The litter is carried by children of the same sex as the deceased, and as the body is carried out of the house, the barrio chapel bell is rung.

general
observations on the life cycle: 20

THE QUESTIONS with which we are here concerned are as follows: (1) What, in summary, are the general qualities of inter-personal relations in Tepoztlán? In other words, what is the Tepoztecan social character? (2) How are the adult attitudes and value systems of Tepoztecans reflected in child training patterns? (3) To what extent does the training of children in Tepoztlán prepare them for adult life? (4) What are the conflict points and inconsistencies in this culture, and how do they affect the lives of men and women?

As we have seen, Tepoztecans value hard work, thrift, practicality, restraint, submission to authority, and the ability to conform. In inter-personal relations, Tepoztecans are detached, individualistic, and sensitive to status differences, with a generalized readiness to be suspicious, negativistic, and even hostile. Gossip, complaint, envy, and criticism are common. Tepoztecans are a constricted people, as seen in their lack of warmth and limited expression of affection, in their attitudes toward sex, and in their general absence of self-expression. Fantasy, imagination, and creativity are at a minimum; although Tepoztecans are turned within themselves, they are not dreamers. They are an indirect people; they frequently rely upon the use of intermediaries and upon formality. Deception also is a sanctioned form of indirection, and the direct expression of aggression is strongly discouraged. Competition between individuals is rare. When competition occurs, it is between groups, thereby giving it a quality of impersonality. Finally, the aspiration level of most Tepoztecans does not place an undue burden on them and does not lead to any marked anxiety.

The patterns of child training in Tepoztlán reflect many of the attitudes and value systems noted above. One of the underlying principles in child rearing is to develop children who are easy to control. Submissiveness, quietness, passivity, and dependence are all encouraged; activity, aggression, demanding, self-gratification, curiosity, and independence are discouraged. This is manifested in the long nursing period, in swaddling and restricting the movements of the child, in the belief that the child must not cry, in the absence of preoccupation with training the child to walk, talk, eat alone, and develop sphincter control.

The great amount of attention given the infant is primarily for the purpose of limiting and protecting him rather than stimulating him. He is not allowed to explore the world about him, to crawl, to touch many objects, and, when older, to ask too many questions. In general, much concern is felt for the safety of the infant, and the belief that infants are delicate is amply reinforced by the high mortality rate. Most infants wear several amulets to ward off illness, the sleeping child's face is covered to protect him from *los aires,* visitors are not encouraged to look at or hold the infant, and children are not taken out into the street more than is necessary.

The same basic principles apply in the training of children from about two to five, with emphasis upon obedience and respect for elders. After a rather abrupt weaning, the child becomes dependent upon older brothers and sisters, or a mother substitute. The illnesses which generally accompany weaning are interpreted to mean that the child is jealous of the new baby, reflecting the sibling rivalry found in many families. Children of this age are usually required to play within the patio; it is not uncommon to see children of three or four being carried, and many are not yet toilet trained. Children are controlled by means of scolding, frightening, shaming, and physical punishment. On the other hand, the young child, especially a boy or a favorite, is indulged in some ways, permitting a greater amount of ego development. Temper tantrums, whims, and complaints against older siblings are often rewarded by adults. After age five, responsibility and work are gradually increased, generally in proportion to the age and physical strength of the child. From this time on, through youth and even marriage, as long as the child lives under the parental roof, he is dependent upon the parents and subject to their authority.

By and large, this type of child training adequately prepares children for adult life in this community. But there are some points of conflict and inconsistencies between theory and practice in the culture. Perhaps the primary area of conflict is in the roles of men and women and in the relations between the sexes. On the whole, men are under much greater pressure than women; they experience more discontinuity in the transition from childhood to adulthood and more contradiction between their ideal and actual social roles. Although boys are more favored than girls and have, in general, more opportunities for ego development, their early training is not conducive to the development of inner strength and ability to dominate, which are required by the ideals of a patriarchal society. We have seen that frequently husbands are only nominally the head of the household, and that they rely upon fear to maintain authority. As men grow older, and as their sexual powers and ability to work decline, their position of dominance is more difficult to maintain. Furthermore, their older wives and grown-up children are more independent and not so easily controlled, and older men receive little social recognition and have little power in the community. It is interesting to note that in regard to favored position, the life cycle of men and women takes an opposite course: Men in early life are in a comparatively favored position, but as they grow older they are weighed down by life situations; women begin with less freedom, lower aspiration levels, and earlier responsibilities, but as they mature after marriage they slowly gain more freedom and often take a dominating position in the household.

One of the discontinuities in the life of men is found in connection with sex. Although sexuality is inhibited all through childhood, young men are subjected to pressure from members of their age group to be sexually active. To have many sweethearts and sexual affairs before and after marriage is expected and admired. In practice, however, relatively few men in Tepoztlán achieve the reputation of being *muy macho*. On the contrary, boys are often timid in courtship and in many cases are initiated in their first sex experience by older girls or women. In the case of women, there is much less inconsistency between childhood training and acceptable adult behavior. Girls are expected to be ignorant of sex before marriage and to behave with fidelity and restraint after marriage. Girls and women who have illicit sexual relations are considered "bad" or "crazy." Women tend to express rebellion and dissatisfaction with their situation by taking a lover. In effect, then, while the sex activity of men is an expression of manliness, in women it is a form of delinquency.

Still another discrepancy between theory and practice in Tepoztecan society is that, despite the greater freedom of men and their higher social status, it is the women who have greater opportunities for social life and appear to be better socialized. Women visit with neighbors and relatives more than men. Their daily trips to the plaza offer an occasion for gossip and news. They attend church more often. This greater socialization begins early in life. While the girls take care of their brothers and sisters, the young boys are out in the fields caring for the animals. Men spend most of their days alone at their work in the fields. Occasions for communal work are few and are almost always accompanied by drinking. Men do not seem to be at ease in groups, unless they are fortified by alcohol.

OBSERVATIONS ON THE CULTURE-PERSONALITY PROBLEM

We come now to the broad problem of the relationship between culture and personality. What light does the Tepoztecan material throw on this problem? In attempting to think this through I have arrived at a tentative reformulation of the problem in terms of some conceptual distinctions which are presented in the following pages.

Whether or not the study of culture throws light upon personality depends in large measure on how we define the terms culture and personality. If the approach to culture is that of the older anthropology which emphasized descriptions of external forms and customs, then one might expect little relationship between culture and personality. People having different forms of dress, speaking different languages, and having different religions may still have many similarities in personality. But if the core of the culture concept is seen as the attitudes and value systems and their manifestation in inter-personal relations, then there is a very close relationship between culture and personality.

A definition of personality presents greater difficulties. Despite the extensive

literature in this field there is still considerable disagreement about basic definitions. One of the key points of difference is whether or not to include behavior in
the definition of personality.[1] Some psychologists like Katz and Schanck,[2] Guthrie,[3] and Young[4] include behavior. Others, like Allport,[5] Newcomb,[6] and Stagner,[7] formally exclude it. Some of our leading anthropologists, like Linton, Gillin,
and Kluckhohn, follow the latter group in excluding behavior from their definition
of personality and have stressed the subjective element, a position which Bidney
has characterized as "idealist, mentalist." Bidney has shown some of the logical
problems raised by creating a duality between culture and personality.[8] It seems
to me that the inclusion of behavior in the definition of personality resolves most
of these problems.

More important than the inclusion or exclusion of behavior in the definition
of personality is the question as to the role given to values in the total personality.
Most contemporary psychological theory considers characteristic mental states,

---

[1] The identical problem is seen in the differences in modern anthropological definitions of
culture. Thus, Linton includes behavior, whereas Redfield leaves it out. Linton writes, "A
culture is the configuration of learned behavior and results of behavior whose component elements are shared and transmitted by the members of a particular society." Ralph Linton, *The
Cultural Background of Personality* (New York and London: Appleton-Century Co., Inc., 1945),
p. 32.

Redfield, on the other hand, views culture as ". . . the conventional understandings expressed
in act and artifact, that characterize societies." Redfield, *Folk Culture of Yucatan,* p. 132.

My own conception of culture follows Linton in including behavior, but I would stress the
system of inter-personal relations.

[2] "Personality is the concept under which we subsume the individual's characteristic ideational,
emotional, and motor reactions and the characteristic organization of these responses." Daniel
Katz and Richard L. Schanck, *Social Psychology* (New York: John Wiley and Sons, 1938), p. 391.

[3] "A man's personality at any given time consists of those modes of his behavior which we
judge will show comparatively strong resistance to change." Edwin R. Guthrie, *The Psychology
of Human Conflict* (New York: Harper and Brothers, 1938), p. 136.

[4] "For our purposes we define personality as the more or less integrated body of habits, attitudes,
traits and ideas of an individual as these are organized externally into specific and general roles
and statuses and internally around self-consciousness and the concept of the self, and around
ideas, values, and purposes which are related to motives, roles, and status. In other words, personality has two aspects: role and status with respect to behavior affecting others, and selfhood,
ego, or life organization with regard to internal motivation, goals and the ways of viewing one's
own and others' behavior. More briefly, it concerns overt *action* and *meaning* as these are oriented
about one's interactions with one's fellows." Kimball Young, *Social Psychology* (New York: F. S.
Crofts and Co., 1944), p. 120.

[5] "Personality is the dynamic organization within the individual of those psychophysical systems
that determine his unique adjustments to his environment." Gordon W. Allport, *Personality, A
Psychological Interpretation* (New York: Henry Holt and Co., 1937), p. 48.

[6] ". . . we shall mean by personality the individual's organization of predispositions to behavior, including predispositions to both directive and expressive behavior." Theodore M. Newcomb, *Social Psychology* (New York: Dryden Press, 1950), pp. 344–45.

[7] Stagner defines personality as ". . . an inner system of beliefs, expectancies, desires, and
values." Ross Stagner, *The Psychology of Personality* (New York: McGraw-Hill Book Co., Inc.,
1948), p. 6. I am grateful to Ross Stagner for helpful discussions in the culture-personality field.

[8] David Bidney, "Toward a Psychocultural Definition of the Concept of Personality," *Culture
and Personality* (New York: Viking Fund, 1949), pp. 31–58.

emotions, and drives as the core of the personality—the most basic determinants of behavior. Attitudes and values are generally placed in the peripheral "layers" of the personality, which presumably are more readily changed. In contrast to this position, I would like to suggest that the value system of an individual is perhaps one of *the* most important determinants of behavior and a most stable component of the total personality. It is the great organizing principle of the personality. To understand the total personality of an individual we must understand the content and quality of his value system, its degree of consistency, its relation to the realities of the environment in which he lives, and the degree to which it is in accord with the accepted cultural values of his society.[9] The approach to personality suggested in the following pages therefore places great weight on the factor of values.

PRIVATE AND PUBLIC PERSONALITY

As I see it, the total personality of an individual is the organization of his bio-physical and psychological states and processes, his characteristic overt action and reaction patterns, and his attitudes and values. For purposes of research and analysis in culture and personality, it is helpful to distinguish between two fundamental aspects of the total personality of an individual; that is, the private personality and the public personality. The underlying principle in this distinction is of a functional nature. The public personality of an individual includes all those aspects of the total personality which are directly and appreciably influenced by the social norms and which, in turn, directly and appreciably influence or determine the social behavior of an individual. The private personality of an individual includes all those aspects which are not sensitive to social norms and which do not directly affect social behavior. The public or private quality of any single component within the total personality is a relative matter; that is, it depends upon the degree and manner in which it affects behavior. The relative nature of this distinction between public and private personality also follows from the fact that the concept "person" is logically dependent upon and, in a sense, implies the concept of society and culture.

The distinction between the public and private aspects of the total personality is not intended to be rigid, for we do not think of these as permanent compartmentalized configurations of traits but rather as two systems, the component parts of which may be interacting. The same trait in the same individual may move from the private to the public category if it becomes directly effective in influencing his social behavior. For example, so long as a person feels great sympathy for mistreated animals but does nothing to express this feeling, then it is part of his private personality. But should he write a poem about dogs or protect stray dogs or join a society for the prevention of cruelty to animals, then this feeling of sympathy is part of his public personality. In addition, we may find that a similarity between

---

[9] Relatively little work has been done on the role of values in the total personality.

two traits which are functioning simultaneously in the private and public personality may be due to some more basic trait which is affecting both.[10]

The traits which are to be considered part of the private or public personality of an individual are in large measure determined by the culture. For example, for most people in our society the dream would be included in the private personality. On the other hand, among the Blackfoot, a Plains Indian tribe, the culture defines the dream as the major source of individual supernatural power—most young men seek dreams to obtain a guardian spirit, and some may buy visions—and the dream directly affects behavior and is part of the public personality. Another cross-cultural example is the relation between temperament and public personality. In a society which places high value on personal success and individual development we might expect that temperament would be a much more important factor in the public personality of individuals than it is in a society like that of the Tepoztecan or the Hopi which emphasizes conformity.[11]

Just as the culture influences the determination of what traits are to be private or public, so we find that the total area of the private and public aspects of the personality may vary by cultures. In a community like Tepoztlán where a much larger segment of behavior is considered private than in a middle-class American community, an equivalent description of the public personality tells much less about the total personality of Tepoztecans than of Americans.

The dynamics of change in the private and public aspects of the personality of an individual are quite different. The private personality is subject to relatively little pressure by the social norms, for either change or conformity. The public personality, on the other hand, is subject to the pressures toward conformity in the form of rewards and punishments. As a result, we would expect to find a wider range of individual differences in the private personality than in the public personality.[12]

Our distinction between private and public aspects of the personality has some

---

[10] It may be said that we are not dealing with a private and public aspect of personality but rather with a private expression of a psychological trait vs. a public expression of a psychological trait. This formulation, though attractive in its simplicity, is not acceptable because it tends toward the conception of traits as static entities which exist independently of their function in a field situation. In this case our categories of private and public define the field. Our conception of personality begins with very broad factors like constitution, psychological processes, and values, which become individual personality traits only in given field situations. For example, if laziness is viewed as a psychological trait, then it is in the person at all times, waiting to be expressed. But even "lazy" men work hard sometimes. If, however, laziness is viewed as a predisposition toward laziness, then a man can be considered as lazy only when he acts lazy. What Newcomb calls a "predisposition" would be the equivalent of our "psychological state" but not of a psychological trait.

[11] This suggests that the great interest of modern psychologists in individuality and in private personality reflects the culture in which they live.

[12] McQuitty has provided us with some evidence for this. See Louis L. McQuitty, "Effective Items in the Measurement of Personality Integration," *Journal of Educational and Psychological Measurements* (in press). I am grateful to Professor McQuitty for making this manuscript available to me.

precedent in the distinction made by psychologists between personal and public attitudes.[13] It is also somewhat similar to what McQuitty is getting at in his distinction between subjective and objective cues in the answering of questions by his subjects. Our distinction differs from the traditional overt-covert dichotomy in that we may include overt private behavior as well as introspection under the private personality. Secret masturbation, for example, would be part of one's private personality, provided it did not directly and appreciably affect the carrying out of one's social roles. Any guilt feelings which might arise from this behavior will of course affect total personality, but so long as it does not significantly affect social behavior it remains part of the private personality.

Our distinction between the private and public aspects of the personality bears some resemblance in terminology to Lewin's distinction between the peripheral and central layers of the personality, or what he calls "the private and non-private personal regions." [14] However, our conception of private and public personality is quite different from Lewin's. His conception of the personality in terms of "layers" is structural rather than functional. His view of the "core" as the most important and stable element in the personality, and of the "periphery" as the least stable, is almost diametrically opposed to our conception of the relation between the private and public personality.

There are some interesting similarities between our twofold distinction of private and public personality and Mowrer's two-factor learning theory.[15] Just as the conception of a single learning process was an oversimplification so is the monistic conception of personality. The relationship between Mowrer's theory and the conception presented here is more than one of analogy. The two formulations dovetail one another. Mowrer's "sign learning" would fall within the private personality. His "solution learning" can be both private or public depending upon the culture, the situation, and the total personality.

Some questions which can only be mentioned now, but which deserve further study concern the different ways in which the private and public personality of an individual can be related, and how these differences affect the quality of the total personality. Are the two equally integrated? Can they be in conflict? To what degree can an individual be disturbed in the private personality without it appreciably affecting the total personality? Can we infer from the public personality of an individual what his private personality is?

In the light of the conception of personality which we have tentatively suggested, the culture-personality problem might be rephrased as follows: What is the rela-

---

[13] Katz and Schanck, *Social Psychology,* pp. 443–44.

[14] Kurt Lewin, "Some Social-Psychological Differences between the United States and Germany" in *Resolving Social Conflicts* (New York: Harper and Brothers, 1948). See especially pp. 20–24.

[15] I am indebted to Professor Mowrer for calling this to my attention. For a full statement of his learning theory, see O. Hobart Mowrer, *Learning Theory and Personality Dynamics* (New York: Ronald Press, 1950).

tionship between (1) public personality and culture; (2) private personality and culture; (3) total personality and culture?[16]

The relationship between the public personality of an individual and the culture is the most obvious one. Viewing culture as an organized system of relationships between individuals in a given society, we see the individual expressing his public personality in the process of living out this system of relationships. The anthropologist in studying inter-personal relations is getting at the individual's public personality and the culture at the same time. This is not to say that the two are identical but that they are both facets of a single complex phenomenon. Neither can be conceived of without the other.

The culture provides the individual with a great part of his public personality in the form of defining social roles and presenting a body of traditions, customs, attitudes, and values. These are absorbed or internalized in varying degrees depending upon age, sex, class, and personal, historical, and accidental factors. We find, therefore, that the public personalities of individuals within a given society share many common elements and, at the same time, contain individual differences. The individual is not a passive agent of culture, and his public personality is by no means a mere reflection or rubber stamp of the culture. Obviously the individual receives more from the culture than he adds to it, but it is equally clear that the culture cannot exist or be perpetuated or changed, except through the expression of the public personalities of individuals.

The relationship between the private personality of an individual and his culture is much less obvious and more difficult to trace. This level of personality seems to be largely determined by many non-cultural factors such as constitution, condition of health, and unique life experiences or what Young called the "personal-social" factors. The cultural factors often function only indirectly by providing the conditions for certain experiences, by encouraging or discouraging practices affecting health, and so on. That the culture plays a *lesser* role in private personality is indicated by the greater variety and uniqueness of private personality components as compared with the public personality. While there are common elements in the private personalities of many individuals, there are fewer of them.

In the light of the distinctions made above, we might ask just what part of the culture-personality problem anthropologists have been reporting in their studies. Moreover, what are they best able to study in terms of their training and the conditions under which most field work in other societies is done? It seems to me that the anthropologist, in practice, has been primarily concerned with the relationship between the public personality and the culture. The explicit recognition of this—and the fact that, by and large, the anthropologist is not studying the private personality and is therefore getting only a limited understanding of the total personality—might help clarify some of the confusion in the culture-personality field

---

[16] I have included this question (3) to indicate the nature and complexity of the problem. However, this point will not be elaborated upon in the following discussion.

and avoid much of the criticism that has been directed at anthropological writing in this field.[17]

In this study, therefore, I have not written about *the* Tepoztecan personality nor have I employed the concepts of "basic personality structure" or "modal personality." By limiting myself to a description of the quality of inter-personal relations I have attempted to get at some of the common aspects of the public personality of Tepoztecans, or what Fromm might call "the social character."

To make reliable and valid statements about the common elements in the total personality of individuals of a given community would require much more detailed and profound information than is available at present in most culture-personality studies.[18] While the Rorschach and other projective tests get at the private component of the personality, comparisons of Rorschach findings with an anthropologist's findings are primarily between (1) private personality and public personality and (2) private personality and the culture—but not between total personality and the culture.

---

[17] Alfred R. Lindesmith and Anselm L. Strauss, "A Critique of Culture-Personality Writing," *American Sociological Review*, Vol. 15, No. 5 (Oct., 1950), pp. 587–600.

[18] It should be noted in this connection that most of the biographies in the anthropological literature are useful primarily for what they reflect about the customs and the culture rather than for what they tell about the private personality. See Clyde Kluckhohn, "Needed Refinements in the Biographical Approach," *Culture and Personality* (New York: Viking Fund, 1949), pp. 75–92.

summary and conclusions: 21

THIS STUDY represents one of the few restudies of a community, in the field of anthropology. The reader who is familiar with the earlier study of Tepoztlán by Robert Redfield will want to know how our findings compare. Such a comparison is made here, not only for a better understanding of Tepoztlán, but also for its broader implications for anthropological method and theory. The questions are: To what extent and in what ways do the results obtained from the independent study of the same society by two anthropologists differ? What are the implications of such differences concerning the reliability and validity of anthropological reporting?

Anthropologists, who like to think that there is an element of science in the social sciences, including anthropology, have often called primitive societies the "laboratory" of the social scientists, where hypotheses about the nature of man and society can be tested. While the experiments and observations of the natural scientist are generally repeated and checked independently by different observers, the reports of anthropologists have to be accepted on their face value, and their reliability has to be judged in terms of the respect for and confidence in the author's integrity, the inner consistency of his work, and the extent to which it agrees with one's own preconceptions.[1] If the analogy with the natural sciences is to be taken seriously, we must develop methods for checking the reliability of our observations and the validity of interpretation. Restudy is one such method. This point has been recognized by a number of anthropologists,[2] but to date there have been very few

---

[1] In view of the increasing and often uncritical use which other social scientists have been making of anthropological data, the problem of reliability assumes much importance. Of course, in these times, when anthropologists are bravely writing about entire nations, it may seem downright heresy to suggest that there is still room for a critical reexamination of some of the methods and approaches used in the studies of the so-called simpler societies. And yet I am certain than many anthropologists and non-anthropologists alike have felt such a need. Bierstedt, for example, in his criticism of some recent anthropological studies of modern communities and nations, has suggested that these studies have stimulated "the growth of scepticism concerning the information which anthropologists have given us about non-literate peoples." See Robert Bierstedt, "The Limitations of Anthropological Methods in Sociology," *American Sociological Review*, LIV (1948), 22–30.

[2] Linton, in discussing the difficulties in studying the covert aspects of culture and the dangers

restudies.[3] The reasons for this are many. Perhaps most important have been the limited funds for field research, the time pressure of studying tribes who were rapidly becoming extinct, the shortage of field workers, the greater appeal in studying a community never before studied, and finally, the lack of emphasis upon methodology.

COMPARISON WITH REDFIELD'S FINDINGS

As has already been pointed out, our study of Tepoztlán was not originally intended as a restudy of Redfield's work but rather as a continuation of it. When the study was begun I did not anticipate that there would be any fundamental differences between our findings. In the course of the work, however, many differences did emerge. These differences range from discrepancies in factual details to differences in the over-all view of Tepoztecan society and its people. Many of the differences have been discussed in the earlier sections of this work. Here I will sum up some of the broader and more fundamental differences in the findings of the two studies.

The impression given by Redfield's study of Tepoztlán is that of a relatively homogeneous, isolated, smoothly functioning, and well-integrated society made up of a contented and well-adjusted people. His picture of the village has a Rousseauan quality which glosses lightly over evidence of violence, disruption, cruelty, disease,

---

involved in making generalizations on the basis of the limited sampling used by most anthropologists, writes, "The only check on such potential sources of error which is possible at the present time is to have each society studied by several investigators. These investigators should work independently and should be as diverse in their own personality configurations as possible." Linton, *Cultural Background,* p. 40.

The need for independent restudies was also suggested in 1933 by Radin, who wrote, "It cannot be too strongly stressed not only that the field ethnologist collects the facts but that his description is most likely to remain the final picture of a given culture, from which no appeal can be made. What more natural than that this semidivine function which has been thrust upon him should make him feel that the facts are peculiarly his, obtained by the sweat of his brow. For any one to question them is not merely an impertinence but a direct aspersion upon his character and veracity. This attitude, particularly prevalent in the United States, that the specific field of inquiry represents an ethnologist's private preserve wherein no one else may hunt has done inestimable harm and frequently has meant that a tribe has been described by only one person. It has sometimes been contended that the dangers attendant upon a tribe's being described by one person have been exaggerated, that, somehow, a description proves itself." Paul Radin, *The Method and Theory of Ethnology* (New York: McGraw-Hill Book Co., 1933), pp. 102–04.

To my knowledge, Margaret Mead is the only modern anthropologist who has expressed serious doubts about the advisability and usefulness of restudies. For her statement, see "The Mountain Arapesh," *Anthropological Papers of American Museum of Natural History,* Vol. 41, Pt. 3 (1949), pp. 296–97.

[3] Many tribes and villages have been studied by more than one investigator, but in most cases the studies have been what might be called additive rather than restudies of the earlier work. In addition there have been restudies by the same investigators, for example, Lynds' *Middletown In Transition* and more recently Redfield's *A Village That Chose Progress.* A field team of husband and wife gives us some independence of observation, and in fact may lead to quite different interpretations. Compare, for example, Reo F. Fortune's impressions of the Arapesh with Mead's.

suffering, and maladjustment. We are told little of poverty, economic problems, or political schisms. Throughout his study we find an emphasis upon the cooperative and unifying factors in Tepoztecan society. Our findings, on the other hand, would emphasize the underlying individualism of Tepoztecan institutions and character, the lack of cooperation, the tensions between villages within the municipio, the schisms within the village, and the pervading quality of fear, envy, and distrust in inter-personal relations.

Now let us consider some of these differences in more detail. Redfield's account of Tepoztlán stresses the role of the communal lands as a unifying factor within the village and the municipio. While this is certainly true it is only part of the story. With the single exception of church lands, communal lands were and are individually operated, and the ideal of every Tepoztecan is to own his private plot of land. Furthermore, the communal lands have been a source of inter-village quarrels, and during the year that Redfield was in Tepoztlán these quarrels resulted in violence. Similarly, Redfield gives the impression that the *cuatequitl,* a traditional form of collective labor, was part and parcel of village life. He described a *cuatequitl* which occurred during his stay as if it were a common and regular occurrence. As a matter of fact, it was the first village *cuatequitl* of importance since the Revolution, and there have been very few subsequent ones. The particular *cuatequitl* which Redfield observed was due to the curious circumstance whereby a local, socialistically oriented political faction, directed from Mexico City by a group of Tepoztecans who were members of the Confederación Regional de Obreros Mexicanos, locally known as the Bolsheviki, revived the traditional *cuatequitl.* Before the Revolution, the village *cuatequitl* was not viewed simply as a voluntary, cooperative endeavor but was also associated with forced labor and imposition by the local *cacique* groups which ruled the village during the Díaz regime. In the colonial period the Spaniards similarly utilized the traditional *cuatequitl* as a source of labor. In short, Redfield's account of the cooperative aspects of village life needs to be modified somewhat in the light of other data. X

Redfield portrayed Tepoztlán as a community of landowners and did not mention a land problem. But we found that over fifty per cent of the villagers did not own private land, and that there was an acute shortage of good land and considerable population pressure in the face of dwindling agricultural resources. Redfield gave a rather glowing picture of Tepoztlán during the Díaz regime as having reached a period of great cultural florescence, but he failed to point out that this was limited to only a few Tepoztecans, and that the vast majority of Tepoztecans were illiterate, desperately poor, landless, and living under an oppressive political regime which forbade them to utilize their own communal resources. In this connection it is interesting to note that Tepoztlán was one of the first villages in the state of Morelos to join the Zapatista revolt against the Díaz regime. Redfield apparently viewed the Mexican Revolution as having had the effect of halting the tendency for the merging of social class differences,[4] but we found that the Revolution had a marked leveling influence, economically, socially, and culturally.

Redfield presented only the positive and formal aspects of inter-personal relations, such as forms of greeting and the respect-relations of *compadres;* he failed to deal with some of the negative and disruptive aspects of village life, such as the fairly high incidence of stealing, quarrels, and physical violence. An examination of the local records revealed that in the year that Redfield lived in the village there were 175 reported cases of crimes and misdemeanors in the local court. Most of these cases were offenses against persons and property. Since not all cases reach the local authorities, this number is indicative of considerable conflict.

Redfield described local politics as a game, but we found that politics was a very serious affair which frequently led to violence. The year Redfield was there, the political schisms culminated in open violence bordering on civil war, and it was this situation which finally resulted in Redfield's leaving the village.

Another important difference between our findings concerns Redfield's delineation of the social structure of the village in terms of what he called the *tontos,* or representatives of folk culture, and the *correctos,* or representatives of city ways. It should be pointed out that Tepoztecans do not conceive of these terms as designations of social classes, in the sense used by Redfield, nor did they twenty years ago. Tepoztecans use the words as descriptive adjectives, with *tonto* meaning stupid, backward, foolish, or ignorant, and with *correcto* meaning well-mannered, well-bred, proper, or correct. The poorest, least educated, and most conservative man may be *correcto* to a Tepoztecan if he is polite and behaves in the accepted manner. Similarly, a well-educated, acculturated man may be called *tonto* if he permits himself to be fooled by others or dominated by his wife. Within any one family, some of the members may be considered *tonto* and others *correcto,* depending almost entirely upon personality traits and manners.

But granting that the degree of exposure to and influence of city ways is an important criterion in making for status differences in Tepoztlán, it is by no means the only one, and certainly not the most significant one in terms of the actual operation of the many status distinctions in the village. Among status distinctions which were then, and are today, more meaningful to Tepoztecans are those of rich and poor, landowners and landless, owners of private lands and holders of *ejidos, ejidatarios* and *comuneros,* farmers in hoe culture and farmers in plow culture, sons of *caciques* and sons of ex-Zapatistas, to mention but a few.

Furthermore, the concept of *tontos* and *correctos,* as social classes representing different cultural levels, led to misunderstanding of the local political situation. The opposing political factions in the village during Redfield's stay were not composed of *tontos* on the one side and *correctos* on the other. The leaders on both sides included highly acculturated and little acculturated individuals, as did the members

---

[4] In discussing the *tontos* and *correctos,* he writes, "The periodic Revolutions afford, it would seem, a mechanism whereby the difference between the classes is from time to time re-emphasized and the tendency for them to merge is checked." Redfield, *Tepoztlán,* p. 205.

at large. A study of the personnel of each of the local government administrations (*ayuntamientos*) from 1926 to 1947 gives no support to Redfield's statement that politics, like the religious fiestas, are in the hands of the *tontos*.

The use of the terms *"tonto"* and *"correcto"* to designate social groups, which did not and do not exist and operate as such, makes much of Redfield's analysis of Tepoztecan society oversimplified, schematic, and unreal. We found a much wider range of custom and belief among the so-called *"tontos"* than was reported by Redfield, and by the same token there was less of a gap between the *tontos* and *correctos*. While Redfield's concept would tend to make for two cultures, we see Tepoztlán as a single culture, with more and less acculturated individuals in close and frequent contact, each influencing the other, as they have for the past four hundred years.

IMPLICATIONS OF OUR DIFFERENCES

More important than the differences in our findings is the question of how to explain these differences. I suppose that in a sense it is inevitable that different students studying the same society will arrive at different conclusions. Certainly the personal factor, and what Redfield has recently referred to as the element of art in social science, cannot be overlooked.[5] Nevertheless the differences in our findings on Tepoztlán are of such magnitude as to demand some further and more detailed explanation.

Some of the differences in our data can be explained by changes which have occurred in the village in the interim of nearly twenty years between our studies. These changes have already been outlined in an earlier publication [6] and are discussed throughout this book. Other differences result from the difference in the general scope of the two studies. This study had the advantage of having Redfield's pioneer work to start with, the assistance of Mexican personnel, more than twice the amount of time for field work, and the development, during the past twenty years, of new approaches and methods, especially in the field of culture and personality. The much greater emphasis upon economic analysis in this study also reflects a fairly recent trend in anthropology. In addition, the fact that this study was based on the testimony of well over one hundred informants, as compared to about a half-dozen used by Redfield, revealed a wide range of individual differences and enabled more thorough checking of data.

Still other differences, such as those summarized in the preceding pages, must be attributed for the most part to differences in theoretical orientation and methodology which in turn influenced the selection and coverage of facts and the way in which these facts were organized. In rereading Redfield's study in the light of my

---

[5] Some sociologists like Mannheim would go even farther. He writes, "It could be shown in all cases that not only do fundamental orientations, evaluations, and the content of ideas differ, but that the manner of stating a problem, the sort of approach made, and even the categories in which experiences are subsumed, collected and ordered, vary according to the social position of the observer." Karl Mannheim, *Ideology and Utopia* (London: Kegan Paul, 1936), p. 13.

[6] See Lewis, "Social and Economic Changes in a Mexican Village," *América Indígena,* Vol. 4, No. 4 (October, 1944).

own work in the village, it seems to me that the concept of the folk-culture and folk-urban continuum was Redfield's organizing principle in the research. Perhaps this helps to explain his emphasis on the formal and ritualistic aspects of life rather than the everyday life of the people and their problems, on evidence of homogeneity rather than heterogeneity and the range of custom, on the weight of tradition rather than deviation and innovation, on unity and integration rather than tensions and conflict.

Redfield's interest was primarily in the study of a single cultural process: the evolution from folk to urban, rather than a well-rounded ethnographic account. He only incidentally considered Tepoztlán in its historical, geographical, and cultural context in Morelos and Mexico, and attempted rather to place Tepoztlán within the broader, more abstract context of the folk-urban continuum.

The questions he asked of his data were quite different from those asked in this study. For example, unlike the present study, he was not concerned with determining just what Tepoztlán is typical of in relation to rural Mexico; nor was he concerned with determining how a study of Tepoztlán might reveal some of the underlying characteristics and problems of Mexico as a whole. Thus, the Revolution in Tepoztlán is not analyzed in terms of its social, economic, and political effects upon the village, nor in terms of what light it might throw upon the nature of the Revolution as a whole, but rather in regard to the more limited question of the emergence of Zapata as a "folk hero." AN OUt-an'- out honky!

CRITIQUE OF REDFIELD'S CONCEPT OF FOLK-URBAN CONTINUUM

Since the concept of the folk society as an ideal type is, after all, a matter of definition,[7] there can be no quarrel with it as such, provided that it can be shown to have heuristic value. On the basis of our study of Tepoztlán, however, I should like to point out a number of limitations I have found in the conceptual framework of the folk-urban continuum, both as a scheme for the study of culture change and for cultural analysis. These criticisms can be discussed under six related points.

(1) The folk-urban conceptualization of social change focuses attention primarily on the city as the source of change, to the exclusion or neglect of other factors of an internal or external nature. So-called folk societies have been influencing each other for hundreds of years and out of such inter-action has come cultural change. As we have seen, the archaeological record in Tepoztlán, as well as in other parts of Mexico, indicates quite clearly a great mingling of peoples and cultures, which dates back at least a thousand years before the Spanish Conquest. Tepoztlán itself

---

[7] It should be noted that Redfield's use of the term "folk" and "folk society" has not always been consistent. In the study of Tepoztlán, he used it sometimes in a non-technical and popular sense, as when he speaks of folk dances, folk music, and folklore. (Redfield, *Tepoztlán*, p. 173.) But for the most part he defines the folk society as an intermediate stage between the truly primitive tribe and the urban community. This position was also taken in his article on "The Folk Society and Culture" in 1940. But in 1947, in another article ("The Folk Society," *American Journal of Sociology*, p. 293) he sets up the folk society as an ideal type which includes the primitive tribal society.

was first conquered by the Toltecs and later by the Aztecs, and with each conquest came new influences, new religious ideas, and new customs.

Another example of non-urban factors in culture change can be seen in the case of Tepoztlán and other parts of Latin America, where the introduction of rural culture elements was at least as far reaching in effect as any changes brought about by later urban influences. Similarly, we find that the Mexican Agrarian Revolution (particularly in its Zapatista phase) was a profound influence for change, but can hardly be classified as an urban influence. It is evident that the folk-urban continuum concept deals with only one of a wide variety of situations which may lead to culture change.[8] In the case of Tepoztlán, to study the urban factors alone would give us only a partial picture of culture change.

(2) It follows that in many instances culture change may not be a matter of a folk-urban progression, but rather an increasing or decreasing heterogeneity of culture elements. For example, we have seen that the incorporation of Spanish rural elements, such as the plow, oxen, plants, and many folk beliefs, did not make Tepoztlán more urban, but rather gave it a more varied rural culture. The introduction of plow culture in Tepoztlán did not eliminate the older system of hoe culture but gave the Tepoztecans an alternative and, in some ways, more efficient method of farming, making for greater heterogeneity in the economic life and in the forms of social relationships.

(3) Some of the criteria used in the definition of the folk society are treated by Redfield as linked or interdependent variables, but might better be treated as independent variables. Sol Tax, in his study of Guatemalan societies, has shown that societies can be both culturally well organized and homogeneous and, at the same time, highly secular, individualistic, and commercialistic.[9] He has also shown that inter-personal relations in a small and homogeneous society can be characterized by formalism and impersonality. His findings are supported by our Tepoztecan study. Moreover, our study shows other possible combinations of variables. Thus, whereas Tax found family disorganization as a concomitant of commercialism, in Tepoztlán the family remains strong, and there is little evidence of family disorganization. Moreover, collective forms of land tenure exist side by side with private land-ownership and individual working of the land.

(4) The typology involved in the folk-urban classification of societies tends to obscure one of the most significant findings of modern cultural anthropology, namely, the wide range in the ways of life and in the value systems among so-called primitive peoples. The folk society as used by Redfield would group together food-gathering, hunting, pastoral, and agricultural peoples, without distinction.[10] Simi-

---

[8] Becker's recent elaboration of his sacred-secular dichotomy, each with numerous subtypes, gives us a much broader typology embracing a wider range of culture change situations. Howard Becker, "Sacred and Secular Societies," *Social Forces*, Vol. 28, No. 4 (May, 1950), pp. 361–75.

[9] Tax, "Culture and Civilization in Guatemalan Societies," *Scientific Monthly*, XLVIII (May, 1939), 463–67; and "World View and Social Relations in Guatemala," *American Anthropologist*, 43 (1941), 22–42.

[10] To apply the term "folk society" to high cultures like that of the Aztecs (Tepoztlán was

larly, it would put into one category societies which are as different culturally and psychologically as the Arunta and the Eskimo, the Dobu and the Ba Thonga, the Zuni and the Alorese, the Dahomey and the Navaho. Indeed, one might argue that the folk-urban classification is not a cultural classification at all since it rides roughshod over fundamental cultural differences, i.e., differences in the ethos of a people. The point is that the attitudes and value systems of folk societies may resemble some urban societies much more than other folk societies. For example, the individualism and competitiveness of the Blackfoot Indians remind one much more of American urban value systems than those of the Zuni.[11] This suggests that the critera used in the folk-urban classification are concerned with the purely formal aspects of society and are not the most crucial for cultural analysis.[12]

What has been said of the folk end of the folk-urban formula applies also to the urban end. Focusing only on the formal aspects of urban society reduces all urban societies to a common denominator and treats them as if they all had the same culture. Thus Greek, Egyptian, Roman, Medieval, twentieth-century American and Russian cities would all be put into the same class.[13] To take but one example, there are obvious and significant differences between American and Russian urban culture, and in all probability these two "urban influences" would have a very different effect upon a preliterate society exposed to them.

It should be clear that the concept "urban" is too much of a catchall to be useful for cultural analysis. Moreover, it is suggested here that the question posed by Redfield, namely, what happens to an isolated homogeneous society when it comes into contact with an urbanized society, cannot possibly be answered in a scientific way, because the question is too general and the terms used do not give us the necessary data. What we need to know is what kind of an urban society, under what conditions of contact, and a host of other specific historical data.

(5) The folk-urban classification has serious limitations in guiding field research

---

part of this high culture area) and at the same time to apply it to simple food-gathering peoples like the Shoshone, robs the term of much of its discriminatory value. Also, to write of a "folk element" in Tepoztlán in 1926 (the so-called *tontos*) as if it were identical with the folk element of the pre-Hispanic days neglects all the cultural influences to which this element had been subjected in the intervening four hundred years and blurs many distinctions which have to be made.

[11] Becker makes a similar observation that "primitive" societies may readily approximate the secular rather than the sacred type of society. He cites the Comanche as an example.

[12] Herskovits has made a similar point in his criticism of the folk-urban classification. He wrote, "In such systems [of classification] the orientation is in terms of categories based on form, rather than problems phrased in terms of process." Melville J. Herskovits, *Man and His Works* (New York: A. A. Knopf, 1947), p. 607.

[13] Herskovits, using African materials, has made a similar criticism. "It is also to be noted that in discussions of the folk society, African data are nowhere taken into account. In West Africa, however, many urban communities are to be found that range from one hundred thousand inhabitants [the approximate size of Merida, Redfield's Yucatán "city"] to over three hundred and fifty thousand. These populations have complex specialized economies exhibiting, as we have seen, the use of money and the presence of profit motivation. Yet in these cities relationships are as personal as in any 'folk society' and religion is the focal aspect of the culture. In short, here we have an anomaly—an anomaly, that is, in terms of the concept of the folk society—of urban, *sacred*, communities." *Ibid.*, p. 606.

because of the highly selective implications of the categories themselves and the rather narrow focus of problem. The emphasis upon essentially formal aspects of culture leads to neglect of psychological data and, as a rule, does not give insight into the character of the people. We have already shown how this approach has influenced the selection, interpretation, and organization of the data in Redfield's study of Tepoztlán.

(6) Finally, underlying the folk-urban dichotomy as used by Redfield, is a system of value judgments which contains the old Rousseauan notion of primitive peoples as noble savages, and the corollary that with civilization has come the fall of man.[14] Again and again in Redfield's writings there emerges the value judgment that folk societies are good and urban societies bad. It is assumed that all folk societies are integrated while urban societies are the great disorganizing force. In his introduction to Miner's St. Denis study, Redfield suggests that the usual view of peasant life "as something to be escaped, an ignominy to be shunned" may be wrong. He finds that the *habitant* of St. Denis has order, security, faith, and confidence, "because he has culture." In another essay ("The Folk Society and Culture" in *Eleven Twenty-Six*), he contrasts the "organization and consistency which gives a group moral solidarity" with "the impaired moral organization of the urban society." Even in his most recent study, which to this writer represents a great departure from his earlier thinking, in that he is less concerned with formalism and categories and more concerned with people, we find the old values reappearing. "Progress" and urbanization now are seen as inevitable, but they are still evil.[15]

Having pointed out some of the limitations of the folk-urban formula let us now

[14] This type of value system is particularly prone to influence the interpretation of whether a given cultural change shall be called disorganization or simply reorganization. Since the concept of disorganization is one of the three key concepts in Redfield's folk-urban hypothesis, it can be seen how directly this value system may affect the interpretation. We are not, of course, objecting to the fact of values per se, but rather to the failure to make them explicit, as well as to this particular value system. Redfield's values suggest what Lovejoy and Boas have called "cultural primitivism," which they define as "the discontent of the civilized with civilization, or with some conspicuous and characteristic feature of it." Arthur O. Lovejoy and George Boas, *Primitivism and Related Ideas in Antiquity* (Baltimore: Johns Hopkins Press, 1935), p. 7.

They show that primitivism has existed in various forms throughout the recorded history of mankind. "Of direct, or even indirect, influence of the classical primitivistic tradition there is probably little. But since the beginning of the present century, Western man has become increasingly sceptical concerning the nineteenth-century 'myth of progress,' increasingly troubled with the misgivings about the value of the outcome of civilization thus far, about the future to which it tends, and about himself as the author of it all; and similar doubts and apprehensions found expression two millenia or more ago. In spite of the more complex and sophisticated general ideology of the contemporary exponents of these moods, there are striking parallels to be observed between certain of the texts that follow [i.e., Greek, Roman, and Indian] and some passages in, e.g., such writings as Freud's *Civilization and Its Discontents* and Spengler's *Man and Technics*." *Ibid.*, p. xi.

[15] Redfield writes, "The people of Chan Kom are, then, a people who have no choice but to go forward with technology, with a declining religious faith and moral conviction, into a dangerous world. They are a people who must and will come to identify their interests with those of people far away, outside the traditional circle of their loyalties and political responsibilities. As such they should have the sympathy of the readers of these pages." Redfield, *A Village That Chose Progress*, p. 178.

see to what extend the trend of change found in our study of Tepoztlán falls within the categories suggested by Redfield in his study *The Folk Culture of Yucatan*.[16] He postulates that with increased urban influences there is greater disorganization, secularization, and individualization. Taking each separately, we shall consider the family first, as an example of disorganization. Redfield summarized the broad trends of change in family organization as follows:

As one goes from Tusik toward Merida there is to be noted a reduction in the stability of the elementary family; a decline in the manifestation of patriarchal or matriarchal authority; a disappearance of institutions expressing cohesion in the great family; a reduction in the strength and importance of respect relationships, especially for elder brothers and for elder people generally; an increasing vagueness of the conventional outlines of appropriate behavior toward relatives; and a shrinkage in the applicability of kinship terms primarily denoting members of the elementary family toward more distant relatives or toward persons not relatives.[17]

The first generalization that can be made in the case of Tepoztlán is that, despite the increased city influences in the last seventeen years, the stability of the nuclear family has not been seriously modified. The family remains strong and cohesive, separations have not noticeably increased, and divorce is all but non-existent. The extended family is relatively weak but continues to serve in cases of emergency. This weakness, however, is not a recent phenomenon. Quarrels between husband and wife and wife-beating occur with some frequency, but this too seems to be an old pattern. The tensions and quarrels within families reflect a type of family organization, as well as Tepoztecan personality, but are not necessarily symptoms of disorganization.

Parental authority remains strong in Tepoztlán, despite the elimination of arranged marriages and the increase in elopements. Parents continue to have control over their children, in many cases even after marriage. As we have seen, about sixteen per cent of all house sites are composed of joint families, and about half of these are extended families in which married sons are treated as children subject to the authority of the parents (*hijos de familia*).

Although about fifty per cent of the marriages now begin as elopements, which flout the authority of the parents, the old form of asking for the girl's hand by the

---

[16] In effect, we are comparing the results of a diachronic study of culture change with that of a synchronic study. Redfield's methodology in *Folk Culture of Yucatan* involved the reconstruction of a historical process from the differential position of four communities on the hypothetical folk-urban continuum. That is, each of the four communities represented a distinct stage in the evolution from folk to urban. It assumed that the communities were similar at some unspecified time in the past, and explained the differences in the degree of secularization, individualization, and disorganization, as a result of urban influences. Redfield had posed a historical problem which he attempted to solve in a non-historical way. In referring to the four monographs on which his book was based, he wrote, "The outlines of historical trends of change . . . might be expected to appear more clearly if carefully prepared histories of local cultures were written. . . . But in none of the four communities studied in the present connection was any systematic effort made to recover the older conditions of the local society by asking informants." Redfield, *Folk Culture of Yucatan*, pp. 341–42.

[17] *Ibid.*, p. 63.

boy's parents continues. In any case, elopements do not lead to disorganization, for most elopements end in marriage, and the couple make peace with their parents. Assuming that elopements are an old trait, as seems to be indicated, here we have a case in which urban influence has intensified an old trait rather than caused its breakdown. Moreover, because Redfield found practically no elopements in Tusik and many elopements in Merida, he associated elopements with urbanism and disorganization. But this assumes what has still to be proved. In Tepoztlán, which is much less urban than Merida, by Redfield's own standards, we find a much higher proportion of elopements than in Merida. Furthermore, in Tzintzuntzan, an even more isolated village, Foster found that ninety per cent of marriages began as elopements. And he cites documentary evidence for the antiquity of this pattern.[18]

The desire of young couples to become independent of their parents and to set up their own homes, which has been indicated earlier, reflects a greater individualism but does not necessarily imply a breakdown in family life. On the contrary, the lesser role of the in-laws and the greater dependence of the husband and wife upon each other, plus the fact that they are each of their own choice, may make for better marriage relations and greater family stability.

Although it is true that some outer forms of respect have been discarded, the fundamental respect status of elders remains. Perhaps the single exception has been the decline in the respect accorded elder brothers. But it is questionable whether the elder brother in Tepoztlán ever enjoyed the special position that he had in Maya society.

We find no evidence for any marked change in the reciprocal behavior of relatives, perhaps because such changes have occurred so far back in history that informants have no memory of them today. As we have said before, the extended family is weak and, so far as we know, has been weak for many generations. The same may be said for the use of kinship terms, which have not changed in recent history. In surrounding villages, which generally conserve older culture elements, kinship terms are used in substantially the same way as in Tepoztlán.

In the examples cited, it is clear that changes have occurred in the village, but these changes do not necessarily imply disorganization. Rather, they involve a new kind of organization or reorganization.[19]

---

[18] Foster, *Empire's Children*, p. 429.

Beals, in another connection, has also called attention to a pattern of change different from that reported by Redfield. Beals writes, "Cherán, like many Indian communities of Mexico, is increasingly influenced by the town and the city. Nevertheless, the process again seems significantly different from those hitherto described by Redfield. In Cherán there is no distinction of *los tontos* and *los correctos*, mestizo and *indio*, or *ladino* and *indio*, although such may exist in some Tarascan towns with an appreciable mestizo population. Nor does the neat diminishing order of city, town, and village hold in this area. Cherán is probably more influenced by Gary [Indiana, U.S.A.], Mexico City, and Morelia [possibly in diminishing order] than it is by Uruapan and Pátzcuaro. Indeed, it is quite probable that fundamentally Cherán is more progressive, more in touch with the modern world, than is mestizo Pátzcuaro with its conscious idealization of a Colonial past." Beals, *Cherán*, pp. 211–12.

[19] Gross in a recent study has made the same point. He writes, ". . . it should be noted that Redfield's concepts of organization and disorganization are subject to a severe limitation. They

The second conclusion in the study in Yucatán showed a clear trend toward secularization.

The conclusion has been reached that the city and town exhibit greater secularization than do the villages. The principal facts offered in support of this conclusion are . . . the separation of maize from the context of religion and its treatment simply as a means of getting food or money; the increase in the number of specialists who carry on their activities for a practical livelihood relative to those that carry on traditional activities which are regarded as prerogatives and even moral duties to the community; the change in the character of the institution of *guardia* whereby from being an obligation, religiously supported, to protect a shrine and a god it becomes a mere job in the town hall; the (almost complete) disappearance of family worship; the decline in the sacramental character of baptism and marriage; the conversion of the pagan cult from what is truly religious worship to mere magic or even superstition; the decline in the veneration accorded the santos; the change in the novena in which from being a traditional form expressive of appeal to deity it becomes a party for the fun of the participants; the alteration in the festival of the patron saint in which it loses its predominant character as worship and becomes play and an opportunity for profit; the separation of ideas as to the cause and cure of sickness from conceptions as to moral or religious obligation.[20]

The data from Tepoztlán does not enable a careful comparison on each of the cited points. However, much of the data is comparable and shows the trend toward secularization noted. The attitude toward corn in Tepoztlán combines both the secular and religious. Certainly corn is viewed as the basic crop, both for subsistence and for trade. But the religious aspects have not been entirely lopped off. The corn is still blessed in the church on San Isidro's day, and some families still burn incense in the home and address a prayer to the corn before planting. Some also make the sign of the cross when planting the first seed. Moreover, on the day of San Miguel, crosses are still placed at the four corners of the milpa to ward off the winds. From informants' accounts, it appears that these customs were more widespread before the Revolution. It is difficult to say how much change has occurred since 1926, for Redfield did not report on this subject.

The study of occupational changes and division of labor in Tepoztlán showed that most of the old "folk specialists" have continued and even increased in number, side by side with the increase in the new specialists. There were more *curanderos, chirimiteros,* fireworks makers and mask makers in 1944 than in 1926, and there seemed to be every indication that these occupations would continue. The only exceptions are the *huehuechiques,* who must be able to speak Náhuatl, and the *chirimiteros,* who are being displaced by the modern band. However, the rate of increase in what Redfield would call the secular specialists has been much greater than that of the "folk specialists." To this extent the independent findings for

force the analysis into an organization-disorganization framework and neglect the possibility that there may exist different levels of organization in cultures. . . ." Neal Gross, "Cultural Variables in Rural Communities," *American Journal of Sociology,* Vol. LIV, No. 5 (March, 1948), pp. 348-450.

[20] *Ibid.,* p. 352.

Yucatán and Tepoztlán agree. But it should be noted that before the Revolution there were more shoemakers, carpenters, saddle makers, and other artisans than in 1926 or in 1944. Were it not that we had specific historical information to explain this phenomenon, we might conclude that with increasing urban contacts there is a decrease in the number of specialists. The reason for this decrease has been, rather, the destruction of many neighboring haciendas which were formerly supplied by labor from Tepoztlán, and the abolition of the *cacique* class which offered a market for the products of the artisans.

In Tepoztlán there does not appear to have been any appreciable decline in the sacramental character of baptism and marriage. At any rate, both are considered important and are standard practices. Despite the legalization of secular marriage, church marriage is still considered the best marriage by most Tepoztecans.

Similarly there is no evidence of any decline in the veneration of the *santos;* the novena continues to be an appeal to the deity rather than a party for fun; the patron saints of the barrios are still regarded as protectors and are worshipped as such. Nor have barrio fiestas become primarily an occasion for profit. In fact, Tepoztecans do not show the marked commercial spirit reported in Mitla by Parsons, and in communities of the Guatemalan highlands by Sol Tax. Unlike Parsons' experiences in Mitla, we were never besieged by questions about the cost of things, nor did we ever witness Tepoztecans haggling among themselves or with strangers.

The third conclusion of the Yucatán study pertains to the trend toward individualization, or individualism as one goes from folk to urban. The specific facts found in the study of the four communities are given as follows:

. . . . The relative decrease in importance of specialized functions which are performed in behalf of the community and the relative increase of specialties discharged for the individual's own benefit; the development of individual rights in land and in family estates; the diminution or disappearance of collective labor and of the exchange of services in connection with civic enterprises and religious worship; the decreasing concern of the family or of the local community in the making and the maintaining of marriages; the becoming less common of the extended domestic family; the lessening of emphasis and of conventional definition of the respect relationships among kin; the decline in family worship and the disappearance of religious symbols expressive of the great family; decrease in the tendency to extend kinship terms with primary significance for members of the elementary family to more remote relatives or to persons unrelated genealogically; the increasing vagueness of the conventional outlines of appropriate behavior towards relatives; the change in the nature of the marriage and baptismal rites so as less to express the linkage of the families and more to concern the immediate involved individuals only; the decline in relative importance of the santo patron of the local community; the suggested relation of the increase in sorcery to the separation of individuals, especially of women from the security of familial groups.[21]

Some of the items listed above were also listed under the categories of disorganization and secularization and have been treated earlier. The development of

---

[21] *Ibid.,* p. 355.

individual rights in land may date back prior to the Spanish Conquest. Cortés and his heirs owned land in Tepoztlán and rented it out to Tepoztecans as early as 1580. In the past twenty or thirty years there have been no changes in the direction of the private ownership of the communal resources. The persistence of the communal resources, which still accounts for over eighty per cent of all the area of the municipio, is impressive.

The trend toward the breakdown of collective labor is seen clearly in Tepoztlán, particularly in connection with the difficulty in getting barrio members to turn out for the plowing and planting of the barrio fields. In 1947, three of the barrios had rented out the land and used the rental for the barrio. On the whole, many of our findings for Tepoztlán might be interpreted as confirming Redfield's more general findings for Yucatán, particularly in regard to the trend toward secularization and individualization, perhaps less so in regard to disorganization.

CULTURE CHANGE IN TEPOZTLÁN

Let us now depart from Redfield's formulation and analyze the changes in Tepoztlán in terms of concrete historical occurrences and their patterns. For this purpose, the history of culture change in Tepoztlán may be divided into three major periods, each with its distinctive characteristics. These periods are (1) from the Spanish Conquest to about 1910; (2) from 1910 to about 1930; (3) from 1930 to the present. The great differences in the lengths of each of these periods correspond, to some extent, to the different rates of change characteristic of each. Furthermore, each period is characterized by changes of a different order.

During the first period, change was on the whole gradual but far-reaching, touching all aspects of life from material culture and technology to social organization, economics, and religion. The changes during this period were the result of outside influence and consisted of the transformation of the culture by the super-imposition of Spanish culture, consisting of both urban and rural elements, on the native culture, with a resultant fusion of the two. During the second period, the changes were caused by a combination of external and internal factors, and changes were more rapid and violent, affecting primarily the social and political organization. The third period was in a sense a continuation of the second, with the changes primarily in the fields of communication, literacy, education, consumption patterns, and values, and with economics, social organization, and religion remaining quite stable. On the whole, but particularly in the field of material culture, the new culture elements in all periods did not supplant but were added to the old, making for a richer and more heterogeneous culture.

FROM THE CONQUEST TO 1910

This period can be divided into two sub-periods: one, from the Conquest to 1810, the colonial period; and two, from 1810 to 1910, the end of the Díaz regime.

The effects of the Spanish Conquest and of Spanish influence during the colonial period were extremely complicated and included both destructive and constructive aspects, disorganization, and reorganization. On the whole, the period was characterized by a sharp population decline due to epidemics, forced labor in the mines of Taxco and Cuautla and on neighboring haciendas, and out migration to escape heavy taxes. Some local industries, such as paper making, pulque manufacture, cotton growing, and weaving declined. Many new culture elements were introduced. In material culture, the most important of these included iron, the plow, oxen, cattle, swine, and other domesticated animals; new food plants and new styles in houses, furnishings, and clothing. Most of these new items were taken up slowly and only by the very small portion of the population that could afford to buy them, generally those of the upper socio-economic group, consisting of the Spaniards, the older *principales,* and their descendants. We have seen that, as late as 1943, less than a third of the families owned plows and oxen.

Some of the elements mentioned above were part of culture complexes which transformed certain aspects of the Indian economy. This point needs to be emphasized because of the tendency, among some students, to view the process of diffusion of Spanish culture in terms of discrete traits. We have shown, for example, that the plow and oxen were more than two traits. Rather they formed part and parcel of a new system of plow culture which involved changes in native concepts of land tenure, in work cycles, in time pressures, in the relation of labor to capital, in the yields, and finally in the effects upon the natural resources.

Other related changes which occurred during the colonial period included the spread of private ownership of land, the practice of renting land, working for wages, the use of money, and the adoption of a European system of weights and measures and the European calendar.

While the documentary evidence for the changes in Tepoztecan social organization during the colonial period is very meager, it might be presumed that the old clan organization broke down and was substituted by the Spanish-type family organization. On the other hand, if we were to judge only from Sahagún's description of family life, which supposedly referred to the pre-Hispanic period, then family life was changed relatively little by the Conquest. In regard to other aspects of the social structure, the evidence is clearer. Class stratification continued, except that a few Spanish and mestizo families took over the leading positions in the newly established local government.[22] The Spaniards introduced their municipal form of government, with locally elected officials and a complicated administrative machinery for the hearing of complaints. Early documents indicate that Indians were elected to office, and that the populace lodged complaints against local officials and haciendas because of the treatment accorded them.

[22] Our findings for Tepoztlán corroborates the findings for Mexico as a whole. For example, Diffie writes, "For the great masses of Mexican people, the Conquest effected no considerable change in the aristocratic and despotic nature of their administration. They had not participated in the government before, and they did not participate after Spanish domination. Before, they were ruled by an hereditary Indian aristocracy; after, they were ruled by Spaniards who took the place of their old chieftains, or who utilized their old chieftains as instruments of Spanish power." Diffie, *Latin-American Civilization,* p. 275.

Probably the greatest changes took place in religion. As we have seen, Tepoztlán was easily converted to Catholicism, at least as far as the adoption of Catholic forms of worship, which were in many respects similar to native forms. The village became a Dominican center for religious instruction after the convent was built in the middle of the sixteenth century. The unity of church and state made the position of the church strong in Tepoztlán throughout the colonial period. The church was supported by taxes collected by the government, and ecclesiastic and secular authorities worked together in administering the population. Some of the best lands went to the church, and by the close of the colonial period the church was the largest landowner in the village. During this period the church was an active agent for culture change, particularly in its efforts to wipe out native beliefs and to establish Christianity. The church also introduced new plants; the first European vegetables brought to Tepoztlán were planted in the churchyard by the priests.

FROM 1810 TO 1910

This period was one of relative stability; the Wars of Independence from Spain seem to have had little effect on Tepoztlán. Colonial forms of life continued, on the whole, and population increased. However, the Reforms of 1857 had great importance in the village, since the church lost most of its lands. These lands were distributed among a small portion of the population, resulting in the growth of a local aristocracy, the *caciques,* who ruled the village throughout the Díaz regime. The church revived much of its power under the support of the *cacique* class, and religious life was active. Although schools were introduced early in this period, they were attended by a privileged few. A small intelligentsia developed, and for a brief period the upper class in Tepoztlán experienced a cultural florescence.

During the mid-eighties, coffee growing and ropemaking were introduced. Toward the end of the century, the railroad was built through the municipio, and Tepoztecans had their first contact with North Americans. Steel plows and wire fencing came with the railroad. This was a time of relative prosperity for the *caciques,* merchants, and artisans. The railroad encouraged the charcoal industry, giving Tepoztecans a new source of income but at the same time seriously depleting forest resources. Public improvements, such as the Municipal Building, the park and bandstand, and streets were constructed or repaired. The hacienda system was at its height, offering employment to hundreds of Tepoztecans and a market for the artisans.

The abuses of the haciendas and the local *caciques* made for discontent and discord. The people were not permitted to use the communal lands for *tlacolol,* and those who opposed the *cacique* rule were sent off to the army or to jail in Quintana Roo. Inter-village strife over the use of the forests for charcoal resulted in violence and bitterness. Finally, the landlessness and poverty of the majority of Tepoztecans led many to participate in the Revolution which was to come.

FROM 1910 TO 1920

Tepoztlán suffered extremely during the years of the Revolution, and village life was completely disrupted. The village was repeatedly occupied by the opposing forces, homes were burned, crops and animals destroyed, and the people completely impoverished and forced to flee. A large number of Tepoztecans had their first contacts with city life at this time. Village population declined markedly, many having lost their lives in battle or as a result of hunger and illness. With the Revolution, the political power of the *caciques* in Tepoztlán was broken, and the old class distinctions were abolished.[23] The church barely functioned during this period and religious life was at a standstill.

FROM 1920 TO 1930

In the ten years after the Revolution, the village struggled back to normalcy. Population increased rapidly as people returned and as living conditions improved. In 1930, constitutional government was established in the state of Morelos, providing for independent municipios and "free" elections. New political factions arose, reflecting the post-revolutionary tension and unrest, which culminated in a minor civil war in Tepoztlán. The many restrictions placed on the church by the new federal government caused the church to shut its doors, so that religious life was again at a minimum. In 1920, the Colonia Tepozteco was established in Mexico City, exposing Tepoztlán to a permanent and active urbanizing influence.

FROM 1930 TO 1945

The changes which occurred in the past twenty years have been far reaching and may be summarized as follows: a rapid increase in population, an improvement in health services accompanied by some decline in the importance of *curanderos*, a marked rise in the standard of living and the aspiration level of the people, the growth of a class of small landowners, the development of a greater variety and specialization in occupations, a decrease in the use of Náhuatl, and a corresponding spread in the use of Spanish, a rise in literacy and the beginnings of regular newspaper reading, and a greater incorporation of the village into the main stream of national life.

The primary influences for change have been the new road, the granting of *ejidos,* and the expansion of school facilities. Corn mills were also important. Be-

---

[23] Here again, the concrete historical data do not follow the logic of the folk-urban continuum. One of the criteria used in Redfield's definition of the folk society is that it is a classless society. As we go toward the urban pole of the folk-urban continuum we might expect greater class differentiation. But Tepoztlán today shows much less class stratification than in 1910, so that we might conclude that Tepoztlán was more of the folk society type today than in 1910. Similarly, the classless society of the future, as envisioned by the socialists, would, according to the folk-urban continuum, have to be considered a folk society. Becker has avoided this difficulty in his sacred-secular dichotomy by setting up subtypes under each category. He distinguishes two types of sacred societies, the folk and the prescribed, each in turn with their subtypes. The socialist society would probably be classified under the sacred-prescribed type.

cause these innovations occurred within such a short period, their effects were mutually reenforcing and the tempo of change was accelerated. The road broke down the barriers of isolation and gave Tepoztlán easy access to new markets; the granting of *ejidos* supplied a somewhat broader land base, thereby increasing production; the corn mills improved the lot of the women and gave them free time which they could devote to commerce and other gainful occupations. The villagers obtained a new source of income from the sale of their *ciruelas* and other fruits which gained commercial value after the means of communication were improved. The road was also responsible for the tourist trade, more frequent social contacts with Cuernavaca, and indirectly the changes in clothing styles. The bus lines have affected village life in more ways than simply that of improving means of communication. They have become a new economic and political force in the village and a new source of conflict. Each line has built up a following of members who have a direct economic interest in their cooperative. The relatives and *compadres* of these members are also involved in the conflict, and the village is again divided into factions. Furthermore, the directors of the cooperatives are beginning to take political control out of the hands of the peasants. The employees of the bus cooperatives now constitute the first important group of non-farmers in Tepoztlán.

The school has been an extremely important agent of cultural change in the village in the past twenty years. As we have seen, enrollment soared from less than 100 in 1926 to over 700 in 1948. The school has increased literacy; has taught the children new standards of personal hygiene and cleanliness; has familiarized them with toilets, running water, and showers; has introduced new games and a spirit of group play lacking before. The school has become the symbol of the new in Tepoztlán; it has made for a greater identification with the nation. The school also has been a great socializing factor. It is breaking down barrio localism and is making for friendships between individuals in different parts of the village. The school has offered new outlets for emotional expression.

PATTERNS OF CHANGE

In the preceding pages we have focused primarily upon the changes which have occurred in each of the major periods considered. But there have also been stable elements which have persisted almost intact, not only during the past twenty years, but since the beginning of the colonial period. This is all the more striking because of the proximity of the village to Mexico City and Cuernavaca. Perhaps the greatest stability has been in agriculture. The tools and techniques have remained essentially the same. Corn and beans are still the major crops. The agricultural economy is still primarily a subsistence economy. Tepoztlán has managed to hold its communal lands throughout this period, primarily because these lands are poor and undesirable to the near-by haciendas. This has been a primary factor in stabilizing Tepoztecan economy, although on a subsistence level with a low standard of living.

The persistence of Náhuatl is also noteworthy and was probably related to the class character of the society. It was primarily *caciques,* merchants, and artisans, who had need of Spanish in their dealings with the outside. The peasants traded among themselves and with the Náhuatl-speaking people of near-by villages. With the change in the class structure, the equalizing of opportunities, the greater contacts with the outside, and the increase in school attendance after the Revolution, the use of Spanish has increased.

It is on the psychocultural level that we find the greatest stability and continuity with the past. The reader who is familiar with the ethnographic literature of Middle America must be impressed with the many similarities in the general quality of inter-personal relations in Tepoztlán, and those reported from more isolated Indian communities in Guatemala. Among some of the similarities are the great value placed on work, the strong ties to the land, the view of farming as the ideal occupation, the persistence of an almost tribal localism, the stability and strength of the family, the continued belief in *los aires, mal ojo,* El Tepozteco, and herbal remedies.

In reviewing the history of cultural change in Tepoztlán since the Spanish Conquest, it is apparent that there is no single formula which will explain the whole range of phenomena. The period of the Spanish Conquest is an example of forced acculturation in which the direction of cultural change was in large measure determined by the conqueror rather than the conquered. The motives of Cortés, who controlled Tepoztlán and the surrounding villages, were to secure Tepoztecan labor for his mines and haciendas and obtain wealth in the form of taxes. He was not concerned with reorganizing Tepoztecan society and certainly was not interested in raising the standard of living. His policy was to interfere as little as possible with native beliefs and practices, except where they directly threatened his interests. As we have seen, he continued the tax system of Moctezuma; he did not alter the native boundaries; he left the Tepoztecans most of their communal lands, taking only the best portions.

It should be noted that many of the traits, such as religion, the calendar, the new system of weights and measures, were essential to the interests of the conquerors. In some cases, the Indians were specifically prohibited from taking on Spanish traits; witness the restrictions placed upon the owning of horses and firearms during the colonial period. Mounted and armed, Indians were obviously a threat to the conquerors.

Another important factor which determined the diffusion of Spanish traits during the colonial period was the inter-marriage of Spaniards with native women. The fact that there were no Spanish women, to teach their culinary and other domestic arts, perpetuated the native cuisine, utensils, and kitchen equipment. Similarly, practices of child rearing remained essentially native. However, the Indian women probably learned many Spanish folk beliefs from their husbands.

In other words, the Conquest affected the work of women much less directly than that of men. The men were forced to leave the village for long periods to work in the mines and haciendas, where they learned European agricultural methods and later introduced them to the village. Here we find a process similar in some respects to the case of the enslavement of the Negro in the New World.[24]

A third factor which conditioned the nature of change in the colonial period was the class structure whereby the Indians or the lower classes were socially isolated from the upper class. This lasted throughout the colonial period and up to the Revolution of 1910.

Another more general factor, which facilitated the diffusion of Spanish culture, was the basic similarities between the native and Spanish colonial cultures. Both were stratified feudal societies, both had a system of communal landholding, in both the religious and social structure was closely interwoven, both had well-developed markets. In addition, they shared many more specific traits, such as the use of flowers with images, pilgrimages to sacred shrines, the use of incense, the concept of lucky and unlucky days, and a host of other items.

Other factors which influenced the diffusion process was the obvious superiority of some Spanish matériel, such as the gun, compared to the bow and arrow; or the tile roof, compared to the thatched roof. Finally, the acceptance of one trait required the acceptance of related traits, as we have seen in some detail in the example of plow culture.

During the nineteenth century most of the changes in the village were in the form of an increasing urbanization of the upper class in the village. However, the more urban culture of this group did not spread widely to the mass of the population primarily because most of the traits were of no practical use and were economically out of their reach. Moreover, unlike the colonial period, there was no new group in the village which stood to benefit by spreading new traits. The only exception to this was a small movement to increase literacy.

The major characteristics of the acculturation process since the Revolution were the increased contacts with the outside, the breakdown of the internal barriers to social mobility, the increase in wealth. In contrast to the colonial period, in which the work of men was primarily affected, it was the work of the women that was affected in this period, by the corn mills, the sewing machines, and the bus lines.

IMPLICATIONS OF CHANGE

What are the implications of the total findings of this study for administrators, social scientists, and others concerned with the problem of improving life in communities like Tepoztlán? In the first place, it is important to recognize that Tepoztecans do not have many of the problems which beset our own modern industrial civilization. In Tepoztlán there is little exploitation of man by man; no single individual or group has power over others. Indeed, the lust for power and prestige motivates few people in this village. Nor are the anxieties and frustrations those which come from living in a highly competitive society, in which the fetish of personal success places a great burden upon the individual.

---

[24] See, for example, Herskovits, *Trinidad Village* (New York: A. A. Knopf, 1947).

But Tepoztecans have their own problems. Their agricultural resources are limited and of poor quality, their technology is backward, and their productivity low. Less than forty per cent are landowners, and holdings are much too small to support a higher standard of living. Moreover, there is no new land available, since the village is surrounded by other municipios with similar problems. It should be emphasized that, on the whole, Tepoztecans have a profound knowledge of their physical environment and have made as good an adjustment to it as might be expected. They are familiar with the advantages of crop rotation and practice it to the extent to which the size of their landholdings permit. They also know the benefits of letting land lie fallow, but again the majority of families do not have sufficient land to practice it. An ancient form of terracing is used to prevent soil erosion, but this is only partially effective, and erosion continues. Perhaps the most important improvement in agriculture would be the use of commercial fertilizer. Corn production could be doubled in many instances, but the high price of fertilizer makes this a difficult innovation. Irrigation and insect control would also be of great benefit to Tepoztlán.

The prospects of solving the agricultural problems through mechanization are slight. The rough and hilly terrain rules out the use of tractors and the very small size of holdings would make it uneconomical. In fact, even plow culture is becoming a burden because of the increased need of capital. As we have seen, some Tepoztecans are turning to the more primitive system of hillside hoe culture in order to avoid the rising costs of the recent inflationary period. But this system is an anachronism in the modern scene. It is further depleting the communal resources and cannot support an expanding population with a higher standard of living. Although the *ejido* program has helped to relieve the agrarian problem it has by no means solved it in Tepoztlán. It is difficult to see how the standard of living can be appreciably raised in such an environment. As the means of communication improve and the aspirations of the people rise, the move to the city will in all probability increase. That this has not occurred on a larger scale before this is an interesting commentary on the Tepoztecan character. Most of the young people are still quite provincial and fear the dangers of the outside world.

Given the objective limitation of Tepoztecan economy and environment, their history of colonial status over a three-hundred-year period, the instability and chicanery of Mexican politics, and the unplanned and haphazard nature of social change due to urban influence, we can better understand the psychology and world view of the Tepoztecans. It is a psychology of living with problems rather than solving them, of constantly adjusting to difficulties rather than eliminating them.[25]

We have seen that in the increased contact with the outside world in recent years, Tepoztecans have taken many new traits of modern life. They now have Coca-Cola, aspirin, radios, sewing machines, phonographs, poolrooms, flashlights, clocks,

---

[25] In a recent paper, discussing Indian and Ladino values, John Gillin has suggested that the drive to manipulate and control the environment was more characteristic of the Ladinos than of the Indians. Following this, Tepoztlán would appear to be more Indian.

steel plows, and some labor saving devices. They also have a greater desire to attend school, to eat better, to dress better, and to spend more. But in many ways their world view is still much closer to sixteenth-century Spain and to pre-Hispanic Mexico than to the modern scientific world. They are still guided by superstition and primitive beliefs; sorcery, magic, evil winds, and spirits still dominate their thinking. It is clear that, for the most part, they have taken on only the more superficial aspects and values of modern life. Can western civilization offer them no more?

Appendixes

A. *AN INTENSIVE SURVEY OF MAIZE IN TEPOZTLÁN*

BY EDGAR ANDERSON

MORE THAN any other crop plant, maize is a sensitive mirror of the people who grow it. There are myriads of varieties and they fall into a few ill-defined races. Any two varieties can cross and frequently do so if they are grown near each other, since maize is naturally cross-pollinated and the wind blows the pollen from one field to another. By their type and their departures from it, fields of maize bear witness to the history of the peoples who are growing them. By their uniformity to type they show the skill of those who selected the seeds. Their beauty, their yield, the purposes for which they are adopted, all portray the attitudes and scale of values of their cultivators.

Maize in Mexico varies from plant to plant, from field to field, from variety to variety, and from region to region. The usual variation in kernel color which is so noticeable to one accustomed to the puritanical uniformity of field crops in the United States, is relatively superficial. It often masks, to American eyes, the fact that an Indian variety may be more morphologically uniform than modern commercial varieties which have been selected for a single color. Of all the characteristics of a variety, the shape of the ear is probably the most significant, but it has been found difficult to measure effectively. The number of rows of kernels, the width of the kernels, the extent to which they are pointed at the apex, and the texture of their starch (from flinty to floury) have proved more reliable (Anderson and Cutler, 1942; Anderson, 1946).

A fairly well systematized method of making standard 25 ear samples from fields or corn cribs has been worked out, the results being condensed into a pictorialized scatter diagram which serves as a record. These diagrams lend themselves to the making of exact comparisons between varieties or regions or cultures. (See Anderson, 1946 and 1948, for details and examples.)

For at least seven hundred years, the maize of western Mexico has been markedly different from that of the Mesa Central. Modern commerce may have blurred this boundary, but it has not obliterated it. The varieties of maize grown in the region west of Guadalajara, for instance, belong to the race which Anderson has named "Mexican Narrow Ear"; those in the vicinity of Mexico City to the race previously designated "Mexican Pyramidal" by Anderson and Cutler. So different are they that not a single ear raised in the one region could be duplicated by one from the other, in spite of the great variability in both areas. The maize of Tepoztlán is of particular interest because it comes from one of the places where the dividing line between these two races is quite sharp. To the north lies the region of Mexican Pyramidal, with its various sub-races and mongrels. To the west and south is a region long characterized by Mexican Narrow Ear, in which various commercial blends of these and other races are now pushing rapidly westward.

Through the cooperation of Dr. Lee Lenz (now of the Rancho Santa Ana Botanical Garden) and of Dr. J. G. Harrar of the Rockefeller Foundation and several of his staff, it was possible to make an intensive survey of the variation in the maize of Tepoztlán. Ninety-eight samples of 25 ears each were taken in the winter of 1947-48, the sampling being distributed as evenly as possible between the various barrios and villages. From each of the seven barrios eight samples were taken, two each from fields in the *cerro,* two each from corrals, two from *texcal* land, and two from *valle* milpas. Similar samples were taken from the seven outlying pueblos, Santiago, Ixcatepec, Ocotitlán, San Juan, Gabriel Mariaca, San Andrés Calera, and Amatlán. From only one of these pueblos was it possible to obtain eight samples; from Gabriel Mariaca there were only four and from the remainder only six each, but they too were reasonably well distributed between the four types of site so that from the municipio as a whole we have 25 *cerro* samples, 25 corral samples, 23 *texcal,* and 25 *valle.* (See Fig. 1.)

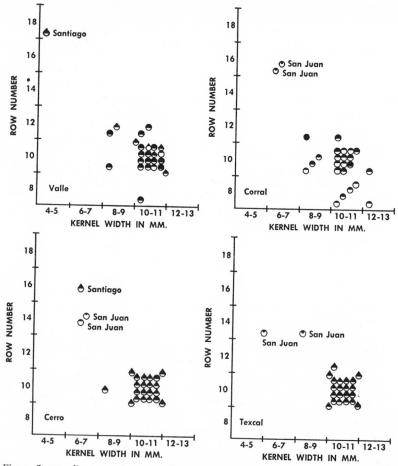

Fig. 1. Scatter diagrams of *cerro, valle, corral,* and *texcal* samples. Each glyph is the average of a twenty-five ear sample. The shape of the glyph indicates how pointed the kernels were on the average. The amount of black in each glyph is roughly proportional to the amount of soft starch in the kernel.

The most outstanding fact revealed by this survey is that the maize of Tepoztlán is surprisingly uniform. It is uniform within many of the samples. As many as 20 ears out of a sample of 25 may be identical in row number and kernel size. It is also uniform between samples. The sample averages for *cerro, valle,* and *texcal* are either identical or differ in only a single detail for virtually all the samples from the municipio. Of the 2,450 ears which were measured, approximately forty per cent fell in the modal cell of the summary chart. That is to say that 995 out of the 2,450 ears had the same row number and kernel size. While there are other native American communities with as great or even greater maize uniformity, such a condition is unusual in much of Mexico, where diverse types, some of them highly differentiated, may be grown in the same village, and even by the same individual.

Furthermore only two samples out of the 98 are good characteristic Mexican Pyramidal, though several of the others show its influence. The modal type, though not typical Mexican Narrow Ear, is closer to that than it is to Mexican Pyramidal. It is 10-rowed, like much of the maize in western Mexico but the kernels are smaller (10-11 mm. in diameter), they are slightly dented on the average, and slightly pointed, suggesting a slight infiltration of Mexican Pyramidal germ plasm. On the other hand, their prevailing uniformity suggests that this contamination may have taken place long ago, since the modal type is now so strongly stabilized. Since the maize of Tepoztlán is so prevailingly uniform, pueblo and barrio differences are most readily discussed by showing the extent to which these differ from the usual type.

One of the villages, San Juan, has an outstandingly different type of maize. It averages fourteen rows, and the kernels are small and flinty. In spite of the higher row number, it shows neither the pointing nor the denting which so frequently accompany high row number in the Mesa Central. All three of these characters (row numbers of fourteen, small kernels, and flinty kernels) are very ancient characters in maize, though not typical for most of Mexico.

One of the other pueblos, Santiago, shows obvious signs of influence from the Mesa Central. We have six samples of maize from this pueblo. Two are typical Mexican Pyramidal, many rowed, pointed dents, one with a modal row number of sixteen, the other of eighteen. Two other samples from this pueblo are intermediate between these and typical Tepoztlán maize, the other two have the usual Tepoztlán mode, but each sample includes several ears with highly dented, sharply pointed kernels, suggesting crosses with Mexican Pyramidal varieties. In one sample from Los Reyes, two from La Santísima, and one from Santo Domingo, a minority of the ears show unmistakable signs of Mexican Pyramidal influence.

There is little differentiation, on the whole, between the maize grown in the *valle,* the *texcal,* and the *cerro* plots, though the *valle* samples are slightly less pointed than the other two, and their averages vary a little more from one to the other. The corral samples, however, show a distinct tendency to be more frequently eight-rowed and to be much less pointed than the other three. This undoubtedly means that the corral maize is a more or less differentiated type. In all probability it is frequently designed to be used as *elotes,* or for other special dishes prepared from maize in the roasting ear stage. There is a general tendency, over much of Mexico, to grow more or less specialized varieties for these purposes, and particularly in western Mexico these *elote* varieties tend to be characterized by a wider kernel and by fewer row numbers, than the ordinary maize of the milpas.

The maize samples may also be used to examine the comparative uniformity of harvested maize in the different barrios and pueblos. Uniformity of maize in Mexico and Central America is a rough measure of the pride and skill with which the maize crop has been selected and grown. Conservative Indian communities, which have preserved their old customs, have the most uniformity, skilled agriculturists are next in order, and the more or less urbanized *pobrecitos,* who have lost much of their Indian tradition, have the most variable maize crops. In this respect there is little difference between the barrios. They all have moderately uniform samples, much more uniform for example than similar samples from S. P. Tlaquepaque (Jalisco). The samples from the barrio of San Pedro are the most uniform of the lot. Among the pueblos, Ixcatepec is outstanding but in the other direction. All six of its samples are variable, two of them so markedly so as to reflect upon the integrity of its agricultural traditions.

B. *THE CERAMIC SEQUENCE OF TEPOZTLÁN*

BY FLORENCIA MULLER

THE STUDY of the potsherds excavated in Tepoztlán during the two field seasons of 1942-43 gave rise to the following hypotheses: (1) Tepoztlán was a frontier town on the peripheral zone of two different types of cultures, one from the Mexican highlands and the other from the coastal lands and the south; (2) Tepoztlán was the entrance for the influences from the valley of Mexico.

The sherds extracted from the excavations fell into six levels, which have been numbered I to VI. The oldest was named Tepoztlán I.

The potsherds of this period showed similarities to those of Xochicalco, Gualupita I and the Cerro del Venado, Chimalacatlan, in the valley of Morelos. During this period, Tepoztlán had relations with Middle Zacatenco and Ticoman of the valley of Mexico. Nevertheless, the presence of other wares indicated trade with the valley of Toluca, as well as with the site of Tres Zapotes of the state of Veracruz. Resemblances were also found with the wares of Monte Alban I, and with the state of Guerrero. Although very little is known of the archaeology of the state of Guerrero, some green stone figurines of Tepoztlán seem to be similar to those from this state.

Evidence. Xochicalco: Orange ware, and red on dark brown. Cerro del Venado: Red on orange and orange ware. Gualupita I: Black and dark brown ware with simple and composite silhouette bowls and jars, figurines D and K of Vaillant's classification. Valley of Mexico—Middle Zacatenco and Ticoman: Buff ware, orange ware, figurines D and C. Monte Alban I: Jar with ribbon handles near lip, green stone *penate*. Valley of Toluca: Matlazinca ware, figurine, type O.

For the next level, or Tepoztlán II, analogies were found with Teotihuacan I and II, Gualupita II, Cerro del Venado, and Xochicalco.

Evidence. Teotihuacan I: Brown ware, dark and light; tripod bowls with flat bottoms, small conical solid supports, cups and figurines diagnostic of this period. Gualupita II: Brown and black ware. Cerro del Venado: Orange ware. Xochicalco: Red on orange ware highly polished.

For the following levels, or Tepoztlán III and IV, relations seemed to have been more important with Teotihuacan, in lesser degree with Xochicalco, Cerro del Venado, and the valley of Toluca.

Evidence. Teotihuacan: Brown ware, orange hard ware with annular supports, slab feet, *incensarios*. Xochicalco: Red on orange, Cerro del Venado: Hard orange ware. Valley of Toluca: Matlatzinca ware with high supports.

The fifth level is the most interesting due to the great variety of types of wares, found during this period, not only in colors but in forms.

The sherds which showed relations with Xochicalco or Cerro del Venada have disappeared. But analogies were found with Coyotlatelco, Colhuacan, Tula, Valley of Toluca, Cholula, the Huasteca area, and other parts of Veracruz. Also relations were found with the wares of the highlands of the Mixteca, Oax, and as far south as Zacualpa, Guatemala.

Evidence. Coyotlatelco: Red on orange or buff, black on red. Azteca I: Black on orange, figurines Azteca I. Valley of Toluca: Matlatzinca ware, red on cream, three armed jars. Cholula: Laca, black on orange ware. Huasteca: White ware, pink ware. Highlands of Veracruz: Fine orange. Mixteca area: Porous orange ware. For the first time spindle clay whorls, chile grinder tripod bowls, *comales* (tortilla griddles) are found. Also the important tripod bowl with effigy supports appeared. This last mentioned ware has a very wide and interesting distribution. In Tepoztlán the characteristic type is the serpent-head support. This same type is found in Zacualpa, Guatemala, as well as in Cholula. Effigy leg supports are found in Alta Verapaz, Guatemala, Monte Alban V, in the Mixteca area of Oaxaca, Isla de Sacrificios, and Cerro Montoso of Veracruz. Other examples of effigy legs are found as far south as Nicoya, Costa Rica; Nicaragua; and the site of Chiriqui, Panama. How much of this distribution was due to trade, or to cultural influences, is hard to determine. Nevertheless, it is a very important element; in some places like Zacualpa and Tepoztlán, it is just as diagnostic of this period as is fine orange or plumbate.

In the last level, or Tepoztlán VI, all these wares have disappeared. The period is dominated by the Azteca wares III and IV with other associate wares of this period, as well as that of the Mixteca area.

Evidence. Valley of Mexico: Black on orange ware Azteca III and Azteca IV, polichrome. Mixteca: Porous orange.

As a summary, it can be stated that Tepoztlán seemed to be located in the peripheral zone of two different types of cultures, one from the highland and the other from the coasts and the south. It was through this site that the highland cultures filtered into the valley of Morelos. During the fifth level, which corresponds roughly to around 900 A.D., this site seemed to have reached its climax. But it declined under the dominance of the Méxicas and their allies during the sixth period. In this period Tepoztlán seems to have lost all its importance to Cuernavaca.

C. ORIGINAL DOCUMENT, INDIOS [1]

TASACIÓN A LA VILLA DE TEPOZTLÁN, DEL MAÍZ QUE SE COGE DE COMUNIDAD. Don Martín Enríquez, por cuanto los naturales de la Villa de Tepoztlán, dan por cuenta haber recogido de las sementeras de comunidad que hicieron el año pasado de mil y quinientos e setenta e nueve mil y cuatrocientas y sesenta fanegas de maíz que al presente dicen valer en el dicho Pueblo, a peso e medio, cada fanega y para enterar a la Caja de su comunidad de cuatrocientos y noventa y ocho pesos y seis tomines de oro común, que perteneció a ella de los dos tomines que se solian recoger de cada tributario por año, para sobras de tributos, conforme a la tasación antigua, es necesario venderse del dicho maíz docientas y cincuenta y tres fanegas que al dicho precio de peso e medio cada fanega, monta trecientos y setenta e nueve pesos e cuatro tomines con los cuales y con ciento y diez e nueve pesos y un tomín que se recogieron de las indias viudas y sol teras de las estancias de Santiago, Santa María Magdalena, Santo Domingo, San Juan, Santa Catalina, San Andrés, sujetas a la dicha Villa. Se entera la dicha comunidad de los dichos cuatrocientos y noventa y ocho pesos y seis tomines y para enterarse lo que cabe a dar y pagar las dichas estancias está repartido en la forma siguiente.

De la estancia de Santiago, veinte pesos y tres tomines el un pesos y siete tomines de quince indias, viudas y solteras que hay en ella a real de cada una y los diez y ocho pesos y medio por lo que cabe a pagar a setenta y cuatro tributarios enteros a dos tomines cada uno y para pagar esta cantidad se han de vender doce fanegas y media de maíz de las setenta y cuatro fanegas que dicen haber recogido en ella, que descontado esto que da en especie, para la dicha estancia, sesenta y una fanega y media del dicho maíz.

De la estancia de Santa María Magdalena veinticinco pesos y dos tomines los dos pesos de diez y seis indias viudas y solteras que hay en ella a real cada una y los veintitres pesos y dos tomines por lo que cabe a pagar a noventa y tres indios tributarios enteros a dos tomines cada uno y para pagar esta cantidad se han de vender quince fanegas y media de maíz de las noventa y tres fanegas que dice haber recogido en ella que descontado esto, queda en especie para la dicha estancia setenta y siete fanegas y media del dicho maíz.

De la estancia de Santo Domingo doce pesos y tres tomines el un peso y un tomín, viudas y solteras, que hay en ella a real cada una y los once pesos y dos tomines por lo que cabe a pagar a cuarenta y cinco tributarios enteros a dos tomines cada uno y para pagar esta cantidad se han de vender siete fanegas y media de maíz, de las cuarenta y cinco que dicen haberse cogido, que descontado esto, queda en especie para la dicha estancia treinta y siete fanegas y media del dicho maíz.

De la estancia de San Juan, nueve pesos y dos tomines los seis tomines de seis indias viudas y solteras que hay en ella a real de cada una y los ocho pesos y cuatro tomines por lo que cabe a pagar a treinta y cuatro tributarios, enteros a dos tomines cada uno y para pagar esta cantidad se han de vender seis fanegas de maíz de las treinta y cuatro fanegas que dicen haber recogido en ella que descontado esto, queda en especie para la dicha estancia veintiocho fanegas del dicho maíz.

De la estancia de Santa Catalina doce pesos y medio, del dicho oro. El un peso de ocho indias viudas y solteras que hay en ella a real cada una y los once pesos y medio por lo que cabe a pagar a cuarenta y seis tributarios enteros a dos tomines cada uno y para pagar esta cantidad se han de vender ocho fanegas de maíz de las cuarenta y seis fanegas que

[1] *Indios*, Vol. 1, Exp. 252. This is presented as a sample of documents used.

dicen haber recogido en ella que descontado esto queda en especie para la dicha estancia treinta y ocho fanegas del dicho maíz.

De la estancia de San Andrés, doce pesos y cuatro tomines el un peso y dos tomines de diez indias viudas y solteras que hay en ella a real cada una y los once pesos y dos tomines por lo que cabe a pagar a cuarenta y cinco tributarios. Enteros, a dos tomines cada uno y para pagar esta cantidad se han de vender siete fanegas y media de maíz de las cuarenta y cinco fanegas que dicen haber recogido en ella que descontado esto, queda, en especie para la dicha estancia treinta y siete fanegas y media del dicho maíz.

De la cabecera veinte y seis pesos y siete tomines, que se recogieron de docientas y cincuenta indias viudas y solteras que hay en ella.

Todo lo cual se ha de meter en la dicha Caja de su comunidad y de ellos se han de pagar los salarios del gobernador y alcaldes, regidores y otros oficiales de su república, conforme a la tasación que tuvieron y lo demas que restare en las cosas necesarias al dicho pueblo con cuenta y razón y atento que el dicho gobernador alcaldes y regidores y otros principales acudieron a la solicitud y beneficio de las dichas sementeras demás de los salarios que han de llevar, se les de y reparta de las mil y ochocientas y una fanegas de maíz que sobran en especie lo siguiente.

Al gobernador treinta fanegas de maíz.	XXX fanegas
A dos alcaldes a diez fanegas a cada uno.	XX fanegas
A seis regidores seis fanegas a cada uno.	XXXVI fanegas
A dos mayordomos dos fanegas a cada uno. [*sic*]	XII fanegas
A dos escribanos seis fanegas a cada uno.	XII fanegas
Al fiscal de la iglesia, diez fanegas.	X fanegas
A veinte cantores de la iglesia a dos fanegas a cada uno.	XL fanegas
A seis alguaciles de las sementeras a cinco fanegas a cada uno.	XXX fanegas
Al alguacil mayor de la cabecera, seis fanegas.	VI fanegas
A doña María Cortés, hija de don Hipólito, cacique, doce fanegas.	XII fanegas
A cuatro hijos de principales que fueron de la dicha cabecera, cinco fanegas a cada uno.	XX fanegas
A diez tequitlatos de la cabecera, cuatro fanegas a cada uno.	XL fanegas
A ocho tequitlatos del barrio de Atenco de la dicha cabecera, cuatro fanegas a cada uno.	XXXII fanegas
A diez tequitlatos del barrio de Teycapan, cada uno cuatro fanegas	XL fanegas
A cinco tequitlatos del barrio de Olac, cuatro fanegas a cada uno.	XX fanegas
A un alguacil y dos tequitlatos, del barrio de Pochitlán cuatro fanegas a cada uno.	XII fanegas
	CCCLXXII fanegas

Por manera que monta el maíz que se reparte entre los susodichos trecientas y setenta y dos fanegas que descontadas de las mil y ochenta y una fanegas sobran, setecientas y nueve, en especie, las cuales se han de meter. En su comunidad para los gastos necesarios y en las fiestas y pascuas del año que celebran y en dar de comer a los religiosos que los fueren a visitar y doctrinar con cuenta y razón y a la dar cada y cuando se les pida y atento que en los sujetos que atrás quedan declarados, se recogio cierta cantidad de maíz, el cual así mismo se ha de repartir en la forma siguiente.

En la estancia de Santiago quedan después de haber pagado lo que han de meter en la comunidad de la cabecera setenta y una fanega y media de maíz de las cuales han de llevar un alguacil y un principal y un tequitlato de la dicha estancia por el cuidado que tuvieron del beneficio de las sementeras cada uno de ellos cinco fanegas que son quince y quedan cuarenta y seis fanegas y media las cuales se han de quedar en la dicha estancia para los gastos necesarios de ella y para dar de comer a los religiosos que los fueren a visitar y no se ha de echar derrama.

En la estancia de Santa María Magdalena después de haber pagado lo que le cabe a la comunidad de la cabecera, les quedan setenta y siete fanegas y media de maíz de las cuales se han de dar a un alguacil un principal y un tequitlato de la dicha estancia quince fanegas a cada uno, cinco y sobran para la dicha estancia y gastos de ella sesenta y dos fanegas y media las cuales han de gastar con cuenta y razón y a la dar cuentas se les pida.

En la estancia de Santo Domingo quedan después de haber pagado lo que les cabe a la comunidad de la cabecera treinta y siete fanegas y media de maíz de las cuales se han de dar siete fanegas y media a un alguacil y un principal y un tequitlato a cada uno dos fanegas y media y quedan para los gastos de la dicha estancia veinte fanegas y media las cuales han de gastar con cuenta y razón para la dar cuando se les pida.

En la estancia de San Juan quedan habiendo después de haber pagado a la comunidad de la cabecera veintiocho fanegas de maíz de las cuales se han de dar a un alguacil, un principal y un tequitlato siete fanegas y media a cada uno, dos y media y quedan líquidas. A la dicha estancia veinte fanegas y media del dicho maíz, los cuales se han de gastar con cuenta y razón.

A la estancia de Santa Catalina, después de haber metido en la comunidad de la cabecera lo que le cupo quedan treinta y ocho fanegas de maíz, de las cuales se han de dar a un alguacil un principal y un tequitlato siete fanegas y media a cada uno dos fanegas y media y queda líquido a la dicha estancia y para los gastos de ella treinta y una fanega y media del dicho maíz, los cuales han de gastar con cuenta y razón para la dar cuando se les pida.

A la estancia de San Andrés le quedan después de haber pagado a la comunidad de la cabecera lo que atrás queda referido treinta y siete fanegas y media de las cuales han de llevar un alguacil, un principal y un tequitlato, que tienen a cargo de la dicha estancia siete fanegas y media por iguales partes y lo restante que son treinta fanegas han de guardar en la dicha estancia para los gastos necesarios de ella sin acudir con cosa alguna a la dicha cabecera.

Y en la manera susodicha se reparte el dicho maíz, y las justicias de su Majestad lo hagan así guardar y cumplir. Fecho en México a veinte días *del mes de julio de mil e quinientos y* ochenta años don Martín Enríquez, por mandado de su Excelencia Juan de Cuevas.

D. FIESTA CALENDAR OF TEPOZTLÁN

Jan. 1. *Fiesta de Divina Providencia*,[1] celebrated in the central parish church: Candles burn in church all night. Members of the Adoración Nocturna keep vigil all night, and confess, and take communion at midnight Mass. Most Tepoztecans attend church on January 1 to petition (*las tres monedas*) the Divine Providence for food, clothing, and shelter for the year. A coin is dropped into the church box for each of the petitions. *Mole* and tamales with pork are eaten by many families; poor families eat tamales made with squash flowers. It is becoming customary for the younger generation to present parents with a small gift on this day.

Jan. 6. *Fiesta of "The Kings,"* celebrated in Los Reyes: The secular aspects of this fiesta consist of the burning of *"toros"* and a *jaripeo*. This is not an important fiesta but popular with the children because they may receive gifts from their parents. This custom was introduced by the Colonia Tepozteca of Mexico City who used to distribute gifts to the poor children of the village.

Jan. 12. *Fiesta of the Virgin of Guadalupe*, celebrated in Santo Domingo: One of the two fiestas of this barrio. It was originally a secondary fiesta honoring the Virgin one month after her Saint Day, but has recently become rather elaborate and costly. The residents of the barrio have boasted that they have enough money to give two fine fiestas and to do fitting honor to the *Virgencita*. There is music and fireworks all the morning of January eleventh. On the twelfth and thirteenth, there is a *jaripeo* and a *torito*.

Following Sunday. *Fiesta of the Virgin of Guadalupe*, celebrated in Gabriel Mariaca: This village is obliged to postpone its festivities because they conflict with the barrio of Santo Domingo. Many Tepoztecans attend this fiesta.

Jan. 20. *Fiesta of San Sebastián*, celebrated in San Sebastián and La Calera: In this case the village of La Calera refuses to postpone its fiesta, so both are given the same day. The only unusual feature of this barrio fiesta is the *brinco* or dance by the *tiznados* or blackfaced dancers. There are usually some fireworks and musicians.

Feb. 2. *Fiesta of the Candlemas*, celebrated in the parish church and at some domestic altars: The raising the child Jesus for the *sacamisa*. A few families set off fireworks, hire musicians, and serve *mole*, chocolate, and cakes to the ceremonial godparents.

Sunday, Monday, and Tuesday preceding Lent.[2] *Fiesta of the Carnaval*, celebrated in the plaza of Tepoztlán: The church is open, but almost no one attends, as the fiesta is now largely secular. This is the most splendid fiesta in Tepoztlán and attracts visitors from far and near. Buses run every half hour on these days, and the local merchants do brisk business. It is estimated that 45,000 pesos were spent by villagers on the Carnaval of 1946. Most of the expenses are incurred in the purchase of new *chinelos* costumes by those who dance, in the buying of new clothing by almost everyone, in drinking and good eating, and in payment of the many bands of musicians who take turns playing. The three large barrios organize *comparsas*, groups of *chinelos* dancers, and compete with each other in the size of the group, elegance of costumes, and endurance in dancing. Most Tepoztecan youths aspire to dance at the Carnaval, and work hard to earn money to buy or rent a costume. The costumes have become more costly and elaborate with each passing year.

---

[1] Our informants did not agree with those of Redfield, who designated this day as the fiesta of *Santa María de Tepoztlán*.

[2] Redfield reported six days of festivities for the Carnaval. During our stay, there were only three fiesta days.

They are made of heavy satin and velvet and trimmings of glass beads, tiny mirrors, sequins, and gold fringe. Some men go to distant cities to purchase the finest materials. The huge hats are also more elaborate, and many are lighted by electric light bulbs placed in the brim and worked by concealed batteries. The cost of a complete *chinelo* outfit was between 100 and 300 pesos in 1944. By 1947, the cost had risen to over 600 pesos. An interesting aspect of the Carnaval is that the masked participants frequently ridicule and caricature popular figures in the village, much to their discomfiture.

Fiesta of Ash Wednesday, celebrated in the parish church: Initiates Lent and brings with it obligations to fast, pray, light candles at the altar, pay *limosnas,* etc. Most Tepoztecans go to church to "take the ash." They believe that the cross made on their foreheads by the priest protects them against sorcery and evil acts of enemies. This belief is strengthened by the fact that the ashes used are those from the burning of old images of holy figures. It is customary for Tepoztecans to bring old images to the sexton to be burned. When Lent begins, the images in the central church and in the chapels are ceremonially covered with purple cloths by men who have inherited the honor from their fathers.

Fiesta of First Friday of Lent, celebrated in Chalma and Jiutepec: Two *mayordomos* in Tepoztlán organize pilgrimages to these holy centers. Each *mayordomo* has a banner with images of the Santo Señor de Chalma and the Santo Cristo of Jiutepec. The pilgrimage to Chalma includes the *pastores,* children who will sing to the image. The group going to Jiutepec includes dancers.

Fiesta of Second Friday of Lent, celebrated in Cuautla: Only a few Tepoztecans attend this fiesta.

Fiesta of Third Friday of Lent, celebrated in Tepalzingo: Because of the fair held at Tepalzingo, many Tepoztecans go, particularly those who wish to buy or sell. *Curanderos* go to purchase herbs from other localities and to sell Tepoztecan herbs; the ropemakers of San Sebastián go to sell ropes. Local merchants go to buy *rebozos,* painted gourds, and curiosities.

Fiesta of Fourth Friday of Lent, celebrated in Tlayacapan: In homage of the *Virgen del Transito.* According to Tepoztecan legend, this image once belonged to Tepoztlán, but in 1770 it was taken to Tlayacapan to be repainted. On the way back the men who carried it became tired and set it down. When they were ready to go on they found the image had become too heavy to lift. This was interpreted to mean that the image wished a temple to be built for her there, and that is why she remained in Tlayacapan. It is believed that the image promised Tepoztlán water so long as Tepoztecans made pilgrimages to Tlayacapan. Thus, it is the custom of many Tepoztecan families to attend this fiesta.

Fiesta of the Sunday after Fourth Friday of Lent, celebrated in Ocotitlán: Only those with *compadres* or friends in Ocotitlán attend this fiesta.

Fiesta of Fifth Friday of Lent, celebrated in Mazatepec and Totolapan: Both towns have important fairs on this occasion. Pilgrimages to Totolapan are organized by the *mayordomía* of Gabriel Mariaca, and to Mazatepec by the *mayordomía* of the barrio of Santa Cruz. Those who go generally take many flowers to sell, especially the *yoloxochitl* (heart flower), and buy in return *petates, rebozos,* dried squash gourds, tamarind, and several types of dried seed.

March 19. *Fiesta of San José,* celebrated in Santa Cruz: The large image of San José is housed in the barrio chapel along with other saints. Since the devotees of this image have been steadily increasing, there is talk of building a separate chapel for the image.

Fiesta of Sixth Friday of Lent or Viernes de Dolores, celebrated in the parish church: Fasting is required. This is the beginning of Holy Week.

Fiesta of Sábado de Dolores, celebrated in the parish church: This is celebrated with holy offices and a Vía Crucis procession.

Fiesta of Palm Sunday, celebrated in the parish church: This is a very important holiday. Tepoztecans take palm leaves to be blessed by the priest. It is believed that blessed palm protects against lightning. Ashes of blessed palm placed upon the head are thought to cure bad headaches. Blessed palm is also placed at the door of the house to prevent fires and being struck by lightning.

Fiesta of Holy Monday and Holy Tuesday, celebrated in the parish church: These are days of great devotion. The religious associations are very active, visiting the church and barrio chapels. Many Tepoztecans choose these days for their annual confession.

Fiesta of Holy Wednesday: Rigorous fasting begins. Meat is not eaten until the Saturday of Glory. Substitute foods are beans, *huauzontle, tortas,* stuffed peppers, fish, *revoltijo,* and lentils. All work must stop through the Sunday of Resurrection. Women prepare tortillas for the rest of the week. In the evening is the vigil of the Lord, the men taking turns all through the night. Women customarily go to church in the late afternoon to pray the thirty-three Credos, one for each year of Jesus' life. It is believed that those who do this will triple their earnings during the year.

Holy Thursday: The church is full on this day. The priest dramatically describes the passion of Christ, and crying on the part of women is common. Not to do so is "to have a cold heart." In the afternoon is the ceremonial foot-washing of the apostles.

Holy Friday: This is the culminating day of Holy Week. Throughout the village there is profound quietude. No one must run or shout or use bad words, so as not to offend the Lord. The men silently drink their *ponche* together while the women, dressed in black, go to church. On this day, children are not to be struck, for "it would be striking the Lord."

Holy Saturday: At 7:00 A.M. the faithful of the village and the municipio go to the church where the priest pronounces the "Gloria in Excelsis Deo." With this all the bells, which have been silent since Wednesday, are rung, and joy spreads through the village. While the bells ring, old men trim their plants so that they will produce more, mothers snip the ends of their daughter's hair to make it grow longer, and children are struck on the legs to make them grow taller. Two or three *comparsas* are organized to dance on this day.

Easter Sunday: Everyone dresses well and goes to Mass. Sometimes the *chinelos* leap in the afternoon. People stand in little groups in the plaza, and men drink a great deal.

April 29. *Fiesta of San Pedro,* celebrated in San Pedro: The only unusual feature of this fiesta is the group of children who dance for San Pedro.

May 1-31. All this month is dedicated to the Virgin Mary, and *rosarios* are held every afternoon. Girls from seven to fifteen years of age dress in white and bring flowers to the Virgin.

May 3. *Fiesta of Santa Cruz,* celebrated in Santa Cruz: This fiesta is celebrated not only in this barrio but in all homes and places having crosses. All crosses are adorned with flowers, especially Bougainvillaea. Incense is burned, and fireworks are set off. This fiesta is also celebrated in Ixcatepec, but is postponed until the following Sunday in deference to the barrio of Santa Cruz. It is one of the best attended fiestas. There are cockfights and visiting dancers from Yautepec and Milpa Alta.

May 8. *Fiesta of San Miguel*, celebrated in San Miguel: This is one of the two annual fiestas of this barrio. As one of the larger barrios, it spends huge sums to have an impressive fiesta.

The following Thursday. *Fiesta of Thursday of the Ascensión*, celebrated in the parish church: This is a movable fiesta, which comes seven weeks after Holy Thursday. Mass is said in the large church, and fireworks are set off. The peasants must rest this day.

Ten days later. *Fiesta of Tlanepantla*, celebrated in Tlanepantla: A favorite fiesta of Tepoztecans, who carry *aguacate, cuajilote,* and *zapote blanco* for sale.

All of June is dedicated to the Sacred Heart of Jesus.

About June 12. *Fiesta of La Santísima*, celebrated in La Santísima: La Santísima, traditional rival of Santo Domingo, organizes an impressive fiesta, with the usual playing of the *chirimía,* and the eating of *mole* and tamales.

June 24. *Fiesta of Day of San Juan*, celebated in San Juan: Boys and girls sing *mananitas* to the image of San Juan at dawn. Then they visit houses where persons named Juan or Juanita live, and they sing *mananitas*. In the afternoon, the young people go out to the fields to seek four-leaf clovers for luck.

June 29. *Fiesta of San Pedro*, celebrated in San Pedro: Similar to other fiestas.

July 16. *Fiesta of Day of Virgin of Carmen*, celebrated in the parish church: All who wear the scapulary of this virgin must attend Mass.

July 22. *Fiesta of Amatlán*, celebrated in Amatlán: Generally only about fifty Tepoztecans attend.

July 25. *Fiesta of Santiago*, celebrated in Santiago: During our visit about 150 persons from Tepoztlán attended.

Aug. 4. *Fiesta of Santo Domingo*, celebrated in Santo Domingo: An important fiesta which lasts three days. A band is hired in Mexico City for greater prestige. There are *toros*, cockfights, dancers, and fireworks.

Aug. 6. *Fiesta of San Salvador*, celebrated in Santa Cruz and Ixcatepec: Follows the usual patterns of barrio fiestas.

Aug. 15. *Fiesta of the Assumption of the Virgin Mary*, celebrated in Tejalpa.

Sept. 8. *Fiesta of the Virgin of the Natividad*, patron of Tepoztlán: This is one of the most important village-wide fiestas, combining pre-Hispanic and Catholic elements. The Catholic ceremony in honor of the Virgin takes place in the church; the honor to El Tepozteco takes place out of doors. A dance to El Tepozteco is held to the accompaniment of the ancient *teponaztle* and a traditional discourse of El Tepozteco in Náhuatl is spoken.

Sept. 28. *Day of the Blessing of the Pericón*, celebrated in the parish church and cornfields: This is an outing day for Tepoztecans who go out into the cornfields to roast fresh corn and place crosses of blessed *pericón* at the four corners of the milpas. Similar crosses are also placed in the homes, for it is believed that on this night the demons are loose, and the evil winds blow hard.

Sept. 29. *Fiesta of Barrio of San Miguel*, celebrated in San Miguel: Follows the tradition of other barrio fiestas.

Oct. 31. *All Saints' Day (Children)*, celebrated in the parish church, in the homes, and at the cemetery: Day in commemoration of dead children. A candle is lighted for the dead child, and incense is burned.[3]

---

[3] See Redfield, *Tepoztlán,* for more detailed description.

Nov. 1. *All Saints' Day (Adults):* Day in commemoration of the adult dead. Food is offered for the dead. The mother of the house says a prayer with the offering. A typical utterance is, "For thee, my son Juan, who has left us here so sad, here we leave thee thy food so that thee will not suffer hunger and so that thee will not forget to aid us in our misery." In this way an offering is made for each dead member of the family. The families then go to place flowers on the graves. "The usual offerings consist of tamales, rice, chicken, chocolate, *mole verde, mamones,* and fruits. . . . All night people keep awake. They pray, and call out the names of the dead. There are torches alight in the streets. The bells on the chapels strike the hours with double strikes. At four o'clock a group of men from each barrio go about asking food for the bell-ringers. People give a tamale and a dish of *mole*. At six in the morning the blessing is given, Mass is said, and the offering is eaten." [4]

Nov. 7. *Octava of the Dead (Children):* Again there is a commemoration of the dead children.

Nov. 8. *Octava of the Dead (Adults):* The offering and the vigil are repeated.

Nov. 9. *Cult of the Dead:* Mass is said in the parish church, and then the priest leads a procession to the cemetery where he prays for the dead. During the remainder of November the priest says Masses for the dead.

Dec. 8. *Fiesta of the Purísima Concepción,* celebrated in the parish church: In addition to the participation of the appropriate *cofradía,* all persons named Concha celebrate this day.

Dec. 12. *Day of the Virgin of Guadalupe,* celebrated in the parish church in Mexico City: The day before, Tepoztecans organize a pilgrimage to Mexico City to do homage to the Virgencita Tonantzin.

Dec. 17. *Days of the Posadas:* The traditional *posadas* begin on this day. The images of San José and the Virgin are borrowed from the large church, and the scenes of asking for lodging at the homes of those who have an image of the child Jesus are re-enacted. [5]

Dec. 24-25 *La Nochebuena,* celebrated in the parish church: In the evening the birth of the child Jesus is celebrated. The usual Catholic ceremony goes on in the church, with a midnight Mass. [6]

---

[4] *Ibid.,* p. 125.
[5] *Ibid.,* pp. 129–31.
[6] *Ibid.*

E. SAMPLE RORSCHACH PROTOCOLS [1]

M. R., Female, 55 Years of Age

[1] The following records have been selected to represent the four age groups discussed in, Chapter 13, "The People as Seen from Their Rorschach Tests," p. 306. The left-hand column represents direct responses to the ink-blot cards; the right-hand column represents answers to inquiries of the tester.

RESPONSE	INQUIRY
I. 15 sec. (1) A butterfly, no? No more. 1 min.	I. (1) (Q) As though it is flying. (Q) Only that it is flying. They like water. They sit down in water.
II. 15 sec. (1) Boxing, isn't it? Fighting, isn't it? What else? No, nothing. 1½ min.	II. (1) They are two boys who are fighting. This is their cap. Here is the face, their shirt.
III. 15 sec. (1) Ah, this is. . . . What could this be? They are skeletons, no? (2) The form of a butterfly, no? 1½ min.	III. (1) (Q) Because they have no flesh. (Q) They are standing and facing each other. (2) (Q) It is red. It is flying.
IV. 6 sec. (1) I don't know this, what could it be? [What does it make you think of?] Who knows? I don't know it. Like the shape of flowers that grow. (2) Or a lyre, isn't it? 1 min.	IV. (1) Here is the flowerpot. It is standing and is where they put the flowers. (2) (Q) The shape.
V. 2 sec. (1) This also is a butterfly. Like those that go—like birds. Only it has its wings extended. 2 min.	V. (1) It is called a bat. It is hairy with little hairs. It is flying.
VI. 60 sec. (1) It is an animal, isn't it? Like the shape. This is a tree. They sit there. 2 min.	VI. (1) This animal sits on this tree. This is the trunk. [What animal?] Who knows. (2 add.) This is like a cross.

M. R., Female, 55 Years of Age—continued

RESPONSE	INQUIRY
VII. 5 sec. (1) It is the shape of like bouquets of flowers that they use for embroidery. 1 min.	VII. (1) This is the shape of a flower they embroider on handkerchiefs. (Q) Only the shape.
VIII. 20 sec. (1) They are animals that go in water. Now they are hanging this way. They are rabbits, I think. What could these animals be? They are cows, aren't they? Walking, no? 2 min.	VIII. (1) Like a castle and these animals are like adornments. (Q) Of cardboard. [If black?] No, they are colored. [Before, you said the cows were walking.] No, they are hanging—they move while hanging.
IX. 10 sec. (1) This is a . . . What is this? Like a lyre? These two are making it, they are holding it with their hands. Yes, these are like lyres. 1½ min.	IX. (1) No. It is a flowerpot with flowers. (Q) (*No answer.*) [If black?] No, if black it would be different.
X. (1) This is the last one. This is like the image of La Santísima Trinidad, isn't it? This is it.	X. (1) It is sitting. This is the dress. On the Santísima the cloak is yellow, and the dress is white. This is her hat? (2 add.) These are flowerpots, decorations for the church.

$$W = 8 + 1$$
$$D = 4 + 2$$
$$\underline{S = 0 + 1}$$
$$12$$

$$M = 1$$
$$FM = 2 + 2$$
$$F = 7$$
$$Fc = 0 + 1$$
$$FC = 2$$
$$\underline{CF = 0 + 1}$$
$$12$$

$$H = 3$$
$$A = 5$$
$$PL = 2 + 1$$
$$Obj = 1 + 1$$
$$\underline{Arch = 1}$$
$$12$$

$$P = 4 + 1$$

C. F., Female, 23 Years of Age

<table>
<tr><td align="center">RESPONSE</td><td align="center">INQUIRY</td></tr>
</table>

I. 10 sec. (1) Isn't it a—how shall I say?—Isn't—it a bat? That is—how?—Opening its wings? I say that he is looking for a place where he can go to rest. How shall I say? (*Laughs.*) This bat is looking for an animal. Then—there are no more.

2 min.

I. (1) (Q) The shape.

II. 26 sec. (1) It looks to me like two rabbits running. Nothing else. I see two rabbits.

2 min.

II. (1) (Q) This is how the shape is. (Q) (*No answer.*)

III. 14 sec. (1) They are two monkeys. They look to me as though they are holding hands. I think there is no more.

1 min.

III. (1) They are holding something. (Q) It is almost the shape. [What kind of a skin do they have?] (*No answer.*)

IV. 27 sec. (1) This also looks like a bat, opening its wing. Nothing else.

1 min.

IV. (1) (Q) The wings are open. (Q) (*No answer.*)

V. 30 sec. (1) It looks to me as though there is a butterfly with its wings open. Nothing more.

1 min.

V. (1) (Q) The shape. [Only the shape?] Nothing else. [Is it dead or alive?] Alive.

VI. 20 sec. (1) It looks like a statue. Nothing else.

1½ min.

VI. (1) It is an angel. [Does the face show?] No, this is the back. [What is it made of?] The statue of stone and this (*base*) of *mezcla* (*mixture of mud and pebbles*).

VII. 23 sec. (1) Two faces looking at each other face to face. (*Peers.*) They have their hands behind. It looks like no more.

1½ min.

VII. They are statues of stone. [What is this (bottom)?] That is the thing on which they are. [This? (connection).] That is where they are connected. (Q) (*No answer.*) [Faces of what?] Of people.

C. F., Female, 23 Years of Age—continued

RESPONSE	INQUIRY
VIII. 19 sec. (1) A flowerpot with flowers. (*Searches.*) Nothing else. 2 min.	VIII. (1) [If this were black would it look the same?] No, the flowers are colored.
IX. 42 sec. (1) Well—this is a tree, round. 1 min.	IX. I see the shape, nothing else. [If it were black, etc.?] It is not because of the colors.
X. 21 sec. (1) This is a branch of flowers, of different colors. Nothing else. 1 min.	X. The whole thing.

W = 8	M = 1	H = 1	P = 3
D = 2	FM = 2 + 2	A = 5	
——— 10	F = 3	PL = 3	
	Fc = 2	Statue = 1	
	CF = 2	——— 10	
	——— 10		

C. G., Female, 15 Years of Age

RESPONSE	INQUIRY
I. 5 sec. (1) Like a bat, no? (2) Other things? Like a butterfly, no? It has no head. (3) This way the wings have the shape of an animal, don't they? They are not clear—I can't say what they are called. 3 min.	I. (1) It has no head. (Q) It is a nocturnal animal. (Q) I don't understand. [Is it dead or alive?] Alive, because it has no head. Here is the head, wings, etc. (2) The wings. It has no head. The body is not shaped well. It is dead because it has no head—only the neck. (3) It hardly shows . . . only half. It has one foot in the air. The wing . . . it is flying, isn't it?

C. G., Female, 15 Years of Age—continued

RESPONSE	INQUIRY

II. 2 sec. (1) Like clowns, isn't it? They have no face. May I say other things here?

II. (1) The face cannot be distinguished. The body, the neck . . . the little hands, the feet are not complete. This is his suit—a dress, this is the waist. (Q) Well, like clay . . . ? (Q) I think—it is dead because the face is not there, and the feet are not complete.

(2) It looks like a little animal. The head is cut and the feet are missing. There is no more, is there? Now, what?

3 min.

(2) Without a head, here is the body. Here are the legs, tail, forefeet. (Q) It is alive, but the feet are missing. Here the bird appears to be flying—but it is not a bird. It seems to me to be standing on rocks. [Do you see the rocks?] Yes, here.

III. 5 sec. (1) They are animals. They are not clear—like some puppets I think (*laughs*).

III. (1) Puppets—made of rags. (Q) They are held hanging from the hands. The little shoes and legs here. The face is not clear. [Is it male or female?] It is male because it has no dress, only a man's suit. (Q) Like in the circus, they are sitting.

(2) A little plant—a bean plant, no? But there are no beans formed.

(3) It looks like a bow, that they wear in the hair, isn't it?

(2) This is the stem. This is the seed—it breaks here to grow.

(3) It is made of ribbon. (Q) The shape. [If black?] Yes, they are of various colors.

(4) It looks like a little bird. There is no body or tail. It is flying, it has wings. Ready.

3 min.

(4) The feet are missing.

IV. 10 sec. (1) It is clear—like—it has a head like a spider, doesn't it? (*Laughs.*) It is not very clear—it has the shape. I cannot—I can't—it is not clear—what shape it has.

IV. (1) (Q) Because it has the flattened thing—the head. It has no body.

(2) There like the head of a butterfly.

(3) Here—I don't know—like shoes—like boots, aren't they? Ready.

3 min.

(2) It has the little horns (*antennae*). It has no body.

(3) They are made of leather.

C. G., Female, 15 Years of Age—continued

RESPONSE

V. 2 sec. (1) Ah! Like a bat, no? It is clear. (*Subject interrupted with a conversation about her younger sisters—about 1½ min.*)

(2) Here . . . what? . . . here, like some animals.

(3) The head like pincers. Oh no, they are the feet, aren't they? (Subject asked, "Did others come for this test? Did my cousin?")

2½ min.

VI. 130 sec. (1) This is like mountains. (*Interruption—5 min.—to look after baby brother.*)

(2) The head—because of the whiskers—these are the wings. (*Laughs.*)

4 min.

VII. 80 sec. (1) A monkey, isn't it? Like Cantinflas (*Mexican comedian*). A caricature—it is a clown, isn't it? Do you know Cantinflas? (*Conversation about little sister.*)

(2) I cannot say what animals they are.

(3) They look like some rabbits, the head . . . rabbit's ears are longer—it is not clear. Do you see this, too?

(4) A fish, isn't it?

7 min.

VIII. 25 sec. (1) It has the shape of a fox. It has very delicate feet, doesn't it?

INQUIRY

V. (1) It is facing the other way. (Q) It is flying. It is the whole bat.

(2) Only half of the body. It is running—the tail and the feet.

(3) Like pincers of iron.

VI. (1) (Q) An animal on rocks. Here is the head looking over there. The feet don't show—they are between. There are rocks all over here. (Q) Because of the shape. (Q) Yes, I think only the shape.

(2) [What type of animal?] I don't know.

VII. (1) Only half the body. This is his cap. It is of clay, it doesn't look alive. It is artificial. (*Subject appears sleepy.*)

(2) (Q) The head and the ears. [How?] It is artificial—because the hands and feet are not well formed. It is made of—like wood, isn't it?

(3) It is also of wood.

(4) No—.

VIII. (1) (Q) It is jumping from one rock to another. [Do you see the rock?] Yes, but it is not this color.

C. G., Female, 15 Years of Age—continued

RESPONSE	INQUIRY
(2) It has the shape of a butterfly—its antennae, and very small head.	(2) No—it is the flower.
(3) A flower, isn't it? Now no more.	(3) The whole is the flower. I don't remember what its name is. [The petals?] No, they don't show. This is the bottom—it has the seed. [If black?] No.
3 min.	

IX. (*Conversation on English. Subject said she wanted to learn it.*) I cannot make it out.
100 sec. (1) Here is a person's head. It is looking, the mouth is open. It has no body.
(2) Like coconut—like slices. Do you know it? Did my cousin Francisca come here, too?
(3) Like a map of South America—but a lot is missing.

8 min.

IX.

(1) One eye shows.

(2) This is the skin.

(3) It is not complete. (Q) I don't know. I cannot say.

X. 1 sec. (1) It looks like a flower.

(2) It looks like some turtles, don't they?

(3) Like a worm, isn't it? The petals of the flower form a worm, no?
(4) Like microbes, no? There are many things here, but they are not clear.
(5) This is like a spider but the head is missing, no?

4 min.

X. (1) These are the petals. This is the stem, and here is where the seeds are. (Q) The shape. [If it were black?] No.

(2) (Q) Because of the head and body they have. [If black?] I think they would. (Q) They are not on the ground. They seem to be jumping—but it doesn't show where.

(3) (Q) It looks dead.

(4) They have eyes. [If they were black?] Yes.

(5) But they aren't—they are artificial. These are the feet.

C. G., Female, 15 Years of Age—continued

W = 3	M = 0 + 2	H = 2	P = 4
D = 19	FM = 6	Hd = 2	
d = 3	F = 21	A = 14	
dd = 4	cF = 0 + 5	Ad = 3	
――	CF = 2	Obj = 3	
29	――	PL = 3	
	29	Geo = 1	
		Food = 1	
		――	
		29	

F. G., Female, 11 Years of Age

RESPONSE

I. 20 sec. (1) A moth.

(2) Some small moths. No others.
1 min.

II. 10 sec. (1) A spider.

(2) A bird.

(3) A butterfly.
1 min.

III. 11 sec. (1) Two dolls.

(2) A horse.
(3) A tree.
1 min.

IV. 14 sec. (1) A toad.

(2) Two scorpions.

INQUIRY

I. (1) The whole thing. Here is the head. (Q) This is the way moths are. (2) (Q) They are this way from a distance.

II. (1) We see them when they are on us because they bite. (Q) It is dead. (Q) Because we do not see live ones, only dead ones. (2) They are two linnets. (Q) This way. (3) Here is the head and the wings.

III. (1) [Describe it.] (*Points out parts.*) They are grabbing two birds. (2) (*Points out parts.*) (3) Here are the stalks (*twigs*). This is the upper part. I don't see the trunk.

IV. (1) It is in water. [Do you see the water?] Yes, here. (2) This is the way they are—?

F. G., Female, 11 Years of Age—continued

RESPONSE	INQUIRY
V. 3 sec. (1) A bat.	V. (1) We have seen them. This is the way they are. (Q) (*No answer.*)
(2) A pig.	(2) (Q) This is the way they are.
(3) Two ducks. Now there is no more.	(3) This is the way they are.
1 min.	
VI. (*Touches card for first time.*) 16 sec. (1) An insect.	VI.
	(1) There are insects that have feet and insects that have wings. (Q) (*No answer.*)
(2) A calf.	(2) This is the way they are. We have two.
(3) Two birds.	(3) These two white things. [What type?] They are eagles.
(4) A butterfly.	(4) (Q) This is the way they are. [Dead or alive?] Alive.
1 min.	
VII. 5 sec. (1) Two clowns.	VII. (1) They have a skirt. They are alive.
(2) Two chickens.	(2) They are resting.
(3) A heart.	(3) The clowns use them. A cardboard figure with feathers, in the shape of a heart.
1 min.	
VIII. 5 sec. (1) Two tigers.	VIII. (1) [Tell me more.] I don't know (Q) They are climbing.
(2) A lion.	(2) Here with wings. (Q) A bird. [Not a lion?] No.
(3) A butterfly.	(3) (Q) The wings. [If black?] No, there are some of this color.
IX. 7 sec. (1) Two roosters.	IX. (1) (Q) This is the way they are. [Would it look the same if black?] There are black ones also and of this color, too.
(2) A tree.	(2) Here is the trunk and here the branches. (Q) It is of this color.
(3) A boy.	(3) (*Points out parts.*) (Q) This is the way they are.
1 min.	

F. G., Female, 11 Years of Age—continued

X. 3 sec. (1) Two spiders.
(2) Two birds.
(3) A face, no more.

1 min.

X. (1) (Q) [No answer.]
(2) (Q) [No answer.]
(3) [Face of whom?] (*No answer.*) [What kind of a face?] (*No answer.*) [Do you like the face?] Yes.

W =	4 + 1	M =	1	H =	3	P = 4
D =	12	FM =	1	Hd =	1	O = 1
d =	4	F =	24	A =	22	
Dr =	8	cF =	0 + 1	Obj =	1	
S =	1	C' =	0 + 1	PL =	2	
	29	FC =	3		29	
			29			

G. R., Male, 55 Years of Age

I. 7 sec. (1) I see—a—body.

1 min.

I. (1) [Of a person or animal?] Of animal—without a head and with wings. (Q) Like a butterfly. (Q) It has the wings extended. (Q) Dead. (Q) I think this because it doesn't have anywhere to move.

II. 11 sec. (1) A part of the body. This part (*hips*). . . . [Do you see anything else?] No.

1 min.

II. (1) It is bone but it is covered with flesh. [If black?] No, not the same.

III. 7 sec. (1) There are some people.

(2) The birds.
No more. The feet are like this.

1 min.

III. (1) They are holding something. It is a woman. (Q) Because of the breast.
(2) It is flying. [If black?] No, it would surely be different. (Q) Well—.

G. R., Male, 55 Years of Age—continued

RESPONSE	INQUIRY
IV. 47 sec. (1) What is this?—There is nothing. What does this mean? (*Laughs.*) 1 min.	IV. (1 add.) This way it is the body—but of an animal. Of the hips. It is the skin. It is extended open, and it was already folded. These are the legs.
V. 4 sec. (1) It is a bat. With its wings extended—yes, a bat. 1 min.	V. (1) It is extended and decaying. It is already open.
VI. 14 sec. (1) A part of the body (*back of neck*), dorsal spine, and this (*hips*). 1 min.	VI. (1) It is an animal. [Which?] The body of, like a cow. (Q) It is the skin. (2 add.) And this is different. It looks like the head of a snake—open. [Open?] But this is the outside.
VII. 40 sec. (1) (*Holds card level with eyes at horizontal plan.*) There isn't anything. (*Laughs.*) 1 min.	VII. (1 add.) The cheekbones.
VIII. 20 sec. (1) They are some animals. Yes, they are animals. (2) And a part of the body. 1 min.	VIII. (1) [What type?] They look like sheep. (Q) The shape. They look as though they are jumping. (2) The back.
IX. 28 sec. (1) This is also a part of the body. (2) Some angels. No more. 2 min.	IX. (1) [What body?] Like a hen which is sitting down. (2) (Q) Because of its wings. [If black?] It would look like a bird.
X. 27 sec. (1) A part of the body. (2) Little animals.	X. (1) It is of an animal. It is open. This is flesh and this is bone. (2) Grasshopper. (Q) The shape and the color.

G. R., Male, 55 Years of Age—continued

RESPONSE	INQUIRY
(3) And a head of a rabbit.	(3) Clear.
(4) The same—some animals.	(4) They are dead because they are hanging. They are rabbits. (Q) The shape.

W = 3	M = 1	H = 2	P = 4
D = 10 + 3	FM = 2	A = 7 + 1	
Dr = 1	m = 1	Ad = 1 + 1	
S = 0 +	F = 5 + 3	At = 4 + 1	
14	Fc = 2	14	
	FC = 2 + 2		
	CF = 1		
	14		

C. G., Male, 32 Years of Age

RESPONSE	INQUIRY
I. 20 sec. (1) This looks like a butterfly.	I. (1) The eyes are here. (Q) It seems to be flying.
(2) This looks like a dog which is up there.	(2) (Q) It is sitting.
(3) Here is a tree.	(3) Only the branches—it is standing on a rock. (Q) Yes, it is a tree and a rock.
(4) A *mogote* (*type of hill*).	(4) Like a hill of rock. (Q) Yes, here. (*Outlines in air.*)
(5) Some fingers.	(5) [How many?] Two. It is pointing with the forefinger, with the hand up.
2½ min.	
II. 30 sec. (1) A lamp—it is white.	II. (1) It is hanging. [What makes it look like hanging?] This looks like a chain. It has a tassel. [Do you see the light?] No, just the lamp.
(2) Here is a pig.	(2) Only the head with ears and a snout.
(3) A dog.	(3) Up to the neck. (Q) It is standing.

C. G., Male, 32 Years of Age—continued

RESPONSE	INQUIRY
(4) A worm (*or caterpillar*).	(4) (Q) It is walking. The body here is turning this way.
(5) A *resplandor* (*something like a reflector behind a light, usually very bright and shining*).	(5) It is a decoration. In the church it is made of silver. [If it were black would it look like a *resplandor*?] Yes.
1 min.	

III. 18 sec. (1) Some dolls.

(2) A pineapple.

(3) A rooster.

(4) Some ducks.

1 min.

III. (1) Here is the head with a cap; two arms, one like this (*up*) and one like this (*akimbo*). This is a foot. (Q) Standing.
(2) It is picked. (Q) Yes, and this is the fruit.
(3) The crest, the beak, the feet. This is a long feather. (Q) It is standing.
(4) (Q) The head here and the tail and feet. (Q) They are standing.

IV. 28 sec. (1) Some rats.

(2) A goat.

(3) A coyote.

1½ min.

IV. (1) (Q) The ears, eyes, mouth, feet. It is standing.
(2) It is sitting. The feet and tail don't show.
(3) Only up to the neck. It is stretching its neck.

V. 15 sec. (1) A bat.
(2) A cat.

(3) A person's face.

V. (1) Flying. (Q) (*Points out parts.*)
(2) It is sitting. The eyes, ears, and nose.
(3) [Man or woman?] Woman. Her eyes, nose, mouth. (Q) She has it up.

VI. 11 sec. (1) A moth. (*Points out parts.*)
(2) A tree trunk.

VI. (1) (Q) Flying.

(2) Just the trunk, this is like a cut log. (Q) (*No answer.*)

RESPONSE

(3) A parrot

1½ min.

INQUIRY

(3) It is stretching its neck.

VII. 10 sec. (1) A butterfly.

(2) Some monkeys.

(3) A dog.

1 min.

VII. (1) [What kind?] Those that fly in the fields. (Q) Flying.
(2) Only the head. Here is the tail and body. (Q) Because it has the shape of a monkey's face. It is sitting.
(3) It is peeping out of a door.

VIII. 80 sec. (1) Some bears.

(2) A doll.

2½ min.

VIII. (1) (Q) It has the shape and face of a bear. (Q) Standing, it is climbing a hill. (Q) Pure pasture. [If it were black, would it?] Yes, of course.
(2) It is sitting.

IX. 29 sec. (1) Dove.

(2) A cat.

(3) A hen.

(4) A *tlacuache* (opossum). That's all.

1½ min.

IX. (1) (Q) Here are the wings. (*Points out parts.*) (Q) It is sitting and the wings are up. [If black?] It would be the same.
(2) It is opening its mouth. Here are the eyes.
(3) (Q) Only the head and neck. It is the crest.
(4) The tail doesn't show. It is sitting.

X. 15 sec. (1) A rabbit.
(2) A coyote.

(3) A chimney.

(4) A pig.

X. (1) Just the head. The nose, ears.
(2) Neither the tail nor the feet show. It is sitting. [If black?] The same.
(3) (Q) It has the shape. It is round.
(4) The head is up. Doing this, it is standing.

C. G., Male, 32 Years of Age—continued

RESPONSE	INQUIRY
(5) A spider. That's all.	(5) (Q) It is climbing up a wall.

2 min.

W = 2	M = 1	H = 1	P = 5
D = 18	FM = 15	Hd = 3	O = 2
d = 6	F = 20	A = 17	
dd = 10	Fc = 1	Ad = 9	
S = 1	‾‾	Obj = 2	
‾‾	37	N = 4	
37		Arch = 1	
		‾‾	
		37	

R. M., Male, 15 Years of Age

RESPONSE

INQUIRY

I. 20 sec. (1) Like a crown, no? [Are there other things?]
(2) Also like a bat.

(3) Like a *chimáyote* (*a winged insect*).
(4) That's all. Ah, as though they are walking with a dead child. Now I see no more.

4 min.

I. (1) A stone crown.

(2) (Q) It is stuck—dead. (Q) The wings and body.
(3) (Q) Its wings are extended. It is flying.
(4) A table adorned with arches of flowers. (*In a child's funeral the body is carried on an adorned table.*)

II. 10 sec. (1) Like the face of a cat.

(2) Like a molar.

(3) Like a butterfly.

(4) The white also? Like a Virgin, this way.
(5) Like a bulb to light . . . Yes.

3 min.

II. (1) It is screaming (*meowing*). (Q) (*The parts.*)
(2) The tooth is spotted with this color.
(3) The wings are out—it is flying. (Q) The shape. (Q) (*No answer.*) [If black?] No, it is red.
(4) The Virgin, crown and dress.

(5) It is hanging. [Do you see the light?] Yes, the same white.

R. M., Male, 15 Years of Age—continued

RESPONSE	INQUIRY
III. 7 sec. (1) Like a mask . . . a . . . the nose, eyes, ears.	III. (1) A mask of a person.
(2) A kiosk.	(2) A bandstand for the musicians in the park.
(3) Three trees.	(3) Here behind.
(4) . . . Like a tie.	(4) (Q) Because of the color.
3 min.	
IV. 12 sec. (1) Skin . . .	IV. (1) (Q) Of a badger. [Which side of skin?] The fair. It is far.
(2) Like a branch of a flower or plant.	(2) (Q) The flower and leaves are thick and have spines (*thorns*).
2 min.	
V. 3 sec. (1) A bat.	V. (1) (Q) The wings are out flying.
(2) A butterfly.	(2) The same.
(3) Two goats with heads down.	(3) (Q) The heads are down.
3 min.	
VI. 30 sec. (*Looked at back of card.*)	VI. (1) (Q) The wings this way, as though it wants to fly.
(1) An owl.	
(2) A canyon.	(2) With water going down with rocks. Here is the water.
	(3 add.) A syringe for children. To give enemas. This is the bottom (*bulb*), and this is the bowl for water.
3 min.	
VII. 60 sec. (1) Two rabbits.	VII. (1) (Q) Looking at each other.
(2) A mushroom.	(2) Just the shape.
(3) Two *señoritas* dancing.	(3) Dancing.
(4) Like a butterfly.	(4) (Q) Alive, with the wings extended.
2 min.	
VIII. 10 sec. (1) A *piñata* (*colorful bowl for sweets on Christmas*).	VIII. (1) With decorations. (Q) Because of the color.
(2) Ah! Two lizards climbing up the rocks.	(2) Clear.

R. M., Male, 15 Years of Age—continued

RESPONSE	INQUIRY
(3) Like a skull . . .	(3) Looks like bones . . . of a person.
(4) A cedar.	(4) A tree.
	(5 add.) Some silks (*in a skein*).

2½ min.

IX. 47 sec. (1) Two animals.
    (2) Like a seat.
    (3) Two rabbits.

   2 min.

X. 26 sec. (1) Two spiders.
    (2) Like a flower.
    (3) Like a flowerpot.
    (4) Two deer.

   3 min.

IX. (1) They don't show.
    (2) Round, of wood.
    (3) Just the heads.

X. (1) Walking.
    (2) (Q) The shape and color.
    (3) A flowerpot with many flowers.
    (4) (Q) They have horns.

W = 12	M = 1	H = 2	P = 4
D = 16 + 1	FM = 5 + 3	Hd = 1	O = 1
dd = 2	m = 1 + 1	A = 11	
S = 3 + 2	FU = 1	Ad = 2	
———	F = 17 + 2	Aobj = 1	
33	Fc = 3 + 1	Obj = 5 + 2	
	FC = 5 + 1	PL = 4	
	———	N = 3	
	33	Art = 1	
		Arch = 1	
		Mask = 1	
		Tooth = 1	
		———	
		33	

J. N., Male, 11 Years of Age

RESPONSE	INQUIRY
I. 3 sec. (1) A bat. (*Long pause.*)	I. (1) (Q) The way it is painted. (Q) Its wings are extended.

1 min.

J. N., Male, 11 Years of Age—continued

RESPONSE	INQUIRY
II. 16 sec. (1) A moth. (*Pause.*) 1 min.	II. (1) It is colored. [Is that what makes it look like a moth?] No. [If it were all black, would it?] No. [What makes it look like a moth?] It is flying.
III. 7 sec. (1) Two people. (2) A little moth. 1¼ min.	III. (1) They look like people because here are their shoes. The hands are as though they are holding a ball. [Men or women?] Men. (Q) No, they look like women because they have shoes with heels. (2) (Q) (*No answer.*) [If black?] No. [Is it because of the color?] Yes. [Tell me more about it.] It is alive.
IV. 15 sec. (1) A lobster. (2) The shape of a worm. 1¾ min.	IV. (1) (Q) It has the face and hands (*claws*) of it. (*Points out parts.*) (Q) Alive. (2) It is stretched out as if it were dead.
V. 7 sec. (1) The shape of a buzzard. 1 min.	V. (1) It is flying.
VI. 26 sec. (1) The shape of a hill. (2) And here there is like an arrow. Nothing else. 1 min.	VI. (1) [Describe the hill.] It is a smooth hill like that one. (*Points to hill in the distance—the hill is made of rock and has no trees or stones and very little vegetation on it.*) (2) The shape of an arrowhead.
VII. 10 sec. (1) A butterfly. (2) And here are some clouds which are rising. 1 min.	VII. (1) (Q) It is alive. (2) [How rising?] Going up in the air. (*Like smoke.*)

J. N., Male, 11 Years of Age—continued

RESPONSE	INQUIRY
VIII. 9 sec. (1) Like two rats.	VIII. (1) Two rats climbing. They are climbing on—like a house. [What kind of a house?] Made of tin.
(2) A butterfly.	(2) (Q) It has colors. [Tell me more.] It is alive. [What makes it look alive?] (*No answer.*)
(3) Like a castle.	(3) No, like a kiosk.
IX. 34 sec. (1) The shape of a cloud.	IX. (1) (Q) Because they are going up. [Is there anything else?] (*No answer.*) [If they were black?] Yes, they would look like clouds.
(2) Like a tree.	(2) [What kind of tree?] (*No answer.*) [Does it have flowers?] No. [Leaves?] Yes, it is green.
1 min.	
X. 6 sec. (1) Like a spider.	X. (1) It is dead. [What makes it appear dead?] (*No answer.*)
(2) Two shapes of rats.	(2) The heads do not show. They are resting.
(3) Two shapes of dogs.	(3) They are running. [If black?] Yes.
(4) Like a worm with a little face.	(4) Here are the feet. It is standing. [Does a worm have feet?] Yes. [If this were black?] No.
1½ min.	

W = 5	M = 1	H = 1	P = 7
D = 14	FM = 3 + 1	A = 13	
dd = 1	m = 0 + 2	Obj = 1	
———	KF = 2	Arch = 1	
20	F = 10	Clouds = 2	
	FC = 4 + 1	N = 1	
	———	PL = 1	
	20	———	
		20	

A. F., Female, 74 Years of Age [2]

RESPONSE	INQUIRY
I. 8 sec. (1) A spot that has . . . Like people.	I. (1) Like a woman without a head. (Q) Don't know. (Q) Her arms are out like this.
(2) A butterfly, no? Now no more.	(2) The whole thing. (Q) Because it looks alive.
1 min.	

II. 11 sec. (1) They look like people—like spots and I never had spots. This is like people—spots.

(2) They look like monkeys, here they are.

(3) Here they are like, like—what are they called—dwarfs. Now there are no more.

3 min.

II. (1) Only it is rounded. The neck is short. They look as though their hands are extended with a dress. They look as though they are still strong.
(2) The same—also has a dress. [What kind of dress?] Like hairy, like clothing—there are many colors. It has a hand like a cat.
(3) The dwarf is like a monkey

III. 15 sec. Only I don't know what thing this is . . .
(1) Resembles people but I don't recognize it. What are they called. Like dead ones, long neck, and thin, skeletons. A pair. The waist is thin, like a fish, thin.

III. (1) (Q) Because people become skeletons. (Q) Like people, but thinner, like skeletons.

IV. 7 sec. (1) I know it in Náhuatl—*tlapahuehuete*. It is an animal like a chicken. It has feathers and many feet, about twenty. They say they are eagles' chickens. Yes, they look like that.

2 min.

IV. (1) They die each year. This one is dead.

---

[2] The following two records are included because they illustrate so well the vitality and strong personality of the older Tepoztecan women. The record of A. F., age 74, is unusually vivid for a person of her years.

A. F., Female, 74 Years of Age—continued

RESPONSE	INQUIRY
V. 15 sec. (1) It is an *abuja del cielo,* bird with feelers and wings.	V. (1) It is a butterfly, yes. Also an *abuja del cielo.* It has its face, its body—it is like a hawk. Here are its feathers. (Q) It is dead.
1 min.	
VI. 18 sec. (1) This is a dragonfly. Its wing is long and its tail is long. They go about here.	VI. (1) It is rounded. It is going. It looks strong. It has spots on it.
1 min.	
VII. 10 sec. (1) I do not know this, who knows what it is? They are like monkeys—little ones. They have a beard and this is the forehead.	VII. (1) This is adornment like a feather. This is the fur. I only see it from a distance, not close.
1 min.	
VIII. 7 sec. (1) This is similar. In Mexicano it is *correcamino* (*prairie chicken or bird*). We see them in the mountains here. They have long legs and necks, and they are thin. Who knows if it is true?	VIII. (1) It has feathers. It is darkish. (Q) It is alive. (Q) It still wants to go on the earth.
1 min.	
IX. 18 sec. (1) This could be a frog. The dirt is here.	IX. (1) Its feet are like bent. They are rounded. Its mouth is long, its eyes white. It is dead. (Q) Its body looks lazy. [If black?] Yes, they are darkish.
1 min.	
X. 17 sec. (1) This looks like some lizards. I don't know why, that is the way they look . . . [Are there other things?] (2) It looks like a chimney. I don't know this (*blue*), only these two.	X. (1) They do things like cut corn or carry away pesos or cloth. They are this color, like coffee. (2) Smoke goes out. They are made of clay bricks and *mezcla* (*rough cement*).
2 min.	

A. F., Female, 74 Years of Age—continued

W = 6	M = 1 + 1	H = 2	P = 2 + 2
D = 5	FM = 2 + 2	Hd = 1	O = 1
Dr = 1	F = 3	A = 9	
$\overline{12}$	Fc = 5 + 1	Obj = 1	
	FC′ = 1	$\overline{13}$	
	$\overline{12}$		

L. N., Female, 52 Years of Age [3]

RESPONSE

I. 4 sec. (1) It looks like a bat.

(2) And it looks like two women.

(3) It is the shape of a bell with its tongue.

(4) And like an eagle with its wings.

(5) And like a dog here.

(6) Like two in this way—like two hills and water splashing.

(7) And it looks like a rope like this (*an arc*).

(8) And like a dog up there; the same on the other side.

(9) Here like a hill and this too.

(10) Here like a flower—the same here.

(11) Like a bell that is divided here (*line*).

(12) There are two divisions with a stick in the middle. The dog looks as though it is lying down—the other is the same. I have finished.

5 ½ min.

INQUIRY

I. (1) (Q) Because it looks like it. (Q) Its wings, feet, and tail. (Q) (*No answer.*) [Does it seem to be dead or alive?] Alive. (Q) It is flying.

(2) (Q) Standing. (Q) She is standing, because her feet are separated.

(3) It is hanging from this stick. [What is it made of?] Bronze—there are no other kind of bells.

(4) (Q) It looks like this (*waves*). It is flying. (Q) Because that is how they are—and its head.

(5) The head is clear. [Do you see eyes?] No. It is looking up.

(6) These are drops of water. [Do you see water on the hill?] No.

(7) (Q) Because it is white and extended.

(8) Same as (5).

(9) Same as (6).

(10) [What kind of flower?] Who knows, only a flower. [Do you see petals?] No—nothing.

---

[3] See fn. 2, p. 482.

L. N., Female, 52 Years of Age—continued

RESPONSE	INQUIRY

RESPONSE

II. 20 sec. (1) Now this? These are two clowns with their hats. They are holding hands. They are sitting. They are holding like this. They are making—like a bench and they have their belts.

There are two. They don't have feet. There are only two hands. They don't have fingers and have a hump. They don't have a face, one does not have a neck, and the other doesn't have a foot. He is dressed in black. The other also in black. And one has his foot doubled and doesn't have his shoulder blanket here. He has his nose like this (*up in the air*). One is short, it looks as though he is dancing. They look like people who are holding hands like this, true, and their pointed hats. They don't have fingers, nor chins, no faces, nor necks. They are talking. They don't have a mouth. They are people wrapped in blankets liks this and have a tricolor (*Mexican flag*) behind. It looks like they are carrying something. They look as though they have faces like a monkey, with their noses. One has shoes and has a narrow waist. He has a shirt. He is putting it on.

11 ½ min.

III. 5 sec. (1) They are dead ones, thin, bare, long mouthed. They look like skeletons of monkeys. It looks as though the leg is not connected. He has a knee. It seems as though there is a stick in between. It has a jacket like this (*out*). It has shoes, the heel very pointed. They are playing with —like two jars. They are bent and

INQUIRY

II. Clear.

III. (1) Clear.

L. N., Female, 52 Years of Age—continued

RESPONSE	INQUIRY
here it is like a thread (*forearm*). They have something here (*chest*). Here in the middle it is like a leg or stockings. The large nose. It looks as though it was torn apart. They have only one foot.	
(2) Underneath there is—like a round hoop.	(2) It is like a bone of this monkey. It is round.
(3) And behind is like a dog.	(3) (Q) With its neck upward. (Q) It has the shape. They are red. (*These could be pots.*)
(4) And the other like a pig (*bank*) with its handle. And the dog is doing this (*praying*)—with its tail.	(4) (Q) It is lying down.
(5) And this is like a fish. And it has a bone here and hands. They have sleeves up to here. He has only one; the other also. Nothing else. He is bending; the other also. They are hunch-backed. Here it is disconnected. It is doing something with its foot. They are divided. They are talking—they are like faces.	(5) It is stretched out, it is upright. Very clear, very clear.
10 min.	

RESPONSE	INQUIRY
IV. I already saw this one. Is this a different one?	IV.
8 sec. (1) This looks like a boar.	(1) (Q) It is standing.
(2) The face of a pig, with its forepaws, and its deformed feet. Also the forepaws are deformed. It has no toes; very thin, they look like threads. It has its feet like this (*out*).	(2) It doesn't have a nose, nor feet.
(3) And underneath like a stick with many little sticks.	(3) The stick is upright.
(4) It looks like an elephant. He has shoulders.	(4) He is standing. He has a lot of hair.
(5) This is like a log of wood.	(5) A log.
(6) He is dressed in flannel.	(6) (Q) Because of the hair. (*The shading*)—it looks like gabardine. Same as (8).
(7) And here like a pot with white flowers in the middle.	(7) It is like a pot of clay.

L. N., Female, 52 Years of Age—continued

RESPONSE	INQUIRY
(8) He is standing—like an animal. It doesn't have a human face, it has the face of the grasshopper. It doesn't have a nose, nor eyes, nor mouth, nor ears. It has hair. They are looking at their feet. Their feet are very long, deformed—long. They have pants like men but the legs are opened. His hand looks like a tie, it is doubled over. Both sides are dark. They are looking. That is all.	(8) He is standing. Everything I see is alive. [What kind of hair?] He has long hair like I do. (*Was very vague in pointing out forms here. Kept mixing up each with what had previously been seen. This accounts for the F- on this card.*)

8 ½ min.

V. 4 sec. (1) This is a bat with its horns and head and wings. The wings are arched and divided. The feet are like a chicken's. It doesn't have toes. It is flying. It is going to rest in a tree. It is a nocturnal animal and goes at night. They go sucking animals. They have large beaks to take out the blood of the animals. It has horns like sticks and whiskers. These lines in the middle are like carvings. Also the feet; the wings are very wide. It also has two shoulders and down there the legs like chickens'. I am very quick, am I not?

V. Clear.

8 min.

VI. 6 sec. (1) Is it a cross?
    (2) They are two dogs. A cross with —like one hand extended.
    (3) Some pigs—like this they are pigs. They look like dogs. They have heads, thick forepaws. They are kneeling.
    (4) Like a candlestick.

    (5) Like a lamp.
    (6) Like a straight stick.

VI. (1) I don't see it.
    (2) Lying down. It has fur.

    (3) Only this part above—with the mouth.

    (4) (Q) No, it is not a candlestick. (4 add.) They are flowers, leaves, and petals.
    (5) It is hanging.
    (6) Clear.

L. N., Female, 52 Years of Age—continued

RESPONSE

(7) Like some dogs that are lying down and sitting. They have one rounded arm; no toes; only one arm.

(8) Looks like two eggs.

(9) It looks as though it is a cloth that I see. It is covered with flowers or wool, as though it is soft.

(10) The whole figure is like a pot with a handle; it is boiling. It looks as though it is hanging from above from a stick. They are divided, one here and the other there.

(11) There is a tie here. No more.

6 min.

INQUIRY

(7) Same as (2).

(8) Clear.

(9) The whole thing.

(10) [Do you see the fire?] No. [What makes you think it is boiling?] The steam is coming out.

(11) No.

VII. 1 sec. (1) They are like rocks—carved rocks.

(2) Like a person with his mouth, his nose, forehead, eyes, head, and braids standing up. It looks like a baby's hat—like smooth stones. They look as though they have cotton attached to the neck. They have hands but no feet. They are connected. They are talking with their mouths. They have hair and eyelashes. They are divided into several parts.

2 min.

VII. (1) [What makes them appear carved?] For these (*shading*).

(2) Underneath is a rock, and this above is the face. [What makes it look like cotton?] Because it is light colored.

VIII. 3 sec. (1) Airplanes with their flags.

(2) Some burros with their four hands (*feet*).

(3) A rat going up. Now it is pulling the airplane. They are climbing on the airplane. They have dog's feet. They are fat, and their feet are thin. They have their head, ears, and mouth.

(4) There are threads here.

VIII. (1) It is shaped like an airplane. It is flying up there.

(2) [Do you see the eyes?] No. [Ears?] Yes. (Q) (*No answer.*)

(3) Same as (2).

(4) Threads, only threads, they are shaped that way.

L. N., Female, 52 Years of Age—continued

RESPONSE	INQUIRY
(5) Lower down are all colored flowers. They are blue, grey, and rose-colored.	(5) Four flowers.
(6) It is a tree with its branches and roots. Like poppies.	(6) [If it were black?] It is colored. The shape, too.
(7) Like a boat—upright—going in water, and above are only little boats. It is divided into three parts. A tree with rats going up and scratching it.	(7) [Do you see the boat clearly?] Yes. (Q) This is how they are.
7½ min.	

IX. 5 sec. (1) It is a tree with—like potatoes.

(2) And above there are—like monkeys.

(3) A shape like of jars, pointed.

(4) And above two pigs.

(5) Looks like deer with horns, ears, mouth.

(6) Like a jar with its flowers.

(7) It looks like a plant—it was planted. (*Like a tree.*) And it has branches with leaves. It looks as though divided into fourths. It has many roots.

(8) It looks like some pointed lambs. Two are carrying something. They have tails. Ready.

3½ min.

IX. (1) (Q) This is how they are, round. [If they were black?] Of course.

(2) (Q) Because of the shape. They are standing.

(3) No.

(4) They are lying down.

(5) (Q) (*No answer.*)

(6) It is standing up. [If it were black?] No.

(7) Same as (1).

(8) Same as (4).

X. 2 sec. (1) Some spiders.

(2) Like a cannon with its balls. The spiders are flying.

(3) And down there is a rabbit.

(4) Some snakes, two with the tails up.

(5) Two hens are standing.

X. (1) They are walking.

(2) Like in the war—the cannon balls. (Q) They are rounded.

(3) It is walking.

(4) They are long and thick and round. They are standing up. [If they were black?] They would be clearer if they were black.

(5) [If they were black?] (*No answer.*)

L. N., Female, 52 Years of Age—continued

RESPONSE

(6) Like a hill.

(7) They look like two dogs who are climbing. They are dark. The tails are arched. The snakes are hanging from above.

(8) Some—like people in a forest. They are holding hands, and there are many little animals.

(9) It is like a tube.

(10) A heart.

(11) And its sticks go upward. Ready.

5 min.

INQUIRY

(6) A hill. [If it were black?] Yes.

(7) Clear.

(8) These people are here with these—like hands. All these are animals. (Q) (*No answer.*) (Q) (*No answer.*)

(*Subject became impatient, and inquiry was discontinued.*)

W = 6	M = 6	H = 4	P = 5 + 1
D = 24	FM = 14	A = 21	O = 7
d = 5	m = 1	Ad = 3	
Dr = 17	F = 25 + 1	Obj = 13	
S = 0 + 3	Fc = 2	N = 4	
52	c = 2	PL = 5	
	C' = 0 + 1	At = 1	
	FC = 0 + 1	Eggs = 1	
	CF = 2	52	
	52		

F. CHILDREN'S GAMES PLAYED IN TEPOZTLÁN

La Marisola (for girls): A circle is formed by players holding hands. One player seats herself in the center. The players move clockwise and sing, while one of the players covers the face of the center girl with a piece of cloth. At this all players run away, and the center player uncovers her face and chases them. The first player caught then goes to the center.

Doña Blanca (for girls): A circle is formed by holding hands. One player, Doña Blanca, is inside the circle, and another, the Hornet, is outside. The circle turns as the players sing: "Doña Blanca is covered with pillars of gold and silver. We will break a pillar to see Doña Blanca." The players drop hands, and the Hornet chases Doña Blanca.

Pares y Nones, or Odds and Evens: A circle is formed with one player in the center. The players hold hands and turn, singing, "We are going to play odds and evens. He who remains alone will lose." At the end of the song players quickly seek a partner and embrace. The one who remains alone goes to the center.

Naranja Dulce, or Sweet Orange: [1] A circle is formed by holding hands. One player is in the center. The circle turns and the players sing:

> Sweet orange,
> Sliced lemon,
> Give me a hug
> I ask of you,
> Play the march, Pecho,
> My heart weeps.
> Farewell, Lady,
> I leave you now.

The players take leave of each other by shaking hands, and another player is then chosen to be in the center.

Gato y Ratón, or Cat and Mouse: A circle is formed. One player, the Mouse, is in the center, and another, the Cat, is outside the circle. The Mouse attempts to leave the circle and return without being caught.

Pan y Queso, or Bread and Cheese: Small circles are drawn for each player except one who goes to the center. This player then asks each player in turn if he will buy bread and cheese. The answer is always no, but meanwhile players are slyly exchanging places. The one in the center can "steal" a circle by being quicker than the players exchanging circles.

Encantados, or Enchanting: A group of players count from one to seven. The one who is number seven is the enchanter, who chases all the players and seeks to enchant them with a tap. A player who has been tapped must stand still until disenchanted by a tap from another player.

Another version of this game is played with two groups, the enchanters and the enchanted. The latter stay on three bases, and seek to run from one base to another without being enchanted by the other side. When all are enchanted, the groups change sides.

A la Roña, or Tag: The one who is "it" or has the *roña* chases the others and tries to pass on the *roña* by touching them.

---

[1] Elsewhere in Mexico this game is part of another called *La Despedida*.

La Penuna and Pinocho, or Long Nose: A player counts the others in the group by saying *penuna, pendos, pentres, pencuatro, pencinco, penseis, pensiete, penocho.* The eighth one drops out, and the counting is renewed, with the eighth one always dropping out. The one player who remains is "it" and is called *"pinocho"* (long nose), and he must chase the others. The first one tagged is then *pinocho.*

A que te Robo un Alma, or Stealing a Soul: The eldest player is first, and all but one of the players line up behind him, holding each other by the waist. The one who steals souls says, "I bet I'll steal a soul from you." The first defender says, "I bet you don't." The former then attempts to pull one of the players out of the line. If he succeeds, he punishes the "soul" by assigning a task such as, "Stay here and guard these ninety cows."

This game is similar to one, Catholic in origin, in which the struggle is between the good angel and the devil. When the devil captured a soul, he sent it to hell.

A la Cebolla, or Onions: All but one of the players seat themselves one behind the other. The remaining one, the buyer, takes a little stick and uses it to examine the head of each "onion" to see whether it is ready to be pulled up. He then attempts to pull out one player, who is held down by the others. If the buyer succeeds, he assigns the "onions" a task as a punishment.

La Campanita de Oro, or the Little Golden Bell: Similar to *London Bridge.* Two players join hands to form an arc. The rest of the players get in line and pass under the arc singing:

> Little golden bell
> Let me pass,
> With all my children
> Who are behind me.

The last one to pass under is held and asked, "With whom do you wish to go?" The player chooses one and lines up behind her. The line continues to pass under the arc and sing until all the players are behind one or the other who form the arc. There is then a tug of war to see which one is the winner. In other parts of Mexico this game appears as part of the *Sea Serpent.*

La Víbora del Mar, or the Sea Serpent: Similar to the *Little Golden Bell.* The chant sung is:

> The serpent, serpent of the sea
> Here it can pass by.
> Those in front run fast,
> Those in back will be left behind;
> A Mexican girl selling fruit:
> Plums, apricots, muskmelons, and
> Watermelons.

The players divide up into two groups, by choosing one of the latter two fruits, and a tug of war determines the winning side.

Qué Flores Somos, or What Flowers Are We: The group divides in half; one group gives the names of flowers to each player. The second group approaches and says, "We have come so that you will sell us a flower." The first group answers, "Yes, tell us which flower to offer." If a flower named belongs to one of the group, that player must run and be chased by one of the other group. If caught, she is assigned a task; if not caught, she returns to her group.

Los Santos Viejos, or the Old Saints: Three players are purchasers; the rest each choose to be a saint, imitating a characteristic pose. The purchasers go from saint to saint examining each to see if they wish to buy it. The saint they decide to purchase runs away. If she is caught by the purchasers, she is given a task to do.

Los Listones, or the Ribbons: Three players are purchasers, the rest are "ribbons," each of a designated color. The three purchasers approach saying, "tan, tan." The others ask, "Who it is? What do you wish?" They answer, "A ribbon." "What color?" is then asked. When a correct color is named, the "ribbon" must run and be chased by the purchaser. If caught, she is punished.

La Mama Cochina, or the Mother Pig: One player is the mother pig who must cook the *atole*. The other players are visitors who ask for an herb. The mother pig says, "Go and pick some." They answer, "We don't want to because of the dog, or coyote," etc. The mother pig then agrees to pick some if they will stir the *atole*. When she leaves, the visitors shout that the *atole* has burned, and they run away followed by the mother pig. She punishes all those caught, by giving them work or by hitting them.

El Perrito Ladrón, or the Thieving Little Dog: The players form one line. One player says, "How many little dogs are there in the oven?" The others respond, "Twenty-one burned ones." "Who burned them?" "The thieving little dog." "Burn them, burn them for stealing." The last one leads the line under the arms of the first, and the line faces the other way, with the second player's arms crisscrossed. After each chant, the line files through until everyone stands with crisscrossed arms.

Spinning Tops (for boys): A circle is drawn on the ground and some coins are placed within. If a top touches a coin and leaves the circle, the player wins the coin. There are several other variations of top games in Tepoztlán.

Marbles (usually for boys): A hole is made and a line drawn at a distance of about two meters. The players throw their marbles, and the one nearest the line is first player. The marbles are then thrown into the hole. If successful, the player gets three points, and his marble is placed a span's length from the hole and directed at other marbles nearby. If another marble is struck, the player wins three points. The first to earn twenty-one points wins one or two marbles.

Kite-flying: Popular among boys.

Games imitating adult life (played by girls and small boys).

A la Casita, or House: Building a house of mud, stones, branches, boxes, and blankets and providing it with furnishings, and often including a father, mother, and children.

A la Comidita, or Cooking: Cooking and eating a meal.

A la Madrina, or Godmother: Acting out all the steps in requesting someone to be godmother, baptizing the child, and feasting afterward.

A la Plazita, or Market Place: Each child sets up a stand of fruits, leaves, etc., and buys and sells each other's wares.

A la Milpa, or Farming: The boys go to work in the fields, and the girls carry food to them.

A la Procesión: A religious parade carrying a saint, candles, and flowers. One child takes the part of the priest.

Al Muertito, or Funeral: Acting out a child's funeral with a doll.

A la Cantina, or Drinking: Selling punch, alcohol, and drinks; becoming drunk, shouting, and falling down like drunkards.

A la Piñata: Several children contribute five centavos each to buy peanuts or candy which is placed in a jar as during the Days of the Posadas. The jar is hung high, and the children try to break it with sticks. The one who breaks it gets a spanking, and all eat the contents.

A los Novios, or Sweethearts: The children divide into couples or sweethearts. One is the mother of the girls. When she sends the girls on errands, they are stopped by their sweethearts. When the girls return home late, they are scolded and spanked by their mother.

Al Vestido, or Dressing Dolls (for girls): Making dresses for dolls out of leaves or bits of cloth.

A los Músicos, or Musicians (usually for boys): Imitating local bands of musicians.

A los Chinelos, or Dancers: Dressing in paper masks and *rebozos* or rags to make costumes and jumping like *chinelos* to their own music.

A los Toros, or Bullfighting: The girls or small domestic animals generally take the part of the bull and the boys, the part of the matador.

A Escuelita, or School: Playing school.

A la Iglesia, or Church: A group of girls make an altar, kneel before it, and place flowers and candles on it.

Al Viaje, or Traveling: Traveling in a train or bus.

Al Doctor, or Doctor: Imitating *curanderos* and local methods of curing with herbs, massages, and cleansings.

NEW GAMES TAUGHT IN SCHOOL.

Futbol, or Soccer Game (for older boys): This game is extremely popular, and some young men continue to play it even after marriage.

Vollibol, or Volleyball (for boys and girls of the upper grades).

Beisbol, or Baseball (for older boys and youths).

Basketbol, or Basketball (for older boys and youths).

Rey de Círculo, or King of the Circle: A large circle of about three meters in radius is drawn on the ground. All players enter the circle and try to push each other out. The last one to remain is King of the Circle.

La Metralla, or the Cannon: Two groups hold hands and form circles, one inside the other. Each circle pushes against the other in an effort to break through.

Qué Pesces Somos, or What Fish Are We: A large outer circle is formed, each player standing inside a small circle. In the center are four players. The outer circle selects the name of a fish and advances slowly saying, "What fish are we?" If one of the inner circle guesses correctly, all players dash to the outer circle to secure a small circle in which to stand. The four who remain with no small circle must go to the center.

Bibliography

ABEL, THEODORA M. "Rorschach Test in the Study of Cultures," *Rorschach Research Exchange and Journal of Projective Techniques,* Vol. XII (1948).

ALLPORT, GORDON W. *Personality, A Psychological Interpretation.* (New York: Henry Holt and Co., 1937.)

ANDERSON, EDGAR. "Maize in Mexico: A Preliminary Survey," *Annals Missouri Botanical Gardens,* 33 (1946), 147-249.

———. "Field Studies of Guatemalan Maize," *Annals Missouri Botanical Gardens,* 34 (1947), 433-67.

ANDERSON, EDGAR and HUGH C. CUTLER. "Races of Zea Maize I: Their Recognition and Classification," *Annals Missouri Botanical Gardens,* 29 (1942), 69-88.

BARLOW, R. H. "The Extent of the Empire of the Culhua Mexica," *Ibero-Americana,* XXVIII (1949), 81.

BEALS, RALPH L. *Cherán, A Sierra Tarascan Village.* Institute of Social Anthropology Publ. No. 2. (Washington, D.C.: Smithsonian Institution, 1946.)

BEALS, RALPH L. and EVELYN HATCHER, "The Diet of a Tarascan Village," *América Indígena,* Vol. 3, No. 4 (October, 1943), pp. 298-301.

BECKER, HOWARD. "Sacred and Secular Societies," *Social Forces,* Vol. 28, No. 4 (May, 1950), pp. 361-75.

BIDNEY, DAVID. "Toward a Psychocultural Definition of the Concept of Personality," *Culture and Personality.* (New York: Viking Fund, 1949.)

BIERSTEDT, ROBERT. "The Limitations of Anthropological Methods in Sociology," *American Journal of Sociology,* 50 (July, 1948), 22-30.

BILLIG, O., JOHN GILLIN, and W. DAVIDSON. "Aspects of Personality and Culture in a Guatemalan Community," *Journal of Personality,* 16 (1947), 153-78; (1948), 328-68.

Carta General del Estado de Morelos. (México, D.F.: Secretaría de Fomento, 1910.)

CHASE, STUART. *Mexico—a Study of Two Americas.* (New York: Macmillan Co., 1931.)

CHÁVEZ OROZCO, LUIS. *Historia Económica y Social de México.* (Mexico, 1938.)

———. "Las Instituciones Democráticas de los Indígenas Mexicanos en la Época Colonial," *América Indígena,* Vol. III, No. 2 (1943), pp. 161-71.

COOK, O. F. "Milpa Agriculture, a Tropical System." (Washington, D.C.: *Smithsonian Institution Annual Report,* 1919.)

COOK, SHERBURNE F. "The Historical Demography and Ecology of the Teotlalpan," *Ibero-Americana,* Vol. XXXIII (1949).

———. "Soil Erosion and Population in Central Mexico," *Ibero-Americana,* Vol. XXXIV (1949).

COOK, SHERBURNE F. and LESLEY B. SIMPSON. "The Population of Central Mexico in the Sixteenth Century," *Ibero-Americana,* Vol. XXXI (1948).

COUTU, WALTER. *Emergent Human Nature, a Symbolic Field Interpretation.* (New York: A. A. Knopf, 1949.)

COVARRUBIAS, MIGUEL. *Mexico South, the Isthmus of Tehauntepec.* (New York: A. A. Knopf, 1946.)

DÁVILA Y PADILLA, M. F. AGUSTÍN. *Historia de la Fundación y Discurso de la Provincia de Santiago de México,* 2nd ed. (Brussels, 1625), p. 617.

DIAZ DEL CASTILLO, BERNAL. *The Conquest of New Spain.* Bk. X.

DIEZ, DOMINGO. *Bibliografía del Estado de Morelos,* No. XXVII. (Mexico: Monografías Bibliográficas Mexicanas, 1933.)

DIFFIE, BAILEY W. *Latin-American Civilization: Colonial Period.* (Harrisburg: Stackpole Sons, 1945.)

DURÁN, FRAY DIEGO. *Historia de las Indias de Nueva España y las Islas de Tierra Firme,* I (Mexico, 1867), 9-11.

Estado de Morelos. Estudios Histórico—Económico—Fiscales Sobre los Estados de la República. (México, Secretaría de Hacienda), II (1939), 42.

FOSTER, GEORGE M. *Empire's Children: The People of Tzintzuntzan.* (México: Imprenta Nuevo Mundo, 1948.)

FROMM, ERICH. *Man for Himself—an Inquiry into the Psychology of Ethics.* (New York: Rinehart and Co., 1947.)

FUENTE, JULIO DE LA. *Yalalag, Una Villa Zapoteca Serrana.* (Mexico: Museo Nacional de Antropología, 1949.)

GAMIO, MANUEL. *Forjando Patria.* (Mexico, 1916.)

———. *La Población del Valle de Teotihuacán,* 3 vols. (Mexico, 1922.)

GROSS, NEAL. "Cultural Variables in Rural Communities," *American Journal of Sociology,* Vol. LIV, No. 5 (March, 1948), pp. 348-450.

GRUENING, ERNEST. *Mexico and Its Heritage.* (New York: Century Co., 1928.)

GUTHRIE, EDWIN R. *The Psychology of Human Conflict.* (New York: Harper and Brothers, 1938.)

HALLOWELL, A. I. "Acculturation Processes and Personality Changes as Indicated by the Rorschach Technique," *Rorschach Research Exchange and Journal of Projective Techniques,* VI (1942), 42-50.

HERNÁNDEZ, FRANCISCO. *Historia de las Plantas de Nueva España,* I (México, D.F.: Imprenta Universitaria), 249.

HERSKOVITS, MELVILLE J. *Man and His Works.* (New York: A. A. Knopf, 1947.)

———, AND FRANCES S. HERSKOVITS. *Trinidad Village.* (New York: A. A. Knopf, 1947.)

IXTLIXOCHITL, FERNANDO DE ALVA. *Obras Históricas,* I (Mexico, 1891), 141.

JIMÉNEZ MORENO, WIGBERTO. "El Enigma de los Olmecas," *Cuadernos Americanos,* Vol. V, No. 5 (Sept.–Oct., 1942), pp. 122-25.

KATZ, DANIEL AND RICHARD L. SCHANCK. *Social Psychology.* (New York: John Wiley and Sons, 1938.)

KLOPFER, B. and D. M. KELLY. *The Rorschach Technique.* (Yonkers, N.Y.: World Book Co., 1942.)

KLUCKHOHN, CLYDE. "Needed Refinements in the Biographical Approach," *Culture and Personality.* (New York: Viking Fund, 1949), pp. 75-92.

KLUCKHOHN, C. and O. H. MOWRER. "Culture and Personality: A Conceptual Scheme," *American Anthropologist,* Vol. 46, 1944.

LA FARGE, OLIVER. *Santa Eulalia, The Religion of a Cuchumatan Indian Town.* (Chicago: University of Chicago Press, 1947.)

LA PIERE, RICHARD T. and PAUL R. FARNSWORTH. *Social Psychology.* (McGraw-Hill Book Co., Inc., 1949.)

LENS, HANS and FEDERICO GÓMEZ DE OROZCO. *La Industria Papelera de México.* (México: Editorial Cultura, 1940.)

LEWIN, KURT. "Some Social-Psychological Differences between the United States and Germany" in *Resolving Social Conflicts.* (New York: Harper and Brothers, 1948.)

LEWIS, OSCAR. "An Anthropological Approach to Family Studies," *American Journal of Sociology*, Vol. LV, No. 5 (March, 1950).

————. "Social and Economic Changes in a Mexican Village," *América Indígena*, Vol. 4, No. 4 (October, 1944).

————. *The Tepoztlán Project: A Report on Administrative Problems.* (Washington, D.C.: National Indian Institute, 1945.)

LHUILLIER, ALBERTO RUZ. *Guía Arquelógica de Tula.* (Mexico, 1945.)

LINDESMITH, ALFRED R. AND ANSELM L. STRAUSS. "A Critique of Culture-Personality Writing," *American Sociological Review*, Vol. 15, No. 5 (Oct., 1950), pp. 587-600. Cultures, Memo. XV (Oxford, England: Oxford University Press, 1938).

LINTON, RALPH. *The Cultural Background of Personality.* (New York and London: Appleton-Century Co., Inc., 1945.)

LOVEJOY, ARTHUR O. and GEORGE BOAS. *Primitivism and Related Ideas in Antiquity.* (Baltimore: Johns Hopkins Press, 1935.)

MACIVER, ROBERT M. and CHARLES H. PAGE. *Society.* (New York: Rinehart and Co., Inc., 1949.)

MALINOWSKI, BRONISLAW. "The Anthropology of Changing African Cultures," *Methods of Study of Culture Contact in Africa.* International Institute of African Languages and Cultures, Memo. XV (Oxford, England: Oxford University Press, 1938).

MANLY, JOHN M. *Canterbury Tales by Geoffrey Chaucer.* (New York: Henry Holt, 1928.)

MANNHEIM, KARL. *Ideology and Utopia.* (London: Kegan Paul, 1936.)

MARTÍNEZ, MAXIMIANO. *Las Plantas Medicinales de México.* (México, D.F.: México Ediciones Botas, 1939.)

McQUITTY, LOUIS L. "Effective Items in the Measurement of Personality Integration," *Journal of Educational and Psychological Measurements* (in press).

MEAD, MARGARET. "The Mountain Arapesh," *Anthropological Papers of American Museum of Natural History*, Vol. 41, Pt. 3 (1949), pp. 296-97.

MENDIETA Y NÚÑEZ, LUCIO. *El Problema Agrario de México*, 4th ed. (Mexico, 1937.)

MENDIZÁBAL, MIGUEL OTHÓN DE. "La Demografía Mexicana," *Obras Completas*, Bk. III (Mexico, 1946).

MINER, HORACE. *St. Denis, a French Canadian Parish.* (Chicago: University of Chicago Press, 1939.)

MIRANDA Y MARRÓN, MANUEL. "Una Excursión a Tepoztlán," *Société Scientifique*, Bk. 23 (1905–06), pp. 22-23.

MOWRER, O. HOBART. *Learning Theory and Personality Dynamics.* (New York: Ronald Press, 1950.)

MULLER, FLORENCIA. *Chimalacatlan, Acta Antropológica*, Vol. 3, No. 1 (March, 1948).

————. *La Historia Vieja del Estado de Morelos.* Unpublished thesis, Museo Nacional, Departamento de Historia y Antropología (México, D.F., 1948).

NEWCOMB, THEODORE M. *Social Psychology.* (New York: Dryden Press, 1950).

OBERHOLZER, E. "Rorschach's Experiment and the Alorese," *The People of Alor* by Cora Du Bois, Chap. XXII. (Minneapolis: University of Minnesota Press, 1944).

OROZCO Y BERRA, MANUEL. *Historia Antigua de la Conquista de México*, 3 (Mexico City, 1880), 24.

PARSONS, ELSIE CLEWS. *Mitla, Town of Souls.* (Chicago: University of Chicago Press, 1936.)

Paso y Troncoso, Francisco del, ed. *Epistolario de Nueva España,* XI (Mexico, 1505–1818). Antigua Librería Robredo de J. Porrúa Hijos, 1939–42.

———. *Papeles de Nueva España,* Vol. 6, Ser. II (Madrid, 1905).

Paul, Benjamin D. "Symbolic Sibling Rivalry in a Guatemalan Village," *American Anthropologist,* Vol. 52, No. 2 (April–June, 1950).

Phipps, Helen. *Some Aspects of the Agrarian Question in Mexico—A Historical Study.* (Austin: University of Texas Press, 1925.)

Radin, Paul. *The Method and Theory of Ethnology.* (New York: McGraw-Hill Book Co., Inc., 1933.)

Ramos, Samuel. *El Perfil del Hombre y la Cultura en México.* (Mexico, 1938.)

Redfield, Margaret Park. "A Child Is Born in Tepoztlan," *Mexican Folkways,* Vol. 4, No. 2 (1928), pp. 102-08.

Redfield, Robert. "The Art of Social Science," *American Journal of Sociology,* 54 (November, 1948), 181-90.

———. "The Cerapha and the Casteyohpa in Tepoztlan," *Mexican Folkways,* Vol. 3, No. 3 (1927), pp. 137-43.

———. *The Folk Culture of Yucatan.* (Chicago: University of Chicago Press, 1941.)

———. "The Folk Society," *American Journal of Sociology,* 52 (January, 1947), 292-308.

———. "The Folk Society and Culture," *Eleven Twenty-Six,* ed. Louis Wirth. (Chicago: University of Chicago Press, 1940.)

———. "Remedial Plants of Tepoztlan: A Mexican Herbal," *Journal of the Washington Academy of Sciences,* 18 (April, 1928), 216-26.

———. *Tepoztlán—a Mexican Village.* (Chicago: University of Chicago Press, 1930.)

———. *A Village That Chose Progress, Chan Kom Revisited.* (Chicago: University of Chicago Press, 1950.)

Redfield, Robert and Alfonso Villa Rojas. *Chan Kom—a Maya Village.* Carnegie Institute Publ. No. 448. (Washington, D.C., 1934.)

Sahagún, Bernardino de. *Historia General de las Cosas de Nueva España,* ed. Pedro Lobredo, Vol. III (Mexico, 1938).

Salinas, Miguel. "La Sierra de Tepoztlán," *Memorias y Revista de la Sociedad Científica,* Vol. XXXVIII, Nos. 9 and 10 (July, 1920).

Seler, Edward. "Die Tempelpyramide von Tepoztlán," *Globus,* LXXIII, No. 8 (February, 1898), 123-29.

Simpson, Eyler N. *The Ejido, Mexico's Way Out.* (Chapel Hill: University of North Carolina Press, 1937.)

Stagner, Ross. *The Psychology of Personality.* (New York: McGraw-Hill Book Co., Inc., 1948.)

Stanislowski, Dan. "Early Spanish Town Planning in the New World," *Geographical Review,* 37 (1947), 94-105.

Steward, Julian. "Some Limitations of Anthropological Community Studies." Paper read at the American Anthropological Association Meeting, 1948.

Tampa, Manuel Carrera S. "The Evolution of Weights and Measures in New Spain," *Hispanic American Historical Review,* Vol. 29, No. I (February, 1949), pp. 12-24.

Tannenbaum, Frank. *The Mexican Agrarian Revolution.* (New York: Macmillan Co., 1929.)

Tax, Sol. "Culture and Civilization in Guatemalan Societies," *Scientific Monthly,* XLVIII (May, 1939), 463-67.

―――. "The Problem of Democracy in Middle America," *American Sociological Review*, Vol. X, No. 2 (1945), pp. 192-99.

―――. "World View and Social Relations in Guatemala," *American Anthropologist*, 43 (1941), 22-42.

THOMPSON, L. and A. JOSEPH. *The Hopi Way*. (Chicago: University of Chicago Press, 1945.)

VALENTINE, J. J. "Mexican Paper," *Proceedings of the American Antiquarian Society*, N. S., I (1880–81), 69.

VELASCO, ALFONSO LUIS. *Geografía y Estadística de la República Mexicana*, Bk. VIII (1890), p. 57.

VELASCO, JUAN LÓPEZ DE. *Geografía y Descripción Universal de las Indias*. (Madrid, 1894.)

VILLA ROJAS, ALFONSO. "Kinship and Nagualism in a Tzeltal Community, Southeastern Mexico," *American Anthropologist*, Vol. 49, No. 4 (Oct.–Dec., 1947), pp. 578-86.

WAGLEY, CHARLES. "The Social and Religious Life of a Guatemalan Village," *American Anthropologist*, Vol. 51, No. 4, Pt. 2 (October, 1949).

WHETTEN, NATHAN L. *Rural Mexico*. (Chicago: University of Chicago Press, 1948.)

YOUNG, KIMBALL. *Social Psychology*. (New York: F. S. Crofts and Co., 1944.)

ZAVALA, SILVIO Y MARÍA CASTELO. *Fuentes para la Historia del Trabajo en Nueva España*, Bk. I (México: Fondo de Cultura Económica, 1939).

DOCUMENTS [1]

Duplicados, Vol. 2, Exp. 311, 31 de octubre de 1588. *Para que al Capitan Rodrigo Jorge se le Cumpla el Titulo que se le Dio de Corregidor de las Cuatro Villas del Marquesado del Valle. . . .*

―――, Vol. 2, Exp. 312, 31 de octubre de 1588. *A la Audiencia de México que Habiendo Llevado Salarios los Tenientes que han Tenido los Corregidores de Cuernavaca. . . .*

―――, Vol. 2, Exp. 313, 31 de octubre de 1588. *Al Virrey de la nueva España y Audiencia de Ella. Que Estando en Terminos del Corregimiento de Cuernavaca de Aquella Tierra Ciertas Minas que se han Descubierto. . . .*

Hospital de Jesús, Leg. 38, Exp. 886, 17 de febrero de 1603. *Testimonios de los Autos Hechos de la Posesion que Aprehendio la Parte del Señor Don Pedro Cortés.*

―――, Leg. 289, Exp. 100. *Proceso de Tepoztlán y Yautepeque.*

―――, Leg. 298, Exp. 7. *La Orden de Instrucciones que han de Guardar los Corregidores y Alcaldes Mayores de las Jurisdicciones del Estado y Marquesado, del Valle de Oaxaca. . . .*

―――, Leg. 312, Exp. 9, 16 de mayo de 1699. *Autos y Diligencias que se han Hecho en Razon de lo que Pagaron los Naturales del Pueblo de Tepoztlán, Jurisdiccion de Yautepec, por no ir al Repartimiento del Real. . . .*

―――, Leg. 340, Exp. 27, 5 de septiembre de 1732. *Testimonio de la Certificacion que en Virtud de Degreto del Excelentisimo Señor Marques de Casa Fuerte, Virrey de Este Reino, Dio Don Benito Gonzalez de Ceballos Contador. . . .*

―――, Leg. 340, Exp. 28, 14 de enero de 1756.

―――, Leg. 356, Exp. 8. *Testimonio del Pedron de 1807.*

―――――

[1] The documents listed here are in the Archivo General y Pública de la Nación, México, D.F.

————, Leg. 376, Exp. 1, 15 de mayo de 1590. *Censo Perpetuo de 40 Pesos Cuernavaca, Rancho de Jaltitlan.*

————, Leg. 402, Exp. 14, 3 de diciembre de 1732. *Tepoztlán: Cuaderno Sobre los Titulos que Presento Antonio de Morales.*

————, Leg. 407, Exp. 3, 24 de febrero de 1592. *Real Cedula Despachada al Virrey y Audiencia de México, Sobre no Haber Puesto en Posesion al Capitan Rodrigo Jorge....*

————, Leg. 407, Exp. 26, 10 de julio de 1782. *Informe Sobre Compostura y Raparos del Palacio de Cuernavaca.*

Indios, Vol. 1, Exp. 1, 12 de febrero de 1574.

————, Vol. 1, Exp. 31, 28 de junio de 1575. *Tasación a la Villa de Tepuztlan.*

————, Vol. 1, Exp. 252, 20 de julio de 1580. *Tasación a la Villa de Tepuztlan, del Maíz que se Coge de Comunidad.*

————, Vol. 2, Exp. 103, 20 de octubre de 1582. *Para que el Alcade Mayor de la Villa de Tepuztlan no Consienta.*

————, Vol. 4, Exp. 377, 23 de marzo de 1590. *Para que el Corregidor de Suchimilco Haga Volver a Don Pablo Fernandez un Caballo.*

————, Vol. 4, Exp. 398, 27 de marzo de 1590. *Licencia a don Jose Hernandez Indio Principal de la Villa de Tepuztlan....*

————, Vol. 4, Exp. 410, 29 de marzo de 1590. *A Pedimento de los de Tepuztlan sobre las Casas que Repararon del Marques del Valle.*

————, Vol. 4, Exp. 434, 2 de abril de 1590, *Auto de Confirmacion sobre le Cuenta que esta Mando Tomar de la Villa de Tepuztlan.*

————, Vol. 4, Exp. 435. *Confirmacion de un Mandamiento que se Dio a los de la Villa de Tepuztlan Para que no se les Pida Servicio para los Panes de Chalco.*

————, Vol. 4, Exp. 436. *Confirmacion de Otro Mandamiento que se Dio a los Dichos Indios de la Villa de Tepuztlan.*

————, Vol. 4, Exp. 539. 30 de abril de 1590. *Para que el Corregidor de la Villa de Cuernavaca, Haga Averiguacion de Ciertas Cases....*

————, Vol. 4, Exp. 565, 15 de mayo de 1590. *Para que el Corregidor de la Villa de Cuernavaca Informe si los Indios de Tepuztlan Tienen Tierras y el Inconveniente que habra en hacer lo que Piden.*

————, Vol. 4, Exp. 715. *Licencia a Don Lucas de Castro, Gobernador de Tepuztlan, para Andar en una Jaca.*

————, Vol. 4, Exp. 728, 20 de junio de 1590. *A Pedimento de los Indios de Tepuztlan.*

————, Vol. 4, Exp. 797, 11 de julio de 1590. *Para que los de Tepuztlan no den mas de Susenta y tres Indios que les Causa dar a Cuatro por Ciento.*

————, Vol. 4, Exp. 789. *Para que se Guarde el Mandamiento aqui Inserto, sobre el Maíz que se Manda Acudir a los de Tepuztlan.*

————, Vol. 4, Exp. 874, 28 de julio de 1590. *A Pedimento de los de Tepuztlan.*

————, Vol. 4, Exp. 911, 14 de agosto de 1590. *A Pedimento de los de Tepuztlan.*

————, Vol. 4, Exp. 940, 9 de agosto de 1590. *Para que no Habiendo Habido Cosa en Contrario, se Guarde el Mandamiento del Virrey Don Martín Enríquez....*

————, Vol. 4, Exp. 962, agosto de 1590. *Para que el Corregidor de Cuernavaca Constando que Francisco de Quintana Duenas Mando Hacer Ciertas Obras....*

————, Vol. 5, Exp. 117, 17 de enero de 1591. *Los Naturales de la Villa de Tepuztlan.*

————, Vol. 5, Exp. 118, 17 de enero de 1591. *Los Naturales de la Villa de Tepuztlan.*

Indios, Vol. 5, Exp. 127, 1591. *Los Naturales de Tepuztlan.*

———, Vol. 5, Exp. 180, 4 de febrero de 1591. *Para que por Esta Vez, se Cobre de Cada Tributario de Tepuztlan en Lugar de la Sementera de Comunidad.* . . .

———, Vol. 5, Exp. 181, 4 de febrero de 1591. *Para que en la Villa de Tepuztlan con una Legua a la Redonda no Entren Ganados.*

———, Vol. 6, Exp. 216, 7 de marzo de 1592. *Los de Tepoztlán.*

———, Vol. 6, Exp. 905, 12 de diciembre de 1594. *Licencia a Damian Alvarez, Indio.*

———, Vol. 6, Exp. 906, 12 de diciembre de 1594. *Licencia a Martín Juarez.*

———, Vol. 6, Exp. 417, 21 de enero de 1592. *A Pedimento de los Naturales del Pueblo.*

———, Vol. 17, Exp. 102, 9 de mayo de 1654. *Para que la Justicia del Pueblo de Tepoztlán Ampare a Comingo de Santiago.* . . .

———, Vol. 18, Exp. 89, 14 de abril de 1655. *Para que la Justicia del Pueblo de Tepoztlán Ampare a los Naturales.* . . .

———, Vol. 18, Exp. 141, 17 de junio de 1655. *Para que la Justicia de la Ciudad de Tepoztlán que Constandole Haber Pagado a los Naturales.* . . .

———, Vol. 18, Exp. 142, 17 de junio de 1655. *Para que la Justicia del Partido de Tepoztlán Guarde y Cumpla los Decretos Despachados en el Juzgado de Indios.* . . .

———, Vol. 18, Exp. 143, 17 de junio de 1655. *Para que la Justicia del Partido de Tepoztlán Ampare a Doña Juana Maria.* . . .

———, Vol. 18, Exp. 163, 19 de julio de 1655. *Para que el Alcalde Major del Partido de Tepoztlán Compela al Teniente, de Quíen se Quejan los Naturales.* . . .

———, Vol. 18, Exp. 272, 2 de Diciembre de 1655. *Vuestra Excelencia en conformidad de Parecer del Señor Doctor Don Andres Sanchez de Ocampo.* . . .

Ramo de Tierras, Vol. 67, Exp. 11, Foja 12, 1591.

———, Vol. 3501, Exp. 1, Cuaderno 4, 1745.

———, Vol. 1499, Exp. 9, Foja 5, 1767.

Index

504

Family studies, xiv; *see* Methodology
Farnsworth, Paul R., 496
Fauna, 4-6, 13, 83
Federal District, 170
Federal troops, 42, 232, 233
Field methods, xi-xxii
Fiestas, 41, 106, 208, 210, 259, 271, 272-73, 287, 458-62
Flora, 4, 6, 13, 82-83, 188; *see* Herbs
Florence, 85
Folk-urban, xi; concept of social change, 432 ff.
Food, attitudes toward, 198-99; classification of, 200; expenditures for, 214 ff.; whims, 357; pre-Hispanic, 83; *see* Diet, Family budgets
Forest conservation, 238; resources, 6-7
Forestry Cooperative, 117, 163
Forestry Department, 41, 116
Fortune, Reo F., 428
Foster, George M., 31n, 303, 356n, 437, 496
Fox, Amelia, x
Fraternales, 109-10, 238, 239, 242, 262; *see* Politics
Free union, 409-10; *see* Marriage
Free village, the, 126-27
Freud, 435n
Friendship, 292-93
Fromm, Erich, 496
Fuente, Julio de la; *see* de la Fuente
Funerals, 416; fees, 269-70

Gabriel Mariaca, 3, 5, 49, 54, 117, 170, 232-33, 450, 458-59
Games, 382, 389-90, 491-94; *see* Sports
Gamio, Manuel, ix, xv, 496
García, Pablo, 235
Genova de la O, 237
Geographical horizons of Tepoztecan, 36-38
Gillin, John, 310n, 421, 447n, 495
God, concepts of, 254, 275-76
Godparents, 368n, 369; *see compadrazgo*
Gómez de Orozco, Federico, 84n, 88n, 496
Gómez, Felipe, 230
Gómez, José, 233
Goodenough Draw-a-Man Test, xx; *see* Psychological tests
Gossip, 294; *see* Rumors
Government, local, 221-26; in sixteenth century, 89; attitudes toward, 43-44
Grace-Arthur Performance Scale, xix
Gross, Neal, 437-38n, 496
Gruening, Ernest, xx, 496

Guadalupe, Virgin of, 232, 459, 462
Guatemala, xxiii, 254, 310, 453-54
Guerrero, xxvi, 45, 133, 135, 158, 161, 163, 178, 227, 230, 453
Guthrie, Edwin R., 496
Gutiérrez, Rafael, 237, 242, 243
Guzmán, Cresenciano, 233

Hacienda, effect on family life, 321; role in Tepoztecan history, xxv; treatment of Tepoztecans on, 94; *see* Atlihuayan, Cinconcuac, Oacalco, San Carlos, San Gaspar, Temixco, Tlaltenango
Hallowell, A. I., 311n, 311-12, 496
Harrar, J. G., 449
Hatch, Spencer, 58
Health services, 42
Heaven, concept of, 277; *see* Religion
Hell, concept of, 277; *see* Religion
Henry, Jules, x
Herbs, 83, 354-55, 357-59, 361, 365, 373, 375-76, 377
Hernández, Francisco, 84-85, 496
Hernández, Tranquilino, 231, 235-37
Herskovits, Melville J., x, 434n, 446n, 496
Hidalgo, Juan, 237-39, 241
History of Tepoztlán, as methodology, xiii ff., xx; economics, 81-97; barrios, 19-23; means of communication, 35; land tenure, 113-19; political, 47-48, 50-51, 221; population, 26-30; municipal, 47-48; stratification, 50-51; religion, 253-63
Hoe culture, 128, 148-54; *see* Agriculture
Holidays, 41; *see* Fiestas
Hospital de Jesús, 21n, 48, 84n, 86n, 89n, 229n, 499
Hostility, 292, 320; *see* Inter-personal relations
Houses, 83, 178-87, 215-16; furnishings of, 178-87, 215-16
House sites, number of, 59; kinship composition of, 60
Huasteca, 453
Huaxtepec, 27, 47, 88, 228, 229
huehuechique, 101, 268, 273
Huemac, 228
Huerta, 237
Huitzilhuitl, 228
Huitzilopochtli, 253
Hulett, J. E., x
Husbands and wives, 319-29; adultery, 323, 328; authority, 320, 325; culture change, 323-24; division of labor, 320-21; ideal

Husbands and wives—(Cont.)
  roles of, 319; poisoning, 324; sex, 325-27, 328; suspicion between, 324, 327, 328; wife beating, 295, 327

Iguala, plan of, 258
Illiteracy, 34
Illness, 377; see *los aires,* Herbs, *chipilez, muina*
Incest, 339
Indios, 21n, 28n, 84n, 86n, 87n, 88n, 89n, 161n, 229n, 230n, 455-57, 499-500
Individualism, 118, 303, 439
Industry, pre-Hispanic, 83, 84, 87, 96; charcoal, 163-65; livestock, 158-63; paper, 89; plums, 165-66; ropemaking, 167-68; see Trade, Economics
Infants, baptism of, 269, 368-69; bathing, 380; dress, 370; eneuresis, 380; favoritism, 374; godparents, 369; illness, 377; jealousy, 377 ff.; masturbation, 381; nursing, 372; nurses, 372; play, 381-82; postnatal care, 360, 361; punishment, 381; sleeping arrangements, 379; status of, 52; swaddling, 371; temper tantrums, 379; toilet training, 375; weaning, 375-78; see Birth, Children
Inflation, effect of, 131; see Economics, Prices
Inquisition, xxiv
Insect control, xv, 138, 141
Inter-American Indian Institute, ix
Inter-personal relations, xvii; and status, 52-58; as seen from Rorschach protocols, 306-18; between cousins, 346; between godparents, 350-52; between husbands and wives, 319-29; between in-laws, 347-50; between siblings, 343-46; general qualities of, 287-306; see Personality
Inter-village, conflict, 163; quarrels, 117-18, 238; trade, 171
Ixcatepec, 3, 4, 6, 8, 21, 159, 162, 268, 450, 460-61
Ixtlixochitl, Fernando de Alva, 228n, 496

Jalisco, 38, 40, 452
Jealousy, 322, 377
Jews, 259
Jiménez Moreno, Wigberto, xxiiin, 227n, 228n, 496
Jiutepec, 45, 210, 234, 459
Jojutla, 36, 170
Juárez, Benito, 258

Kaplan, B., 311
Katz, Daniel, 421n, 424n, 496
Kelly, D. M., 310n, 496
Kindergarten, 383; see School
Kissing, 402-03
Klopfer, B., 310n, 496
Kluckhohn, Clyde, 421, 426n, 496

Labastida, Bernabel, 231, 233
Labastida, Esequiel, 231
Labor, collective, 108-11; in colonial period, 85-88; relations, 55, 56, 299; shortage, 112; see *cuatequitl*
Ladinos, 305, 310-11
La Farge, Oliver, 305, 496
Lancaster Society, xxv
Land, communal, 114-18; *ejido,* 120-23; ownership, xviii, 101, 118-23, 424; problem, 96, 447; rental, 123-24; resources, 6; titles, 114, 118; values, 124-25; see Agriculture, Land tenure, Economics
Language and literacy, 33-34
La Piere, Richard T., 496
La Santísima, 77, 78, 93, 119, 121-23, 134, 149, 160, 206, 223, 231, 235, 451, 461
League of Agrarian Communities, 40, 242
Lens, Hans, 84n, 88n, 449, 496
Lewin, Kurt, 424, 496
Lewis, Oscar, xiv, xv, 306n, 431n, 497
Lewis, Ruth M., x, xix, xx, 306n
Leyva, Francisco, xxv
Leyva, Patricio, 231, 233
Lhuillier, Ruz A., 227n, 228n, 497
Life cycle, 353-427; adolescence, 394-98; birth, 358-60; childhood, 378-93; courtship, 399-405; death, 414-17; discontinuities, 420; infancy, 367-78; marriage, 405-10; observations on, 418-27; old age, 411-14
Lima, Francisco, ix
Lindesmith, Alfred R., 426n, 497
Linton, Ralph, 421, 427-28n, 497
Literacy campaign, 40; see Books, Newspapers
Livestock, 158-63; cattle, beliefs about, 162-63; cattle, care of, 158, 161; cattle, ownership of, 159-60; donkeys, ownership of, 159-60; hogs, ownership of, 159-60; horses, ownership of, 159-60; mules, ownership of, 159-60; prices of, 162; stealing of, 158-59.
López de Velasco, 27

Pulque, 254
Punishment, 334 ff., 381

Quarrels, 226-27, 347-48
Quetzalcoatl, 228
Quintana Roo, 95, 230-31, 233, 442
Quiroz, Julio, 234
Quiroz, Luis, 237

Race prejudice, 53
Radin, Paul, 428n, 498
Railroad, xxv, 35
Ramo de Tierras, 114n, 501
Ramos, Samuel, 303n, 498
raptos, 407
Receptoría General de Rentas del Estado, 144
Recreation; *see* Diversion
Redfield, Robert, x, xi, xviin, xx, 8n, 12n, 19, 20, 23n-26, 34, 35, 56, 57, 77, 85n, 93, 103-09, 107n, 125-26, 132, 142, 169, 183, 184, 186, 201n, 228n, 229n, 235, 273n, 280n, 305, 353n, 356n, 360n, 361n, 421, 428-36, 432n, 434n, 435n, 436n, 443n, 458n, 461n, 462, 498
Reform Laws of 1857, 115
Reid, Margaret, x
Relación, 21, 47n, 48, 50n, 81-84, 84n, 88n, 114n, 253, 256, 405n
Religion, 253-83; and status, 57; associations, 258, 266-67; church finances, 269-72; church organization, 263-69; colonial period, 254-58; cults, 44; expenditures, 217; images, 185; independence period, 258-60; fiesta cycle, 272-73, 458-62; pre-Hispanic elements, 255-56, 275-81; revolutionary period, 260-63; practices and beliefs, 256, 267, 273-83; polytheism, 253, 254, 255, 278; *see* Catholic Church, Protestants, Confession, *rezanderos,* Nuns
repartimiento system, 22, 229
Respect, 322, 329, 346, 350-52
Revillagigedo, 28n
Revolution; *see* Mexican Revolution
rezanderos, 261, 266, 269, 415-16
Rich and poor, 93, 109, 174-77
Ritual, in agriculture, 137; *see* Religion
Road, 35; *see* Means of communication, Culture change
Rodríguez, Juan Z., 249
Rodríguez, Prisciliano, 258
Rojas, Demetrio, 231
Rojas, Gabriel, 234

Rojas, José D., 235
Rojas, Mariano, 235
Rojas, Mariano Jacobo, xxiv-xxv
Ropemakers, 101
Ropemaking, 167-68
Rorschach test, xix; sample protocols, 463-91; results, 306-18
Rumors, xvi

sacamisa, 369
Sahagún, Bernardino de, xxiin, 253, 331-32, 498
Saint Miguel, 140; *see* San Miguel
Saints, 277-78; *see* Fiesta calendar
Salaries, 223
Salinas, Miguel, 85n, 498
Salteaux Indians, 311-12
San Andrés, 3, 5, 57, 170, 450
San Antonio, 162
San Carlos, hacienda of, 94-95
Sánchez, Refugio, 231, 233
Sánchez, Timoteo, 234
San Gaspar, hacienda of, 94, 114
San Isidro, 136-37, 140
San Juan, 3-5, 8, 45, 47, 90, 117, 170, 239, 450-51, 461
San Miguel, barrio of, 24, 25, 77, 78, 106, 119-23, 134, 149, 160, 206, 223, 461
San Pedro, barrio of, 22, 23, 25, 77, 78, 111, 119, 121-23, 134, 149, 160, 163, 198, 206, 223, 236, 268, 278, 452, 460, 461
San Sebastián, barrio of, 22-25, 53, 57, 77, 78, 104, 111, 119, 121-23, 134, 149, 160, 163, 167, 206, 223, 236, 259, 458
Santa Catalina, 90
Santa Cruz (large), barrio of, 19, 23, 25, 77, 111, 119-23, 134, 149, 160, 206, 236, 259, 268, 459-61
Santa Cruz (small), barrio of, 23, 77, 119, 129n, 121-23, 134, 149, 160
Santa Eulalia, 305
Santiago, 3, 4, 6, 8, 46, 90, 239, 450-51, 461
Santo Domingo, barrio of, 19, 21, 23-25, 77, 78, 87, 119, 121-23, 134, 149, 160, 206, 223, 231, 238, 451; village of, 3, 4, 6, 8, 47, 117, 461
Schanck, Richard L., 421n, 424n, 496
School, 38, 43, 92, 210, 273, 287, 291, 307; enrollment, 384; registration, 104
Seler, Edward, 228n, 498
Seventh Day Adventists, 57, 58
Sewing machines, 173, 186